To: Del

Thank you for all your
love & support. You were
there when being LGBTQ+ wasn't
easy. I value the stories
you've shared with me regarding
your experiences.

LGBTQIA+ history
is
American History!

Praise for *Our Gay History in Fifty States*

"This informative collection of stories and facts helps bring to life the experience of LGBT people in all parts of our country. It shows that everyday people from all walks of life can become heroes and make significant contributions to our community. These stories can inspire anyone looking to make a difference in their own corner of the world."

—Andrew Park, former Director of International Programs at the Williams Institute, UCLA School of Law, and founder of the Center for Lesbian and Gay Civil Rights in Philadelphia

"Our Gay History in Fifty States is a fantastic road trip. From surprises to familiar faces/spaces, Zaylore Stout's book is important knowledge for the twenty-first century. LGBTQIA+ history is everyone's history."

—Kirstin Cronn-Mills, author of *Beautiful Music for Ugly Children* and *LGBTQ+ Athletes Claim the Field: Striving for Equality*

"Colorful, dynamic, and engaging, Our Gay History in Fifty States *is packed with fascinating anecdotes and inspiring history. This book makes me want to take a road trip to visit every place it mentions! A celebration of the diversity and complexity of the many American LGBTQ communities and individuals that have enriched this country's history,* Our Gay History in Fifty States *is a powerful and essential new resource."*

—Noam Sienna, *A Rainbow Thread: An Anthology of Queer Jewish Texts from the First Century to 1969*

OUR GAY HISTORY IN FIFTY STATES

OUR GAY HISTORY

HISTORY

in

STATES

ZAYLORE STOUT

TO MY CHOSEN FAMILY:

Thank you for your years of love, support, patience, and compassion.
I would not be the man I am today but for you all being in my life.

TO LGBT+ YOUTH:

You matter! You have always mattered and always will matter,
regardless of where you live in this country.

TO THE ALLIES:

Your voice makes a difference. Keep using it to push toward a
more loving and inclusive world for everyone.

ISBN 13: 978-1-63489-257-5
Library of Congress Catalog Number: 2019907148
Printed in the United States of America
First Printing: 2020

23 22 21 20 19   5 4 3 2

Cover and interior design by Mayfly Design.
Illustrations by Alexandra Bye and Chelen Ecija.

Wise Ink Creative Publishing
807 Broadway St. NE, Suite 46
Minneapolis, MN 55413
wiseink.com

To order, visit itascabooks.com or call 1-800-901-3480.
Reseller discounts available.

CONTENTS

FOREWORD

By Judy Shepard, president of the Matthew Shepard Foundation

Read more about Matthew Shepard and the Matthew Shepard Foundation on pages 333 and 334.

Three years in a row, starting when he was eight, my son Matt dressed as Dolly Parton for Halloween. And he was pretty good at it—like Parton herself, he was fun and loving, and he never thought one human being should ever be worth less than someone else. Many people have big hearts, but no one's was quite like his.

Years later, when I was living in Saudi Arabia and Matt was back in America, he called to tell me something. "I'm gay," he said. It was the middle of the night, because he never quite did get the hang of the time zone difference.

I had a feeling this conversation was coming. I can't say why I thought he might be gay—it was just a feeling. "What took you so long to tell me?" I responded. It was vital to me that he knew how much I loved him, that nothing would change because he was gay. Then I wondered to myself, "Why *did* he wait so long?"

In the years since my husband, Dennis, and I started the Matthew Shepard Foundation, I've come to know many people who waited much longer to come out to their parents, their friends, and the world than Matt did. And some never have, making it far into their sixties and seventies with their "big secret" hidden. They fear being rejected by the people they love, by strangers with hateful agendas, and even by others in the LGBT+ community. Their hopes and dreams, heartaches and joys are hidden from the world, entombed by these fears. I am thankful Matt was able to be himself and that I was able to know and love him for everything he was.

The goal of our foundation is to replace these currents of rejection with rivers of acceptance. We aim to end the hatred and ignorance that still exist in our society today, and to inspire compassion, acceptance, and understanding. We are here to make LGBT+ people—especially children—feel like they belong and are loved, not despite their identities, but because of them. In this world we're creating, the Matthew Shepard Foundation might one day no longer be needed. Just the same, this book, *Our Gay History in Fifty States*, will be an inspiration and validation to everyone that they belong in their own lives just as they are, whoever they are.

When I first met Zaylore Stout at the 2017 Twin Cities Quorum National Coming Out Day luncheon, I knew his mission was the same as mine. At the luncheon, Zaylore told me about the intersectional aspects of his own identities, and about his dreams of uniting the LGBT+ community and ending the infighting that often distracts us from our deep commonality and most important goals. I've come to know him even more during the years he's been writing *Our Gay History in Fifty States*, a historical and factual foundation on which to build a proud and productive community that's accepting of all identities on the LGBT+ spectrum, including race, ethnicity, religion, age, body type, ability, occupation, and more. I was deeply touched when he told me his biggest inspiration for taking on this project was my son Matt. We're lucky and honored to be among the many LGBT-centered nonprofits receiving proceeds from the sales of this book.

Reading through *Our Gay History in Fifty States*, I think about what this book could mean to a young person who doesn't see or know where to find people in history like themselves—people struggling with who they are, how they will fit into their own lives, how they will contribute to the world around them—and thinks they don't matter because of it. I think about what it could mean to people outside the LGBT+ community who ignore or even disparage it for the same reason. And I think about how different the world would be if those LGBT+ kids and everyone else had been raised to understand that the LGBT+ community is as old as America itself.

This book shares many of the contributions the LGBT+ community has made, across almost every aspect of society throughout America's history. For the LGBT+ community, *Our Gay History in Fifty States* will be part of the personal journey from fear and shame to pride and acceptance. And for those outside the LGBT+ community, this book will help start the conversation about understanding. Ignorance is our enemy. My hope is that this beautiful, carefully researched book filled with truth and love will not only educate and validate the LGBT+ community, but also enlighten and inspire everyone who opens it.

No one book can capture every story from LGBT+ history, but this one does an excellent job giving everyone from the LGBT+ community a seat at the table. By design, not everyone in this book is a political leader, famous actor, or honored martyr. Many icons of LGBT+ history are just ordinary people fighting daily, in ways large and small, for the love, dignity, and equality they deserve but have been long denied.

Our lives today will be the history of tomorrow. Be who you are. You belong here. Please join us—we've been saving a seat for you.

INTRODUCTION

TUMULTUOUS TIMES

From the moment people hear about *Our Gay History in Fifty States*, the first question I'm often asked is, "What inspired you to write this book?" To begin to tell the story, it's important to know the context of the times. During one of my many road trips from California back to Minnesota, the idea for this book started to take shape.

I grew up and lived about a mile away from the Disneyland Resort in Orange County, California, as a youth and moved to Minneapolis, Minnesota, for law school at the University of St. Thomas in 2007. I graduated three years later, passed the bar exam, and returned to Pasadena to help with the family business.

At law school, the issue of same-sex marriages had reached a fever pitch in my home state. In 2004, San Francisco Mayor Gavin Newsom performed same-sex marriages, which were subsequently annulled by the courts. This case and others eventually made their way to the California Supreme Court, which ruled on May 15, 2008, by a 4–3 vote, that Proposition 22 was unconstitutional. Proposition 22 was a law enacted by California voters in March 2000 that prevented marriage between same-sex couples.

Proposition 8 (also known as Prop 8) was a California ballot proposition and a state constitutional amendment that passed in November 2008. It defined marriage as between one man and one woman. From June 15, 2008, through November 4, 2008, an estimated fifteen to twenty thousand same-sex couples married in California. Many of us assumed these marriages would remain valid after the passage of Proposition 8, because laws are rarely applied retroactively. But there was concern and confusion regarding whether these marriages would or could be instantaneously annulled by the courts. Litigation on this issue continued.

On November 6, 2012, voters defeated Minnesota's Amendment 1 by a margin of 51.5 to 47.5 percent, with a 1-percent abstention margin. The proposed amendment to the state constitution would have banned same-sex marriage in Minnesota. The defeat of Amendment 1 made Minnesota the first state in the nation to defeat a constitutional amendment to limit marriage to heterosexual couples and was a monumental

victory for the LGBT+ community. Minnesota began recognizing same-sex marriages performed in other jurisdictions on July 1, 2013, and began issuing marriage licenses to same-sex couples on August 1 of that year. In a surprise action in June 2013, a federal appeals court bypassed a standard waiting period and lifted the hold on the trial judge's order that declared Proposition 8 unconstitutional. Then on June 26, 2013, the US Supreme Court, in the *United States v. Windsor* case, struck down section 3 of the Defense of Marriage Act, ruling that legally married same-sex couples were entitled to federal benefits. The high court also dismissed a case involving California's Proposition 8.

Throughout this period, Russia's LGBT+ rights record began to overshadow the 2014 Winter Olympics in Sochi. The county enforced a law banning the promotion of so-called "gay propaganda" to minors. On February 7, 2014, Russian authorities arrested more than a dozen LGBT+ rights advocates for protesting in Saint Petersburg and Moscow just before the opening ceremony. Transgender former Italian parliamentarian Vladimir Luxuria was arrested twice during the Sochi games after she publicly promoted LGBT+ rights. Similar protests occurred around the world, including in the United States.

Local tensions fired up as sponsors faced the difficult choice of whether to pull their support from Boston's St. Patrick's Day parade. The event to date draws more than one million spectators to South Boston, yet had traditionally not allowed gay groups to march. The decision led to politicians such as Boston Mayor Martin Walsh and Representative Stephen Lynch to declare they would not participate in the parade. These acts of

defiance, protests, and shifts in policy framed the lens through which I started to conceive of this book while road-tripping alone from Los Angeles to Minneapolis.

REFLECTIONS

When I think of road trips, I think Americana: open roads, convertibles, amber waves of grain. I think of Yosemite National Forest, Old Faithful, the Grand Canyon, and Mount Rushmore—all the great American symbols. But most of all, I think of freedom.

On March 15, 2014, my GPS routed me northeast toward Las Vegas, then on to Salt Lake City. I'd made the Las Vegas trip many times; it's only a short four-hour drive from Los Angeles, without traffic. For some reason, my best friend Tony Johnson was unable to join me on this trip. So, instead of our usual routine of listening to music and cracking jokes during the three-day ride, this trip would just be me, alone with my thoughts.

I stopped at Stateline, on the border separating California from Nevada, known for its streets lined with casinos. I wanted to try my hand at winning a few bucks at the roulette wheel and a few slot machines. I don't recall winning anything, but I started taking photos

to document my voyage. I wanted to capture the first state line I had crossed.

I love listening to public radio while in the car. It helps me stay up to date with current events while on long drives or while stuck in traffic. The sad part, however, is that radio signals don't always cooperate, especially in more remote areas—the areas I call "Rush Limbaugh talk radio territory." So, I'd listen to public radio for as long as I could until the signal would fade. More often than not, I'd scroll around only to find Rush, Christian radio, and a few Spanish-language channels. I am more Buddhist than anything, and my Spanish skills had fallen off after long periods of nonuse. While in these radio dead zones, I'd turn the radio off altogether.

When I crossed into Arizona, the first thing that came to mind was Arizona Governor Jan Brewer and her infamous heated exchange with then-President Barack Obama on the tarmac. I suddenly pictured a quick collage of what first came to mind when I thought of Arizona.

After a quick drive through the Mount Bangs pass, I entered Utah. My feelings were still raw regarding the Church of Jesus Christ of Latter-day Saints' money, impact, and influence in the passage of Proposition 8 in California. I thought, *What happened to the separation between church and state? What happened to freedom from religion, especially the religion of others?* I

metaphorically shook my fist at the sky, demanding answers. *Why do they hate us so much? What's with these red states and red counties?* Clips of the documentary *8: The Mormon Proposition* scrolled through my mind as I realized I would be spending the first night of this road trip at the epicenter of the entity most committed to eliminating marriage equality for gay Californians. At my next gas station stop, I envisioned a collage representing what came to mind when I thought of Utah.

I continued on my drive toward Salt Lake City, pondering the "Great Migration" of LGBT+ folx from conservative rural areas to more urban liberal areas. The explanation was simple. Those of us raised in an area not welcoming of "our kind" are left with few choices but to migrate to a city—or if you're lucky, a state—that does. Today, thirty states actively do not protect LGBT+ Americans. Our community wants to live where we don't have to worry about being fired, kicked out of our residences, sent to conversion therapy, physically harmed, unable to adopt, and persecuted for using the "wrong" restroom. So, we move to destinations where we have protections, often leaving conservative cities and towns across the country with limited to no interactions with LGBT+ people and voices. People tend to fear the unknown and fall back on stereotypes and media interpretations of the marginalized. The same applies here. Peoples' hearts and minds can begin to change once they have no choice but to see, interact with, and hear our stories told in our voices.

I arrived in Utah with little to no fanfare. I checked into my hotel early enough to take myself on a walking tour around the city. I was only a few blocks from downtown Salt Lake City when I headed to the most obvious place, Temple Square. The town was clean yet desolate. There were barely any people on the sidewalks or cars on the streets. By now, I had seen both the Los Angeles and San Diego temples, but never up close and personal. The Salt Lake Temple was beautiful and was in no way ominous, as I had initially anticipated. I found a great local restaurant to try out (thanks, Yelp), then I was off to see what gay life was like in the city. I hit two spots before landing at a final location that had one of my greatest weaknesses: a pool table. The locals were friendly, as you'd expect at any gay bar. However, I remember being surprised that so many people were there. If the Mormons held such hatred toward the LGBT+ community, why were all these LGBT+ people here?

The next day, I got on the road bright and early, not knowing when or where I'd end my day. Before too long, I crossed into Wyoming. Matthew Shepard immediately came to mind. I wondered, *Where would I go if I wanted to lay flowers where Matthew was tied to a fence by his attackers?* Unfortunately, I was in another dead zone, so I was unable to try looking up the location. I quickly pulled over to snap a photo at the continental divide sign. Wow, was it cold. The wind whipped right through me. Before long, I was back on the road when the unthinkable happened: my car broke down about forty-five minutes outside of Casper, Wyoming.

The tow truck driver was friendly and dropped me off at the Meineke repair shop on Cy Avenue. The shop needed to order a part and my car wouldn't be ready to go until the following day. Ugh! I booked a room at the Super 8 because it was only a few blocks away. I later learned that the demographics of Casper was around 1 percent African American, which made sense. I did not see one Black person my whole time there. However, everyone was friendly and cordial. Yet, I still had Matthew and what happened to him on my mind.

I was back on the road the following day with a nice dent in my credit card for the significant auto repair costs. I badly needed a pick-me-up, so I decided to go

Mount Rushmore was amazing. I had hoped to catch a glimpse on my drive up the mountain, but there was no such luck. You can see it only once you've arrived. I spent as much time outside as my body would allow, because it was still March and snow was on the ground. I didn't realize at the time that the monument was only over seventy years old. For some reason, I thought it was much older. While gazing at the faces of George Washington, Thomas Jefferson, Theodore Roosevelt, and Abraham Lincoln, my mind came back to the concept of freedom. When this country was founded, my people, African Americans, weren't free. I thought about equality. Women were also not equal to these men. The presidents etched in those rocks weren't thinking of freedoms for people like me while they lived, and here we are, I thought, more than 238 years later, still fighting for freedom.

to Mount Rushmore. I've always been a lover of American history and the political system. I remember being asked in grammar school, "What do you want to be when you grow up?" My enthusiastic reply, "A chef or a Supreme Court justice!" Really? A Supreme Court justice? What kid thinks that? This kid did.

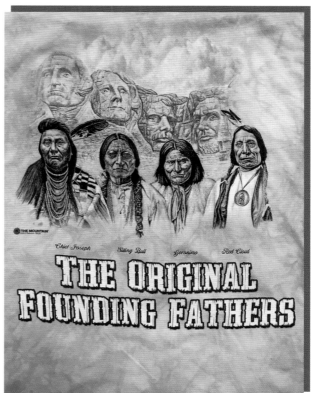

In the gift shop I purchased a few things, including a postcard I would send to my grandmother, Bertha, in St. Louis. I was happy to see there was a Native American section. It wasn't lost on me that we were on stolen lands previously inhabited by over five hundred

Native American tribes. I learned about them and Black history through my family outside of my formal school education. I snapped a photo of a T-shirt showing the original founding fathers being Chief Joseph, Sitting Bull, Geronimo, and Red Cloud. I couldn't bring myself to buy the shirt, despite really wanting it, because I had just spent more than a thousand dollars on those unexpected auto repairs. I texted the photo to my best friend, who always touted his Creek tribal ancestry. I knew he'd appreciate it. It was then that I shared my idea of an LGBT+ history book that would highlight people, places, and things state-by-state. He loved it. We even planned to go on a road trip someday to all the places in the book. Once I arrived in Minneapolis, I downloaded a fantastic photo I had taken of a rainbow lion. That photo became my phone's screensaver for more than a year to remind me of the journey and to also remind me of how our community needs to stay strong.

IT'S TIME

Fast-forward to November 11, 2017. I had since moved back to Minneapolis with my partner, Ore, and I had become involved in several local LGBT+ causes. I was serving on the board for RECLAIM, a nonprofit that provides mental health services to transgender and non-binary youth regardless of their ability to pay. I was fighting on behalf of students in my local community, St. Louis Park, for the passage of a Gender Inclusion Policy through the school district. My law practice led

me to represent two separate clients who had been discriminated against in the workplace solely based on their HIV+ status, a transgender client outed by their boss and LGBT+ business owners looking to be included in supplier diversity programs. My firm became the first in Minnesota to receive certification through the National Gay & Lesbian Chamber of Commerce, and I remained an active member of Quorum, the Twin Cities LGBT+ Allied Chamber of Commerce, and now serve on its board of directors.

I was given the honor to speak at the Midwest's largest National Coming Out Day luncheon alongside Judy Shepard. I was extremely nervous. Though I had presented about legal matters countless times, to share my coming out story in such a public forum was something else entirely.

While writing my speech, I couldn't hold back the necessary critique of the LGBT+ community. Just like the broader community, we have racists, sexists, homo- and transphobes; we shame people based on weight, age, and disabilities too. Lesbians and gays are not always 100 percent welcoming to bisexual and transgender community members. And don't get me started about the community's vocal opinions about those who identify as asexual or queer. I kept trying to write a happy, uplifting speech, but my conscience wouldn't let me do it. I wrote what was in my heart about my story, my journey, then asked for attendees to challenge themselves and others to be more inclusive of each other. Below is an excerpt from my speech:

I'm committed to every letter within the LGBTQIA community, and not just with the letter that I identify. Those within our community who identify as BTQIA should receive the same love and support from our community as the L and the G. It shouldn't be more difficult to come out as bi or trans to your gay friends than it is to come out as gay or lesbian to your straight friends.

I was taken aback when Judy Shepard echoed some of my sentiments in her speech. She shared that it was one of the saddest things when she learned there was not equality and acceptance within the LGBT+ community. She described seeing a hierarchy within the community that needed to change. I couldn't agree with her more. I realized that she was speaking on the nineteenth anniversary of her last few days with Matthew. I was heartbroken and knew that whatever I was doing wasn't enough, given what Judy and Dennis Shepard were doing and going through for our community.

Within days, I reached out to my dear friend Dara Beevas, cofounder of Wise Ink Creative Publishing. I asked her out to lunch so I could get her honest assessment regarding my book idea. I knew that as a friend, Dara would "give it to me straight," and I had a feeling this book was something that needed to happen. In the end, I decided that gay, lesbian, bisexual, transgender, queer, nonbinary, intersex, asexual, 2-Spirit, and youth, especially those in conservative states and counties, need to know that people like them have lived in every state in this country and have made an impact on our country's history. I hoped that every reader would find at least one entry they could personally identify with. If this book gives one young person hope, encourages one family to accept their child for who they are, encourages one parent not to throw their child into the street, I'll feel this project was worthwhile. Finally, LGBT+ history is currently taught in only two states, California and New Jersey. Join me in helping to increase the number of states doing so. The rest is, as they say, history. Now I present to you *Our Gay History in Fifty States*.

AUTHOR NOTES

THE TITLE

We understand this title may suggest a more limited scope than the book actually covers. This book is not only about gay and lesbian people, but everyone within the LGBT+ community. We've chosen the title because the history we are highlighting started with the "gay rights movement." There was a time that this umbrella term provided aid and comfort to anyone who was not accepted by the dominant culture. Without those early pioneers, we likely wouldn't be fighting collectively for the full inclusion of bisexual, transgender, queer, questioning, nonbinary, intersex, pansexual, asexual, and 2-Spirit persons. The title is not meant to exclude any in our community, and we hope this explanation provides some clarity regarding why it was selected.

THE SCOPE

OGH50S is not intended to be a comprehensive overview of the entire LGBT+ experience from our country's founding to present. Instead, this book is meant to provide a historical snapshot of each state's individual history seen though an inclusion and equity lens. Extra attention was paid to ensure this book is as representative and as diverse as the LGBT+ community we all know and love. Our goal was to have at least one entry within this book that everyone could identify with regardless of their race, gender, sexual orientation, gender identity, class, weight, color, politics, education, geographic location, religious beliefs, physical abilities, ethnicity, gender, or nationality, among other factors.

There are some amazing people who've made great contributions towards full LGBT+ inclusion who are not in this book. That is in no way meant as a slight to any of them. This book grew by a hundred pages from its original inception. We felt it was important for *Our Gay History in Fifty States* to be not just a who's who of the community, but also for it to uplift those unsung champions for the cause. Even with our limited space within these pages, some of the stories of these amazing people are being shared on our various social media pages @gay50states.

THE TERM "QUEER"

Queer is a controversial term that means different things to different people. For older generations, queer was a derogatory term used to hurt anyone who didn't "fit in." Younger generations have reclaimed it as a self-affirming umbrella term. We encourage reclaiming ourselves and our lives on our own terms. So, this book will use the term queer in this positive fashion (thanks, millennials!).

BIRTH STATE

People always wonder how were able to secure information on so many LGBT+ people in so many conservative states. This was a threshold challenge we addressed from the very beginning. LGBT+ people are born in every part of our great country, and were it not for societal pressures, discrimination, and violence, they may have chosen to stay in their hometowns. We wanted to honor this fact, so each honoree's contributions have been credited to the state of their birth. For those historical figures whose stories were not fully preserved over time, or those living today who remain factually inaccessible, our best attempt was made at placing them in their home state. Those who were born outside of the country were listed under the state in which they currently live or have made the most impact in their great lives.

OUTING

As you probably know, it wasn't always legal for people to be LGBT+ within the United States. Over most of our country's history, you could be arrested, sent to a mental health institution, subjected to conversion therapy, excommunicated from your place of worship, fired from your job, and/or kicked out of your home either by your family or your landlord simply by identifying or being perceived to be LGBT+. Even as of this writing in May 2019, the following is true:

- 26 states have no explicit prohibitions for discrimination based on sexual orientation or gender identity in state law regarding employment.
- 26 states have no explicit prohibitions for discrimination based on sexual orientation or gender identity in state law regarding housing.
- 27 states have no explicit prohibitions for discrimination based on sexual orientation or gender identity in state law regarding public accommodations.

- 36 states, plus the District of Columbia, have no explicit prohibitions for discrimination based on sexual orientation or gender identity in state law regarding credit and lending.
- 16 states have no explicit prohibitions for discrimination based on sexual orientation or gender identity in state law regarding state employees.

So, yes, even today there are significant potential ramifications for people to be out about either of these things. It's still not safe to be out in all parts of the US. But being out to the public has no bearing on one's true identity. The people highlighted within this book have either self-identified at some point in their lives as LGBT+, or engaged in conduct, confided in family members/lovers/friends, or disclosed in their personal/private writings that they were LGBT+. We've outed no one by publishing their names and stories within this book.

OUR GAY HISTORY IN FIFTY STATES

NORTH EAST

CONNECTICUT

PEOPLE

Faisal Alam *(Frankfurt, Germany)* established the Al-Fatiha Foundation, an organization for LGBT+ Muslims and allies, in 1997 at the age of nineteen. Of Pakistani heritage, Alam was raised in Connecticut and struggled to reconcile his gay identity with Islam. Al-Fatiha ("the opening") began as an email listserv among a small group of people; over time, it grew to over eight hundred members with chapters spanning the US, the UK, Canada, and South Africa, and held an annual conference for its members. Although Al-Fatiha has long since disbanded, Alam has continued his global queer Muslim advocacy via the National Religious Leadership Roundtable, the Muslim Alliance for Sexual and Gender Diversity, and more. In 2011, he was honored to attend President Barack Obama's White House iftar dinner during Ramadan.

Joseph Alsop *(Avon, CT)* was a writer, perhaps best known for the nationally syndicated *New York Herald Tribune* column "Matter of Fact," which he wrote from 1945 to 1974. Alsop was a closeted gay man, though his identity came close to being exposed while he was working with the CIA during the Cold War. On a trip to Moscow in 1957, Alsop fell for a honey trap when a Soviet agent seduced and had sex with him in a hotel room. The KGB photographed the interaction and threatened to expose Alsop as a homosexual if he didn't reveal US secrets. Alsop ignored their demands and chose instead to reveal his mistake to relevant

Brian Anderson

American authorities, thus protecting his career and reputation. The 2012 David Auburn play The Columnist, which originally starred John Lithgow, dramatizes Alsop's life and his Moscow scandal.

Brian Anderson *(Groton, CT)* is a professional skateboarder who came out as gay in a 2016 *VICE Sports* documentary. In response to people asking why he didn't come out earlier, he said he was scared to as a young adult and stayed closeted due to concerns that it would negatively affect his career. Now, Anderson advocates against his fellow skaters using the word "fag," a word that made him feel he couldn't talk about his

> **"** I think of myself as an artist who happens to be transgendered. Being a creative person is the most important, vital part of my identity as a human being. That being said, it's hard to create any kind of meaningful work if you're not living authentically—so coming out and transitioning was an important step for me to take, if only because it meant I was no longer filtering myself in such a destructive way.
>
> —Namoli Brennet, interview with Monika Kowalska, *The Heroines of My Life*, 2014 **"**

identity when he was younger. Anderson was named *Thrasher* magazine's 1999 Skater of the Year, and has skated with companies such as Toy Machine, Girl, and his own 3D Skateboards.

Namoli Brennet *(Waterbury, CT)* is a folk-rock musician. Since releasing her first album, *Boy in a Dress*, in 2002, Brennet has produced thirteen albums—all self-released on her own labels, Girls Gotta Eat Records and Flaming Dame Records. Brennet's music has been featured on NPR and PBS and in the 2009 Emmy-winning documentary *Out in the Silence*, which centers on a gay teen struggling through life in rural Pennsylvania. Brennet plays fifteen different instruments, has been nominated four times at the OUT-music awards, and was named to the first class of the Trans 100 in 2013.

Caitlin Cahow *(New Haven, CT)* is an Olympic Women's Ice Hockey player who earned a bronze and a silver medal in the 2006 and 2010 Olympics. Cahow studied at Harvard and at Boston College Law School; she retired in 2013 following complications due to a concussion. That year, President Obama selected her and tennis legend Billie Jean King, both openly lesbian athletes, to represent the US at the Winter Olympics in Sochi, Russia—a clear rebuke of Russia's longstanding anti-LGBT+ policies.

Elizabeth Gilbert *(Waterbury, CT)* is a writer best known for her 2006 bestselling memoir *Eat, Pray, Love*. Gilbert revealed in 2016 that she and her husband were separating; a few months later, she announced online that she was in a relationship with Rayya Elias, her best friend. Elias had been diagnosed with terminal cancer, prompting Gilbert to fully recognize her feelings for Elias; the two had been friends since 2000, when Gilbert first had her hair cut by Elias. Gilbert and Elias had a commitment ceremony in June 2017, and Elias passed away in January 2018. Gilbert's other writings include *The Signature of All Things* (2013), *Big Magic: Creative Living Beyond Fear* (2015), and *City of Girls* (2019).

Devin Grayson *(New Haven, CT)* is a bisexual comic book writer known for DC's *Nightwing*, *Batman: Gotham Knights*, *The Titans*, and more. Grayson wrote the 2001 DC Vertigo series *User*, which focused on a young woman playing a male character in an online RPG as a means to explore her gender identity; it was nominated that year for the GLAAD Media Award for Outstanding Comic Book. "I love to preach tolerance, but truthfully I'm the least tolerant person I know. I cheerfully write off bigots, dogmatists, and hypocrites without a second thought," she told CBR.com in 2007.

Adrian Adolph Greenberg *(Naugatuck, CT)*, who often went only by his first name, was a costume designer for 1930s and 1940s films such as *The Wizard of Oz* and *Romeo and Juliet*. Early in his career, Adrian

Caitlin Cahow

Elizabeth Gilbert

> *Being who I am—including the bisexuality—has made my life rich and engaging and full of love and amazing people. Any community that can't see value in that is not a community in which I have any interest or investment.*
>
> —Devin Grayson, CBR.com, 2007

wanted to avoid being recognized as Jewish, so he eventually dropped his last name and took his father's first name to become Gilbert Adrian, though he soon became mononymous. Over his thirteen-year career with Metro-Goldwyn-Mayer, he designed costumes for over 250 films. To spite rumors that he was gay, Adrian married Janet Gaynor—who was also rumored to be gay—in 1939. They had one son, Robin, and remained married until Adrian's death in 1959. Adrian's legacy lives on today in the iconic design of Judy Garland's red-sequined ruby slippers in *The Wizard of Oz.*

Jennie June *(Connecticut)* was one of the earliest known transgender autobiographers. Assigned male at birth in 1874, June changed her name and switched to feminine pronouns relatively early in life. She went on to publish two books, *Autobiography of an Androgyne* (1918) and *The Female Impersonators* (1922), which detail her struggle to physically express her identity and advocate for societal acceptance of homosexuality. June documented her castration in her late twenties, as well as her weekly urge to go "at night to a lonely quasi-abandoned graveyard, throw myself on the grass-covered graves, and write in an agony of tears and monas, and beseech my Creator by a miracle then and there to take away my perverted instinct and make a virile man of me," she wrote in *Autobiography of an Androgyne.*

David LaChapelle *(Hartford, CT)* is a photographer and videographer known for his pop art take on celebrities. LaChapelle was bullied in school for being gay, and ran away to New York at age fifteen. There he met Andy Warhol and, after being mentored by him, quickly gained popularity within the art community. His repertoire includes photos of Michael Jackson as

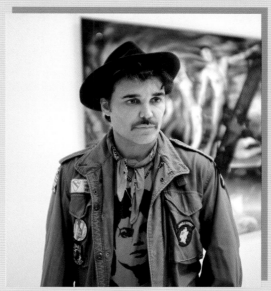

David LaChapelle

the Archangel Michael, Tupac posed as Christ, and various kitschy depictions of figures such as Madonna, Lady Gaga, and more. LaChapelle has produced a catalog of music videos, from Gwen Stefani's "Rich Girl" to Elton John's "Goodbye Yellow Brick Road."

Peterson Toscano *(Stamford, CT)* is a Quaker comedian. Toscano has described his coming out journey as long and complicated; he spent seventeen years in and out of gay conversion therapy, but eventually learned to accept himself for who he is and, in his words, "tumbled out of the closet." Toscano is a staunch advocate of climate change issues, a theme he writes into his comedic routines. He and his husband, writer Glen Retief, lead the Sunbury, Pennsylvania, chapter of the Citizens' Climate Lobby. Toscano was featured in the 2005 documentary *Fish Can't Fly*, which explores the experiences of lesbian or gay people of faith.

💡 QUEER FACTS

Connecticut decriminalized sodomy in 1971, following Illinois ten years prior. Nineteen other states followed suit in the 1970s, though they were typically motivated by updates to criminal justice policies modernized for the times.

The Connecticut Gay Men's Chorus (CGMC), founded in 1986, was the state's first performing arts organization comprised of openly gay men. While the chorus now invites men of all identities to join, its mission is to bridge the divide between the LGBT+ community and the general public. CGMC partners with other community arts organizations in its mission for social change, and donates 10 percent of its proceeds toward LGBT+ causes, such as AIDS outreach and youth support.

Connecticut legalized same-sex civil unions in 2005, also the second state to do so, following Vermont. In 2008, the state legalized same-sex marriage, again the second in line, after Massachusetts had legalized it in 2004.

Transgender birth certificate amendments were made more accessible in 2015 with the passage of HB 7006. The bill overrode previous legislation that required trans people to provide proof of having received gender-affirming surgery in order to change the gender on their birth records. The Senate and House passed the bill with overwhelming support, with votes of 32–3 and 126–8, respectively.

> 66
>
> *Who would have thought that my entire reputation as a designer would rest on Joan Crawford's shoulders?*
>
> —Adrian Adolph Greenberg, 1942
>
> 99

Deborah Waxman *(West Hartford, CT)*, in 2014, became the first female rabbi and first lesbian to lead a Jewish congregation and seminary. She is president of the Reconstructionist Rabbinical College in Pennsylvania, a congregational union and seminary. Waxman came of age as the Jewish Conservative movement was moving toward giving Jewish girls the same opportunities as boys, regarding things such as education and bat mitzvah ceremonies. She holds an MA in Hebrew from the Reconstructionist Rabbinical College and a PhD in American Jewish history from Temple University.

Michael Wigglesworth *(Yorkshire, England)* moved to New Haven, Connecticut, at the age of seven and went on to become a prominent Puritan minister in the original American colonies. Wigglesworth struggled intensely with his homosexuality, especially while working as a tutor at Harvard. His life is well documented in the diaries he left behind. In one entry, he refers to himself as an "object of God's loathing"; in several others, he is agonized by a series of sexual dreams and nocturnal emissions that plagued him. He was also a poet, most successful with his work *The Day of Doom*, a rumination on God's judgment and the inevitability of most people going to hell.

📍 PLACES

The Northeast Women's Musical Retreat (NEWMR) *(Cornwall, CT)* was an annual music festival held in the Berkshires from 1981 to 2000 on Labor Day weekend. Christine Pattee, an activist with the New Haven Women's Liberation Movement, founded the festival with thirteen other women in 1981, basing it off the Michigan Womyn's Music Festival. Attendees chose between three levels of "Amazon camping" and were expected to bring their own wares for shared vegetarian meals. Maxine Feldman, Judy Sloan, and Alix Dobkin were among the inaugural performers.

The Park West *(Hartford, CT)* was the site of a series of 1971 protests after lesbian patrons were ejected from the gay bar for not dressing femininely. The Kalos Society, a local LGBT+ activist group, organized the protest, which lasted several days until the bar's management ceded to the group's demands for equal treatment.

The Primus House *(Hartford, CT)* was the home of Rebecca Primus, a Black school teacher in the 1800s. Growing up on 20 Wadsworth Street, where the house is located, Primus was born to a grocer father and a dressmaker mother. After the Civil War, high school education complete, Primus established a school for formerly enslaved people in Maryland, later renamed the Primus Institute. While in Hartford, Primus met Addie Brown, another free Black woman, and the two began a passionate relationship documented in their extensive written correspondences. Though both women married men, their affection for each other lasted until Brown died of tuberculosis at age twenty-nine. "If you was a man, what would things come to? They would come to something very quick," Brown wrote to Primus in 1865.

👤 PEOPLE

Elena Delle Donne *(Wilmington, DE)* is a professional basketball player, Olympic gold medalist, and children's book author. Delle Donne attended the University of Delaware and played basketball for the school's team, the Blue Hens, from 2009 to 2013. During this time, Delle Donne developed Lyme disease. Though occasionally slowed by the disease, she maintained a successful college basketball career and was drafted into the WNBA by the Chicago Sky in 2013. In 2016, Delle Donne won a gold medal at the Olympics, and that same year announced her engagement to her girlfriend, Amanda Clifton, in *Vogue*. Delle Donne uses her free time to support a number of causes, including the Lyme Research Alliance and Special Olympics. Since 2017, she has played for the Washington Mystics.

Jesse Ehrenfeld *(Wilmington, DE)* is a physician and combat veteran. Ehrenfeld earned a Bachelor of Science from Haverford College, an MD from the University of Chicago, and a Master of Public Health from Harvard University. While serving a tour in Afghanistan in 2014, Ehrenfeld worked on the short documentary *Transgender, at War and in Love*, which received a 2016 Emmy nomination. He currently practices at Vanderbilt University in Nashville, Tennessee, where he lives with his husband. He specializes in anesthesiology and clinical informatics.

Raúl Esparza *(Wilmington, DE)* is a singer and stage, television, and voice actor. Esparza received bachelor's degrees in drama and English from New York University's Tisch School of the Arts. Best known for portraying the New York Assistant District Attorney Rafael Barba in *Law & Order: Special Victims Unit*, he has been nominated for multiple Tony awards in his career, including Best Actor in a Play and Best Actor in a Musical. He has also narrated several audiobooks. Esparza came out as bisexual in 2006 in the *New York Times*.

Sarah McBride *(Wilmington, DE)* is a transgender rights activist and the National Press Secretary of the Human Rights Campaign. During her final term as president of the American University student government

> *So many artists I admire are bisexual. I knew a lot of gay men growing up. There didn't seem to be anything wrong with it as long as it was someone else, but not me.*
>
> —Raúl Esparza, *New York Times*, 2006

Sarah McBride

in 2012, she came out as transgender in the student newspaper the *Eagle*. After graduation, McBride became an influential activist for transgender rights. In 2013, Delaware passed the Gender Nondiscrimination Act, guaranteeing equal legal and employment protections to all people regardless of gender identity. During the signing ceremony, McBride was thanked for her advocacy of the Act. McBride made headlines again when she became the first openly transgender person to speak at a major party convention by addressing the 2016 Democratic National Convention.

Marshall "Kirk" McKusick *(Wilmington, DE)* is a computer scientist best known for his work on the program BSD UNIX. McKusick received a BS from Cornell University as well as two MS degrees and a PhD in computer science from the University of California–Berkeley. His work on BSD UNIX at Berkeley made it possible for computers to efficiently locate files after they have been saved and closed. McKusick's husband, Eric Allman, is an influential programmer in his own right and developed the technology that made it possible to send files between computers over email. McKusick and Allman are open about their relationship and support and advocate for gay individuals in their field, often wearing pink triangles on their badges at conferences to show their support.

Aubrey Plaza *(Wilmington, DE)* is an actor, comedian, and producer best known for her role of April Ludgate on the sitcom *Parks and Recreation* from 2009 to 2015. After attending the Tisch School of the Arts at New York University, Plaza began her acting career by

Aubrey Plaza

💡 QUEER FACTS

Delaware's first openly gay mayor was John Buchheit, elected in Delaware City in 2011. Running as an independent, he defeated the small town's sitting mayor by thirty votes, with a total of 198 votes. Buchheit and his partner own the restaurant Crabby Dick's, a facetious seafood chain serving items such as crab balls and Seaman sauce, located in Delaware City and Rehoboth Beach.

Delaware legalized same-sex marriage via legislative action on July 1, 2013. Civil unions had been legal in the state since 2011; by 2013, Delaware was the eleventh state to legalize gay marriage. HB 75 passed in the state's General Assembly by 23–18 and in the Senate by 12–9.

The first legal victory against LGBT+ discrimination in Delaware was won by James Welch in 1992. Welch, a cofounder of the Gay & Lesbian Alliance of Delaware and nurse who led the state's first HIV/AIDS testing program in the 1980s, was barred from the position of AIDS director within Delaware Health and Social Services. As a result of the ruling, DHSS added sexual orientation to the classes protected by the state.

Sterilization was legalized in Delaware in 1923, primarily targeting people with mental illnesses or disabilities. Delaware amended the law in 1929 to require sterilization for repeat criminals of three times or more; at the time, sodomy was considered an illegal act. The state had performed 783 sterilizations by 1948. While sterilization has become unpopular over time and sodomy has been legal since 1972, involuntary sterilization laws still remain in Delaware.

> *Unfortunately, LGBTI health is just not something that historically has been taught in medical schools. And when I got to Vanderbilt, there was a desire on the part of our students to learn more and be better prepared to serve patients. And so the school institution embraced that and said, you know, we ought to be doing better. It is a disservice to our students and to our patients not to provide the right kinds of opportunities to integrate this content into our training programs.*
>
> —Jesse Ehrenfeld, interview with Fei Wu, *Fei's World*, 2017

joining the Upright Citizens Brigade Theater. Plaza has starred in several major motion pictures, including *Scott Pilgrim vs. the World*, *The To Do List*, and *Ingrid Goes West*. In a 2016 interview with *The Advocate*, Plaza came out as bisexual, stating that she grew up knowing several LGBT+ people in her family.

 # PLACES

The ACLU of Delaware *(Wilmington, DE)* was established in 1961 as a local affiliate of the national ACLU. Its programs focus on legal and legislative advocacy, as well as media outreach, to mobilize voters and legislators against bills and other efforts that threaten civil liberties. The ACLU-DE's website includes a Know Your Rights page, which spotlights a person's rights while attending protests, for example, or while simply existing as an LGBT+ student. In 2018, the ACLU-DE campaigned against proposed changes to Regulation 225, a nondiscrimination policy that required parental approval for students to self-identify their gender and race. Although the amended regulation initially passed, it was shelved in August 2018.

AIDS Delaware *(Wilmington and Rehoboth Beach, DE)* is the state's first and largest AIDS Service Organization. Originally founded in 1982 as the Gay and Lesbian Alliance of Delaware (GLAD), an organization active in HIV prevention and support, it changed names in 1984. AIDS Delaware serves people living with HIV/AIDS with a yearly AIDS walk, case management services, status testing, support groups, and more.

CAMP Rehoboth *(Rehoboth Beach, DE)* is a nonprofit LGBT+ service organization based in a year-round gay resort and beach town. It strives for community well-being by providing the education and tools necessary to promote civil rights, develop space for community organizations, and foster economic growth via fundraising for local nonprofits. Since its founding in 1991, the organization has been volunteer-run.

The Delaware Human Relations Commission *(Wilmington, DE)* enforces fair housing and equal accommodations. The agency protects against all forms of identity discrimination, including national origin, familial status, disability, age, and source of income. Among its many services, the commission mediates identity-related disputes, including hate crimes and police conflicts. It also investigates housing discrimination complaints, conducts fair housing and equal accommodations seminars, and participates in community events to promote fair housing.

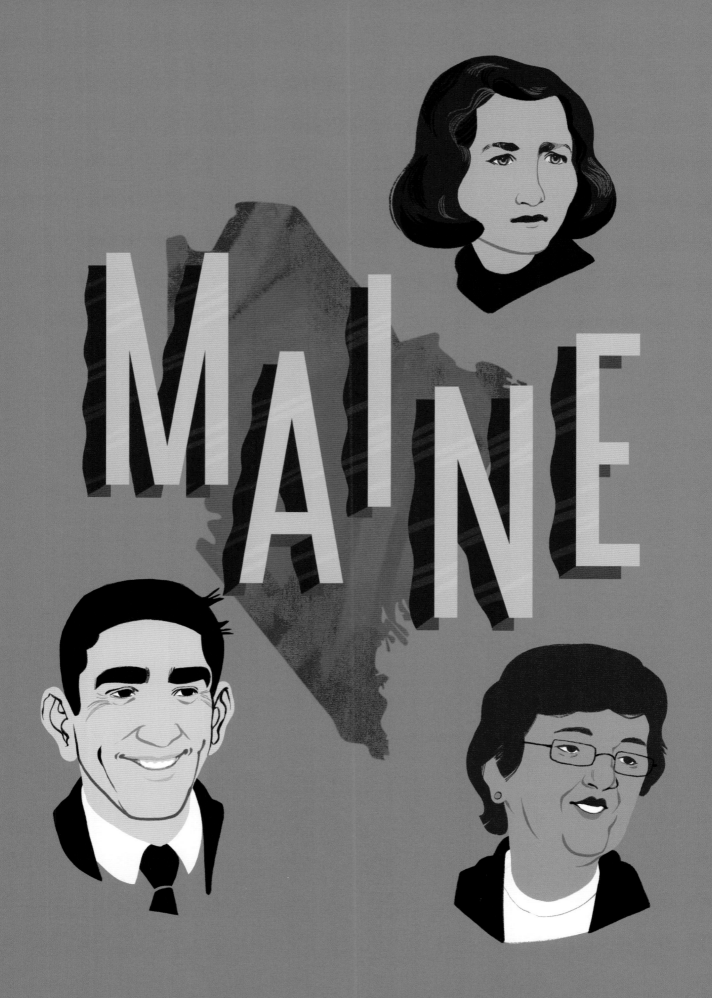

PEOPLE

> **For me, being a gay leader is about more than coming out of the closet. It's about helping the community move forward. Today, as the youngest gay legislator in the county, I'm keenly aware of what it takes to get to this point.**
>
> —Ryan Fecteau, accepting the Youth Innovator of the Year Award at TrevorLIVE, 2015

Ian Harvie

Ryan Fecteau *(Biddeford, ME)* is a Democratic politician and member of the Maine House of Representatives. Elected in 2014 at the age of twenty-one, Fecteau is the youngest openly gay state legislator in the country. Fecteau completed a degree in political science and theology at the Catholic University of America in Washington, DC, before running for office. His legislative work has focused on senior citizens, strengthening public education, and improving economic opportunities. Now in his third term, Fecteau represents District Eleven and serves as the Assistant House Majority Leader. He also runs the Perkins Cove Pottery Shop in Ogunquit, Maine.

Ian Harvie *(Portland, ME)* is an actor and stand-up comedian. After landing his first stand-up gigs in 2002, he moved to Los Angeles four years later to be a regular opener for the comedian Margaret Cho. Though he knew he was transgender at an early age, Harvie has said he didn't have the language for his identity for many years. As such, he came out to his parents twice: first as gay and again as transgender in his thirties. In 2017, Harvie starred in a video letter to Hollywood written by Jen Richards that advocated for fair casting practices for transgender roles. Now a solo comedian and television actor, Harvie's comedy challenges the traditionally masculine and sex-centered themes of stand-up. He made his acting debut in 2014 as Dale on the Amazon TV series *Transparent*.

Donna Loring *(Penobscot Indian Island Reservation, ME)* is an author, radio broadcaster, and tribal representative of the Penobscot Nation. Loring attended Glen Christian Academy before joining the Women's Army Corps in 1967; Loring she served as a communications specialist at Long Binh Post during the Vietnam War. She later attended the Maine Criminal Justice Academy, serving as a police chief and the first female director of security at Bowdoin College. In 1998, she became the Penobscot Nations Representative to the Maine state legislature for seven years. During that time, she sponsored a 2001 law requiring the teaching of Native American history and culture in Maine schools. After leaving the legislature, she became president of the educational nonprofit Seven Eagles Media Productions.

> We've had such a long history of being marginalized and being sort of looked down on, and the fact is, if people knew who we were and the contributions we've made to this state and the talents we all have . . . There's just so much that the majority of society does not know about us.
>
> —Donna Loring on tribal representation in the legislature, *Bangor Daily News*, 2008

Donna Loring

Edna St. Vincent Millay

before attending Vassar college. During her career in New York, Millay expressed her bisexuality openly and wrote controversial poems depicting female sexuality. In 1923, Millay married Eugen Boissevain, an outspoken feminist who gave up his professional pursuits to help manage Millay's growing literary career. Millay died of a heart attack in 1950 at the age of fifty-eight. Her home in Austerlitz, New York, is a designated national historical landmark.

Edna St. Vincent Millay *(Rockland, ME)* was one of the most successful and renowned poets of the twentieth century, known for works such as *A Few Figs from Thistles* and *The Harp-Weaver* and the play *Two Slatterns and a King*. As a child, Millay was described as a tomboy and often asked to be called Vincent. Millay was raised by her mother, Cora, who divorced Millay's father due to his financial irresponsibility. Cora looked after the cultural education of her daughters, and Millay won several poetry awards for young people

Howard Solomon *(Bowdoinham, ME)* is an artist, academic, and former professor of history and LGBT+ studies. Solomon taught some of the first college history courses on sexuality, beginning at New York University and later at Tufts University in Massachusetts. His research and classes often focused on marginalized sexual identities. Upon retirement in 2009, Solomon began his career as a found-object and collage artist, examining the ways in which social views of religion, myth, sexuality, and gender affect our perception of them. His work has been shown throughout Maine

QUEER FACTS

Charles Howard was murdered in July 1984 by three teenagers. While yelling homophobic threats and slurs, the teenagers chased Howard and threw him over the State Street Bridge in Bangor, Maine. Howard could not swim and drowned in the Kenduskeag Stream. This event sparked outcry from the gay rights movement and led to an increase in civil rights activism in the state. Howard's murder has been memorialized in several works of literature, including a poem by Mark Doty and a scene in Stephen King's *It* that depicts a similar hate crime.

Doe v. Regional School Unit 26, sometimes known as *Doe v. Clenchy*, was a 2014 Maine Supreme Court case—the first state court ruling protecting transgender students' rights to access bathrooms matching their gender identities. Nicole Maines, a transgender teenager from Portland, was barred access to the female bathroom in her middle school—and later, her high school—due to parental complaints. With the support of the Maine Human Rights Commission and the GLTBQ and Legal Advocates and Defenders (GLAD), Maines's family sued the school district. In June 2014, the Maine Supreme Court ruled that Maines's rights had been violated under the Human Rights Act.

Pride Portland is a ten-day annual festival hosted by Pride Northwest, a nonprofit that encourages positive diversity and promotes education on the history and accomplishments of the LGBT+ community. Pride Portland is the largest LGBT+ celebration in the region. The festival is volunteer-run and brings together people from the greater Portland area to raise awareness of LGBT+ issues, foster community, and celebrate the accomplishments of the LGBT+ movement.

and Massachusetts, and he splits his time between his hometown and New Orleans.

# PLACES

Blackstones *(Portland, ME)* is the city's oldest gay bar. Opened in 1987 ("Hangovers installed and serviced since 1987," its website declares), Blackstones quickly became a social center for Portland's LGBT+ community. The bar is an active supporter of Pride Portland!, the organization that hosts the city's annual pride festival, and has hosted fundraisers and food and toy drives for the city.

"Camp" Camp *(Kezar Falls, ME)* is a summer camp for LGBT+ adults. It includes social events and traditional camp activities such as mountain biking, art classes, sailing, canoeing, and softball. "Camp" Camp was started in 1997 by Bill Cole, a former camp director and volunteer in the American Camping Association. After attending a men's weekend retreat, Cole came up with the idea for a camp retreat for gay adults. Since its founding, the camp's attendance has risen from eighty campers per year to several hundred.

Maine TransNet *(Portland, ME)* is a nonprofit that facilitates support groups for transgender people and allies throughout Maine. As part of its mission, Maine TransNet provides social networking avenues and public dialogue surrounding the needs and rights of transgender individuals. The organization also provides training, advocacy, and education on transgender culture and sexual health to the community.

Ogunquit, Maine, is an artists' colony town in York County that has become a regular vacation destination for LGBT+ tourists. Ogunquit is home to several LGBT-owned hotels, restaurants, bars, and nightclubs. It also claims one of the top-rated beaches in the country. In 2016, Ogunquit was hailed by *Bloomberg* magazine as a premier vacation destination in Maine.

MARYLAND

👤 PEOPLE

Jack Andraka *(Crownsville, MD)* is notable as the inventor of a tool to detect pancreatic, ovarian, and lung cancer, which he created in 2013, when he was sixteen. After a relative died from pancreatic cancer, Andraka resolved to find a way to detect cancers in their earlier stages. He researched independently and submitted the idea proposal to many scientists, hoping he would convince one to let him use their lab. Anirban Maitra, a pathologist from Johns Hopkins University, was the only scientist to respond. The tool won Andraka the grand prize at the 2012 Intel International Science and Engineering Fair. A local newspaper dubbed him a "gay wunderkind," and he went on to study engineering at Stanford University, where he won a Harry S. Truman scholarship in 2018.

Jack Andraka

Kevin Clash *(Baltimore, MD)* is a puppeteer best known for his characters like Elmo from *Sesame Street* and multiple Muppets such as Clifford and Leon in *The Jim Henson Hour*. Clash was interested in puppeteering from an early age. His mother taught him to sew and his father helped him build sets, which sparked some criticism from his mother's friends. Clash went on to become the senior Muppet coordinator for *Sesame Street* as well as a coproducer for the "Elmo's World" segment. Clash, as a Black man, likes to defy preconceptions people have of professional puppeteers. He is the subject of a 2011 documentary called *Being Elmo: A Puppeteer's Journey.* Clash won one Primetime Emmy Award and twenty-seven Daytime Emmy Awards in his

Kevin Clash

Sesame Street is the epitome of children's television. It has continued to maintain the successful structure that was established in the beginning. Through its amazing research department, teaching has been made fun. This, the heart and humor works, for children and adults alike; that's why I'm very honored to be a part of it.

—Kevin Clash, *Sesame Street* press release, 2010

career; he left *Sesame Street* in 2012. He came out as gay in November 2012.

Divine (Harris Milstead) *(Baltimore, MD)* was an actor and drag queen. Milstead struggled with his weight all his life, but as Divine, he was embraced as an iconic and campy performer. He led an extravagant lifestyle as a young adult, throwing many parties and charging all his expenses to his father. Milstead destroyed the invoices before his father had a chance to see them. Milstead then began to star in his former classmate John Waters's films, including *Female Trouble* (1974) and *Pink Flamingos* (1972), raunchy comedic roles that displeased his parents and caused them to disown him, socially and financially. Milstead also released a number of albums over his career, including *The Story So Far . . .* (1984) and *Maid in England* (1988). At the peak of his career, he starred in *Hairspray* (1988) as Edna Turnblad and Arvin Hodgepile, but died from a heart attack two weeks after the film's release. Milstead always thought of himself not only as a drag queen but as an actor, saying, "I don't do Judy Garland or Mae West, and I'm not a female impersonator. I'm an actor."

Maya Marcel-Keyes *(Darnestown, MD)* is a queer activist and daughter of the conservative politician and multi-time presidential and congressional candidate Alan Keyes. In 2005, at the age of nineteen, Marcel-Keyes spoke at a Equality Maryland rally, her first public appearance as an out activist. Having been disowned by her own parents after coming out, Marcel-Keyes dedicated her activism to LGBT+ homeless youth. "[Y]ou can't overlook the fact that there are kids who are fighting just to stay alive and they are a big part of the community. It's a massive problem that never gets attention," she told *Metro Weekly* in 2005.

Angel McCoughtry *(Baltimore, MD)* is a WNBA athlete and Olympian. McCoughtry graduated from the University of Louisville holding the record for the highest scorer and rebounder on its women's basketball team. In 2009, she joined the Atlanta Dream as the number-one pick in the WNBA draft. She won two gold medals on the USA women's basketball team—one in 2012 and one in 2016. McCoughtry came out on social media in 2015, saying, "All I know is that love is a great feeling and that God is Love."

Yes, we been discriminated against! We lost friends! Family members are upset! They said I disgraced my religion! One thing I do know is that LOVE is a great feeling!

—Angel McCoughtry, Instagram, 2015

DeRay Mckesson

DeRay Mckesson *(Baltimore, MD)* is a former school administrator and activist instrumental in the Black Lives Matter movement in Ferguson, Baltimore, Milwaukee, and New York. After the 2014 murder of Michael Brown, Mckesson drove from Minneapolis to Ferguson to participate in the protests and live-tweeted his experience. He recorded himself being tear-gassed, the arrival of armored police vehicles, and the shots fired outside the Ferguson Police Department. With other activists, he helped publish the newsletter *This Is the Movement*, which independently reported the events in Ferguson. Mckesson used his Twitter account to organize protests, make political commentary, and tweet inspirational messages. In 2018, Mckesson published *On the Other Side of Freedom: The Case for Hope*, a memoir of his involvement with BLM. One of the impetuses for the book, he says, was his sexuality: "I know that I'm a gay black man every time I come into a space, and what does that mean to be in movement spaces or other spaces where people are homophobic, but like me. I wanted to write about that."

Shane Ortega *(Patuxent River, MD)* is the one of the first openly transgender people to serve in the military, serving in the army's Twenty-Fifth Infantry Division in Oahu, Hawaii. As of 2015, he could not renew his flight certification because although his government-issued IDs state he is male, the army still records him as female. Ortega has served in two combat tours in Iraq and one combat tour in Afghanistan. Ortega's mother, a lesbian, also served in the military under Don't Ask, Don't Tell, and Ortega is an advocate for the policy's repeal. Ortega says his father and uncle were also servicemembers, who instilled in him the will to serve, even with the military's official ban on transgender soldiers.

Felicia Pearson *(Baltimore, MD)* is an actress and rapper best known for playing a character of the same name on *The Wire*. Pearson has also appeared in *Chi-Raq, Anthony Bourdain: No Reservations*, and *Love & Hip Hop*. Her 2007 memoir, *Grace After Midnight*, covers her difficult upbringing in foster care as well as her five years in prison for second-degree murder when she was fifteen. Pearson is open about her sexuality and public about her relationship with J. Adrienne on *Love & Hip Hop*. After the murder of Freddie Gray in Baltimore, Pearson spoke out about police violence in her home community, condemning the city for closures of schools and recreation centers in Black neighborhoods, saying that these issues "should be personal to everyone."

Adrienne Rich *(Baltimore, MD)* was a feminist poet and essayist. Her first collection of poetry, *A Change of World* (1951), was selected by W. H. Auden for the Younger Poets prize at Yale. While it was well regarded, it wasn't until the 1960s that Rich's work took on a more confrontational tone, critiquing women's role in society, racial injustice, and the Vietnam War. In 1970, she left her husband and later began a relationship with the Jamaica-born writer and editor Michelle Cliff. Rich was offered but refused the National Medal of the Arts in 1997, protesting that art "is incompatible with the cynical politics of [the Clinton] administration." Along with Audre Lorde and Dr. Gloria I. Joseph, Rich cofounded the Women's Coalition of St. Croix.

Darren Star *(Potomac, MD)* is a writer, producer, and director of TV programs such as *Sex and the City, Melrose Place*, and *Beverly Hills, 90210*. Star is Jewish and has traveled to Israel to learn about their television industry

> *I wanted to tell relevant stories. On 90210, Kelly dated a boy who struggled with his sexuality. It was a small storyline, but it was important for me to start that conversation early in the series.*
>
> —Darren Star, *Variety*, 2015

Darren Star

with a group of other Jewish creatives from Hollywood. He likes to write about groups of friends who support each other and share some common experience. Star has not been afraid to criticize the television industry, noting how common it is for networks to cancel shows before the audience has a chance to build a relationship with the show's characters by saying, "None of the shows I did were big hits in week one, week two, week three; they took a while."

Anne Strasdauskas *(Baltimore, MD)* was a Baltimore County Sheriff from 1998 to 2002, one of the first openly lesbian sheriffs in the country. In the 1998 election, Strasdauskas defeated the incumbent, Norman M. Pepersack, who had fired her a year prior when she worked as a police officer because she turned her radio in four days late. During the election, Pepersack released confidential documents about Strasdauskas's time as a police officer, and she took him to court. Two weeks before the election, thieves stole her pickup truck, removed the campaign placards from the outside, searched the interior, and rubbed it clean of fingerprints. The townspeople did not respond well to the corrupt politics and elected Strasdauskas as county sheriff. She served until 2002, when the sheriff's department released a report of twenty-three misconduct allegations that dated back to 1990, although Strasdauskas has denied many of them.

John Waters *(Baltimore, MD)* is a film director and writer best known for *Hairspray* (1988) and *Pink Flamingos* (1972). Known for his kitschy style, Waters has been referred to by admirers as the "pope of trash." Waters met Harris Milstead (a.k.a. Divine) when they were teenagers and formed a creative partnership that lasted until Milstead's death in 1988. Waters hosts an annual Christmas stage performance called *A John Waters Christmas,* where he gives his insights and opinions on the holiday. Waters said he sends 1,900 signed Christmas cards every year, and that "if you ever sell mine on eBay, not only will you never get one again, my friends will burn down your house on Christmas Eve." The state of Maryland hosted a John Waters day on February 16, 1985, and a John Waters Week in Baltimore in 1988. In 2018, the Baltimore Museum of Art hosted an exhibit called "Indecent Exposure" in honor of Waters's work. Waters has said that he's never afraid

> *It wasn't until I started reading and found books they wouldn't let us read in school that I discovered you could be insane and happy and have a good life without being like everybody else.*
>
> —John Waters, interview with the *Onion, The Tenacity of the Cockroach,* 2012

John Waters

to try something new, because that's what his audience expects of him, but, "It's easy to shock people. It's much harder to make 'em laugh."

Y-Love (Yitz Jordan) *(Baltimore, MD)* is a hip-hop musician. His songs feature a variety of languages, including Arabic, Hebrew, Aramaic, and Latin. A former Hasidic Jew, though neither of his parents are Jewish, Jordan began to practice freestyling to help him memorize religious texts while he studied at Ohr Somayach yeshiva in Jerusalem. One of his former rabbis, Meir Fund, told Jordan that his music would

QUEER FACTS

Former Navy SEAL and trans activist Kristin Beck ran for Congress in Maryland in 2016. Originally from Pennsylvania, Beck served as a SEAL for twenty years and won twenty-nine medals, including a Purple Heart. She did not come out while in the military because she feared retaliation, although she had a small boat off the coast of Coronado, where she dressed in women's clothing between deployments. She married a woman, and together they had two children. When Beck came out to her wife, she left Beck and took their children with her. In 2011, Beck retired from her military career and decided to live as her true self. Beck is the subject of the 2014 CNN documentary *Lady Valor*, which details her military past and her coming out, including a scene where she confirmed her transgender identity on *Anderson Cooper 360*. Although she lost her congressional campaign, her activism didn't stop there—in 2017, Beck publicly shamed President Trump for his announcement of a ban on transgender service members in the military. Beck relates her journey as a transgender person to something many people go through on a smaller scale: a conflict of identity. "You get this pressure to be one thing or another, to be binary. In a way, it's not that different from anyone. My conflict is just a lot more visual."

Giovanni's Room Open Mic is a reoccurring event hosted by the Gay, Lesbian, Bisexual, and Transgender Community Center of Baltimore. It is a safe space for gay vendors (including chefs and artisans) and performers to showcase their skills and support one another. The open mic occurs the first Friday of every month and features comedians, dancers, singers, and rappers.

Margaret L. "Maggie" McIntosh is a politician in the Democratic Party and a former public school teacher for the Baltimore City district. Originally from Kansas, McIntosh first joined the Maryland House of Delegates in 1992 before becoming the first woman in Maryland to serve as the majority leader in the House of Delegates. McIntosh received multiple awards for her work as an effective legislator, including the Dorothy Beatty Memorial Service Award from the Women's Law Center and the Chair's Award from the Mautner Project, an organization dedicated to lesbian health.

Maryland's statewide LGBT+ protections have increased dramatically since the start of the twenty-first century. The state banned discrimination based on sexual orientation in 2001. In 2012, voters legalized same-sex marriage, and the law became effective in 2013. The year 2012 also brought a ban on housing discrimination on the basis of sexual orientation and gender identity. In 2014, the state banned discrimination based on gender identity. Maryland also made gay conversion therapy illegal for those under eighteen, effective in 2018.

The death of Marcus Rogers, a transgender activist, occurred six days after his Baltimore apartment was set on fire in 2006. In his autopsy, doctors determined that it was not only the fire, but blunt force trauma that led to his death. Prosecutors on the case released the suspect, Zukael T. Stephens, due to a clerical error that dropped the murder charges; he was later re-arrested by police. A jury ruled that there was not enough evidence to convict Stephens of the murder, though surveillance footage placed him at the scene of the crime and showed him rushing to leave the building moments before people realized there was a fire.

The LGBTQ Heritage Initiative began in 2011, providing tours and education functions on places of historical significance to Baltimore's LGBT+ community. It supported the publication of the book *LGBT Baltimore* and has held walking tours of Charles Village and Mount Vernon. It has partnered with Baltimore Black Pride, the GLCCB, and Baltimore Queerstories for various exhibits and events.

The murders of Mia Henderson and Kandy Hall occurred in Baltimore six weeks apart in the summer of 2014. The women were both Black and transgender, and were stabbed to death. Henderson was the sister of Reggie Bullock, who at the time played for the NBA's LA Clippers; she was murdered just five miles away from where Hall was killed. The original police report for Hall's murder referred to her with male pronouns, which Aaron Merki, director of the Free State Legal Project, described as inappropriate. The murders sparked local conversations about police relations with the LGBT+ community and the vulnerability of Black transgender people to violent crimes, particularly in the Baltimore area, where another transgender woman named Kelly Young was shot to death a year earlier.

never spiritually enrich anybody; Jordan responded that banning any genre of music does not benefit the Jewish community. In 2008, Jordan released his first album, *This is Babylon.* He came out as gay in 2012 and said he struggled to reconcile his sexuality with his religious past until he realized, as he said, "It's God's will to be gay." Jordan's music has a following in Israel, and he hopes it helps young Jewish people embrace their identities.

 PLACES

Cafe Hon and Hon Bar *(Baltimore, MD)* are located in the same building and owned by the same people. The kitschy decor was inspired in part by John Waters and his love for Baltimore; the outside of the restaurant is adorned with a giant pink flamingo that spans two levels of the building. Waters featured Thirty-Sixth Street, the site of the restaurant, in several of his films, including *Hairspray.* Cafe Hon hosts the annual HonFest, an homage to the culture of Baltimore. The owner of the cafe, Denise Whiting, has trademarked the word "hon," although John Waters has denounced HonFest, saying that the term is "used up. It's condescending now."

The Gay, Lesbian, Bisexual and Transgender Community Center of Baltimore *(Baltimore, MD)* is a nonprofit that catalogs local LGBT+ history and supports educational and social functions. It has its own LGBT+ history project, a collection of videos of LGBT+ community members who describe the area's LGBT+ history and their activism. The GLCCB also organizes volunteers for Baltimore Pride, offers HIV testing and support groups for those struggling with substance issues, and hosts family nights and open mics.

Johns Hopkins Hospital *(Baltimore, MD)* is where sex researcher Dr. John Money conducted the infamous 1967 "John/Joan" case study, an effort to prove that gender is the result of nurture, not nature. The experiment involved a pair of twin eight-month-old boys, David and Brian Reimer. David had received a botched circumcision; under Money's supervision, the child was castrated, given cosmetically female genitalia, and raised as a girl. The twins saw Money for regular appointments as they aged, and were instructed to enact sexual positions with each other and with Money in an effort to train David early into his sexual identity—methodology that is nowadays considered assault. Money hailed his experiment as a success, but Reimer asserted his identity as a male when he turned fourteen. In 2004, Reimer died by suicide at the age of thirty-eight after decades of identity-related depression and struggle. Money died two years later at eighty-four, having achieved a number of awards for his work, though his research is largely criticized as intersex infant genital mutilation today.

Leon's Backroom *(Baltimore, MD)* is the one of the oldest gay bars in Maryland. It opened in 1957 and has since been visited by multiple celebrities, such as Joan Rivers and Liberace. When the bar first opened, men would be asked at the door if they were a friend of Dorothy, a code phrase used to identify gay patrons. Prior to its 1957 iteration, the bar had been running since the 1890s and survived as a speakeasy during Prohibition; it takes its names from its 1930s owner, Leon Lampe. After World War II, the space became a haven for artists and beatniks, a mixed gay and straight crowd.

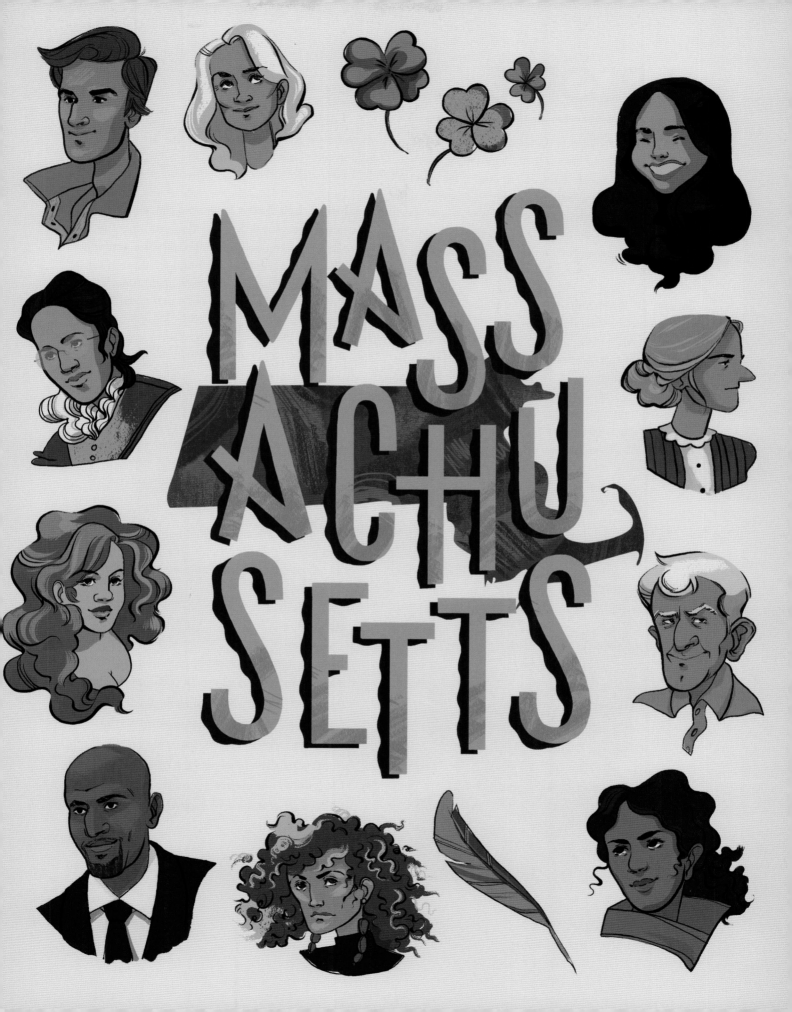

👤 PEOPLE

John Amaechi *(Boston, MA)* was the first NBA player to come out as gay. Amaechi disclosed his identity in his 2007 memoir *Man in the Middle* and discussed his career interactions with homophobic NBA players and figures. Amaechi began his basketball career playing for Penn State in the early 1990s, then went on to play for the Cleveland Cavaliers, Orlando Magic, and Utah Jazz.

Susan B. Anthony *(Adams, MA)* was a women's suffrage pioneer. Serving as president of the National American Woman Suffrage Association (now known as the League of Women Voters), she paved the way for the 1920 passage of the Nineteenth Amendment, which granted women the right to vote. Anthony was an abolitionist who was part of the Underground Railroad, working with Harriet Tubman and friend Frederick Douglass. Historians have suggested that Anthony had romantic relationships with women, including her longtime friend and fellow activist Elizabeth Cady

Stanton. Her 1906 New York Times obituary described how in the 1850s Anthony had attempted to popularize bloomers—a Turkish style of dress with visible pants underneath—but abandoned it after being subject to ridicule.

Katharine Lee Bates *(Falmouth, MA)* was an American songwriter best known for authoring the anthem "America the Beautiful" in 1893. She graduated from Wellesley College in 1880 and went on to teach there. Bates and her partner, who lived together for twenty-five years, have often been described as "intimate lesbian partners," while others describe their arrangement as a Boston marriage. Bates was inducted into the Songwriters Hall of Fame in 1970.

Leonard Bernstein *(Lawrence, MA)* was a composer and conductor best known for *West Side Story* and for his tenure as the musical director of the New York Philharmonic. Bernstein dabbled in many genres, from orchestra to ballet and opera. While Bernstein was known by some to be gay, he still married a woman, Felicia Montealegre, a Chilean actress. "You are a homosexual and you may never change . . . I am willing to accept you as you are, without being a martyr," she wrote to him in the early 1950s as a plea for them to marry. Bernstein briefly abandoned Montealegre for

John Amaechi

One day some of the other teachers and I decided to go on a trip to 14,000-foot Pike's Peak. We hired a prairie wagon. Near the top we had to leave the wagon and go the rest of the way on mules. I was very tired. But when I saw the view, I felt great joy. All the wonder of America seemed displayed there, with the sea-like expanse.

—Katherine Lee Bates

Leonard Bernstein

another man when she was diagnosed with cancer later in life. He died in 1990 at the age of seventy-two.

Holly Boswell *(Washington, DC)* created the transgender symbol in 1993 and is credited as being the first person to coin the term "transgender." She also founded the Phoenix Transgender Support Group in Ashville, North Carolina, and the Tree House, a retreat center for gender and spirituality, in Black Mountain, North Carolina. Boswell wrote several essays on gender, including "The Transgender Alternative" (1990), "The Transgender Paradigm Shift toward Free Expression" (1997), and "The Spirit of Transgender" (2000). She died in 2017 at age sixty-six.

John Boswell *(Boston, MA)* was a gay historian at Yale University. His books *Same-Sex Unions in Pre-Modern Europe* (1994) and *Christianity, Social Tolerance, and Homosexuality* (1980) were widely regarded for their scholarship on the intersection between Christianity and homosexuality; the latter won a National Book Award in 1981. Boswell received his PhD at Harvard in 1975; while teaching at Yale, he helped found what later became the Research Fund for Lesbian and Gay Studies. Boswell either read or spoke

seventeen languages, including Icelandic and Persian. He died of AIDS complications in 1994 at forty-seven.

Marie Equi *(New Bedford, MA)*, who lived from 1872 to 1952, was a medical doctor of the Old West. Equi was also an anarchist, and performed abortions and provided birth control decades before either was legal. She was eventually jailed for sedition and for protesting World War I. Equi allegedly was enamored with birth control activist Margaret Sanger and sent her many one-sided letters. Eventually, Equi met Harriet Frances Speckart, with whom she adopted and raised a child.

Raffi Freedman-Gurspan *(Intibucá, Honduras)* was appointed to the White House staff by President Obama in 2015, the first openly transgender person to fill such a role. Raised in Brookline, Massachusetts, by an adopted Jewish family, she was also appointed by Obama to the US Holocaust Memorial Council. Freedman-Gurspan has worked for the National Center for Transgender Equality and as an LGBT Liaison for the city of Somerville, Massachusetts.

Angelina Weld Grimké *(Boston, MA)* was a poet and playwright. Her father, Archibald Grimké, was the vice president of the NAACP, and her great aunts, Angelina and Sarah Grimké, were prominent abolitionists and suffragettes. Growing up in a mixed-race family of civil rights and gender equality activists prepared Grimké for a literary career alongside famous creatives of the Harlem Renaissance. Grimké's most famous work, *Rachel*, protested racial violence and was written on behalf of the NAACP. Though little is known of her private relationships, she is widely considered to have been a lesbian or bisexual, as she often wrote love poems to female subjects.

Boston marriages describe a relationship wherein two women cohabitate, often (but not always) asexually. The term arose from the 1886 Henry James novel *The Bostonians*, which portrays two wealthy women who live together in Boston, Massachusetts. In the nineteenth and early twentieth centuries, many lesbian relationships were publicly cloaked as Boston marriages to avoid speculation.

Hurley v. Irish American Gay, Lesbian, and Bisexual Group of Boston was a 1995 US Supreme Court case ruling that allowed the exclusion of LGBT+ participation in the St. Patrick's Day parade as a matter of free speech. In 1993, the GLIB was barred from participating in a Boston-area St. Patricks' Day parade held by the South Boston Allied War Veterans Council. After the GLIB sued, several courts ruled that the Veterans Council had a right to exclude the GLIB, as the group's message conflicted with the messaging of the private group in charge of the event. After the ruling, the Veterans Council did not allow LGBT+ marchers to participate in the parade until 2015. The Council briefly reversed course in 2017, but reopened to LGBT+ members within several days due to negative backlash.

Intersex Awareness Day marks the anniversary of a demonstration held in Boston on October 26, 1996. Activists from the former Intersex Society of North America attended an American Academy of Pediatrics conference to share their experiences and denounce nonconsensual genital surgery. Intersex Awareness Day was first founded in 2004 by Betsy Driver and Emi Koyama, and has since spread in recognition across the world. Intersex Solidarity Day was founded in 2005 and is held on November 8.

Massachusetts legalized same-sex marriage in 2003, the first state to do so, following the ruling of *Goodridge v. Department of Public Health.* Mitt Romney, then governor of Massachusetts, immediately called for a constitutional amendment to define marriage has only between a man and woman, but none arose. It would be years before another state legalized same-sex marriage—Connecticut was the second, following in 2008.

Wicked Queer is an annual LGBT+ film festival hosted annually at theaters throughout the Boston area. Formerly known as the Boston LGBT+ Film Festival, the event was founded in 1984 by film programmer George Mansour. It survives today, completely staffed by volunteers, to the benefit of all levels of film lovers.

Rita Hester *(Boston, MA)* was a Black transgender woman. On November 28, 1998, Hester was found on the floor of her apartment, stabbed twenty times in the chest. She later died at the hospital due to cardiac arrest. Her murder devastated the Boston transgender and Black LGBT+ communities, and inspired what is now the Transgender Day of Remembrance. TDOR takes place annually on November 20 to memorialize those who have been killed as a result of suicide and transphobic hate crimes.

Piper Kerman *(Boston, MA)* is a bisexual woman and author of the bestselling 2010 memoir *Orange is the New Black*. In 2013, the memoir was adapted as a Netflix show of the same name, which went on to win several Emmys. *Orange is the New Black* recounts Kerman's romantic involvement with a heroin dealer for whom Kerman laundered money and trafficked drugs. She pleaded guilty and served a thirteen-month sentence in a minimum-security prison. Since her release, she has advocated on behalf of women in prisons as a board member of the Women's Prison Association, PEN America Writing for Justice Fellowship, and more.

PLACES

The History Project *(Boston, MA)*, founded in 1980, is a volunteer-run organization that seeks to research and document the history of the Massachusetts LGBT+ community. It hosts up to twenty online and physical exhibits per year, such as *Black & Gay in Black & White*, which features the work of Boston-area Black LGBT+ photographers. In 1998, the History Project published *Improper Bostonians*, a book of influential local LGBT+ icons.

interACT *(Sudbury, MA)* fights for the legal rights of intersex children. Founded in 2006 as Advocates for Informed Choice, the organization stands firmly against intersex infant genital mutilation. Its website provides resources on intersex research, medical policies, and court cases, as well as brochures and information targeted to teachers, friends, parents, and doctors. Read more about interACT's executive director, Kimberly Zieselman, under Vermont.

Playland Café *(Boston, MA)*, opened in 1937, was Boston's oldest gay bar before it closed in 1998. From the 1960s to the 1970s, its neighborhood, a district known for its adult entertainment as much as its crime and prostitution, was nicknamed the Combat

Provincetown, Massachusetts

Zone. Robert David Sullivan, a reporter for the *Boston Globe*, remembered the Playland Café for its "sketchy clientele, banged-up piano, and year-round Christmas lights." In 1998, an undercover police operation stripped the bar of its entertainment license and the café closed permanently. Formerly located at 21 Essex Street, its building was demolished in 2011.

Provincetown, Massachusetts, is a popular LGBT+ vacation destination. Nicknamed P-Town, it was also the first place the pilgrims landed in 1620. P-Town established ties with the queer community in Greenwich Village, New York, in the early twentieth century; in the mid-1960s and '70s, the town saw an influx of hippies, which contributed to the town's high LGBT+ population and to its reputation as a queer artists' colony.

> *My Jewish identity and family played an enormous role in shaping the individual I am today. Torah, tzedakah, and tikkun olam are essentially the Jewish education I received at Temple Israel in Boston and at home. The importance of social action and taking responsibility of the welfare of those less fortunate in our midst was drilled into me by parents and Jewish educators from an early age.*
>
> —Raffi Freedman-Gurspan, interview with MyJewishLearning.com, 2016

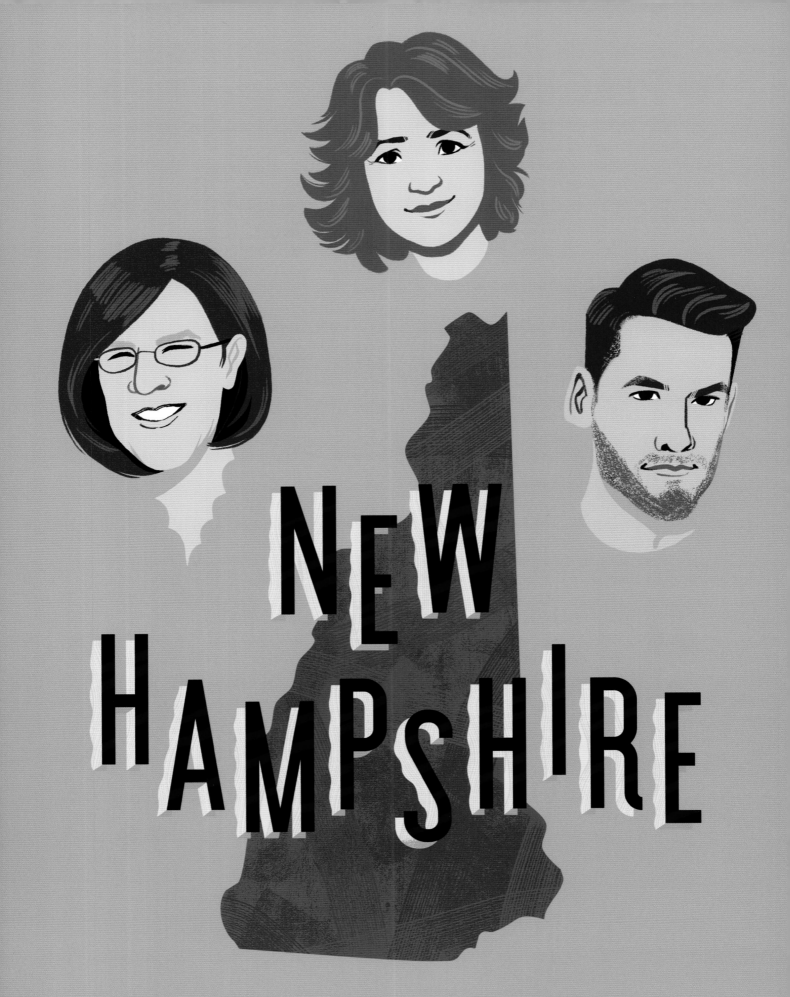

NEW HAMPSHIRE

⊖ PEOPLE

Raymond Buckley *(Keene, NH)* is an American politician and chair of the New Hampshire Democratic Party. In 2007, Buckley became the first openly gay person to serve as chair of a major party, serving the New Hampshire Democratic Party. Buckley has been politically active since the age of eight, when he began canvassing for local elections. In 1986, he won his first election, becoming a New Hampshire House Representative; he served in the House until 2004.

Randy Harrison *(Nashua, NH)* is an openly gay American actor who began his television career playing the character Justin Taylor in the American version of the TV series *Queer as Folk*. Harrison has since acted in several films and theatrical productions, including a role in Broadway's *Wicked*, as well as the hit TV show *Mr. Robot*.

Maura Healey *(Hampton Falls, NH)*, the Attorney General of Massachusetts, was elected to her second term in 2018. She is the first openly gay person to hold the position. Healey attended Harvard College before earning a JD from Northeastern University School of Law. Between her two degrees, she spent two years playing professional basketball in Austria. She then worked in the Middlesex District Attorney's Office as a criminal prosecutor before working eight years as an attorney at a large international law firm.

Sean Patrick Maloney *(Sherbrooke, Quebec, Canada)* is an attorney and politician. Raised in Hanover, New Hampshire, Maloney secured his BA and JD from the University of Virginia before going on to work as a White House staff secretary under President Bill Clinton. In 2013, he won a seat to the US House of Representatives for New York's eighteenth congressional district, becoming the state's first openly gay person elected to Congress. Maloney married Randy Florke in June 2014, making Maloney the second member of Congress to legally marry their same-sex partner while in office. Maloney and Florke had been together since 1992.

Patricia Racette *(Manchester, NH)* is a Richard Tucker Award–winning operatic soprano. During her tenure, Racette has performed with the Opéra National de Paris, the Royal Opera in London, Opera Australia, the Boston Symphony Orchestra, the Chicago Symphony Orchestra, and the San Francisco Symphony, among many others. In 2017, she won a Grammy Award for Best Opera Recording for her performance in the Los Angeles Opera's production of *The Ghosts of Versailles*. Racette married fellow opera singer Beth Clayton in 2005, and the couple considers New York their second home after Santa Fe, New Mexico.

Maura Healey

> 66
>
> *I'm proud of who I am. I'm proud of the fact that for the first time in our country's history we will have a gay attorney general. I am certainly proud that this barrier has been broken.*
>
> —Maura Healey, the *Boston Globe*, 2014
>
> 99

The first openly gay senator to serve in the New Hampshire Senate was David Pierce. Pierce served three terms in the New Hampshire House of Representatives, from 2006 to 2012, and two years in the New Hampshire Senate, from 2012 to 2016. After not seeking reelection in 2012, he ran for his senate seat again in 2018, but lost.

Gerri Cannon is one of thirteen openly transgender people elected to school boards across the US. Originally from Massachusetts, Cannon was elected in November 2017 to the Somersworth, New Hampshire, school board. She was previously a PFLAG New Hampshire chairperson and board member, as well as a Freedom NH Steering Committee member.

One of the earliest written defenses of homosexuality in the English language was the manuscript *Millions of Queers (Our Homo America)* written by the World War II veteran and New Hampshire native Allen Irvin Bernstein. The manuscript, which was rediscovered in 2010 by Drexel University associate professor Randall Sell, presents a libertarian argument against the criminalization and stigmatization of homosexuality. It is also notable for its casual use of terms such as "homo" and "queer" several decades before they were reclaimed by LGBT+ groups of the 1990s. The text also provides important insight into the gay culture of the 1920s and '30s.

Women Singing OUT! (WSO!) is a female musical group based in Portsmouth, New Hampshire. It is dedicated to music that inspires, heals, and promotes visibility for the LGBT+ community. WSO! boasts a diverse group of members from various backgrounds, spiritual traditions, political values, and gender identities. WSO! hosts two concerts each year in winter and late spring, as well as many smaller musical events throughout the year.

⊙ PLACES

Equality Health Center *(Concord, NH)* is a nonprofit health care facility bringing quality health care, education, and advocacy for sexual and gender-affirming services to New Hampshire. The center was founded as a safe abortion clinic in 1974, one year after *Roe v. Wade*, under the name New Hampshire Women's Health Services. It was later renamed Equality Health Center to better reflect its commitment to broad health care services for men and members of the LGBT+ community.

The MacDowell Colony *(St. Peterborough, NH)* is an artists' colony. Founded in 1906 in memory of the composer Edward MacDowell, the colony's mission is to provide an inspiring environment to artists from a wide range of perspectives and demographics. The MacDowell Colony has provided space and inspiration to many of America's greatest artists, including novelist James Baldwin and composer Leonard Bernstein.

Paul Goodman's grave *(North Stratford, NH)* is located in the Stratford Center Cemetery. Goodman was an openly bisexual writer, critic, philosopher, psychotherapist, and founder of Gestalt therapy. Educated at City College in New York and a faculty member of the Black Mountain College in North Carolina, Goodman was noted for his frank honesty as well as his unapologetic openness about his sexuality. He died of a heart attack in New Hampshire in 1972.

Seacoast Outright *(Portsmouth, NH)* is an LGBT+ youth group. The group provides a safe space for LGBT+ youth to explore issues around sexual orientation and gender identity. Seacoast Outright hosts events to raise visibility of LGBT+ issues, including the largest annual event Portsmouth PRIDE. The group celebrated its twenty-fifth year of service in 2018.

NEW JERSEY

⊖ PEOPLE

Dolores Alexander *(Newark, NJ)* became the executive director of the National Organization of Women (NOW) in 1969, though she resigned a year later over the homophobia perpetuated by NOW founder Betty Friedan and other straight feminists. While working as a reporter for *Newsday* in 1966, Alexander interviewed Friedan for a piece and became immersed into activist feminism. In 1972, Alexander and her partner opened the world's first feminist restaurant, Mother Courage, in New York's Greenwich Village. Her lesbian feminism continued long into her career as she spoke around the country on behalf of the women's movement, founded Women Against Pornography, joined the board of the National Association for the Repeal of Abortion Laws, protested the *New York Times*'s segregation of classified ads, and more. She died in 2008 at the age of seventy-six.

Kwame Anthony Appiah *(London, England)* is a New York University philosophy and law professor. Born in London, where his father was a Member of Parliament, Appiah was primarily raised in Ghana. His teaching career spans several prominent American universities prior to NYU, including Harvard and Princeton. A prolific writer, Appiah's works span genres from the autobiographical *In My Father's House: Africa in the Philosophy of Culture* (1992) to the philosophical *The Ethics of Identity* (2005) and the novel *Another Death in Venice* (1995). His partner, Henry Finder, is the editorial director of the *New Yorker*.

Michael Ausiello *(Roselle Park, NJ)* is the president and editorial director of TVLine.com, an entertainment news site. Ausiello began as a writer in 1997 for the magazine *Soaps in Depth* and later for TVGuide.com and *Entertainment Weekly*. He can be seen in a handful of television cameos over the years, on shows including *Gilmore Girls*, *Veronica Mars*, and *Scrubs*. His 2017 memoir, *Spoiler Alert: The Hero Dies*, chronicles his relationship with his partner, photographer Kit Cowan, who died of cancer in 2015. In 2018, he and producer J. J. Abrams began writing a show based on Ausiello's youth as a closeted, TV-obsessed child.

Ben A. Barres *(West Orange, NJ)* was a neuroscientist at Stanford University. Barres's research established that glial cells in the brain play a vital role in synapses, neurological degeneration, and Alzheimer's disease. Barres transitioned in 1997, some time after having a double mastectomy as the result of breast cancer. After his transition, he noted the extra respect he gained as a man in science, an experience that further motivated him to advocate for women in the field. "Ben Barres gave a great seminar today, but then his work is much better than his sister's," he once overheard a colleague say. While at Stanford, he also chaired the neurobiology department and directed the Masters of Science in Medicine program. He died from pancreatic cancer in 2017 at the age of sixty-three.

Richard Berkowitz *(Newark, NJ)* is a safe-sex advocate and the subject of the 2008 Daryl Wein documentary *Sex Positive*. Berkowitz attended Rutgers University in the 1970s, where he was active in LGBT+ rights demonstrations. For a time, he worked as an S&M hustler. Berkowitz was a longtime vocal proponent of condom use, though he was not taken seriously until the 1980s AIDS epidemic. As the epidemic flared, he published educational materials on safe sex, such as a booklet called *How to Have Sex in an Epidemic*. *Sex Positive* sought to remind viewers of the importance of safe sex during a time when AIDS diagnoses were on the rise after the memories of the 1980s had faded.

Raphael Bostic *(Delran, NJ)* became the president of the Federal Reserve Bank of Atlanta in 2017, the first Black and openly gay man to do so. Bostic earned degrees in economics from Harvard and Stanford in 1987 and 1996, respectively. He then went on to work for the Federal Reserve Board of Governors, served two stints in the US Department of Housing and Urban Development, and taught at the University of Southern California.

Cason Crane *(Lawrenceville, NJ)* made history in 2013 as the first openly gay mountaineer to climb to all Seven Summits. He called his mission the Rainbow Summit Project, which raised over $100,000 in donations for the Trevor Project, in memory of a friend Crane lost to suicide in high school. Crane achieved his goal within the year, and photographed himself with

> *As we wrote in* **How to Have Sex in an Epidemic,** *safe sex is about more than preventing AIDS. The promotion of PrEP conveniently overlooks all the other sexually transmitted viruses and infections, like primary syphilis, herpes, chlamydia, gonorrhea, non-specific urethritis, CMV, etc., that PrEP does nothing to protect you from, but which condoms often can.*

—Richard Berkowitz, *Huffington Post*, 2013

> *If sexual issues are not brought up in the Scouting environment—and in my experience they never were, until an outside party publicized my homosexuality—that's all the more reason that it should not matter if some members happen to be gay.*

—James Dale, *Washington Post*, 2013

Shaun T. Fitness

a rainbow flag at the summit of each mountain as he reached it.

James Dale *(Middletown, NJ)* is an activist known for the lawsuit *Boy Scouts of America v. Dale*, which challenged the Boy Scouts exclusion of gay members. Dale was an active Boy Scout in the 1980s and was awarded an Eagle Scout badge, the BSA's highest honor, his freshman year of college. In 1990, while Dale was a junior and president of the Rutgers Lesbian/Gay Alliance, his BSA membership was terminated because of his identity; he sued the BSA two years later. While the New Jersey Supreme Court held that Dale was unlawfully expelled and should be readmitted, the BSA appealed the case to the US Supreme Court, which overturned the state court's ruling in 2000. It wasn't until 2013 that the BSA began loosening its restrictions on the identities of its members, first allowing homosexual boys, then transgender boys and cisgender girls over the following years.

Julie Decker *(Summit, NJ)* is the author of the 2014 book *The Invisible Orientation: An Introduction to Asexuality*. In addition to writing and vlogging as an asexuality spokesperson, Decker also writes science fiction and fantasy for people of all ages. Decker is particularly outspoken about corrective rape, something she and many other asexual people are subject to. "When people hear that you're asexual, some take that as a challenge," she told the *Huffington Post* in 2013. "They think that you really want sex but just don't know it

> *Many contemporary feminists talk about the many feminisms there are—meaning that no one analysis of gender, class, race, religion, nationality fits all. I agree with that. But I also think that if these many feminisms were overlayed one upon the other, there would be certain clusters of issues that appear everywhere but in different forms that often disguise the similarities. One feminist analysis doesn't fit all, but I believe there is a meta-theory that encompasses it all.*
>
> —Marcia Freedman, *Haaretz.com*, 2010

yet. For people who perform corrective rape, they believe that they're just waking us up and that we'll thank them for it later."

Shaun T. Fitness *(Camden, NJ)* is a fitness expert known for programs such as Insanity, Hip Hop Abs, Focus T25, and more. His workout videos have sold over eight million copies. Fitness is also a dancer, and has performed with celebrities such as Mariah Carey and Aaron Carter, as well as in stage theater and films such as 2006's *Bring It On: All Or Nothing*. His approach to personal fitness is notably relaxed: "Some fitness professionals eat lettuce and chicken and they're on a really strict diet. For me, I eat whatever I want. I eat 85 percent healthy and 15 percent fun," he told *People* in 2015.

Malcolm Forbes *(Englewood, NJ)* was a multimillionaire and editor-in-chief of *Forbes* magazine. An unapologetic capitalist and businessman, Forbes loved to flaunt his wealth with private jets, a motorcycle collection, and a seventieth birthday party worth $2 million. He wrote a book about his love of material objects, *More Than I Dreamed: A Lifetime of Collecting*, wherein he mixed his own biography with descriptions of his many coveted belongings, from expensive toys to Fabergé eggs. Forbes loved hot air balloons and broke multiple world records for ballooning. After his death in 1990, *OutWeek* magazine published a story detailing how Forbes had been closeted all his life. The article stated that Forbes regularly invited male waiters at the Forbes townhouse and galleries to his private jacuzzi, where would pay each man $100 regardless of whether or not he decided to have sex with

Barney Frank

him. Georg Osterman, who worked in communications at *Forbes*, told *OutWeek* that he had a sexual relationship with Forbes for the "experience." Forbes likely remained closeted because many of his closest political affiliates and colleagues were conservative, such as Richard Nixon and Henry Kissinger, who both attended his funeral.

Barnett "Barney" Frank *(Bayonne, NJ)* served in the Massachusetts House of Representatives between 1979 and 2013. Frank lived with anxiety that revealing his gay identity would derail his political career, although he came out to much public support in 1987. In 1989, a scandal erupted involving Frank and a prostitute named Steve Gobie, whom Frank had first hired in 1985 and continued to employ for other domestic tasks. Gobie continued running a prostitution ring partly out of Frank's home, though Frank was unaware of it and was not charged with any criminal behavior—his career continued unscathed by the controversy. Frank retired in 2013 and is known as one of the wittiest members of Congress; he claimed to have been unable to read the 1998 report of the President Clinton and Monica Lewinsky scandal, complaining, "Too much reading about heterosexual sex!"

Marcia Freedman *(Newark, NJ)* is an activist who in 1967 immigrated to Israel, where she helped found the country's feminist movement in the 1970s. There, she was a member of Knesset, the Israeli Parliament, though she decided not to run for reelection in 1977 due her party's treatment of female candidates; she became a founding member of the Women's Party instead, though it did not receive enough votes to gain representations in the Knesset. During her term in the Knesset, Freedman came out as a lesbian, a fact she often had to hide due to the country's culture at the time. Freedman soon returned to America and became the president of American Jewish Alliance for Justice and Peace (Brit Tzedek v'Shalom) from 2000 to 2007.

Gina Genovese *(Newark, NJ)* was elected in 2006 as the mayor of Long Hill, New Jersey, becoming the first openly gay mayor in the state. Genovese ran for governor in 2017, though she lost the election. She is the founder and executive director of Courage to Connect NJ, a nonprofit that aims to consolidate redundant local government practices. In the 1980s, Genovese was a member of the Women's Tennis Association, though she quickly retired due to injury. Since 1983, she has run Gina's Tennis World, coaching and developing young players.

Allen Ginsberg *(Newark, NJ)* was a Beat Generation poet. While studying at Columbia University in the 1940s, Ginsberg befriended Jack Kerouac, Neal Cassady, and William S. Burroughs—fellow writers who went on to define the Beats. Ginsberg's 1955 poem "Howl" (considered a manifesto for the following

Allen Ginsberg

decade's sexual liberation movement) and the homoerotic content of his poetry drew eyes to his work in a time when sodomy was still illegal. With the rise of his profile came his activism, as he actively demonstrated against the Vietnam War and the CIA in the 1970s and the Reagan administration in the 1980s. His major writings include *Iron Horse* (1973), *Mind Breaths* (1978), *White Shroud Poems* (1986), and more. Ginsberg died of cancer at age seventy in 1997.

Whitney Houston *(Newark, NJ)* was a bestselling singer known for classic 1980s and 1990s multimillion-selling hits such as "How Will I Know," "I Wanna Dance with Somebody," and her cover of Dolly Parton's "I Will Always Love You." Houston was the daughter of Aretha Franklin's backup singer Crissy Houston and the first cousin of Dionne Warwick, and spent her early career years backing up singers such as Chaka Khan. In her later years, Houston became known for her turbulent 1992 marriage to singer Bobby Brown and for her struggles with drug dependency. She died in 2012 at the age of forty-eight, having drowned in a bathtub as the result of drug use and heart disease. Houston was long speculated to be a lesbian or bisexual based on her close relationship with her childhood friend and assistant Robyn Crawford, but in 1999 she told *Out*

Whitney Houston

magazine, "[That] ain't me. I know what I am. I'm a mother. I'm a woman. I'm heterosexual. Period." In his 2016 memoir, *Every Little Step*, Brown confirmed that Houston was indeed bisexual.

Dario Hunter *(New Jersey)*, born in the 1980s to an Iranian, Muslim father and African American mother, is considered the first Muslim-born person to be ordained as a rabbi. After earning a BA in history from Princeton and a JD from the University of Detroit, Hunter was ordained as a rabbi in 2012. Hunter lives in Youngstown, Ohio, where he serves on the local board of education. In 2019, he announced his 2020 presidential bid as a member of the Green Party.

Marsha P. Johnson *(Elizabeth, NJ)* was an activist and drag queen who participated in the 1969 Stonewall riots. In the 1970s, Johnson and Sylvia Rivera founded Street Transvestite Action Revolutionaries (STAR) and STAR House for homeless gay and trans youth. Johnson was well known in the Greenwich Village gay community and beyond—her renown caught the eye of artists such as Diana Davies and Andy Warhol, and she became the subject of some of their work. Johnson's body was found in the Hudson River soon after the 1992 Pride parade; police declared her death a suicide, which is doubted by those who knew her.

She is the subject of the 2017 Netflix documentary *The Death and Life of Marsha P. Johnson*, which reinvestigates her death.

Orlando Jordan *(Salem, NJ)* began his career as a WWE wrestler in 1999. In 2002, he earned the Maryland Championship Wrestling title; in 2005, he claimed the WWE US Championship title after defeating John Cena. While Jordan had been out about his bisexuality in his personal life, it was revealed publicly in 2006 after fans discovered his private Myspace page. When asked if he thought his fellow wrestlers would have an issue competing against him because of his identity, he replied, "Too bad!"

Arnie Kantrowitz *(Newark, NJ)* founded the Gay and Lesbian Alliance Against Defamation (GLAAD) in 1985, along with fellow activists Darrell Yates Rist and Vito Russo. Together, they sought to combat the negative portrayal of LGBT+ people that was prevalent in the media during the AIDS epidemic of the time. Kantrowitz is a writer, known for his 1977 memoir *Under the Rainbow: Growing Up Gay*, one of the first gay memoirs printed by a major publisher, as well as the 2005 biography *Walt Whitman: Gay and Lesbian Writers*.

Alfred Kinsey *(Hoboken, NJ)* was a bisexual biologist and sexologist famous for developing the Kinsey scale of sexual orientation. After earning a biology PhD from Harvard, he moved to Indiana University

> *I was no one, nobody, from Nowheresville until I became a drag queen. That's what made me in New York, that's what made me in New Jersey, that's what made me in the world.*
>
> —Marsha P. Johnson

> *What I remember in seeing it as a young man was not only how funny it was but also how subversive it was in its way. It's subversive in the fact that the gay people are the heroes and the straight people are the villains.*
>
> —Nathan Lane on *Le Cage aux Folles*, the inspiration for *The Birdcage*, the *Morning Call*, 2017

in 1920 to study the reproduction of gall wasps. Two decades later, IU asked him to teach a course on marriage—there, he began collecting the sexual histories of his students, which ballooned into larger research on human sexuality. He soon published the Kinsey Reports (*Sexual Behavior of the Human Male* in 1948 and *Sexual Behavior of the Human Female* in 1953), which revealed the spectrum of orientations between hetero-, homo-, and bisexuality and established the commonality of them. The reports also refuted the era's notion of women as nonsexual beings, though Kinsey never lived to see the sexual liberation movement that rose in the wake of his work; he died of pneumonia in 1956 at the age of sixty-two. He is estimated to have interviewed over eighteen thousand people regarding their sexual habits. IU is home to the Kinsey Institute for Research in Sex, Gender, and Reproduction, which he founded in 1947.

Jason Klein *(East Brunswick, NJ)* in 2013 was named president of the Reconstructionist Rabbinical Association, becoming the first gay man to lead a national rabbinical association. Previously, Klein was a Hillel rabbi at the University of Maryland. "It's great when role models look and act like us and have certain common experiences, values, and ideals," he told *New Jersey Jewish News*. "It can be helpful, especially for some who still feel they are on the margins rather than in the forefront of leadership."

Marc Kushner *(Livingston, NJ)* is an architect and founder of the website Architizer, a social marketplace for architectural projects. Kushner earned a master's in architecture from Harvard in 2004 before starting Architizer in 2009 with $2 million in seed money he raised from family and friends. Kushner is the cousin of Jared Kushner, Ivanka Trump's husband. In 2012, he married Chris Barley, a fellow architect.

Nathan Lane *(Jersey City, NJ)* is a stage, film, and TV actor known for his roles in *The Lion King*, *The Birdcage*, and *The Producers*. Born Joseph Lane, he adopted the name Nathan from the role he had played in *Guys and Dolls* to distinguish himself from another actor who shared his birth name. Lane never hid his sexuality while he established his career, but avoided roles that would typecast him as a gay actor; after the murder of Matthew Shepard, however, he was motivated to publicly announce his sexuality. In 2015, he married fellow actor Devlin Elliott, after dating for eighteen years.

Thomas Lanigan-Schmidt *(Linden, NJ)* is an artist who participated in the 1969 Stonewall riots. Lanigan-Schmidt's art is at once both kitschy and baroque, using sparkly household materials such as foil or tinsel to create lavish-looking rat or cockroach sculptures, or a collage of Paula Deen in the style of the Madonna, for example. Over the years, his work has been featured in institutions such as the Metropolitan Museum of Art and the Whitney Museum of American Art, and he was taught at New York's School of Visual Arts. In 2009, President Obama honored

Nathan Lane

Fran Lebowitz

Because of her witty writing style, she has frequently been compared to Dorothy Parker. Lebowitz, who was a frequent guest on *Late Night with David Letterman* and *Law & Order*, is known for her cold exterior and her distinct wardrobe of suits and cowboy boots.

Lanigan-Schmidt for his participation in the Stonewall riots on the event's fortieth anniversary.

David Lat *(Bergenfield, NJ)*, of Filipino descent, is the founder and editor-at-large of Above the Law, an online source for legal news. Lat earned an English degree from Harvard in 1996 and went on to earn his JD from Yale, where he served as the vice president of the Federalist Society. He clerked for a federal appeals judge before starting the anonymous and irreverent blog Underneath Their Robes, which featured gossip about the judicial community. His career has spanned work as a federal prosecutor, litigation associate, and law clerk, and Lat has written for publications such as the *New York Times* and the *Washington Post*. Lat is married to fellow attorney Zachary Shemtob.

Fran Lebowitz *(Morristown, NJ)* is an iconic lesbian writer and cultural commentator. After being expelled from school, moving to New York, and working odd jobs, she was hired as a columnist at Andy Warhol's *Interview* magazine in the 1970s. She published three comedic essay collections in her career, including 1978's bestselling *Metropolitan Life* and 1981's *Social Studies*.

Amanda Lepore *(Cedar Grove, NJ)* is an iconic transgender model and singer, known for her cartoonish Marilyn Monroe–esque appearance. Assigned male at birth, Lepore knew from a young age that she was female; as a young teen, she and a friend started go-go dancing at a nearby club, where Lepore traded outfits for hormone pills with a fellow trans dancer. At seventeen, Lepore married a man ten years her senior, whose father had a crush on her and paid for her gender-affirming surgery. Lepore eventually fled her marriage and moved to New York in the 1990s, where she worked as a nail technician and dominatrix. Photographer David LaChapelle discovered her during this time and turned her into one of his most well-known muses. Lepore released her debut EP, *Introducing . . . Amanda Lepore*, in 2005, and her memoir, *Doll Parts*, in 2017. "I like women who transform themselves. It's what I do. My high is looking fabulous," she told the *Observer* in 2017.

Kermit Love *(Spring Lake, NJ)* was a puppeteer and costume designer most known for his work on *Sesame Street*. Love created the iconic costumes for Big Bird, Oscar the Grouch, and the Cookie Monster—he was so particular about how the Big Bird costume was handled, that he often flew with the costume in its own seat. Although he shares a name with Kermit the Frog,

Amanda Lepore

Love insisted he was not the inspiration for the character's name. Prior to joining the show, Love made a name for himself designing dance costumes for performers such as George Balanchine and Twyla Tharp. He died in 2008 at the age of ninety-one, survived by his partner of fifty years.

Jim McGreevey *(Jersey City, NJ)* was the governor of New Jersey from 2002 until 2004. McGreevey resigned in 2004, revealing simultaneously that he was gay and that he had used his power to secure a $110,000 job as a homeland security adviser for his secret lover. He went on to seminary school with the intent of becoming an Episcopal priest, but his priesthood application was rejected. He later found work and his calling as a spiritual counselor at the Hudson County Jail for women. McGreevey is the subject of the 2013 Alexandra Pelosi HBO documentary *Fall to Grace*.

Tracey Norman *(Newark, NJ)* was the first Black trans model to appear on a box of Clairol hair coloring in the 1970s—though she had kept her identity a secret at the time. Norman began her modeling career in 1975 when she booked a gig with *Vogue Italia*. Shortly

thereafter, she signed a contract with Avon and Clairol to be the face of the No. 512, Dark Auburn in the Born Beautiful hair color line. Norman's career flourished in the 1970s; in 1980, while she was on a shoot for *Essence* magazine, the hairdresser's assistant discovered and spread word that Norman was transgender. Because of taboos against trans women, Norman's pictures were not published and her modeling career came to an end.

Kate Pierson *(Weehawken, NJ)* is a singer and musician known as the frontwoman of the 1970s and 1980s group the B-52s. Pierson has collaborated with numerous artists over her career, including the Ramones, Iggy Pop, Blondie, and more. She has made a modest number of film and TV appearances, including as a member of the BC-52s in the 1994 film *The Flintstones*. Pierson and her wife, Monica, operate and designed Kate's Lazy Meadow Motel in New York's Catskill Mountains, a retro-style cabin getaway, and Kate's Lazy Desert Airstream Motel in California's Mojave Desert.

Keith Rabois's *(Edison, NJ)* career as a technology executive spans roles at PayPal, LinkedIn, and Square, among others. Rabois is a member of the PayPal Mafia, a circle of former PayPal employees who have gone on to establish other prominent Silicon Valley businesses, including Elon Musk, Peter Thiel, and Max Levchin. His early investments and mentorship have helped guide platforms such as Yelp, YouTube, and Lyft to success. In 2013, Rabois resigned as COO of Square due to sexual harassment accusations from a man he had dated and encouraged to apply for a job at Square, where the man was eventually hired.

Kevin Spacey *(South Orange, NJ)* is an actor, producer, and singer whose career peaked when he won his first Academy Award for Best Supporting Actor for *The Usual Suspects* (1995) and later an Academy Award for Best Actor for *American Beauty* (1999). Spacey won a Tony Award in 1991 for his role in *Lost in Yonkers* and later hosted the 2017 Tony Awards. Later that same year, Spacey became embroiled in a sexual assault scandal. *Rent* actor Anthony Rapp accused Spacey of assaulting him in 1986, when Rapp was fourteen and Spacey was twenty-six. Spacey tweeted an apology to Rapp, but also used the opportunity to confirm

Darren Young

longstanding speculation that he is gay. He was met with immediate criticism for attempting to deflect Rapp's accusation, demonstrating what is perhaps the only incorrect way to come out. Since then, as many as fifteen men have accused Spacey of sexual assault, and Spacey's main character on Netflix's *House of Cards* was written off the show.

Joel Weisman *(Newark, NJ)* was the first doctor to identify the pattern of illnesses that eventually became known as AIDS. In 1980, Weisman was working as a doctor in California when he noticed three male patients who all had the same symptoms. He referred them to Martin Gottlieb at UCLA, who had other patients with the same symptoms. The two doctors partnered on a report of the illness, which was published by the Centers for Disease Control and Prevention in 1981 and was considered the first official documentation of AIDS. Weisman, a gay man himself, became a vocal AIDS activist, founding AIDS Project Los Angeles and educating his patients about safe-sex practices. He died in 2009 from heart disease at the age of sixty-six.

Darren Young (Fred Rosser) *(Union, NJ)* was a WWE wrestler from 2005 to 2017. Young came out as gay in 2013 while still an active wrestler, a first in the wrestling world. That year, he was named Inspirational

> *The linkages we have to make when we celebrate that I can marry after twenty-two years of being together that this comes from movements—the civil rights movement, the women's movement—and those were the legal justification for us to be considered equal and have the right to be married.*
>
> —Helen Zia, speech at the University of Maryland–Baltimore County, 2014

Wrestler of the Year by *Pro Wrestling Illustrated*, a title he holds in addition to two IWF Heavyweight championships, among others. In 2018 he described his coming out to ESPN, saying, "Cher was actually the first person to contact me on social media. She told me her friend was a big wrestling fan and that my story made him courageous enough to come out to his family." Inspired, Young dedicated his platform to LGBT+ advocacy, partnering with the Trevor Project and Los Angeles's Covenant house to help prevent teen suicide and aid homeless youth.

Helen Zia *(Newark, NJ)* is an award-winning journalist. Born to immigrants from Shanghai, China, Zia attended Princeton University amidst the first class of women to graduate in 1973. Zia was living in Detroit at the same time as the 1982 murder of Vincent Chin, a hate crime that solidified her commitment to advocacy journalism. She went on to write for publications such as the *New York Times*, *Washington Post*, and more; Zia was the executive editor of *Ms.* magazine for three years until 1992, when she quit to move to San Francisco to be with the woman who eventually became her wife. Her first book, *Asian American Dreams: The Emergence of an American People*, was published in 2000; her latest, *Last Boat out of Shanghai: The Epic Story of the Chinese Who Fled Mao's Revolution*, was published in 2019.

PLACES

Garden State Equality *(Asbury Park and Montclair, NJ)* is New Jersey's statewide LGBT+ community advocacy and education organization. Established in 2004, GSE is also the state's largest LGBT+ organization. It focuses on programming and support for youth, transgender people, and seniors while seeking racial, economic, and social justice. GSE's current initiatives include partnering with HealthSherpa to provide access to affordable health care that includes HIV screenings and mental health support, as well as Pledge and Protect, which offers workshops and support for the aging LGBT+ community.

Gay Activists Alliance in Morris County (GAAMC), founded in 1972, is the state's longest-running LGBT+ group. GAAMC meets weekly and asks for members to bring a small monetary donation to each program. Online, it offers a Pride Guide—resources for all issues related to mental health, finances, legal counseling, spirituality, theater, and more.

Hudson Pride Center *(Jersey City, NJ)* advocates for the LGBT+ and HIV/AIDS communities in Hudson County. In addition to cohosting the area's annual

QUEER FACTS

Jersey City offered trans-inclusive health care benefits in 2015, the first area of the state to do so. The benefits include services such as gender-affirmation surgery, and offer guaranteed care to transgender people in a time when they are still often denied care based on their identities. According to the city's health care providers, the cost of adding such benefits was relatively small: only about a tenth of the previous cost. Cities such as San Francisco, Portland, and Austin offer similar benefits.

The New Jersey Gay Men's Chorus is a volunteer choir in the New Jersey and Pennsylvania areas. For over twenty-five years, the NJGMC performs an annual concert series, as well as various community performances. It also collaborates and travels with other 170 choruses associated with the Gay and Lesbian Association of Choruses (GALA) network.

Rutgers student Tyler Clementi died by suicide in September 2010 by jumping from the George Washington Bridge in New York City. Clementi had come out as gay after graduating high school, and went on to Rutgers excited to embrace his identity. One night, Clementi had asked his roommate for privacy because he had a date; though his roommate excused himself, he left his webcam on and later shared online the video of Clementi being intimate with his date. The ensuing cyberbullying and planned second video by his roommate led Clementi to take his life days later, at the age of eighteen. The Tyler Clementi Foundation was founded in his memory and aims to stop all forms of harassment and bullying.

Same-sex marriage was legalized in New Jersey in October 2013, following the ruling of *United States v. Windsor*, which mandated that same-sex marriages receive the same benefits as heterosexual ones. Civil unions had been legal in the state since 2007; *Garden State Equality v. Dow* argued that gay marriage must be legalized in order to comply with the *Windsor* ruling, thus overturning the marriage ban.

Transgender student protections were passed in 2017 with the help of GLSEN, a national LGBT+ anti-harassment organization with chapters in central, northern, and southern New Jersey. The measure laid the foundation for a nondiscriminatory school environment for transgender students, ensuring their rights to use bathrooms that correspond with their identities and to be called by their proper names and pronouns.

Pride festival, it offers services spanning support groups, HIV/STI prevention, gender-affirming service referrals, and an LGBT+ intern program for social workers. The center also provides numerous training workshops, including LGBT+ sensitivity training.

The Pride Center of New Jersey (Highland Park, NJ) first opened its doors in 1994 with the goal of providing a safe space for members of the LGBT+ community. The center offers a place to meet new people, access community resources, and explore one's identity in a comfortable, welcoming environment. Its active social calendar includes a variety of support groups and events, such as bowling, karaoke, and even computer coding lessons. The Pride Center is focused on improving the health of the LGBT+ community, and offers online resources for people who want to learn more about living a healthy LGBT+ lifestyle.

Walt Whitman's grave (Camden, NJ) is located in Harleigh Cemetery. Whitman designed the mausoleum himself, and observed the construction of it years before his death—the stone tomb is set into a small hill, and a commemorative plaque added after his passing stands at the path up to its gate. Whitman paid for the tomb using funds his friends had raised to buy him a summer cottage. His immediate family is buried alongside him.

Walt Whitman's New Jersey home (Camden, NJ) is the only property the poet ever owned. He moved there in 1884 after suffering a stroke, and remained there as his health steadily declined until his death in 1892. The house, located on Mickle Street, was a clapboard row house Whitman called his "little old shanty." Whitman's companions there included his brother, George; a teenager named William Duckett, who is considered to have been his lover; and a man in his thirties named Horace Traubel, who helped Whitman with his errands and was also speculated to have been his lover. Today, the house is preserved as a museum, holding Whitman's belongings much as they were before his death. Read more about Walt Whitman under New York.

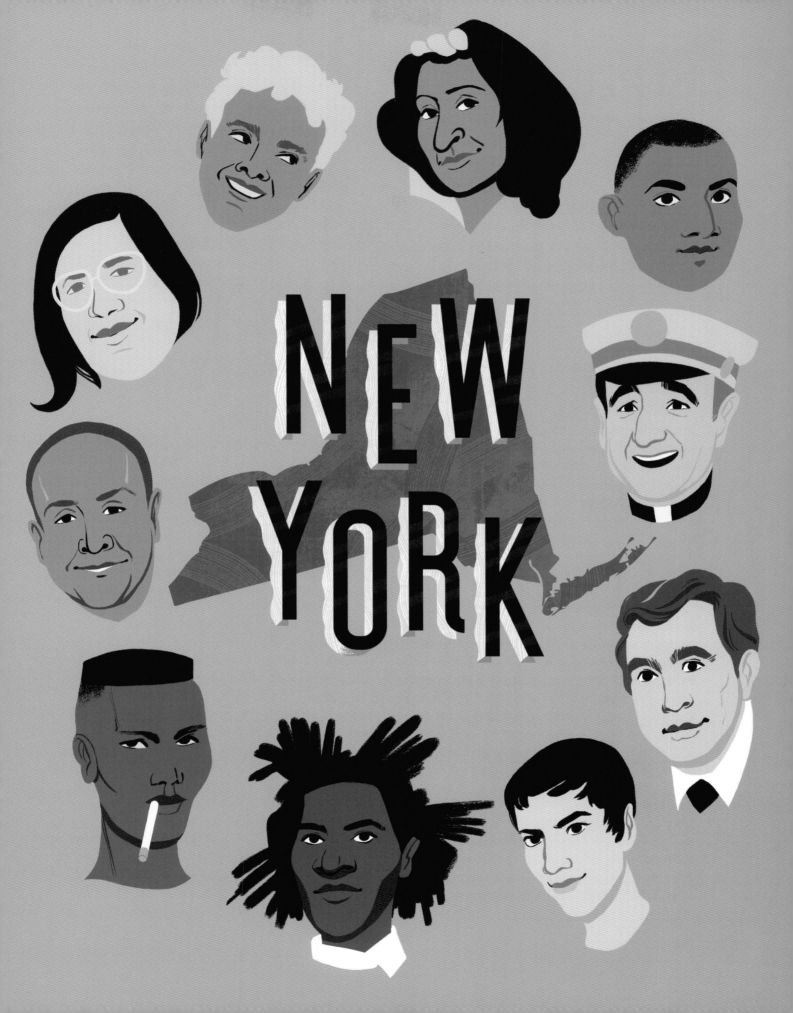

NEW YORK

PEOPLE

> " To be a Negro in this country and to be relatively conscious is to be in a rage almost all the time. So that the first problem is how to control that rage so that it won't destroy you. "
>
> —James Baldwin, "The Negro in American Culture," *Cross Currents*, 1961

James Baldwin

James Baldwin *(Harlem, NY)* was an author and activist who wrote, amongst many other notable works, *The Fire Next Time* (1963) and *Giovanni's Room* (1956). Baldwin grew up poor and spent a lot of time in the library as a teenager. Later, he began to work as a preacher, where he developed his voice as a writer. Baldwin lived in Greenwich Village while working as a freelance writer before moving to Paris to gain perspective on American culture and to live more freely as a gay man. His first book, *Go Tell It on the Mountain* (1953), was a fictionalized representation of his religious upbringing and his struggles with his stepfather. Baldwin's writing focused on themes of racial politics, homosexuality, identity, and equality—themes that moved people with his added emotional, historical, and philosophical depth. *The Fire Next Time,* a work about the struggle for racial equality, became so popular that *TIME* magazine put Baldwin on the cover of its May 1963 issue. Baldwin died of cancer in 1987 at the age of sixty-three.

Jean-Michel Basquiat *(Brooklyn, NY)* was a popular 1980s artist known for his colorful, graffiti-style paintings. After high school, Basquiat began to focus on street art. He signed his art SAMO (for "Same Old Shit"), and before long, it drew media attention. Though he spent some time homeless, he began to show his work in galleries and became associated with the neo-expressionist and punk art movements. Basquiat began to do more gallery shows throughout the '80s; of Haitian and Puerto Rican heritage, he often showcased art that featured Black celebrities and dealt with African Diaspora. In the mid-'80s, Basquiat released a series of collaborations with Andy Warhol. Throughout his career, he received praise from *Artforum,* the *Village Voice,* and the *New York Times.* Basquiat struggled to deal with his instant fame, and at times resented the art establishment. He died of an overdose in 1988, when he was twenty-seven years old. In her 2010 memoir *Widow Basquiat*, Jennifer Clement, his former partner, described his sexuality as multichromatic, saying, "He was attracted to people for all different reasons. They could be boys, girls, thin, fat, pretty, ugly. It was, I think, driven by intelligence. He was attracted to intelligence more than anything . . ."

Wilson Cruz *(New York, NY)* is an actor known best for his role as Rickie on the 1990s teen drama *My So-Called Life.* Cruz began acting from an early age, starring in plays such as *Cradle of Fire.* When he came out as gay, his family kicked him out of their home. His character on *My So-Called* Life experienced a similar story, and when those episodes aired, Cruz did PSAs

Wilson Cruz

advocating for gay homeless teens. Cruz has also appeared in shows such as *ER, 13 Reasons Why,* and *Star Trek: Discovery.* Cruz is Puerto Rican and advocates for Puerto Rican visibility in the media against whitewashed beauty ideals. "My identity is my sword in the fight against prejudice and I hold it high—like a torch," he said in 2013 while hosting the GLAAD Media Awards.

Countee Cullen *(New York, NY)* was a famous poet and singer of the Harlem Renaissance. He was raised by his grandmother, who died when he was a teenager. After her death, he lived with Reverend Frederick Cullen, who served as his guardian and mentor, and who went on to become the president of Harlem's chapter of the NAACP. Cullen won a number of poetry contests while he attended college at NYU, and later earned a graduate degree from Harvard in 1927. He won a Guggenheim fellowship and published a number of books of successful poetry, including *Caroling Dusk* and *Color.* In 1928, Cullen married Nina Yolande DuBois, the daughter of W. E. B. DuBois, in an extravagant wedding, a major social event of the time. Yet some of Cullen's poems showed a suspicious attitude towards heterosexual love, and it was rumored that he was homosexual. Cullen, who excelled in white academia, believed that art could unify Black and white people,

and respected the white English and American literary canon. Cullen believed that the value of poetry was primarily aesthetic and not political, and commended poets of all races according to that value system. Nevertheless, he remained committed to racial equality, and race was a theme of many of his poems.

Alan Cumming *(Aberfeldy, Scotland)* is an actor, singer, and activist. Interested in acting from an early age, Cumming often played out spy stories alone in his backyard. He described his childhood as "backwards," as his father was very strict and he didn't feel free to be playful until he was older. Cumming has starred in multiple critically acclaimed plays, including *Hamlet* in London, where he played Hamlet, and *The Seagull* on Broadway; he won a Tony in 1998 for his role in *Cabaret.* Cumming also has a long history as a film and television actor, including roles in *Spy Kids, Broad City, Sex and the City, Doctor Who,* and *Frasier.* Cumming has received many awards, including the ACLU/NYCLU Freedom Award, the PETA Humanitarian Award, and the HMI Community Excellence Award. The Queen made him an official Officer of the British Empire in 2009 for his work in entertainment and for his human rights activism. Cumming's 2014 memoir, *Not My Father's Son,* was a *New York Times* bestseller. He lives in New York city with his husband, Grant Shaffer, an illustrator and photographer.

Clive Davis *(New York, NY)* was a music producer and executive, founder of Arista Records, and president of Columbia Records. Over the course of his career, he signed talent such as Bruce Springsteen, Billy Joel, Aerosmith, Pink Floyd, Whitney Houston, Patti Smith, and Sarah McLachlan. In 1985, Davis was diagnosed with AIDS. He became an advocate for AIDS research, hosted concerts that benefited AIDS organizations, and won a Humanitarian Award from the American Foundation for AIDS Research in 1998. He came out as bisexual in his 2013 autobiography, *The Soundtrack of My Life.* He is in the 2000 Rock and Roll Hall of Fame, and also won the Trustees Lifetime Achievement Award at the 2000 Grammys.

Guillermo Díaz *(New York, NY)* is an actor most recently known for his role of Huck on the TV show *Scandal.* Since 1994, Díaz has acted in dozens of film

Guillermo Díaz

Nyle DiMarco

and television roles, including *ER*, *Stonewall*, *The Sopranos*, and *Weeds*; he has also appeared in music videos for Britney Spears, Beyoncé, and Jay-Z. Díaz was named to the Out100 in both 2013 and 2017, for being, in his words, "a gay Latino, doing my thing very matter-of-factly. . . . We have a lot of work to do, and I am ready to stand up for our rights, or take a knee."

Chris Dickerson *(New York, NY)* is a professional bodybuilder. He grew up in Alabama, a child of Mahala Dickerson, the first Black female lawyer in the state. In 1970, he became the first Black person to win the Amateur Athletic Union's Mr. America Contest and the first openly gay winner of the IFBB Mr. Olympia contest. Dickerson gained more public attention in 1980, when he faced Arnold Schwarzenegger in a pose-off. Dickerson later won the title of Mr. Olympia in 1982 through the International Federation of Bodybuilding and Fitness, making him the oldest person ever to win that competition. He holds multiple IFBB Grand Prix titles, only a fraction of the mass of titles he accumulated during his bodybuilding career that spanned from the 1960s to the 1990s.

Nyle DiMarco *(Queens, NY)* is an activist, model, and actor. As a Deaf person in a family with other Deaf members, DiMarco's first language was ASL. In 2015, he won the title award of *America's Next Top Model*, the first deaf person and the second male model to win

the competition. DiMarco is signed with Wilhelmina Models, and has also worked as a Broadway producer. DiMarco has other television credits that include Hulu's *Difficult People* and Sundance Now's *This Close*. His nonprofit, the Nyle DiMarco Foundation, seeks to provide Deaf children with education and opportunities so they can succeed in any field they choose. DiMarco has also worked with the United Nations to promote its 2030 Sustainable Development Goals.

Betsy Driver *(Buffalo, NY)* is the cofounder of the website Bodies Like Ours, an online community for intersex people. Driver, along with Emi Koyama, also founded Intersex Awareness Day on October 26, 2004 (read more in Massachusetts). In 2017, she was elected to the Borough Council of Flemington, New Jersey, the first intersex person to hold an office in the US and the second worldwide, after Australian mayor Tony Briffa.

Harvey Fierstein *(Brooklyn, NY)* is a producer and actor. He created a series of plays about a gay drag queen called the *Torch Song Trilogy,* for which he won two Tony awards in 1983. Fierstein also wrote the book for *La Cage aux Folles,* an adaption of the French film of the same name, which earned him another Tony in 1984. Fierstein soon moved from stage to film and television roles, such as narrating the Oscar-winning documentary *The Times of Harvey Milk*. Fierstein contributed voiceover work to shows such as *The Simpsons*, *Family*

Guy, and *BoJack Horseman,* and appeared on *Cheers* and *Murder, She Wrote* and in *Mrs. Doubtfire.* Fierstein has always been proud of his sexuality, and earned a GLAAD Award for Visibility in 1994 when he was the first gay person to play a gay character on a sitcom (*Daddy's Girls*).

David Geffen *(Brooklyn, NY)* is a music agent and film producer. Geffen worked with musicians such as the Eagles, Jackson Browne, and Joni Mitchell, and in 1980 signed John Lennon's last recording contract. In 1994, he cofounded the film production company Dream-Works SKG; prior, he had produced the 1986 film *Little Shop of Horrors* and 1989 TV series *Beetlejuice.* When he was misdiagnosed with bladder cancer in 1976, Geffen donated millions to medical charities, universities, and foundations, including a $100 million scholarship fund to UCLA's medical school. Prior to coming out as gay in 1992, Geffen had dated celebrities such as Cher and Marlo Thomas.

Lesley Gore *(Brooklyn, NY)* was a singer famous for 1960s hits such as "It's My Party," "You Don't Own Me," and "Sunshine, Lollipops, and Rainbows." She starred as Pussycat in the 1967 TV series *Batman,* and received an Academy Award nomination for Best Song in the 1980 film *Fame.* Gore came out as a lesbian in 2005 while hosting the LGBT+ PBS show *In the Life.* Gore died of lung cancer at sixty-eight in 2015, and producers continue to use her music in films and television shows today.

Brenda Howard *(Bronx, NY)* was an activist for the rights of women, bisexuals, and the LGBT+ community. Howard organized the Pride march that recognized the first-year anniversary of the Stonewall riots, the Christopher Street Liberation Day March. One of the first Pride marches, it earned Howard the nickname "Mother of Pride." Howard went on to work for the Gay Activists Alliance, the Gay Liberation Front, and the Coalition for Lesbian and Gay Rights. The police arrested Howard multiple times for her social justice work, though it did not diminish her passion for advocacy. Howard founded an Alcoholics Anonymous chapter for bisexual people, and helped found the New York Area Bisexual Network. She regularly advocated for those who suffered from HIV/AIDS. In honor

> *And today when I sing that song—I don't know, maybe it's after the Anita Hill hearings and a number of other things that seem to be happening in our world—'You Don't Own Me' takes on a whole other set of meanings for me now.*
>
> —Lesley Gore, *NPR*, 1991

of her work, PFLAG gives the Brenda Howard Award to activists who have made notable contributions to bisexual rights.

Tab Hunter *(New York, NY)* rose to fame as an actor in the 1950s, when he was known as "the Sigh Guy" for his good looks. As a teen, Hunter joined the Coast Guard, but was soon discharged for being too young. After a brief stint as a riding instructor, he decided to pursue acting. His first film was *The Lawless* (1950), but it wasn't until his next role in *Island of Desire* (1952) that his image as dreamy love interest was cemented. Throughout his career, Hunter starred opposite Hollywood starlets such as Linda Darnell, Natalie Wood, and Sophia Loren. In the mid-1950s, Hunter began to release music as a singer, landing a few songs on the Top 40 charts. Throughout his fame, tabloid magazines constantly speculated about his sexuality. In 2005, Hunter released a memoir, *Tab Hunter Confidential,* writing about his struggle to keep his sexuality secret while embracing fame.

Marc Jacobs *(New York, NY)* is a fashion designer and founder of his own brand, Marc Jacobs. Jacobs attended Parsons School of Design in the early 1980s. His final collection of clothes in college, a line of sweaters that his grandmother hand-knitted, earned him several awards and a job at the label Sketchbook. Jacobs began to design more successful collections, and received CFDA's Perry Ellis Award for New Fashion Talent in 1987, the youngest designer to do so.

Marc Jacobs

Jacobs designed a collection of grunge wear for Perry Ellis in 1992, marking a creative turn in his career. Although critics loved the collection, Perry Ellis fired Jacobs because it did not sell. Jacobs cites the experience as the first time he stayed true to his intuition, and said that being fired made him seem like a rebel in the fashion industry. He launched Marc Jacobs International Company a year later. In 1997, he became the creative director for Louis Vuitton, where, over the course of a decade, he increased the label's profit by 400 percent. He left Louis Vuitton in 2013 to focus on the Marc Jacobs brand. In 2018, Jacobs proposed to his boyfriend, model Charly Defrancesco, with a flash mob at a Chipotle.

Grace Jones *(Spanish Town, Jamaica)* is a model, actress, and singer. She grew up in Jamaica, where she was raised by her disciplinarian grandparents who would sometimes ask her to climb trees to pick out her own branch so they could whip her. Her grandparents served as inspiration for some of her fiercest characters, but she left them when she was thirteen to live with her parents in Syracuse, New York. At eighteen, she began to model, working for top designers such as Yves Saint-Laurent, Kenzo Takada, and Guy Bourdin. She moved to Paris and started singing with model Pat Cleveland—Jones later signed to Island Records and released hit albums such as *Portfolio* (1977) and

> **We didn't start the sexual revolution but I think we gave it a good kick in the pants!**
>
> —Christine Jorgensen

Nightclubbing (1981). Her numerous nightclub hits garnered her a large gay following, exacerbated by her often masculine and/or androgynous appearance. Though she has been publicly linked to many male partners, Jones has long been rumored to have had private relationships with women. Regardless of her sexual orientation, her gender nonconforming appearance has resulted in her serving as an icon for many within the LGBTQ+ community.

Christine Jorgensen *(Bronx, NY)* was a transgender entertainer, author, and veteran. Too short to qualify for a combat position, she served as a clerk in the military until she was honorably discharged in 1946 due to an illness. Jorgensen went on to study photography, and at the same time learned about hormone therapy experiments on animals, which inspired her to seek hormone therapy and gender-affirming surgery in Europe. She chose the name Christine in honor of her surgeon, Dr. Christian Hamburger, who in the early 1950s performed her surgeries at no cost and gave her hormones. Once Jorgensen returned to the US, the tabloids picked up her story and launched her to fame. She embraced fame and began to perform in nightclubs, notably singing "I Enjoy Being a Girl." She tried to marry but was denied a marriage certificate because her legal status was still male. Though she was open and positive about her transition, she was not a supporter of the women's rights movement because she believed women were already liberated.

Dr. Gloria I. Joseph *(New York, NY)* is a professor, psychologist, counselor, activist, and cofounder of the Women's Coalition of St. Croix in the US Virgin Islands. Raised in New York City by West Indian parents, Joseph first studied at New York University before achieving an MS in psychological services at the City College of New York. For many years, Joseph worked as a guidance counselor and school psychologist before earning a PhD in educational psychology from Cornell University. She became a professor of social science at Hampshire College in Amherst, Massachusetts. Joseph was the longtime partner of Audre Lorde until Lorde's death in 1992.

Mychal Judge *(Brooklyn, NY)* was a priest and humanitarian. After graduating from St. Joseph's Seraphic Seminary in 1954, he became an ordained priest in 1961 at the Franciscan Monastery, going on to serve in churches in Massachusetts, New Jersey, and New York City. In the late 1980s, Father Mychal opened a ministry dedicated to those who suffered from AIDS. He visited patients in hospitals, performed funeral services, and worked with the Dignity chapter (an LGBT-supportive organization) of his local church. He also participated in several gay pride parades. Father Mychal took his vow of chastity seriously, but engaged in romantic communications with both men and women over the course of his life. He identified himself as gay in his personal journals and to others. In 1992, he became a chaplain for the New York Fire Department, touching the lives of many families. He died during the September 11 attacks, when he ran to the World Trade Center to say the last rites for a firefighter. His was the first official death recorded on 9/11, and 2,800 people attended his funeral four days later.

Frankie Knuckles *(Bronx, NY)* was a DJ and house musician. Knuckles grew up listening to jazz and began to play in clubs such as the Gallery in New York with his friend Larry Levan in the 1970s. Knuckles worked at the club Continental Baths until it closed, then moved to Chicago, where he DJed at the Warehouse. He started his own club, the Power Plant, and began to produce his own music, rising to fame in the house music scene. Knuckles teamed up with David Morales to start Def Mix Productions back in New York City. He started to release his own albums through Virgin Records, such as *Beyond the Mix* (1991) and *Welcome to the Real World* (1995). Knuckles has a place in the Dance Music Hall of Fame, and won a Grammy in 1997 for Remixer of the Year. He died in 2014 due to diabetes complications at age fifty-nine.

Michael Kors *(Long Island, NY)* is a fashion designer and founder of the fashion label of the same name. Born as Karl Anderson, Kors, born as Karl Anderson, was given the option to change his whole name by his mother when she married his stepfather, Bill Kors. He studied at the Fashion Institute of Technology, but left as soon as the clothing store Lothar's began buying his designs; his sales soon expanded to Bergdorf Goodman. Kors went on to design for Celine in France, then left to focus on his own brand full-time. Kors has designed garments for a range of celebrities, including Michelle Obama's dress for her first White House photo portrait in 2009. He appeared as a judge on *Project Runway* from 2004 to 2016, and has also appeared on *The Apprentice* and *Gossip Girl*. Kors has received multiple awards from the Council of Fashion Designers of America, including its Lifetime Achievement Award. Kors married fellow designer Lance LePere in 2011.

Lady Gaga (Stefani Germanotta) *(New York, NY)* is a singer and actress known for LGBT+ rights activism. Early in her career during an interview with Barbara Walters she stated she 'd had sexual relations with both men and women. She attended NYU's Tisch School of the Arts in 2003, but dropped out to focus on her music career. She began to write songs for other artists at Sony/ATV while she experimented with her own artistic vision for herself as a performer. After providing vocals to one of Akon's songs, he recognized her talent and signed her to his record label, KonLive. She then started

Lady Gaga

to work on her first album, *The Fame,* which came out in 2008 and won a Grammy. The Monster Ball, Lady Gaga's second tour, became one of the highest-grossing tours of all time. Lady Gaga's 2011 album *Born This Way* received three Grammy nominations. In addition to music, she has also acted in the 2015 TV series *American Horror Story: Hotel,* for which she won two Golden Globes, and the 2018 film *A Star is Born,* which won an Oscar for Best Original Song for "Shallow."

Audre Lorde *(New York, NY)* was a writer, professor, and feminism and civil rights activist. Lorde wrote the classic feminist text *Sister Outsider* in 1985, among many other celebrated works, which have created space for discussions of racism, sexuality, and class. Lorde challenged the issue of racism in feminist thought and emphasized the interrelation between forms of oppression. Lorde was an influential activist for civil rights movements and attended the March on Washington in 1963. In 1991, she was named New York State Poet Laureate. Lorde was diagnosed with breast cancer in 1978 and with liver cancer in 1985. She spent the final six years of her life in St. Croix in the US Virgin Islands, the home of her partner, Dr. Gloria I. Joseph, before dying in 1992.

Kate McKinnon *(Seacliff, NY)* is a comedian and actress best known for her role on *Saturday Night Live* since 2012. She graduated from Columbia University, where she studied theater and cofounded an improv group called Tea Party. McKinnon starred on the *Big Gay Sketch Show,* which aired from 2007 to 2010 on Logo TV. During the same time, she performed stand-up in New York, most notably at the Upright Citizens' Brigade Theatre. McKinnon has starred in a number of films, including *Ghostbusters, The Spy Who Dumped Me,* and *Office Christmas Party.* She has done voice work in animations like *Nature Cat, Family Guy, Finding Dory,* and *The Simpsons.* McKinnon has two Emmy Awards and an American Comedy Award, and has been nominated for a Critics' Choice Award.

Wentworth Miller *(Chipping Norton, England)* is an actor who grew up in Brooklyn, New York. The product of a mixed-race marriage and a stellar high school student, Miller went on to attend Princeton University, where his experience in the a capella group the

Princeton Tigertones made him realize his love for performing. He moved to Los Angeles to work in production, but decided to build a career as an actor instead. He began acting in small roles on TV shows such as *ER* and *Buffy the Vampire Slayer,* but his major break happened after the 2003 film *The Human Stain.* Two years later, Miller landed a major role in the television show *Prison Break,* which earned him many award nominations, including a Golden Globe and three Teen Choice Awards nominations. He came out as gay in a 2013 letter posted on GLAAD's website opposing Russia's treatment of its gay citizens.

Michael Musto *(Brooklyn, NY)* is an actor and journalist. He began writing at the *Village Voice* in 1984, penning gossip columns as well as pieces about art, fashion, and gay culture. Known for his humorous, personal, and self-deprecating writing style, Musto has been a regular writer for the *New York Times,* the *Daily Beast,* and *Out* magazine. He is also well known for his obsession with camp films, and has made a number of film cameos and small roles over his career, including in *The Smurfs* (2011) and the *Vamp Bikers* series.

Willi Ninja *(Queens, NY)* was a dancer and drag ball performer who came into the public eye after the 1990 documentary *Paris is Burning.* He was known by many as the grandfather of vogue dancing. Ninja grew up dancing, raised by a mother who was supportive of his sexuality. As an adult, Ninja started the House of Ninja, a dance group that took in young LGBT+ people and mentored them in the Harlem drag ball scene, which invented voguing. Ninja embraced his androgyny, and frequently performed in elaborate jewelry, makeup, and a moustache. He added signature sharp movements to the vogue dance, which he taught and perfected throughout his life. He went on to train models and began his own agency in 2004 called EON, which stands for Elements of Ninja. Ninja was diagnosed with HIV in 2003, and died in 2006 at forty-five years old.

Cynthia Nixon *(New York, NY)* is an actress, most well known for her role as Miranda Hobbes on *Sex and the City.* She has many credits as a Broadway actress in productions such as *Angels in America, The Women, The Real Thing,* and *The Rabbit Hole,* for which she won a Tony Award in 2006. Nixon has also received a

Grammy Award, a Theatre World Award, a Los Angeles Drama Critics Award, and an Emmy Award for Best Supporting Actress for *Sex and the City*. In 2018, she ran for governor of New York, but lost to incumbent Andrew Cuomo. Nixon is passionate about issues such as LGBT+ and women's rights and public education. Nixon is married to activist Christine Marinoni.

Rosie O'Donnell *(Commack, NY)* is a comedian and actress. After first appearing on the TV show *Star Search* in 1984, O'Donnell grew her audience by appearing on the 1986 sitcom *Gimme a Break!* and in movies such as *A League of Their Own*, *Sleepless in Seattle*, and *Beautiful Girls*. From 1996 to 2002, she hosted *The Rosie O'Donnell Show*, which won multiple Emmy Awards. Shortly after the show ended, O'Donnell came out as a lesbian, stating, "I'm a dyke!" That year, she was named Person of the Year by *The Advocate*. In 2006, O'Donnell moderated *The View* for one season, boosting its ratings with her controversial opinions; she rejoined *The View* in 2013. O'Donnell has several children and is a philanthropist for several child-centered causes, with foundations such as Rosie's For All Kids Foundation and Rosie's Theater Kids.

Anthony Perkins *(New York, NY)* is an actor most recognized for his role as Norman Bates in Alfred Hitchcock's 1960 film *Psycho*. Perkins was an only child, and his father, Osgood Perkins, was also an actor. His first film was *The Actress,* which came out in 1953, and he continued to work in film until his death in 1992 from AIDS-related pneumonia. According to Tab Hunter's 2005 autobiography, the two were romantically involved in the 1950s. Perkins discovered he had AIDS from a 1990 article in the *National Enquirer,* after it illegally tested his blood and published the discovery. "I have learned more about love, selflessness, and human understanding from the people I have met in this great adventure in the world of AIDS than I ever did in the cutthroat, competitive world in which I spent my life," he wrote in a public statement shortly before his death.

Sylvia Rivera *(Bronx, NY)* was a transgender activist and one of the leaders of the Stonewall Riots. Rivera wore makeup from a young age, much to the dismay of her grandmother. She had a very difficult childhood, as she ran away from home when she was eleven

> *Marsha and I fought a lot for the liberation of our people. We did a lot back then. Marsha and I had a building on Second Street, which is called STAR House. And when we asked the [gay] community to help us, there was nobody to help us. We were nothing. We were nothing! And now we were taking care of kids that were younger than us.*
>
> —Silvia Rivera, 1989 interview with Eric Marcus, *Making Gay History* podcast

years old to live on Forty-Second Street amongst drag queens and sex workers. Rivera increased the visibility of trans people early in the gay rights movement, when trans people were not always welcome. Rivera was unafraid of arrest in her activism, and on one occasion tried to climb through the window of a government building while politicians inside discussed a gay rights bill. Rivera was involved in many early gay rights organizations, from the Gay Activists Alliance to her own organization cofounded with Marsha P. Johnson, Street Transvestite Action Revolutionaries, which provided shelter to homeless LGBT+ adolescents. Even though the gay rights movement often excluded her, she continued to fight, saying that she wouldn't stop until "our community [is] given the respect we deserve." Rivera died in 2002.

Eleanor Roosevelt *(New York, NY)* was a humanitarian and a First Lady of the United States. In 1905, she married Franklin D. Roosevelt, who later became the thirty-second US president. Early in her career, Roosevelt volunteered with the American Red Cross in World War I and joined the Women's Trade Union League and the League of Women Voters. She was the first First Lady to hold a press conference, and regularly held them exclusively for female reporters because women were not typically allowed to attend the conferences. Roosevelt reportedly had an affair with Lorena Hickok, a reporter from the Associated Press. Hickok lived at the White House for part of FDR's presidency, during which time Hickok and Roosevelt exchanged intimate letters—Hickock's estate released them to the public ten years after Hickok's death. Roosevelt traveled across the nation as an advocate for many human rights causes, and she shared thoughts from her travels with her husband and with the American public in a newspaper column called "My Day," which had an audience of four million people. After her husband's death, Roosevelt helped draft the Universal Declaration of Human Rights while she served as the chair of the Human Rights Commission of the United Nations General Assembly. She died in 1962 at the age of seventy-eight.

Felipe Rose *(Brooklyn, NY)* is a member of the Village People, a music group known for hits such as "YMCA" and "Macho Man." Rose started his entertainment career while performing in New York clubs in a Native American headdress, an homage to his Lakota roots. When the music producer Jacques Morali saw Rose's performance, he envisioned him as part of the costumed group that later became the Village People, named after the LGBT+ community of New York's Greenwich Village. The Village People won the American Music Award for Favorite Band in 1978, the only year to feature disco as a category. Rose released his first solo single, "Trail of Tears," in 2002. He is passionate about teaching Native American history in schools, and has his own record company, Tomahawk Records. He was inducted to the Native American Music Awards Hall of Fame in 2008.

Vanessa Selbst *(Brooklyn, NY)* made history in 2015 as the top-ranking player on the Global Poker Index. She was the first woman and openly gay person to hold the title. Selbst was a math prodigy in high school and earned the title of Essex County Calculus Champion. She later attended Yale, where she was a member of the Queer-Straight Alliance and played rugby. She started to play poker online and in person, analyzing the math behind the game. After her mother died when she was twenty, Selbst began to play poker more seriously to cope with the loss. She earned seventh

place in her first World Series of Poker tournament in 2006, and in 2013 she won the PokerStars Caribbean Adventure $25,000 High Roller event. She went on to win the World Series of Poker three times. Selbst's foundation, Venture Justice, advocates for economic and racial equality. Now with a Yale Law School degree and mostly retired from poker, she works for the hedge fund Bridgewater Associates.

Maurice Sendak *(Brooklyn, NY)* is most well known for writing and illustrating the children's book *Where the Wild Things Are,* which won a Caldecott Medal in 1964. Though he wrote for children, he was not afraid to delve into dark themes and imagery. In his 1970 book *In the Night Kitchen*, for example, a little boy falls into a vat of cake batter and is almost baked alive. Sendak felt that peril loomed in his life from an early age, as World War II and the Holocaust deeply affected him as a young, gay, Jewish boy. He spent a lot of his childhood drawing, and as a young adult built window displays for the toy store FAO Schwartz. He went on to illustrate books for Harper & Row, and eventually began working on his own books. Many consider Sendak to be one of the best children's books authors of the twentieth century. Amongst other awards, he won the National Medal of the Arts and the Hans Christian Andersen Award for Illustration. Sendak died in 2012 at the age of eighty-three.

Parvez Sharma *(New Delhi, India)* is a film director and writer. He directed the documentaries *A Sinner in Mecca* (2015) and *A Jihad for Love* (2007), both of which deal with the intersection of identity, homosexuality, and Islam. Film festivals around the world have featured his documentaries, which are critically acclaimed and controversial. Organizations such as GLAAD, Amnesty International, and the Human Rights Watch have all honored Sharma's work; in 2018, he earned a Guggenheim Fellowship. Now living in New York, Sharma is the author of the 2017 memoir *A Sinner in Mecca: A Gay Muslim's Hajj of Defiance.*

C. Riley Snorton *(Bronx, NY)* is a professor, writer, and academic whose work focuses on cultural studies, communication, gender and sexuality, pop culture, Africana studies, and transgender theory. Snorton earned his PhD from the University of Pennsylvania in 2010 and has received postdoctoral fellow-ships from Harvard University and Pomono College, as well as a fellowship from the National Endowment for the Humanities. His first book is titled *Nobody is Supposed to Know: Black Sexuality on the Down Low* (2014), and he is also the author of *Black on Both Sides: A Racial History of Trans Identity* (2017). He has taught at Northwestern University, Cornell University, and at the University of Chicago. In 2014, BET listed Snorton as one of the top ten transgender people you should know.

Keith St. John *(White Plains, NY)* is a politician and lawyer, and the first openly gay Black person to be elected to public office. He studied public policy at Harvard and Duke University, where he earned his graduate degree, and earned his JD from Cornell Law School in 1985. Soon after, he began working in social security disability law and in family law in Albany, New York, and was elected to the Albany Common Council a year later. St. John worked as a regional coordinator on President Bill Clinton's 1992 campaign, and went on to counsel the New York State Senate Democratic Conference. He also served as the Director of Ethics on the New York State Joint Commission on Public Ethics. St. John has a number of awards, including the Root/Stimson Community and Professional Service Award from the New York Bar Association, and the Progressive Leadership Award from Citizen Action.

Octavia St. Laurent *(Brooklyn, NY)* was an actress and drag queen who was featured in the 1990 documentary *Paris is Burning.* St. Laurent was a showstopper in the Harlem drag ball scene that created voguing, which Madonna later brought to the mainstream. After *Paris is Burning,* St. Laurent became a public persona and starred in other documentaries such as *Octavia Saint Laurent: Queen of the Underground* (1992) and *How Do I Look* (2006). Though St. Laurent was assigned male at birth and was not born with intersex genitalia, she identified as intersex rather than transgender—"I'm not trying to be a woman. Just beautiful," she told *Dazed* in 2009, her last interview. She embraced elements of both the masculine and the feminine, and said that she was arrested many times for her gender-nonconformity. She died of cancer in 2009 at the age of forty-five.

I feel that those two experiences of being an outsider in another culture but also then identifying so strongly with all these other outsiders who were agitating for their rights and their freedom against the old world order was something that really connected with me.

—Urvashi Vaid on moving from India to the US during the 1960s, Provincetown Community TV, 2010

Urvashi Vaid *(New Delhi, India)* is a lawyer, LGBT+ rights activist, and founder and CEO of the Vaid Group LLC, which advocates for justice and inclusion in public policy. Now living in New York, she has served as the executive director of the LGBTQ Task Force and at Columbia Law School as director of the Engaging Tradition Project at the Center for Gender and Sexuality Law. Vaid has worked with the ACLU's National Prison Project to advocate for HIV/AIDS awareness and health care in prison. In 2009, *Out* magazine named Vaid one of the fifty most influential people in America.

Luther Vandross *(New York, NY)* was an R&B and soul singer. Over his career, Vandross wrote and performed songs with famous musicians such as David Bowie, Bette Midler, Whitney Houston, Diana Ross, and Aretha Franklin. Vandross was nominated for his first Grammy in 1981 for the album *Never Too Much,* though his first Grammy win came in 1990 for his song "Here and Now." In 1994, he did a duet with Mariah Carey called "Endless Love." That same year, he released the number one track "Always and Forever," an R&B cover of the original by Heatwave, which earned Vandross his fourth Grammy nomination of the year. Over the course of his life, he won eight Grammys and received thirty-three Grammy nominations. His most successful album, *Dance with My Father,* came out in 2003 after

Luther Vandross

Vandross suffered a stroke, and reached number one on the Billboard 200. Vandross had diabetes and struggled with dramatic fluctuations in weight due to emotional eating. He died in 2005 at the age of fifty-four. Though Vandross never came out publicly while he was alive, Patti LaBelle controversially confirmed rumors about his homosexuality in 2017, saying that he struggled with potentially disappointing his mother or his female fans.

Gore Vidal *(West Point, NY)* was an author and screenwriter known for his fascination with politics and his very public life. He ran for office twice, regularly engaged in public spats with other celebrities, and was even offered a role on *The Tonight Show* by Johnny Carson. Vidal had a passionate romance with one of the best athletes in his high school, Jimmie Trimble. After Trimble died in World War II, Vidal never had another romantic connection that was as satisfying. Trimble inspired Vidal's novel *The City and the Pillar,* a coming-out story that scandalized many people upon its release in 1948. Vidal, convinced he had alienated himself in the literary world, went on to write television dramas, including *Visit to a Small Planet*, which he later adapted into a Broadway play. Paul Newman, Eleanor Roosevelt, and other celebrities supported Vidal in his 1960

> *It is a paradox of the acquisitive society in which we now live that although private morals are regulated by law, the entrepreneur is allowed considerable freedom to use—and abuse—the public in order to make money.*
>
> —Gore Vidal, "A Manifesto," *Esquire*, 2008

run for Congress, although he did not win. During this time, he wrote *Julian,* which many people consider to be the crown jewel of his career. He also developed many political rivalries, notably when he called William F. Buckley a "crypto-Nazi." Despite the controversies that riddled his career, Vidal received a lifetime achievement award at the 2009 National Book Awards. He died in 2012 at the age of eighty-six.

Bruce Vilanch *(New York, NY)* is a comedian who wrote jokes for many hosts of the Academy Awards beginning in 1991, and also wrote for the Emmy Awards and Tony Awards. Vilanch has many television and film acting credits, including *The Eric Andre Show* and *Bosom Buddies*, and the role of Edna Turnblad in the 2003 Broadway production of *Hairspray*. Vilanch is known for his signature look: a ragged mop of dirty blonde hair paired with thick-rimmed, colorful glasses and a sassy T-shirt. Bette Midler recruited Vilanch to write jokes for her after she was impressed with his 1970 review of one of her early shows in the *Chicago Tribune*, and he went on to write for other comedians such as Joan Rivers. Vilanch regularly attends LGBT+ charity events and has won two Emmy Awards.

Hida Viloria *(New York, NY)* is an activist for intersex and nonbinary rights. They grew up as a queer child of Latinx immigrants. Their 2017 memoir, *Born Both: An Intersex Life*, was nominated for a 2018 Lambda Literary Award. They also cofounded the Intersex Campaign for Equality (IC4E), which fights policies that

> *It's a radical act of ending our oppression. It's saying: We're not ashamed. And we're so not ashamed that we're going to share who we are. We're going to step out proudly as intersex people, even though we're getting the message that we should never want to admit that's what we are.*
>
> —Hida Viloria on Intersex Awareness Day, *INTO*, 2017

discriminate against intersex people and promotes educational opportunities and equality for intersex people. Viloria frequently consults for other human rights organizations, such as the United Nations, Lambda Legal, and the Human Rights Watch. Viloria is featured in the early ISNA film *Hermaphrodites Speak* as well as in the 2012 documentary *Intersexion*. In April of 2017, they received the second US intersex birth certificate ever issued. They continue to work as a nonbinary pioneer.

Abby Wambach *(Rochester, NY)* plays soccer for the US women's national team. Wambach attended the University of Florida, where she played for the Gators and became the team's leading scorer. In 2002, she was drafted while still in college to play for the Washington Freedom, where she helped her team win the Founders Cup III. She has scored more goals internationally than any other player, and has two Olympic gold medals. In 2012 FIFA named her their Women's World Player of the Year, and in 2015 *TIME* magazine named her on its list of one hundred most influential people. Her memoir, *Forward*, was a 2016 bestseller. In 2015, Wambach retired from soccer.

Jann Wenner *(New York, NY)* is a cofounder of *Rolling Stone* magazine. His father described him as a "cruel" child, and as an adult he developed a reputation that didn't stray far from his father's original assessment.

He flattered and bullied his way to favorable positions throughout high school and college, where he started to write about music and drugs. When Wenner started *Rolling Stone* after college, it was an almost immediate success, catering to younger audiences that other publications ignored. Yet some of Wenner's methods drew scrutiny, as he regularly let stars edit their own articles. He also took out personal vendettas in his magazine, such as giving Paul Simon little coverage because he had dated Wenner's ex, Denise Kaufman. Wenner married Jane Schindelheim, a socialite from New York who was critical to the success of *Rolling Stone*, but had gay affairs his whole life, and finally left Schindelheim to come out publicly in 1995. A biography about Wenner, *Sticky Fingers*, came out in 2017 and highlights his many escapades with drugs, sex, and rivalries. It also cements his status as a legend in music journalism and as a talented, if spiteful, editor. He no longer speaks to Joe Hagan, the man he convinced to write his biography—Wenner says it is because the book is flawed, but Hagan says it's because Wenner couldn't stand lacking control over the book. His companies have won numerous National Magazine Awards, the Oscars of the magazine business.

Walt Whitman *(West Hills, NY)* was a Romantic-era poet and writer. Born in 1819, Whitman loved to read from an early age. He worked in the printing industry as a teenager, then became a teacher, and later a journalist. He worked for many publications, including the *Long-Islander* (his own paper) and the *Brooklyn Freeman*. Whitman released his first book of poetry in 1855, *Leaves of Grass,* which he revised and republished multiple times during his lifetime. Many fellow writers, including Ralph Waldo Emerson, praised *Leaves of Grass* and Whitman's unique writing style. Many Americans think of Whitman as one of the most important poets in the English literary canon. While Whitman

> *I exist as I am, that is enough.*
>
> —Walt Whitman, "Song of Myself," 1892

Walt Whitman

never came out as gay, some of his poems (notably the *Calamus* series) refer to same-sex relationships, and biographers suspect he had a long-term romantic relationship with a man named Peter Doyle.

H. Sharif "Herukhuti" Williams *(Brooklyn, NY)* is an academic, activist, and writer. Williams is a faculty member at Goddard College and professor at CUNY School of Professional Studies, and has received fellowships through the Lambda Literary Foundation as well as the National Endowment of the Humanities. In 2012, Williams founded the Center for Culture, Sexuality, and Spirituality, which publishes an online journal called *Sacred Sexualities.* Williams explores the intersection of sexuality, colonialism, and race in many of his works, including his speech at a 2018 New York City Pride Rally and his play *My Brother's a Keeper,* which explores Black bisexuality and activism. He also produced the 2019 documentary *No Homo | No Hetero* about Black sexual fluidity.

 PLACES

The AIDS Memorial *(New York, NY)* is a monument in memory of the 100,000+ people in New York who have died from AIDS, and in honor of the activists, health care professionals, and friends and family who fought for those suffering from it. Located in the northwestern corner of St. Vincent's Triangle, it stands on a section of the former property of St. Vincent's Hospital. In 2011, Brooklyn-based Studio a+I won the competition to design the memorial, and it was dedicated on December 1, 2016. The monument features a white triangular structure with a central fountain and benches, and has phrases from Walt Whitman's poem "Song of Myself" engraved on the pavement.

The Ali Forney Center *(New York, NY)* is the largest LGBT+ homeless center in the US. It serves approximately 1,400 youth per year via a scattered-site housing program and a drop-in center, which provide youth with the tools they need to live independently. AFC's namesake was a gender-nonconforming youth who left home at thirteen and entered the foster care system, where he was abused. By the age of fifteen, Ali (sometimes known as Luscious) was living on the streets, and he was tragically murdered in Harlem in December 1997. AFC was founded in 2002 by Carl Siciliano, who still serves as its executive director. In 2015, AFC broke ground on the new Bea Arthur Homeless Shelter, funded by actress Bea Arthur, who left money for the shelter in her will.

The Alice Austen House *(Staten Island, NY)* was home to Alice Austen, a prominent photographer, founder of the Staten Island Garden Club, and a lesbian. Austen took photos at the beginning of the twentieth century and documented how New York City changed as it welcomed immigrants. The Alice Austen House shows both Austen's photography and the work of current photographers. Listed on the National Register of Historic Places, the house's entry was amended to include her sexuality due to the advocacy of the NYC LGBT Historic Sites Project. The house is open to the public.

Audre Lorde's house *(Staten Island, NY)* is the former home of writer Audre Lorde, where she lived with her children and partner from 1972 to 1987. During her time there, she spoke at the National March on Washington for Lesbian and Gay Rights and cofounded Kitchen Table: Women of Color Press. She also wrote *The Black Unicorn* and *The Cancer Journals*, amongst other works, and taught English at John Jay College.

The Bayard Rustin Residence *(New York, NY)* is the former home of civil rights advocate Bayard Rustin, who lived there from 1962 to 1987. Rustin was a Black Quaker who promoted nonviolent activism on issues such as economic, social, and racial justice. In 1963, Rustin organized the March on Washington for Jobs and Freedom, where Martin Luther King Jr. delivered his "I Have a Dream" speech. In the mid-1980s, Rustin advocated for the New York City Gay and Lesbian Rights Bill. He lived with his partner, Walter Naegle, who still lives at the residence on West Twenty-Eighth Street.

The Bethesda Fountain (Angel of the Waters) *(New York, NY)* was unveiled in Central Park in 1873, sculpted by Emma Stebbens, the first woman and first lesbian to receive a major sculpture commission in New York. The Angel of the Waters was the only sculpture commissioned during the creation of Central Park, and was an homage to the new Croton Aqueduct system that brought fresh water to New York in response to a cholera epidemic. It honored health and healing, drawing inspiration from the Gospel of John, which (in part) says, "For an angel went down at a certain season into the pool and troubled the water, whosoever then first after the troubling of the water stepped in, was made whole of whatever disease he had." Tony Kushner featured the sculpture in the final scene of his 1993 Pulitzer Prize–winning play *Angels in America* about AIDS and homosexuality in the 1980s.

Bluestockings Bookstore *(New York, NY)* is a collectively owned LGBT+ bookstore and fair-trade café staffed by volunteers. In addition to LGBT+ literature, Bluestockings also stocks books on climate change, politics, race studies, gender studies, and capitalism, amongst other subjects. Founded in 1999 by Kathryn Welsh, the store takes its name from "bluestocking," an eighteenth-century term for an educated woman.

The Callen-Lorde Community Health Center *(New York, NY)* provides health care to the LGBT+ community, regardless of patients' financial situations. Named after singer Michael Callen and writer Audre Lorde, the center began when the St. Mark's Community Clinic and the Gay Men's Health Project merged in 1983. In addition to physical and dental health services, the Callen-Lorde Community Health Center offers mental health assistance at the Thea Spyer Center.

Cherry Grove *(Fire Island, NY)* was a resort and safe haven for gay writers, businesspeople, and celebrities going back to the 1940s. Physically isolated from the mainland of Fire Island, the narrow strip of land was a secluded place where LGBT+ people did not have to fear persecution from the law, their workplace, or their families. It was also the site of the Cherry Grove Community House and Theater, one of the oldest LGBT+ theaters in the US and on the National Register of Historic Places. Cherry Grove is the third place relevant to LGBT+ history to receive government recognition as a landmark.

Christopher Street *(Greenwich Village, New York, NY)*, the site of the Stonewall Riots, has historically been a hub of LGBT+ culture since the 1960s. Drag queens—notably, Marsha P. Johnson—began to frequent the Christopher Street piers in the 1960s to avoid police persecution. In 1966, the Mattachine Society invited reporters to a tour of local bars to see which ones would still serve them after they revealed they were gay. The year after the Stonewall Riots, Christopher Street was the site of the first gay pride march in New York, Christopher Street Gay Liberation Day. In 1973, an LGBT+ bookstore, Oscar Wilde bookshop, opened on Christopher Street, followed by many other LGBT+ businesses. The first HIV/AIDS housing center, Bailey House, opened on Christopher Street in 1986. LGBT+ culture and life began to subside in the 1990s as the demographics of the neighborhood changed. Today, Christopher Street is an affluent neighborhood that harbors luxury businesses, but its legacy remains. In Germany, Berlin's Pride is often called CSD, which stands for Christopher Street Day.

Eleanor Roosevelt's home *(Hyde Park, NY)*, nicknamed Val-Kill after a neighboring stream, is a modest home on a picturesque property where Eleanor Roosevelt lived after her husband, Franklin Roosevelt, died in 1945. FDR first purchased the property in 1911, and over the years the Roosevelts hosted picnics on the land. Val-Kill also served as a site to revive old methods of crafting and farming under the name Val-Kill Industries, which inspired elements of the New Deal.

Val-Kill Industries was started by Eleanor Roosevelt and her friends Marion Dickerman and Nancy Cook, a lesbian couple who lived at the cottage year-round. Val-Kill is now a National Historic Site.

The Gay Men's Health Crisis (GMHC) *(New York, NY)* provides health care to those living with HIV/AIDS. The organization began as an AIDS hotline in 1982, and received one hundred calls the first night the line opened. It also provides education and resources for AIDS prevention, as well as legal aid, vocational training, nutrition information, and mental health services.

Hamilton Lodge *(Harlem, New York, NY)*, located at 111th Street and Seventh Avenue, was the site of the Hamilton Lodge Ball, which started the New York tradition of drag balls. Drag balls were held all over the country, and were a safe space for LGBT+ people to celebrate, socialize, drink, and dance. Most of the participants of the Hamilton Lodge Ball were Black. The first ball was held in 1869, and over the years drew scrutiny from organizations such as the Committee of Fourteen, which found the balls immoral and scandalous because of their high energy and the prominence of drag queens. Over time, the balls grew to harbor activism and advocacy.

The Hudson River at West Village Piers *(New York, NY)* was where Marsha P. Johnson's body was found on July 6, 1992. Though police ruled her death a suicide, those who knew her claimed she was murdered. She was forty-six. Read more about Johnson under New Jersey.

James Baldwin's home *(Harlem, New York, NY)*, on 131st Street and Fifth Avenue, is where the author lived from 1965 until his death in 1987. There, he wrote the essay "Here Be Dragons" and the book *Just Above My Head,* amongst other works. The site is marked by a plaque.

Julius' *(New York, NY)* was the site of the Mattachine Society's iconic 1966 "sip-in," where they invited the press to follow them around to bars to see which ones refused them service on the basis of their sexuality. At the time, the law prohibited bars from serving people they knew were gay. Although Julius' was a gay bar, the police had recently raided it and the bar refused to serve the Mattachine Society alcohol. From this event launched the court case that struck down the law banning bars from serving homosexuals.

The Lesbian Herstory Archives *(Brooklyn, NY)* are home to the largest collection of objects pertaining to lesbian history. Joan Nestle, Deborah Edel, Julia Stanley, Sahli Cavallaro, and Pamela Oline founded the archive in 1974, along with a newsletter in 1975. The archives contain news articles, documents pertaining to LGBT+ organizations, books, media, and many other materials dating as far back as the 1800s. The Lesbian Herstory Archives host a Pride book sale every June, and are completely run by volunteers.

The Leslie Lohman Museum of Gay and Lesbian Art *(SoHo, New York, NY)* is a library visual arts collection of more than twenty-two thousand pieces. All materials relate to LGBT+ art, themes, and history. The museum offers free field trips for NYC public schools, as well as classroom residencies and other opportunities for educators.

The LGBT Community Center *(New York, NY)* supports LGBT+ arts, education, health, and community. It moved into its current building on West Thirteenth Street in 1984 and opened its library in 1991. It hosts fundraisers, such as the Center Dinner, to raise money for LGBT+ organizations. It also connects people to resources for adoption, health, suicide prevention, insurance enrollment, and legal assistance, among others. More than six thousand people visit the LGBT Community Center every week.

The National Women's Hall of Fame *(Seneca Falls, NY)* is a historical project and museum that highlights notable women throughout history. Many of the women honored here were lesbian or bisexual, though that facet of their identities is not typically mentioned. Seneca Falls is often credited as where the women's rights movement began, as it was the site of the first Women's Rights Convention in 1848. The National Women's Hall of Fame began in 1969 and holds induction ceremonies to honor new women whose achievements have greatly contributed to American art, culture, and politics, amongst other areas.

QUEER FACTS

ACT UP (the AIDS Coalition to Unleash Power) was formed in 1987 to demand better handling of the AIDS crisis. The organization was created by people who wanted to take action and still avoid the traditional leadership structure of most organizations, instead choosing to work as a collective. ACT UP is known for its powerful demonstrations to attract attention to the crisis and inspire change. Its first demonstration, only three weeks after formation in March 1987, took place on Wall Street in protest of Big Pharma's poor management of AIDS medication. Soon after, the FDA announced it would quicken its drug approval process.

The Audre Lorde Project is a community group for lesbian, gay, bisexual, transgender, two-spirit, and gender nonconforming people of color. It is located in the Fort Greene neighborhood of Brooklyn, in the parish house of the Lafayette Avenue Presbyterian Church, where it has been since 1996, two years after its founding. The group exists so that LGBT+ people of color can fight a history of discrimination and other forms of oppression.

AVEN (Asexual Visibility Education Network), founded in 2001, hosts the world's largest online asexual community and archive of asexuality resources. The organization aims to create public acceptance and discussion of asexuality and to facilitate asexual community growth. It also provides resources for family and friends of asexual people. AVEN occasionally offers a survey on its forum to collect information on the asexual community and posts results on its website. Its quarterly newsletter and magazine, *AVENues*, features works from the community.

BiNet USA is the oldest advocacy organization in the United States for bisexual people; it also advocates for the bi+ community (pansexual, fluid, queer-identified, and unlabeled people). BiNet was founded in 1987 after a group of bisexuals marched in the 1987 March on Washington for Gay and Lesbian Rights—it was the first time a national group of bisexuals gathered, and they decided to form a national organization. The organization was originally called NABN (the North American Bisexual Network) but eventually changed its name to BiNet. The group promotes bisexual community and visibility, and recently paired with GLAAD to sponsor #BiWeek.

The first intersex birth certificate was issued on December 15, 2016, to New York resident Sara Kelly Keenan. Keenan, who was fifty-five at the time, struggled with gender issues from early in her life. When tested at age sixteen, she was shown to be genetically male with female genitalia and mixed reproductive genitalia. Even after surgery and female hormone replacement therapy to try to "make her biologically female", she never felt completely comfortable. After New York allowed Keenan to correct her birth certificate, others have been allowed to legally change the sex on their birth certificates to intersex, as long as they can provide documentation from a doctor.

The first Pride parade was held on June 28, 1970, commemorating the one-year anniversary of the Stonewall Riots. Deciding that real progress for LGBT+ rights required more visibility, a group of activists at an LGBT+ conference voted to organize a parade. Although it didn't have floats or music, it also didn't enforce a strict dress code, which was new for the era. The organizers referred to it as a pride parade to try to encourage the community to be more confident in their identities; the official slogan of the parade was "Say it loud, gay is proud." The activists also encouraged other states to host similar parades; Chicago, Los Angeles, and San Francisco participated that same week. The New York City parade was a resounding success with thousands of marchers, which solidified the Stonewall Riots as a significant turning point in LGBT+ history and inspired decades of LGBT+ pride events.

Giovanni's Room is a 1956 novel by James Baldwin. It tells the story of a bisexual American living in France. Critics received the novel well, and it remains an important piece of writing because of its complex treatment of the protagonist's sexuality. The novel is notable among Baldwin's works for being one of only two fictional works by him that feature only white characters.

The God of Vengeance, a 1923 play by Sholem Asch, caused a scandal when it debuted in New York City. The play had toured through Europe successfully and even did well in New York when it was performed in its original Yiddish. Once the show was translated to English and moved to a more prominent theater, however, it drew negative attention because it featured a lesbian kiss. Quickly after the move, the play's producer and entire cast were arrested on charges of obscenity. The producer, Harry Weinberger, was a lawyer and defended the group in court, successfully winning his appeal.

Harvey Milk High School was founded in 1985 as a place for displaced LGBT+ youth to earn their GEDs, but in 2003 it became an official public high school in New York. The school is small; when it expanded into a public high school, it had about one hundred students. There is some controversy about having a school dedicated to students based on their sexuality—critics argue that this is segregation and that it's sexual bias to divide students by their sexual orientation or gender identity. Since the controversy arose, the school has stopped accepting only LGBT+ students. It is still LGBT-centered, but does not explicitly deny non-LGBT+ students.

Housing Works is a New York City nonprofit fighting AIDS and homelessness by providing work, health care, legal services, and housing for those affected by AIDS. The organization was founded in 1990 by four members of ACT UP. Housing Works believes that addressing housing concerns will prevent further spread of AIDS and help those already affected live better lives. It funds its programs with profits from its bookstore cafe, online shop, and thrift shops.

The Human Rights Watch's intersex research was completed in 2013, bringing public attention to body-altering surgeries performed on intersex individuals before they are old enough to give consent. The fifty-nine-page report recommends parents and hospitals not commit to any surgical procedures on intersex individuals. It also states that intersex people can live full and healthy lives without surgery and gives specific messages to the American Medical Association, the World Health Organization, and the American Academy of Pediatrics, amongst other institutions.

The Ithaca Statement on Bisexuality was issued in June 1972 by a group of Quakers attending the Friends General Conference. The statement, published in *The Advocate*, was supportive of bisexuality, and is considered the first public statement on bisexuality from a religious or political group.

Lambda Legal is a nonprofit legal service that defends the rights of LGBT+ people. Originally founded in 1973 by a group of volunteers, their first case was for themselves: their application for nonprofit status was denied by the city, and the group had to appeal in order to achieve nonprofit status. They won their case, thus launching a successful string of legal cases. Lambda Legal was co-counsel in *Obergefell v. Hodges*, the landmark case that won same-sex couples the right to marriage. Lambda Legal continues to provide free legal services to LGBT+ people across the country.

The Mattachine Society and Daughters of Bilitis New York chapters were founded in the 1950s. The Mattachine Society (a group supporting the rights of gay men) chapter was started in 1955 by Tony Segura and Sam Morford, and the Daughters of Bilitis (a group supporting the rights of lesbian women) chapter was started in 1958 by Barbara Gittings and Marion Glass. Both organizations were early supporters of LGBT rights and referred to themselves as homophile groups.

The New York State Liquor Authority Ban took effect in New York after the end of Prohibition, stating that bars could have their liquor licenses revoked if they "permit [their] premises to become disorderly." Police used this law to revoke the licenses of bars that knowingly served LGBT+ patrons as early as 1939. The SLA continued to patrol bars to make owners feel like they were under constant surveillance, tension that set the stage for the Mattachine Society's 1966 sip-in and the Stonewall Riots.

NewFest promotes LGBT+ films, including the annual New York LGBTQ Film Festival that takes place every October. Founded in 1988, NewsFest was formed to connect LGBT+ artists with their audiences. NewFest also promotes other year-round events, such as film screenings and after-school programs.

The Oscar Wilde Memorial Bookshop was the first LGBT+ bookstore in the US. Opened in 1967 by Craig L. Rodwell, an influential gay rights activist, the space was intended to be a community gathering place that carried materials promoting a positive perception of the LGBT+ community. Rodwell named his bookstore after Oscar Wilde because he was a recognizably gay literary figure, calling it "A Bookshop of the Homophile Movement." The store closed in 2009 after switching through four different owners following Rodwell's death in 1993.

PFLAG (Parents, Families and Friends of Lesbian, Gay, Bisexual and Transgender People) is a nationwide advocacy group for LGBT+ people and their families. Founded in 1973 in New York, the organization now has over five hundred chapters across the country with a total of more than 250,000 members and supporters. PFLAG works with schools to make sure they're safe for LGBT+ students, provides support services to families, and works with corporations and community groups to help straight people understand the daily lives of LGBT+ people.

The Quaker Emergency Committee of New York City, the first social welfare agency for gay people, was opened in 1945 by Quakers who empathized with youths who were arrested on charges of same-sex relationships. It was active for nine years until internal disagreements led to the organization's dissolution, but many members went on to work with other LGBT+ organizations.

Richards v. US Tennis Association was a 1977 case filed by tennis player Renée Richards after she was not allowed to compete in the US Open because she refused chromosome testing. During the Tennis Week Open, twenty-five female athletes declined to participate after they learned that Richards would compete, feeling it was unfair for a transgender woman to compete in a women's athletic event. Richards won her case and went on to have a successful tennis career as one of the first openly trans athletes. Now retired, she currently works as an ophthalmologist.

SAGE, founded in 1978, provides advocacy and support for the elderly LGBT+ community. Inspired by Stonewall, a group of advocates began providing support for elder LGBT+ folks because they thought they weren't getting enough support. SAGE has been running for over forty years and continues to provide valuable nationwide service. The organization runs the National Resource Center on LGBT Aging, advocates for LGBT+ elders, provides training for care professionals to understand LGBT+ care, and contributes to housing programs.

Same-sex marriage became legal in New York on June 24, 2011, when Governor Andrew Cuomo signed the Marriage Equality Act. New York began performing marriage ceremonies for same-sex couples a month later. This made New York the sixth state and the seventh jurisdiction to legalize same sex marriage.

The Silence = Death Project was a 1987 initiative that spread AIDS awareness. The project distributed posters with a pink triangle symbol, the same symbol Nazis used in concentration camps during World War II to identify homosexuals. The LGBT+ community turned the pink triangle into a positive icon of its movement by flipping the triangle to face upright. The posters served as a reminder of the suffering LGBT+ people faced throughout history by relating Nazi persecution of gay people to the AIDS epidemic. The posters later became associated with the ACT UP organization.

The Sylvia Rivera Law Project, named for the transgender activist and veteran of the Stonewall riots, was founded in 2002 by attorney and transgender civil rights activist Dean Spade. The organization is a nonprofit legal aid society that serves low-income or people of color who are transgender, intersex, or gender-nonconforming, and aims to eventually end discrimination and violence toward these identities. The group's staff and board is always at least half transgender and at least half people of color.

The Trevor Project was founded in 1998 by Peggy Rajski, Randy Stone, and James Lecesne. The producers Rajski and Stone and performer Lecesne came together to produce an Academy Award–winning short film about a young man named Trevor who was struggling with his sexual identity. After realizing that resources to help kids like Trevor didn't currently exist, the trio decided to take action. On the night the film premiered on HBO, the Trevor Lifeline was launched—the first national crisis intervention and suicide prevention lifeline for LGBT+ teens and youth. This blossomed into what is known today as the Trevor Project, which offers a variety of life-affirming resources for LGBT+ people ages twenty-five and under. The organization maintains crisis intervention lines, chats, and texts, offers suicide prevention training, conducts research about suicide, and more. The Trevor Project is headquartered in New York and California.

Vogue was a style of dance created in 1960s Harlem by the Black and Latinx LGBT+ community in the drag ball scene. Vogue began as a dance battle between different dance troupes known as "houses." The dancers were considered more skilled if they could portray "realness," or effectively mimic heterosexuality, and the winner of a competition was the dancer who threw the best "shade." Its exaggerated movements mimicked white glam culture, subverting the performative nature of gender. Voguing included pantomiming, sharp movements, catwalks, and complicated hand movements. It came to mainstream attention when Madonna appropriated it in the 1980s, and in the documentary *Paris is Burning*. It has also influenced fashion and the choreography of multiple pop stars, and sparked international voguing movements in places such as Russia and New Zealand as a symbol of LGBT+ resistance and pride.

The Stonewall Inn

Our Gay History in 50 States

St. Vincent's Catholic Medical Center *(Greenwich Village, New York, NY)* was a teaching hospital home to the second AIDS ward in the US (the first was in San Francisco). St. Vincent's was the closest hospital to the World Trade Center during the September 11 attacks and treated many wounded in the incident. The hospital closed in 2010, five years after filing for bankruptcy with a total debt of $700 million, and the building was demolished in 2013. St. Vincent's had a long history of treating the homeless and the poor, and as its neighborhood grew wealthier, its residents started to seek treatment at different hospitals. Operating since 1849, the hospital had treated many patients during the cholera epidemic of the time as well as patients from the *Titanic* sinking in 1912.

The Stonewall Inn *(Greenwich Village, New York, NY)* was the site of the famous Stonewall Riots, which incited gay rights movements around the world. The six-day riots started on June 28, 1969, when police raided the inn. At the time, bars were not allowed to serve LGBT+ people, and those suspected of doing so were raided for "disorderly" behavior. The police regularly arrested LGBT+ people for offenses such as wearing less than three pieces of gender-conforming clothing or holding hands. LGBT+ people sought places away from police brutality in gay bars that were often controlled by the mafia—the Stonewall Inn, one such place, was run by the Genovese family, who operated without a liquor license and bribed the NYPD to stay away. Though the police still occasionally raided Stonewall, an officer would usually tip off the owners beforehand. During the first night of the Stonewall Riots, there was no tip, and the police arrested thirteen people. Many of the patrons stayed near the bar and began to riot once they witnessed police brutality against a lesbian. The police shut themselves inside the bar, along with a reporter and those arrested, while the crowd outside tried to burn the inn to the ground. President Barack Obama designated the Stonewall Inn as a National Historic Landmark in 2016 for its crucial role in the fight for LGBT+ equality.

Studio 54 *(New York, NY)* was an iconic LGBT+ nightclub founded in 1977 by Steve Rubell and Ivan Schrager. The club was known for its sexy staff, its over-the-top special effects, and the velvet door rope policy where owner Rubell picked who could enter. Holding two thousand people at a time, Studio 54 was frequented by a host of celebrities, including Truman Capote, Salvador Dalí, Divine, Calvin Klein, Liza Minelli, Andy Warhol, Valentino, and Yves Saint-Laurent. The Roundabout Theatre Company bought the space in 1998.

Transy House *(Brooklyn, NY)* was a shelter for displaced and homeless transgender and gender-nonconforming people from 1995 to 2008. Rusty Moore and Chelsea Goodwin ran Transy House, located in the former home of activist Sylvia Rivera. The house could shelter thirteen people at a time. It also served as a center of transgender rights activism, as both Goodwin and Moore participated in the Metropolitan Gender Network and the National Transgender Advocacy Coalition. Transy House was inspired by the former STAR House, created by Sylvia Rivera and Marsha P. Johnson during the 1970s as a safe space for homeless transgender young people.

PENNSYLVANIA

PEOPLE

I just want to become a woman as quickly as possible, that's all. . . . I'll become a citizen of anywhere I can receive that treatment I need and be operated on.

—Carlett Brown Angianlee, *Jet*, 1953

Lee Daniels

Carlett Brown Angianlee *(Pittsburgh, PA)* was a US Navy veteran who, in the 1950s, wanted to become the first Black person to undergo gender-affirmation surgery. While in the Navy, Angianlee corresponded with Eugene Martin, a US sergeant stationed in Germany, whom she knew from childhood and had fallen in love with. In order to obtain gender-affirmation surgery, Angianlee made plans with a doctor based in Germany and intended to become an expat in order to be with Martin. After leaving the military, Angianlee made a living as a shake dancer and drag queen, and by selling her blood. In 1953, she was barred from leaving the country due to owing back taxes to the government; it is unknown if she ever made it to Germany.

Deborah Batts *(Philadelphia, PA)* was, in 1994, nominated by President Bill Clinton to the US District Court in New York. She was the first Black, openly lesbian judge to hold the position. In 2012, Batts achieved status as a senior judge on the court, and continues to serve. She earned her JD from Harvard Law School in 1972; in 1984, she became the first Black faculty member of Fordham Law School in New York, where she worked until beginning her tenure as a judge.

Ilene Chaiken *(Elkins Park, PA)* is a television producer and writer most known for *The L Word*. She developed the script for the Hulu adaptation of *The Handmaid's Tale*, and has produced programs including *Empire*, *Black Box*, and *The Fresh Prince of Bel-Air*,

amongst others. In the male-dominated entertainment industry, Chaiken sees her gender and her sexuality as strengths. She is married to LouAnne Brickhouse, and they live together in Los Angeles. They are animal lovers, members of the Los Angeles Zoo, and have an amicable relationship with a neighborhood raven, James, and his partner, Margaret.

Lee Daniels *(Philadelphia, PA)* is a producer and director known for the TV show *Empire* and the films *The Butler* (2012) and *Precious* (2009). As a child, Daniels's father often beat him for expressing femininity, and spurning him motivated Daniels to come out as gay. Later, Daniels attended Lindenwood University in Missouri before moving to Los Angeles in 1980, where he worked in casting for Prince's films *Purple Rain* and *Under the Cherry Moon*. Daniels's work has received multiple accolades, including six Academy Award nominations for *Precious*, which won Best Adapted Screenplay and Best Supporting Actress for Mo'Nique.

Candace Gingrich *(Harrisburg, PA)* is the associate director of the Human Rights Campaign's youth and campus engagement program. They are also the half-sibling of former Georgia Representative Newt Gingrich, and became politically active and outspoken against his conservative views on homosexuality when Newt was elected Speaker of the House in 1995.

Billy Porter

"

I had to come out to my mother three times over a twelve-year period, but I first came out to her when I was sixteen. It didn't go over so well, because I grew up in the Pentecostal Church. It was a very strict environment. She has since done a lot of work and has really blown my mind. She has learned about my life and has changed her mind.

—Billy Porter, TheaterMania.com, 2013

"

While Newt ran on a platform of LGBT+ tolerance, Candace fired back, telling the New York Times, "For him to say we should be tolerated, that still allows for us to be fired merely for being gay or lesbian, and that's not tolerance, that's discrimination. I want him to understand that discrimination is wrong." Gingrich identifies as a genderqueer lesbian and lives with their partner, Illinois Representative Kelly Cassidy.

Keith Haring *(Reading, PA)* was a prominent graffiti and pop artist in the 1980s. Haring held his first exhibition at the age of nineteen in what is now the Pittsburgh Center for the Arts. He then spent time hitchhiking the country selling anti-Nixon T-shirts before arriving in New York City in 1978 to attend the School of Visual Arts. Though his work was at times considered "low art" by critics, Haring became an influential artist, promoting awareness of issues such as the AIDS epidemic, drug addiction, and apartheid. Haring often used his work to advocate for gay causes, including promoting safe sex. Haring tested positive for HIV/AIDS in 1988 and died one year later. His legacy is preserved by the Keith Haring Foundation, which supports nonprofits related to children in need and to AIDS research.

Billy Porter *(Pittsburgh, PA)* began his entertainment career on Broadway, performing in shows such as *Grease* (1994) and *Jesus Christ Superstar* (1998). As a talented vocalist with multiple albums, Porter soon made the jump to film, landing roles in *The First Wives Club* (1996), *Law & Order* (2004), and *Pose* (2018). Porter starred as Lola in the 2013 Broadway iteration of *Kinky Boots*, which earned him a Tony Award for Best Actor in a Musical and a Grammy for Best Musical Theater Album, among several other accolades.

Bayard Rustin *(West Chester, PA)* was a civil rights leader and political activist who advocated for nonviolence and gay rights. As a student, Rustin attended two of the oldest predominantly Black institutions in the country, Wilberforce University and Cheyney State Teachers College, though he did not graduate from either. After moving to New York City, Rustin taught English, performed in several musical acts, and became active in antiracist politics. A close mentor to Martin Luther King Jr., Rustin pushed for nonviolent civil protest during the civil rights movement of the 1950s and '60s and helped found the Congress of Racial Equality and the Southern Christian Leadership Conference. Despite his influential presence in social and political movements, the fact that Rustin was openly gay often forced him to work out of the public eye. Rustin died at age seventy-five in 1987. Ronald Reagan praised him that year for his conviction in the civil rights movement; in 2013, Barack Obama awarded Rustin a posthumous Presidential Medal of Freedom.

Andy Warhol *(Pittsburgh, PA)* was an influential artist, director, and producer. Being diagnosed at a young age with a neurological disorder led Warhol to escape through celebrity magazines and comic books. He adopted many personas in college, eventually graduating from the Carnegie Institute of Technology with a degree in pictorial design. After years of working in advertising, Warhol opened an art studio in New York City called the Factory. There, alongside his more widely known pop art, Warhol displayed art with homosexual themes, erotic photography, and films depicting gay culture. In response to criticism against his work, he stated, "Of course, people said the Factory was degenerate just because 'anything went' there, but I think that was really a very good thing." In 1968, Warhol barely survived an assassination attempt when Valerie Solanas, a radical feminist and author of the *SCUM Manifesto*, shot him at the Factory. Warhol died years later at the age of fifty-eight in 1987 from complications following gallbladder surgery. He was buried in his native Pittsburgh.

Ethel Waters *(Chester, PA)* was a renowned jazz, blues, and swing singer, who also frequently performed as an actor on Broadway stages. Before launching into a career famous for recordings such as "Stormy Weather," "Cabin in the Sky," "Taking a Chance on Love," "Dinah," "Heat Wave," and "I'm Coming Virginia," Waters was just a seventeen-year-old girl celebrating her birthday at a local Philadelphia nightclub in 1913. That night, her friends persuaded her to sing two songs, so impressing the audience that she was offered to work at the Lincoln Theatre in Baltimore. Waters married three men in her lifetime, and was in a relationship with dancer Ethel Williams, with whom she performed under the name the Two Ethels. Waters went on to star in the 1950 TV show *Beulah*, the first Black actor to star in her own show. In 1961, Waters appeared in an episode of *Route 66*, which earned her an Emmy nomination in 1962—she was the first Black woman ever to be nominated.

Edith Windsor *(Philadelphia, PA)* was the lead plaintiff in *United States v. Windsor*, the 2013 US Supreme Court case that ruled it unconstitutional to interpret marriage laws as only applying to heterosexual unions. That year, Windsor skyrocketed to LGBT+ fame, and was honored as the runner-up for *Time* magazine's

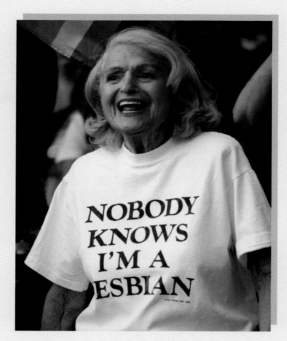

Edith Windsor

person of the year. Windsor held a master's degree in mathematics from New York University, and spent her career as a computer programmer for IBM. After ending her brief marriage with a man, she became engaged to a woman in 1967—their engagement lasted forty years, until they married in Canada in 2007. Windsor's wife died two years later, and Windsor married again in 2016. She died in 2017 at the age of eighty-eight.

PLACES

The Delaware Valley Legacy Fund *(Philadelphia, PA)* is a community foundation that provides grants to nonprofit LGBT+ organizations. The DVLF was founded in 1993 in response to the need for reliable support to LGBT+ organizations within the Greater Philadelphia area. The DLVF supports four key community areas: civil rights, arts and culture, education, and health and human services. Since its founding, the DLVF has distributed around $1 million in grants.

Giovanni's Room *(Philadelphia, PA)* is the country's oldest LGBT+ bookstore. Founded in 1973 by Dan Sherbo, Tom Wilson Weinberg, and Bern Boylethe, its

QUEER FACTS

Annual Reminders occurred yearly in the 1960s on July 4, beginning with a 1965 LGBT+ rights demonstration at Philadelphia's Independence Hall. East Coast Homophile Organizations (an alliance of regional organizations such as Daughters of Bilitis and the Mattachine Society) organized the demonstration as an "annual reminder" that many people, such as the LGBT+ community, still lacked equal protection and rights under the Constitution. The demonstrations continued annually for five years, and were honored on the fiftieth anniversary of the first demonstration during the Philadelphia Pride Festival.

Pennsylvania's first gay lawmaker was Brian Sims, who, since 2012, has served in the House of Representatives. Originally from Washington, DC, Sims had previously worked as an attorney, Chairman of the Gay and Lesbian Lawyers of Philadelphia, and president of Equality Pennsylvania. In 2013, Sims introduced the bill that legalized same-sex marriage in Pennsylvania. Later that year, he garnered support for the Employment Non-Discrimination Act, which encompassed anti-LGBT+ discrimination, although the act has yet to be passed.

Philadelphia's Gayborhood was honored in 2007, when the city's mayor dedicated thirty-six rainbow street signs to signify the neighborhood. The area, which saw an influx of LGBT+ community in the 1950s, lies in Washington Square West between Pine Street, Walnut Street, Eleventh Street, and Broad Street. While many cities are home to explicitly queer communities, the Gayborhood is considered among the first to be officially recognized.

Philadelphia scored 100 on the Municipal Equality Index by the Human Rights Campaign in 2018. Its nondiscrimination laws, employment policies, municipal services, law enforcement policies, and leadership on LGBT+ equality added up to its perfect score. While it did lose points for lacking inclusive workplaces, it scored bonus points in protecting LGBT+ youth from conversion therapy and providing city services to LGBT+ people who are homeless, elderly, HIV-positive, and more.

name is an homage to James Baldwin's book of the same name. During the 1980s, Giovanni's Room provided support for people during the AIDS epidemic by producing cartoons about safe sex and working with a nearby clinic to provide medical material to customers. When owner Ed Hermance retired in 2014, the store closed with an uncertain future; a few months later, it reopened under new ownership as the Philly AIDS Thrift @ Giovanni's Room, a combination book and thrift store.

The William Way LGBT Community Center *(Philadelphia, PA)* is a nonprofit that advocates for the well-being and acceptance of the LGBT+ community. Founded in 1974 as the Gay and Lesbian Community Center of Philadelphia, it originally contained a library and archives and hosted classes, support groups, and a small theater. After moving to several locations, the center purchased a building it named the William Way LGBT Community Center, named after the man who was the driving force behind the center's success in the 1980s. The current iteration hosts community services such as peer counseling, educational classes, and space for local arts and culture programs. It also hosts the John J. Wilcox Jr. Archives, an extensive collection containing regional LGBT+ historical documents and artifacts.

RHODE ISLAND

⊘ PEOPLE

Anne Bogart *(Newport, RI)* is a prominent theater and opera director. Bogart earned an MA from New York University's Tisch School of the Arts in 1977 and went on to work as a theater director, teacher, playwright, and essayist. Bogart is a director of the Saratoga International Theater Institute (SITI) Company, which she founded in 2002 with Tadashi Suzuki. SITI Company teaches improvisational acting and dancing techniques now used widely in college theater programs. Bogart has received numerous awards for her work in theater, including two Obies, a Guggenheim Fellowship, and several honorary degrees from distinguished universities. Bogart is married to Rena Chelouche Fogel, whom she married three times: once in Paris, again in New York so her daughter could attend, and once more when same-sex marriage was legalized.

Wendy Carlos *(Pawtucket, RI)* is a musician and film composer. Carlos is best known for her work in electronic music and for scoring the films *A Clockwork Orange* and *The Shining*. Carlos caught onto music early, starting piano lessons at the age of six. By sixteen, she had mastered several instruments, including the organ. Carlos studied physics and music at Brown University before earning a master's in music composition at Columbia University. In 1979, Carlos came out as transgender in a *Playboy* interview—until then, Carlos had avoided performing publicly. Carlos called the response to her coming out "tolerant or, if you wish, indifferent," and soon began to perform again for the public.

Alexander Chee *(South Kingston, RI)* is a writer best known for his 2016 novel *The Queen of the Night*. Chee is also an editor at several publications, including the *New Republic* and the *Virginia Quarterly Review*. Chee attended the Iowa Writers' Workshop and went on to teach there as well as at the New School University, Columbia University, and Dartmouth College. Chee, an openly gay Korean American writer, writes about his experience living in San Francisco in his 2018 essay collection *How to Write an Autobiographical Novel*.

Kate Fagan *(Warwick, RI)* is an *ESPN* writer and author of the *New York Times* Sports and Fitness bestseller *What Made Maddy Run*. The daughter of a professional basketball player, Fagan herself lettered in basketball at the University of Colorado–Boulder. Fagan began her journalism career covering the Philadelphia 76ers for the *Philadelphia Inquirer*. In addition to her written work, she also appears as a panelist on the ESPN shows *Around the Horn* and *Outside the Lines*. In 2018, she married Kathryn Budig.

Israel David Fishman *(Westerly, RI)* was a librarian who founded the Task Force on Gay Liberation, via the American Library Association, in 1970. Now known as the ALA's Gay, Lesbian, Bisexual, and Transgender Round Table (GLBTRT), it is dedicated to providing free information about and to the LGBT+ community. Fishman attended the City College of New York before earning a master's in library sciences at Columbia University. Fishman came up with the idea of the Task Force on Gay Liberation after attending the 1970 American Library Association meeting in Detroit. By the next year, TFGL members received national attention for their demonstrations and outcry regarding their work. Though he lost his job as a librarian at Upsala College in New Jersey because of it, Fishman continued to lead the TFGL for several years before studying at the Gay Community Services Center in Los Angeles. Fishman died in June of 2006.

Bob Hattoy *(Providence, RI)* was an environmental and gay rights activist. Hattoy began working on

> **Why is it so loud when you cry from grief? Because it must be loud enough for the missing one to hear, though it never can be. Loud enough to scale the sky and the backs of angels, or to fall through the earth to where they rest.**
>
> —Alexander Chee,
> *The Queen of the Night*, 2016

environmental issues and rent control in the office of Los Angeles city councilman Zev Yaroslavsky, then moved to the Sierra Club as its director from 1981 to 1992. He became the first openly gay person with AIDS to address a national political convention when he spoke against President George H. W. Bush's AIDS policies at the 1992 Democratic National Convention. Hattoy died in 2007 at the UC Davis Medical Center from complications related to AIDS.

Van Johnson *(Newport, RI)* was an actor, singer, and dancer. Johnson began his acting career in 1936 in the Broadway production of *New Faces* before moving to Hollywood to pursue film acting. Due to a car accident en route to filming, Johnson avoided being drafted and was able to star in several popular movies during the 1940s. By 1945, he was ranked second on the list of Top 10 box office stars; he went on to appear in productions such as *I Love Lucy*; *Murder, She Wrote*; *Yours, Mine and Ours*; and *The Purple Rose of Cairo*. Because of rumors surrounding his sexuality, Johnson was encouraged to marry actress Eve Abbott, with whom he shared a brief and unhappy marriage before their divorce in 1960. Though he struggled to get away from the boy-next-door image he gained from his wartime career, Johnson continued a moderately successful film and theater career until his death in 2008.

Caitlín R. Kiernan *(Dublin, Ireland)* is a former academic and an author of science fiction and weird fiction, including ten novels, several comic books, and over two hundred works of short fiction. She has

Caitlín R. Kiernan

received numerous awards for her work, including winning the Bram Stoker Award and World Fantasy Award twice. Kiernan was influenced by the literary interests of her mother, who read her Poe and Stoker at an early age. She also claims influence from several other authors of fantasy and weird fiction, including J. R. R. Tolkien, Shirley Jackson, and H. P. Lovecraft. Kiernan is openly transgender and bisexual and lives in Providence, Rhode Island.

H. P. Lovecraft *(Providence, RI)* was a prominent writer of horror and weird fiction in the early twentieth century. Lovecraft is best known for developing the

QUEER FACTS

The first panel of the Project AIDS Quilt was sewn for Marvin Feldman of Providence, Rhode Island, who died in 1986 from AIDS-related illnesses. The Quilt serves as a visual reminder of the AIDS epidemic and commemorates the lives of those who died of AIDS. Activist Cleve Jones, who helped organize the candle-light march honoring Harvey Milk and George Moscone following their assassinations, conceived of the idea. The quilt was first displayed in 1987 on the National Mall during the National March on Washington for Lesbian and Gay Rights.

Fricke v. Lynch was a 1980 state court case that ensued when student Aaron Fricke was barred from attending his high school prom with a male date. In response, Fricke sued the school board, and the court ruled that Fricke's first and fourteenth amendment rights were violated. The *Fricke v. Lynch* decision marked one of the first courtroom victories for LGBT+ youth issues. Following the ruling, Fricke appeared regularly on television programs to promote and defend LGBT+ rights. His 1981 memoir, *Reflections of a Rock Lobster*, tells the story of Fricke's youth and the aggression he faced due to his sexuality.

The Newport Sex Scandal was a 1919 US Navy investigation into allegations of illicit sexual behavior of Navy personnel at the Newport Army and Navy YMCA. Led by then–Assistant Secretary of the Navy Franklin Roosevelt, undercover investigators sought to have sex with fellow naval personnel in order to identify offending parties. Anyone who was arrested was then asked to incriminate others. This method of entrapment, and Roosevelt specifically, were later condemned as "reprehensible" by the US Senate's Committee on Naval Affairs. The case drew wide criticism from the media; the *New York Times* covered it with the headline "Lay Navy Scandal to Franklin D. Roosevelt, Details are Unprintable."

> *I want to emphasize that it was that shift in my consciousness*—that I would no longer be afraid—*that led me to bring about the birth of this Task Force, this miracle, this incredible tool/weapon for social change and liberation.*
>
> —Israel David Fishman, speech at the twenty-fifth anniversary of the GLBTF, 1995, *Liberating Minds: The Stories and Professional Lives of Gay, Lesbian, and Bisexual Librarians and Their Advocates* by Norman G. Kester

genre of cosmic horror, exemplified in the short stories that make up his Cthulhu Mythos, now a major thematic influence on games and literature. Many regard Lovecraft as asexual, due in large part to reflections of his wife Sonia Lovecraft after his death. Relatively unknown in his lifetime, his work had widespread influence on later writers and artists, including Guillermo del Toro, Stephen King, and Jorge Luis Borges. Lovecraft has become a controversial figure due to recent increased awareness of his outspoken anti-Semitic writings and views regarding race.

 PLACES

The LGBTQ Center at Brown University *(Providence, RI)* provides education, programming, and support services to LGBT+ students, faculty, staff, and friends in the campus community. Established in 2004, the LGBTQ Center promotes changes in the university and local community leading to more inclusive and social justice–centered environments. The center sponsors the Brown Safe Zone, a campus-wide initiative for local residents to visibly identify themselves as LGBT+ allies and supporters.

Rhode Island Pride *(Providence, RI)* is a festival celebrating LGBT+ rights and accomplishments in Providence, Rhode Island. First held in 1976 with only seventy-five participants, the festival attendance has grown to over 60,000 people. City leaders initially blocked the festival, but the original Rhode Island Pride organizers successfully sued the city to allow it to take place. Rhode Island Pride also includes the only nighttime illuminated Pride parade in New England.

Youth Pride, Inc. *(Providence, RI)* is a support and advocacy organization that works to end homophobia and transphobia while helping young adults struggling with identity-related issues. Founded in 1992 as an extension of the Greater Rhode Island YWCA, the group quickly outgrew its YWCA space and became a nonprofit in 1994. Youth Pride, Inc., now hosts an Annual Rainbow Party in the fall, using the proceeds to fund its programs and services, such as support groups, community dinners, and its annual GSA conference.

VeRMoNT

PEOPLE

Carleton Carpenter (*Bennington, VT*) is an openly bisexual film, television, and stage actor who is best known for his roles in Hollywood hits such as *Three Little Words* and *Two Weeks with Love*, both of which debuted in 1950. Carpenter starred in these films alongside Debbie Reynolds, and their duet "Aba Daba Honeymoon" was the first soundtrack recording to become a top-of-the-chart gold record. In 1953, Carpenter withdrew from film to focus on stage and radio acting.

Justin Chenette (*St. Albans, VT*) was elected as a Maine State Representative at the age of twenty-one in 2012, becoming the youngest legislator in Maine, as well as the youngest gay legislator in the nation. Before graduating with a degree in broadcasting from Lyndon State College, Chenette got his start in politics as a youth ambassador for Barack Obama's first presidential run. In 2016, Chenette was elected to the Maine Senate. *The Advocate* honored him on its 2013 40 Under 40 list; "I didn't want to wait 30 years and be told

> "
> *I think that our country and voters believe in equality. They want all of our LGBT neighbors, brothers, sisters, parents, kids to be welcomed, accepted in workplaces and in the community. . . . The message of our campaign is 'stronger together,' and an important part of being stronger together is welcoming the LGBT community.*
>
> —Robert Mook on Hillary Clinton's 2016 presidential campaign slogan, TheGeorgiaVoice.com, 2016
> "

I couldn't change the system," he told the magazine. "One day, being different won't be a headline."

Robby Mook (*Sharon, VT*) was the campaign manager for Hillary Clinton's 2016 presidential run, making him the first openly gay manager of a major presidential campaign. *Mother Jones* described Mook in 2015 as a "political nerd who lives and dies by data and nuts-and-bolts organizing." He has worked with CNN as a political commentator, and with Harvard Kennedy School to help election officials prevent interference from foreign hackers.

Charley Darkey Parkhurst (*Sharon, VT*), also known as "One-Eyed Charley" or "Six-Horse Charley," was an American stagecoach driver, farmer, and rancher in California. He was born in 1812 and raised as a girl in an orphanage. Later in his youth, he ran away and took on the name Charley, living as male. As a stable hand, he learned how to handle horses, and eventually drove coaches drawn by multiple horses. In 1849, he set his sights on California and joined the Gold Rush, where he became known as a skilled stagecoach driver. Parkhurst was possibly the first anatomically female individual to vote in a presidential election in California in 1868. He died of tongue cancer at the age of sixty-seven. Parkhurst's female anatomy was discovered posthumously, and records indicate he had given birth earlier in life.

Patty Sheehan (*Middlebury, VT*) is an American professional golfer who won six major championships and thirty-five LPGA Tour events. She won several high school and amateur state championships before even starting her successful professional career in 1980, and was one of the first LPGA players to come out as a lesbian. Sheehan adopted two children with her partner, Rebecca Gaston. Now in her sixties, she spends her time hosting the Patty Sheehan & Friends tournament, which raises money for women and children's charities.

Kimberly Zieselman (*Burlington, VT*) is the executive director of interACT, a Massachusetts-based organization fighting for the legal rights of intersex children. When she was fifteen, Zieselman's parents and doctor told her she had to have surgery to remove

Patty Sheehan

her potentially cancerous female sex organs. At the age of forty-one, she obtained her medical records and discovered it was a lie; her undescended testes had been removed instead. Zieselman has focused inter-ACT as an intersex children's advocacy organization and has consulted on projects such as the MTV show _Faking It_, which featured one of the first intersex main characters on TV. She holds a JD from Suffolk University Law School and has served as a member of the Human Rights Network and the UN Women LGBTI Reference Group.

 PLACES

Andrew's Inn _(Bellows Falls, VT)_ was a seemingly all-purpose gay community space, functioning as a hotel, bar and restaurant, and disco. The inn operated from 1973 to 1984 as a haven for Vermont's rural LGBT+ culture. Green Mountain Crossroads hosts an online oral history of Andrew's Inn, including dozens of audio recordings from people who remember what it was like to visit and live there.

Camp Outright _(Starksboro, VT)_ is a residential summer camp for LGBT+ teens and young adults. Established in 1989, the weeklong program puts a queer spin on traditional summer camp programming. Campers enjoy all the quintessential camp activities—swimming, boating, archery, campfires—and can also attend LGBT+ justice workshops. The camp is generally held in mid- to late August. All bathrooms are gender-liberated, and camper sleeping arrangements are based on age or common interest rather than gender. Camp Outright also hosts a winter reunion in February for campers to keep in touch between summers.

Faerie Camp Destiny _(Chester, VT)_, since 1993, is Vermont's largest gathering of Radical Faeries, a movement that emerged in the 1970s and '80s in rejection of heteronormativity and gender conformity. Its website describes the camp as "a three-season intentional community in southern Vermont that hosts gatherings and educational offerings to help queer people cope and heal from a hostile Default World." Five to ten full-time faeries live onsite, and housing is provided by community-built cabins and a yurt. The camp also hosts gatherings of fifty to seventy people in the summer.

Pride Center of Vermont _(Burlington, VT)_ is the state's most comprehensive LGBT+ community center. Founded in 1999, the center has since grown its programs and services to be a fundamental part of the queer community in the area. It has a lending library with over three thousand volumes, a full calendar of events, free rapid HIV testing, a Center Space with community computers and free wi-fi, and several volunteer opportunities. It is also the root organization of the state's annual Pride parade and festival.

QUEER FACTS

5.3 percent of Vermonters identify as LGBT+, according to a February 2017 Gallup poll, making Vermont the state with the highest proportion of LGBT+ residents. Washington, DC, led the list at 8.6 percent, and South Dakota closed the list at 2 percent. The study surveyed over 400,000 Americans and showed a generalized increase in LGBT+ self-identification across all states since a similar poll in 2012, especially among millennials.

Charity Bryant and Sylvia Drake were a lesbian couple in the late 1700s and early 1800s, notable for the unusual amount of documentation of their relationship. The two met in 1806 and fell in love; soon after, they built a house in Weybridge, Vermont, and set up a tailoring business. Bryant's nephew, the poet William Cullen Bryant, described their relationship in terms that recall today's modern contours of queer intimacy and affection: "In their youthful days, they took each other as companions for life, and . . . this union, no less sacred to them than the tie of marriage, has subsisted, in uninterrupted harmony, for more than forty years." Rachel Hope Cleves, American-Canadian historian, examines their relationship in her 2014 book *Charity and Sylvia: A Same-Sex Marriage in Early America*.

The first transgender gubernatorial candidate was Christine Hallquist, who ran for governor of Vermont in 2018. Hallquist ultimately lost to the Republican incumbent, after facing months of death threats that caused her to alter her campaign publicity. Prior to her run for governor, Hallquist was the CEO of Vermont Electric Cooperative. She came out as transgender publicly in 2015, though she was open about her identity early on in her relationship with her wife and children.

A third gender option on driver's licenses was introduced in early January 2018. The Vermont Department of Motor Vehicles implemented a new computer system that allows the option for citizens who do not identify as male or female. Allowing for a third gender option on state IDs would make Vermont the first East Coast state to offer it, and the third state overall, after Oregon and California. The announcement of what exactly the third option will be is expected in July 2019.

The University of Vermont (UVM) Gay Dance occurred in 1975 in Burlington, Vermont. John Krowka, then-president of the newly formed UVM Gay Student Union, organized the dance. It was heralded as a success by the *Vermont Cynic* student newspaper, which reported that there was little to no negative response from the wider community. The reporter who covered the event concluded his article by saying, "For the sake of love and liberation, let's hope public reaction and attitudes remain that way."

Vermont became the first state to legalize same-sex marriage though legislative rather than judicial ruling in September 2009. Republican Governor Jim Douglass did initially veto the law, but state legislature overrode it in a 100 to 49 vote. Vermont was also the first state to allow same-sex civil unions a decade earlier in 2000. At the time, this was seen as groundbreaking and controversial, but it quickly became the conservative approach that many states used to recognize same-sex relationships without implementing full marriage equality.

The VT Bear Film Festival is an annual event celebrating gay bears and their admirers. The clothing-optional festival is located in the foothills of the Green Mountains, and is billed as "an occasion for guys to eat, drink, and be merry . . . and see some great films too." Most attendees stay at the festival grounds, which serve as an independent camping facility, for the duration of the festival. The films shown include shorts, features, documentaries, and others from all genres. The festival, which is open to participants over age eighteen, occurs in mid-August and includes a barbeque and dance party.

⊖ PEOPLE

Tallulah Bankhead *(Huntsville, AL)* was a film, television, and stage actress. Her father was Alabama congressman William Bankhead. She started to get roles in silent films in 1918 after she submitted her photo to a movie fan magazine. She then transitioned to the Broadway stage for the play *Squab Farm*, written by Frederic and Fanny Hatton. Next, Bankhead starred in a series of plays in London, where she specialized in sex dramas. After appearing abroad, she returned to Hollywood to film *My Sin* and *Devil and the Deep*, as well as Hitchcock's *Lifeboat*. Later in her career, she guest-starred as a villain in the 1960s *Batman* television series with Adam West. Bankhead was known for her wild image and sexual interest in both men and women. She is quoted as saying, "My father warned me about men and booze, but he never mentioned a word about women and cocaine."

Nell Carter *(Birmingham, AL)* was an actress known for her performance in the sitcom *Gimme a Break!* and her Tony award–winning performance in the 1978 Broadway musical *Ain't Misbehavin'.* She got her start in show business as a child when she sang on a local gospel radio show. She married George Krynicki, a union that lasted from 1982 to 1989. During her life, she was involved in AIDS activism after her brother, Dr. Bernard Taylor, died from the disease. In 1999, Carter performed and recorded a concert titled "Misbehavin'!" with the San Francisco Gay Men's Chorus in her brother's honor. She died in 2003 due to complications from diabetes. After her death, it was revealed that Carter had a romantic relationship in the mid-1990s with a woman, Ann Kaser, and that they had lived together in Beverly Hills. Kaser was her heir and the custodial parent of her two sons, Joshua and Daniel. Carter was also survived by her daughter Tracey.

François Clemmons *(Birmingham, AL)* is an actor and opera singer most known for his role as Officer Clemmons on *Mr. Roger's Neighborhood.* This role made him one of the first Black people to have a recurring role on American television. Clemmons received a bachelor of music degree from Oberlin College, master of fine arts from Carnegie Mellon University, and an honorary degree of doctor of arts from Middlebury College. He is also a renowned opera star with over seventy opera roles in his career, including the recording of *Porgy and Bess* in 1973 for which he won a Grammy. Though he was openly gay in 1968 when he started his role as Officer Clemmons, Mr. Rogers, his mentor, told him that he needed to keep his sexuality out of the public eye due to fear of the public controversy that might occur from having a Black gay character on a children's television program, in keeping with the norms of the era. He is now a professor of music at Middlebury and currently writing his autobiography, *DivaMan: My Life in Song.*

Tim Cook *(Robertsdale, AL)* is a business executive and industrial engineer. Cook was baptized at a Baptist church and earned a bachelor of science in industrial engineering from Auburn University, then a master of business administration from Duke University's Fuqua School of Business. Cook joined Apple as its senior vice president in 1998. His early investment in flash memory helped bring about the iPod Nano, iPhone, and iPad. Two months before Steve Jobs's death in 2011, Cook became the CEO of Apple. He publicly came out as gay in *Bloomberg* in 2014, making him the first openly gay CEO of a Fortune 500 company. In the article he stated, "I'm proud to be gay, and I consider being gay among the greatest gifts God has given me." In March 2015, Cook shared that he planned to donate his entire stock fortune to charity upon his death.

Tim Cook

Laverne Cox *(Mobile, AL)* is an actress and LGBT+ activist. She graduated from Marymount Manhattan College, where she studied theater. It was during this time that she came out as transgender. Cox starred on and produced the show *TRANSform,* where she gave makeovers to cisgender women. She is best known for her Emmy-nominated ongoing role as Sophia Burset in *Orange Is the New Black.* She has used her media presence to advocate for transgender rights, spreading her message through a number of outlets, including newspaper articles, television interviews, and public speaking engagements. Cox is the first openly transgender person to ever win a Daytime Emmy Award in Outstanding Special Class Special as executive producer for *Laverne Cox Presents: The T Word.*

Angela Davis *(Birmingham, AL)* is a writer, lesbian, radical feminist, and former member of both the Communist Party and the Black Panther Party. As a young girl, her family moved to a predominantly white neighborhood, followed by other Black families, which angered her white neighbors and caused them to try to segregate the neighborhood. Some white people in the area even bombed the homes of their Black neighbors. Davis attended a segregated school and knew the four girls killed in the 1963 Birmingham Church Bombing. She earned a degree in philosophy in France before she returned to the States to work as an activist in the Civil Rights Movement. She received a PhD in Marxist philosophy from UC San Diego in 1967. Around this time, she joined the Che-Lumumba Club and associated with the Blank Panthers. Sometimes viewed as a controversial figure, Davis was the third woman ever listed on the FBI's most-wanted list. She became a respected philosophy professor and wrote about prisons, racism, and feminism. Her books include *Women,*

Laverne Cox

Culture, and Politics; *Are Prisons Obsolete?*; and *Abolition Democracy: Beyond Empire, Prisons, and Torture.* She has been a professor at UCLA, San Francisco State University, and currently UC Santa Cruz. She also ran as the Communist Party's candidate for vice president in 1980 and 1984. Davis came out as a lesbian in 1997 in *Out* magazine. In 2017, Davis was a featured speaker and honorary cochair at the Women's March on Washington after Donald Trump's inauguration.

 PLACES

Auburn University *(Auburn, AL)* erupted in controversy in 1992 when a Gay and Lesbian Association (GLA) attempted to get chartered but was denied by the student government with a vote of 23–7. When the ACLU threatened legal action against Auburn, the school's administrators gave the GLA its charter. This enraged many students, who gave a petition of twelve

I think the importance of doing activist work is precisely because it allows you to give back and to consider yourself not as a single individual who may have achieved whatever but to be a part of an ongoing historical movement.

—Angela Davis, *Frontline,* 1997

☉ QUEER FACTS

Alabama's first college Gay Student Union was formed on January 13, 1983, at the University of Alabama. They initially had twenty-four members who were dedicated to statewide gay rights activism. During its first year, the union organized speaking engagements in an attempt to engage in dialogue with their detractors while also establishing a gay resource library. The union has since changed its name to Spectrum.

The *Gay Lesbian Bisexual Alliance v. Sessions* court case of 1992 was initiated by a gay University of South Alabama student and the ACLU against the university over the denial of funds for the school's GLBA as a result of the 1992 law that banned state funding to gay groups. In 1996, Judge Myron Thompson found the law unconstitutional and struck down the ban.

Promo-No-Homo was a law passed in Alabama in 1992, similar to others around the country, stating that students in public schools must be taught that homosexuality is unacceptable and illegal. Despite homosexuality being legal since 2003, the law remains in effect today, though in February 2018 the Senate Education Policy Committee voted to delete the phrase.

V. L. v. E. L took headlines as it went to the US Supreme Court in 2016. In 2015, the Alabama Supreme Court denied a lesbian woman visitation rights of children she had previously adopted in Georgia once she had separated from her partner, the biological parent of the children. The US Supreme Court reversed the state court's decision, restoring her parental rights to her children.

---

thousand signatures to the board of trustees, asking to rescind the GLA's charter. The Alabama House of Representatives issued a resolution that expressed their support of the students who opposed the club.

An Auburn University student fired shots at GLA students *(Auburn, AL)* with a pellet gun from a third-floor window of Noble Hall in January 1992 while the GLA students were putting up posters condemning the student government's decision above. The shooter was only required to pay a $99 fine. On February 8, 1992, four hundred people protested the shooting on Auburn's campus. In direct response to the controversy, the state legislature banned the spending of state money on gay groups in 1992.

The Southeastern Lesbian, Bisexual, and Gay Conference controversy *(Birmingham, AL)* started in February 1996 at the University of Alabama–Birmingham, where the conference was slated to take place. The event was a forum for LGBT+ issues and had an estimated three hundred participants. Due to the 1992 law that forbid state-funded

facilities from being used for activities that promoted sexual behavior violating "sodomy and sexual misconduct laws," Alabama Governor Fob James accused the event of violating the law. Despite political controversy, Jeff Sessions (the state's attorney general at the time) stated that while the event violated the law, the law itself had no penalty or enforcement procedure, so nothing could be done. The conference proceeded as planned.

The Supreme Court of Alabama *(Montgomery, AL)* issued an order against gay marriage in 2015 shortly after the United States Supreme Court decision in *Obergefell v. Hodges* legalized same-sex marriage across the US. The chief justice of the Alabama Supreme Court at the time, Roy Moore, ordered that same-sex marriage licenses not be issued in the state. This sent counties in disarray, with some giving licenses to same-sex couples, some only to straight couples, while others issued no marriage licenses at all. The Alabama Court of the Judiciary suspended Roy Moore without pay for the rest of his term for his actions against the US Supreme Court's ruling.

ARKANSAS

⊖ PEOPLE

Joe Brainard *(Salem, AR)* was a fine artist, costume designer, set designer, comic artist, and poet. He was born in 1941 in Salem, but spent much of his childhood in Tulsa, Oklahoma. As a child, he showed a lot of artistic talent and even designed dresses for his mother. As an adult, he moved to New York City, where he began his career as an artist. He began to socialize with the New York School community, where he met and collaborated with other notable artists such as Frank O'Hara and Anne Waldman. Brainard spent a lot of time playing with different art mediums, from collages to comics, and believed in art for the fun of making it rather than any serious ideology. His most well-known works include his autobiographical poem series *I Remember* and a series of illustrated comics called *The Nancy Book*. He died in 1994 from AIDS and pneumonia.

James Bridges *(Paris, AR)* worked in the film industry as an actor, producer, screenwriter, and director in Hollywood. He was born in 1936 and attended the University of Central Arkansas, after which he moved to Hollywood. There, he briefly worked as an actor before he became a screenwriter for the television show *Alfred Hitchcock Presents*. His work on the show earned him an Emmy nomination in 1963 and an Edgar Award from the Mystery Writers of America in 1966. Bridges went on to write the Marlon Brando western *Appaloosa* (1966) and directed a stream of popular films in the 1970s and '80s, including *The Paper Chase*, *The China Syndrome*, and *Urban Cowboy*. In 1988 he said in an interview, "I think it's a fallacy that you have to be young to be hip. It's bullshit." Bridges had a romantic relationship with

> **"**
> *If I'm as normal as I think I am, we're all a bunch of weirdos.*
>
> —Joe Brainard, *The Collected Writings of Joe Brainard*, 2012
> **"**

his longtime film collaborator Jack Larson starting in the late 1950s. The two lived together until Bridges's death from intestinal cancer in 1993.

Wade Davis *(Little Rock, AR)* is a football player and advocate for LGBT+ and women's rights. He was born in Little Rock in 1977 but grew up in Shreveport, Louisiana. His football career began in college, when he played for Weber State University. Davis went on to play for the Tennessee Titans and the NFL's Europe League. In 2003, he injured himself in training camp, ending his professional football career. Throughout his time in the NFL, Davis attempted to conceal that he was gay from his teammates due to fear of professional scorn. However, starting in 2006, he joined the New York Gay Flag Football League and went on to win three consecutive Gay Bowls from 2006 to 2008. Davis was the first LGBT+ inclusion consultant for the NFL and does similar consulting work for private companies like Google, Viacom, and Netflix. Davis also campaigns for gender equality with organizations such as Planned Parenthood, *Ebony* Magazine, and even the United Nations.

Wade Davis

I believe I owe all the best parts of my adulthood to embracing my imperfections and showcasing them.

—Beth Ditto, *The Guardian*, 2007

Beth Ditto

Beth Ditto *(Searcy, AR)* is a punk rock musician. She was born in Searcy in 1981 and moved to Olympia, Oregon, after high school. There, she joined the feminist punk scene as a singer in the band Gossip. Her music regularly features critiques of homophobia, such as her single "Standing in the Way of Control," which Gossip wrote about Republican opposition to gay marriage. In 2006, the British magazine *NME* named her the number-one person on its Cool List, making her the first woman ever to receive the title. In 2012, she released her memoir, *Coal to Diamonds,* and the following year she married her longtime partner, Kristin Ogata. In 2017, Ditto released her first solo album, *Fake Sugar.*

Ed Madden *(Newport, AR)* is a poet, activist, literary critic, radio producer, and professor. He grew up on a rice farm in Newport, and later secured a BA from Harding University in English and French and a PhD in literature from the University of Texas–Austin. His books of poetry include *Signals* (which received the South Carolina Poetry Book Prize in 2007) and *Nest*. In 2015, he was honored as the poet laureate of Columbia, South Carolina. Madden works for the University of South Carolina as an English professor and director of the Women's and Gender Studies program. He has also served as the president of the South Carolina Gay and Lesbian Pride Movement, and was the executive producer of *Rainbow Radio: The REAL Gay Agenda*, a South Carolina–based, gay-themed radio talk show.

Rae Nelson *(Little Rock, AR)* came out as transgender while she served in the Navy Reserve and attended a nursing program focused on transgender health at the University of Arkansas. Despite the support of her academic community and Navy Reserve commander, higher-ups refused to allow Nelson to continue in the navy. Instead, they put her in the Individual Ready Reserve, where she remained inactive for the rest of her contract. She is now the deputy director of the Arkansas Transgender Equality Coalition and has resisted a proposed bill to ban transgender people from the public restrooms consistent with their gender identities. At the capitol, Nelson told state legislators, "Trans women of color are dying every year and you're worried about what bathrooms we use? You're trying to disenfranchise us even more." Nelson continues her social justice work as an activist with Black Lives Matter of Little Rock, where she advocated for police accountability and an independent investigation after the shooting of Roy Lee Richards by a LRPD officer.

Kathy Webb *(Blytheville, AR)* was Arkansas's first openly gay state representative in the state House of Representatives, where she served from 2007 to 2013. During her time there, the Sierra Club and the Arkansas Advocates for Children and Families honored Webb with awards for her philanthropic work. Webb is a graduate of the University of Central Arkansas and has also studied at Harvard's Senior Executives in State and Local Government program. Webb has since served on the board of directors for the City of

Arkansas and became the city's vice mayor in 2017. She successfully proposed and implemented LGBT+ anti-discrimination legislation for Little Rock in 2015. Before her life in politics, she was a restaurateur. Amongst other ventures in the hospitality industry, she opened Lilly's Dim Sum, Then Some in Little Rock. Combining her love of public service with her love of food, she also serves as the Executive Director of the Arkansas Hunger Relief Alliance.

PLACES

The Arkansas State Capitol *(Little Rock, AR)* was where a statewide anti-sodomy law and House Bill 32 passed, barring gays and lesbians from equal employment and housing opportunities. It is the site of the 2017 protests against House Bill 1986 and Senate Bill 774, which proposed that people could only access the bathrooms that match the sex on their birth certificate as noted at birth, with no options to legally change their sex. It was the site of numerous other

QUEER FACTS

Arkansas's 1977 anti-sodomy law was passed in direct response to the outcome of the James Black and Willie Henderson case involving sexual conduct while in a jail's drunk tank in February 1976. The state's sodomy law had expired on January 1 of that year, so Judge Jack Hold, Sr. found that the two had not committed a criminal act. The prosecutor, Wilbur Bentley, said he feared the city jail would become "a gay bar." Later, state representative Bill Stancil introduced House Bill 117, which would make bestiality and sodomy equal as a class C felony, punishable with up to ten years in prison. The bill was later amended to make sodomy a misdemeanor, punishable by one year in prison. It passed the state senate unanimously with Senator Milt Earnhard saying that the bill was "aimed at weirdos and queers who live in a fairyland world and are trying to wreck traditional family life." Governor David Pryor signed the bill into law on March 28, 1977, despite protest from the ACLU, Quaker, and LGBT+ communities.

The Equal Care for Equal Lives Conference occurs annually in Little Rock, Arkansas, focusing on educating healt hcare professionals and community members about issues the state's LGBT+ community faces. It provides resources for identifying the

roadblocks that stand in the way of the LGBT+ community's access to equitable and affordable health care, with a special focus on youth and the elderly.

Gay and Lesbian Students Association v. Gohn. In 1983, the University of Arkansas–Fayetteville student senate denied funding to the Gay and Lesbian Students Association, which sought money to show a series of gay films and host gay speakers. The student senate stated that they could not fund a program that promoted an illegal act, and many students demonstrated in support of defunding the club. The GLSA sued Lyle Gohn, the vice chancellor of the university's student services, and a higher court eventually ruled that the GLSA's First Amendment rights had been violated, as its funding was denied based on the matter of the GLSA's content.

The Ross Dennis editorial controversy began on January 5, 1978, when Dennis published an editorial in the *Lincoln Ledger* criticizing Anita Bryant, an outspoken opponent to gay rights. Dennis and the *Ledger* faced backlash; many pastors criticized the paper and its editors and threatened to boycott it if the editorial was not retracted. Dennis apologized for the editorial in the next issue of the paper and was fired a month later.

protests for LGBT+ rights throughout the years, such as a "kiss-in" that took place in 2016 in response to the state leaders' lack of response to the Pulse Orlando nightclub shooting.

Fayetteville Women's Center *(Fayetteville, AR)* was an organization on the Fayetteville University of Arkansas campus that offered a safe space for women. The organization was funded largely by the university, but also by private donors. It offered health services, resources for relationship violence, a sports group, and a meeting place for a group of lesbian students who called themselves the Lesbian Rap Group. Disputes between the Lesbian Rap Group and the Women's Center over the goals of the organization led to the Lesbian Rap Group changing its name to Razordykes. The Razordykes were outspoken about rights for lesbian women, and their events inclined the school to cut funding for the Women's Center. After the wife of a prominent banker received an invitation to one of the Razordykes' events, the tension between the Women's Center and the Razordykes grew, as state legislators put pressure on the university to close the Women's Center. The Women's Center struggled to keep funding and eventually closed in 1980. The story of the Women's Center highlights how the movement for LGBT+ rights and the women's movement were periodically at odds with one another, and sometimes not seen as sharing common goals. It is also part of a history of a lack of support from the University of Arkansas for members of the LGBT+ community; in 2017, they suspended university health care coverage for gender dysphoria–related treatments.

Yellowhammer Farm *(Madison County, AR)* was a woman-only communal farm and safe space for lesbians from 1974 to 1980. Yellowhammer Farm was founded by Trella Laughlin and Patricia Jackson, who named it after the yellowhammer bird common in the area. They advocated for women's land rights, organic farming, and feminism, and protested the use of the herbicide 2,4,5-T, the active component of Agent Orange, which was used to clear plants during the Vietnam War and sparked controversy about its safety to human health. The harsh living conditions of the farm, along with personal disputes, eventually led to its dissolution. Laughlin stated that she no longer believed in separatism but wanted to continue to resist imperialist ideology.

> *When Cubans have true freedom to vote, speak, travel and love—then we can talk about planning conferences and celebrating the successes of the island's leadership. For now we simply mourn its victims and pray for actual rights—not blood-stained press releases and staged pictures.*
>
> —Herb Sosa, *Washington Blade*, 2014

Other Latina Longings, won the Alan Bray Memorial Book Prize and was a Lambda Literary finalist.

Joe Saunders *(Fort Lauderdale, FL)* made history in 2012 as one of two openly gay people elected to the state House of Representatives, the first two in Florida's history. David Richardson of Miami Beach was the other elected representative. Saunders had previously worked with Equality Florida as a field director, then rejoined in 2017 as a senior political director. After losing his reelection campaign in a 2014 red wave, Saunders joined the Human Rights Campaign as a field director.

Elizabeth Schwartz *(Miami Beach, FL)* is a lawyer and LGBT+ advocate. Her work has focused on securing the right for same-sex couples to marry, as well as to adopt children. In 2014, Schwartz's work with the National Center for Lesbian Rights representing six same-sex couples helped overturn Florida's ban on same-sex marriage. With law expertise in the realm of family planning, Schwartz also handled Florida's first same-sex divorce case. Schwartz has received numerous awards and recognitions throughout her career, including being named by the National LGBT Bar Association as a best lawyer under 40 in 2010.

Nadine Smith *(Panama City, FL)* is the CEO of Equality Florida, an organization fighting against LGBT+ and gender discrimination. Smith founded the organization in 1997; prior to that, she cochaired the 1993 March on Washington and in 1991 ran for Tampa City Council, the first openly gay Black person to do so. Currently, Smith also chairs the US Commission on Civil Rights Florida Advisory Committee.

Herb Sosa *(Miami, FL)* founded the Unity Coalition, an organization bringing equality to Florida's Latinx/ Hispanic LGBT+ community, in 2002; he now serves as president and CEO. Since 2003, Sosa has also served as the publisher and editor-in-chief of *AMBIENTE* magazine, the first LGBT+ publication available in English, Spanish, and Portuguese. He has received numerous awards and recognitions; in honor of his community work, Miami Beach declared Herb Sosa Day one day in 2009.

LJ Woolston *(Miami, FL)* is a nonbinary trans-pan-queer social worker. Woolston is a homeless service liaison for the Alliance for GLBTQ Youth. Via the organizations SunServe and Pridelines, Woolston also works on Project SAFE, the first and only program in Miami-Dade County serving LGBT+ youth experiencing or at risk of homelessness. They are currently working to expand Project SAFE into the Diana Hemingway Foundation, named after Woolston's late partner, Diana Hemingway. Hemingway died by suicide in 2016 out of fear of homelessness and an inability to have stable income as she was a trans woman, an open sex worker, and also had difficulties stemming from her neurodivergence. Woolston recollects Hemingway's trauma of experiencing homelessness throughout her life, and wishes to honor her through the foundation.

Pedro Zamora *(Havana, Cuba)* was an AIDS activist and cast member of the 1994 season of MTV's *The Real World* in San Francisco. Zamora discovered his HIV status in 1989 at the age of seventeen after donating blood. His ensuing advocacy for AIDS prevention among young people culminated in him testifying before Congress in 1993, validating the need to allocate federal funds to HIV/AIDS programs in schools. "If you want to reach me as a young man—especially a young gay man of color—then you need to give me information in a language and vocabulary I can understand and relate to," he said. On *The Real World*, Zamora's commitment ceremony to his partner, Sean Sasser, was the first televised same-sex event of its type. Zamora died in November 1994 at the age of twenty-two, just hours after the season finale of *The Real World* aired.

⊙ PLACES

Aqua Foundation for Women *(Miami, FL)* is a non-profit founded in 2004 that seeks to empower lesbian, bisexual, and transgender women. The Aqua Foundation receives financial support from their Aqua Girl fundraising event, private sector donations, grants, and individual donations. It awards grants to other organizations that focus on issues such equality, education,

and LGBT+ support, and provides a scholarship and mentorship program. The Aqua Foundation supports a number of events such as TransCon, the LGBTQ Family BBQ, and Aqua's LBT Emerging Leadership Conference.

Key Largo *(Lockhart, FL)* was the largest lesbian bar in the nation when it opened in 1988. It operated on two and a half acres of land with a building around fifteen thousand square feet. Previously, the space had been a country bar named Margo's.

LGBT Collections at the University of Southern Florida Libraries *(Tampa, FL)* is a collection of documents and artifacts pertaining to LGBT+ history. The collection includes a four-thousand-year-old Sumerian tablet as well as a collection of queer literature, an Asian male nude collection, a collection on lesbian rights, and a collection on sex in advertising. It was founded in part by David Johnson, an associate professor of history with a focus on gender and sexuality. He is the author of the 2004 book *The Lavender Scare,* which was later made into a documentary.

The Palace

> *I went to Penn, where I got very involved in civil rights issues like race relations, pro-choice, and homelessness. I was the kind of activist student who would do things like staple wire coat hangers to trees with signs that said, 'This is not a surgical instrument.'*
>
> —Elizabeth Schwartz, *LGBTQ Nation*, 2010

Palace *(Miami Beach, FL)* is a gay bar famous for its extravagant drag shows. Palace opened in 1988 under the original name the Fruit Palace. It served a variety of fruit cocktails, and began to offer drag shows as the location became popular with the local gay community. Palace is near to what is known as South Beach's "gay beach," and has remained a social gathering space for the LGBT+ community. In 2016, Palace put on a special drag performance to commemorate the victims of the Pulse shooting in Orlando. The bar's tagline is "Every queen needs a palace."

Pearl's Rainbow *(Key West, FL)* was a lesbian-owned, formerly female-only hotel founded by Heather Carruthers in 1989. The hotel offered amenities such as two hot tubs, a pool that allowed skinny-dipping, and complimentary breakfast. In 2010, the hotel began to allow male patrons, as Carruthers cited tough economic circumstances. Pearl's Rainbow still stands but is called the Southernmost Inn.

Stonewall National Museum and Archives *(Fort Lauderdale, FL)* is a collection of over thirty thousand items that pertain to LGBT+ history. Some objects in the collection are contemporary, and some are over a century old. The collection was created in 1973 by a Florida Atlantic University student named Mark Silber. Ellen DeGeneres, Neil Patrick Harris, Nathan Lane, and other celebrities have all donated objects to the archives. It hosts events and exhibits year-round, such as a special exhibit to document the Pulse Nightclub shooting. It also hosts readings, group discussions, and an annual fundraising gala, and offers lesson curriculums for teachers.

Villa Casa Casuarina/Versace Mansion *(Miami Beach, FL)* is the former home of fashion designer Gianni Versace, where he lived from 1992 until he was murdered in 1997. Versace's boyfriend of fifteen years, Antonio D'Amico, found his body on the steps outside the mansion after he was shot. D'Amico said of their relationship, "We lived as a natural couple. . . . He never tried to hide who he was." Versace's murder, at the hands of a twenty-seven-year-old gay man named Andrew Cunanan, is the subject of the 2018 season of *American Crime Story* called *The Assassination of Gianni Versace*, which won multiple Emmys. The mansion itself was built by Alden Freeman in 1930. Once Versace purchased it, he did $32 million worth of renovations and demolished the historic hotel next door to build a garden and pool. Versace threw many parties with famous guests such as Madonna, Elton John, Naomi Campbell, and Sting. The mansion is now a restaurant and hotel.

Vizcaya Museum and Gardens *(Miami, FL)* is a museum and queer space known for elaborate parties and events. It houses precious artworks, statues, and tapestries from Venetian palaces. The museum was previously known as Villa Vizcaya when it was the estate of James Deering, the Deering McCormick-International Harvester heir, from 1916 until his death in 1925.

Villa Versace

Over the past three years, I fell deeply in love with a beautiful soul named Diana Hemingway. When this began as a hookup on November 18, 2013 (forever named our sexy-versary), I had no idea that I would fall in love with her. She told me that she had hunted me, that I was her prey. She called herself the Huntress. And so yes, I suppose I was hunted. And I have no regrets about being her prey, even now.

—LJ Woolston, in memory of Diana Hemingway,
InLoveThatNeverDies.wordpress.com, 2017

Villa Vizcaya

Wilton Manors

Deering was rumored to be gay, to the point that one newspaper called him "the prissy bachelor who preferred bourbon to women" in 1961. Around the early 1920s, the artist and architect Paul Chalfin lived in the estate with his boyfriend, Louis Koons. Chalfin is responsible for much of the current aesthetic of the museum, which draws its inspiration from different Italian cities. The Vizcaya Museum served from 1984 to 2010 as the venue of the White Party, a Health Crisis Network fundraising event to support people who live with HIV/AIDS. The gardens boast both contemporary sculptures and Renaissance and Baroque era works, and the interior is full of antique Italian furniture, artwork, and unique architectural elements.

Wilton Manors, Florida, is a city with the second most concentrated population of gay residents in the United States—14 percent of the population, according to the 2010 census. The gay population of Wilton Manors tends to consist of middle-aged people and families, and is home to many LGBT-owned businesses. The city's first gay mayor was elected in 1988, and the City Commission had a gay majority as of 2018. Wilton Manors has an LGBT+ community center called Pride Center at Equality Park, and also hosts the annual Stonewall Street Festival & Parade.

> My greatest challenge in life has been to become an entire person. We fragment people, especially minorities, because we assume it's easier to deal with specific problems if we compartmentalize behavior. Well, I could deal with the fact that I was gay. I could deal with my being a Latino man in America. I could deal with having been sexually abused as a kid. And I could deal with having HIV and AIDS. But I couldn't deal with them together at the same time. And you have to if you ever want to become a whole person.

—Pedro Zamora, *POZ*, 1994

QUEER FACTS

Aqua Girl is an annual event for the LGBT+ community hosted by the Aqua Foundation for Women. Typically lasting several days, the event is a celebration and fundraiser that benefits the health, opportunities, and equality of women in the LGBT+ community. The proceeds go to the Aqua Foundation for Women, which in turn supports different health and education initiatives for LGBT+ women through grants, scholarships, and programming. The event began in 1999, when Alison Burgos and the producer Shescape launched the event as a fundraiser for breast cancer. It was an incredible success with over eight hundred attendees, and inspired Burgos and other producers over the years to continue the celebration as the annual Aqua Girl event. Events at Aqua Girl include themed dance parties, beach days, brunches, and more. It occurs in the fall in the South Beach area.

The Democratic National Convention of 1972 occurred at the Miami Beach Convention Center. The party's nominee for president, George McGovern, was one of the first politicians to court LGBT+ voters. Though he planned to run on a platform of gay liberation, the Democratic Party rejected the idea out of fear that it was too progressive to win a presidential

Miami Beach Convention Center

election. At the convention, activists Jim Foster and Madeline Davis gave nationally televised speeches about gay rights that energized the movement for LGBT+ equality across the nation. During the summer of the convention, many LGBT+ people from all around the country came to participate in various events and political demonstrations that solidified the reputation of Miami, particularly the South Beach, as a place where the LGBT+ community could thrive.

The Walt Disney World Resort has offered couples commitment ceremonies from all walks of life since 2007. When same-sex marriage was legalized by the Supreme Court of the United States in 2015, Disney's Fairy Tale Weddings & Honeymoons began offering Disney Weddings to same-sex couples.

Gay adoption was outlawed in Florida in 1977, in part because of the success of Anita Bryant's "Save Our Children" campaign. The law made Florida the first state to explicitly ban same-sex adoption. State senator Alan Trask and the state senate's president, Curtis Peterson, supported the same-sex adoption ban; it remained in effect until the *In re: Gill* case, which Martin Gill and the ALCU brought to the circuit court in 2007 in order to adopt two children he had fostered with his spouse. Judge Cindy S. Lederman declared the same-sex adoption ban discriminatory and unconstitutional, but the state of Florida appealed her decision. In 2010, the district court ruled in favor of Judge Lederman's original ruling, and same-sex adoption has been legal in Florida ever since.

The Gay Pride Protest at Winter Park occurred in Orlando in 1988 when the city refused to grant a permit to the Gay Pride Winter Park event. We the People, a gay and lesbian activist group, organized a protest, which drew about fifty people. Shortly after their protest began, a counter-protest arrived, including eleven members of the KKK.

The Johns Committee (a.k.a. the Florida Legislative Investigation Committee) was a state government group that investigated and persecuted Black people, suspected communists, and LGBT+ people. The committee (named after Senator Charley Johns, the first chairman of the group) aimed to find such people, interrogate them, and strip them of their credentials and employment, as it believed they posed a threat to the state. Active from 1956 to 1965, the group began in response to *Brown v. Board of Education*, investigating members of the NAACP, tapping phone lines, and going so far as to break up the slumber party of a teenage girl in its hunt for Black activists, LGBT+ people, and communists. In 1964, the group released "Homosexuality and Citizenship in Florida" (the "Purple Pamphlet"), a report that contained sexual photographs, lewd terminology, and sections that condemned homosexuality with an unprofessionalism that embarrassed the state. The report ultimately led to the group's downfall; though Florida continued to persecute suspected homosexuals, it disbanded the Johns Committee in 1965. In 1993, Florida's State Legislature released documents from the Johns Committee, which are available to the public through the Florida Memory State Libraries & Archives.

Key West Fantasy Fest is an annual celebration for adults known by many as a gay Mardi Gras. It consists of parties, street fairs, home decorating challenges, parades, and costumed events that draw people from all over the country. The first Fantasy Fest took place in 1979 and began as a costumed parade. Over the years,

the event has grown to include multiple events throughout Key West. Many of the proceeds benefit nonprofit organizations that work to promote LGBT+ equality.

Loving Committed Network was an Orlando-based organization and an extension of Gay Pride Week that catered to women. Le June Perrin, Carolyn Dorton, Sherri Goyette, and Donna Coleman started LCN in 1984 to remedy the fact that most Gay Pride Week events were for men. To achieve their goal, the LCN events excluded men and sparked a rivalry between the organization and Gay Community Services, which had a majority male staff. The LCN published a newsletter called the *LCN Express*, which ran up until the mid-1990s and covered political and cultural issues of concern to lesbians at the time of publication.

The Mariel Boatlift of 1980 was a wave of around 125,000 Cuban immigrants who arrived in Miami. Dubbed "Marielitos," the Cubans fled Fidel Castro's communist revolution because of economic pressure and violence. After many tried to escape Castro's government by breaking into a Peruvian embassy in Havana, Castro declared that anyone who wanted to leave could depart from Cuba's Port of Mariel, so long as they supplied their own boats. Many of the refugees were people Castro's government deemed undesirable, such as criminals, the mentally ill, and homosexual and gender-nonconforming people. As a result of their arrival in Miami, the visibility of LGBT+ people and culture in South Florida increased. While the Marielitos still faced discrimination and imprisonment in large numbers, the Mariel Boatlift set a new precedent in

Mariel Boatlift

the US immigration system: Homosexuals could now immigrate to the US as long as they did not explicitly confess their homosexuality to immigration officials. It wasn't until the Immigration Act of 1990 that the US could no longer officially deny an immigrant because of sexual orientation.

The Metropolitan Community Church is an LGBT+ congregation that was one of the first churches to perform same-sex marriages. It was founded by Florida native Troy Perry in 1968, and since then has been a strong advocate for social justice and inclusion. Though it started in California, the church has grown to the size of 250 congregations in twenty-six countries. MCC seeks to be a liberating religious force that gives people a sense of community and encourages them to reach their potential. As of 2018, there were eighteen MCC churches in Florida, in places ranging from Tampa to Orlando. The Tampa branch of MCC was established in 1971 and was the first LGBT+ organization of any kind in the city. The Joy Metropolitan Church in Orlando was the first LGBT+ church in Central Florida, and had been meeting since 1979, though it received a charter from MCC in 1983.

Miami Beach's first Pride parade occurred in June 1972, although the first official Miami Beach Gay Pride (established by the Miami Beach Gay Business Development) wasn't until 2009, from which point it occurred annually. The 1972 parade was actually an organized protest on Lincoln Road against Miami's cross-dressing ban, although the march was simultaneously communal and celebratory. Two weeks after the protest, a federal court ruled against the cross-dressing law. The protest was among many organized LGBT+ rights events that occurred in the summer of 1972 in anticipation of the 1972 Republican and Democratic national conventions, which both took place at the Miami Beach Convention Center.

Nondiscrimination laws do not exist in Florida (as of the date of this publication). About 40 percent of Florida cities allow people to be fired or evicted because of their sexual orientation or gender identity. Nonetheless, poll data shows that 75 percent of state residents would approve of a statewide nondiscrimination law prohibiting discrimination against LGBT+ people.

Miami Beach Pride

One of Florida's most prominent bisexual activists was Alan Rockway, a psychologist. In 1977, he coauthored an LGBT+ nondiscrimination ordinance, which passed by popular vote in Dade County. The ordinance was publicly opposed by the "Save Our Children" campaign led by Anita Bryant, former Miss Oklahoma and a brand ambassador for the Florida Citrus Commission. In response, Rockway initiated a "gaycott" of Florida orange juice until Bryant's ambassador contract was canceled. Rockway notably cofounded BiPOL, a bisexual activism group, in California in 1983, and also two of the country's first LGBT+ mental health programs in Florida and California. The Rockway Institute, an LGBT+ research center, was founded in his memory in 2007 at Alliant University in San Francisco. Rockway died of AIDS in 1987.

OneOrlando Alliance is a united coalition of LGBT+ advocacy organizations throughout Florida, including the ACLU of Central Florida, the Gay & Lesbian Lawyer Association of Central Florida, the First Congregational Church of Winter Park, the Orlando Gay Chorus, Planned Parenthood of Greater Orlando, the GLBT Center of Central Florida, and Equality Florida, amongst others. The OneOrlando Alliance helps finance nonprofits and assists in community outreach on behalf of LGBT+ organizations.

Orlando's 1970s gay bar scene was helmed by entrepreneurs Mike Hodge and Bill Miller. The pair, along with three other gay bar owners, became known as the Gay and Lesbian Gang. Hodge and Miller's bars included the Palace Club, Diamond Head, and El Goya. In 1975, they bought and reopened Parliament House, which still operates today as one of the oldest gay resorts in the country. Miller died in 1987 at the age of fifty-three due to AIDS. Hodge refused to allow their friends to conceal Miller's cause of death, instead using it as an opportunity to educate the community. Hodge died in 1992 at the age of forty-eight, also from AIDS.

OUTSHINE Film Festival (previously known as MiFo) is a series of annual film screenings that promote LGBT+ artistry, visibility, and pride. The festival rose out of the 2015 merging of the Miami Gay & Lesbian Film Festival, which began in 1998, and the Fort Lauderdale Gay & Lesbian Film Festival, which began in 2008. The OUTSHINE Film Festival is one of the earliest LGBT+ festivals of the year and sets the tone for the rest of the LGBT+ film community.

The Pulse nightclub shooting in Orlando was a hate crime and act of terrorism that occurred on June 12, 2016. Forty-nine people were killed and fifty-three others injured—an estimated third of the people inside the club, most of whom were Latinx. Many people were unable to escape and could only leave the club around 5:00 a.m., when a SWAT team entered the building and killed the shooter after a three-hour standoff. Governor Rick Scott initially declared the shooting as a terrorist attack with no mention of the LGBT+ and the Latinx communities, whom he finally acknowledged two days later with a tweet that read, "We pray for our LGBT community. Our Hispanic community. Our state. Our nation. This was an attack on every American. We are #OrlandoStrong." The shooting was both the deadliest hate crime against the LGBT+ community and the second deadliest shooting in the US to date (the first being the 2017 concert shooting in Las Vegas). Pulse is now closed. The owners of Pulse created the one-PULSE Foundation, which built the Pulse Interim Memorial on the former site of the club and created a task force of volunteers to advise the organization as they build the Pulse Museum to commemorate the victims and all those affected by the shooting. We honor those who lost their lives by naming them here:

> Stanley Almodovar III, Amanda Alvear, Oscar A. Aracena-Montero, Rodolfo Ayala-Ayala, Alejandro Barrios Martinez, Martin Benitez Torres, Antonio D. Brown, Darryl R. Burt II, Jonathan A. Camuy Vega, Angel L. Candelario-Padro, Simon A. Carrillo Fernandez, Juan Chevez-Martinez, Luis D. Conde, Cory J. Connell, Tevin E. Crosby, Franky J. Dejesus Velazquez, Deonka D. Drayton, Mercedez M. Flores, Peter O. Gonzalez-Cruz, Juan R. Guerrero, Paul T. Henry, Frank Hernandez, Miguel A. Honorato, Javier Jorge-Reyes, Jason B. Josaphat, Eddie J. Justice, Anthony L. Laureano Disla, Christopher A. Leinonen, Brenda L. Marquez Mc-Cool, Jean C. Mendez Perez, Akyra Monet Murray,

Pulse nightclub

> Kimberly Morris, Jean C. Nieves Rodriguez, Luis O. Ocasio-Capo, Geraldo A. Ortiz-Jimenez, Eric Ivan Ortiz-Rivera, Joel Rayon Paniagua, Enrique L. Rios Jr., Juan P. Rivera Velazquez, Yilmary Rodriguez Solivan, Christopher J. Sanfeliz, Xavier Emmanuel Serrano Rosado, Gilberto Ramon Silva Menendez, Edward Sotomayor Jr., Shane E. Tomlinson, Leroy Valentin Fernandez, Luis S. Vielma, Luis Daniel Wilson-Leon, and Jerald A. Wright.

Reading Queer is a Miami literary organization that promotes queer literary culture through the annual RQ Literacy Festival and the RQ Writing Academy. It also offers a queer writers residency program and has hosted a queer film series called the O Cinema Literary/Film Salon Series. Neil De La Flor, a gay writer and teacher, started Reading Queer in 2013 and served as one of the editors of the organization's 2018 poetry anthology, *Reading Queer: Poetry in a Time of Chaos*.

The "Save Our Children" campaign was an anti-gay campaign spearheaded by Anita Bryant, a singer, evangelical, former Miss America contestant, and spokesperson for the Florida Citrus Commission. Bryant founded "Save Our Children" in response to Dade County's 1976 nondiscrimination ordinance, which made it illegal to discriminate against someone based on their sexual orientation. Bryant's "Save Our Children" campaign collected 64,304 signatures to add the repeal of the nondiscrimination ordinance to the next ballot, 54,304 more than the minimum required

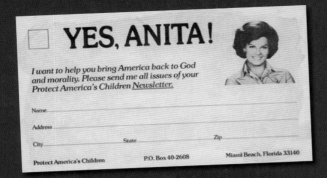

A flyer from the Save Our Children campaign

to do so. In 1977, the people of Dade County voted the nondiscrimination ordinance out of law and violence against LGBT+ people subsequently increased. Bryant said, "Homosexuals cannot reproduce biologically, but they have to reproduce by recruiting our children." The "Save Our Children" campaign also rallied popular support around a law that banned same-sex adoption and another that explicitly banned same-sex marriage. After the effectiveness of the "Save Our Children" campaign in Florida, Bryant took the campaign nation-wide and used it to support discriminatory legislation in other states, such as California, where she had notable influence over state legislator John Briggs, who sought to prohibit homosexual teachers from working in public schools. Yet as Bryant gained supporters, LGBT+ people and allies began to protest her wherever she went. Comedian Jane Curtin regularly impersonated Bryant on *Saturday Night Live*, and Virginia's first gay rights protest occurred after one of Bryant's concerts. While Bryant gave a television interview, a protestor threw a pie in her face, to which Bryant responded, "Well, at least it's a fruit pie," and began to pray for him as the protestor licked whipped cream off his fingers. Back in Florida, Alan Rockway, one of the authors of the Dade County nondiscrimination ordinance, began a "gaycott" of orange juice that inspired gay bars in Florida and around the country to stop serving orange juice. The Florida Citrus Commission, under pressure from the gaycott, fired Anita Bryant.

TransArt Festival is a Pride Month art festival that includes visual media, performance art, and literary works by transgender artists throughout the US. Since its founding in 2014, it has taken place on Miami Beach, at Wilton Manors, and in the Little Haiti neighborhood. The festival, cochaired by Aryah Lester and Morgan Mayfaire, seeks to showcase the many dimensions and talent of the transgender community and to connect transgender artists to the world and to each other.

We the People was a gay and lesbian activist organization based in Orlando and founded by Beth Raps, Jim Ford, and Saviz Shafaie in 1988. The group contributed to gay pride events and organized protests—see the entry above on the Gay Pride Protest at Winter Park.

The White Party is a celebration and fundraiser every November to benefit HIV/AIDS research. The White Party is not exclusive to Florida, but Miami's White Party has been a staple event in the local LGBT+ community since 1984, when Frank Wager and Jorge Suarez founded the local event. The White Party has since raised millions of dollars for the Health Crisis Network, which is now known as Care Resource. It was held at Villa Vizcaya up until 2010 and has since been held at numerous other venues. Partygoers dress in white while attending extravagant dance parties and performances. Over the years, the White Party has attracted celebrity guests such as RuPaul, Calvin Klein, and Madonna.

The YES Institute is an organization dedicated to the prevention of anti-LGBT+ violence and suicide, founded in 1995 by Martha Fugate and Connie Barden. The two wanted to train educators and professionals to become comfortable speaking about LGBT+ issues and to effectively promote the safety of all LGBT+ people. Since then, the institute has offered counseling and education to tens of thousands of people, helping to create safe, stable environments for the LGBT+ community, whether at home, school, or the workplace.

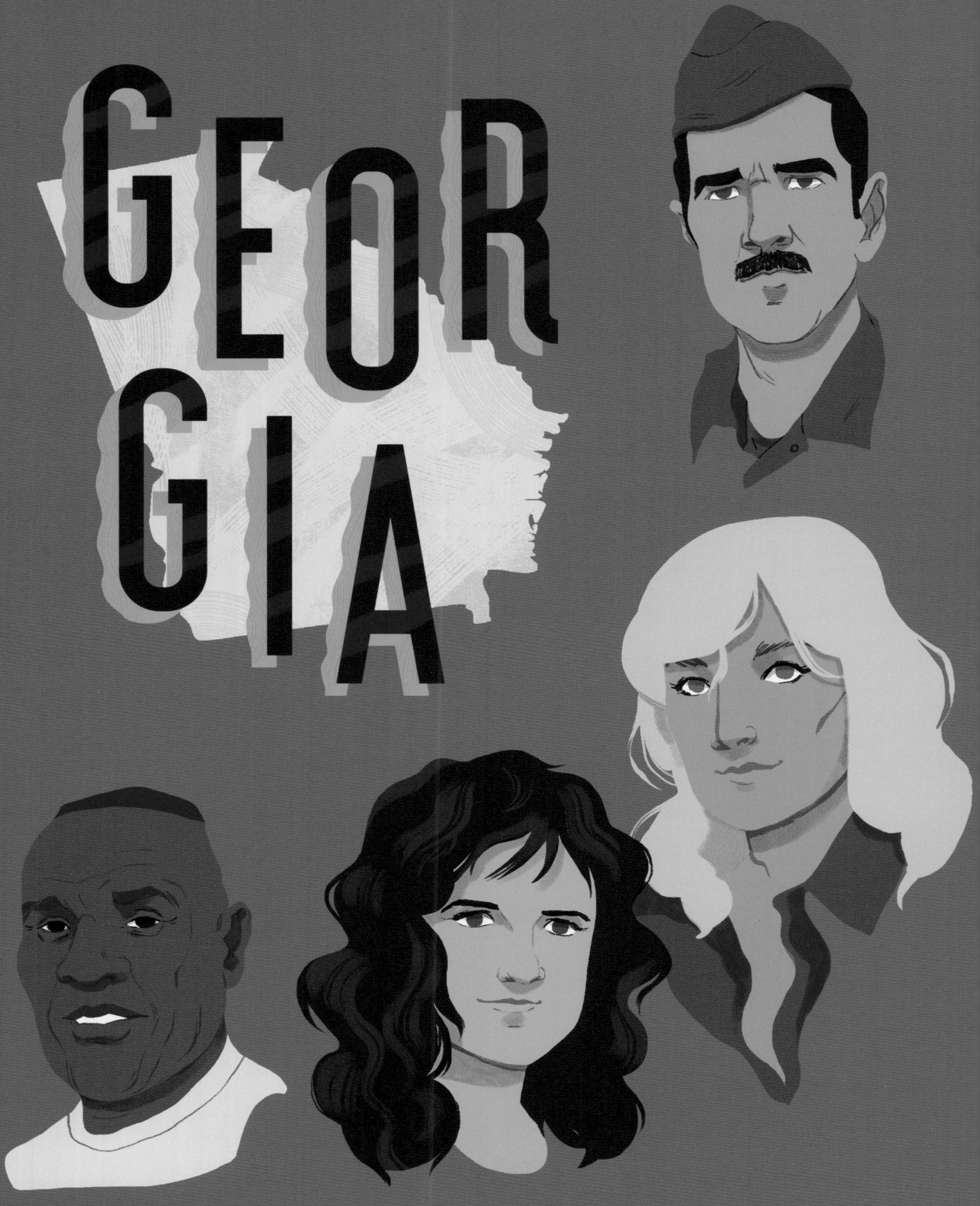
GEORGIA

👤 PEOPLE

Alan Ball *(Marietta, GA)* is a screenwriter and producer, most well-known for the 1999 film *American Beauty*, as well as for the HBO series *Six Feet Under* and *True Blood*. For his work, Ball has won an Oscar, an Emmy, and a Golden Globe, among many other awards and nominations. In 2008, he was named among the OUT100.

Laura Jane Grace *(Fort Benning, GA)* is the frontwoman of the punk rock band Against Me!. Formed in 1997 in Florida, the band has produced seven studio albums and built a reputation for politically motivated and anarchist music. Following Grace coming out as a trans woman in 2012, the band released 2014's *Transgender Dysphoria Blues*, an intimate catalog of Grace's experiences with gender dysphoria. She also performs with the solo act Laura Jane Grace and the Devouring Mothers, and in 2016 cowrote her memoir *TRANNY: Confessions of Punk Rock's Most Infamous Anarchist Sellout*.

Lawrence D. Mass *(Macon, GA)*, a physician and writer, cofounded the nonprofit Gay Men's Health Crisis in 1982. A year prior, Mass wrote the first news reports on what was to become the AIDS epidemic.

Mass's career in medicine spanned from anesthesiology to addiction care, all while writing for publications such as *New York Native* and the *Huffington Post*. Mass lives in New York with his partner, GLAAD cofounder Arnie Kantrowitz.

Leonard Matlovich *(Savannah, GA)*, an Air Force Technical Sergeant, became the first military servicemember to disclose his homosexuality. After being discharged, he was offered his position back in exchange for ceasing homosexual activity; he declined. Matlovich's LGBT+ activism also included establishing a memorial to Harvey Milk in Washington, DC; forcing Northwest Airlines to end its ban on flying people with AIDS; and fighting against California's Proposition 6, a ban on LGBT+ teachers. See the entry about his gravestone in the Congressional Cemetery under *Washington, DC*.

Little Richard (Richard Wayne Penniman) *(Macon, GA)* is a singer, musician, and the self-proclaimed king and queen of rock 'n' roll. In 1956, Richard's first single, "Tutti Frutti," reached number two on the Billboard R&B chart, and he went on to record hits such as "Long Tall Sally" and "Good Golly, Miss Molly." On stage, Richard is known for his stage persona, vigorous dancing, and thick makeup—elements that inspired future musicians from Elvis to Liberace to Prince. With well over three hundred singles to his name, Richard was inducted to the Rock & Roll Hall of Fame in 1986. While he has sometimes referred to himself as an

Laura Jane Grace

> **"**
>
> *Where are you supposed to go when you no longer feel welcome in the places you turned to because you didn't feel welcome anywhere else?*
>
> —Laura Jane Grace, *Tranny: Confessions of Punk Rock's Most Infamous Anarchist Sellout*, 2016
>
> **"**

Little Richard

 It was widely rumored that I had AIDS, or that I was HIV-positive. Which is not the case. I didn't answer those rumors for a long, long time because I felt like making a big deal out of saying no would stigmatize people who are HIV-positive.

—Michael Stipe, *Newsweek*, 1994

omnisexual, in 1995, he told *Penthouse* magazine: "I've been gay all my life and I know God is a God of love, not of hate."

Roy Simmons *(Savannah, GA)* was a professional football player. He played for the New York Giants starting in 1979, and then for the Washington Redskins in 1983, playing all the way to 1984's Super Bowl XVIII and retiring shortly thereafter. When Simmons came out as gay in 1992, he was only the second retired NFL player to do so. Simmons was also the first NFL player

to reveal his HIV-positive status, and died from the illness in 2014 at the age of fifty-seven.

Michael Stipe *(Decatur, GA)* is the singer-songwriter for R.E.M. A self-described queer artist, Stipe's roles include film producer, music video director, visual artist, and philanthropist. He has been nominated for multiple Grammy awards, and won three Grammys in 1991 with R.E.M. for the song "Losing My Religion." The band was inducted into the Rock & Roll Hall of Fame in 2007.

moved to Mississippi after college to participate in the Civil Rights Movement, to write, and to teach. Her work deals with themes of sexism, racism, and violence. She writes novels, short stories, poetry, and nonfiction, and has sold more than fifteen million copies of her books. Her work has been taught in many American history and literary history courses in high schools and colleges across the country.

⊙ PLACES

The National Association of Black and White Men Together (NABWMT) *(Atlanta, GA)* formed its Atlanta chapter in 1981. While its national presence has spread, Atlanta remains its largest individual chapter. NABWMT's task is to combat racism in the LGBT+ community by fostering a multiracial and multicultural organization. The group's website offers resources such as gay-friendly doctors and businesses, and the group hosts in-person events such as potlucks, bowling outings, and more.

Raven-Symoné

Raven-Symoné *(Atlanta, GA)* is an actress, singer, songwriter, television personality, and producer. She first appeared on television on *The Cosby Show* in 1989, then in 2003 on the Disney Channel's *That's So Raven*. From 2015 to 2016, she was a host of the talk show *The View*. Raven stirred controversy in 2014 for shirking labels related to her sexual and racial identities. "I don't want to be labeled gay," she said. "I want to be labeled as a human who loves humans."

Alice Walker *(Eatanton, GA)* is a writer best known for her novel *The Color Purple*. Walker won a Pulitzer Prize and a National Book Award for the book, becoming the first Black woman to win either award. When she was a child, her brother accidentally shot her right eye with a BB gun. Her injury helped inform her writing, and her mother gave her a typewriter to practice when she could no longer complete other household tasks. Though she grew up in Georgia in an area where black people did tenant farming, she

The Otherside Lounge *(Atlanta, GA)*, a local gay and lesbian nightclub, was bombed in February 1997. Five people were injured; a second bomb meant to detonate once first responders appeared at the site was discovered and detonated without harm. The bombing was claimed by an anti-abortion activist group called Army of God, which also bombed an abortion clinic in 1997. Investigators later charged Eric Rudolph with these bombings, as well as Atlanta's 1996 Olympic bombing, which killed one person and injured over a hundred.

Pride School Atlanta *(Atlanta, GA)* opened in 2016 with the mission to provide LGBT+ educators, students, and families with a learning environment free of homophobia and transphobia. Cofounded by Christian Zsilavetz, the K-12 school was the culmination of his dream, which started when he was working at a private school as a closeted transgender man. Due to declining enrollment and the difficulty of serving students outside the Atlanta area, the school closed in 2018.

America's first openly lesbian Black legislator is Simone Bell. Originally from Detroit, Bell was elected as a Democrat to the Georgia House of Representatives in December 2009, and served the Fifty-Eighth District until November 2015. Bell was Georgia's second openly gay member of the General Assembly; the first was Democrat Karla Drenner, elected in 2000.

Atlanta Black Pride Weekend (ABPW) started in 1996 and is touted as the world's largest pride celebration for African American LGBT+ people. The festivities occur the week of Labor Day, with an annual $65 million economic impact on Atlanta's economy. Over seventy-five thousand people attended in 2017. Atlanta is widely regarded as being a "Black Gay Mecca" due to its largely visible Black LGBT+ community and vibrant, urban gay nightlife.

The *Bowers v. Hardwick* decision of 1986 was upheld by the US Supreme Court, allowing Georgia's sodomy laws to stand on the grounds that the Constitution does not cite "a fundamental right to engage in homosexual sodomy." Justice Byron White stated that "the act of consensual sodomy is not protected under the fundamental right to privacy or any right protected under the United States Constitution." Georgia's sodomy law was later struck down in 1998 by the State Supreme Court in the case of *Powell v. State*. All sodomy laws were overturned by the US Supreme Court case *Lawrence v. Texas* (2003).

The Indigo Girls are a folk-rock group. Amy Ray and Emily Saliers formed the group as Emory University undergrads in 1985, though the two had grown up and performed together under the name Saliers & Ray. The band's 1989 album *Indigo Girls* went double platinum, and in 1990 won a Grammy for Best Contemporary Folk Recording. Since 1985, the pair have released fifteen studio albums. The two are lesbians and regarded as icons of the LGBT+ rights movement.

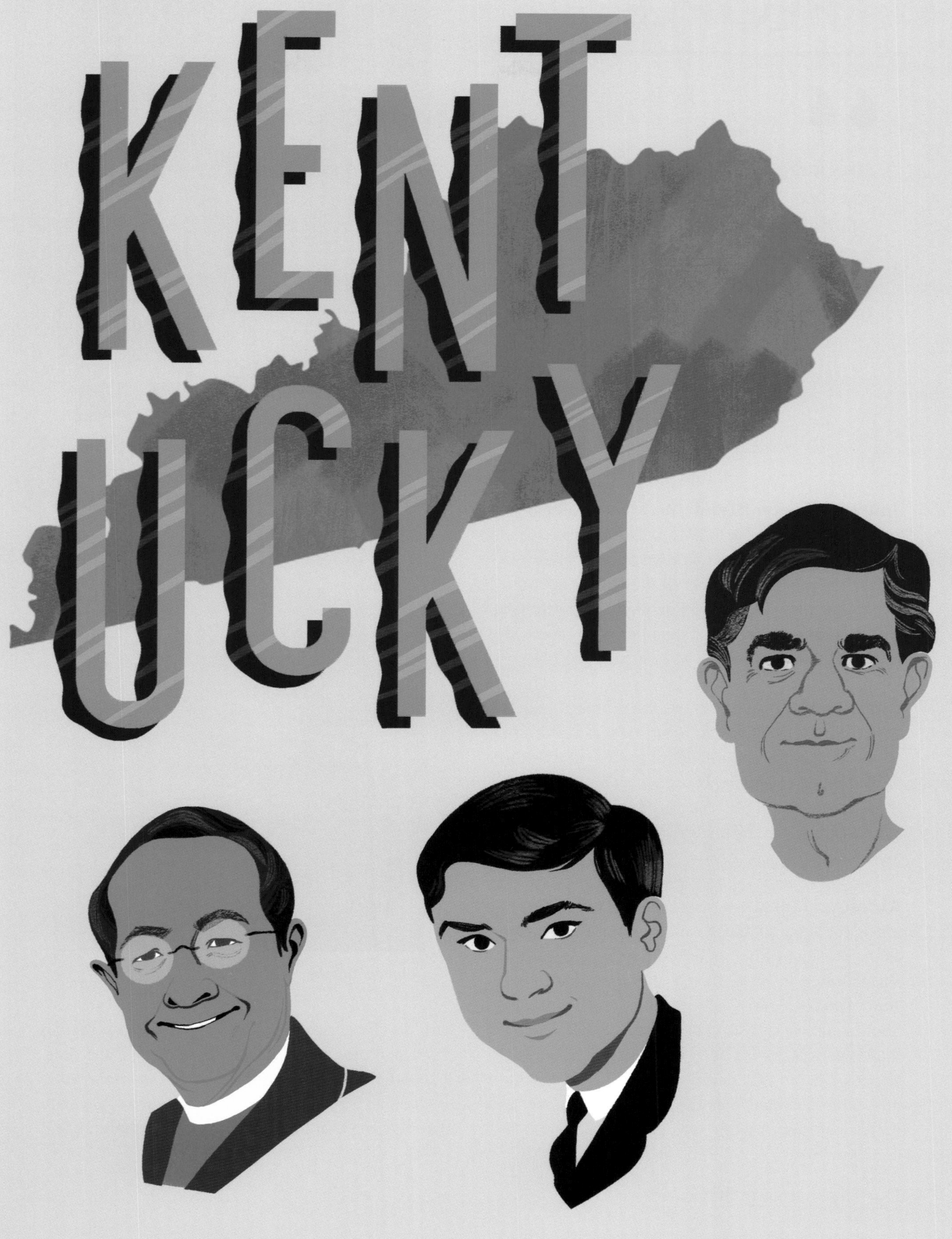
KENTUCKY

⊖ PEOPLE

> " I feel for the first time in my life I'm at peace, I am at peace with myself. . . . The torment that I lived with day and night, 24-7, which never goes away for anyone who deals with transgender issues, is now over. "
>
> —JoAnne Wheeler Bland, *Kentucky Educational Television*, 2015

Tommy Kirk

JoAnne Wheeler Bland *(Sonora, KY)* is a transgender lawyer and activist. In 2014, she worked to create a gender identity nondiscrimination policy for Kentucky colleges as a board member of the Kentucky Council for Postsecondary Education on Equal Opportunities. She also serves as a board member of the Kentucky Fairness Association.

Tommy Kirk *(Louisville, KY)* rose to prominence in the 1950s and 1960s as a child actor. He was featured on *Mickey Mouse Club* and a series of popular films including *Old Yeller*, *The Shaggy Dog*, *Swiss Family Robinson*, and *The Misadventures of Merlin Jones*. In 2006, Disney inducted Kirk into the Disney Legends, its version of a hall of fame.

Abraham Lincoln *(Hodgenville, KY)*, the sixteenth president of the United States, is primarily recognized as the president who abolished slavery and was later assassinated in 1865. Despite his marriage to Mary Todd Lincoln, much speculation has been raised about whether Lincoln was gay or bisexual. Lincoln's marriage to Mary has been documented as a fraught one, as Lincoln was emotionally detached from her and often traveled away from home for extended periods of time. Lincoln was known to share a bed

Abraham Lincoln

with his close friend Joshua Speed for years, though it was common for people to share beds at the time. A 2004 book by C. A. Tripp titled *The Intimate World of Abraham Lincoln* asserts that Lincoln was gay, and also suggests that he slept with his bodyguard, David

Derickson. Tripp's thesis was supported by the historians and academics Jean H. Baker, Michael B. Chesson, and Carl Sanburg.

Joan Osborne *(Anchorage, KY)* is a multi-Grammy-nominated artist who came to prominence as a musician in 1995 with her hit "One of Us." Since then, she has released over seven studio albums. Osborne's regard in the LGBT+ community began when he joined the 1997 Lilith Fair concert tour, which attracted a number of lesbian concertgoers based on its all-female lineup. Osborne has described herself as sexually fluid, telling the *Huffington Post* in 2016, "I have never really seen sexuality so easily defined that you can label yourself and say, 'This is who I am. This is what I like. Period. End of sentence.'"

Gene Robinson *(Lexington, KY)* was the first openly gay Episcopal Church bishop. He wrote the 2013 book *God Believes in Love: Straight Talk About Gay Marriage* and gave the invocation at President Obama's 2009 opening inaugural event. After retiring in 2013, Robinson moved to Washington, DC, to join the Center for American Progress as a senior fellow. In 2018, he presided over a funeral service for Matthew Shepard on the twentieth anniversary of his being beaten to death

for being gay in Wyoming. "Many of you have been hurt by your own religious communities, and I want to welcome you back," Robinson stated during the service, welcoming back to the Church anyone who had left it because of their identity.

Patricia Todd *(Richmond, KY)* became the first openly gay elected official in Alabama when she was elected to represent Birmingham in 2006. Despite being a politician in one of the most socially conservative states, she advocates for progressive issues, focusing on social justice, education, and HIV/AIDS. After determining

Gene Robinson

💡 QUEER FACTS

The Kentucky State Fair ham auction protest took place in 2015. The Kentucky Farm Bureau, an insurance company known for its anti-LGBT+ policies, hosted the charity auction and breakfast. Members of the Kentucky Fairness Campaign purchased tables at the auction to draw attention to the bureau's discriminatory policies; they stood in peace and silence, but were quickly arrested. As of 2018, the group was still fighting a lawsuit against the state, claiming that its First Amendment rights were violated at the protest.

A lesbian health forum sparked controversy at the 2002 Fifth Annual Women's Health in Kentucky Conference. The University of Kentucky hosted an hour-long panel on lesbian health, resulting in two Republican state senators, Dick Roeding and Charlie Borders, threatening to cut funding to the University of Kentucky.

Miller v. Davis involved Kim Davis, a Rowan County clerk who denied marriage licenses to same-sex couples in 2015, citing her religious beliefs. Two same-sex couples and two straight couples, represented by the ACLU, sued Davis. Judge David Bunning ruled that as a public official, Davis had the responsibility of following the orders of the US Supreme Court, which had mandated equal protection for same-sex couples earlier that year. Davis was thus found in contempt of court and jailed for five days.

> *You walked into this institution that's never had anybody like you. It's Alabama. I was prepared for the worst. But you know, I've never heard anybody make any crude remark. Everybody's always been very respectful.*
>
> —Patricia Todd, *Associated Press*, 2018

not to seek reelection in 2018, Todd reflected on her career, stating, "Alabama has only passed one anti-gay bill since I've been in office, but we've killed every other one, bathroom bills and all, that have come up."

Gus Van Sant *(Louisville, KY)* is an openly gay producer, writer, and director. He has made critically acclaimed films, many featuring overt themes of homosexuality, including *My Own Private Idaho*, *Good Will Hunting*, *Elephant*, and *Milk*. In 2017, he directed the first episode of the TV series *When We Rise*, which chronicled the gay rights movement in the United States, beginning with the Stonewall riots in 1969. His films have earned him several Oscar nominations and wins at the Cannes Film Festival.

⦿ PLACES

Hazard Pavilion *(Hazard, KY)* was the location of the 2011 Hazard Pavilion Protest. On June 10, 2011, two disabled gay men were asked to leave the Hazard Pavilion public pool due to a public display of affection. The men were told by staff to "go read the Bible." The Kentucky Equality Federation organized a protest at the Hazard Pavilion, demanding an apology and reassignment of the offending staff.

Kingdom Come State Park *(Cumberland, KY)* is where Kevin Pennington was taken on April 4, 2011, after being kidnapped and beaten by Jason and Anthony Jenkins because of his sexual orientation. Pennington's four assailants pleaded guilty to violating the Matthew Shepard and James Byrd Jr. Hate Crimes Prevention Act, becoming the first people in the nation to be successfully charged under this provision.

The Rowan County Courthouse *(Morehead, KY)* is the infamous location where County Clerk Kim Davis defied a federal court order and denied same-sex couples their marriage licenses following the June 26, 2015, US Supreme Court decision in *Obergefell v. Hodges*. The incident became a political flashpoint as Davis was jailed for her refusal to follow the court order.

LOUISIANA

PEOPLE

Ti-Grace Atkinson *(Baton Rouge, LA)* is a feminist activist and writer. The "Ti" in her name comes from her Creole roots, derived from the French *petit*. Atkinson has a doctorate in philosophy from Columbia University. When she read Simone de Beauvoir's *The Second Sex,* she was so inspired that she wrote to Beauvoir, who told her to reach out to Betty Friedan, the author of *The Feminine Mystique.* Friedan, one of the founders of the National Organization for Women (NOW), encouraged Atkinson to join, and Atkinson eventually became president of NOW's New York City chapter. She left the organization after one year because she did not believe they took a strong enough stance on abortion rights, amongst other issues. Atkinson started her own organization, the Feminists, which she described as practicing radical feminism. She believed lesbian relationships were a political stance against the institutions of marriage and love, and was famously quoted saying, "Feminism is the theory, lesbianism the practice." She taught at Harvard and Tufts University, but in her retirement has focused on activism relating to housing costs.

Big Freedia *(New Orleans, LA)*, the Queen of Bounce, is a rapper and musician. Her music career began in 1999, when she toured as a backup dancer for Katey Red, a transgender bounce artist. Among her many collaborations, Freedia has worked with RuPaul, Drake, Lizzo, and Beyoncé (Freedia is featured in the iconic 2016 music video for "Formation"). Freedia and other New Orleans bounce artists have created and popularized a number of dance moves, most notably the twerk; in 2013, Freedia set a Guinness World Record in New York when a crowd of over three hundred people twerked simultaneously. Born Freddie Ross, Freedia identifies not as trans but as a gay man indifferent to pronouns—"It doesn't matter to me either way whether you call me 'he' or 'she.' . . . My pronoun is 'me,'" Freedia said in 2018.

Truman Capote *(New Orleans, LA)* was a famous writer best known for his book *In Cold Blood*, which pioneered the true crime genre. His friend Harper Lee, author of *To Kill a Mockingbird*, encouraged the project and helped Capote investigate the murders of the Clutter family. Capote was born in New Orleans, where he wrote his first book, *Other Voices, Other Rooms*. During his childhood, he felt abandoned by his eccentric parents, who regularly sent him to live with other people. He later changed his last name to that of his stepfather, Joe Capote, who adopted him. He spent the first years of his career as a copy editor for the *New Yorker,* although it would not initially publish his own work. Capote was a lively and entertaining personality who described his sensitive nature as one of the reasons he used drugs and also why he was a good writer. He is also known for writing *Breakfast at Tiffany's,* which was later made into a film starring Audrey Hepburn.

Failure is the condiment that gives success its flavor.

—Truman Capote, "Self Portrait," 1972

Truman Capote

Ellen DeGeneres

Tony Kushner

Although he spent much of his childhood in New York and his later years in California, he regularly returned to New Orleans. His ashes sold for $43,750 at an auction in 2016 from the estate of his friend Joanne Carson, former wife of Johnny Carson.

Ellen DeGeneres *(Metairie, LA)* is a talk show host, comedian, and television personality best known for the *Ellen DeGeneres Show* that has aired on CBS since 2003 and won over twenty Daytime Emmy awards. DeGeneres first garnered attention for her comedy routine in the late 1970s, and eventually won the award for Showtime's Funniest Person of the Year in 1982. She went on to television roles in shows such as *Open House* and *Ellen.* She came out as gay in 1997, making her eponymous sitcom character on *Ellen* the first gay lead character in US television history. She has been a judge on *American Idol,* hosted the Academy Awards twice, and has several of her own shows in addition to her talk show, including *Ellen's Design Challenge, Little Big Shots,* and *Ellen's Game of Games.*

Tony Kushner *(Lake Charles, LA)* is a renowned playwright and screenwriter. He attended college at Columbia University and New York University. He is the

> **I was born gay, just as I was born black.**
>
> —Don Lemon, interview with Joy Behar, 2011

recipient of numerous awards, including an Emmy, the Pulitzer Prize for Drama, two Tony Awards, and a National Theater Award. His most well-known work is a seven-hour long, two-part play about the AIDs epidemic called *Angels in America: A Gay Fantasia on National Themes.* Kushner contributed screenplays to Steven Spielberg's *Munich* and *Lincoln*, and has also written a children's book with Maurice Sendak.

Don Lemon *(Baton Rouge, LA)* is an Emmy Award–winning journalist who came out as gay in his 2011 memoir, *Transparent.* Lemon majored in broadcast journalism at Brooklyn College in New York; he also studied at Louisiana State University. Throughout his career, Lemon worked as a journalist in many cities,

☻ QUEER FACTS

The first transgender person to earn an engineering degree from Louisiana State University was Reed Erickson. Originally from Pennsylvania, Erickson was a philanthropist who pioneered early research into transexuality. Because Erickson transitioned after college, he is often noted as the first woman to graduate from LSU's engineering program. He started the Erickson Educational Foundation in 1964 in order to fund some of the first research on the transgender experience—this included the work of Dr. Harry Benjamin and the opening of the first gender clinic at Johns Hopkins University. Erickson also financed the work of ONE in Los Angeles, one of the country's oldest LGBT+ support organizations. Erickson's transition set the legal precedent for gender transitions in Louisiana, first with his name change in 1963 and then with his sex change in 1965. Later in life, Erickson moved to Mexico in a house he called the Love Joy Palace, where he lived with his family and pet leopard, Henry. He died at the age of seventy-four with an estimated net worth of $40 million.

Hate Crime Laws have been more progressive in Louisiana than other areas of the South. In 1997, Louisiana became the first Deep South state to pass legislation that prohibited hate crimes based on sexual orientation. In 1998, New Orleans became one of the first cities in the nation to give discrimination protections based on gender identity.

The New Orleans chapter of Daughters of Bilitis, a national lesbian rights organization formed in the 1950s in San Francisco, opened in the 1970s. The organization began as a place for lesbians to socialize away from discrimination, and then became an activist organization. It was the first lesbian civil and political rights organization in the United States.

Southern Decadence started as a costume party by a group of friends in August 1972 and has turned into a world-famous gay celebration attracting over 200,000 participants. The party generates an estimated $250 million for the city. The celebration is mostly concentrated in the French Quarter, although it has smaller gatherings outside of the area. It is New Orleans's largest gay street fair and begins the Wednesday before Labor Day.

Don Lemon

including New York, Birmingham, Philadelphia, St. Louis, and Chicago. After working for MSNBC and NBC, in 2006 Lemon began working with CNN. Lemon's reporting has garnered him widespread attention, notably when President Obama referred to Don Lemon's interview with a 106-year-old voter in his acceptance speech after he won the 2008 election. Lemon has hosted CNN's *New Year's Eve Live* from New Orleans, and has his own show, *CNN Tonight with Don Lemon*. In addition to his Emmy, Lemon also won an Edward R. Murrow award for his coverage of the 2002 Beltway sniper attacks in the Baltimore-Washington metro area.

PLACES

Café Laffitte in Exile *(New Orleans, LA)* is one of the oldest gay bars in the US, and is open 24-7. It was established in 1933 after the end of Prohibition, and over the years has welcomed distinguished visitors such as Truman Capote and playwright Tennessee Williams. The bar hosts a famous disco party every Sunday night called the Trash Disco, but also offers a more relaxed atmosphere with an upstairs bar and balcony.

Fat Monday Luncheon *(New Orleans, LA)* is considered the oldest large-scale LGBT+ event in Louisiana and dates back to 1949. It began as a small gathering at Brennan's Restaurant, when Bob Demmons declared one of the out-of-town Mardi Gras goers "Queen of the Luncheon." Currently, the luncheon is hosted at Arnaud's Restaurant, where one out-of-town visitor and one local guest are crowned queen every year. A number of awards are also given to partygoers throughout the event, and a parade goes from the breakfast to the Queen's Reception at a different location in the afternoon. The Fat Monday Luncheon attracts hundreds of attendees every year.

LGBT Community Center of New Orleans *(New Orleans, LA)* is an organization that was established in 1992 as the Lesbian and Gay Community Center. It has tracked hate crimes against members of the LGBT+ community since 2000, and hosts an annual Trans Day of Remembrance. After Hurricane Katrina, it hosted a collective of related organizations to assist members of the community during the recovery period. The LGBT Community Center remains a safe space for members of the LGBT+ community; advocates for economic and racial justice and gender equality; and helps its members find resources to start their own supportive projects.

Truman Capote's apartment *(New Orleans, LA)* is where the renowned author wrote his first book, *Other Voices, Other Rooms.* Capote referred to New Orleans as "like a hometown," because it is where he was born and spent the first three years of his life. As a child, his mother would lock him in a room at the Hotel Monteleone, where she left him for long periods of time. Another place of significance to Capote is the St. Louis Cathedral, which he attended in his youth.

The UpStairs Lounge *(New Orleans, LA)* was a gay bar and the site of arson in 1973 that killed thirty-two people. St. Mark's United Methodist Church was the only church that held a memorial service, and the governor at the time, Edwin Edwards, refused to acknowledge the deaths from the incident. A man named Roger Nunez reportedly confessed to multiple people that he started the fire. He was also the subject of a police investigation into the incident, though he never served jail time. The attack is the second-largest killing of LGBT+ people in the US, after the Pulse Nightclub shooting in Orlando in 2016. The fire is the subject of two documentaries, *UpStairs Inferno* and *The UpStairs Lounge Fire.*

MISSISSIPPI

⊖ PEOPLE

James Richmond Barthé *(Bay St. Louis, MS)* was a painter and sculptor born in 1901. He is considered the first Black sculptor of the modern era to achieve success in the US. The rural area of Bay St. Louis allowed him to enjoy a peaceful, artistically focused childhood. At age fourteen, Barthé left school after contracting typhoid fever. He worked odd jobs until a pastor noticed his talent and encouraged him to apply to art school. At twenty-three, he was accepted to the Art Institute of Chicago, where he studied for four years while living with his aunt Rose. Barthé moved to New York City in 1930 and opened a studio in Harlem, where he made a name for himself as a sculptor during the Harlem Renaissance and the Great Depression. In 1950, he moved to Ocho Rios, Jamaica, where he produced his largest sculptures before moving to Europe and eventually back to California. Barthé had several short-lived gay relationships.

Lance Bass *(Laurel, MS)* was raised in a conservative Southern Baptist environment, where he had to keep his sexuality private. Nevertheless, he has said he had a happy childhood. At the age of eleven, he was encouraged to sing in a show choir called the Mississippi Show Stoppers, which performed at state fairs and various political functions. In his junior year of high school, Bass was contacted by Justin Timberlake, who was looking for another singer for the pop group NSYNC. Bass auditioned for the role and was accepted, so he left school to move to Orlando and work with the band full time. NSYNC became the biggest pop act of its time in 2000 when the album *No Strings Attached* sold over a million copies in one day. The band went on indefinite hiatus in 2002. Later, Bass moved on to other media work, including television acting, film production, and a season on *Dancing with the Stars*. In 2006, he publicly came out as gay in *People* magazine. He describes his coming out as a positive experience and has been proud to be a role model for fans.

Cat Cora *(Jackson, MS)* was raised in a family of restaurateurs, and was strongly influenced by her father and grandfather and their Greek cultural background. By the age of fifteen, she was already ambitious enough to have drafted a business plan for her own restaurant, which she presented to her father and grandfather. After studying exercise physiology and biology at the University of Southern Mississippi, she enrolled in New York's Culinary Institute of America. She has built a successful career combining her passion for food, ambitious business acumen, and enthusiastic personality. In addition to her signature restaurants, including Ocean by Cat Cora, Cat Cora's Kitchen, and Kouzzina,

Lance Bass

> **"**
>
> *Bullying is killing our kids. Being different is killing our kids and the kids who are bullying are dying inside. We have to save our kids whether they are bullied or they are bullying. They are all in pain.*
>
> —Cat Cora, *Larry King Live* web exclusive, 2010
>
> **"**

Tennessee Williams

in the early 1950s, but continued struggling with alcohol and drug use, and with frustration that audiences did not connect with his later works. He sank deeper into a depression after 1963 when his romantic partner, Frank Merlo, died. Twenty years later at the age of seventy-one, Williams died alone in a hotel room, having choked on a plastic bottle cap.

PLACES

Grace House *(Jackson, MS)* is a nonprofit that provides temporary and semipermanent housing for homeless people living with HIV and AIDS, and women in recovery from chemical dependency. The organization has grown from a single house to multiple services, including permanent housing for some residents, rent assistance for others, and a ninety-day transitional apartment program for women in recovery for chemical dependency. Grace House also provides health education, counseling, and a food pantry for the HIV+ community.

Lighthouse Community Church *(Biloxi, MS)* in its own words is an "ALL inclusive, fully LGBTQIA+ affirming, progressive, and independent worship community in the Anglican tradition, serving the MS Gulf Coast." This church provides a variety of religious and community services, including worship services, potlucks, weddings, and seasonal celebrations catering to the LGBT+ community in the area.

PFLAG of Jackson, Mississippi *(Jackson, MS)*, is the Jackson chapter of Parents, Families & Friends of Lesbians and Gays (PFLAG), a national organization that provides support, education, and advocacy to LGBT+ populations and allies in the community. Jackson PFLAG holds monthly meetings the second Tuesday of each month. The organization also provides information for youth outreach and provides general information on political topics that affect the LGBT+ community.

Rumors *(Shannon, MS)* was a gay bar and one of the subjects of the documentary *Small Town Gay Bar*, released in 2006 by Canadian film producer Malcolm Ingram. The film was a success, as it honestly depicted the way LGBT+ communities can form even in remote, socially hostile areas. Rumors closed in 2010. In 2013, a lesbian from Memphis, Tennessee, wanted to reopen the bar on its former spot, but was met with unconcealed hostility from both the local government and homophobic townspeople, and was unable to reopen the bar.

The Spectrum Center *(Hattiesburg, MS)* was established in 2014 near the University of Southern Mississippi, and serves as a resource center for the area's LGBT+ community. The Center is a meeting place for support and discussion groups for trans and gender-nonconforming people. It also provides HIV testing free of charge. The Center hopes to add new amenities and functions such as a community kitchen and housing for homeless LGBT+ youth in emergency situations. The Spectrum Center hosts events, marches, and gatherings throughout the year to promote LGBT+ pride, community education, and a sense of social unity.

Tennessee Williams Home & Welcome Center
(Columbus, MS) is Tennessee Williams's first home and a national literary landmark. It was almost torn down in the 1990s before it was relocated to Main Street and preserved as a tourist destination. It is the site of the annual Tennessee Williams Celebration, and is thought to have been a creative influence on his work.

QUEER FACTS

The first prosecution of a gender-based hate crime occurred in 2015 when Joshua Vallum, twenty-nine, killed Mercedes Williamson, a seventeen-year-old transgender girl. The two had dated in 2014 and he knew she was transgender, which she did not disclose to many people. Vallum was active in a street gang, the Almighty Latin Kings and Queens Nation. When a friend found out that Williamson was transgender, Vallum feared retribution from the gang and decided to murder her. They met one night in his car—he stabbed her, then beat her to death with a hammer. He was arrested and pled guilty to the murder, claiming he had not known she was transgender and claiming a "gay panic" defense. Because he effectively admitted he killed her because of her gender identity, federal prosecutors were able to convict him under the 2009 Matthew Shepard and James Byrd Jr. Hate Crimes Prevention Act. This was the first time someone had been prosecuted under the act for violence against a transgender person. Vallum was fined $20,000 and sentenced to forty-nine years in prison.

The Religious Liberty Accommodation Act, also known as House Bill 1523, was a statewide act that allowed discrimination over sexual orientation and sexual identity on religious grounds. It was a response to the 2015 decision by the US Supreme Court that ruled it unconstitutional to deny marriage to same-sex couples. HB 1523 passed by a wide margin. On June 30, 2016, a day before it was to take effect, District Court Judge Carlton Reeves filed a preliminary injunction in an attempt to strike down the law. On June 23, 2017, the Fifth Court of Appeals lifted the injunction, allowing the law to go back into full effect. The US Supreme Court refused to take the case any further. Since December 2016, six states and over a dozen cities have banned nonessential, publicly funded travel to Mississippi in protest of HB 1523. Britain and the European Union both issued traveler's warnings, advising LGBT+ tourists not to visit Mississippi while HB 1523 remains law.

A transgender student graduated Pass Christian High School on May 18, 2018. Jorden Blosser was the first openly transgender person to graduate from the school. He described how his struggles with his identity led to depression and a severe eating disorder that resulted in his withdrawal from Gulfport High School. He was homeschooled for the rest of his freshman year. He transferred to Pass Christian High the following year, but it was not until his junior year that he came out as male to his classmates. After some initial struggles, he found them supportive, and was able to focus on school and personal development. He graduated with a 3.5 GPA and was accepted at Berea College in Kentucky.

A twelve-year-old bisexual boy died by suicide in Southaven, Mississippi, in March 2018. Andrew Leach's sixteen-year-old brother found his body hanging in his family's garage with his suicide note. He had revealed at school that he thought he might be bisexual, and his classmates tormented and bullied him. Southaven Middle School claimed a zero-tolerance policy for bullying, but harassment of Leach escalated until he was terrified that "he wouldn't make it out" of a bathroom.

NORTH CAROLINA

PEOPLE

Clay Aiken *(Raleigh, NC)* first gained public attention when he placed second on the 2003 season of *American Idol*. Aiken's first album, *Measure of a Man*, sold over two million copies in its first month. In 2008, Aiken made headlines again for coming out as gay in *People* magazine. His career has expanded beyond music into Broadway performances, activism work with UNICEF and the National Inclusion Project, and even a stint on Donald Trump's *The Celebrity Apprentice* in 2012. Aiken was in the spotlight again in 2014, when he ran for Congress as a Democrat in North Carolina, but lost to incumbent Republican Renee Ellmers.

Isadora Cerullo *(Raleigh, NC)* is a lesbian American rugby player. A child of Brazilian immigrant parents, Cerullo holds dual citizenship. She was recruited to play on the Brazilian women's national rugby sevens team after graduating from Columbia University in 2013. At the 2016 Rio Olympics, Cerullo's team lost against Australia—but at the end of the game, her partner, Marjorie Enya, walked onto the field and asked Cerullo to marry her. "I wanted to show people that love wins," Enya said.

Chris Hughes *(Hickory, NC)* is a gay entrepreneur who cofounded Facebook and directed President Obama's digital campaign in 2008. In 2012, the Harvard graduate became a major shareholder of the *New Republic* magazine and joined the staff as its publisher and editor in chief; he sold the magazine four years later. In 2016, Forbes named Hughes number twenty-eight on its list of America's Richest Entrepreneurs Under Forty. Hughes is married to Sean Eldridge, the former director of the Freedom to Marry campaign.

Moms Mabley *(Brevard, NC)*, born Loretta Aiken, was a Black lesbian stand-up comic in the 1950s and '60s. Born March 19, 1894, she came out at the age of twenty-seven, becoming one of first openly gay comedians. Her routines were known to be raunchy, and she often wore housedresses and appeared toothless while performing. At the height of her career, Moms performed at Harlem's Apollo Theatre, earning $10,000 a week. She eventually reached a more mainstream, white audience and performed at Carnegie Hall in 1962 and on TV comedy shows including *The Ed Sullivan Show* and *The Smothers Brothers Comedy Hour*. "Every comedian has stolen from me but Jack Benny," she once said. She died in 1975 at the age of seventy-seven.

Stephen Rhodes *(Goldsboro, NC)* was the first openly gay NASCAR driver. He began his career at age eight as a go-kart racer, winning thirty-one out of fifty-five races in his first year. Rhodes came out at the age of seventeen in 2001, one year before his NASCAR career began. He competed in the NASCAR Late Model Stock Division, Camping World Truck Series; in 2003, he finished eighty-seventh overall. In 2018, speaking to whether he thought his fans cared about his sexuality, he told *Queerty*, "Most NASCAR fans don't care either way, as long as it doesn't affect my ability to drive."

There is actually a statistic that more athletes are coming out after what happened, and even Rio has the highest number of 'out athletes' ever. So maybe we'll hear about more athletes being more comfortable, just being themselves and proud of who they are. I hope so.

—Isadora Cerullo, *Associated Press*, 2016

Jacob Tobia

Evan Rachel Wood

Jacob Tobia *(Raleigh, NC)* is a genderqueer LGBT+ activist with a degree in human rights advocacy from Duke University. In 2016, Tobia developed *Queer 2.0*, a video column for NBC News that focused on in-depth exploration of queer issues. Tobia was recognized on the OUT100 in 2016 and *Forbes*'s 30 Under 30 list in 2018. Their memoir *Sissy: A Coming-of-Gender Story* was published in 2019.

Evan Rachel Wood *(Raleigh, NC)* is a bisexual actress best known for her roles in film and television such as *Westworld*, *Across the Universe*, and *Thirteen*. Born in 1987, Wood began acting around 1994 in several made-for-TV films, but in 1995 landed a role on the CBS horror show *American Gothic*. She is widely remembered for her role in the 2005 Green Day music video for "Wake Me Up When September Ends." In 2011, Wood revealed that she is bisexual via Twitter.

PLACES

The Durham Judicial Annex *(Durham, NC)* is where a vigil was held in 1981 in response to the murder of Ronald "Sonny" Antonevich. On April 12 of that year, Sonny and three friends were sunbathing at a popular gay swimming spot on Little River near Durham. They were approached and beaten by two young men who shouted anti-gay slurs. Antonevich, unable to move due to a physical disability, sustained critical injuries

The Carolina Gay Association was founded in 1974 at the University of North Carolina–Chapel Hill, the first such organization in the state and one of the oldest in the country. In 1976, it began publishing the *LAMBDA* newsletter, one of the nation's oldest student-run LGBT+ publications. The organization became increasingly politically active through the AIDS crisis and is today called the Gay, Lesbian, Bisexual, Transgender, Straight Alliance (GLBTSA).

Gay marriage was legalized in North Carolina in October 2014. Judge Max O. Cogburn Jr. ruled in the lawsuit *General Synod of the United Church of Christ v. Cooper*—in which the church challenged the constitutionality of North Carolina's existing anti–gay marriage laws as a restriction of its religious freedom—that banning same-sex marriage is unconstitutional. The case was notable for the several religious groups that supported the United Church of Christ in favor of overturning the state's ban.

The HB2 "bathroom bill" passed in North Carolina in March 2016 and required transgender people to use restrooms corresponding with the gender identity noted on their birth certificates. The bill was proposed in response to a Charlotte ordinance that allowed transgender people to use the restroom that corresponded with their gender identity. The bill became a national flashpoint, with celebrities and major organizations (including the NBA, NCAA, Bruce Springsteen, Maroon 5, Demi Lovato, and Nick Jonas) who cancelled shows and championship games in the state in protest. The bill was partially repealed in April 2017.

qnotes was a small monthly newsletter founded in 1983. Three years later, it was reborn as a monthly print newspaper. Today, it exists as a biweekly print publication focusing on LGBT+ arts, education, and news in North and South Carolina.

to his head and organs, and died in the hospital three days later. Sonny's assailants were charged with his murder; during their court proceedings, the vigil held in Sonny's memory outside the courthouse set the precedent for LGBT+ community protests and parades for years to come.

The Gay and Lesbian Pulp Fiction Collection

(Durham, NC) of Duke University's Rubenstein Library includes an extensive collection of lesbian pulp novels published in the 1950s and '60s. The collection also houses hundreds of gay male mysteries, police stories, and pulps under the Drewey Wayne Gunn and Jacques Murat Collection of Gay American Pulps. The books, featuring graphic cover art and campy and salacious plots, were sold as popular novels in drugstores, giving straight and queer people a view into a world they might not otherwise have access to.

The UNC Oral History Project *(Charlotte, NC)* is

an extensive archive documenting Charlotte's LGBT+ history. The project began in 2016 and is helmed by community volunteers, as well as UNCC's Atkins Library staff. Its goal is to document the history and culture of the area's LGBT+ community in a region of the country where it often goes overlooked.

PUERTO RICO

⊖ PEOPLE

> *I refuse to accept the assertion of any historian who erroneously believes that women have no right to use their freedom without being considered corrupt or immoral.*
>
> —Luisa Capetillo, *Influencias de las ideas modernas*, 1916

> *I want to try to be the best role model I can be for kids who might look into boxing as a sport and a professional career. I have and will always be a proud Puerto Rican. I have always been and always will be a proud gay man.*
>
> —Orlando Cruz, *USA Today*, 2012

Ana Irma Rivera Lassén

Luisa Capetillo *(Arecibo, PR)* made waves in 1915 when she wore men's clothing publicly in Puerto Rico while organizing tobacco workers. It's unclear to what degree her "crossdressing" was an expression of gender identity as opposed to her rejecting sexism, or whether it was a mixture of the two. She was arrested for crossdressing; in court, she told the judge, "Your Honor, I always wear pants," and lifted the hem of her dress to reveal them underneath. The charges against her were ultimately dropped. Capetillo was a prominent labor organizer in Puerto Rico, fighting in particular for fair wages and safe working conditions for women. A thought leader in anarchist philosophy, she wrote a book in 1909 titled *Mi opinión sobre las libertades, derechos y deberes de la mujer* (*My opinion about the rights, liberties, and responsibilities of women*) that promoted ideas of women's equality and free love. Aurora Levins Morales and Leslie Feinberg have both written extensively about this historic woman.

Orlando Cruz *(Yabucoa, PR)* became, in 2012, the first active American professional boxer to come out as gay. In 2013, Cruz was among the inaugural inductees to the National Gay and Lesbian Sports Hall of Fame. As of 2016, Cruz was the number-two ranked junior lightweight in the World Boxing Organization. That year, he dedicated a fight against Alejandro Valdez to the victims of the Pulse nightclub shooting; four of Cruz's friends were murdered in the massacre. Cruz defeated Valdez in seven rounds while sporting rainbow-colored shorts.

Cecilia La Luz *(San Juan, PR)* is an activist and radio producer. She founded and serves as president of Saliendo del Clóset, which offers support and mental health resources to the LGBT+ community. La Luz runs a radio program of the same name. She also founded the United Organization for Equality to develop public policy, combat homophobia, and educate the LGBT+ community. In 2011, she founded Centro Comunitario LGBTT De Puerto Rico, an LGBT+ community center.

Ricky Martin (Enrique José Martín Morales) *(San Juan, PR)* is a singer often regarded as the king of Latin pop. Martin performed with the boy band Menudo in the 1980s, and released his debut solo album in 1988.

Ricky Martin

Puerto Rico and the United States. Negrón-Muntaner is a professor of English and comparative literature at Columbia University, where she also founded the Latino Arts and Activism Collection at the school's library. Some of her writing includes *Puerto Rican Jam: Rethinking Colonialism and Nationalism* (1997), *Boricua Pop: Puerto Ricans and the Latinization of American Culture* (2004), and *The Latino Media Gap: The State of Latinos in US Media* (2014).

Ana Irma Rivera Lassén *(San Juan, PR)* was the first Black woman and the first lesbian to head the Bar Association of Puerto Rico. Elected in 2012, she was also the third woman to hold the position. In the 1980s, Rivera Lassén sued a judge and won when she was refused entry into court in pants, as opposed to a dress or skirt. Rivera Lassén's activism career is long and decorated with awards, including the Medalla Senatorial Capetillo-Roqué from the Puerto Rican Senate, which she was awarded in 2003 for her work on behalf of women's rights.

While popular in Puerto Rico for years, Martin captured worldwide attention with his 1999 single "Livin' La Vida Loca" off his first album in English, *Ricky Martin*. In 2010, Martin came out as gay on his website, a decision he said was inspired by his twin sons, born in 2008. "I am very blessed to be who I am," he wrote.

Frances Negrón-Muntaner *(San Jan, PR)* is a prominent scholar of Latino studies. Her works explore colonialism, race, gender, and sexuality, primarily in

Pedro Julio Serrano *(Ponce, PR)* founded Puerto Rico Para Tod@s, an organization supporting the island's LGBT+ community, in 2003. Serrano's activism has spread far, leading to roles at the Human Rights Foundation, the National Latino/a Lesbian and Gay Organization (LLEGÓ), and Freedom to Marry's Voices for Equality. He is both HIV-positive and a cancer survivor. In 2007, Serrano made front-page headlines across Puerto Rican publications for kissing his then-boyfriend at the island's capitol. "Gay Love Shakes the Capitol," one headline read.

💡 QUEER FACTS

The La Comay boycott, in late 2012 and early 2013, was led by Pedro Julio Serrano. It began when Serrano was ridiculed for homosexuality by Antulio Santarrosa, the host of WAPA TV's *SuperXclusivo* program, via a puppet named La Comay. Activist Carlos Rivera called for protest via Facebook, and Serrano quickly joined. The movement brought together more than seventy thousand people to cancel the program due to its homophobia, sexism, racism, and other forms of intolerance. Companies such as Coca-Cola, Walmart, and Ford pulled their sponsorships from the show, and Santarrosa resigned within a month.

> *The struggle for social justice is never one that is done unilaterally. We have to confront oppression from every angle because the root of oppression is the same for sexism, racism, homophobia, classism—for any type of intolerance, it's the same root.*
>
> —Pedro Julio Serrano, *The Odyssey Online*, 2016

PLACES

Centro Comunitario LGBTT de Puerto Rico *(San Juan, PR)* was founded in 2011 by Cecilia La Luz, who also serves as the executive director of the center. La Luz has said the center helps a population known to be "excluded, marginalized, and whose rights are constantly being stepped on." It remains the only LGBT+ center in Puerto Rico.

The Comunidad de Orgullo Gay *(San Juan, PR)*, founded in 1973, was the first gay rights organization in Puerto Rico. Created in response to the 1969 Stonewall Riots, the group sought political action and resistance to LGBT+ discrimination. Also called Casa Orgullo, it shuttered in 1976. Today, it is listed in the National Register of Historic Places for its initiation of Puerto Rico's gay liberation movement.

Puerto Rico's first LGBT+ monument *(San Juan, PR)* was erected in Third Millennium Park in June 2016, shortly after the massacre at Pulse nightclub in Orlando, Florida. Twenty-three of the forty-nine people gunned down were from Puerto Rico; their names are engraved on a plaque at the monument. Following the names, an inscription reads, "This tribute to life strengthens our commitment to fight hate—the product of homophobia—with love and respect. Our slogan resounds in all our hearts: Love is love, is love, is love . . ."

SOUTH CAROLINA

⊖ PEOPLE

Dorothy Allison *(Greenville, SC)* is a writer whose work focuses on themes of feminism, trauma, and sexuality. Allison was the first person in her family to earn a high school diploma. She was raised by a single mother, who gave birth to Allison at the age of fifteen and worked as a waitress. Allison's notable works include the novels *Bastards Out of Carolina* and *Cavedweller;* a short story collection, *Trash;* and a collection of poems titled *The Women Who Hate Me.* Allison is the recipient of the American Librarian Association Prize for Lesbian and Gay Writing and two Lambda Literary Awards, among other honors. She serves on the board of the Fellowship of Southern Writers.

Anita Cornwell *(Greenwood, SC)* is an author whose work deals with themes of feminism, sexuality, and race. Cornwell graduated from Temple University in 1948 with degrees in journalism and social sciences. At some point in her life, Cornwell realized she wasn't comfortable around straight men and that the state of relationships between men and women is "atrocious." She believes in allowing everyone their full identity expression, regardless of expectations for dress and behavior. Cornwell became interested in the women's movement early on, and has said that Black women have always been feminists because they had to be. In 1983, she wrote her first collection of essays, *Black Lesbian in White America.* She has also written for *Feminist Review, Gay Alternative, Labyrinth, National Leader, Los Angeles Free Press,* and *The Negro Digest.*

Andy Dick *(Charleston, SC)* is an actor and comedian. He is best known for hosting *The Andy Dick Show* on MTV, and also his displays of public drunkenness, during which he has licked, mooned, and groped unsuspecting people. Dick has said that he licked Carrie Fisher at a roast, and was forcibly removed from *Jimmy Kimmel Live!* after he wouldn't stop touching Ivanka Trump. Dick has sought treatment for substance abuse. He has starred as himself in episodes of *Arrested Development* and *Family Guy.* Dick played Kramer in the 1999 film *Inspector Gadget* and multiple different characters on *The Ben Stiller Show* in the early 1990s.

Andy Dick

LGBT youth are actually up to eight times as likely to commit suicide as compared to their straight peers if they come from an unaccepting environment. So I'm really excited to partner with [the Trevor Project] and I hope it will be a great year of social change.

—Erin O'Flaherty, *Good Morning America*, 2016

Erin O'Flaherty *(Florence, SC)* was crowned Miss Missouri in 2016 and was the first openly gay contestant in the Miss America pageant. When she was thirteen, one of O'Flaherty's friends died by suicide. The experience deeply affected O'Flaherty, and she uses her platform to support the American Foundation for

Suicide Prevention and the Trevor Project, reaching LGBT+ youth specifically. O'Flaherty hopes that her accomplishments overshadow her sexual orientation, and that one day it will not be remarkable for an LGBT+ person to compete in Miss America.

Rembert S. Truluck *(Clinton, SC)* was a pastor and writer. He was raised Baptist and earned his Master of Theology from the Southern Baptist Theological Seminary in Kentucky. He is most known for his writings on religion and sexuality, such as *Invitation to Freedom,*

💡 QUEER FACTS

A man named Joshua Esskew was beaten in April 2011 in the parking lot of a convenience store in Rock Hill. A group of five men threw a beer bottle at Esskew, and when he responded, they beat him severely. Surveillance cameras recorded the assault, and LGBT+ advocacy groups from across the nation responded in outrage. The assailants were arrested and charged with assault, though their crimes were not considered hate crimes, as sexually motivated crimes did not qualify under South Carolina law at that time.

M. C. v. Aaronson was a 2017 legal settlement regarding infant genital surgery. In 2006, a sixteen-month-old child named M. C., who was born with ambiguous genitalia, received intersex genital-mutilating surgeries because the state believed it would increase M. C.'s adoptability. After being adopted, M. C. grew to identify as male, opposite of what the surgery intended. In 2013, the Crawfords, his adoptive parents, sued the department of social services, arguing that it violated M. C.'s constitutional rights. This was the first case of its kind in the United States and the first time an intersex person was awarded monetary damages for the damage inflicted upon their body during nonconsensual cosmetic procedures. The Crawfords were awarded $440,000 in a settlement.

The murder of Sean Kennedy occurred in 2007 in Greenville, when Stephen Andrew Moller stopped his car to ask Kennedy for a cigarette as he left a bar. Moller then got out of his car, called Kennedy a homophobic slur, and punched him so hard that it broke bones in his face and separated his brain stem from his brain. Kennedy died in the hospital. Kennedy's mother Elke started the Sean's Last Wish Foundation

to advocate for LGBT+ rights and safety. The court sentenced Moller to five years in prison, though he served only one year before he was released.

South Carolina Black Pride (SCBP) started in 2006, then called Black/Latino Gay Pride. SCBP unifies and serves Black LGBT+ people and allies in the state, and became a nonprofit in 2009. SCBP has six Pillars of Pride that set the foundation of its mission, goals, and aspirations for the Black LGBT+ community: education, community involvement, youth and young adults, health and wellness, political foundation, and LGBT+ unity. SCBP holds its yearly pride event in August.

South Carolina's same-sex marriage ban passed in 2006. It amended the state constitution to explicitly state that marriage should be between one man and one woman, with no other partnerships officially recognized by the state. The amendment had the support of 78 percent of voters, and remained in effect until the US Supreme Court legalized gay marriage in 2015.

University of South Carolina Upstate assigned the book *Out Loud: The Best of Rainbow Radio* to its 2014 incoming freshman class. The book, edited by Ed Madden and Candace Chellew Hodge, is a collection of essays about the first LGBT+ radio show in South Carolina. After USC Upstate announced its selection, the South Carolina House of Representatives threatened to cut $17,172 of funding to the school. The controversy pushed two students, Marniqua Tomkins and Laketra Cureton, to start their own advocacy group on campus, SPEAK, and another student, Cody Owens, to a Guide to Personal Evangelism in the Gay Community (1993) and *Steps to Recovery from Bible Abuse* (1997). Truluck believed that Christianity could help gay and lesbian people recover from internalized homophobia and advocated against religious oppression. He died in 2008 at the age of seventy-four.

Thomas Jefferson Withers *(York County, SC)* was a politician and judge who served in the South Carolina Court of Appeals. While studying at South Carolina College in 1826, Withers wrote a series of romantic and sexually explicit letters to James H. Hammond, who would go on to become a politician aligned with the Confederacy. Withers did not enjoy his time in college, which he described as time "murdered." He reached the height of his political career when he served as a delegate for the seven seceded states of the South in 1861. With a team of fifty other delegates, he helped construct the plan for the provisional government for the new Confederacy, which they hoped would be independent from the US government. Withers married Elizabeth Boykin, and together they had eight children, though the first four died from scarlet fever in infancy.

 **PLACES**

College of Charleston Libraries *(Charleston, SC)* houses an archive on LGBT+ history that started as the independent project of librarian Harlan Greene.

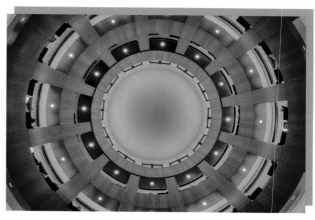
College of Charleston Libraries

A graduate student helped expand his collection, and a $200,000 grant from the Dorothy and Gaylord Donnelley Foundation gave the library financial resources to take the collection further. The archive project has an oral history component, as well as a collection of historic documents such as photographs and personal papers.

Middleton Place plantation *(Charleston, SC)* held the first statewide meeting of the South Carolina Equality Coalition in 2002. There, activists from all over the state met to discuss how to best advocate for LGBT+ South Carolinians. The meeting led to the formation of a statewide coalition to coordinate LGBT+ activism, now called the South Carolina Equality Coalition (SCEQ). Middleton Place is a historic landmark and garden that seeks to preserve the stories of the slaves who formerly worked on the grounds.

> *I feel some inclination to learn whether you yet sleep in your Shirt-tail, and whether you yet have the extravagant delight of poking and punching a writhing Bedfellow with your long fleshen pole—the exquisite touches of which I have often had the honor of feeling?*
>
> —Thomas Jefferson Withers, letter to James H. Hammond, 1826

TENNESSEE

⬤ PEOPLE

Calpernia Addams *(Nashville, TN)* is a transgender icon. She served as a Hospital Corpsman with the navy and United States Marine Corps and came out as transgender during her last year of service. Her personal and tragic love story was showcased in the movie *Soldier's Girl*. In 1999, while working as a performer, Addams began dating PFC Barry Winchell. Word of their relationship spread at Winchell's Army base, where he was harassed by fellow soldiers and ultimately murdered.

Calpernia Addams

The trial resulted in widespread press and a formal review of the US military's Don't Ask, Don't Tell policy.

Eden Atwood *(Memphis, TN)* is an intersex artist, jazz musician, actor, activist, teacher, mother, and co-creator of the Interface Project website. The Interface Project emphasizes that "No Body Is Shameful" and encourages intersex people to record videos to provide representation for intersex people who have yet to find community and support.

Miley Cyrus *(Franklin, TN)* is a pansexual singer and actress best known for her role as the titular character on *Hannah Montana* and her songs such as "Wrecking Ball" and "Party in the USA." While her identity has publicly evolved over time, she has also described herself as androgynous and gender fluid. Cyrus has been a fierce supporter of LGBT+ inclusion through her art and philanthropy. In 2018, Cyrus married her longtime partner, actor Liam Hemsworth; they have since divorced.

Megan Fox *(Memphis, TN)* is a bisexual actress and model. She is best known for her roles in the movies *Transformers*, *Jennifer's Body*, and *Confessions of a Teenage Drama Queen*. "I have no question in my mind about being bisexual," she told *Esquire*.

Leslie Jordan *(Memphis, TN)* is a comedian and actor. He appeared in the 1996 stage performance *Sordid Lives*, and again in its 2000 film adaptation. Jordan has made numerous TV guest appearances on shows ranging from *Star Trek*, *Ally McBeal*, and *Monk* to *Ugly Betty*, *Desperate Housewives*, and *American Horror Story*.

The gay rights movement was not started by people who wore a pink T-shirt one day on gay pride day and went back to a closeted office job. It was started by drag queens, transsexuals, and street people who were totally flamboyant and lived their lives flamboyantly and didn't have a conservative place to retreat to and got shit on all the time. Don't ever try to subtract drag queens from gay rights history; you will fail.

—Lady Bunny, *Edge Media Network*, 2013

A 67,000+ signature petition was delivered to lawmakers in 2016, asking them to veto Tennessee's proposed bathroom legislation. High school students Jennifer Guenst and Henry Seaton delivered the petition to the governor's office. The petition included signatures from six thousand members of clergy or people of faith.

The "Don't Say Gay" bill (also called the Classroom Protection Act) of 2011 would have prevented pro-LGBT+ discourse in school classrooms from kindergarten to eighth grade. It also would have required school teachers and counselors to notify a student's parents if the student were suspected or confirmed to be gay. The bill was originally approved by the Tennessee Senate in 2011, but was debated for two years before failing in the House in 2013, on the grounds that the K-8 curricula did not include sex education.

Know Your Rights, also known as the LGBT+ Toolkit, is a website that lists rights for any member of the LGBT+ community. Tennesseans are encouraged to read up on their rights. The toolkit is also a helpful guide for any information on changing legal names or genders and a resource to report discrimination or violence against members of the community.

Tanco v. Haslam was a 2013 lawsuit that eventually became included in the landmark US Supreme Court case *Obergefell v. Hodges*. Four same-sex couples had been married in other states before moving to Tennessee, which did not legally recognize their marriages. Tennessee Judge Trauger ruled in favor of the plaintiffs but also stated that case would not allow other same-sex marriages to occur in the state of Tennessee. In 2015, the US Supreme Court determined in *Obergefell v. Hodges* that same-sex marriage is legal.

Leslie Jordan

Megan Fox

People are realizing that being gay is just as defining as the color of our skin and it's not a choice. I'm really encouraged. I think in my lifetime we will achieve equality. I'm honored to be a part of it.

—Leslie Jordan, interview with *Today.com*, 2008

Jordan's recurring role as Beverly Leslie on *Will & Grace* won him an Emmy for Best Guest Actor in 2006.

Lady Bunny *(Chattanooga, TN)* is a comedian and drag queen known for her iconic and extravagant blonde wigs. Lady Bunny cofounded the drag festival Wigstock in 1985 in New York, which has survived since then despite a few hiatuses. While attending Georgia State University, she befriended RuPaul Charles, and the two worked together as go-go dancers. The pair moved to New York in 1983, in time going on to record a couple singles. Bunny appeared in RuPaul's *Drag U* and RuPaul's *Starrbooty*, as well as HBO's *Sex and the City*, *Dragtime*, *The Out List*, and more. Performing has been her main career for over two decades, and Bunny also works as a DJ in New York.

Bessie Smith *(Chattanooga, TN)*, known as the Empress of the Blues, was a popular 1920s and '30s blues singer. Recording over 160 songs during her career, Smith is most known for songs such as "Downhearted Blues," "St. Louis Blues," and "Empty Bed Blues"—three songs that have since been recognized by the Grammy Hall of Fame award. Although she was married to a man, Smith was known for her infidelity with the women who toured with her, including Lillian Simpson. In the 2015 HBO film *Bessie*, Queen Latifah played the title character.

Rebecca Young *(Lynnville, TN)*, with the assistance of the ACLU of Tennessee, filed a lawsuit in 2015 when she was publicly reprimanded and censored by the school system for wearing a shirt that read "Some people are gay, get over it!" ACLU-TN legal director Thomas H. Castelli stated, "Students have a First Amendment right not only to be out at school, but to an education free from such discrimination and harassment." The case reached a settlement in 2016 when the school district revised its dress code to allow pro-LGBT speech.

PLACES

Clarksville, Tennessee, was named the best town in the state for LGBT+ families by Movoto.com. Located about an hour northeast of Nashville, the town of 145,000 was ranked first based on its already established community of LGBT+ families. Johnson City, Chattanooga, Franklin, Memphis, Knoxville, and Nashville round out the list in that order.

East Tennessee Faith for Equality is an organization of congregations and clergy members united for LGBT+ justice. The group's website lists congregations welcoming to same-sex couples in various ways: sanctioning participation, performing marriages, and ordaining to the clergy, among others. Depending on one's faith or beliefs, this list includes welcome places to practice. Among its other local and national resources include links to summer camps, university LGBT+ groups, pride fests, and more.

US VIRGIN ISLANDS

PEOPLE

Emile Griffith *(St. Thomas, USVI)* was a bisexual world welterweight and middleweight boxing champion who won 337 world championship rounds. Born in 1938, he worked as a stock boy in New York City, working largely with women's hats before being encouraged to start boxing by trainer Gil Clancy. Griffith's career was haunted by the death of his opponent Benny Paret, who died from his injuries ten days after their 1962 match. But it was his relationships with men and his support of the Hispanic gay crowd in New York City that drew condemnation from the boxing community. Reflecting on his career, Griffith has said, "I keep thinking how strange it is . . . I kill a man and most people understand and forgive me. However, I love a man, and to so many people this is an unforgivable sin; this makes me an evil person."

Janelle Sarauw *(St. Thomas, USVI)* is the youngest female senator and the first openly LGBT+ lawmaker in the US Virgin Islands. Elected for her first term in a 2017 special election, Sarauw was reelected for her second term in November 2018. Sarauw earned an MA in organizational leadership from Gonzaga University, and has served the US Virgin Islands as an educator at her alma mater, Charlotte Amalie High School, as

> **"**
>
> *We live in a conservative area, and there are gay people in government, but there is a 'don't ask, don't tell' policy, and I don't want to live like that—I want to be free. . . . My intent is to not really give people an option to like me or not. I'm going to tell you who I am and you're going to respect in that regard.*
>
> —Janelle Sarauw, *NBC News*, 2018
>
> **"**

well as a part-time professor of political science at the University of the Virgin Islands. Along with her work promoting the territory's workforce, environment, culture, economy, and youth population, Sarauw has remained an active advocate for LGBT+ rights in a socially conservative area. After her election, she stated, "My intent is to not really give people an option to like me or not. I'm going to tell you who I am and you're going to respect me in that regard."

PLACES

Liberty Place *(St. Croix, USVI)* is a nonprofit organization that hosts a safe and supportive space for young Virgin Islanders with questions about sexual identity and orientation. Founded in 2012 in response to the murder of a young boy, Liberty Place now supports outreach programs for LGBT+ rights and awareness, petitions for hate crime legislation, and hosts support groups in the community. Liberty Place is a member of the larger Eastern Caribbean Alliance for Diversity and Equality, which supports and strengthens the capacity of local LGBT+ and human rights organizations.

St. Croix Pride *(Frederiksted, St. Croix)* held the first LGBT+ Pride parade in the island's history in 2018. St. Croix Pride's mission is to use education, advocacy, and celebration of diverse communities to work toward a future where all people enjoy equal rights and lives free of discrimination. Despite the threat of a mass shooting made on Facebook, the parade continued without incident, aided by the protection of the police and FBI. Several local politicians attended, including the congressional delegate Stacey Plaskett and the gubernatorial candidate Albert Bryan.

Virgin Islands National Park *(St. John, USVI)* expanded by twelve acres in 2017 with the help of a $1.275 million donation from Jon Stryker. Originally from Michigan, Stryker is an American billionaire, architect, and philanthropist who advocates for social and environmental causes. He founded the Arcus Foundation, which advocates for LGBT+ social justice, as well as the conservation and respect of natural spaces.

Between the 1960s and 1980s, St. Thomas was seen as a gay mecca for its number of gay bars and restaurants that accepted and catered to gay clientele. The community supported many gay artists and cultural events up until the late 1980s, when several hurricanes and the onset of the AIDS epidemic significantly impacted gay-owned and gay-friendly businesses on the island.

The fourth annual Caribbean Women and Sexual Diversity Conference was hosted on St. Croix in 2016. Over fifty stakeholders gathered to discuss LGBT+ issues and attend presentations from internationally recognized educators and speakers. The conference was started by Kenita Placide, the Eastern Caribbean Coordinator for the Caribbean Forum for Liberation and Acceptance of Genders and Sexualities (CariFLAGS).

> *I see LGBT rights as part of the spectrum of human rights—the freedom to define your relationships, the freedom to define yourself and how you present yourself to the world. I think those are basic freedoms. . . . People don't realize that there is just one country in Africa where homosexuality is protected by the constitution. They don't know that there are seven countries in the world where homosexuality is punishable by death. When people hear those facts, it becomes much easier to see the connections between human rights and LGBT rights.*
>
> —Jon Stryker, *Synergos*, 2008

Virgin Islands National Park

The Women's Coalition of St. Croix *(Christiansted, St. Croix)* is a nonprofit organization dedicated to supporting and empowering survivors and people impacted by domestic violence, sexual assault, dating violence, and stalking. It began in 1981 when Audre Lorde, Adrienne Rich, and Dr. Gloria I. Joseph organized a symposium for women writers. During the symposium, a discussion was held addressing the problem of violence against women. The attendees went on to conduct workshops for volunteers and offer services to survivors at police stations and hospitals. This group later became the Women's Coalition of St. Croix. WCSTX offers free, confidential assistance in English and Spanish, and is open to people of all gender identities and sexual orientations.

VIRGINIA

⊖ PEOPLE

Kevin Aviance *(Richmond, VA)* is a performer and musician. Aviance began performing in the club scene in Washington, DC, before moving to Miami and joining the House of Aviance (where he adopted the name as his own) ballroom community. He then moved to New York City, where he became a staple in the club community, cultivating the reputation of a "revered freak" as a bald drag performer. Aviance appeared in the 1999 movie *Flawless* and released his debut album, *Box of Chocolates*, that same year. Several of Aviance's singles have been top hits on the Billboard Dance chart and led to collaborations with Whitney Houston and Janet Jackson. In 2006, he was violently attacked in a hate crime during Pride Month, but he still took part in the parade later that month.

Tona Brown *(Norfolk, VA)* is a vocalist and violinist. In 2014, she became the first African American transgender woman to perform in Carnegie Hall and to perform for a United States president. Early in her career, she toured with the Tranny Road Show, a group of transgender performers. Brown also appeared in the Netflix show *City Lightz* and starred as La Principessa in the opera *Suor Angelica*.

Sally Miller Gearhart *(Pearisburg, VA)* was the first openly lesbian professor to receive tenure at a university. Gearhart began her teaching career in Texas but didn't feel comfortable living as a lesbian there, so she moved to San Francisco, where she felt she could live more openly. She was hired in 1969 by San Francisco State University, where she helped found one of the country's first women and gender studies departments. She also worked with Harvey Milk to defeat Proposition Six, which would have banned California public schools from discussing LGBT+ topics. Gearhart is now a professor emerita of San Francisco State University.

Greta J. Harris *(Danville, VA)*, since 2013, has been the president of the Better Housing Coalition, Richmond, Virginia's largest nonprofit housing organization. Harris has worked for better housing in the country for over thirty years and has helped raise over $250 million in real estate throughout her career. Harris came out as gay in the 1990s amid concern it would harm her relationship with the community, but has since described the experience as "blessedly successful." In 2016, the Virginia Tech Black Alumni Association declared her Philanthropist of the Year.

Zakia McKensey *(Richmond, VA)* is an activist and founder of the Nationz Foundation. McKensey has worked for various organizations to educate and advocate for the HIV/AIDS community, but in 2012, she decided to do more for the community and started her own nonprofit organization to provide greater support. The Nationz Foundation offers HIV testing, condom distribution, employment assistance, and a food pantry. Having struggled with health care during her own transition, McKensey makes a point to offer aid to trans people seeking health care programs. McKensey hosts an annual pageant to raise funds for the foundation.

> **"** Not everyone is going to like you or appreciate you, but in the end, it doesn't matter. I am still doing what I was put on this planet to do. My primary focus is to share the works of African American composers, and to do as much research as possible, to find hidden gems, and perform them on concert stages. After all, it's my music that will live on, long after I leave my earthly body.
>
> —Tona Brown, *Out*, 2014 **"**

George Quaintance (*Alma, VA*) was a pulp artist known for his homoerotic images of men. Quaintance studied art in New York in 1920 and began working in advertising. Soon, he moved to illustrate for pulp magazines, creating the homoerotic fantasy paintings for which he became known, although the magazines were only sold discreetly. Although homosexual relationships were not socially acceptable in his time, Quaintance normalized images of homosexuality by placing them in classic or historical settings (such as Greek gods bathing). Borrowing also from the pin-up aesthetic, Quaintance was a founder of the "macho" gay aesthetic. He died of a heart attack in 1957 at the age of fifty-five.

Danica Roem (*Manassas, VA*) is one of the first openly transgender politicians to be elected in a US state legislature. Roem worked as a journalist for over a decade before running for office in 2017 as the Democratic candidate for District 13 in Virginia's House of Delegates. Her candidacy was particularly vicious because the incumbent candidate was known for his anti-LGBT+ beliefs and specifically targeted Roem's gender identity in campaign ads. Roem won her election with over 53 percent of the vote.

B. Scott (*Franklin, VA*) is a transgender actor, blogger, vlogger, and pop culture influencer. Scott's career originally began in 2005 with his blog, which he later relaunched in 2007 on his website, www.LoveBScott. com. That year he began to make YouTube videos, some of which went viral and gained him millions of followers. He has also acted in shows such as *The Skinny* on LOGO and *DTLA* on Netflix, and hosted the 2013 BET Awards preshow.

Dr. Walter Sheppe (*Hopewell, VA*) was a biologist and professor. He completed his doctorate in zoology in 1958 and began teaching across Zambia, New York, and Virginia. Sheppe was an early advocate for the LGBT+ movement, beginning his advocacy in 1959. He worked to add sexual orientation to the nondiscrimination policy at the University of Akron and founded its LGBT Union. When he died in 2017, Sheppe left a sizable donation to the Gay Community Endowment Fund of Akron Community Foundation.

People are going to label you anyway, but the one that bugs me the most is when they say, 'One of the funniest female comedians.' There's no 'funniest male comedians.' You're either a funny comedian, or you're not!

—Wanda Sykes, *The Denver Post*, 2012

I feel like we are in some scary times. But I do not feel that the major things we have accomplished, they will take back. We have a lot of power and influence; [we need to] get out of that mindset that your vote doesn't matter. That goes back to education, making sure that people know the power of voting, and understand about writing your senators, and your delegates and congressmen, so you can make a difference.

—Zakia McKensey, *GayRVA.com*, 2018

Wanda Sykes

Benjamin Banneker Boundary Stone

Wanda Sykes *(Portsmouth, VA)* is a comedian, actor, and producer. She began her career as a government employee, but after doing stand-up for a talent show 1987, she was hooked on the world of comedy. She began touring and built a successful career, with writing and performing credits in *The Chris Rock Show*, *Last Comic Standing*, *Ice Age*, and *The Wanda Sykes Show*. In 2009, Sykes was both the first Black woman and the first gay person to perform at the White House Correspondent's Dinner. Sykes has won four Emmys and a GLAAD award.

PLACES

The Benjamin Banneker Boundary Stone *(Arlington, VA)* marks the boundary between Virginia and Washington, DC. The stone also serves as a monument to the legacy of Benjamin Banneker, a free Black man who was instrumental in the initial planning of Washington, DC. Banneker helped place fourteen stones used to mark the edges of the city, including the stone that now serves as a memorial for Banneker. Some historians believe that Banneker was gay because he never had any relationships with women and was known to have made some comments alluding to the fact that he had a "guilty passion." The stone is a National Historic Landmark.

The Block *(Richmond, VA)* was a roving area of downtown Richmond friendly to the LGBT+ community in the 1950s and '60s. The Block included a few streets with various gay bars. Restrictive sodomy and liquor sale laws at the time made these bars frequent targets of the authorities. Because of this, the Block wasn't at a consistent geographical location and instead occasionally moved between streets. The popularity of the Block ended once the LGBT+ community gained more legal leeway and explicitly gay bars were established.

The Gay Community Center of Richmond *(Richmond, VA)* provides a safe place for LGBT+ groups to meet. The center opened in 2008, helmed by the Richmond Gay Community Foundation. For more information on the combination of those two groups, see the Diversity Richmond entry under Queer Facts. The center is an event space that also hosts an art gallery dedicated to the work of LGBT+ people.

The Backstreet Café shooting occurred in Roanoke, Virginia, in 2000 when Ronald Edward Gay walked into the Backstreet Café, a gay bar, ordered a beer, and began to shoot people. Police charged Gay with first-degree murder. The shooting killed one person and injured six others. The incident could not be charged as a hate crime because, at the time, Virginia's hate crime legislation did not include sexual orientation. Nonetheless, Gay received four life sentences.

Bostic v. Schaefer is the case that legalized gay marriage in Virginia in 2014. In 2013, Timothy Bostic and Tony London sued Virginia for equal marriage rights, which eventually turned into a class-action lawsuit representing fourteen thousand LGBT+ couples in the state. The attorney general at the time, Mark Herring, announced that he would not defend the marriage ban because he believed it was unconstitutional. Upon appeal, the District Court found the ban to be unconstitutional, and the Fourth Circuit Court also ruled against the law. When the US Supreme Court denied to review the case in 2014, it essentially legalized gay marriage in all the states under the Fourth Circuit, including Virginia.

Diversity Richmond represents the combined forces of the Richmond Gay Community Foundation and the Gay Richmond Community Center. The group primarily works to provide funding for local LGBT+ organizations (including those mentioned here, such as the Richmond Triangle Players, the Health Brigade, Side by Side, and Equality Virginia). Over the years, it has raised more than $850,000.

Doe v. Commonwealth's Attorney of Richmond was an unsuccessful case that attempted to fight Virginia's sodomy laws in 1976. Virginia had observed sodomy laws, which were still common throughout the country in the 1970s , since 1610. The case eventually made it to the US Supreme Court, which ruled to uphold the state's laws. While the law is still in place in Virginia, it has not been enforced since 2003, when the Supreme Court ruled that sodomy laws were unconsti-

Equality Virginia was founded in 1989 as Virginians for Justice. Equality Virginia is a statewide nonpartisan education, outreach, and advocacy organization seeking equality for LGBT+ Virginians. It works to connect people with elected officials, engage with the business community, increase transgender visibility, strengthen communities, and create inclusive schools. Its website has links to resources about being new to Virginia as an LGBT+ person as well as coming out, needing support, being trans, being an ally, legal advice, looking for a faith community, and more.

The first LGBT+ chair of the board of trustees of a major American university was Jeff Trammell, who served as rector at the College of William & Mary. He was also the first LGBT+ member of William & Mary's board of visitors, as well as the first LGBT+ member of the board of trustees of the Association of Governing Boards of Universities and Colleges. Trammell, originally from Florida, has worked as a lawyer and has been involved in many political campaigns. He married his long-term partner in 2013 on the steps of the US Supreme Court, with retired Supreme Court justice Sandra Day O'Connor presiding over the ceremony.

Robin Gorsline was a minister for the Metropolitan Community Church in Richmond for over a decade. Originally from Michigan, Gorsline created social change through religion and helped found both the Alliance of Religious Individuals Supporting Equality (ARISE) and People of Faith for Equality in Virginia (POFEV). A passionate writer, he currently runs three blogs that address faith, politics, and sexuality, sometimes through poetry. Gorsline lives in Maryland with his husband.

Side by Side, formerly the Richmond Organization for Sexual Minority Youth (ROSMY), is a group dedicated to providing a safe space for LBGT+ youth. The group was founded in 1991 and has since expanded to offer youth programming, leadership training, scholarships, counseling services, peer support groups, and even an annual alternative prom. Each year, this group

The Skip Two Periods newsletter was founded by a separatist group of lesbian women called First Fridays. The women gathered and held retreats to talk about women's rights and lesbian history. The newsletter ran from 1983 to 1988.

Virginia's first openly gay elected official was Jay Fisette, who was elected to the Arlington County Board in 1997. Fisette, originally from Pennsylvania, worked in the 1980s with the Arlington Gay and Lesbian Alliance and was the director of a nonprofit clinic specializing in HIV/AIDS. In 1993, he ran for a seat on the Arlington County Board but lost by only 206 votes. He ran again in 1997 and won, going on to serve five terms in office. In 2013, he was named Best Elected Official by *Arlington Magazine*.

Jay Fisette

The Health Brigade, formerly the Fan Free Clinic *(Richmond, VA)*, was founded in 1968 as a community clinic to serve marginalized communities. The clinic was Virginia's first free clinic and is known for being on the forefront of modern medical issues. It was an early supporter of oral contraceptives and provided health care to those with AIDS/HIV as early as the 1980s. It also provides care for transgender people. In 2018, it celebrated its fiftieth anniversary of providing care for the local community.

The LGBTQ History Collection *(Roanoke, VA)* is a permanent archive at the Roanoke Public Library, established by the Southwest Virginia LGBTQ+ History Project. In addition to its collection of oral history and physical objects, the collection has an online archive that can be found on the Southwest Virginia LGBTQ+ History Project's website. The organization founded both the online and the physical archives in December 2015 with the help of Roanoke College, Roanoke Diversity Center, and Roanoke Public Libraries.

Nationz Foundation *(Richmond, VA)* was founded by activist Zakia McKensey. The nonprofit works to edu-

cate and provide resources for the local LGBT+ community, with a focus on HIV/AIDS education and awareness. Its main focus is to increase the overall wellness of the local community by offering HIV testing, condom distribution, referral services to other health care providers, employment assistance, and a food pantry.

Richmond Triangle Players (RTP) *(Richmond, VA)* is an LGBT+ community theater. Founded in 1993, the group has produced hundreds of plays that explore LGBT+ topics such as gender, sexual orientation, equality, and identity. It collaborates with other theaters, cultivates new works, and hosts internationally acclaimed artists.

The Trade Winds *(Roanoke, VA)* opened in 1953 and was the oldest gay bar in Roanoke. Though described by former patrons as "shady," it was also one of the first places gay people could be themselves. The Trade Winds provided a space for people to organize and was subject to a boycott itself in 1971 after it failed to properly address the assault of a patron outside the bar. The Trade Winds shuttered in 1983, unable to keep up with competition from other gay bars.

QUEER FACTS

Intersex Awareness Day was first recognized on October 26, 2017, by the federal government in Washington, DC. Its press release stated: "When those most marginalized in society are afforded equal protection and opportunity, global security and stability are strengthened. Increased recognition, understanding and awareness of intersex persons and their human rights strengthens democracy for all."

The Guild Press, owned by Herman Lynn Womack, mostly published periodicals for a gay, male audience. In 1960, former FBI director J. Edgar Hoover began a crusade against erotic media in an effort to staunch the rising rate of sex crimes. As part of his initiative, the postmaster general J. Edward Day filed a lawsuit against Guild Press, citing thirty-one counts of obscenity. Womack took the case (*Manual Enterprises v. Day*) to the Supreme Court, which issued a 6–1 decision in 1962, stating that the magazines were not obscene and that Womack could continue to distribute them by US mail. Justice John Marshall Harlan said that the erotic images of men "cannot fairly be regarded as more objectionable as many portrayals of the female nude that society tolerates." The ruling was one of the first LGBT+ victories in the US Supreme Court and meant that nobody could charge gay and lesbian publications for obscenity.

The High Heel Drag Queen Race is an annual local event on the Tuesday before Halloween. The race is held on Seventeenth Street by Dupont Circle and is a chance for locals to show off elaborate costumes. It is followed by festivities at local restaurants and bars, notably JR's Bar & Grill, the site of the first race. In 1986, two men in drag raced each other to the bar to see who would be the first to do a shot, and over the years more and more people participated. Once spectators began to join, the police asked the queens to officially organize the event, and the High Heel Drag Queen Race has become a DC staple ever since.

L. Page "Deacon" Maccubbin and Jim Bennett were the second couple to obtain a domestic partnership in Washington, DC. Maccubbin, originally from Virginia, is a gay activist who contributed to multiple LGBT+ advocacy institutions such as the Washington Area Gay Community Council, the Lambda Literary Award, and the Community Building, a meeting place for many anti-war and social justice groups. Maccubbin founded Capital Pride, an event attended by hundreds of thousands of people annually. He is a veteran who joined the Gay Liberation Front in DC while he was still an active servicemember. Maccubbin got the nickname "Deacon" when he became an ordained minister through the mail while he served time in jail for destroying his draft order. Maccubbin also founded the famous LGBT+ bookstore chain Lambda Rising and has owned other LGBT+ bookstores such as the Oscar Wilde Bookstore in New York, which he saved from closing.

The Lavender Scare was an era of federal prosecution of LGBT+ government employees that began in the late 1940s and intensified in the 1950s. In a climate of fear and suspicion of homosexual relationships, the US Park Police began to arrest homosexual individuals in 1947. On April 27, 1953, President Eisenhower signed Executive Order 10450, which allowed government agents to terminate LGBT+ federal employees on a massive scale—but they had already begun to be persecuted and fired due to Senator Joseph McCarthy. McCarthy, in his search for communist federal employees, compiled a list of 205 suspected communists. The list included the names of two suspected homosexuals and helped popularize the idea that homosexuality and communism were related, as homosexual employees were vulnerable to blackmail by communist agents in order to hide their sexualities. Nobody ever proved that homosexual employees were in any way primed to betray their country, but the ruthless termination continued as federal agents pressured all government employees to give up their homosexual coworkers. EO10450 remained active until President Clinton repealed the policy in 1995. An estimated five to ten thousand people lost their jobs due to the Lavender Scare.

The Mattachine Society's DC branch, one of the first gay rights organizations in the area, was founded by Frank Kameny. Originally from New York, Kameny also organized some of the earliest gay and lesbian rights protests against national sodomy laws. He earned a doctorate in astronomy from Harvard University, despite putting his studies on hold to serve in World War II. Later, he was fired from his job with the US Army Map Service and prohibited from working for the government on the grounds of "sexual perversion." Kameny took the government to court, appealed its decision that his firing was lawful, and then took the issue to the US Supreme Court, who denied his case. Kameny took matters into his own hands and through his work in the Mattachine Society began to change popular attitudes about homosexuality. He toted the slogan "Gay is Good" in the 1960s, and on one occasion demanded the microphone at an American Psychiatric Association meeting to shame its classification of homosexuality as a mental illness. He founded the Gay and Lesbian Activist Alliance, the National Gay Task Force, and the National Gay Rights Lobby, and became the first gay commissioner of the DC Commission on Human Rights.

The National LGBT Chamber of Commerce (NGLCC) was founded in 2002 by Justin Nelson and Chance Mitchell to expand economic opportunities for the LGBT business community. To this day, the NGLCC is the only national advocacy organization of its kind. The NGLCC is the exclusive third-party certifying body for LGBT Business Enterprises (LGBTBEs), which is now comprised of the nation's 1.4 million LGBT business owners. Those enterprises add $1.7 trillion to the national economy each year. Additionally, the NGLCC is the leading public policy advocate working to include certified LGBT businesses in procurement opportunities at the federal, state, and local level. NGLCC Global is expanding its reach to five continents, bridging economic opportunity and LGBTI human rights worldwide.

The Rainbow History Project is a nonprofit organization that archives documents, photographs, and other media pertaining to LGBT+ history in the DC area. The Rainbow History Project also offers walking tours, presentations, and research assistance. It hosts the Community Pioneer Award, which has recognized individuals who have made important contributions to the local LGBT+ community since 2003.

Sophie's Parlor is a women's radio show billed as "By womyn, about womyn, for everybody." On air since 1972, when it began as a Georgetown University radio program, the show is considered one of the longest-running in the country. The two-hour segment airs every Wednesday at three o'clock on WPFW, showcasing music and conversation borne out of the second-wave feminism movement.

him front-page coverage in the *New York Times* and *Time* magazine. Leonard continued LGBT+ activism until his death, for which he arranged to have a special gravestone. The stone was made from the same granite as the Vietnam Veterans Memorial Wall and has two pink triangles that reference the symbols the Nazis used to mark gay people in concentration camps. The stone is labeled "A gay Vietnam veteran," rather than Matlovich's name. Below it, the epitaph famously reads: "When I was in the military they gave me a medal for killing two men and a discharge for loving one."

Nob Hill Restaurant *(Washington, DC)*, between 1957 and 2004, was one of the country's longest-running Black gay bars. Born in a time when segregation was legal, Nob Hill was originally established in 1953 as a safe, private meeting space for queer Black men before opening publicly four years later. As DC's nightlife grew and diversified, the restaurant remained steadfast as a low-key and somewhat highbrow nighttime establishment, attracting older men who felt uncomfortable among the younger crowds and earning the nickname "Snob Hill." After closing in 2004, the space reopened as a neighborhood bar called the Wonderland Ballroom.

WEST VIRGINIA

I am comfortable in my own skin. People can either jump on the Christy Martin bandwagon or jump off.

—Christy Martin, *AfterEllen.com*, 2011

Box, where she met celebrities such as F. Scott Fitzgerald and Cole Porter. Smith taught future King Edward VIII how to dance the Charleston and "the Black Bottom." In Paris, she started her own club, Chez Bricktop, in 1926, which hosted musicians from Duke Ellington to Jascha Heifetz. Before World War II, she moved to New York and went on to open other clubs all around the world in cities such as Mexico City and Rome. Early in her career, Bricktop had an affair with the singer Josephine Baker. She died at the age of ninety in 1984.

PLACES

Fairness West Virginia *(Charleston, WV)* is the state's largest LGBT+ advocacy organization. The organization advocates for statewide legislation to protect LGBT+ citizens and offers help to municipalities hoping to pass their own ordinances. FWV also publishes newsletters on the state of queer affairs in the state. Jan Rader (see listing under Queer Facts), the first female fire chief in the state, serves as a board member.

Guesthouse Lost River *(Lost River, WV)* is located in an unincorporated town known by residents of the area as a queer-friendly rural weekend getaway. Guesthouse opened in 1982 as a gay retreat near Lost River State Park; in the following years, the amount of real estate sold to gay couples significantly increased.

Despite its location in a conservative county, the town of Lost River is home to a small number of other queer-owned businesses and hosts many gay wedding receptions.

Living AIDS Memorial Garden *(Charleston, WV)* is a garden that commemorates those who lost their lives to AIDS. Established in 1998 just outside the State Capitol Complex, the garden is run by a nonprofit of the same name. A brick path goes through the garden, which is surrounded by a wrought-iron fence. Some bricks bear the names of donors or of those who died from AIDS, and others bear inspirational messages.

Marshall University Lambda Society *(Huntington, WV)* is a student-run LGBT+ rights coalition that focuses on community service. Located in the basement of the university's Memorial Student Center, the group was founded in 2015.

Rainbow Pride of West Virginia *(Charleston, WV)* is a nonprofit organization that provides educational and social support to LGBT+ people and their allies. The group runs a number of meetings and events throughout the year, including an annual pride parade and a pageant called Mr. & Miss Pride of West Virginia. Rainbow Pride has been in operation for over twenty years.

Ravenswood *(Ravenswood, WV)* was ranked the gayest city in West Virginia in 2019 by RoadSnacks.net. The city has a gay household population of 2.32 percent (about 1,377 households), based on data from the US Census. Ravenswood is followed by Clarksburg, Wellsburg, Dunbar, and Milton.

Thurmond, West Virginia, was the smallest town in the US to pass an LGBT+ anti-discrimination ordinance. In 2015, the town's five residents all voted in favor of the ordinance. They wanted to send the message that West Virginia is welcoming to LGBT+ people, from the largest town to the smallest.

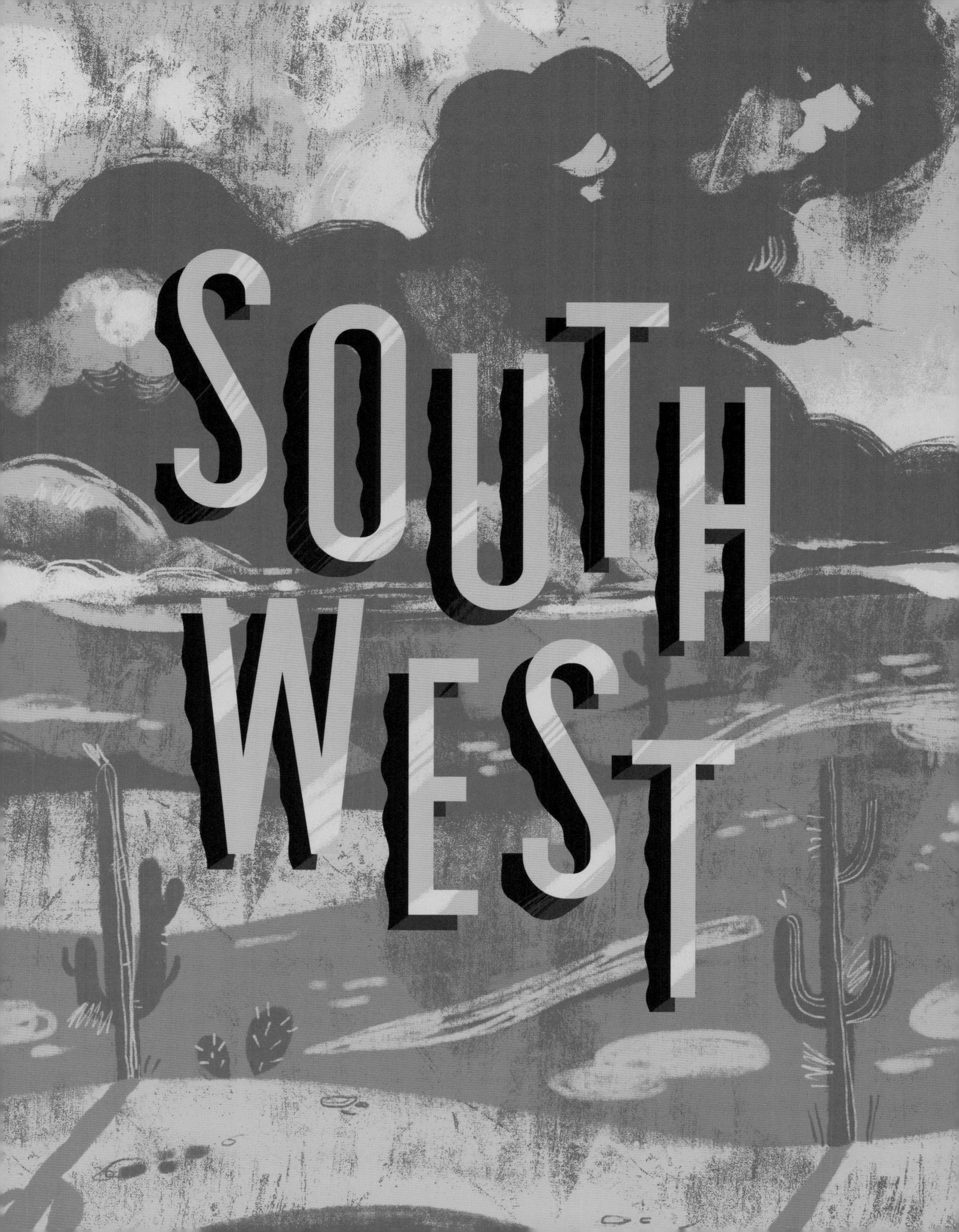
SOUTH
WEST

ARIZONA

⊖ PEOPLE

Gabriel Arana *(Nogales, AZ)* is a journalist who has worked for the *Daily Beast,* the *Nation, Salon, The Advocate, The Atlantic,* the *New York Times* and the *Huffington Post.* He is an editor at the *American Prospect.* He has a BA in linguistics from Harvard University and a master's degree in linguistics from Cornell University. In 2012, he wrote a report on gay conversion therapy called "My So-Called Ex-Gay Life," which caused Dr. Robert Spitzer of Columbia University to renounce his 2001 study that gave gay conversion therapy credibility. Spitzer issued a formal apology to the gay community for the damage his study caused.

Ken Cheuvront *(Phoenix, AZ)* was the first openly gay man elected to the Arizona State House of Representatives in 1994. He represented the Fifteenth District. He later became the Democratic leader of the Arizona House from 2001 to 2002, and was elected to the state senate in 2002 by a margin of 63 percent. Cheuvront has said that because of his family's long history in Arizona, he was worried that they would shame him for associating their name with his homosexuality. Despite his anxiety, he made a name for himself in Arizona politics, and his parents were supportive. Outside of politics, he started a restaurant called Cheuvront Wine & Cheese Cafe, which operated from 2003 to 2013.

Matt Dallas *(Phoenix, AZ)* is an actor most often recognized for his role as the star of *Kyle XY,* a show on ABC Family. *People* magazine named him one of the Sexiest Men Alive in 2006. He came out publicly on Twitter in 2013 by announcing his engagement to Blue Hamilton, a Grammy-nominated music executive. In 2015,

When queer people speak out, the country listens.

—Gabriel Arana, *Them,* 2018

Matt Dallas

they adopted a son named Crow. Dallas's other roles include the soldier whom Katy Perry mourns in her music video for "Thinking of You," Pastor John in the horror film *Along Came the Devil,* and Max in *You, Me & the Circus.*

Ruben Gonzales *(Phoenix, AZ)* is the vice president of the LGBTQ Victory Institute, an organization working to build a diverse network of public leaders to further LGBT+ equality. Gonzales's twenty-year career in the nonprofit sector has included work with the National Council of La Raza, where he established an annual LGBT+ Latinx reception, as well as GLAAD. *The Advocate* named Gonzales one of its 40 Under 40 in 2013 in honor of his leadership as an LGBT+ Latino.

Daniel Hernandez *(Tucson, AZ)* is a politician and a person who believes in public service. As a young man, he volunteered for Hillary Clinton's 2008 presidential campaign. Then he began to intern for Representative Gabrielle Giffords. When Giffords was shot during a "Congress on Your Corner" event in Tucson in 2011, he ran through the crowd to stop her wound from bleeding. President Obama credited Hernandez with saving her life, and led the memorial crowd of fourteen thousand people in a round of applause for Hernandez's heroism. Hernandez went on to become a cofounder of the state's LGBTQ Caucus and in 2016 was elected to serve in the Arizona House of Representatives. His first bill removed the sales tax from diapers, baby formula, and feminine hygiene products. He has also spoken out against gun violence and is a believer in reproductive rights.

Helen Jacobs *(Globe, AZ)* is an athlete who has won nine tennis Grand Slam titles. She is credited with making it popular for women to wear shorts instead of skirts on the tennis court. Jacobs was also one of only five women to work as a commander in US Navy Intelligence during World War II. She has been inducted into the National Gay and Lesbian Sports Hall of Fame and the International Tennis Hall of Fame. Jacobs has written a number of books, mostly about sports, including *Famous Women American Athletes* and *The Tennis Machine.*

My-King Johnson *(Phoenix, AZ)* is a football player who played for the University of Arizona Wildcats as defensive end. He is the first openly gay, active NCAA Division I football player. He says that he understands why his sexuality made national headlines, but said, "It's going to be so amazing when it's not a shock." Before college, he held Tempe High School's all-time sack record and was his team's captain when he was a senior.

Ben Patrick Johnson *(Tucson, AZ)* is a voice actor, activist, and author. He has done voice work for numerous trailers, movies, and television shows, including *Philomena, The Peanuts Movie,* and *My Little Pony: The Movie.* He has written five books, including *If the Rains Don't Cleanse,* which was inspired by his mother's experience as a Christian missionary in the Congo in the 1950s, and *In and Out of Hollywood,* a novel that explores the dark side of the entertainment industry.

> *It's not new for me. So, it's just new for everybody else.*
>
> —My-King Johnson, Pac-12 Networks, 2017

Ben Patrick Johnson

Monica Jones *(Phoenix, AZ)* is a transgender activist who worked to overturn Arizona's prostitution "manifestation" law, which criminalizes acts that indicate "an intent to commit or solicit an act of prostitution." Because of the law's vague wording, people had been stopped for waving at cars or asking if someone was a police officer. Jones says police profiled her as a prostitute based on her identity as a transgender woman of color. One day after speaking out against Project ROSE (a city program to arrest sex workers in order to "save" them), an undercover officer offered Jones a ride and tried to solicit her for sex. She warned him about the Project ROSE stings, and after he wouldn't let her out of the car, she asked him if he was a police officer. He arrested her for manifesting. While the charges against her were ultimately dropped, the manifestation law remained in place. Jones also works with the Sex Workers Outreach Project.

Bill Kennedy *(Phoenix, AZ)* is a basketball referee for the NBA. He has also officiated in the CBA, the WNBA Finals, and fifteen years of Arizona high school sports. Before attending Arizona State University, in high school he was named 1985 Knight of the Year. Kennedy came out in 2015 after Rajon Rondo, a Los Angeles Lakers player, referred to him with a homophobic slur. Though many people close to Kennedy were already aware of his identity, he came out publicly so that he could "send a message to young men and women in sports that you must allow no one to make you feel ashamed of who you are." In his free time, Kennedy enjoys singing karaoke.

Jason F. Sellards *(Mesa, AZ)*, also known as Jake Shears, is the cofounder and lead singer of the band Scissor Sisters. When the band first started out, Shears worked as a go-go dancer in New York City to, in his words, "get attention." Within two years of the Scissor Sisters performing in the US and the UK, they had sold three million records. Shears came out in his teens to the dismay of his parents, who threatened to remove him from school. As a student he was bullied, which was the subject of his video for the It Gets Better Project. Now, he says that his parents are supportive and that his dad even makes clothes for him. His first song as a solo artist, "Creep City," came out in 2017, and his first solo album, *Jake Shears*, came out in 2018. Shears's autobiography, also released in 2018, is called *Boys Keep Swinging*.

Jacques Servin *(Tucson, AZ)*, also known as Andy Bichlbaum, is one of the members of the Yes Men, an activist group that performs pranks to showcase corporate power and corruption. In 2016, the group impersonated a Pfizer spokesperson to announce to activists that Pfizer would lower the price of over one hundred medicines to show how easily the company could do the right thing. Confusion over whether or not the announcement was real forced the company to deny the claim. Pfizer said that it was open to an honest discussion with patients, though it ignored the demands of protestors with HIV and cancer outside its corporate headquarters. Earlier in his career, Servin was fired from his job as a software engineer at Maxis for inserting the image of two men in bathing suits kissing in the game *SimCopter,* which nobody noticed until the game's release. Servin said he did it to counter his "aggressively heterosexual" boss, who filled the game with scantily clad women. Servin is one of the subjects of the documentaries *The Yes Men* (2003) and *The Yes Men Fix the World* (2009).

Jacques Servin

When it comes down to it, Barry Goldwater says it best: "It doesn't matter if the guy in the foxhole is gay or straight. It's whether they can shoot straight." It also doesn't matter what's between their legs. Can they perform the job?

—Amanda Simpson, *Out Coast*, 2017

Amanda Simpson *(Tucson, AZ)* is the Vice President for Research and Technology at Airbus. In 2010, she accepted an appointment by President Obama to the US Department of Commerce, making history as the first transgender person to be appointed by a president. Her other roles have involved working for the United States Department of Defense and the US Army Office of Energy Initiatives. Simpson has flown planes for over twenty years and is a certified flight instructor. She also has degrees in business administration, engineering, and physics.

Kyrsten Sinema *(Tucson, AZ)* is a Democratic politician. As a child, her family struggled financially and was once even homeless. Sinema was elected to the US Senate in 2018 to replace Jeff Flake after his

Kyrsten Sinema

Tony Tripoli

retirement, the first time Arizona had elected a Democrat to the US Senate since 1988. She is the first openly bisexual senator, and was also the first openly bisexual person elected to Congress, where she served as US representative for Arizona's Ninth District starting in 2012. She had previously served Arizona in 2004 as a state representative and then as a state senator in 2010. She is known for compromising to achieve her goals, something her fellow Democrats have criticized and something she talks about in her book, *Unite and Conquer: How to Build Coalitions That Win and Last.*

Tony Tripoli *(Phoenix, AZ)* is a producer and comedian. He is best known for producing *Fashion Police* with Joan Rivers as well as *Joan & Melissa: Joan Knows Best?* and *In Bed with Joan.* He starred as himself in *Kathy Griffin: My Life on the D-List, Entertainment Tonight,* and *Million Dollar Matchmaker.* Tripoli said that his parents always wanted him to be himself, but that they encouraged him to learn how to deal with bullies early on; his mother later said, "I totally pulled that one out of my ass." Joan Rivers was his mentor and, according to Tripoli, tried to set him up with older, rich men who had not much life left to live. His career now focuses on stand-up comedy.

Dot Wilkinson *(Phoenix, AZ)* is a renowned athlete with spots in both the Softball Hall of Fame and the Bowling Hall of Fame. Born in 1921, she joined her softball team, the Phoenix Ramblers, at the age of eleven and remained active in softball until 1965. Wilkinson and her team won national titles in 1940, 1948, and 1949. During this time, she managed the Ramblers, as well as a real-estate office. She later transitioned to professional bowling, and in 1963 won the Women's International Bowling Congress singles. A biopic about her life called *Extra Innings* came out in 2015.

Mia Yamamoto *(Poston, AZ)* is a lawyer and activist who was born in a World War II Japanese American internment camp. She served in the army from 1966 to 1968 and was honored with the National Defense Service Medal, the Army Commendation Medal, and the Vietnam Campaign Medal. Yamamoto said that she found inspiration in other LGBT+ members of the army, though she herself was not yet out. After graduating UCLA Law School and starting work as a lawyer, she could finally afford therapy, which helped her come to terms with her gender identity and begin living as a woman. She is an advocate for racial equality

A 1975 Same-Sex Marriage License was successfully obtained by Sam Burnett and Tony Secuya in Arizona, who were subsequently married in a private ceremony at their home. Their license was later ruled void and labeled a legal error by a local judge. Secuya was quoted saying that he wanted an official license "showing that we are for each other enough to be permanently bonded."

The Arizona Gay Rodeo Association (AGRA) was formed in 1984 in Phoenix following the crowning of Tish Tanner as Miss Reno National Gay Rodeo in 1982. Arizona became the first state to host a gay rodeo. AGRA is one of the five founding members of the International Gay Rodeo Association (IGRA).

The mayor of Tempe from 1994 to 2004 was Neil Giuliano, who, in 1996, received a letter from a voter that threatened to tell the public he was gay if he did not do so himself. After he came out, he received hundreds of supportive letters from gay people to whom his authentic public identity was meaningful. Originally from New Jersey, he was raised in a Republican household and was a Republican himself until 2008, when he

Neil Giuliano

changed his political affiliation to the Democratic Party. His memoir, *The Campaign Within: A Mayor's Private Journey to Public Leadership*, speaks candidly about the sexual abuse he suffered as a child and a depressive phase he went through in college, when he considered suicide. Giuliano went on to work as the CEO of the San Francisco AIDS Foundation from 2010 to 2015. He is now an activist and public speaker for LGBT+ issues.

The Mecham Recall Committee was established in 1987 to recall Arizona Governor Evan Mecham, who was openly homophobic and racist. Mecham wanted to cancel state funds to officiate Martin Luther King Jr. Day, and also said he agreed that working women promoted lesbianism and caused divorce. Ed Buck, a gay Republican, led the recall efforts, and gained enough petition signatures for a recall election to be scheduled in 1988. However, that year, Mecham was impeached for failing to disclose a number of loans he had taken out from both private and public funds for his campaign and for personal use. Rose Mofford became Arizona's first female governor as she was next in the order of succession, which the state Supreme Court said took precedence over the recall, effectively cancelling the election.

Phoenix Gay Pride is a nonprofit organization that began in 1981. It strives to bring visibility and self-esteem to Arizona's LGBT+ community through educational services, social services, and fun events. It runs the Arizona LGBT+ History Project and offers scholarships and community grants to college students and local nonprofits.

The Pride of Phoenix was a gay periodical first published in 1977. The paper featured an illustration of a group of lions at the top corner of the first page, and it covered gossip, news, and events. *The Pride of Phoenix* sometimes published ads warning readers about the homophobic agendas of some political candidates. It also contained a classified section, explicit photo ads, and opinion pieces. Some issues are preserved online in the BJ Bud Memorial Archives.

The Radical Faeries is a countercultural spiritual movement that theorizes about queer consciousness. The group was founded by gay activist Harry Hay in 1979. More than two hundred men showed up to the first Spiritual Conference for Radical Faeries, which was held outside Benson, Arizona. The Radical Faeries believe that homosexuality is a meaningful facet of evolution, that gay people are gifted with special abilities including healing and creating beauty, and that gay people are a gift to humanity. It is an anti-authoritarian movement that encourages its members to reach their full potential and serve as visionaries for the future of society.

The Tucson Gay Newsletter was founded and published in 1976 by Bob Ellis, George Rederus, and Barney Robles. It was later renamed the *Tucson Observer* and *Observer Weekly*. Seeking to inform and unite Tucson's LGBT+ community, the two-page first issue advertised a variety of restaurants, bars, and a bath house. The publication shuttered in 2013.

and LGBT+ rights. She was a cofounder of the Multicultural Bar Alliance and also served as the president of the Japanese American Bar Association. Lambda Legal awarded her the Liberty Award, and she also has a Golden Key Award and a Harvey Milk Legacy Award.

PLACES

307 Lounge

307 Lounge *(Phoenix, AZ)* was a drag and cabaret venue, formerly known as Ray's Buffet in the 1940s. In the 1970s, the owners, Mike Elrod and a partner, reinvented it as a gay bar. 307 Lounge relocated three times after it first opened.

The BJ Bud Memorial Archives *(Tempe, AZ)* at the Arizona State University Library honor Harlene "BJ" Bud, a lesbian and LGBT+ rights grassroots activist in the 1970s through the early 1990s. Born in Chicago, Bud was instrumental to the creation of Arizona's first LGBT+ pride parade in Phoenix in 1981. She also founded an LGBT+ newspaper called *Sundays Childe*, which covered community events and legislation concerning gay rights. In her later years, she brought visibility to the AIDS crisis in Arizona. Bud died in 1996 after a long battle with cancer. She was so integral to the LGBT+ rights movement in Arizona that, in 2015, ASU created an archive for significant documents related to LGBT+ history in the state.

Kaye's Happy Landing Buffet *(Phoenix, AZ)* was a gay bar that first opened in 1941. Many speculate that the World War II era inspired the bar's name. It was owned and operated by lesbian Kay Elledge, who ran the business until her death in 1977.

Nourishing Space *(Tucson, AZ)* was a safe space for women of all sexualities, started by Kittu Riddle. It was a 165-acre desert ranch where women could go to find solitude, peace, and time to reflect on their lives. They built cabins on the land that they wired with electricity, and it fostered a sense of self-reliance amongst the women who stayed there. Riddle offered counsel to every woman who came, but was on her own journey of self-discovery, and kept the vision of Nourishing Space as one of collective learning.

Tucson LGBTQ Museum *(Tucson, AZ)* was founded in 1967. It holds a collection of photographs, documents, memorabilia, and other artifacts pertaining to LGBT+ history in the Tucson area, with a huge virtual collection organized by decade. The museum exists primarily online but has roving physical exhibits.

⊖ PEOPLE

Cris Alexander *(Tulsa, OK)* was a photographer based in New York City. Born as Allen Smith, he changed his name on the advice of a spiritualist who promised him success. Shortly after, he got a job as a radio announcer before moving to New York City. Alexander enjoyed a moderately successful acting career on the side, but his most successful work was as a photographer of the New York social scene. Alexander lived with his partner, Shaun O'Brien, for eighteen years before they were able to marry in 2011, when same-sex marriage was legalized in New York. He passed away the next year at the age of ninety-two.

Melanie Gillman *(Tulsa, OK)* is a queer nonbinary artist and writer. Their work can be seen anywhere from book covers and illustrations to posters and product labels. Gillman also writes and illustrates several web-based cartoons and graphic novels, such as the comic *As the Crow Flies*, which tells the story of a thirteen-year-old queer girl dealing with layers of racial and gendered prejudice while attending a restrictive Christian youth camp. Gillman's cartoons provide presentations of queer and nonbinary characters with agency.

Roberta Knie *(Cordell, OK)* was a soprano who sang at the Metropolitan Opera as well as several famous European opera houses. She began her music career at the University of Oklahoma, where she studied under the guidance of the renowned soprano Eva Turner. Knie was best known for her performances of Wagner on record and stage. In 1982, she was inducted into the Oklahoma Hall of Fame. She ended her opera

> *I'd have gotten very hungry if I'd just been an actor.*
>
> —Cris Alexander, *Interview*, 1980

career when she was diagnosed with detaching retinas aggravated by singing, stating, "I'd rather read than sing." She continued to give vocal lessons until her death in 2017.

Kelly Mantle *(Oklahoma City, OK)* made film history by becoming the first gender-fluid actor submitted to the Academy Awards under both best supporting actor and best supporting actress categories. Upon graduating the University of Oklahoma, Mantle had a brief theater career in Chicago before moving to Los Angeles to pursue television and movie acting. Mantle is an active member of the Los Angeles music scene and has also appeared on several TV shows, including an episode of *RuPaul's Drag Race* and *NYPD Blue*.

Billy Tipton *(Oklahoma City, OK)* was a jazz musician of the 1930s and '40s. Assigned female at birth, Tipton began dressing as a man after high school and took on the name Billy Lee Tipton. It is unknown whether he did this for personal or professional reasons, though

Kelly Mantle

Tipton had found himself shut out of several bands due to his gender prior to taking on the name. Though never officially married, Tipton had been in serious relationships with five women who considered themselves married to him. His birth gender assignment was not discovered until after his death in 1989 at the age of seventy-four. After Tipton's family made his identity public, his story went on to inspire several theatrical works, including the opera *Billy*, the play *Stevie Wants to Play the Blues*, and the musical *The Slow Drag*.

⊙ PLACES

The Dennis R. Neill Equality Center *(Tulsa, OK)* is the home of Oklahomans for Equality, a community organization that promotes intersectional advocacy. It hosts educational programs, arts programs, and community events, including the Equality Gala, Rainglow Run, and the Tulsa Pride Festival.

Freedom Oklahoma *(Oklahoma City, OK)* is a nonprofit advocacy organization for the Oklahoma LGBT+ community. Freedom Oklahoma hosts the annual Equality Run, a fundraiser that promotes awareness of anti-LGBT+ legislation. The organization also hosts an annual College Summit, which invites students and faculty from Oklahoma universities to meet and discuss LGBT+ issues.

PFLAG Oklahoma City *(Oklahoma City, OK)* is a local chapter of the national organization PFLAG, which provides educational tools, advocacy, and peer support to the LGBT+ community. Its work includes monthly support groups, individual visits, hosting social events, development trainings, and referrals to specialized support agencies.

⊙ QUEER FACTS

The first act signed by eleveneleven, Ellen DeGeneres's record label, was Greyson Chance, a musician and former YouTube star. Chance rose to stardom in 2010 by covering the Lady Gaga song "Paparazzi" for his sixth-grade talent show in Edmond, Oklahoma. He was signed to eleveneleven after performing on *The Ellen DeGeneres Show*, and released his first album, *Hold On 'til the Night*, in 2011. Chance came out at the age of nineteen, encouraging others to take the time to find "self-confidence, self-acceptance, and self-love."

National Gay Task Force v. Board of Education began in 1978 when Oklahoma passed a law allowing teachers to be fired based on their sexual orientations. The National Gay Task Force, a nonprofit advocacy group formed only five years earlier, filed a class-action lawsuit to the state court. When the case was carried to the US Supreme Court in 1985, it upheld the Tenth Circuit's decision that the law was unconstitutional in a 4-4 decision.

Since the 1980s, OkEq (Oklahomans for Equality) has sponsored major LGBT+ social events and high-profile speakers, including launching one of the first Pride picnics. During the 1980s HIV/AIDS epidemic, OkEq organized to send medical professionals to conferences in order to return with updated knowledge on prevention and treatment. This work developed into Northeast Oklahoma's first HIV clinic, which later became the nonprofit H.O.P.E. (Health Outreach, Prevention, and Education).

The Rainglow Run is a charity running event during the Tulsa Pride Festival hosted by the advocacy group Oklahomans for Equality (also referred to as OkEq). The proceeds of the run go toward funding the Pride Festival and OkEq's outreach and advocacy programs.

⊖ PEOPLE

Alvin Ailey *(Rogers, TX)* was a choreographer who popularized modern dance and spearheaded the movement to increase African American participation in twentieth-century concert dance. His dance company, the Alvin Ailey American Dance Theater, founded in 1958 in New York, strives "to further the pioneering vision of choreographer, dancer, and cultural leader Alvin Ailey" and to use "the beauty and humanity of the African American heritage . . . to unite people of all races, ages, and backgrounds." Ailey's 1960 masterpiece *Revelations* is one of the best-known works of modern dance performance. The choreography draws on "his 'blood memories' of Texas, the blues, spirituals, and gospel." In 2014, President Barack Obama awarded Ailey a posthumous Presidential Medal of Freedom. Ailey died of AIDS in 1989 at the age of fifty-eight.

Eric Alva *(San Antonio, TX)* was one of the most important figures in the movement to repeal Don't Ask, Don't Tell in the United States military. Alva joined the Marine Corps in 1990, serving until March 2003, when he lost his right leg in a landmine explosion, becoming the first casualty of Operation Iraqi Freedom. He was awarded a Purple Heart and was an instant celebrity as the war's first injured soldier. In 2006, he joined the Human Rights Campaign in its effort to repeal DADT. In 2011, the movement achieved its goal and succeeded in lifting the prohibition. Alva disclosed his motivation for serving in the military and for fighting for the rights of the LGBT+ community in 2017, saying, "At nineteen, when I took that oath to defend this country against all enemies foreign and domestic, it meant every single walk of life. That meant every individual, whether male or female, young or old, whether gay or straight, whether black or white, whether Hispanic, whether able-bodied, disabled. . . . Those rights don't belong to just the selected few."

Gloria Anzaldúa *(Rio Grande Valley, TX)* was an American scholar, best known for her semi-autobiographical book *Borderlands/La Frontera: The New Mestiza*, a work of both prose and poetry that explores the borders between Latinx and non-Latinx people, men and women, heterosexuals and homosexuals, and others. She wrote about the concept of linguistic terrorism

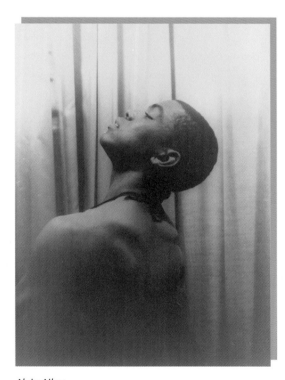

Alvin Ailey

Gloria Anzaldúa

in her influential essay "How to Tame a Wild Tongue." Anzaldúa identified as multi-sexual, alongside her identities as multi-racial and multi-ethnic, although she spoke of herself as a lesbian in much of her writing. She is an essential author of postcolonial feminism and Chicana cultural theory. Anzaldúa died in 2004 at the age of sixty-one.

Marshall Applewhite *(Spur, TX)* was the infamous leader of the Heaven's Gate religious group that shocked the world with its 1997 mass suicide, which resulted in the deaths of thirty-nine people. Much of the dogma to which the cult adhered originated from Applewhite's troubled relationship with his own sexuality. In 1970, before founding the cult, Applewhite was fired from his position as a music professor for having sex with a male student. Afterward, he sought cures for his homosexuality. Much of the Heaven's Gate religion emphasized celibacy and the suppression of sexual urges. Members of the cult were required to adopt similar clothing and haircuts, regardless of gender, to reinforce the group's nonsexual status. Before the suicide, Applewhite and seven others underwent voluntary surgical castration.

Mack Beggs *(Euless, TX)* rose to prominence as a high school wrestler in 2017 when he won the Texas Class 6A girls' state championship. He was the first transgender wrestler to win a Texas high school state championship. Although he wanted to compete amongst boys, state law required that he wrestle against those of the gender he was assigned at birth. In February 2018, Beggs won his second state championship. Beggs went on to college at Life University in Georgia, where regulations allow him to wrestle in the men's division.

Willmer "Little Ax" Broadnax *(Houston, TX)* was a transgender mid-century gospel quartet singer. Born in 1916, Broadnax moved to California in the 1940s and quickly gained success as a gospel singer. He formed the quartet Golden Echoes with his brother, which found popularity in the 1950s and '60s. Until his death in 1992, only his co-performer knew his identity as a transgender man.

Mo Cortez *(San Angelo, TX)* is an intersex activist and cofounder of the Houston Intersex Society. As a child, Cortez and his family fought against doctors and child protective services in order to raise him male and avoid surgery to make his genitalia present as female. In 2017, he consulted on SB 1342, a proposed bill in Texas that would have provided protections for intersex people, such as preventing nonconsensual genital surgeries. The bill did not pass the State Affairs Committee.

Tom Ford *(Austin, TX)* is a fashion designer, director, screenwriter, and producer. Ford is known for the luxury brand that shares his name, and for directing the films *A Single Man* and *Nocturnal Animals*, both of which were nominated for Academy Awards. Ford later moved to New York to study architecture at the Parsons School of Design. Soon after, he changed his major to fashion design. He later worked for Gucci as a designer and creative director before launching his own brand. He met his husband, Richard Buckley, a former editor-in-chief at *Vogue*, in 1986 at a fashion show. They have one son.

Todrick Hall *(Plainview, TX)* is a singer, actor, dancer, choreographer, director, drag queen, songwriter, and YouTube celebrity. Hall first found success on *American*

I think there are a lot of people who are afraid to be who they are, and if I have to sacrifice a little bit of fame and a little bit of success because I'm being 100 percent truthful with who I am, hopefully that will create a paved way for someone else.

—Todrick Hall, *Huffington Post*, 2016

Texas   175

Idol, where he made it to the semi-finals. Hall later found success once again by writing and performing songs on YouTube. Alongside his successful online following, Hall has since helped choreograph and direct many notable music videos, including one for Beyoncé's song "Blow," and has served as a guest judge on *RuPaul's Drag Race*.

Janis Joplin *(Port Arthur, TX)* was one of the most noteworthy musical artists of her generation. Born in 1943, Joplin's musical career began in 1966, when she joined the band Big Brother and the Holding Company. The band released two albums, including *Cheap Thrills* in 1968. After breaking up with the band, Joplin released two albums as a solo artist. Her fourth album, and last before her death in 1970, was titled *Pearl* and peaked at number one on the Billboard 200, staying there for nine weeks. The album was also certified quadruple platinum. Joplin, in the words of *Vanity Fair* writer Sheila Weller, is remembered as "the merry, bawdy, rowdy middle-finger-giver to rectitude and thoughtfulness." Joplin had relationships with both men and women. In August 1969, she performed at Woodstock in front of hundreds of thousands of fans. A year later, she died of a heroin overdose in Los Angeles at the age of twenty-seven.

Barbara Jordan *(Houston, TX)* was a lawyer and professor of political ethics. In 1967, she was the first African American elected to the Texas State Senate since 1883, and the first Southern African American woman elected to the United States House of Representatives. She also served one day as acting governor of Texas on June 10, 1972, making her the first African American to serve as governor of a state. Jordan famously delivered an impassioned attack of the Watergate scandal on the House floor, where she stated that though she had originally been left out of the Constitution, "my faith in the Constitution is whole, it is complete, it is total, and I am not going to sit here and be an idle spectator to the diminution, the subversion, the destruction of the Constitution." She also served as chairwoman of the Commission on Immigration Reform in the mid-1990s, speaking out against a proposal to deny automatic citizenship to children born to illegal immigrants in the United States. Jordan met her partner, Nancy Earl, on a camping trip in the 1960s. They lived

John Cameron Mitchell

together for twenty years, and Earl aided Jordan in her health issues later in life. Jordan died from pneumonia in January 1996 at the age of fifty-nine.

John Cameron Mitchell *(El Paso, TX)* is an actor, writer, and director who is best known for originating the lead role in the musical *Hedwig and the Angry Inch*, and for directing the films *Shortbus* and *Rabbit Hole*. Mitchell came out publicly in 1992 and has explored sexuality and gender in many of his roles in film and theater. He is a Radical Faerie and a cofounder of the Mattachine party series in New York City. In 2017, he hosted the Gotham Awards for independent film.

Annise Parker *(Houston, TX)* was the mayor of Houston from 2010 to 2016. She was the city's second female mayor, and one of the first openly gay mayors of a major US city. Before her term as mayor, Parker worked in the oil and gas industry and co-owned a bookstore named Inklings Bookshop. She has also served on the board of directors of the Holocaust Museum Houston and the advisory board of the Houston Zoo, among several other positions. In 2018, she became the president and CEO of the Victory Fund, a

Annise Parker

political organization that works to elect gay, lesbian, and transgender candidates to public office.

Jim Parsons *(Houston, TX)* is an American actor best known for his role in the CBS sitcom *The Big Bang Theory*. In the series, he plays Sheldon Cooper, a theoretical physicist with a genius-level IQ and a complete lack of social skills. He has received four Primetime Emmy Awards in recognition of his performance on the show and has also appeared in Broadway dramas and in film, including a supporting role in the 2016 film *Hidden Figures*. Parsons lives in New York and is married to art director Todd Spiewak. When asked about their relationship, Parson responded, "If we're inspiring at all, it's that we're a very average, normal, just-moving-right-along-with-our-lives kind of people. . . . I've never considered my relationship with Todd to be an act of activism. Rather simply, it's an act of love, coffee in the morning, going to work, washing the clothes, taking the dogs [out]—a regular life, boring love."

Robert Rauschenberg *(Port Arthur, TX)* was one of the most important artists of the twentieth century. A member of the Neo-Dada and Abstract Expressionism movements, Rauschenberg is most famous for his 1959 works *Monogram* and *Canyon*. With these, Rauschenberg originated the genre (and coined the term) for "combine paintings." These artworks cross mediums and incorporate objects from the everyday world,

Jim Parsons

The artist's job is to be a witness to his time in history.

—Robert Rauschenberg

such as clothing, newspaper clippings, furniture, or even, in the case of *Monogram*, a stuffed goat with a rubber tire around its midsection. Rauschenberg was sexually fluid; although he married a woman (whom he divorced three years later) and had a child with her, his romantic relationships with other men were not unknown to his peers in the art community. In some contexts, exhibiting an artist's works with no reference to their sexuality is fine, but in Rauschenberg's case, said *Slate* writer Mark Joseph Stern in 2013, "ignoring orientation amounts to curatorial malpractice." Rauschenberg's paintings were forged in queerness and can only be understood in the context of a homosexuality that existed before the advent of the gay rights movement.

John Rechy *(El Paso, TX)* is a novelist, memoirist, playwright, and literary critic whose work often focuses on issues surrounding gay culture. Rechy attended Texas Western College before joining the US Army. Though he applied to study at Columbia University under Pearl S. Buck, his application was declined, and he later enrolled at the New School in New York under the Random House editor Hiram Haydn. Rechy often wrote about his life with unflinching honesty, and many of the events in his novels are drawn from his personal experiences. This includes being arrested at the 1959 L.A. Cooper Do-nuts Riot for fighting against police harassment of LGBT+ citizens, as well as his struggles with drug addiction later in life. Rechy's 2018 novel *After the Blue Hour* won the Lambda Literary Award for Gay Fiction.

Michelle Rodriguez *(San Antonio, TX)*, an award-winning actor, is best known for her appearances in the *Fast and the Furious* franchise. Rodriguez's breakthrough was in the 2001 film *Girlfight*, for which she won several awards. Her other notable roles have also been in the action genre, such as James Cameron's *Avatar* and the TV series *Lost*. When asked about her sexuality, Rodriguez reportedly responded, "I've never walked the carpet with anyone, so they wonder: What does she do with her vagina? . . . I've gone both ways. I do as I please. I am too fucking curious to sit here and not try when I can. Men are intriguing. So are chicks."

Michael Sam *(Galveston, TX)* became briefly famous nationwide in 2014 when he was drafted by the St. Louis Rams, becoming the first openly gay person to be drafted into the NFL. President Obama commended him, "From the playing field to the corporate boardroom, LGBT Americans prove every day that you should be judged by what you do and not who you are." Unfortunately, following a series of disappointing performances in pre-season games, the Rams dropped Sam from its roster in favor of undrafted rookie Ethan Westbrooks. Sam retired from professional football, citing his mental health, in 2015.

> *I'm not afraid to tell the world who I am. I'm Michael Sam: I'm a college graduate. I'm African American, and I'm gay. I'm comfortable in my skin.*
>
> —Michael Sam, *ESPN*, 2014

Michelle Rodriguez

Michael Sam

Justin Simien *(Houston, TX)* is a film director, screenwriter, and producer known for the film *Dear White People,* the Netflix Original Series of the same name, and the film *Rings.* Growing up, Simien had to hide his sexuality as well as his music interests, which he has said were "a recipe for being a total outcast for a black kid in the South." He has called his time at Houston's High School for the Performing and Visual Arts as the most formative years of his life, and afterwards studied film at Chapman University in California. There he began working on the script that would become *Dear White People.* The film and Netflix series both question the hard labels placed on Black Americans and challenge the notion that there is one African American experience. Simien has expressed a similarly complex view of his own life, stating, "Yes, I'm black; yes, I'm a man; yes, I'm gay; but really, truly, I'm more than all of those things. But at the same time, to function in the world, I do need these identities."

Sheryl Swoopes *(Brownfield, TX)* is a former professional basketball player. She became the first person signed on to the WBNA upon its creation in 1996 and was named one of the league's Top 15 Players of All Time in 2011. A three-time Olympic gold medal winner, Swoopes played for the Houston Comets from 1997 to 2007. In 2005, she announced that she was gay. In an interview with the *New York Times,* she said, "I was at a point in my life where I am just tired of having to pretend to be somebody I am not. I was basically living a lie. For the last seven, eight years, I was waiting to exhale." Her coming out helped pave the way for other prominent athletes to openly express their sexualities while competing in athletics.

Tommy Tune *(Wichita Falls, TX)* is an actor, singer, theatrical director and producer, choreographer, and dancer. His work has won him ten Tony Awards, including the Lifetime Achievement Award, and he was awarded the National Medal of Arts in 2003. Tune began dancing lessons at the age of five and by high school was directing and choreographing his school's musicals. Upon graduation, he enrolled as a performing arts major at the University of Texas. His first major success was as a performer and choreographer on *Seesaw* in 1973, for which he won a Tony Award for best featured actor. He has remained a renowned and

Tommy Tune

influential member of the New York arts scene, and for a time opened his own art gallery. He wrote about his experience being openly gay in the theater community in his memoir *Footnotes.*

Alok Vaid-Menon *(College Station, TX)* is a gender-nonconforming performance artist, writer, educator, and entertainer. They cocreated Dark Matter, a trans South Asian performance art duo, with Janani Balasubramanian. Speaking on the topic of gender, Vaid-Menon has said, "I live my life in a way that interrupts gender in all aspects . . . how I dress, how I think, how I desire. I try to imagine a world where I and everyone else isn't gendered." Vaid-Menon is Indian American and was raised Hindu. Their latest book, a poetry chapbook titled *Femme in Public,* was published in 2017.

Lupe Valdez *(San Antonio, TX)* served as sheriff of Dallas County from 2005 to 2017, and was the Democratic nominee in the 2018 Texas gubernatorial election. When elected, she was the nation's only Latina sheriff and one of the first openly gay sheriffs of Texas. Born into a family of eight children, Valdez later enrolled in Southern Nazarene University, where she earned a

Circle of Friends, the first gay society in Texas, was founded in 1965 by Phil Johnson, a historian of LGBT+ history who also founded the Dallas Gay Historic Archives. The Circle of Friends worked with straight allies to prevent harassment and discrimination and to protect gay people from Texas's openly hostile legal and social environment. With the circle, Johnson held the first gay pride parade in downtown Dallas in 1972. In 1994, the archive was absorbed by the AIDS Resource Center.

Dallas Buyers Club is a 2013 biographical film of the early days of the HIV/AIDS epidemic. In the 1980s, when medications had shown some efficacy in treating the disease but were not yet approved by the FDA, several communities established Buyers Clubs. These groups pooled members' collective buying power, enabling them to purchase the medicines, such as peptide T, that they needed to survive before these drugs became affordable and legal. One such buyers club, founded by Ron Woodroof of Dallas (who was not himself gay) became known as the Dallas Buyers Club. The final years of Woodroof's life were the basis of the 2013 film, starring Matthew McConaughey and Jared Leto.

Hugh Callaway and Thanh Nguyen were attacked in October 1991 by three assailants while walking in Reverchon Park in Dallas. Callaway was seriously injured, and Nguyen was killed after Corey Butler, the primary perpetrator, shot him. Despite the attackers using anti-gay slurs during the offense, prosecutors refused to try the case as a hate crime. Butler was sentenced to life in prison and will be eligible for parole in 2026. Callaway still lives in Texas. Anti-LGBT+ hate crimes have posed a significant threat to sexual and gender minorities in Texas; between 1993 and 1995, there were eight brutal murders of gay men in the state, only a small portion of crimes against LGBT+ Texans.

Lawrence v. Texas is a 2003 US Supreme Court case that struck down sodomy laws in Texas, as well as several other states. In September 1998, just outside Houston, police responded to a phony tip reporting a weapons disturbance in a private residence. They entered the residence at around 11:00 pm. with weapons drawn and discovered John Lawrence, the owner of the apartment, and Tyron Garner, a friend, engaged in consensual anal sex. The two men were subsequently arrested on charges of deviant sexual acts. Lawrence and Garner were jailed overnight, and their ensuing prosecution and appeals eventually grew into a case presented before the United States Supreme Court. In a 6–3 decision delivered by Justice Anthony Kennedy, the court ruled that the Texas statute against sodomy was unconstitutional.

"No Promo Homo" laws gained attention in the late 2010s, as Texas is one of several states where it is illegal for teachers to discuss homosexuality and LGBT+ history. Even after the 2003 case *Lawrence v. Texas*, Texas educators were still required to inform their students that "homosexual conduct is not an acceptable lifestyle and is a criminal offense." In June 2017, Houston's local news station KHOU11 ran a story on the subject when Richard Carranza, the superintendent of Houston's Independent School District, the largest in Texas and seventh largest in the country, proposed amending the public curriculum to better reflect the history of Texas's African American, Latino, and LGBT+ communities. While the laws remain in Texas, states such as California and New Jersey have implemented mandatory LGBT+ units in their curricula.

The Texas Gay Conference was first held in June 1974, sponsored by the Fort Worth/Dallas Metroplex Gay Council. The yearly gathering ran until 1982, rotating between cities throughout the state and inviting national speakers. The original organizers argued that "if we as gay people are to assume our rightful place as equal, responsible citizens of this nation, we must first develop our knowledge and understanding of ourselves, including our strengths and weaknesses, our differences and our similarities." Some of the proposed Workshops and Idea Exchange sessions included "Gay Prisoner Rights," "Dealing with Public Officials," "Religion and the Homosexual," and "The Crisis of Coming Out." Many of the conference programs and associated clippings are available online in the JD Doyle Archives.

> But people who came here for a better life, get picked up for a broken tail light or speeding, who make as many mistakes as the rest of us Americans make . . . We should just leave them alone.
>
> —Lupe Valdez, *Huffington Post*, 2018

degree in business administration. She earned a master's degree in criminology from the University of Texas at Arlington, and later enlisted in the army, where she achieved the rank of captain. She worked in US Customs and Border Protection and the Department of Homeland Security before serving as a sheriff. On the issue of border security, she has said, "People who came here for a better life get picked up for a broken tail light or speeding, who make as many mistakes as the rest of us Americans make . . . which one of us who has no sin can cast the first stone?"

Babe Didrikson Zaharias *(Port Arthur, TX)* was a successful athlete in golf, track, baseball, and several other sports. In addition to winning two gold medals for javelin in the 1932 Olympics, she was also the first woman to qualify for the Los Angeles Open men's golfing tournament, but she was not allowed to play, as the event was intended only for male golfers. After divorcing wrestler George Zaharias, Babe was later linked (albeit privately) with golfer Betty Dodd. Zaharias died in 1956 at the age of forty-five due to colon cancer. The Associated Press named her Woman Athlete of the Year six times between 1931 and 1954, and in 1999 declared her the greatest woman athlete of the twentieth century.

PLACES

The Babe Didrikson Zaharias Museum *(Beaumont, TX)* preserves the legacy of the multi-sport athlete Mildred "Babe" Didrikson Zaharias. The museum is open to the public, and also operates as the city's visitor center. The museum houses Zaharias's awards, newspaper clippings, photographs, and fan correspondences. Its proceeds go toward scholarships for female students at Lamar University.

The Houston Intersex Society *(Houston, TX)* is an intersex advocacy and educational organization founded in 2012. THIS has hosted local and national workshops and seminars, and in 2015 succeeded in getting Houston's city hall to illuminate its building for Intersex Visibility Month. The group's founders, Mo Cortez and Koomah, also collaborated on a 2017 intersex protections bill with Senator Sylvia Garcia, although the bill did not pass.

The Lesbian, Gay, Bisexual and Transgender (LGBT) Archive *(Denton, TX)* at the University of North Texas collects and curates primary source material documenting the history of LGBT+ communities in the South and Southwest regions. While most scholarship on LGBT+ history focuses on urban communities, the LGBT Archive saves and preserves records of Southern and Southwestern LGBT+ communities that are not often studied or portrayed in media. The archive includes letters, newspaper clippings, photographs, diaries, records of organizations, and scrapbooks, which have been used for research and material in documentaries and feature films, as well as in academic research papers.

The LGBT History Research Collection *(Houston, TX)* at the University of Houston collects materials recording the history of the city's LGBT+ community. The collection bears witness to the area's rich history of social, cultural, and political activism. It also houses records for many local LGBT+ services, including the nonprofit HIV prevention and education organization AIDS Foundation Houston, as well as back issues of *OutSmart* magazine, Houston's monthly LGBT+ publication.

Mary's, Naturally *(Houston, TX)* (sometimes referred to as Mary's Lounge or just Mary's) was a gay bar that opened in 1968. At the time of its closing in 2009, it was the oldest gay bar in Houston, and the second oldest in the state. Its story began when Joe Anthony bought the bar, previously called Tommy's, and brought in go-go boys for entertainment. In the bar's early days, it was tradition for patrons' underwear to be hung from the ceiling. The owners never adopted a dress code, unlike many gay bars of the time, but the bar did adopt a cat, named Mr. Balls, as its mascot. The bar was a frequent target of police raids and harassment against its LGBT+ patrons. From 1978 to 1980, the bar was raided by police in the days leading up to Gay Pride Week. The building is now a coffee shop named Blacksmith, and several Mary's artifacts can be viewed at the Gulf Coast Archive and Museum.

Pink Dolphin Monument *(Galveston Island, TX)* in R. A. Apffel Park is the first monument in the southern United States to celebrate gender and sexual minority communities. The figure of the pink stone dolphin, mined from red limestone in Corpus Christi and designed by artist Joe Joe Orangias, takes inspiration from the historical Pink Dolphin Tavern as well as the LGBT+ activist group the Pink Posse. It was unveiled in July 2014 and is open to the public.

Robert's Lafitte *(Galveston, TX)*, the oldest gay bar in Texas, opened in August 1969, the summer of the Stonewall Riots. As advertised on their website, "Whether you're just looking for a great place to hang out and enjoy some great cocktails and ice-cold beers or want to check out a fantastic female impersonator show, Lafittes is the place to be any day or night of the week on Galveston Island!" Regular programming includes weekend drag shows, Tuesday karaoke, and the Shipwreck Talent Contest, hosted by Fifi LaMoore.

⊖ PEOPLE

Urooj Arshad *(Karachi, Pakistan)* is a Muslim LGBT+ activist. Arshad's family immigrated to Chicago when she was a teenager. After coming out in college, she realized she didn't feel connected among white LGBT+ people and also didn't have a space where she could reconcile her two identities as a queer Muslim. So, she cofounded the Muslim Alliance for Sexual and Gender Diversity, which gives a voice to the American Muslim LGBT+ community. She works for Advocates of Youth (a group that educates on sexual health) as the Director of International Youth Health and Rights Programs. Arshad's advocacy has been recognized with the Latino GLBT History Project's Mujeres en el Movimiento Award, the National Queer Asian Pacific Islander Alliance's Community Catalyst Award, and the Young Women of Color HIV/AIDS Coalition's We Speak Award.

Paris Barclay

Paris Barclay *(Chicago, IL)* is an award-winning director who has directed television shows such as *ER*, *NYPD Blue*, *Glee*, *Lost*, *CSI*, *House*, and *Sons of Anarchy*. Barclay has also directed music videos for stars such as Janet Jackson, Bob Dylan, and LL Cool J. He has won two Emmys, three NAACP Image Awards, four Peabody Awards, and two Humanitas Prizes. In 2013, Barclay was elected as the President of the Directors Guild of America (DGA), becoming its first Black, gay president.

Albert Cashier *(Clogherhead, Ireland)* was a transgender man who fought for the Union Army during the Civil War. Assigned female at birth, he began living as Albert Cashier when he moved to Illinois as an adult. After Cashier was discharged from the army, he continued living as a man and worked various handyman jobs. In 1913, a doctor discovered he was anatomically female; a year later, Cashier was committed to a mental institution and was forced to live the rest of his life

> ❝
>
> *I want to tell her that when she comes out as queer at 19, around the time of her father's passing, she will find very little empathy within the white LGBTQ community at her college. She will find that her experiences as a recent immigrant from Pakistan, and her fear about the consequences of family finding out that she is queer, won't be relatable for others. While many around her will speak casually about having LGBTQ members in their families, she will not even be able to think of 'LGBTQ' and 'family' in the same sentence.*
>
> —Urooj Arshad in a love letter to herself, *Bustle*, 2019
>
> ❞

> *Words have power, and I strongly feel this power can be used to control people's actions or, more specifically, how people respond to the intersex diagnosis. If you present intersex as a medical problem known as a disorder of sex development, you're likely to warrant a medical response that's medically unnecessary but also irreversible. As one of my participants shared with me, 'I'm not disordered.'*
>
> —Georgiann Davis, XYSuZ.com, 2016

> *The only way we can get anyplace is by being together. . . . Gay people have to get in there just like anybody else. We have to work. We need more businesses. Scientists, chemists, things like that. If we could get more gay people in our politics, I think it would help a lot. . . . And be honest and caring. Try to love people. Have a happy life if you can in this crazy world.*
>
> —Ruth Charlotte Ellis

as female. However, when he died, his gravestone recognized him as Albert Cashier.

Pamela K. Chen (*Chicago, IL*) was the first lesbian Asian American woman to be appointed as a federal judge when she was nominated by Barack Obama in 2013. Chen had been a practicing civil rights attorney since 1986, and spent the first five years of her career in the private sector before transitioning to work in public service. She now resides over the District Court for the Eastern District of New York. She is only the second Chinese American woman to serve as a federal judge.

Georgiann Davis (*Chicago, IL*) is the president of InterACT, as well as a sociologist working to raise awareness of the intersex community. Davis was born intersex, but her doctors hid this fact from her until she was an adult. She received her doctorate in sociology in 2011 from the University of Illinois–Chicago. Davis now works as an associate professor at the University of Nevada–Las Vegas. Her 2015 book *Contesting Intersex: The Dubious Diagnosis* examines the medical and social impacts of how our society views intersex individuals..

Ruth Charlotte Ellis (*Springfield, IL*) was the oldest surviving open lesbian. Born in 1899, Ellis came out when she was a teenager and eventually moved to

Detroit with her longtime partner. Their home became a safe space for the LGBT+ community in the 1940s, especially for Black LGBT+ people at a time when they were frequently discriminated against in bars. Ellis ran her own print shop and had a passion for photography and painting. As she aged, Ellis became famous within the LGBT+ community for being the oldest out lesbian. In 1999, a documentary about her life came out, called *Living with Pride: Ruth C. Ellis @ 100*. Ellis died at age 101 in 2000, achieving her goal of living into the new millennium.

Edward Gorey (*Chicago, IL*) was an author and illustrator. Over his career, Gorey wrote over one hundred books and illustrated over sixty works by other authors. He was known for his macabre yet funny stories, with titles such as *The Gashlycrumb Tinies* and *The Headless Bust: A Melancholy Meditation on the False Millennium*. Gorey, who defined his style with crosshatched line drawings, also worked as a set and costume designer for Broadway and the ballet. In his youth, Gorey attended Harvard, where he lived with the poet Frank O'Hara. Gorey often avoided labeling his sexual identity when asked in interviews, and in a 1980 interview described himself as "reasonably undersexed" and asexual. His purposely tongue-in-cheek book *The Curious Sofa: A Pornographic Work*, published under the pseudonym Ogdred Weary, contains sexual scenarios featuring fully clothed, flat-chested, and genital-less illustrations. He died in 2000 of a heart attack at age seventy-five.

Miss Major Griffin-Gracy *(Chicago, IL)* has been a transgender activist since the Stonewall Riots. During the 1970s, early in her activism, Griffin-Gracy was often imprisoned, which led her to become vocal for incarcerated trans women. In 2005, Griffin-Gracy joined the organization Trans Gender Variant and Intersex Justice Project (TGIJP), and eventually became its executive director. After retiring in 2015, she remained active in the community with a project called the House of GG's, a safe space for trans women. In 2018, Griffin-Gracy was awarded the Susan Hyde Award for Longevity in the Movement, celebrating her forty years of service.

Lorraine Hansberry *(Chicago, IL)* was a lesbian playwright and activist. She is most well known for her play *A Raisin in the Sun*, which premiered on Broadway in 1959. The play was the first written by a Black person to be produced on Broadway, and Hansberry was also the youngest American and the first Black playwright to win the New York Drama Critics' Circle Award for Best Play. She married writer Robert Nemiroff in 1953, and divorced in 1964; the two remained friends and continued to creatively collaborate. In 1965, Hansberry died of pancreatic cancer at the age of thirty-five. Before her death, she wrote anonymous letters to *The Ladder*, a lesbian magazine, about her struggles as a closeted lesbian married to a man.

Rock Hudson *(Winnetka, IL)* was a Hollywood actor known for playing the leading man in films through the 1950s and '60s. Appearing in over sixty films in his career, Hudson is most known for co-starring with Elizabeth Taylor in the 1956 film *Giant* and for his roles in *A Farewell to Arms* and *Pillow Talk*. In 1985, Hudson became seriously ill and released a statement that he had AIDS, becoming the first major celebrity to publicly announce an AIDS diagnosis. He died later that year. Although he never publicly announced it, Hudson is believed to have been gay.

Jim Kolbe *(Evanston, IL)* was a member of the Arizona House of Representatives for twenty-two years,

Jim Kolbe

from 1985 to 2007. During the vote for the Defense of Marriage Act of 1996, some LGBT+ groups pushed Kolbe to acknowledge he was gay and support the act. While Kolbe did eventually publicly state he was gay (becoming the second openly gay Republican member of Congress), he ultimately voted against the Defense of Marriage Act. In 2000, Kolbe was the first openly gay speaker at a Republican National Convention. Kolbe married his longtime partner in 2013.

David Kopay *(Chicago, IL)*, a former NFL player, was one of the first professional athletes to come out as gay. During Kopay's nine-year NFL career, he played for the San Francisco 49ers, the Washington, DC team, and the Green Bay Packers before retiring in 1972. Kopay publicly came out in 1975 in order to provide an accurate public representation of what it means to be a gay athlete. The football industry proceeded to shun Kopay, and he found it impossible to find a job related to football. Instead, he found work at a flooring company for the remainder of his career. Kopay's 1977 memoir about his experience as a gay NFL player, *The David Kopay Story: An Extraordinary Self-Revelation*, was a *New York Times* bestseller. In 2007, Kopay announced an endowment of $1 million to the University of Washington's Q Center to help make the future for LGBT+ youth better than what he experienced.

Lynnell Stephani Long *(Chicago, IL)* is an intersex activist, educator, photographer, and paramedic. She works to spread intersex awareness in order to prevent genital mutilation against intersex children, and to end the stigma around being intersex. She began

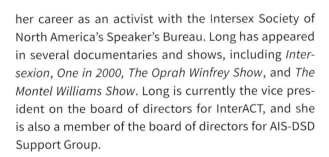

CeCe McDonald

Suze Orman

her career as an activist with the Intersex Society of North America's Speaker's Bureau. Long has appeared in several documentaries and shows, including *Intersexion*, *One in 2000*, *The Oprah Winfrey Show*, and *The Montel Williams Show*. Long is currently the vice president on the board of directors for InterACT, and she is also a member of the board of directors for AIS-DSD Support Group.

CeCe McDonald *(Chicago, IL)* is a Black transgender woman and advocate for prison reform. In 2012, McDonald was on the way home from the grocery store in Minneapolis with some friends when she was verbally attacked by a group of people near a bar who yelled racist, homophobic, and transphobic slurs. When McDonald argued back, a woman from the group attacked her with a shattered glass, cutting her face. McDonald defended herself with scissors and ended up killing one of the men. She was sentenced with manslaughter and three and a half years in a Minnesota prison. Although the state allowed her to receive her full hormone treatment during her sentence, she was forced to serve time in a men's prison. Since her release in 2014, McDonald has focused her activism on prison reform, and worked with Laverne Cox to release the 2016 documentary *Free CeCe* about her story.

Ifti Nasim *(Faisalabad, Pakistan)* was a gay poet and activist raised in Pakistan, where he hid his sexual identity to fit in with cultural norms. But in his early twenties, he moved to Chicago because he thought he would be more accepted. There, Nasim became active in the LGBT+ community, and his house became a local safe space. He founded Sangat Chicago, a South Asian LGBT+ organization, in 1986. In 1994 he published *Narman* (the Persian word for "hermaphrodite"), a collection of LGBT+ poetry. *Narman* is considered the first work written in Urdu to openly discuss the LGBT+ community. He published two more poetry collections in his career, and was inducted into the Chicago Gay and Lesbian Hall of Fame in 1996. Nasim died in 2011 at the age of sixty-five.

Suze Orman *(Chicago, IL)* is a finance expert and media professional. She worked as a financial advisor for an investment company before eventually starting her own company in 1987. She has since written nine books, all of which are bestsellers. Orman hosted her own show on CNBC for thirteen years, earning eight Gracie Awards. Orman has also had shows on PBS and HSN, and has made numerous guest appearances on other shows—she's been on *The Oprah Winfrey Show* twenty-nine times, *Larry King Live* thirty times, and appeared on *The Simpsons*. Orman is married to her manager, Kathy Travis.

Pidgeon Pagonis *(Chicago, IL)* is an intersex activist and filmmaker. They are a national leader in the fight for intersex rights, speaking and lecturing on intersex education and advocacy. Their biography was featured in the 2012 documentary *Intersexion*, and in 2017 they created *The Son I Never Had*, a short autobiographical documentary. Pagonis also works with the youth advocacy group interACT. They are currently working on a new documentary, as well as a photo series about intersex people of color called *Physical Record*.

Jennifer Pritzker *(Chicago, IL)* is a transgender philanthropist. Assigned male at birth, she was born into the Pritzker family, one of the wealthiest in the country. Pritzker serves as the president and CEO of TAWANI Enterprises, which is home to the Pritzker Military Museum and Library and the Pritzker Military Foundation. She served twenty-seven years in the Army and National Guard until her retirement in 2001. When she transitioned to female in 2013, she became the world's first transgender billionaire. Pritzker has since focused a part of her philanthropy on transgender-related causes, such as her $3 million donation to the University of Minnesota's Program in Human Sexuality in 2017, which the university used to establish the National Center for Gender Spectrum Health. A Republican, Pritzker has been outspoken about her political party's support of the military transgender ban. "When the GOP asks me to deliver six- or seven-figure contributions for the 2020 elections, my first response will be: Why should I contribute to my own destruction?" she wrote in the *Chicago Tribune* in 2019, questioning her support of her own party.

Richard Pryor *(Peoria, IL)* was a stand-up comedian and actor known for telling hard-hitting jokes that pulled from his experiences with racism, addiction, and disease. Pryor occasionally appeared on television shows, such as *The Ed Sullivan Show* and *Broadway Tonight*, as well as his own program, *The Richard Pryor Show*. He also had a strong presence in film, acting in almost fifty movies, such as *The Busy Body*, *Wild in the Street*, and *Superman III*. Pryor married seven times. Several people close to him, including his last wife, have said Pryor was open about his bisexuality but didn't consider himself bisexual. In his 1995 autobiography, *Pryor Convictions: And Other Life Sentences*, Pryor mentioned having a brief relationship with a transgender woman. He died in 2005 at age sixty-five.

Robert Reed *(Highland Park, IL)* was a television actor most notable for his role as Mike Brady, the father in *The Brady Bunch*. He also played roles in the television shows *Roots*; *Rich Man, Poor Man*; *The Defenders*; and *Medical Center*. He was nominated for three Emmys. Later in his career, Reed taught Shakespeare for the drama department of the University of California–Los Angeles. Reed hid his gay identity to avoid potentially harming his career. He died in 1992 after suffering from colon cancer and AIDS.

⊙ PLACES

The Chicago Tribute Marker of Distinction for Burr Tillstrom *(Chicago, IL)* is located at 1407 West Sherwin Avenue, his former home. Tillstrom was a famous puppeteer and creator of the show *Kukla, Fran & Ollie*. The show was hugely successful, winning five Emmys and dozens of other awards. Prior to this success, Tillstrom performed puppet shows in the window of his house for neighborhood children. He was gay and in a long-term relationship with the show's costume designer, Joseph Lockwood Jr.

The Chicago Tribute Marker of Distinction for Margaret C. Anderson *(Chicago, IL)* is located at 837 West Ainslie Street, the site of Anderson's former home. In 1997, Chicago Tribute Markers of Distinction were placed around Chicago in places important to the city's various historical figures. Anderson was hugely impactful in the literary scene as a publisher and an editor, and she founded the literary magazine the *Little Review* in 1914. Over the years, the magazine published authors such as Ezra Pound, Gertrude Stein, William Carlos Williams, and James Joyce. Anderson was a lesbian and co-edited the magazine with her lover, Jane Heap.

QUEER FACTS

The Chicago LGBT Hall of Fame is an organization and event that recognizes significant people and organizations in the LGBT+ community. Founded in 1991 by a commission of the city's government, the organization is run by the Friends of the Chicago LGBT Hall of Fame, a volunteer-run nonprofit. Each year's inductees fall into in three categories: Individuals (LGBT+ people who have contributed to the community), Organizations (organizations that have supported the LGBT+ community), and Friends (non-LGBT+ people who have supported the community). Annually, the Chicago LGBT Hall of Fame hosts the induction ceremony and has a float in the city's Pride parade.

Illinois was the first state to repeal anti-sodomy laws in 1961, when the state passed a considerable revision to the state's criminal code, following the recommendation of the American Law Institute. However, at the same time, Illinois also banned public "lewd fondling or caressing of the body of another person of the same sex," specifically calling out same-sex couples. Two years later, the legislation changed the wording to refer to either sex.

The Society for Human Rights, the first LGBT+ organization in the US, was founded in 1924 by the veteran Henry Gerber. During World War I, Gerber served in Germany, where he learned about the country's rising embrace of the LGBT+ community. When he returned to the US, Gerber started the Society for Human Rights, modeled after a similar society in Germany, with the goal of decriminalizing sodomy. Only six members large, the society published the first known LGBT+ periodical, *Freedom and Friendship*. But the group quickly met trouble. In 1925, Gerber's home was raided and three members, including Gerber, were arrested. While the chargers were eventually dropped, Gerber lost his job and his life's savings, and the society quickly ended. Still, Gerber continued to be active in the LGBT+ community. Gerber's Chicago home at 1704 North Crilly Court is now recognized as a National Historic Landmark.

The Henry Gerber House *(Chicago, IL)* is a national historical landmark, particularly in LGBT+ history. It is the location of the founding of America's first LGBT+ organization, the Society for Human Rights, and the first LGBT+ newsletter, *Freedom and Friendship*. It was designated as a historic landmark in 2015.

The Jane Addams Hull House Museum *(Chicago, IL)* honors the achievements of Jane Addams, a feminist, suffragette, activist, and pioneer. A champion of those living in poverty, people of color, women, and the LGBT+ community, Addams helped found both the National Association for the Advancement of Colored People and the American Civil Liberties Union. She cofounded the Hull House in 1889 as a settlement house meant to build a community that brought together the rich and poor members of the community. In 1931, Addams was the second woman ever to win the Nobel Peace Prize. Addams was a lesbian and in a long-term relationship with one of the women who lived in the Hull House. The museum is dedicated to continuing to address the causes that Addams championed.

INDIANA

⊖ PEOPLE

Ray Boltz *(Muncie, IN)* is a contemporary Christian musician. His song "Thank You," which won the 1990 Song of the Year prize at the Gospel Music Association Dove awards, rocketed him to fame within the Christian contemporary music genre. Since his debut album in 1986, Boltz has sold more than 4.5 million records. Boltz came out as gay in a 2008, sparking controversy among his Christian fans. Since then, he has found a home within the Metropolitan Community Church in Florida, where he continues to write, record, and perform, despite having withdrawn from the CCM scene.

Pete Buttigieg *(South Bend, IN)* rose to national attention with his campaign for the 2020 presidential election. In 2011 at age twenty-nine, Buttigieg was elected as the mayor of South Bend, a position he used to build a more inclusive and accepting community. He was reelected to the position in 2015. Buttigieg served in the Navy Reserve during the Afghanistan war, and spent his early career as a management consultant. He lives with his husband in South Bend.

James Dean *(Marion, IN)* was a popular 1950s actor, famous for portrayals of troubled teens in films such as *Rebel Without a Cause* (1955) and *East of Eden* (1955).

James Dean

Dean's charm and charisma onscreen skyrocketed him to fame just out of the gate in his short-lived film career. Though he only starred in a few films, in 1999 the American Film Institute listed him as one of the top twenty-five male stars of the Golden Age of Hollywood. Dean died in a car crash in 1955; he was twenty-four. Although Dean only publicly dated women, rumors since his death have romantically linked him to men such as Marlon Brando, William Bast, Clifton Webb, and more. "Well, I'm certainly not going through life with one hand tied behind my back," Dean once said of his sexuality.

Ernestine Eckstein drew the eye of historians after her appearance in an iconic 1965 photograph of a protest against homosexual discrimination in front of the White House. Eckstein stands off to the side with her picket poster, one Black woman amid a crowd of white protesters. Openly lesbian, Eckstein made history in 1996 by being the first Black woman featured on the cover of *The Ladder*, a lesbian magazine publication. Eckstein was a leader in the lesbian and gay rights movements of the 1960s, and brought valuable experience from her involvement with the Civil Rights Movement to her position as vice president of the New York chapter of Daughters of Bilitis.

Steve Ells *(Indianapolis, IN)* is the founder of Chipotle Mexican Grill. Initially, Chipotle was a means to

> ❝
> *You see, I feel that the homophile movement is only part of a much larger movement of the erasure of labels. And I think the right of a person to dress as he chooses must necessarily follow when we expand our own philosophy of bringing about change for the homosexual.*
>
> —Ernestine Eckstein, Making Gay History podcast
> ❞

an end—Ells's real dream was to open a fine-dining restaurant. However, Chipotle took off, expanding from just three locations in 1996 to well over two thousand today. Ells, an openly gay man, was recognized by the *Wall Street Journal* in 2017 as the year's top innovator in the food industry. He stepped down as CEO that year. Under Ells's leadership, Chipotle has been an active sponsor of many local Pride events, and has openly boycotted the Boy Scouts of America because of its past ban on LGBT+ members.

Will Geer *(Frankfort, IN)* was an actor perhaps best known for his role as "Grandpa" Zebulon Walton on the hit television show *The Waltons* (1971–1981). In the 1930s, Geer met and eventually dated Harry Hay, a gay rights activist. Geer held workshops for young actors and performances of Shakespeare at his home, called Theatricum Botanicum, named after a lauded botany textbook. After Geer's death, the home was transformed into a professional repertory theater by a group of dedicated actors, and it now provides educational programs and musical events for the community. Geer had a long television career, appearing in shows such as *Gunsmoke*, *Bonanza*, *Bewitched*, and *Starsky & Hutch*.

Andrea Jean James *(Franklin, IN)* is a transgender activist and the founder of GenderMedia Foundation, an organization dedicated to improving how transgender teens are portrayed in the media. James has produced and directed several productions, including short films such as *Casting Pearls* and *Transproofed*, which deal with transgender casting and dating, re-

spectively. James has also consulted other stars with writing and portraying transgender characters, including Felicity Huffman on the film *Transamerica*, which won multiple awards.

Cleve Jones *(West Lafayette, IN)* is a human rights activist who cofounded the San Francisco AIDS Foundation in 1983. Jones was mentored by well-known LGBT+ activist Harvey Milk, for whom Jones worked as a student intern at Milk's City Hall office for many years. In 1987, Jones founded the NAMES Project AIDS Memorial Quilt, a piece of community folk art that memorializes and commemorates the lives of AIDS victims. Jones has written two books, including his memoir, *When We Rise* (2016), which was heralded by *Publisher's Weekly* as an "inspiring reminder that one can go from 'daydreaming about sex and revolution' to making them reality."

We need to recommit to sticking together, first of all. The LGBTQ community has to all come together and not have factions that I think we are splitting into.

—Andrea Jean James,
BoingBoing.net, 2017

Thousands of people reading these names on this patchwork of placards up on that wall. And I thought to myself, 'It looks like some kind of quilt,' and when I said the word 'quilt' I thought of my great-grandma. . . . And it was such a warm and comforting and middle-American traditional-family-values sort of symbol, and I thought, 'This is the symbol we should take.'

—Cleve Jones, *NPR*, 2016

Adam Lambert *(Indianapolis, IN)* is an openly gay singer. Lambert was the runner-up on the 2009 season of *American Idol*; later that year, he released his debut album, *For Your Entertainment*, launching a music career that has since amassed over 3 million albums and 5 million singles sold worldwide. In recent years, Lambert has performed as a member of the 1980s rock band Queen under the moniker Queen + Adam Lambert. Lambert has performed in a number of minor acting roles on TV shows such as *Pretty Little Liars*, *Glee*, and *The Rocky Horror Picture Show* (2016).

John Charles Chenoweth McKinsey *(Clinton County, IN)* was a mathematician known for his contributions to mathematical logic and game theory. McKinsey was a Blumenthal Research Fellow and a Guggenheim Fellow, and worked for a small research group that eventually became RAND Corporation. Though McKinsey was openly gay and had made his years-long relationship known to his coworkers, he was fired in 1951 by the FBI, who saw him as a security threat. McKinsey argued that he was in no danger of being threatened with disclosure because he was so open about his homosexuality, but his superiors would not listen. McKinsey went on to teach at Stanford University after leaving RAND. He died by suicide in 1953 at the age of forty-five.

Ryan Murphy *(Indianapolis, IN)* is a Hollywood director and producer, famous for shows such as *American Horror Story* and *Glee*. He was interested in film from an early age, and served as president of a Meryl Streep fan club during his high school years. In addition to four Emmy awards, Murphy holds a plethora of television accolades, and was given a star on the Hollywood Walk of Fame in 2018. Though Murphy is known for approaching his content with a sometimes polarizing attitude, he is extremely self-aware of the effect he has, and says, "My work, for good or for bad, is about mixing lightness with darkness." He and his husband, David Miller, have been married since 2012 and have two children.

Cole Porter *(Peru, IN)* was a prolific Broadway songwriter in the early 1900s. Raised in an extremely affluent family, Porter started violin and piano lessons at age six, and had discovered his proclivity for music and

Ryan Murphy

songwriting by the time he turned eight. He went on to study at Yale, and wrote over three hundred songs during that time. While studying at the Harvard Graduate School of Arts and Sciences in 1916, Porter debuted on Broadway with a musical comedy called *See America First*. Porter's career advanced slowly, gaining enough traction by 1949 that he took home the first-ever Tony Award for Best Musical for *Kiss Me, Kate*. Porter led a vibrant Hollywood lifestyle, filled with all-male parties and a variety of gay love affairs. By the end of his life, he had written music for over twenty different Broadway shows, many of which were later turned into films, such as *Anything Goes*, *Can-Can*, and *The New Yorkers*.

Sandra Spuzich *(Indianapolis, IN)* was a professional golfer. In 1982, she was the oldest player to ever win two LPGA events in the same year, with the Corning Classic and the Mary Kay Classic. Spuzich was known for her dedication to the sport and perseverance in the face of initially discouraging odds. Her wife, Joyce Kazmierski, a former LPGA Tour professional as well, later described Spuzich as easygoing, with "a great sense of humor." Spuzich and Kazmierski, who met at the US Open, were fittingly married in 2015 on a porch overlooking a golf course. Spuzich died two months later at the age of seventy-eight.

Bali White *(Indianapolis, IN)* is a transgender human rights activist. White, a research fellow at the National Institutes of Health, has worked extensively in the public health arena, advocating for health care for sexual and gender minorities (SGM). Some of her accomplishments include coordinating the transgender programing for Housing Works in New York; serving on the board of directors for the Sylvia Rivera Law Project, and developing HIV prevention strategies at Lutheran Medical Center. In 2013, White was invited to the White House as an emerging LGBT+ leader from the New York Department of Health.

PLACES

The Chris Gonzalez Library & Archives *(Indianapolis, IN)*, with over seven thousand books, videos, and other reference material, stand as a testament to the rich history of Indiana's LGBT+ community. Curated by Michael Bohr, the collection is primarily comprised of donated material. The archives were formerly housed by the Health Foundation of Greater Indianapolis; in 2017, a partnership between Indy Pride and the Indianapolis Public Library relocated the collection to the Indianapolis Central Library.

💡 QUEER FACTS

The Bag Ladies is an HIV/AIDS fundraising organization based in Indianapolis. Every year around Halloween, participants dress in drag and go on a bus tour of Indiana's bars, raising support for the fight against HIV/AIDS by entertaining other patrons. At the end of the night, whoever has raised the most money is crowned Bag Lady Queen. The fun has since expanded into the Bag Lady Queen Pageant, which is held before the tour each year. While the bus tour is the Bag Ladies' most popular event, they host several other events throughout the year, often partnering with other organizations.

> *Because of the lack of education on AIDS, discrimination, fear, panic, and lies surrounded me.*
>
> —Ryan White, *Associated Press*, 1988

Ryan White of Kokomo, Indiana, was a thirteen-year-old boy who contracted HIV through a blood transfusion for hemophilia in 1984. White was not gay, and his story received national attention for its uniqueness at the time, bringing new light to the HIV/AIDS epidemic. Despite facing intense discrimination from the surrounding community, as well as a doctor's warning that he had only six months to live, White lived five years longer than predicted and advocated tirelessly for victims of HIV/AIDS. White died in 1990 at the age of eighteen. That year, following his death, Congress passed the Ryan White Comprehensive AIDS Resources Emergency (CARE) Act, solidifying his legacy as a boy who brought desperately needed awareness to this national health issue.

The Screamer was Indianapolis's earliest known gay publication, running from 1966 to 1967. It featured poetry, recipes, and humorous anecdotes from contributors. One of the oldest dated copies of the magazine can be found at the Chris Gonzalez Library & Archives, which also houses other historic LGBT+ publications such as *The Works*, which published similar content.

Indiana Historical Society, home to the Indiana LGBT Collecting Initiative

Lindley Hall, home of the Kinsey Institute

The Indiana LGBT Collecting Initiative *(Indianapolis, IN)*, launched by the Indiana Historical Society in 2014, collects and preserves the LGBT+ history and culture of Indiana. Its collection of recorded and transcribed oral histories fill gaps in the current written history, and is filled with dozens of donated photos and other material. The initiative also hosts a traveling LGBT+ history exhibit.

James Dean's grave *(Fairmont, IN)* is located in Park Cemetery. The heartthrob actor died in 1955 at the age of twenty-four due to a racing accident. The city of his burial, Fairmont, hosts an annual James Dean Festival and also opened the James Dean Gallery at the Fairmont Historical Museum in 1988. Read more about Dean under "People."

The Kinsey Institute *(Bloomington, IN)* at Indiana University was named for Dr. Alfred Kinsey, whose research on human sexual behavior earned him the nickname "father of the sexual revolution." The institute promotes research on sexuality and relationships, and publishes scholarly content every year, much of which can be explored on its website. The Kinsey Institute has an extensive collection of materials concerning the history of sex, including everything from print and art material to films. Read more about Dr. Kinsey under New Jersey.

The Tri-State Alliance (TSA) *(Evansville, IN)* serves the LGBT+ communities of southwestern Indiana, western Kentucky, and southern Illinois. Though TSA's primary focus is social service and education, it offers a variety of opportunities for the LGBT+ community, including LGBT+ youth groups, free confidential and anonymous HIV testing, and events such as Pride Prom and Pride Picnic. TSA doesn't shy away from engaging with the media or other organizations; it offers training through speaker's bureaus, provides a monthly newsletter, hosts guest speakers, and continually works with local media to discuss and solve LGBT+ issues.

IOWA

Laura Duffy

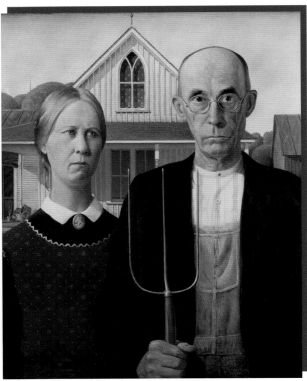

American Gothic *by Grant Wood*

Laura Duffy *(Des Moines, IA)* was appointed by President Barack Obama in 2010 as a US Attorney for San Diego. Duffy was believed to be only the second open lesbian US Attorney. Prior to her appointment, she spent her career as a federal prosecutor, notably working on cases against the infamous Arellano-Felix drug cartel. "I take to heart even the possibility that my being open about my orientation may lessen the stigma or apparent limitations even one individual feels," she told *Voice of San Diego* in 2010.

Roy Halston *(Des Moines, IA)* is a fashion designer known mononymously as Halston. Halston attended Indiana University and the Chicago Art Institute before moving to New York to work with the milliner Lilly Dache in 1958. He later opened his own couture house in 1968, and quickly rose to fame in the 1970s as a fashion icon. His designs, which were made for everyday people as well as celebrities, were known for their sleek lines and minimalist style. For nearly ten years, Halston had an on-again/off-again relationship with the artist Victor Hugo, who worked as a window dresser in his couture house. Halston died of AIDS-related illness in 1990 at the age of fifty-seven.

Sagan C. S. Lara *(Cedar Rapids, IA)* is a disabled intersex and transgender activist. They are a board member of the Minnesota Transgender Health Coalition and have helped establish the Minnesota support and advocacy group MinneOrchids. Lara offers informational presentations on intersex issues to organizations in the Twin Cities area, as well as digital presentations to organizations across the country.

Grant Wood *(Anamosa, IA)* was a renowned painter and art professor at the University of Iowa. Born in 1891, Wood moved with his family to Cedar Rapids ten years later after his father's death. Upon graduating high school, Woods enrolled in the Minneapolis School of Design, Handicraft, and Normal Art. He later attended the University of Iowa and the School of the Art Institute of Chicago, after which he briefly joined the army at the end of World War I. Initially drawn to impressionism, Woods quickly moved into American regionalism and became famous for his 1930 painting *American Gothic*. Toward the end of his life, Wood was accused of homosexuality. Wood denied these claims, but his unhappy marriage and the homoerotic symbolism in many of his paintings have led several art

> " I feel compelled to acknowledge the special pride I feel as the great-grandson of slaves to be here today at this institution whose founders were active participants in our country's abolitionist movement. That change may require great courage and creativity, rigorous thinking, hard work and significant sacrifice, but it can occur.
>
> —Raynard Kington, *Wisconsin Gazette*, 2010 "

> " That issue is an intersection of civil rights, r-i-g-h-t-s, and religious rites, r-i-t-e. It's the unhappy intersection of both. For the community, I certainly believe everybody needs to be equal.
>
> —Richard Eychaner, *Des Moines Register*, 2016 "

critics and biographers to purport Wood was indeed gay. Wood died of pancreatic cancer in 1942 at the age of fifty.

 PLACES

The Alice French House *(Davenport, IA)* was added to the National Register of Historic Places in 1983. The house is not considered architecturally significant, but has become historically significant through its connection to French. French, who was a lesbian and a fiction writer who wrote under the pen name Octave Thanet from 1878 through 1910, was published widely in places such as *Harper's* and *The Atlantic*. She also published twenty-one books, including her most famous novel, *The Man of the Hour*. French lived with her partner, Jane Allen Crawford, at 321 East Tenth Street for over fifty years.

The Blazing Saddle *(Des Moines, IA)* is the city's oldest gay bar. Known as the "gay Cheers", the Blazing Saddle was founded in 1983 by Bob Eikleberry to provide a safe gathering place for the LGBT+ community.

University of Iowa

The bar is now open 365 days a year, rain or shine. Despite several economic upsets in the area, the Blazing Saddle has remained a popular watering hole for locals since its opening.

The LGBTQ Resource Center at the University of Iowa *(Iowa City, IA)* provides cross-cultural education, development opportunities, and social justice workshops for students and faculty. It also offers an informal space for gatherings, group meetings, and studying throughout the school year. In 2016, the center celebrated ten years of service with a new and updated student space.

QUEER FACTS

The Annual LGBTQ Senior Summit spotlights issues surrounding senior living and caregiving in the LGBT+ community. The summits have been held annually since 2015 by One Iowa, an LGBT+ organization dedicated to advancing equality in Iowa through education, trainings in health care and law enforcement, and providing resources to the LGBT+ community.

The first openly gay Black person to serve as a US college president is Raynard Kington, who became president of Iowa's Grinnell College in 2010. Dr. Kington's career has been committed to inclusive leadership and fair decision making, and he has established programs aimed at integrating post-graduation career goals into academic achievement. He has also promoted the creation of the Grinnell Prize, for individuals who have brought positive social change in their field. Grinnell College itself has a history of commitment to social justice issues since its founding by abolitionists in 1846.

The first openly gay man to run for a voting seat in Congress was Rich Eychaner in 1984. A Republican, Eychaner is also a business owner, politician, and LGBT+ rights activist. Along with several other business ventures, Eychaner—who is from Illinois but is based in Iowa—owns a minor league affiliate of the Chicago Cubs.

The first openly transgender professor in Iowa was Deirdre McCloskey. McCloskey was raised in Ann Arbor, Michigan, and attended Harvard for her undergrad and graduate degrees in economics. Now retired, McCloskey's work has included writing on conservative economic theories, rhetoric of economics, and economic history. McCloskey, who was assigned male at birth, made headlines in 1995 when she came out as transgender while teaching economics and history at the University of Iowa. In 2000, she began teaching at the University of Illinois–Chicago, and went on to become a distinguished professor of economics and history. Since her transition, McCloskey has been an outspoken advocate of LGBT+ rights and organizations.

The Sisters of Perpetual Indulgence is a street performance group and satirical religious order that uses drag performances to promote and raise money for sexual tolerance. In 1976, an Iowa City convent loaned old habits to the performing group the Sugar Plum Fairies for a production of *The Sound of Music*. Upon moving to San Francisco, the Sugar Plum Fairies became the Sisters of Perpetual Indulgence and began performing in habits in public spaces to raise money for AIDS and LGBTQ related causes. The organization now boasts houses, or Orders, around the world. In 1987, the Sisters of Perpetual Indulgence reunited in Iowa City to celebrate their founding.

Deirdre McCloskey

The Sisters of Perpetual Indulgence

The University of Iowa, in 1970, became the first university to allow an LGBT+ student group. The following year, the University of Iowa's Gay Liberation Front became the first gay student group recognized by an American university.

Varnum v. Brien was a 2009 Supreme Court case that made Iowa the first Midwestern state to legalize same-sex marriage. In 2005, six same-sex couples in Polk County filed a lawsuit after being denied marriage licenses. Two years later, the Polk County District Court struck down the state's ban on same-sex marriage, declaring it unconstitutional. The decision was later appealed to the Iowa Supreme Court, and the Iowa Supreme Court upheld the ruling in a unanimous vote another two years later.

Vivian Boyack and Alice Dubes met as children in their hometown of Yale, Iowa. In 1947, they moved together to Davenport, Iowa, working as a school teacher and bookkeeper, respectively. They made news in 2014, at the ages of 90 and 91, when they were able to marry after seventy-two years together.

Only three in 10,000 want to cross the boundary of gender, a few of them in your own city neighborhood or small town. Gender crossing is no threat to male-female sex ratios or the role of women or the stability of the dollar.

—Deirdre McCloskey, *Crossing: A Memoir*, 1999

Prairie Lights *(Iowa City, IA)* is Iowa City's largest bookstore. Founded in 1978 as a small "garden" for books, Prairie Lights has grown into a two-story building and now boasts an extensive selection of LGBT+ titles. The bookstore also hosts a coffeehouse on its second floor.

The University of Iowa LGBTQ Clinic *(Iowa City, IA)* provides full-service health care to LGBT+ patients. Founded in 2011, the clinic provides exams, hormone therapy, breast augmentations, and counseling. In conjunction with the University of Iowa's law school, the clinic also provides legal advice to transgender patients regarding identification and insurance.

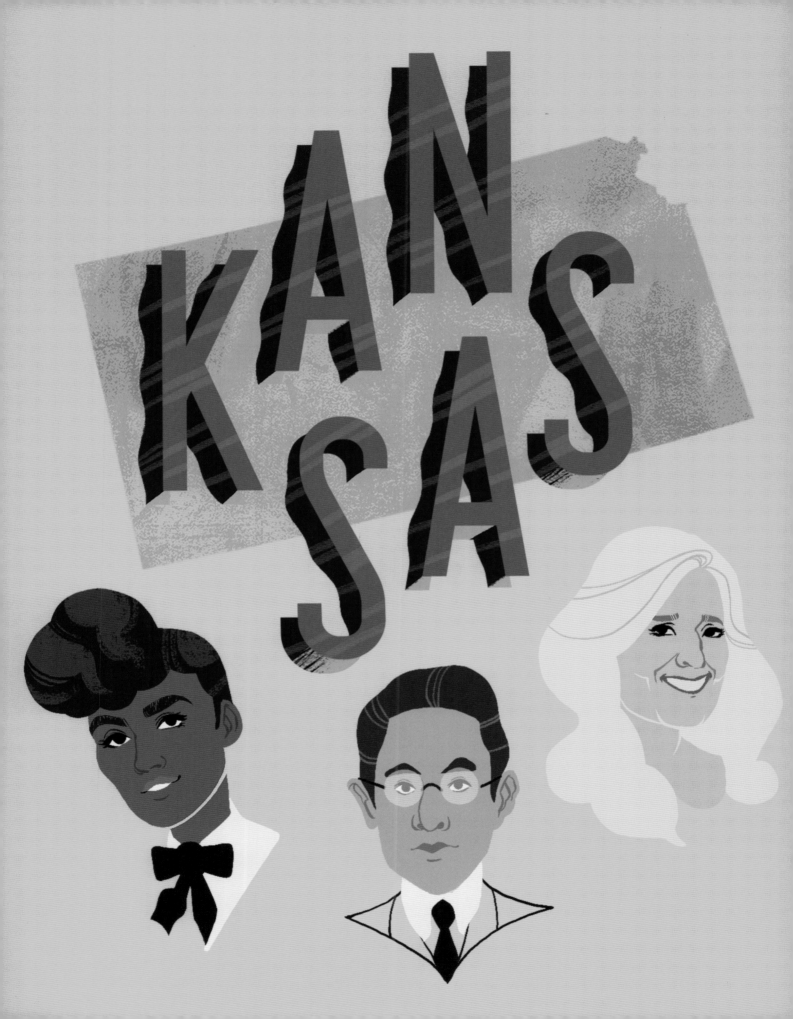

👤 PEOPLE

Gilbert Baker *(Chanute, KS)* was raised by his grandmother in Parsons, Kansas. As a gay man, Baker engaged in gay rights activism throughout his life and created the rainbow flag in 1978 while living in San Francisco. Baker's flag originally consisted of eight colors (hot pink, red, orange, yellow, green, turquoise, indigo, and violet). Baker served in both the US Army and the Sisters of Perpetual Indulgence. He was a friend of Harvey Milk and considered California his home because of the welcome he found in San Francisco.

Ruby Dandridge *(Wichita, KS)* was a bisexual actor best known for her voice acting on the radio show *Amos 'n' Andy*. Because she was a black American, most of her television and film roles were those of maids, cooks, and other domestic help. She was also known for playing airheaded characters. Later in her life, she performed nightclub acts and supported the careers of her two daughters. After her marriage to a man ended, she had a long-term relationship with the actress Geneva Williams.

Melissa Etheridge *(Leavenworth, KS)* is a singer-songwriter and activist. She came out publicly in 1993 and has been an active gay rights advocate since. In 2004, she was diagnosed with breast cancer, which she also publicly discussed. A year later, she performed a tribute to Janis Joplin at the Grammy Awards while still bald from chemotherapy; the performance later inspired a verse in India.Arie's song "I Am Not My Hair." Etheridge's discography spans from 1988 to 2016 and earned her two Grammy Awards for best female rock vocal performance and an Academy Award in 2007 for best original song.

Gilbert Baker

> ❝
> *It came from such a horrible place of murder and holocaust and Hitler. We needed something beautiful, something from us. The rainbow is so perfect because it really fits our diversity in terms of race, gender, ages, all of those things. Plus, it's a natural flag—it's from the sky.*
>
> —Gilbert Baker, MoMA.org, 2015
> ❞

Melissa Etheridge

> *The first time someone said, 'Hey, you saved my life,' it really changed perspectives for me. It means so, so much to hear that. You can't ever take that away from me. Each time one of us came out, it gave us strength. It wasn't so scary.*
>
> —Melissa Etheridge, *Philadelphia*, 2014

Janelle Monae

Alan L. Hart *(Halls Summit, KS)* was an influential doctor, researcher, and novelist. Hart was also one of the first transgender men to undergo gender-affirming surgery. Hart's was the first documented transgender male transition in the United States. His surgery occurred around 1917 at the University of Oregon Medical School, and he lived the rest of his life as a man. Hart married his first wife, Inez Stark, in 1918 and his second wife, Edna Ruddick, in 1925. Hart pioneered the use of X-ray photography in tuberculosis detection, which helped implement early TB screening programs that greatly reduced the prevalence of the disease. He also wrote four novels that are now seen as containing autobiographical themes of medicine and sexuality.

Cornell Gunter *(Coffeyville, KS)* was an R&B singer and musician who played with the Flairs, the Coasters, and the Platters, with whom he released hits such as "Yakety Yak" and "Charlie Brown." Three years before his death in 1990, he was inducted into the Rock & Roll Hall of Fame with the Coasters, who in 1959 were the most popular Black music group in the United States. Gunter was gay and was known for his flamboyant stage presence.

Koomah is an artist and educator. Born in Japan and raised between Kansas and Texas, Koomah is intersex, trans, queer, and genderfluid. These many identities are centered in Koomah's art, which spans all media from performance art to film. Koomah is the founder of the Houston Intersex Society (THIS). In 2017, Koomah

was also a proponent of Texas Senate Bill 1342, which sought to ban nonconsensual genital surgery on intersex minors. "Our lives are not a tragedy. Whether a person has had surgery or hasn't, there are folks that are very happy with their bodies," Koomah said of intersex people to Texas Medical Center News in 2017.

Janelle Monáe *(Kansas City, KS)* is a singer and actor. Monáe came out as pansexual in 2018 with the release of her third album, *Dirty Computer*. In the accompanying visual album, Monáe is seen in a primary romantic relationship with actress Tessa Thompson. Previously, Monáe had stated that she only dates androids and made other comments obliquely referring to the fact that she is queer. Also an actress, Monáe has appeared in films such as *Hidden Figures* and *Moonlight*. She is both a Screen Actors Guild Award winner and multi-Grammy nominee.

Virgil A. Richard *(Anthony, KS)* was a US Army General and outspoken critic of Don't Ask, Don't Tell. Richard came out in 2003 after retiring from his thirty-two years of service; the year also happened to be the tenth anniversary of the Don't Ask, Don't Tell policy. He died in 2013 at the age of seventy-six, and is survived by three children and his partner of sixteen years.

QUEER FACTS

The first same-sex marriage in Kansas took place on November 18, 2014, during a one-week window when the Supreme Court declined to hear appeals in two Tenth Circuit Court of Appeals cases legalizing same-sex marriage across the Tenth Circuit. Although the ruling was directed toward Utah and Oklahoma, same-sex marriages were momentarily legal in Kansas, which is within the same jurisdiction. The window closed when the Kansas Supreme Court issued an injunction to halt the issuance of marriage licenses in the state, but not before one same-sex couple was issued a license. Joleen Hickman and Darci Bohnenblust were legally married in Manhattan County. Hours later, the Kansas Supreme Court issued its stay. No more same-sex couples would be married in Kansas until the US Supreme Court issued its opinion in *Obergefell v. Hodges* in 2015.

A postage stamp promoting The Wizard of Oz

The Phoenix Society was Kansas City's first LGBT+ organization and published its own magazine, *The Phoenix*. It served LGBT+ people across Kansas City in Missouri and Kansas. In 1968, the Phoenix Society also created the Phoenix House, Kansas City's first LGBT+ community center. The Phoenix Society was largely made up of gay men, although there were women members. The society is credited for making Kansas City an important city in the early gay rights struggle, and an LGBT+ friendly city today.

Planting Peace started as a foreign aid NGO but became involved in LGBT+ rights in 2013 when cofounder Aaron Jackson saw a house go up for sale across the street from the Westboro Baptist Church. The group raised $81,000 to purchase the house and painted it the colors of the LGBT+ rainbow flag. Today, it continues to use the space for LGBT+ advocacy, countering the message of the Westboro Baptist Church and hosting pro-LGBT+ events and fundraisers. The organization's current projects include deworming children in Guatemala and operating an orphanage in Haiti.

Wichita Pride is an annual festival in the last weekend of September. The festival began in 2005, and now features traditional Pride activities, such as performances, parades, and parties, as well as advocacy rallies and family-friendly activities.

The Wizard of Oz was a film released in 1939. It was based on the novel by L. Frank Baum and starred Judy Garland, who later became seen as a gay icon. Much of her work on *The Wizard of Oz*, and other MGM films at the time, was later described as campy. In the film, Garland's character, Dorothy, befriends a Cowardly Lion, who is described as a "sissy"; many critics argue this character is coded as gay. Gay men used the term "friend of Dorothy" first as a coded and then as a slang term for themselves. There are several *Wizard of Oz* attractions in Kansas, including the OZ Museum in Wamego and Dorothy's House and the Land of Oz in Liberal.

Matthew Vines *(Wichita, KS)* is an activist and author. Vines is a gay man and a Christian who wrote *God and the Gay Christian* and founded the Reformation Project, which works to change church teaching on sexual orientation and gender identity. In 2012, he gave a speech entitled "The Gay Debate: The Bible and Homosexuality," in Wichita. The speech was recorded and went viral, gaining one million views and launching Vines's career. Vines was publicly critiqued by much older theologians because he was young and very publicly made the case for a biblical interpretation that supported LGBT+ people.

Genevieve Waller *(Wichita, KS)* is a queer artist who grew up in Kansas and created *Rainbow in Reverse: Kansas Queer History*, an art exhibit honoring LGBT+ history in Kansas. Waller's work focuses on camp aesthetic and photograms (cameraless photos). Waller currently lives in Colorado. She hosts a college radio show called *The Violet Hour*, assembles history exhibitions for the Colorado LGBT History Project, is part of the Denver Silent Film Festival, and is a member of the Secret Love Art Collective. She is an expert on Kansas LGBT+ history.

 # PLACES

The Equality House *(Topeka, KS)* was founded in March 2013. Planting Peace (see entry under Queer Facts) purchased the house across the street from the notorious anti-LGBT+ Westboro Baptist Church. The exterior of the house was painted the colors of the rainbow flag by veteran Mike McKessor. The building was initially used as housing for Planting Peace volunteers. In 2017, the house became the organization's main office, and serves as a community center, hosting a variety of LGBT-friendly events, including drag shows, fundraisers, open houses, and weddings. In October 2016, the house was vandalized with graffiti and was shot at. Planting Peace did not remove or repair the vandalism, and it is now displayed as part of the house.

The State Hotel *(Kansas City, KS)* hosted the first national meeting of LGBT+ rights activists in February 1966. Three years before the Stonewall riots, the North American Conference of Homophile Organizations (NACHO) held a two-day conference at the hotel. The event was peaceful, so it didn't gain the national attention that Stonewall did. The hotel no longer exists, but in honor of this historic event, Kansas City placed a bronze historical marker at the hotel's former location in 2016.

Transgender House *(Topeka, KS)* is also run by Planting Peace and opened in June 2016. It neighbors the Westboro Baptist Church and the Equality House. Community members got the idea for the house after the Equality House was painted the colors of the Transgender Flag each year for Trans Day of Remembrance. An eight-year-old transgender girl named Avery Jackson spearheaded the fundraising efforts, and the organization was able to purchase the house as a permanent landmark for transgender people. Avery Jackson also became well-known after her mother made a viral video about the joys of raising a transgender child.

QUEER FACTS

Crossroads, Michigan's first transgender organization, was founded in 1977 by Grace Beacon and was originally intended for crossdressers. Crossroads was a transgender peer and social support group with chapters in Flint and Detroit, and was one of the first of its kind in the country.

East Lansing's nondiscrimination ordinance passed in March 1972, making the city the first in the US to ban LGBT+ hiring discrimination. A group of university students known as the Gay Liberation Movement campaigned for further protections after the ordinance was passed, including more rights for gay citizens in housing, employment, and public services. This set Michigan apart from the rest of the nation, which had yet to put forward such measures.

General Motors publicly apologized in 1990 for an official video made for GM employees in which a man referred to non-US-made vehicles as "little faggot trucks." Outcry from the San Francisco Board of Supervisors caused the automobile manufacturer to apologize and remove the phrase from the video after stating that an outside company filmed the video.

Hotter Than July, an annual Detroit event, is the oldest black Pride event in the Midwest. It was founded in 1996 by Kevin Griffin, Johnny Jenkins Jr., and Curtis Lipscomb, all members of Detroit Black Gay, Inc. Now, Detroit Black Pride Society and LGBT Detroit collaboratively host the festival and showcase a wide variety of events, including a candlelight vigil, an art show, a jazz brunch, a film festival, live music and entertainment, and a parade along the Detroit River.

The Michigan Gay Rodeo Association (MIGRA), a nonprofit founded in 1994 by the owner of Diamond Jim Bar, hosts charity rodeo competitions, including the Greater Motown International Rodeo, an amateur gay rodeo. The rodeo, which is also open to allies, is designed to raise money for local charities such as the Southeast Michigan Food Gleaners, the Ruth Ellis Center, and the Mr. Friendly Project.

The Michigan Womyn's Music Festival (MWMF) was a famous and highly controversial festival held in Oceana, Michigan, from 1967 to 2015. The MWMF was initially started by sisters Lisa and Kristie Vogel, along with their friend Mary Kindig, as a music and camping festival run completely by women. Throughout the years, the festival hosted many feminist and lesbian performers such as Tracy Chapman, Indigo Girls, Tribe 8, and Team Dresch. However, a series of increasingly extreme prohibitions caused huge schisms within the MWMF community. In 1990, the festival organizers issued a statement banning S&M, and in 1991, transgender festival-goer Nancy Burkholder was asked to leave the festival, citing a policy of including only "women-born-women." The MWMF leaders defended the decision to kick out Burkholder and declared MWMF a space for only cis women following this incident, which led to a boycott from a variety of LGBT+ organizations, including GLAAD, HRC, the National LGBTQ Taskforce, and the National Center for Lesbian Rights.

The Radicalesbians was an early feminist activist and consciousness-raising group founded in Ann Arbor by University of Michigan students in the 1970s. Members included academics Marilyn Frye and Gayle Rubin, who authored many popular early feminist texts and founded the Ann Arbor feminist bookstore the Book Co-Op. The Radicalesbians' collectively written

University of Michigan–Ann Arbor

The Woman-Identified Woman challenged people to reconsider their conceptions of lesbianism. This paper was presented at the opening session of the Second Congress to Unite Women in 1970 and helped shape future activism.

Scott Amedure's *The Jenny Jones Show* appearance in 1995—during which he confessed a crush on one of his male acquaintances, Jonathan Schmitz—eventually made national news. The segment never aired, because three days after its taping, a drunken Schmitz shot and killed Amedure at Lake Orion. Schmitz was initially found guilty of murder in 1996, but the case was overturned and re-tried in 1999. Schmitz was found guilty of the same verdict and was sentenced to twenty-five to fifty years in prison; he was released in 2017.

Who Wants Cake? is an LGBT+ theater troupe in Detroit that has operated out of the Ringwald Theater since May 2007. It was named the 2008 and 2009 "Best Theatre Group" in Channel 4's Vote 4 the Best contest, and has won "Best Theatrical Ensemble" multiple times from *Real Detroit Weekly*'s Best of Detroit. The group's name was inspired by an episode of Comedy Central's *Strangers with Candy* series, starring Amy Sedaris.

The Ruth Ellis Center *(Highland Park, MI)* is an LGBT+ space for homeless youth. The center—founded by Ruth Ellis, a Black lesbian—is one of the largest in the nation. It provides short- and long-term housing for LGBT+ youth in foster care or the juvenile justice system, as well as HIV prevention and education services, counseling, trauma-informed health care, and more.

Saugatuck and Douglas, Michigan, have become popular destinations for gay vacations. Sometimes referred to as the "Fire Island of the Midwest," Saugatuck housed a private nude beach in the 1800s, where gay men would gather, shaping Saugatuck's gay-friendly reputation. To continue the foundation of an LGBT-friendly community, the Art Institute of Chicago's summer program, Ox-Bow, brought in artists and creatives in 1910 and later established a residency program in the area. The two towns are now home to more than 140 gay-owned businesses.

Transgender Michigan *(Ferndale, MI)* advocates on behalf of transgender people by creating coalitions that "unify and empower" the community. It also hosts the Transgender Michigan Help Line, a 24/7-access line for those who need support. Although it is headquartered in Ferndale, Transgender Michigan has statewide chapters in areas such as Kalamazoo, Jackson, Lansing, Traverse City, and more.

Saugatuck, Michigan

MINNESOTA

◉ PEOPLE

Ann Bancroft *(Mendota Heights, MN)*, in the 1986 Steger International Polar Expedition, was the first woman to travel from Canada to the North Pole over ice. She made the journey via dogsled, with seven male colleagues and forty-nine male dogs. In 1993, Bancroft became the first woman to travel to both the North and South Poles over ice when she led the American Women's Expedition on a 660-mile ski journey to the South Pole. In 2001, Bancroft and explorer Liv Arnesen, via sailing and skiing, became the first women to cross Antarctica. Between her expeditions, Bancroft was a special education teacher in the Twin Cities, and has worked with the Special Olympics, the Learning Disabilities Association, Wilderness Inquiry, and the Girl Scouts, amongst others. Bancroft, who is openly gay, spearheads the Ann Bancroft Foundation.

David Bromstad *(Cokato, MN)* is an interior designer, most known for his work with HGTV. A graduate of the Ringling School of Art and Design, Bromstad began his career at Disney Destinations and Universal Studios. He won the first season of *HGTV Design Star* in 2006, and returned to host the series in 2012. Bromstad has hosted the HGTV series *Color Splash*, *DIY Insider*, and *My Lottery Dream Home*, and owns his own namesake design firm.

William Brandon Lacy Campos *(Duluth, MN)* was a writer and activist. Campos was a codirector of Queers for Economic Justice, and served on the board of the Audre Lorde Project. An avid poet, Campos hosted the Naked Poetry series on YouTube. His collection *It Ain't Truth if it Doesn't Hurt* was published in 2011. Campos, who was HIV positive, also ran a blog called *Queer, Poz and Colored: The Essentials*. He was also a model and spokesperson for Volttage.com, a dating site for people with HIV. Campos died in 2012 at the age of thirty-five.

James Chalgren *(Mankato, MN)* was the founder and former director of the Alternative Lifestyles office at Minnesota State University in Mankato (now known as the Jim Chalgren LGBT Center). When he opened the

> " Gay people have special needs and concerns which most cannot afford to share with the straight community. For the most part, straight community service agencies have no background, knowledge, or skills with gay issues. Gay people have reported negative treatment at straight agencies. Gay people within the agencies themselves must remain hidden to retain their jobs.
>
> —James Chalgren, 1977; *Land of 10,000 Loves*, Stewart Van Cleve, 2012 "

office in 1977, it was Minnesota's first LGBT+ resource and community center, and the second LGBT+ resource center in the country. In 1985, he went on to cofound the Aliveness Project for those living with HIV/AIDS. Two years later, Chalgren started a grassroots movement to advocate for a nondiscrimination ordinance in Mankato after two gay men were murdered nearby, though it did not pass. His writings have been published in *Lavender Magazine,* the *GLC Voice,* and *Gaze,* amongst others. Chalgren died of liver failure in 2000 at age forty-eight, and Minnesota State University created the Jim Chalgren Award in his honor, for faculty who make significant contributions to LGBT+ rights.

Margaret Chutich *(Anoka, MN)* is a lawyer and judge with expertise in employment discrimination, environmental law, and labor law. From 2011 to 2016, she served as a judge on the Minnesota Court of Appeals, and was appointed in 2016 by Governor Mark Dayton as a Minnesota Supreme Court justice. She was the first openly gay or lesbian person to serve on the Minnesota Supreme Court. She is a former director for the YWCA in Minneapolis, former assistant dean of the University of Minnesota's Humphrey School of Public Affairs, and is a member of the Advisory Council for the Advocates for Human Rights.

Margaret Chutich

Margaret Cruikshank *(Duluth, MN)* is an academic and lesbian feminist writer. Cruikshank has published numerous anthologies of writing by lesbian authors, including 1982's *Lesbian Studies: Present and Future* and 1984's *New Lesbian Writing.* She has taught at a number of different schools, including City College in San Francisco and the University of Maine. She is now an associate of the University of Maine's Center on Aging, and her book *Learning to be Old: Gender, Culture, and Aging* discusses the politicization and taboos around the topic.

Tori Fixx *(Minneapolis, MN),* one of the first hip-hop musicians, started as a DJ in the mid-1990s when he performed at parties for Prince at Paisley Park in Chanhassen, Minnesota. In addition to joining the hip-hop group Rainbow Flava, Fixx released seven solo albums between 1998 and 2008. Sometimes referred to as the "godfather of gay rap," Fixx's music represented the LGBT+ community in a genre known for homophobia.

James Hormel *(Austin, MN)* was the first LGBT+ person to serve as a US Ambassador. President Bill Clinton appointed Hormel as the US Ambassador to Luxembourg in 1999. Conservative senators and Christian groups opposed his appointment, calling him pro-pornography and anti-Catholic, and claiming those traits would impede his work in the deeply Catholic Luxembourg. Luxembourg officials responded by publicly welcoming Hormel. Hormel has worked as an LGBT+ advocate through the UN's Human Rights Commission, the Democratic National Convention, the AIDS Emergency Fund, and the San Francisco AIDS Foundation. Hormel, a vegetarian, is an heir to Hormel

Deli Meats; he serves as the chairman of Equidex, Inc., Hormel's investment and philanthropic organization.

Chi Chi LaRue (Larry David Paciotti) *(Hibbing, MN)* is a drag queen and adult filmmaker. Adult material fascinated LaRue from an early age, when he stole lewd magazines, threw them in a swamp out of shame, and then dug them out to preserve them. When he was older, he started performing in drag as Chi Chi LaRue at gay clubs as half of the duo the Weather Gals. LaRue then moved to Los Angeles to work as a sales representative in the adult film industry before becoming a director. In 1988, his directorial debut was *FLEXX.* Since then, LaRue has gone on to direct over four hundred films, such as *Total Corruption*, *Fly Bi Night,* and *Wrong Side of the Tracks.* A vocal advocate of safe sex, LaRue is the subject of the 2001 documentary *Sex Becomes Her: The True Life Story of Chi Chi LaRue.*

Prince Rogers Nelson *(Minneapolis, MN)* was a musician and performer. When he was nineteen, in 1978, he released his first album, *For You.* His second, *I Wanna Be Your Lover* (1980), reached number eleven on the Billboard 100 list. Over his career, he released many hits such as "Little Red Corvette," "When Doves Cry," and "Purple Rain," the title track of the soundtrack of the movie of the same name. An uncontainable and prolific

Prince

> *Aboriginal people have recognized those who possess the sacred gifts of the female-male spirit, which exists in harmony with those of the female and the male. They have traditional, respected roles within most Aboriginal cultures and societies and are contributing members of the community. Today, some Aboriginal people who are two-spirit also identify as being gay, lesbian, bisexual or transgender.*
>
> —Richard LaFortune, interview with Crisosto Apache, LGBTQ Issues' Racial Equity Campaign

musician, Prince notably coined what became known in music as the "Minneapolis sound," and assembled a wave of local funk bands including the Time, Vanity 6, and the Revolution. Though Prince's romantic relationships were only publicly linked to women, his flamboyant stage costumes and sexually liberated lyrics built his reputation as a gender-bending icon. In 1987, he opened his recording studio, Paisley Park, in Chanhassen, Minnesota. He died there in 2016 at the age of fifty-seven.

Hieu Minh Nguyen *(St. Paul, MN)* is a queer Vietnamese American poet. Nguyen's collections *Not Here* (2018) and *This Way to the Sugar* (2014) have garnered him recognition as a finalist for the Lambda Literary Award and the Minnesota Book Awards. His poetry and writing have been published by *Poetry* magazine, *Buzzfeed*, the *Indiana Review*, and more. Nguyen is a 2018 recipient of the Poetry Foundation's Ruth Lily and Dorothy Sargent Rosenberg Poetry Fellowship.

Danez Smith *(St. Paul, MN)* is a Black, queer poet and cohost of the *VS* podcast from the Poetry Foundation. Many award-winning works include the chapbook *hands on ya knees* (2013); *[insert] Boy* (2014), which won the Lambda Literary Award and the Kate Tufts Discovery Award; and *Don't Call Us Dead* (2017), a National Book Award finalist. Smith has received fellowships from places such as Cave Canem, Voices of Our Nation, and the McKnight Foundation. Smith is open about their HIV-positive status in their work, which has been featured in publications such as the *New York Times*, *Best American Poetry*, and *Ploughshares*.

Joseph Steffan *(Warren, MN)* is a lawyer and gay activist. While attending the US Naval Academy in Annapolis, he was expelled shortly before graduating because he had come out as gay to his fellow cadets. Steffan sued the US Department of Defense to be reinstated in the navy, claiming that his declaration of homosexuality was not enough to prove he had actually had a homosexual relationship. The Defense Department never reinstated him. However, in 1993, the court ordered the US Naval Academy to grant Steffan his diploma, stating the military could not discriminate against people on the basis of their sexual orientation (although Don't Ask, Don't Tell followed that ruling in 1994.) Steffan wrote about his experience in his 1992 memoir *Honor Bound: A Gay American Fights for the Right to Serve*. He went on to graduate law school at the University of Connecticut, where he led an initiative to ban military recruitment on campus.

Jacob Reitan *(Mankato, MN)* is the founder of the Soulforce Equality Ride. While in high school, he founded the Gay/Straight Alliance Club, and went on to attend Harvard Divinity School and the University of Minnesota School of Law. In 2006, he partnered with Soulforce to create the Equality Ride, a bus tour of colleges with homophobic and transphobic policies, with the intent to advocate for LGBT+ equality. In 2006, Reitan also started the Right to Serve campaign, which encouraged LGBT+ youth to protest the military's Don't Ask, Don't Tell policy. In 2006, *The Advocate* listed Reitan among its People of the Year, and *Out* magazine included Reitan on its OUT100 list.

PLACES

The Bridge for Youth (*Minneapolis, MN*) finds shelter for runaway and homeless youth. It began as an initiative of Sister Rita Steinhagen in 1970, when it first offered shelter only to girls. It later expanded its services to everyone. The Bridge for Youth helped found MARYS, a key supporter of the National Runaway and Homeless Youth Act. The Bridge for Youth works to improve relationships between youth and their families through counseling, operates a crisis shelter, hosts a twenty-four-hour call and text hotline, rents housing to formerly homeless minors, and provides many other services. The Bridge for Youth runs a weekly support group for LGBT+ teens called *So What If I Am.*

Indigenous Peoples Task Force (IPTF) (*Minneapolis, MN*) is an HIV education and service organization for Minnesota's Native American community. Founded in 1987, it seeks to prevent HIV and to deliver treatment to Native Americans living with HIV/AIDS. It also provides housing and case management services, and integrates traditional healing methods into its programs.

The Jean-Nickolaus Tretter Collection in Gay, Lesbian, Bisexual and Transgender Studies (*Minneapolis, MN*) is a collection of LGBT+ materials housed at the University of Minnesota's Elmer L. Andersen Library. It contains files from Michael McConnell, records from the Minnesota AIDS Project, and a large two-spirit collection. Materials in the library represent over fifty-eight languages. The collection is also home to the Transgender Oral History Project, and has won a national Diversity Award from the Society of American Archivists.

Just Us Health (*St. Paul, MN*) became an LGBT+ health care organization in 2018 with the merger of the Minnesota AIDS Project and the Rainbow Health Initiative. Physicians and health advocates from Minnesota founded the Rainbow Health Initiative in 2001 to expand the conversation around LGBT+ health care beyond HIV/AIDS. In 2016, RHI was a finalist for the Bush Foundation's Prize for Community Innovation.

OutFront Minnesota (*Minneapolis, MN*), an LGBT+ equality organization, has lobbied for key pieces of LGBT+ rights legislation, such as the 1993 nondiscrimination amendments to the Minnesota Human Rights Act. OutFront's many initiatives include the Anti-Violence Program, Legal & Trans Justice, and LGBT+ equity training for workplaces.

Pride Institute (*Eden Prairie, Minneapolis, and Rochester, MN*) is a health center that provides mental health services and substance abuse treatment. Founded in 1986, the institute does not serve LGBT+ people exclusively, but it makes competence in LGBT+ care a priority, and the majority of its clients are LGBT+ people. Pride Institute offers both inpatient and outpatient services.

Quatrefoil Library (*Minneapolis, MN*) maintains and protects materials related to LGBT+ culture and history. In the mid-1970s, David Irwin and Dick Hewetson founded the library, which they named after James Barr's book *Quatrefoil,* one of the first books to positively depict homosexuality. Irwin and Hewetson collected so many books that they could no longer personally store them. Matthew Stark, then the executive director of the Minnesota Civil Liberties Union, invited the Quatrefoil Library to the MCLU's new building, and they began publicly lending books for the first time. The library grew until it had to move again, and in 1987 it found its new home at the Richards Gordon School in St. Paul. In 2013, it relocated to the Spirit on Lake Building in South Minneapolis. The library contains magazines, newspapers, newsletters, sound recordings, over one thousand DVDs, and over ten thousand books.

RECLAIM (*St. Paul, MN*) increases access to mental health support so that queer and trans youth (ages twelve to twenty-six) can reclaim their lives from oppression in all of its forms. RECLAIM provides individual and group therapy to youth and families, develops gender-competent IPOC practitioners, and partners in community through training and education at the intersection of gender and racial justice. RECLAIM also leads Project CLEAR (Consent Leads to Empowered Affirming Relationships), which supports queer and trans youth (ages eleven to twenty-four) in the Twin Cities to identify, prevent, and heal from sexual violence and unhealthy relationships.

◉ QUEER FACTS

Baker v. Nelson was a 1972 appeal to the US Supreme Court filed by Jack Baker and Michael McConnell when they were refused a marriage license by Hennepin County. The US Supreme Court dismissed the appeal. *Baker v. Nelson* set the precedent for all other states that wanted to legally ban same-sex marriage, until the US Supreme Court overturned its ruling with *Obergefell v. Hodges*.

Bisexual Organizing Project (BOP) is a nonprofit that seeks to build visibility and community among bisexual, pansexual, fluid, and bi+ people in the upper Midwest. In 2012, BOP commissioned the *Bisexual Community Needs Assessment*, which states key ways that organizations should continue meeting the needs of the bisexual community. BOP hosts the annual BECAUSE Conference, which invites bisexual, pansexual, fluid, and bi+ people (and their allies) to attend a variety of workshops around non-monosexual empowerment.

CeCe McDonald was the victim of a 2011 Minneapolis hate crime. One night, McDonald—a Black transgender woman and activist—and friends walked to a grocery store. As they passed a bar, a group of white patrons began shouting slurs, and a woman smashed a glass in McDonald's face, cutting through her salivary gland. McDonald walked away from the confrontation, but soon realized she was being followed by Dean Schmitz, the man who had shouted slurs at her. When Schmitz grabbed her, she stabbed him with a pair of scissors in her bag, ultimately killing him. McDonald faced a murder charge and eighty years in prison. The judge did not find Schmitz's criminal history nor his swastika tattoo relevant, and did not establish his attack as a hate crime. The judge sentenced McDonald to forty-one months in a men's jail for second-degree murder, of which she served nineteen months. McDonald is the subject of the 2013 Laverne Cox documentary *Free CeCe*. In 2014, *The Advocate* named McDonald to its 40 Under 40 list, and the Harvey Milk LGBT Democratic Club awarded her its Bayard Rustin Civil Rights Award.

District 202 was a nonprofit for LGBT+ youth. When it opened in 1993, District 202 offered a community center with a library and an espresso bar. Throughout the 1990s, District 202 grew in popularity, with over twelve thousand office visits in 1997. When the internet began providing a communal space for LGBT+ people, and when high schools began offering more gay/straight alliances, the need for a LGBT+ youth center decreased. As the number of its visitors dwindled, District 202 closed its drop-in center in 2009. It continued to offer programs in the Twin Cities, until in 2012 it became a part of the Family Partnership.

The first bisexual club in the US was Bi Alliance, a University of Minnesota support and community group for bisexuals. Founded in 1967, the club also published a newsletter.

The first Black transgender woman elected to public office was Andrea Jenkins when she was elected to the Minneapolis City Council in 2017. She had previously worked on the campaign of Robert Lilligren and served as an aide to city councilmember Elizabeth Glidden. Jenkins, originally from Chicago, received a 2014 Bush Fellowship, which she used to establish the Transgender Issues Work Group. As an oral historian, Jenkins contributed over two hundred interviews to the Tretter Transgender Oral History Project at the University of Minnesota Libraries.

The first city to pass a transgender nondiscrimination ordinance was Minneapolis. The city's 1975 ordinance banned discrimination on the basis of "having or projecting a self-image not associated with one's biological maleness or one's biological femaleness." The ordinance gave transgender people the legal right to use the bathroom corresponding to their gender identities, as well as protections on the job market, in education, and in housing.

The first International Two Spirit Gathering was hosted by the Minneapolis Native community in 1988. Activist Richard LaFortune was key in organizing

Andrea Jenkins

Phillipe Cunningham

one of the first openly transgender men elected to public office anywhere in the United States. Originally from Illinois, Cunningham went to college at DePaul University and became a special education teacher in Chicago Public Schools. His move to Minneapolis resulted in his mayoral appointee to the Youth Violence Prevention Executive Committee, and his later role as a senior policy aide to Mayor Betsy Hodges.

The first openly gay woman to become CEO of a Fortune 500 company is Beth Ford. Ford became CEO of Land O'Lakes, a Minnesota-based company, in 2018. At the time, she was one of only twenty-five women on the list. Ford was born in Iowa and served as COO of Land O'Lakes before being promoted to CEO. She lives in Minneapolis with her wife and three daughters.

The first openly transgender NCAA Division 1 athlete was Kye Allums, who is also an activist and artist. He came out as transgender in 2010, while attending George Washington University and playing for its women's basketball team. Afterward, he began advocating for the transgender community in speeches at high schools and colleges nationwide. Allums founded the I Am Enough campaign, a platform for LGBT+ people to share their stories and build confidence in their identities. Actor Laverne Cox featured Allums in her 2014 documentary *The T Word.* In 2015, Allums was inducted into the National Gay and Lesbian Sports Hall of Fame. Though he was not born in Minnesota, he grew up there, and graduated from Centennial High School in Circle Pines.

the event, which has since become a recurring celebration that includes a water ceremony, prayer, a pow-wow, and drag performances. The event gives LGBT+ Native Americans a space to affirm the intersections of their identities away from predominantly white LGBT+ spaces such as gay bars and clubs. The International Two Spirit Gathering is a traveling event and has occurred in cities from Tucson to Montreal.

The first major city with two transgender city councilmembers, in 2017, was Minneapolis. Andrea Jenkins was elected to Ward 8, and Phillipe Cunningham was elected to Ward 4. Phillipe Cunningham was

The first same-sex couple to marry was Michael McConnell and Jack Baker. When a Hennepin County clerk denied their application for a marriage license in 1970, they appealed through the Minnesota Supreme Court. The court dismissed their claim, but before it could ban statewide same-sex marriage, McConnell and Baker applied for another marriage license in Blue Earth County. To get the license, McConnell legally adopted Baker so that Baker could change his name to the gender-neutral Pat Lynn McConnell. Michael then applied for the license alone and in person; assuming Pat to be a woman, the Blue Earth County clerk granted the couple a marriage license in 1971. While the National Archives agrees the couple is the first same-sex marriage, others debate the legality of their marriage because it occurred long before Minnesota legalized same-sex marriage in 2013. Baker and McConnell are still married today, and released *The Wedding Heard 'Round the World: America's First Gay Marriage* in 2016.

The first state to reject a same-sex marriage ban was Minnesota. In 2012, the Amendment 1 ballot initiative stated, "Only a union of one man and one woman should be valid or recognized as a marriage in Minnesota." LGBT+ organizations such as Minnesotans United for All Families, OutFront Minnesota, Project 515, and Freedom to Marry drove public opposition to the amendment. Voters struck down the amendment with 51.19 percent of the vote.

Lavender Magazine, a biweekly print and online publication, began in 1995. The free magazine contains articles relevant to the LGBT+ community on a diverse range of subjects, such as style, news, entertainment, and nightlife. *Lavender* also organizes LGBT+ community events. In 2016, the Minnesota Magazine & Publishing Association awarded *Lavender* Magazine of the Year.

The longest-serving LGBT+ state representative was lesbian Karen Clark, who was born in Oklahoma and raised in Rock County, Minnesota. She served the Minnesota legislature from 1980 until her retirement in 2018. During her career, Clark advocated for environmental protection, LGBT+ equality, and human rights protections for illegal immigrants.

The second openly gay player in Major League Soccer is Collin Martin, who was born in Maryland and plays for the Minnesota United. He came out

A scene from the Twin Cities Pride parade

publicly on Twitter in 2018, in line with his team's Pride Night, though he had been openly gay in his personal life long before making the announcement.

The Twin Cities Gay Men's Chorus started in 1981, when it was called the Twin Cities Men's Chorus. In 1991, it changed its name to what it is today. The chorus is the fourth-largest gay men's choir, with over 150 active members. It aims to improve gay visibility, build community, and fight homophobia with a high level of musical integrity. The chorus has released several albums, including *Hand in Hand* (1995), *Angels* (2002), and *The 25th Anniversary Collection* (2006).

Twin Cities Pride is an annual Pride festival at the end of June. The earliest Twin Cities Pride march was organized in 1972 by a group of activists. The first official Gay Pride Parade and Festival happened in 1976, however, as the initiative of Tim Campbell, the editor for the *GLC Voice*.

MISSOURI

⊙ PEOPLE

Josephine Baker

Josephine Baker *(St. Louis, MO)* was a dancer and entertainer. Born into a poor family, Baker babysat white children and waitressed starting around age thirteen. She got her start in showbusiness by touring the US with comedy sketch groups, then began working as a chorus girl. She soon moved to Paris, where she attained celebrity status—and career success—for her personality, style, and poise. She briefly returned to the US in 1936 to film *Ziegfeld Follies,* but American audiences did not give her the same positive reception. After World War II, the French government gave Baker a Medal of Resistance and made her a Chevalier of the Legion of Honor for her work smuggling messages to the resistance and performing for French troops. Baker married four times and adopted twelve children of different nationalities in order to prove that different races could live in harmony. Biographers generally consider Baker to have been bisexual, even though she once drove her own son out of the house when he came out as gay. Baker took many female lovers when she was young, including artist Frida Kahlo and the French writer Colette. An HBO film about her life, *The Josephine Baker Story,* was nominated for five Emmy Awards in 1991.

Danielle Bunten Berry *(St. Louis, MO)* was a transgender computer programmer and game designer. She spent much of her childhood caring for her younger siblings and playing board games with them, experiences she later applied to the video games she designed. Berry predicted video games would become multiplayer at a time when game designers focused on single-player games. While working for Electronic Arts in the 1980s, she designed *M.U.L.E.,* which became a classic video game. Berry's use of modems to create multiplayer gaming experiences opened the door for the multiplayer games common today. She also designed *Seven Cities of Gold,* and though it was not in her signature multiplayer style, it was a huge success because of its user-friendliness. Berry underwent gender-affirming surgery in the early 1990s, a few years before she died of lung cancer in 1998 at forty-nine. Just before her death, the International Game Developers Association awarded Berry a lifetime achievement award for her visionary contributions. The Academy of Interactive Arts and Sciences added her to its Hall of Fame in 2007.

Betty Berzon *(St. Louis, MO)* was a therapist and LGBT+ rights activist. She was closeted for much of her life, and dropped out of Stanford University after another woman made advances towards her. Berzon later started her own bookstore, Berzon Books, in Hollywood. When it closed, she became severely depressed and ended up hospitalized, an experience that led her to study psychology at UCLA. Berzon found success as a therapist, and was instrumental in founding the LA Gay & Lesbian Center, one of the first LGBT+ social service agencies. Berzon also organized the first gathering of gay and lesbian members of the American Psychological Association in 1971 in order to declassify homosexuality as a mental illness, a feat they achieved two years later. Through her activism, Berzon gradually became comfortable with her lesbian identity, and became one of the first openly gay mental health professionals. She authored several LGBT+ self-help books, and penned an autobiography called *Surviving Madness, a Therapist's Own Story,* which won a Lambda Literary Award in 2002. Berzon died of cancer in 2006.

Brian Bond is an LGBT+ and environmental activist. Bond spent six years as the executive director of the Gay and Lesbian Victory Fund, which supports the campaigns of openly LGBT+ political candidates. He worked for the Obama Administration as a deputy director for the White House Office of Public Engagement, then as the associate administrator for public engagement and environmental education at the Environmental Protection Agency. In 2019, Bond became the executive director of PFLAG National, a leading LGBT+ rights organization.

Keith Boykin *(St. Louis, MO)* is a former White House aide for President Bill Clinton. Boykin is a founding member of the National Black Justice Coalition and was also its first board president. In 2006, Boykin co-hosted *My Two Cents* on BET; he has made multiple appearances on news shows such as *CNN Tonight, At This Hour, Erin Burnett OutFront,* and *CNN Newsroom.* He is the author of the book *For Colored Boys Who Have Considered Suicide When the Rainbow is Still Not Enough* (2013), which won the Stonewall Award from the American Library Association.

William S. Burroughs *(St. Louis, MO)* was a Beat writer. Burroughs was raised in an upper-class family, graduated from Harvard, and then moved to New York

to explore its gangster scene on his parents' dollar. There, Burroughs became addicted to heroin and met Allen Ginsberg and Jack Kerouac. After Burroughs married Joan Vollmer Adams, the couple moved to Texas to live on a farm, and then to Mexico after the police pursued Burroughs for his drug use. He wrote his first book, *Junkie* (1953), around this time. During a game, Burroughs shot Adams in the head and killed her. Burroughs said he never would have become a writer if it weren't for the "lifelong struggle" he gained from that incident. He then moved back to the US, where Ginsberg and Kerouac helped publish his first major literary success, *Naked Lunch* (1959). Burroughs had sexual relationships with men throughout his life, though never a long-term relationship. In 1971, he wrote *The Wild Boys,* in which he fantasized about an exclusively male society; his unpublished 1950s novel *Queer* centered on drugs and a same-sex relationship.

George Washington Carver *(Diamond, MO)* was a botanist and writer. Born into slavery during the Civil War, Carver liked spending time in the woods and collecting flowers and rocks, which he said "was considered foolishness . . . to waste time on flowers." As a young adult, Carver worked as a cook to pay for his tuition at Simpson College in Iowa. He went on to become the first Black faculty member of Iowa State

George Washington Carver

Andy Cohen

Agricultural College, where he earned his master's degree. Among Carver's many scientific contributions, he discovered that peanuts had a restorative effect on soil's nutrient content. He also developed over three hundred uses for peanuts, including peanut-based paper and soap. Carver's biographers believe he was bisexual. In 1943, at age seventy-nine, Carver fell down a flight of stairs and died shortly after. He is in the USDA Hall of Heroes, the National Inventors Hall of Fame, and the Hall of Fame for Great Americans. Carver's face is on the US half-dollar coin, and a national monument and national park stand in his honor in Newton County, Missouri.

Andy Cohen *(St. Louis, MO)* is a television host and producer. He is most well known as the host of *The Real Housewives* series on the Bravo network. He also hosts his own show, *Watch What Happens Live with Andy Cohen,* where he plays games and chats with celebrities. Cohen has served as the vice president of Bravo, as well as the network's executive vice president of development and talent. He won a Primetime Emmy in 2010 for the reality show *Top Chef,* and has seventeen total Primetime Emmy nominations. Though many people have openly scrutinized his parenting as a single gay father, Cohen has been quick to shut down all criticism and show the world that single fathers are capable parents.

Masen Davis is an LGBT+ activist. For eight years, Davis was the executive director of the Transgender Law Center, and went on to manage the State Agencies Project at the Gill Foundation, which lobbies for state legislation that supports the LGBT+ community. Davis is a founder of the FTM Alliance of Los Angeles, the first organization specifically for female-to-male transgender people. He also advocated for California's School Success and Opportunity Act, a 2013 bill allowing transgender students to use facilities corresponding to their gender identities. As of 2017, Davis is the CEO of Freedom for All Americans.

Thomas Anthony Dooley III *(St. Louis, MO)* was a Catholic author and doctor. He worked as a medical corpsman in the US Navy during World War II, then enrolled at the St. Louis University School of Medicine. Dooley could not find a residency after graduating because he had been a poor student, so he returned to the Navy. He was soon deployed to Vietnam, where he assisted Operation Passage to Freedom, which relocated people from North Vietnam to South Vietnam. Dooley wrote the book *Deliver Us from Evil* about his experience; it became a popular piece of anticommunist rhetoric and was posthumously revealed to be a propaganda initiative by the CIA. Although the Navy forced Dooley to resign because he was gay, Dooley went on to advocate for international medical missions. He established clinics in Laos, where people called him Thanh Mo America, or Dr. America. Dooley also founded the Medical International Corporation (MEDICO), which funded worldwide medical missions. He died from skin cancer in 1961 at age thirty-four. That year, President Kennedy cited Dooley as one of his inspirations in establishing the Peace Corps.

Melvin Dwork *(Kansas City, MO)* was an interior designer and LGBT+ activist. While serving in the Navy hospital corps, Dwork fell in love with a fellow service member. They wrote letters to each other, but the military intercepted their letters and soon discharged Dwork for homosexuality. He went on to study at the Parsons School of Design in New York, where he found success as an interior designer. After some time working for other designers, he started Melvin Dwork Interiors in 1950. The International Design Hall of Fame inducted Dwork in 1993, the same year his longtime partner passed away. Dwork continually fought his dishonorable discharge from the Navy, with the help of the Servicemembers Legal Defense Network. In 2011, he finally succeeded, and the Board for Correction of Naval Records changed his discharge to honorable. He died in 2016 at age ninety-four.

Leslie Feinberg *(Kansas City, MO)* (pronouns: she/her and zie/hir) is the author of the 1993 LGBT+ classic novel *Stone Butch Blues*. As a young activist, Feinberg helped organize labor, anti-war, and human rights rallies such as the March Against Racism in Boston in 1974. She also worked as a journalist for *Workers World* and edited its Political Prisoners column for fourteen years. Feinberg's other popular writings include *Rainbow Solidarity in Defense of Cuba*, *Trans Liberation: Beyond Pink or Blue*, and *Drag King Dreams*. When Feinberg died in 2014 at age sixty-five from complications with Lyme disease, her last words were, "Remember me as a revolutionary communist."

Langston Hughes *(Joplin, MO)* was a Harlem Renaissance poet and writer. In 1925, Hughes was working as a hotel busboy in Washington, DC, as a young adult when the poet Vachel Lindsay came to stay at the hotel. Hughes slipped some of his poetry into Lindsay's bag. The poems impressed Lindsay, who encouraged Hughes to continue writing. The next year, Hughes attended Columbia University and published his first book of poetry, *The Weary Blues*. He graduated from Lincoln University in 1929, then published his first

Langston Hughes

> *Then it was that books began to happen to me, and I began to believe in nothing but books and the wonderful world of books—where if people suffered, they suffered in beautiful language, not in monosyllables, as we did in Kansas.*

—Langston Hughes, *The Big Sea*, 1940

novel, *Not Without Laughter,* the following year. One of the first Black writers to earn a living solely from his writing, Hughes's writings speak to everyday Black experiences. Some of his writings, such as 1943's *Jim Crow's Last Stand*, influenced civil rights leaders in the 1950s and '60s. Though Hughes was private about his personal life, many of his biographers believe he was gay and/or asexual. Hughes alluded to his attraction to men in his work, including love poems addressed to anonymous men such as "F. S." and "Beauty." Hughes died in 1967 at age sixty-five.

David Jay *(St. Louis, MO)* is the founder of the Asexual and Visibility Education Network (AVEN). Since AVEN's start in 2001, the site has grown to over eighty thousand members and has worked to normalize asexuality to the point where the Diagnostic and Statistical Manual of Mental Disorders no longer classifies it as a disorder. He regularly speaks about the distinction between intimacy and sexuality, and advocates for a society that is more focused on building human connections than it is on sex. Jay has been featured in media outlets such as the *New York Times* and *CNN,* and in the 2011 documentary *(A)Sexual.*

John Kander *(Kansas City, MO)* was a Broadway songwriter and music director. His first role on Broadway in the late 1950s was as a pianist for *West Side Story.* He wrote his first musical, *A Family Affair,* in 1962. Around that time, he met lyricist Fred Ebb, with whom he developed a professional partnership that created

> Sexuality is only one lens to view intimacy, our bodies, power, physical touch, etc. In order to really understand these things, we need to also see them through other lenses and we need to talk openly about our diverse experiences. That is the best way to discover them.
>
> —David Jay, *The Rumpus*, 2011

successful musicals such as *Chicago, Cabaret*, and *Curtains.* The duo's works have won three Tony Awards, two Grammy Awards, an Emmy, a Laurence Olivier Award, and two Oscar nominations.

Michael Kearns (*St. Louis, MO*) is known as one of the first openly gay Hollywood actors. He came to mainstream attention in the 1970s after his boyfriend published a novel called *The Happy Hustler* with Kearns's face on the cover, and suggested that Kearns pose as the real author on his publicity tour. Kearns embraced the role, going so far as to pretend the book was autobiographical and famously showing up drunk to an interview with Tom Snyder. As a television actor, Kearns has appeared in guest roles on shows such as *The Waltons*, *Cheers*, and *Murder, She Wrote.* Kearns, who is HIV positive, is also a theater actor and has worked on many projects related to HIV/AIDS. In 1984, he cofounded Artists Confronting AIDS, which helps artists with HIV/AIDS-related projects.

Rebecca Bauman Kern (*Colombia, MO*) is a grassroots intersex activist who has worked with organizations such as the Intersex Society of North America and InterACT. She is the former president of Androgen Insensitivity Syndrome—Differences of Sex Development, where she was also a member of the executive board. Kern seeks to help intersex people form supportive connections with one another. Through her work, she has granted scholarships to intersex people and effectively fundraised for intersex-supporting organizations.

John McDaniel (*St. Louis, MO*) is a Broadway producer and composer. McDaniel is most known for leading the live band and writing the theme song for the late 1990s/early 2000s *The Rosie O'Donnell Show,* for which he was music director for six years. His work on the show earned him several Daytime Emmy nominations. McDaniel was the musical director for the 1994 theater production of *Grease!*, where he met Rosie O'Donnell, who played Rizzo. His other various Broadway credits for producing, arranging, conducting, and more include shows such as *Annie Get Your Gun, Chicago*, and *Brooklyn: The Musical.*

Thomas Morgan III (*St. Louis, MO*) was a journalist and editor. A 1973 journalism graduate of the University of Missouri, he served in the US Air Force and went on to write for publications such as the *Miami Herald*, the *Washington Post,* and the *New York Times.* He also worked as a White House aide for presidents Nixon and Ford. Morgan was the treasurer of the National Association of Black Journalists for six years starting in 1983, and in his time more than quadrupled its membership and increased its assets from $50,000 to $1 million. In 1989, he became the first gay president of the National Association of Black Journalists, but it wasn't until 2005 that he established its Lesbian, Gay, Bisexual, and Transgender Task Force and started its Ethel Payne Fellowship for Black journalists to visit and report on Africa. In 1995, the National Association of Black Journalists awarded Morgan a lifetime achievement award, and in 2005 he was inducted into the National Lesbian and Gay Journalists Association Hall of Fame. Morgan died at age fifty-six in 2007 due to AIDS-related illness.

Steven Reigns (*St. Louis, MO*) is a teacher, poet, and therapist. With degrees in both creative writing and psychology, he has taught writing workshops to LGBT+ teens, seniors, and those living with HIV/AIDS. The first poet laureate of West Hollywood, Reigns has received fourteen Artist in Residency grants from the Los Angeles County Department of Cultural Affairs. *The Advocate* named Reigns on its 2015 People to Watch list. Reigns works as a therapist in Los Angeles, where he specializes in marriage and family counseling,

> *Heterogeneity in decision-making and problem-solving groups potentially produces better decisions through a wider range of perspectives and more thorough critical analysis of issues. News organizations that continue to rely on the old chestnut that they can't find talented minorities to work for them need to engage in some honest soul-searching to find the reasons why. The truth is, the best talent is going to those news organizations or industries that reward and promote them.*
>
> —Thomas Morgan III, "The Bottom Line: The Economic Case for Diversity," *Kerner Plus 25: A Call for Action*, 1993

addiction therapy, sexual issues and sexual orientation, and therapy for clients dealing with HIV/AIDS. His current project, the Gay Rub, collects rubbings from LGBT+ historical markers, signs, tombstones, cenotaphs, plaques, and monuments.

Ted Shawn *(Kansas City, MO)* was a founding father of modern dance. Shawn originally studied to be a minister, but he fell ill and became physically paralyzed. He began to dance in order to recover, and in doing so found his passion. After marrying Ruth St. Denis in 1914, the two began Denishawn Company and School, one of the first modern dance schools. Denishawn trained many influential dancers, such as Martha Graham and Charles Weidman, but the company dissolved when the couple separated in 1930. Shawn soon started his own dance company, Ted Shawn and His Men Dancers, which trained out of a farm called Jacob's Pillow. In 1941, Shawn started the Jacob's Pillow Dance Festival and continued training dancers at the farm. Later in life, Shawn became more open about his homosexuality, and developed correspondences about it with people such as Dr. Alfred Kinsey and the poet Edward Carpenter. Shawn died in 1972 at age eighty.

Helen Stephens *(Fulton, MO)* was an Olympic sprinter. Although Stephens's schools did not offer athletic teams for girls, her physical education teacher, W. Burton Moore, saw her potential and agreed to train her. When Stephens was sixteen, Moore took her to St. Louis to compete against Stella Walsh, a 1932

Helen Stephens

Olympic gold medalist; Stephens beat Walsh's time with a 6.6-second fifty-meter dash. In the 1936 Berlin Olympics, Stephens took home two gold medals. The first was for an 11.5-second hundred-meter sprint, which set the world record for the next twenty-four years. Stephens set another world record with her second gold medal, for which her team won the 400-meter relay race in 46.9 seconds. Stephens, a lesbian, famously turned down a sexual advance from Adolf Hitler during the Berlin Olympics. Later, Stephens became the first woman to start her own semi-professional basketball team. She competed in the Senior Olympics multiple times, and at age sixty-eight, she could run a hundred-meter dash only four seconds slower than her time at eighteen years old. The 2004 biography *The Fulton Flash: The Life of Helen Stephens*, by Sharon Kinney Hanson, details her life story.

Nick Verreos *(St. Louis, MO)* is a fashion designer. He was a contestant on season two of *Project Runway.* He founded his own fashion label, NIKOLAKI, alongside David Paul in 2001. Verreos and Paul became cochairs of Los Angeles's Fashion Institute of Design & Merchandising in 2018. Verreos is the author of 2016's *Passion for Fashion: Achieving Your Fashion Dreams One Thread at a Time,* which offers business advice for young designers aspiring to start their own fashion lines.

Chely Wright *(Kansas City, MO)* is a country singer. She sang throughout her childhood, and in her senior year of high school, Wright performed at the Ozark Jubilee in Branson, Missouri. Wright signed to the Mercury/Polygram label in 1993, and landed her first top 40 hit, "Shut Up and Drive," in 1997. Over her career, Wright has won a number of awards, including Top New Female Vocalist from the Academy of Country Music and the Vanguard Award at the OUTmusic Awards. In Wright's 2010 memoir, *Like Me*, she said she knew she was a lesbian since she was nine, but that she felt immense pressure to hide it, and once almost died by suicide. She came out in order to show other LGBT+ people they do not need to live in shame. She was one of the first openly gay country music stars with national fame.

 # PLACES

Clementine's *(St. Louis, MO)* was once one of Missouri's longest-running gay bars. Located at 2001 Menard Street, it opened in 1978 and welcomed all subcultures of the LGBT+ community. Though other St. Louis gay bars predated Clementine's, it was one of the first to be open about its identity during a time when many gay bars operated discreetly. Clementine's was proud of the community it served, and even had the ashes

The Grove

of a drag queen, Midnight Annie, placed inside of its walls. When Clementine's closed in 2014, the Missouri History Museum, in partnership with the LGBT History Project, preserved key artifacts from the bar.

The Grove *(St. Louis, MO)* is a neighborhood home to many LGBT+ owned businesses. In the 1950s, locals knew the area as Adams Grove, a commercial neighborhood. The rise of more LGBT+ businesses in the 1980s, such as Attitudes Night Club, transformed the Grove from merely a business district to a lively entertainment district. Today, it is home to many cafes, clubs, and tattoo shops.

JJ's Clubhouse *(St. Louis, MO)* is a bear and leather bar. Operating since 2000, it hosts the annual Mr. Midwest Leather Competition and is also home to the group Show Me Bears, a gay men's group whose yearly Hibearnation community event draws more than five hundred visitors. In 2019, the owners of JJ's Clubhouse put the bar up for sale, as the surrounding neighborhood continued to see LGBT+ venues close in favor of more mainstream establishments.

Naiad Press *(Weatherby Lake, MO)* is one of the oldest and largest publishers of lesbian literature. Couple Barbara Grier and Donna McBride founded the press in 1973 with $2,000. They each worked a day job for almost ten years before they were able to take salaries from the press. In 1983, Naiad Press sold more than four hundred thousand copies of its biggest commercial success yet, *Curious Wine* by Katherine Forrest. The

QUEER FACTS

#BOOM is an LGBT+ magazine. Since 2014, *#BOOM* reports on local and national politics, advocacy, and community issues. In 2016, it received a Missouri Award for Excellence for its coverage of the Miss Gay Missouri America pageant.

The first transgender person on the cover of *National Geographic* was nine-year-old Avery Jackson of Kansas City, Missouri. Avery began her transition when she was four years old. "I don't care if I'm transgender. I'm just out there, a normal human being changing the world," she said. Her mother, Debi, runs the website Trans-Parenting.com, which encourages parents to remain open about their children's gender identities. It provides information about medical, mental health, and school resources for trans children.

Queer Eye, a Netflix show that debuted in 2018, centered its second season in Missouri. The rebooted show has been lauded for its dedication to serving people in rural Southern towns, converse to the New York City–based original series in the early 2000s. Fab Five member Bobby Berk, though born in Texas, was raised in Mount Vernon, Missouri.

QFest St. Louis is an annual film queer film festival held by Cinema St. Louis since 2010. Typically held in April and early May at the Tivoli Theatre, the festival shows a mix of classic and contemporary films with LGBT+ themes, such as the queer Japanese New Wave classic *Funeral Parade of Roses* (1970) or *Tucked* (2018).

The St. Louis LGBT History Project is an ongoing initiative to preserve materials related to the LGBT+ history of St. Louis. It began in 2007 as a blog by Steven L. Brawley, and grew as the community contributed to the project. The project contributes to the collections of Washington University, the Missouri History Museum, and the State Historical Society of Missouri.

Vital VOICE is Missouri's premier LGBT+ magazine. Jim Thomas began the magazine in 1981 at Pride St. Louis as an eight-page newsletter. At the time, the staff published the paper under the title *Gay News Telegraph,* which later changed to *Lesbian and Gay News Telegraph.* It covered political issues and advances in activism along with arts and culture pieces. In 2000, under new ownership, the name changed to what it is today. *Vital VOICE* was sold again in 2009 and was given a lighter tone and expanded distribution. It is now a glossy publication that includes entertainment, art, op-ed, and political writing.

The world's oldest drag queen is Bonnie Blake, according to the St. Louis LGBT History Project's research. Blake turned ninety in 2018. Before moving to St. Louis as a teenager, Blake began borrowing his sister's dresses when he was around six years old. Blake is a Korean War veteran and earned a Purple Heart in 1951. He runs and lives above an antique shop in St. Louis called John's Furniture and Antiques. Other drag queens credit Blake as paving their way, as he began performing in drag at a time when men could be arrested for wearing women's clothing.

press later relocated to Tallahassee, Florida, and in 2003 Grier and McBride sold it to Bella Books.

PrideCenter *(St. Louis, MO)* hosts the city's annual Pride festival. First held in 1980, Pride St. Louis includes nightlife events such as the Big Gay Soiree, as well as family-friendly activities at the St. Louis City Museum or the parade. PrideCenter, located on Chouteau Avenue, is a registered LGBT+ safe space and con-

dom distribution site. It hosts a cyber center to offer internet access to those who need it for homework and job applications, and also offers a lending library of LGBT+ materials.

Shameless Grounds *(St. Louis, MO)* is a sex-positive cafe and library. Shameless Grounds calls itself a "radically inclusive" atmosphere where members of the LGBT+ community are free to meet and mingle. It has

A scene from Pride St. Louis

spaces to host workshops and meetings, as well as a sex-positive library containing materials that are philosophical, political, historical, medically informative, and raunchy, including many LGBT+ titles. Shameless Grounds also hosts Queer Caucus, a monthly LGBT+ discussion group.

Tennessee Williams's homes are both located in St. Louis, where he grew up. Though Williams was born in Mississippi, his father took a job as a shoe salesman in St. Louis, and the family first lived in an apartment on Westminster Place. That apartment was the setting for Williams's autobiographical play *The Glass Menagerie*. During his teenage years, the family moved to another home on Enright Avenue.

The Transgender Institute *(Kansas City, MO)* provides therapy services to people going through gender transition. It offers standard therapy, vocal feminization and masculinization services, mentoring, life coaching, and fellowships for graduate students. The Transgender Institute was founded by the counselor Caroline Gibbs.

QUEER FACTS

The 1997 wedding of a lesbian couple in Omaha resulted in the defrocking of the United Methodist minister who wed them. Jimmy Creech, the minister, was tried by the church. Although he was eventually acquitted, he was asked to leave Omaha. Creech went to North Carolina, where, in 1999, he performed a wedding ceremony for another gay couple and the church withdrew his credentials of ordination. Although Creech is straight, he has continued dedicating his career to combine faith and the LGBT+ community by working for SoulForce, creating Faith in America, and helping to create the Dallas Principles.

Driskell v. Homosexuals was a 2015 case in which Sylvia Driskell, a sixty-six-year-old Nebraska resident, sued all homosexuals in the world. In her seven-page handwritten letter, Driskell asked the judge to rule on whether homosexuality is a sin. She chose to represent herself, citing no legal precedent and instead quoting from the Bible and Webster's dictionary. The case drew a lot of media attention but was dismissed entirely by the judge, who cited its inappropriateness for the courts.

Gay Freedom was a newsletter created by the Omaha Gay Freedom League in 1972. The newsletter included comics, editorial letters, current LGBT+ events and groups, political updates, calls to action, legal ads, and more. Read this excerpt from the first issue: "We have a lot of work to do—changing laws, opening minds, providing services, growing, having fun, and fighting sexism in every form! But, as our treasurer said at an early OGFL meeting, we'll have a lot working for us with the gay community on our side. Gay is free! Gay is good! Join us!"

The Imperial Court of Nebraska (ICON) is a drag competition that began in 1980. A member of the International Court System network, ICON elects its own Emperor and Empress each year. ICON also sponsors a scholarship, maintains archives with the UNO library system's Queer Archive, and raises money for various funds. ICON has raised over $1 million for various charities.

Meredith Bacon was the first out transgender professor at the University of Nebraska–Omaha, and the first known transgender person to be elected to a university faculty position in the US. She has served three terms as the Faculty Senate president. Dr. Bacon, originally from New York, has also worked with the Nebraska AIDS Project and the National Center for Transgender Equality. UNO offers the Dr. Meredith Bacon Lavender Maverick Award to those who contribute to LGBT+ causes.

The Nebraska AIDS Project (NAP), founded in 1984, is a health promotion and education organization that grew out of the HIV/AIDS crisis. It is the only local AIDS organization in the state and also supports parts of Iowa and Wyoming. Its work includes HIV testing, public education, support groups, legal assistance, social/caseworker support, and crisis assistance.

Nebraska repealed its sodomy law in 1977. At this time, many states were removing their sodomy laws in a wave of changing criminal codes, but Nebraska's legal change was more dramatic than most. The governor immediately vetoed the change, but the legislature then voted to override the governor's veto with exactly two thirds of the vote. The sodomy laws were officially repealed in 1978.

Queer People of Color (QPOC) Nebraska provides a community and role models for queer youth of color. The organization was founded by Dominique Morgan (a musician) and Jakeen Fox. QPOC Nebraska is open to anyone supportive of its mission. In 2017, the group cohosted a Youth Diversity Leadership Summit. It also plans various social events.

Ryan Grigsby and Jaron Luttich made national news in 2000 when *Rolling Stone* published an article about them being gay fraternity members at the University of Nebraska–Lincoln. Grigsby was a senior in Sigma Nu and Luttich was a junior in Chi Pi. While the article ("Coming Out on Fraternity Row") meant to put a positive spin on Grigsby's identity, the *Daily*

Nebraskan ran a follow-up piece describing the teasing Grigsby faced from his fraternity brothers, and how no one in the fraternity was allowed to comment on the original piece.

Star City Pride is one of the largest Pride events in Nebraska. Founded in 2006, the nonprofit's annual two-day event includes a pageant, live music, food, and family-friendly activities. Star City Pride also hosts a golf tournament, a volleyball tournament, dinners, and fundraising events.

Stewart v. Heineman ruled that same-sex parents could adopt children. Since 1995, the Nebraska Department of Health and Human Services had a policy preventing same-sex couples from fostering or adopting children. In 2015, *Stewart v. Heineman* made its way to the district judge, who ruled that sexual orientation could not be used to prevent otherwise qualified people from fostering. The State of Nebraska appealed this ruling, but in 2017 the Supreme Court reaffirmed the original ruling.

NORTH DAKOTA

PEOPLE

Jennifer Baumgardner

Jennifer Baumgardner *(Fargo, ND)* is a feminist activist. Much of her activism has been on the grassroots level, and has tackled destigmatizing conversations around abortion and rape. Her 2004 "I Had an Abortion" project involved wearing a T-shirt with that slogan printed on it; feminists such as Gloria Steinem wore the shirts while discussing their own experiences having abortions. In 2008, her "It Was Rape" project followed the same model. Baumgardner is the author of several books, including *Look Both Ways: Bisexual Politics* (2007) and *Abortion & Life* (2008), which are credited as third-wave feminist literature. In 2018, she became the editor in chief of the *Women's Review of Books*; previously, she had been a publisher at Feminist Press and editor at *Ms.* magazine.

Randy Boehning *(Hankinson, ND)* served in the North Dakota House of Representatives from 2003 to 2018. Prior, he was the chair of the Republican Party in District Twenty-Seven, and a construction superintendent. Boehning has a long history of voting against

LGBT+ rights. In 2015, Boehning voted against an LGBT+ nondiscrimination bill, and received word that he would face retaliation from a fellow lawmaker if he did not come out or support the bill. Boehning's consequence came later that year when he was outed not by a politician but by a man on Grindr to whom Boehning had sent a photo of himself. After the incident, Boehning said it was a relief to no longer hide his sexuality, but that it complicated his political life as a representative of a conservative district.

Joshua Boschee *(Minot, ND)* is a politician and a member of the Democratic Party. In 2012, he was elected to serve in the North Dakota House of Representatives, and in 2016 was re-elected for another term. As a representative, Boschee has also served as the state Minority Leader. Boschee works as a realtor and is active with organizations such as the Special Olympics, the American Red Cross, and the United Nations Commission for Social Development. He formerly served as the president of the FM Coalition for Homeless Persons.

Joseph-Katrina Koesterman *(Fargo, ND)* is a transgender activist and filmmaker. With a degree in film studies and production from Minnesota State University–Moorhead, she edited and directed *In Front of Us: The Invisible Problem,* a short documentary about homelessness after the North Dakota oil boom. The film was shown at the 2015 South Dakota Film Festival. In 2017, Koesterman organized International Transgender Remembrance Day in Moorhead, Minnesota, and in 2018 she became the president of Tristate Transgender.

> I think it opens up a lot of options for people who identify as nonbinary. It is a little more humanizing. I'm glad we finally have the option to identify as ourselves on our IDs.
>
> —Joseph-Katrina Koesterman on Minnesota's third gender option for IDs, *Valley News Live*, 2018

Ari Shapiro

Ari Shapiro *(Fargo, ND)* is a host of *NPR*'s "All Things Considered." In 2001, Shapiro began at NPR as an intern; in 2015, he became a host of the radio show. Prior, Shapiro also worked as NPR's correspondent for the White House, the Mitt Romney presidential campaign, international affairs in London, and more. His many accolades include recognition by the Columbia Journalism Review, the American Bar Association, and the Daniel Schorr Journalism Prize.

PLACES

Dakota OutRight *(Bismarck, ND)* is an LGBT+ advocacy organization that focuses on education, increasing visibility, and building community. OutRight organizes Bismarck's annual pride celebration, which includes a river cruise and live performances. Dakota OutRight also hosts regular LGBT+ discussion and reading groups, and has partnered with the North Dakota Human Rights Coalition, Equality Counts North Dakota, and the Faith Forward Network.

Heartbreakers *(Williston, ND)* is a gay bar and former strip club. After the mid-2000s oil boom, the culture of Williston declined, leading to an epidemic of harassment against women. In response, the Williston City Council rescinded the erotic dance licenses from Heartbreakers and the other strip club in down. So, Heartbreakers decided to reopen as a gay bar. At the time, it was the only gay bar in the state. In July 2015, Heartbreakers hosted Williston's first Pride event. Amidst speculation that Heartbreakers was only a gay bar to defy the town's ban on erotic dancing, the bar's former owner, Jared Holbrook, said the space was simultaneously for the LGBT+ community and the general population. In 2018, a Williston city attorney revoked the bar's liquor license because of an increasing number of assaults and police calls.

The North Dakota Human Rights Coalition *(Fargo, ND)* works to take legislative action against human rights violations. The coalition has a wide range of members and member organizations—such as Dakota OutRight and the Equality Federation—that advocate for different human rights initiatives affecting the lives of North Dakota citizens. In 2018, NDHRC and its partner organizations held the first ever North Dakota LGBTQ Summit.

The North Dakota Safe Zone *(Fargo, ND)* provides LGBT+ sensitivity training to increase cultural competency. Faye Seidler started North Dakota Safe Zone with the help of Jared Kellerman, the Rape and Abuse Crisis Center, the Pride Center, and other community members. The NDSZ has trained a variety of private

Damron v. Damron and ***Jacobson v. Jacobson*** were two North Dakota Supreme Court decisions that affected the ability of homosexual parents to adopt children. In 1981, the court ruled on *Jacobson v. Jacobson*, deciding that homosexual parents could not adopt children because the children might endure "the slings and arrows of a disapproving society." Then, in 2003, Valerie Damron's ex-husband, Shawn Damron, sued her for custody of their children because she was in a lesbian relationship and the children might suffer mistreatment because of it. There was no evidence of anybody mistreating the children, but the court ruled in favor of the father. Valerie Damron appealed the decision with help from the ACLU's Lesbian and Gay Rights Project. The court granted her custody of her children, and in doing so struck down its previous ruling in *Jacobson vs. Jacobson*. The court said, "To the extent that *Jacobson v. Jacobson* can be read as creating such a presumption, it is overruled."

Mrs. Nash was a transgender woman who died in 1879. She lived her life as an aid to the US Seventh Cavalry under the direction of Colonel George Armstrong Carver. She joined the cavalry in Kentucky and followed them to Fort Lincoln, North Dakota. Mrs. Nash did laundry, delivered babies, cooked, and tailored the uniforms of the officers. She was vague about her past, and told Colonel Carver's wife, Libbie, that she was from Mexico and had two children. While at Fort Lincoln, Mrs. Nash's husband stole her money and left her. She found social support with the other women and remarried to a man named Noonan. In 1878, Noonan departed Fort Lincoln on a military mission against a Native American tribe, and in his absence Mrs. Nash became sick. She feared death and asked her friends not to allow the coroner to clean and dress her body once she died. When the time came, her friends ignored her request and discovered she was transgender. Upon Noonan's return, he was so socially ostracized that he shot himself in the heart.

North Dakota banned same-sex marriage in 2004. The director of the North Dakota Family Alliance, Christina Rondeau, led a measure put the ban on the ballot. The question of whether or not to restrict marriage to heterosexual couples received overwhelming voter support for keeping marriage between a man and a woman. Seventy-four percent of voters, or 68,586 people, voted in favor of the ban.

North Dakota's first Pride Week was held in 1984 at a Fargo bar called My Place, owned by Lenny Tweeden. A local paper said the event drew a "mellow number" of people, and that people danced next to a jukebox. Then-mayor Jon Lindgren said it was ignorant to declare a "Homosexual Awareness Week" because such celebrations were for professional accomplishments or societal contributions. The annual Fargo-Moorhead Pride Parade would not start until 2001.

North Dakota's gender ID laws allow one to change the gender on their driver's license and birth certificate. Changing the gender on a driver's license requires a letter from a physician or therapist that includes the phrase "gender role transition has been completed" to assert one has gone through gender therapy according to the World Professional Association for Transgender Health Standards of Care. Surgical changes are not necessary. However, to change the gender on a birth certificate, one must provide a letter from a physician asserting one has surgically transitioned.

North Dakota's sodomy laws made the act a criminal offense punishable by prison in Dakota Territory in 1862. In 1877, Dakota Territory increased the sodomy prison sentence from one year to ten. When North and South Dakota split in 1889, North Dakota expanded the legal definition of sodomy to include oral sex, and in 1895 expanded the definition further to ban oral sex, anal sex, necrophilia, bestiality, and seeking knowledge of any of those actions. In 1973, North Dakota repealed its sodomy laws against consensual sexual acts.

The only North Dakota city with LGBT+ nondiscrimination laws is Grand Forks. Grand Forks passed this law in 2013. Several other cities have non-

discrimination ordinances that protect people from discrimination based on sexual orientation, but those laws apply only to government employees. There are no statewide protections against LGBT+ discrimination. A statewide nondiscrimination bill passed the Senate in 2015, but was rejected by the House.

> *I feel very lucky to have a platform where people listen to what I have to say. But I hope I would not be terribly different without that megaphone, knowing that we all have the ability to set an example to others through the way we live.*
>
> —Ari Shapiro, *OUT*, 2016

businesses, government offices, hospitals, therapists, schools, shelters, and churches.

The Pride Collective and Community Center *(Fargo, ND)* is a safe space for LGBT+ people. The center houses a library of materials pertaining to LGBT+ rights and history, hosts fundraisers and events, and partners with local organizations.

Pride Minot *(Minot, ND)* is dedicated to fostering LGBT+ community in Minot. Since 2013, the organization has sought to grow diversity, visibility, and LGBT+ pride. It offers educational services, entertainment, events, and more.

The Ten Percent Society *(Grand Forks, ND)* is the oldest LGBT+ community organization in the state. In 1982, it started at the University of North Dakota to serve the faculty, staff, and students of the university and city. The society advocates for legislation supportive of the LGBT+ community, particularly nondiscrimination laws. In 2013, the society partnered with the UND Law Clinic to establish citywide protections for LGBT+ people. That same year, the group helped pass the Safe Housing Ordinance, which bans LGBT+ housing discrimination. The Ten Percent Society also hosts movie nights and monthly drag shows.

Tristate Transgender *(Grand Forks and Fargo, ND)* is a transgender rights and community organization that primarily serves North Dakota, South Dakota, and Minnesota. It hosts support meetings at Pride Collective in Fargo twice a month and also hosts an annual Trans Support Summit and Gala.

⊖ PEOPLE

Leelah Alcorn *(Kings Mills, OH)* was a transgender teenage girl who, in 2014, took her own life by walking into traffic on the Interstate 71 highway. After she came out as trans at age fourteen, her religious parents removed her from school, took away her internet access, and sent her to a series of Christian therapists who discouraged her transition. When she was seventeen, she published her suicide note on her Tumblr blog, and it went viral after her death. Alcon's death sparked international conversations about transgender youth and conversion therapy. Her note ended with the statement: "My death needs to mean something. My death needs to be counted in the number of transgender people who commit suicide this year. I want someone to look at that number and say 'that's fucked up' and fix it. Fix society. Please." After Alcorn's death, her mother continued to refer to her with male pronouns to the press, and insisted that she was a good parent and that she loved her child unconditionally. Interstate 71 has since been memorialized in Leelah's name with a sign where she stepped into traffic.

Natalie Clifford Barney *(Dayton, OH)* was a poet and playwright. During her childhood, she had an encounter with Oscar Wilde when he shooed some bullies away from her and then consoled her with a story. She described this as her "first great adventure." She later moved to Paris, where she lived as an expatriate and encouraged women to write. Her first collection of poetry, *Quelques Portraits: Sonnets de Femmes*, was published in 1900. Barney founded a Women's Academy (L'Académie des Femmes) as a counterpoint to the Académie Française, which did not allow women on its ruling counsel. She was an open lesbian by the age of twelve and wrote feminist lesbian love poems that shocked readers and stirred controversy. She famously said, "My queerness is not a vice, is not deliberate, and harms no one." Barney started a weekly literary salon and was attended by writers and artists such as Gertrude Stein and Truman Capote. Dayton installed a plaque in her honor, the first in the state's history to mention a person's sexual orientation.

> "If the immutable character of sex is contested, perhaps this construct called 'sex' is as culturally constructed as gender; indeed, perhaps it was always already gender, with the consequence that the distinction between sex and gender turns out to be no distinction at all."
>
> —Judith Butler, *Gender Trouble*, 1990

Natalie Clifford Barney

Judith Butler *(Cleveland, OH)* is a scholar and queer theorist who contributed to the idea that gender is socially constructed, not predetermined, and is displayed through behavior. She pioneered the revelation that sex and gender were not inherently linked, and believed that linking the two was a key proponent of heterosexist culture that imposes expectations on our desires based on our gender identities. She has

Judith Butler

Tracy Chapman

published many books but is perhaps best known for *Gender Trouble: Feminism and the Subversion of Identity*. She was an important thought leader in the realm of cultural theory, especially in the United States, and remains so today. She studied philosophy at Harvard and went on to teach at prestigious institutions such as Johns Hopkins University and the University of California–Berkeley.

Tracy Chapman *(Cleveland, OH)* is a musician and activist. She grew up in poverty, raised by her mother. When she was eleven years old, she learned how to play the guitar; she later wrote her first songs as a teenager. Her most well-known songs include "Fast Car," "Give Me One Reason," and "Talkin' 'Bout a Revolution." She has won four Grammy awards, including Best New Artist and Best Rock Song. Chapman has worked with the American Foundation for AIDS Research, as well as Amnesty International and Cleveland's elementary schools. Chapman was in a relationship with the writer Alice Walker in the mid 1990s, but is private about her personal life.

Elle Hearns *(Columbus, OH)* is an activist, speaker, and writer. She began organizing as a youth in Columbus and later became a cofounder of the Black Lives Matter network. She has written articles in support of the movement that have appeared in the *Huffington Post* and *Ebony*, amongst other publications. She has also worked for GetEQUAL, an organization focused on LGBT+ liberation. Hearns, as a transgender woman, is the Executive Director of the Marsha P. Johnson

Institute, which advocates for the physical safety and empowerment of transgender people.

Trace Lysette *(Dayton, OH)* is an actor who started working in entertainment as a drag queen in Columbus. She is best known for her role as Shea in Amazon's original series *Transparent*. Assigned male at birth, Lysette transitioned after she moved to New York to act and perform, though the first roles she auditioned for were cisgendered. Lysette credits her first major role to an episode of *Law & Order: Special Victims Unit*, where she played a sex worker in season fourteen. She felt the need to come out of the closet after the murder of a transgender woman, Islan Nettles, who died in Lysette's neighborhood in New York. Lysette realized that she could only have a positive impact on the trans community if she lived, in her words, "out loud and . . . visibly." She serves as an activist for the queer community in New York City and uses her platform to bring awareness to transgender issues in the US, including sexual harassment toward transgender actors in the entertainment industry.

James Obergefell *(Sandusky, OH)* was the plaintiff in *Obergefell v. Hodges*, the landmark US Supreme Court decision that legalized gay marriage. A Cincinnati resident, Obergefell married John Arthur in Maryland

Trace Lysette

in 2013. Arthur was terminally ill with ALS and Obergefell filed a lawsuit to force their home state of Ohio to recognize him as the surviving spouse on Arthur's death certificate. In 2015, the Supreme Court ruled in *Obergefell v. Hodges* that state bans on same-sex marriage were unconstitutional, thus requiring all fifty states and US territories to issue marriage licenses to same-sex couples. With Pulitzer Prize–winner Debbie Cenziper, he is the coauthor of *Love Wins: The Lovers and Lawyers Who Fought the Landmark Case for Marriage Equality.*

Rupert "Twink" Starr *(Mt. Sterling, OH)* is a World War II veteran who was later honored with a Combat Infantry Badge and a Bronze Star. He fought in the 106th Infantry Division on the frontlines of the Battle of the Bulge, one of the bloodiest battles of the War. When his colonel learned he had attended business school, he pulled Starr from the battle to supervise twenty-two sergeants at Division Headquarters. Later, he returned to the frontlines to restore communications, but in his absence, the Germans surrounded the division's headquarters. Twink had to sneak past the German army to assure those inside the headquarters that relief was on the way. On his way back, German soldiers captured him and took him as a prisoner of war. He spent four months in German prison camps before the Russian army liberated him. After the War, he worked as a realtor and an advocate for LGBT+ rights, specifically for

the repeal of the Don't Ask, Don't Tell policy. He lived with his partner, Allan Wingfield, for fifty-three years.

John Yang *(Chillicothe, OH)* is a journalist, one of a small handful of openly gay television correspondents. He graduated cum laude from Wesleyan University in 1980 and went on to work for a number of publications, including the *Boston Globe*, *Time*, the *Washington Post*, and the *Wall Street Journal*. Later in his career, Yang moved to television journalism, working for ABC and NBC, where he was a correspondent for *NBC Nightly News with Lester Holt*. He famously covered the Bush campaign, the Al Gore campaign, the 9/11 attack on the World Trade Center, and the first year of the Trump presidency. Currently, he works as a correspondent for *PBS NewsHour*. Yang is the recipient of an Edward R. Murrow award as well as a George Foster Peabody Award.

David "Dolly Divine" Zimmer *(Harrisburg, OH)* was a leader in Ohio's LGBT+ community and a drag queen known as Miss Dolly Divine. Zimmer founded a yearly event called the Halloween Berwick Ball, which began in 1964. To avoid police raids, guests only found out about the event's location by calling a number the day of. In the 1980s, the Berwick Party House and Restaurant became the regular venue. Zimmer performed comedy and music routines in elaborate costumes that made him well-known as a gifted entertainer. Elements of his costumes are part of the Ohio History Connection.

⚙ QUEER FACTS

Black Queer & Intersectional Columbus (BQIC) provides a safe space and supportive programs for black LGBT+ people. Founded in 2016 by Dkeama Alexis and Ariana Steele, BQIC publishes a zine and has organized protests and spoken word nights. The organization hopes to set up a mentoring program for youth, and regularly seeks community participation.

Oven Productions is a nonprofit that showcases talented lesbian and feminist art and media. It began in 1975 and has since supported many concerts, films, and exhibits amongst other creative ventures. Oven Productions has hosted the Annual Womyn's Variety Show since 1975, which features song, dance, drama, and poetry, and is open to those who identify as women. The first variety show was held in a church basement, and it has also been held at synagogues. Oven Productions has additionally hosted women-only dance parties and consistently promotes new voices and creativity at its events.

The Red Party was a large annual circuit party for the LGBT+ community in Columbus. It was the invention of a visual artist named Corbett Reynolds who was credited with bringing popularity to circuit parties all across the nation. These dance parties, such as the Red Party, were themed events that lasted one day and often raised money for LGBT+ organizations. They included performances, extravagant costumes, and art. Reynolds said he chose the theme of red because it is "the color of passion, both in love and creativity." The last Red Party was in 2001, dubbed the Red Fetish. Reynolds died of a heart attack in 2002.

Sistah Sinema is a nationwide organization that screens films featuring LGBT+ women of color. Deidre McPherson founded the Cleveland chapter of the organization in 2012, and it has since hosted dozens of screenings at nonprofit venues on a monthly basis. McPherson has said that Sistah Sinema events "provide a much-needed space for attendees to gather safely and have their voices expressed, heard, and supported," and that "it's important for all people to see themselves represented in mainstream media."

◉ PLACES

Hingetown and West Twenty-Ninth Street *(Cleveland, OH)* are the former center of Cleveland's gay culture, featuring clubs, bars, gay businesses, and a gay/lesbian community center. In recent years, the neighborhood has become gentrified, and new businesses and higher prices have made the area less accessible to the LGBT+ community that used to frequent the area. After the Striebinger Block came under new ownership, the gay businesses that existed before were replaced by new ones, like a juice bar, a cycling studio, and a pet store. The new owners also evicted the men who lived upstairs from the businesses, and the gay pride flag that used to fly on the corner of the block was removed and replaced by the Ohio City flag. Nevertheless, a plaque on West Twenty-Ninth Street honors the former site of Cleveland's first gay community center.

The Wright-Patterson Air Force Base *(Dayton, OH)* was one of the bases where the US State Department began the Lavender Scare, or the purge of queer people, in the 1950s. Once someone was suspected of homosexuality, that person would be pressured to reveal the identities of other LGBT+ people. The threat of dismissal for lesbianism also ensured that female employees in the military were kept under strict control. During the era, around two thousand military personnel were fired every year nationwide for their sexuality.

SOUTH DAKOTA

PEOPLE

> *As queer people of color in queer communities, a lot of times our issues are more than just marriage and we are walking in a lot of different worlds at various times. How do you help to create a more inclusive queer movement that can be expansive enough to hold all of its members?*
>
> —Coya White Hat-Artichoker, interview with Matthew Lewis, University of Wisconsin–Madison Multicultural Student Center, 2013

Angie Buhl *(Aberdeen, SD)* became the first openly LGBT+ public official in South Dakota when she was elected to the state legislature in 2011. Buhl, who is bisexual, was twenty-five at the time, and was also the youngest woman to ever serve in the state's senate. During her tenure, she was the Senate Democratic Caucus chair. Before her political career, Buhl was a nonprofit consultant for organizations such as Equality South Dakota.

Coya White Hat-Artichoker *(Rosebud Reservation, SD)* is a two-spirit queer Indigenous person and activist. She is a member of the First Nations Two Spirit Collective and has worked with the GLBT Host Home Program to secure housing for homeless queer youth. A poet and writer, Hat-Artichoker's work has appeared in places such as the *Huffington Post*. In 2010, her work with her organization Sacred Circle, which sought to end violence against Native American women, landed her recognition on *The Advocate*'s 40 under 40 list.

> *Nobody was buying it, 'oppressed cultural minority.' They didn't want to be a minority. They wanted to be like everybody else. Gay people didn't want to be an oppressed cultural minority.*
>
> —Chuck Rowland, interview with Eric Marcus, *Making Gay History*

Chuck Rowland *(Gary, SD)* was a cofounder of the Mattachine Society in Los Angeles in 1950, which focused on protecting and improving the rights of gay men. Prior, Rowland was a World War II veteran and returned to America to work with the American Veteran's Committee. In 1982, Rowland founded the Celebration Theater in Los Angeles, an award-winning theater company dedicated to telling the stories of the LGBT+ community. It is still in operation.

Jesse Taylor *(Kimball, SD)* was a former basketball player at Dakota Wesleyan University. When he came out in 2014, he became the first openly gay athlete in South Dakota. "For the longest time I didn't understand how I could be gay and be an athlete. I had never heard of a gay athlete growing up," he wrote on OutSports.com in 2015.

PLACES

The Black Hills Center for Equality *(Rapid City, SD)* is a virtual LGBT+ organization. While it has no physical location, BHCFE aims to be an educational and networking space in the local community. Some of its regular events include support groups, the Big Gay Prom, and Black Hills Pride.

QUEER FACTS

House Bill 1008 was introduced in South Dakota in January 2016. It would have restricted bathroom and locker room use for transgender students to match their gender assigned at birth, not their gender identity. The bill initially passed both the state House of Representatives and the state Senate, but was vetoed by Governor Dennis Daugaard. A veto override failed the following day.

Melissa Eidson and Misty Collins were issued the first same-sex marriage license in South Dakota on June 26, 2015, just hours after the US Supreme Court legalized same-sex marriages in all fifty states. The couple are both nurses and live in Rapid City, South Dakota, and received the blessing of their parents and their children before heading to the courthouse.

Randy Rohl and Grady Quinn, in 1979, were the first two openly gay people to attend a prom together. Rohl was a seventeen-year-old senior at Lincoln High School in Sioux Falls; he arrived with his date/friend, twenty-year old-Quinn, just in time for the last dance. The school's principal, Fred Stephens, told the *Washington Post*, "Homosexuals have rights too; you have to accept that."

The two-spirit identity was coined in the early 1990s by activist Beverly Little Thunder of the Standing Rock reservation in North and South Dakota. Though the term varies from tribe to tribe, two-spirit identity goes back centuries, as these people have often held influential and revered positions in their tribes, such as healers or shamans.

Brookings, South Dakota, is considered one of the most gay-friendly cities in the state. Brookings has a human rights commission, nondiscrimination laws in city employment, and an LGBT+ liaison to the city government and the city's police department. The city also provides benefits for city employees' same-sex partners and offers transgender-inclusive health care benefits.

Sioux Falls Center for Equality *(Sioux Falls, SD)* has supported and advocated for the area's LGBT+ community since 2000. Its successes include teaming up with the ACLU to defeat a 2016 transgender bathroom bill. In recent years, the center has refocused its efforts to supporting Sioux Falls Pride, with the goal of making Sioux Falls not just a safe place for LGBT+ people but a welcoming one.

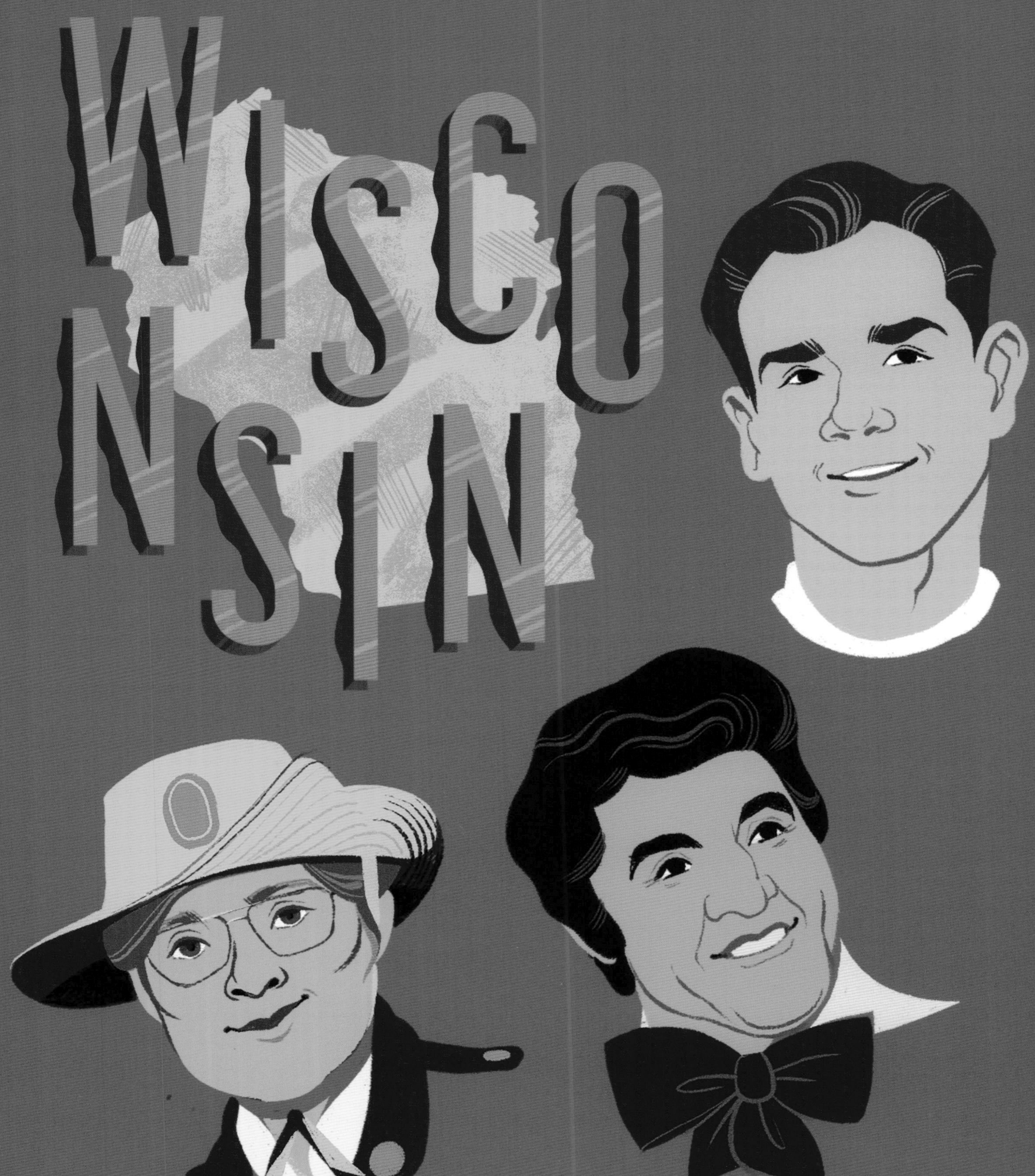
WISCONSIN

⊖ PEOPLE

Tammy Baldwin *(Madison, WI)* is the first openly gay woman elected to the United States Congress (1998) and the first openly LGBT person elected to the United States Senate. Baldwin got her start in politics in 1992, when she won a seat in the Wisconsin State Assembly, representing the seventy-eighth district; she was re-elected twice to the position. She succeeded David Clarenbach, who came out as gay in 2001, years after leaving politics. When she was elected to Wisconsin's House of Representatives in 1998, she was also the first woman to represent the state in Congress. In the 2012 US Senate election, Baldwin defeated Thompson, Wisconsin's former governor and the longest-serving person to hold that position; Baldwin was reelected in 2018.

Miriam Ben-Shalom *(Waukesha, WI)* is a noted military LGBT+ rights activist. She began serving in the Army in 1974 and later become a staff sergeant. In 1976, Ben-Shalom was honorably discharged from the military because of her sexuality. Ben-Shalom took her case to court, where the Chicago Court of Appeals ruled in her favor. She was reinstated to the military in 1978, becoming the first person to be reinstated after being discharged for their sexual orientation. However, when she went to re-enlist after completing her initial tour of duty, the Army refused; when Ben-Shalom took her case to the Supreme Court, they refused to hear the case. Ben-Shalom was no longer able to serve in the military. Since then, Ben-Shalom has been an active supporter of military gay rights. She protested the Don't Ask, Don't Tell policy, and stood next to President Barack Obama when he signed the law repealing it. She is the founder of American Veterans for Equal Rights, and in 2005 received the Stonewall Award.

Mary Cheney *(Madison, WI)* is the daughter of former Vice President Dick Cheney. Cheney has some experience working in politics, helping with her father's election campaigns in both 2000 and 2004. In 2006, Cheney released her autobiography, *Now It's My Turn: A Daughter's Chronicle of Political Life*. Since then, she has worked in the private sector, helping to found BKM Strategies, which eventually merged to form New Troy Strategies, a strategic communications firm. She married her wife in 2012.

Maria Zoe Dunning *(Milwaukee, WI)* is the only openly gay military personnel allowed to remain on active duty after being indicted during the Don't Ask, Don't Tell policy. Dunning initially came out during a political rally

Tammy Baldwin

> **"**
>
> *It takes tremendous time and energy and emotional toil to pretend you're something you're not, or to try to fit into something that's not authentic. Being in the military and keeping a secret, pretending I was straight, it takes a daily toll. It's death by a thousand tiny cuts.*
>
> —Maria Zoe Dunning, Stanford Graduate School of Business, 2018
>
> **"**

after the election of President Bill Clinton because she believed that he would repeal the ban on openly gay military personnel. During the rally, she gave a speech stating, "I am both a naval officer and a lesbian, and I refuse to live a lie anymore." Dunning was initially discharged from her position in the Navy Reserves. However, when Clinton legalized the Don't Ask, Don't Tell policy, Dunning was tried under the new rules. She argued that her statement simply identified her as a lesbian but didn't actually confirm that she partook in "homosexual conduct," which was the grounds for termination. The military accepted this loophole and dropped the charges against Dunning, allowing her to continue to serve. Since then, Dunning has been awarded the Extraordinary Public Service Award and was present when President Barack Obama ended the Don't Ask, Don't Tell Policy. She still continues activism work.

Christopher Fons cofounded the Milwaukee chapter of the AIDS Coalition to Unleash Power (ACT UP). He was an active supporter of all LGBT+ and women's rights but was most prominently a voice for AIDS activism. He received the Community Activist Award from Progressive Milwaukee in 1994. After years of fighting his own personal battle with AIDS, he passed away in 1995 at the age of twenty-seven.

Wladziu Valentino Liberace *(West Allis, WI)* was a world-renowned pianist famous for his glitzy outfits and the huge candelabra he kept onstage during his performances. Known mononymously as Liberace, his musical style combined both classical and pop influences.

Liberace

Over the years, he had his own TV shows, a stage show in Las Vegas, and numerous frequently sold-out tours. During the peak of his fame, *The Liberace Show* was watched by over thirty-five million viewers, and he even performed with Elvis Presley. Liberace was never publicly out as a gay man, but numerous news reports and lawsuits aimed to prove he was gay. Some believe he never publicly came out in an effort to maintain the

QUEER FACTS

AB-70, Wisconsin's gay rights law, an LGBT+ nondiscrimination bill, passed in Wisconsin in 1982. The first iteration of the law was introduced in 1967 by Lloyd Barbee; various other activists and organizations, including local religious groups, mobilized to fight for it. When it finally passed, heavily driven by state assemblymember David Clarenbach's support, Wisconsin was the first state to pass such a law. A year later, the state also passed a law legalizing same-sex sexual relationships.

The Argonauts Leather Club in Green Bay is Wisconsin's oldest gay organization. A gay leather/levi social club, the Argonauts is known for its social activities, such as monthly club nights or annual dinners. It holds three state leather/levi titles, including Wisconsin Leather/Levi Daddy, Wisconsin Leather/Levi Daddy's Boy, and Mr. Northwoods. The club is also known for its charity work and has raised money for a number of local LGBT+ programs.

Donna Burkett and Manonia Evans were part of a national wave of lawsuits in various US states that argued for gay marriage equality. In 1971, the lesbian couple applied for a marriage license in Milwaukee County. When they were refused, they took their case to court, arguing that homosexual couples deserve the same marriage rights as heterosexual couples. The case was ultimately dismissed in 1972, but it connected Wisconsin to the larger national movement for marriage equality.

The first MAGIC Picnic, a political march held by LGBT+ activists, was held in 1989. MAGIC stands for Madison Area Gay Interim Committee and was formed as a local response to national LGBT+ movements. The group organized two local marches (one in 1989 and again in 1991) to energize and motivate the local LGBT+ community. This movement has been connected to the political success that LGBT+ candidates and programs have had in the area (including electing the first openly lesbian congresswoman). Since then, the program has progressed into the current iteration of the OutReach Pride Parade.

strength of his mostly female fanbase. In 1987, Liberace passed away from complications of AIDS.

Jamie Nabozny *(Ashland, WI)* won a legal case that stated that public schools had a duty to provide a safe educational experience to all students, including those who are LGBT+. While he was in middle and high school, Nabozny was severely bullied, once to the point that he ended up in the hospital. When Nabozny and his parents complained to the school district, it refused to do anything to help the situation. Instead, Nabozny was forced to leave the school for his own safety. In 1996, Nabozny decided that he didn't want other students to suffer as he did and sued the school for not better protecting him. With the help of Lambda Legal, he won his case against the school; the courts agreed that all students (including LGBT+ students)

deserve a safe educational experience. In 2010, Nabozny's struggles were chronicled in a teaching documentary titled *Bullied*. He currently travels the country to speak about his experiences.

Ashton Whitaker *(Kenosha, WI)* is a transgender man who in 2018 won a discrimination lawsuit against his high school. Whitaker's high school had refused him to use the men's restroom, referred to him using female pronouns, and even suggested that he wear a green band on his wrist to identify him as transgender. Whitaker sued the school with the help of the Transgender Law Center. In 2016, during Whitaker's senior year at high school, a Federal District Court granted an injunction in favor of Whitaker, allowing him to use the men's restroom. Now a college student, Whitaker settled with the Kenosha Unified School District outside of court.

> "The idea of using the girls restroom was humiliating and there was no way I could do it. If I were to use the gender-neutral restrooms, I would also stand out from everyone else with a big label on me that said 'transgender.'
>
> —Ashton Whitaker,
> *New York Times*, 2018

 # PLACES

The Clarenbach House *(Madison, WI)* is where former Wisconsin State Assemblymember David Clarenbach lived between 1977 and 1982, when he authored and helped push the nation's first gay rights bill through the state legislature. Later pioneers in Madison's LGBT+ community lived there as well, including Jim Yeadon, who became the first openly gay person elected to the Common Council in Wisconsin and the fourth openly gay elected official in the US in 1977. The house symbolizes a lineage of out elected officials in Wisconsin. The city is currently working to get historical landmark status of the property.

The Mint Bar *(Milwaukee, WI)* was an iconic, long-standing gay bar. When it originally opened in 1949, it was referred to as a "male bar." The location was small but had a strong presence in the LGBT+ community; however, it was located on valuable real estate, and was eventually sold to allow for the construction of the Bradley Center arena in 1986. The bar moved to a new location in the Harbor View neighborhood, where it stayed until it closed in the early 1990s.

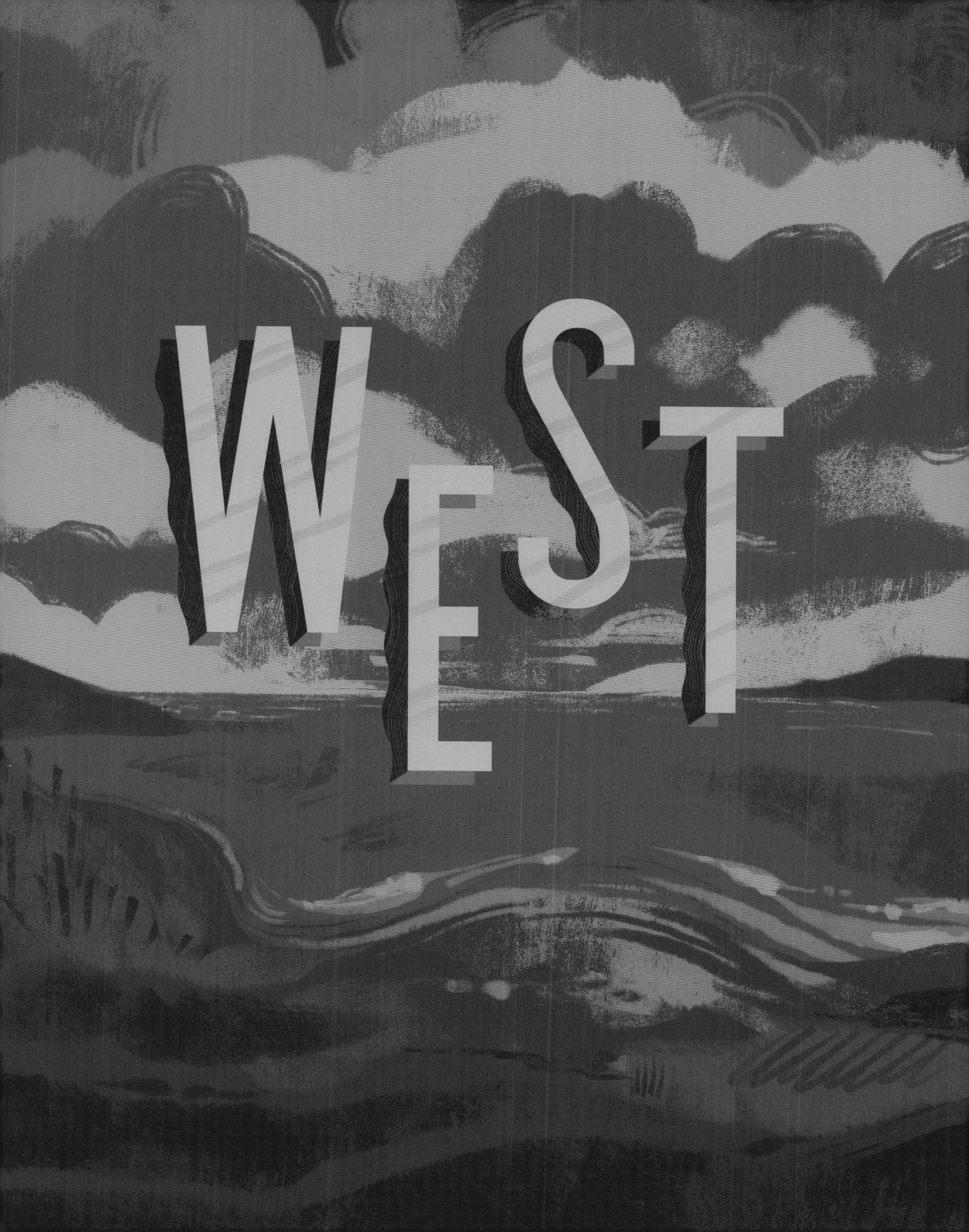
WEST

PEOPLE

Callan Chythlook-Sifsof *(Girdwood, AK)* is an Olympic snowboarder who placed third at the World Cup in 2007 and competed in the 2010 Olympics. Chythlook-Sifsof was injured in the 2012 season, and although she was a close contender for the 2014 Olympic team, she didn't make the team. Despite this, she was inspired to speak up during the 2014 Sochi Olympics during the controversy around Russia's anti-gay laws, and came out in her stand against discrimination.

Christopher Constant was one of the first two gay men ever elected to the Alaskan government. In 2017, Constant was elected to the Anchorage City Assembly. Constant's other career accomplishments include serving as the president of the Fairview Community Council and working as the grants and contracts director for a nonprofit substance abuse and behavioral health treatment provider. He is also a licensed real estate professional.

Jenny Irene Miller *(Nome, AK)* is a gay, two-spirit artist who works to represent the complication of identity. Miller is an Iñupiaq, a Native Alaskan tribe, but she used to pass as white; she also used to suppress her LGBT+ identity. In college, Miller learned more about Native people's concepts of being two-spirit, which helped her identify with it and with her own Native culture. In 2016, Miller began a project called *Continuous*, in which she takes portraits of Indigenous LGBT+ Alaskans to start conversations, build community, and end discrimination. Miller is a leader of Aurora Pride, a local two-spirit organization.

Felix Rivera was one of the first two gay men ever elected to the Alaskan government when he was elected to the Anchorage City Assembly in 2017. Rivera began working in politics when he was the student body president of Alaska Pacific University; after graduating, he began working as a consultant for the mayor's office. He currently sits on the board of directors of three nonprofits. Rivera is the Assembly's only non-white representative.

PLACES

The Identity Center of Anchorage *(Anchorage, AK)* is an LGBT+ center supported by Identity, Inc. The center was established in 1977 and was originally called the Alaska Gay Community Center; in 1983, it changed

Callan Chythlook-Sifsof

It's almost a blessing that the Olympics are happening in Russia and these issues are coming out. It gives the world a chance to view it and it gives athletes a chance to voice their opinions about it and to show every country in the world that this is not OK.

— Callan Chythlook-Sifsof, Towleroad.com, 2014

☿ QUEER FACTS

Alaska legalized same-sex marriage in 2014. That year, the Ninth Circuit Court of Appeals (which has jurisdiction over Alaska and most other Western states) ruled in favor of legalizing same-sex marriage in cases from Nevada and Idaho. After the US Supreme Court refused to hear appeals on these cases, the rulings set a binding precedent in the region, and same-sex marriage was legalized. On October 12, 2014, a district court judge ruled Alaska's ban on same-sex marriage unconstitutional, officially overturning the ban.

Ballot Measure 2, which amended state legislature to define marriage as only between a man and a woman, was passed in 1998 in response to the ruling of *Brause v. Bureau of Vital Statistics*. The Alaska Supreme Court subsequently cited the measure as grounds to overturn the ruling of *Brause*; thus, same-sex marriage remained illegal.

Johnny Ellis

Brause v. Bureau of Vital Statistics was a 1998 Alaska Superior Court case. The case was filed in 1995 after Jay Brause and Gene Dugan sought a marriage license using a loophole with the gender-neutral language of Alaska's marriage laws at the time, but were denied. The judge ruled in the couple's favor, stating that the law's existing language made it unconstitutional to uphold marriage as only available to heterosexual couples.

The first same-sex marriage in Alaska occurred on October 13, 2014, in Barrow. There was supposed to be a three-day wait period after the October 12 ruling before any same-sex marriages could be performed. However, the wait period didn't align with Kristine Hilderbrand and Sarah Ellis, whose families could only attend their wedding if it was held during the wait. The couple's request to waive it was granted, and they married on October 13, 2014, becoming the first known same-sex couple to marry in the state.

Johnny Ellis served in the Alaska House of Representatives from 1986 until 1992, then in the Alaska State Senate from 1993 to 2017. Originally from Springfield, Missouri, he spent his career serving as both the Senate Majority and Senate Minority Leader. In 2016, Ellis came out as gay shortly before retiring from politics; he hid his sexuality during his career to avoid potentially limiting his effectiveness in serving his constituents.

An LGBT+ anti-discrimination law passed in Anchorage in 2015. The ordinance made it illegal to discriminate against the LGBT+ community in housing, employment, and public accommodations. Assemblymen Bill Evans and Patrick Flynn coauthored the law. A similar anti-discrimination proposal was on the ballot in 2012, but was not passed by voters.

Proposition 1 was a 2018 bill to limit transgender bathroom rights, proposed partly in an attempt to repeal some of Anchorage's 2015 anti-discrimination measures. Prop 1 would have required people to use only the public restrooms that matched the gender they were assigned at birth, but it was defeated by the city's voters. The ACLU declared the victory the first of its kind regarding anti-transgender bathroom bills.

In order for our Native communities to heal, we need to acknowledge and honor the gender diversity within our Native peoples. Everyone is entitled to their happiness and shouldn't be afraid to express who they are or who they love. Now this sounds like a fictional utopia. But I just hope everyone will be able to be prideful in who they are and not have to hide any elements of their identity.

—Jenny Irene Miller, *Anchorage Daily News*, 2016

its name to the Identity Center. The center hosts support groups, meetings, and a library. Its programming also supports a youth arts showcase, Pride prom, weekly transgender community meetings, and more. Identity, Inc. organizes the city's annual PrideFest.

Mad Myrna's *(Anchorage, AK)* is a gay bar that's been in business for almost twenty years. The bar was named after the founder's drag persona, and still hosts weekly drag shows. It is a safe space for LGBT+ people to gather, and hosts fundraisers and camp theater; it has also been known to hold political events. The bar was renovated in 2018.

Being gay is not a choice. I know that. But I did make a choice to deny this part of my personal life and just not share that. . . . I've always had great friends and supporters and wonderful staffers, and my satisfaction was in accomplishments and helping other people who needed help. But yes, it was lonely.

—Johnny Ellis on whether he regrets remaining closeted for most of his career, *Anchorage Daily News*, 2016

AMERICAN SAMOA

PEOPLE

> *Life is meant to be lived in your truth. . . . When we hide in the shadow of doubt and fear, we will never see the beauty of light and the love of the days ahead. I am living my truth and by doing so, I am seeing the beauty and love of people.*
>
> —Arrianna Princess Haserota Auva'a, *Samoa Observer*, 2018

> *Most fa'afafine have to dress and act as men in order to advance. I broke that. It wasn't easy. I was the first one dressed as a woman to elevate myself in a professional way. Now they don't ridicule anyone.*
>
> —Dr. Vena Sele on her career achievements, *Seattle Gay News*, 2010

Arrianna Princess Haserota Auva'a is a fa'afafine member of the US Army. She lived in Samoa for years as a fa'afafine public figure, appearing on radio shows, Samoan movies, and pageants. After President Obama repealed Don't Ask, Don't Tell in 2011, Auva'a enlisted in the army openly as fa'afafine. Although she was originally told to live and work as male, she eventually worked with her command team to transition to female. While other American Samoa fa'afafine have enlisted, Auva'a is the first known to swear in while presenting as female.

Vena Sele is a fa'afafine activist. Dr. Sele flouted traditional expectations for fa'afafine to work as caretakers, and instead received her education in America. She returned to Samoa to work at the American Samoa Community College, where she was the dean of student services and eventually the college's president. In the early 1980s, she also founded the philanthropic Island Queens Pageant. Now, Dr. Sele lives in Seattle, working to bring awareness and acceptance of the fa'afafine community. Dr. Sele is also active with the United Territories of Polynesian Islanders Alliance (UTOPIA).

To'oto'oali'i Roger Stanley was the founder and president of the Samoa Fa'afafine Association from 2006 to 2017. She studied policy development at the National University of Samoa and became an advocate for the rights of fa'afafine and faafatama people in the community—specifically in the church, as many young fa'afafine and faafatama people come from conservative Christian families. While Stanley was originally from Samoa, her impact had a global reach. Stanley also advocated for a more inclusive global LGBT+ rights movement that recognizes the diversity of sexual orientation and expression in cultures worldwide. Stanley died in January 2018.

PLACES

Samoa Fa'afafine Association *(Apia, Samoa)* is a nonprofit that advocates for the rights and visibility of fa'afafine and faafatama people in American Samoa. SFA holds an annual Fa'afafine Week event, which connects people to resources for getting tested for HIV/AIDS, builds community pride, educates health care professionals on fa'afafine and faafatama needs, and educates the press on how to cover fa'afafine and faafatama issues. The SFA also hosts the Fa'afafine Industry Variety Awards, which recognize people who have made notable contributions to fa'afafine and faafatama advocacy.

⚲ QUEER FACTS

Fa'afafine is a gender in Samoan culture. The term translates to "in the manner of a woman," and refers to biological males who perform typically female roles in their families. Being fa'afafine is not synonymous with being transgender. About 1 to 5 percent of American Samoans identify as fa'afafine.

Faafatama is a gender in Samoan culture. It refers to biological females who express themselves in ways culture generally codes as male, or to biological females who are attracted to other females. Being faafatama is not synonymous with being transgender.

The only US territory where gay marriage is still illegal is American Samoa. Samoa is officially a Christian state; nearly 100 percent of Samoans are Christian. Because of this, when the US legalized gay marriage in 2015, Samoa protested, citing religious impropriety. All other American territories voluntarily agreed to uphold the ruling.

Samoan Queer Lives was a book edited by Dan Taulapapa McMullin and Yuki Kihara, published in 2018. The book is a collection of stories, personal essays, and transcribed interviews with and about Samoan queer people, told through their own voices. The collection was entirely written and edited by Samoan queer people and attempts to speak directly to the community.

The Society of Fa'afafine in American Samoa (SOFIAS) promotes visibility, pride, and awareness about fa'afafine people. It also aims to blend Western influence and the traditional cultural place of fa'afafine. SOFIAS financially supports the Fatu o Aiga Convalescent Home for the Elderly and Disabled and hosts an annual beauty pageant. Its motto is "Ia e Ola Malamalama I lou Fa'asinomaga," which translates to "Be of virtue and pride in your identity."

> *Being a fa'afafine is at times both a blessing and a challenge. A blessing in the sense that fa'afafine play fundamental roles of service within the family, church, [and] village unit. Fa'afafine play a significant role in the rearing and raising of children, caretaking responsibilities for the elderly and disabled. Many of our fa'afafine do well in education and employment and thus provide financial sustenance to families and the many obligations attributed to being a Samoan.*
>
> —To'oto'oali'i Roger Stanley, OutRightInternational.org, 2017

PEOPLE

Billie Joe Armstrong *(Oakland, CA)* is a musician best known as the frontman of the band Green Day. The band kickstarted the success of the pop-punk genre with its 1994 album *Dookie*, which has sold over twenty million copies to date, and experienced a career resurgence with 2004's *American Idiot*, a rock opera inspired by the political climate of the Bush administration. Armstrong identifies as bisexual; he said in an interview, "I think people are born bisexual, and it's just that our parents and society kind of veer us off into this feeling of 'Oh, I can't.' They say it's taboo. It's ingrained in our heads that it's bad, when it's not bad at all. It's a very beautiful thing."

Drew Barrymore *(Culver City, CA)* made her acting debut as Gertie in Steven Spielberg's *E.T. the Extraterrestrial* at the age of six. She had a difficult upbringing, as her father, the actor John Drew Barrymore, was an abusive alcoholic. Barrymore herself developed substance abuse issues before she was twelve. When she was fourteen, her mother sent her to an institution, and afterwards Barrymore legally separated from her parents. She cleaned toilets and worked in restaurants until she was able to fight her way back into the film industry. She has starred in films such as *Scream*, *Donnie Darko*, *Never Been Kissed*, *Charlie's Angels*, and *Grey Gardens*, for which she won a Golden Globe. She has her own production company, Flower Films, and has directed and produced several films, including 2009's *Whip It*. In 2003, Barrymore publicly revealed her bisexuality in an interview with *Contact* magazine.

Brian Boitano *(Mountain View, CA)* is a professional figure skater who won a gold medal for his performance in the 1988 winter Olympics, and has also won six national titles at the professional level, amongst his more than fifty titles. The Tano Triple, his signature jump, is one few other skaters can perform. Boitano has had many televised skating appearances, including his own television special *Canvas of Ice,* and also starred in the 1990 television movie *Carmen on Ice,* for which he won an Emmy. Boitano skated for the US Olympic team in 1984, 1988, and 1994. In 1997, he published a critically renowned book on skating called *Boitano's Edge: Inside the Real World of Figure Skating.* Boitano founded the nonprofit Youth Skate, which finances skating lessons in San Francisco for children

> " *Then I hit puberty and it confused me. I felt incredibly uncomfortable. I hated what was happening to my body, but I also realized I had this attraction to women so I just made the assumption that I was a lesbian, and that's why I felt this way. At first I was relieved, but as time went on, the older I got, I felt I didn't fit into that identity and I didn't know what was wrong with me.*
>
> —Chaz Bono, the *Daily Beast*, 2011 "

Chaz Bono

who would not otherwise be able to skate. Boitano also enjoys cooking, and in 2009 had his own show on the Food Network called *What Would Brian Boitano Make?* Boitano came out as gay in December 2013 in conjunction with his appointment to the 2014 Winter Olympics in Sochi, Russia.

Chaz Bono *(Los Angeles, CA)* is an actor and LGBT+ activist. Bono, whose parents are Cher and Sonny Bono, has appeared on *American Horror Story*, *Where the Bears Are*, *The Bold and the Beautiful*, and *The Sonny and Cher* Show. Assigned female at birth, Bono came out as a lesbian in the mid-1990s, and began officially transitioning around 2009 at the age of forty. In his 2011 memoir *Transition*, as well as the documentary *Becoming Chaz*, he discusses his experiences as a transgender man. He publicly advocates for LGBT+ rights, and talks openly about his gender-affirming surgery and his experience with gender identity.

Sara Beth Brooks *(Sacramento, CA)* is the founder of Asexual Awareness Week, an international campaign to raise awareness of the nuances of the asexuality spectrum. Since 2010, Asexual Awareness Week has been a platform for legitimizing asexuality amidst the hostility it sometimes receives in the LGBT+ community. As a result, organizations such as the National LGBTQ Task Force, GLAAD, and the Trevor Project have since developed ace inclusivity. In 2015, Brooks was invited to the White House to participate in a discussion around bisexual policy.

Glenn Burke *(Oakland, CA)*, who played for the Los Angeles Dodgers and the Oakland Athletics in the 1970s, was the first gay Major League Baseball player.

> *Prejudice drove me out of baseball sooner than I should have, but I wasn't changing.*
>
> —Glenn Burke, *New York Times*, 1994

Burke tried to hide his sexuality from his fellow players for years, withdrawing socially and becoming an aggressive player to overcompensate. Eventually, he was outed to members of his team, who began acting paranoid around him, especially in the locker room. The tension culminated when the Dodgers traded Burke to the Athletics, denying they did so because of his sexuality. Burke soon left the Athletics due to an injury and retired from the MLB altogether, though he went on to play in the Gay Softball League. He said of quitting major league baseball, "If I thought I could be accepted, I'd be there now. It is the first thing in my life I ever backed down from. No, I'm not disappointed in myself, I'm disappointed in the system." He died from AIDS-related illness in 1995 at the age of forty-two.

David Campos *(Puerto Barrios, Guatemala)* served two terms on the San Francisco Board of Supervisors starting in 2008, only one of two openly gay board-members. During this time, he fought for universal health care for city residents, ensured the fair legal treatment of undocumented children through due process, and issued an ordinance to equalize pay for San Franciscans regardless of race or gender. In 1999, Campos worked as San Francisco's Deputy City Attorney and was the lead legal counsel during the San Francisco Unified School District's desegregation. In 2017, Campos became the Deputy County Executive for Santa Clara County.

RuPaul Andre Charles *(San Diego, CA)* is a celebrity, singer, drag queen, and host of the Emmy Award–winning reality competition show *RuPaul's Drag Race.*

RuPaul

> *'I am gay'—those three words are a violation of Title 10 of the US code. . . . It's an immoral code, and it goes against every single thing that we were taught at West Point with our honor code. The honor code says that a cadet will not lie, cheat, steal—*
>
> —Daniel Choi,
> *The American Prospect*, 2014

Margaret Cho

He moved to Georgia when he was fifteen and studied theater at the North Atlanta School of Performing Arts. He also worked as a used-car salesman for his brother-in-law while dancing in clubs on the side before moving to New York City in 1987. In the early 1990s, he received international attention for his hit song "Supermodel (You Better Work)." After skyrocketing to fame, RuPaul went on to release several studio albums, serve as spokesperson for MAC Cosmetics, and appear in numerous films and TV shows. *GuRu*, his humorous collection of personal philosophies, was published in 2018. "We're born naked, and the rest is drag," RuPaul has said.

Margaret Cho *(San Francisco, CA)* began performing stand-up in the early 1990s, when she won a contest to open for Jerry Seinfeld. In 1994, she landed a starring role in the ABC sitcom *All-American Girl*, but struggled with the lack of creative freedom the show allowed her to have. While the sitcom lasted only one season, Cho went on to release more comedy albums such as *I'm the One That I Want*, *Notorious C.H.O.*, and *Revolution*, which earned a Grammy nomination for Best Comedy Album. Cho has made numerous large and small film and TV appearances, in shows such as *Sex and the City*, *Drop Dead Diva*, *30 Rock*, and more. Cho is openly bisexual; as a teen, she initially thought she was a lesbian because of how her classmates had bullied her. "I don't know using 'bisexual' is right because that indicates that there's only two genders, and I don't believe

that. . . . Maybe 'pansexual' is technically the more correct term but I like 'bisexual' because it's kind of '70s," she told the *Huffington Post* in 2018.

Daniel "Dan" Choi *(Tustin, CA)* is an activist and a former army lieutenant who graduated from the United States Military Academy at West Point in 2003. In 2009, Choi came out as gay on an episode of *The Rachel Maddow Show*. As a result, the military discharged Choi and sent him a bill for $2,500 in unearned pay. It also brought him to court, attempting to sentence him to six months in prison for "failure to obey." Choi's trial continued even after the government repealed Don't Ask, Don't Tell in 2011. Choi protested DADT in a number of ways: he handcuffed himself to the White House fence, spoke out in the media, and started a hunger strike. "What kind of officer or leader would I be if I gave up?" Choi has said. He was present when President Obama officially signed the repeal of DADT.

Belo Cipriani *(Guatemala)* is a writer and disability activist. In 2007, Cipriani was the victim of a hate crime while he was walking through an LGBT+ neighborhood in San Francisco. The attack left him blind, but served as the source for his 2011 critically acclaimed memoir, *Blind*.

Now based out of Minnesota, Cipriani is the founder of Oleb Books, a press dedicated to elevating the representation of writers with disabilities. Also the founder of the accessibility consulting group Oleb Media, Cipriani has worked with Apple, Google, Wells Fargo, and other corporations to increase accessibility for employees with disabilities.

Jason Collins *(Northridge, CA)* is a former NBA basketball player who was also the first active athlete in the US's four major sports leagues to come out as gay. He played with jersey number 98 to commemorate Matthew Shepard's murder in 1998. In 2013, Collins went public with his sexuality in a *Sports Illustrated* article. After he came out, he worked to create an accepting culture within the NBA so that other gay players would feel comfortable enough to come out. Collins was invited to the LA Lakers' first Pride Night game in 2018, where the team honored him with the Laces of Unity. He retired from professional basketball in 2014, ending a career that began in 2001 and spanned many

Jason Collins

teams, including the New Jersey Nets, Boston Celtics, Washington Wizards, and Brooklyn Nets.

Patrisse Cullors *(Los Angeles, CA)* is an artist, activist, and cofounder of the Black Lives Matter movement. During her childhood, she encountered police brutality, which later became fuel for her activism. At sixteen, Cullors came out as queer. She graduated from the University of California–Los Angeles, where she studied religion and philosophy, in 2012. Her performance piece *STAINED: An Intimate Portrayal of State Violence* sparked the creation of her nonprofit, Dignity and Power Now, which advocates for the rights of incarcerated people. Cullors is the co-author of the 2018 *New York Times* bestselling book *When They Call You a Terrorist: A Black Lives Matter Memoir*. She has received numerous awards for her work, including the Defender of the Dream Award from the AFL-CIO Executive Council Committee on Civil and Human Rights, the Justice Award from the National Center for Lesbian Rights, and a Revolution Award for Freedom from the ImageNation Cinema Foundation.

Isadora Duncan *(San Francisco, CA)* was a ballet dancer and the founder of the modern dance movement. A free-spirited person and performer, Duncan danced with bare feet and unrestrictive clothing. Born into a poor family in 1877, Duncan began giving dance

Isadora Duncan

lessons at the age of five to financially support her mother. At the age of ten, she dropped out of school. Duncan once compared ballet dancers to puppets, and her unique style drew the attention of wealthy patrons who hired her to perform at their garden parties. Her first theater performance, in 1902 in Budapest, sold out. By opening dance schools across countries such as Germany, France, and Russia, Duncan cemented her worldwide image as an influential choreographer. Her relationships never lasted long, and she had bisexual affairs with both men and women. In 1927, age fifty, Duncan died in a car accident in France when her long, draping scarf got caught in the wheels of the car and dragged her out of it. *"Adieu, mes amies, je vais à la gloire!"* ("Goodbye, my friends, I go to glory!") were reportedly her last words.

Beth Elliott *(San Francisco, CA)* was a 1970s transgender activist who cofounded an LGBT+ group called the Alice B. Toklas Memorial Democratic Club. Elliott was the first officer younger than twenty-one to serve as vice president of a Daughters of Bilitis chapter, yet the DOB later expelled her in Elliott in 1973 because she was a transgender woman. Elliott faced endless transphobia in her activism, as cisgender women of the time considered trans women to be infiltrators of the feminist movement. Shortly after being ousted from the DOB, for example, people protested Elliott's musical performance at the West Coast Lesbian Conference. She went on to join the committee for sexual law reform for the state of California, aiding its lobby for the state's repeal of sodomy laws. In 2005, she independently released the record *Buried Treasure*, citing her folk music style as a blend of Melissa Etheridge and Lucinda Williams.

Megan Ellison *(Santa Clara County, CA)* is a film producer and founder of Annapurna Pictures. Ellison's father is Larry Ellison, the third-wealthiest man in the country and cofounder of the software company Oracle. Ellison has produced critically acclaimed films such as *Zero Dark Thirty*, *If Beale Street Could Talk*, *Vice*, and *True Grit*. She has a reputation for producing films that other studios won't finance, especially those with edgy plots and stars. Ellison is openly gay, though she remains private about her personal life.

I wrote Vice Versa *mainly to keep myself company because I thought that although I don't know any gay gals now, by the time I finish a couple of these magazines I'm sure I will. I was such a little optimist.*

—Edythe Eyde, *Making Gay History*, interview with Eric Marcus

Edythe D. Eyde *(San Francisco, CA)* was an author, editor, and songwriter. Professionally, she went by the pen name Lisa Ben, an anagram for "lesbian." She self-published her magazine *Vice Versa,* considered the first US lesbian magazine, in 1947. Because it was illegal to send LGBT+ materials through the mail, Eyde hand-delivered issues to her subscribers. She later worked as a journalist for the lesbian magazine *The Ladder.* Eyde also worked with the Daughters of Bilitis and wrote folk songs such as "I'm Going to Sit Right Down and Write My Butch a Letter." Eyde died in 2015 at the age of ninety-four.

Jodie Foster *(Los Angeles, CA)* first began her acting career in childhood on the 1968 show *Mayberry R.F.D.* But it wasn't until her role as a prostitute in the 1976 Martin Scorsese film *Taxi Driver* that Foster rose to fame, following an Oscar nomination. At the time, she was fourteen years old. She continued acting in films such as *Freaky Friday* and *Candleshoe* during adolescence, then attended Yale University to study literature. While in college, she was stalked by John Hinckley, who attempted to assassinate Ronald Reagan in 1981 to impress her. Foster won her first Oscar in 1989 for *The Accused* and her second in 1992 for *The Silence of the Lambs.* Although Foster had spent most of the 1990s in a relationship with a woman and had publicly referenced her identity often, she officially came out as a lesbian at the Golden Globes in 2013 during her acceptance speech for the Cecil B. DeMille Lifetime

Jodie Foster

Alicia Garza *(Los Angeles, CA)* is an activist and a co-founder of the Black Lives Matter movement. She attended the University of California–San Diego, where she studied anthropology and sociology. Garza was raised by a single mother, and started her activism career as an advocate for reproductive rights. She has served as a high-level leader in multiple organizations such as the National Domestic Workers Alliance, the School of Liberation and Unity, Black Organizing for Leadership and Dignity, Right to the City Alliance, and People Organized to Win Employment Rights. After the 2012 shooting of Trayvon Martin, Garza became the first person to use the phrase "Black lives matter." Garza has won many awards for her activism, including the Harvey Milk Democratic Club's Bayard Rustin Community Activist Award, which she won twice.

Achievement Award. The following year, she married actress Alexandra Hedison.

Robert Garcia *(Lima, Peru)* is a civil rights attorney and politician. Garcia graduated from Stanford Law School, where he served as an editor of the Stanford Law Review. He founded the Council of the City Project, a nonprofit legal advocacy and social justice group specializing in environmental and economic justice. In his other advocacy work, Garcia has worked with the Development Team for the National Park Service Healthy Parks initiative and as a lawyer for the NAACP Legal Defense and Education Fund. Garcia was a 2010 recipient of the President's Award from the American Public Health Association.

Todd Gloria *(San Diego, CA)* is a California State Assembly member. Passionate about public service—from improving infrastructure to solving homelessness—Gloria has served his community in a number of positions, from San Diego Housing Commissioner to City Council President. During his time as Interim Mayor of San Diego in 2013, he wrote the city's Climate Action Plan. Gloria, who is openly gay, is a longtime advocate of LGBT+ rights; in college at the University of San Diego, he worked to include sexual orientation in the school's nondiscrimination ordinance. He is now vice chair of the California Legislative LGBT Caucus.

Jennicet Gutiérrez *(Tuxpan, Jalisco, Mexico)* is a transgender rights activist and community organizer.

I say this to people all the time: The reason that we created Black Lives Matter in that way is because we wanted to build a sense of empowerment and self-determination. Early on in the development of Black Lives Matter, we set up some social media pages that we intended to offer information about anti-black racism and state-sponsored violence, so people really understood what it looked like concretely in our present time.

—Alicia Garza, *The Cut*, 2017

Todd Gloria

When she was fifteen, Gutiérrez moved from Mexico to California. She the community organizer for Familia: Trans Queer Liberation Movement, which advocates for the rights of trans, queer, nonbinary, incarcerated, and immigrant Latinx people. In 2015, Gutiérrez interrupted President Obama's Pride Month speech to demand an end to US deportation of LGBT+ immigrants, who are regularly mistreated by immigration officers. The president asked her to leave, and the incident made national news. The following week, Immigration and Customs Enforcement (ICE) said it would respect the gender identities of immigrants and place them in the proper facilities, though Gutiérrez remained skeptical that it followed through.

Harry Hay *(Sussex, England)*, in 1950, founded the Mattachine Society, an early LGBT+ rights movement activist and support group. Though Hay started it with a group of seven gay men, within three years the society drew the interest of tens of thousands of LGBT+ people across California, organizing them at the grassroots level to demand their rights. Hay and his cofounders were radical communists, but McCarthyist attitudes of the era caused the group to quickly temper its beliefs out of fear of the government. In 1953, Hay and his cofounders resigned, turning the Mattachine

Society over to more conservative leadership. In 1979, Hay founded the Radical Faerie movement, which sought to define a unique homosexual spirituality. Hay was associated with numerous romantic partnerships with men; though he adopted two children while married to a woman, his longest relationship was with the inventor John Burnside.

Sylvester James *(Los Angeles, CA)* is a singer known simply as Sylvester. As a teenager, Sylvester sang in his church choir, but left his home and his religion after being shamed for his sexuality. He began performing rock covers under the name Sylvester and the Hot Band, lacking immediate success. Influenced by soul and gospel, Sylvester began making music with the gospel singers Izora Rhodes and Martha Wash in 1976. With their successful 1978 LP *Step II*, which featured the number-one singles "Dance (Disco Heat)" and "You Make Me Feel (Mighty Real)," James began experimenting with disco and electronic music. He performed in nightclubs, and his falsetto voice and elaborate costumes made him a legend in the San Francisco gay community. Over his career, he achieved five gold records and one platinum. James died of AIDS-related illness in 1988 at the age of forty-two.

Gloria Johnson *(Los Angeles, CA)* was an LGBT+ and women's rights activist. She was an active early 1970s member of the National Organization of Women, where she served as a chapter president and also as a state board member. A passionate advocate for the Equal Rights Amendment, Johnson once served jail time for civil disobedience after the amendment was defeated. She also fiercely opposed the Briggs Initiative, which sought to ban gay and lesbian teachers from California's public schools. Throughout her life, she supported the campaigns of numerous female politicians and served as a mentor to many young women. Johnson worked for the County of San Diego as a social worker for the AIDS Case Management Program and went on to become the cochair of the California Democratic Party LGBT Caucus, amongst her other roles at LGBT+ activist organizations.

Sara Kelly Keenan *(Santa Cruz, CA)* is the first person to hold an official intersex birth certificate, which she fought for and won in New York City. Keenan is also the first California resident and second US citizen to change her legal gender to nonbinary; Keenan also uses she/her pronouns. She was born with Swyer Syndrome, and her parents decided to surgically alter her body before she was old enough to decide for herself. Her two legal genders, intersex on her birth certificate and nonbinary in California, are evidence of the lack of consensus regarding gender classification within the government. Now retired, Keenan is a former paralegal.

Billie Jean King *(Long Beach, CA)* is a professional tennis player and activist with thirty-nine Grand Slam titles. King began playing tennis in middle school, and confronted inequality at an early age when a photographer told her she couldn't be in the junior tennis players' photo because she wore shorts and not a traditional skirt. She went on to become the number-one female tennis player in the world, a title she held for five years. King advocated for equal award money for male and female tennis matches, and as a result the US Open became the first major sports tournament to offer equal prize money regardless of sex. Her advocacy for equal pay in sports also led to the famous 1973 match called the "Battle of the Sexes," when King played against Bobby Riggs and beat him 6–4, 6–3, and 6–3. The match drew ninety million viewers. Despite her heroic win, King lost all her endorsements when she was outed as a lesbian in 1981. Never one to give in to setbacks, King continued her successful career and six years later entered the International Tennis Hall of Fame. King helped form the Women's Tennis

Billie Jean King

Association, and also founded World TeamTennis and the Women's Sports Foundation. The USTA National Tennis Center in Queens, New York, was dedicated to King in 2006, making her the first female athlete to have a major sports venue named after her.

Ricardo Lara *(Commerce, CA)* became the insurance commissioner of California in 2019, thus also becoming the first openly gay person elected to a statewide office in California. Prior, Lara had been a state senator since 2012. Lara attended San Diego State University, where he studied journalism and Chicano studies. He has spent his career advocating for immigrant rights, for children's health care with the Health4All Kids Act, and for clean air with the Super Pollutant Reduction Act. Lara is passionate about low-emission transportation, multilingual education, and financial assistance for low-income students pursuing higher education.

Louise Lawrence *(Berkeley, CA)* was a transgender activist. Lawrence is widely remembered as a uniting force within the early transgender community; she mentored Virginia Prince, inspiring her to do the same. She also worked with sexologist Alfred Kinsey and researcher Harry Benjamin to raise awareness of transgender people in the fields of medicine and psychology. When Prince launched *Transvestia* magazine in 1960, Lawrence's address book served as the magazine's first subscription list. A transgender history project called the Louise Lawrence Transgender Archive is named in her honor.

Hans Lindahl *(San Francisco, CA)* is a genderqueer intersex writer and cartoonist. They have served as the communications director for InterACT, where they cofounded the #4intersex campaign, which focuses on policy action as it regards intersex rights. Lindahl's illustrations focus on microaggressions they have experienced from medical professionals, as well as intersex educational booklets.

Greg Louganis *(El Cajon, CA)* is an Olympic diver and humanitarian. He first competed in the Olympics in 1976, when he was sixteen. That year, he won a silver medal for the ten-meter platform event. Although he could not compete in the 1980 Olympics because of the US boycott against Russia, he went on to win two

> *I'm 56, a gay man, living with HIV, happily married. Who would have imagined that back in the 1980s? I also did some research and found that General Mills is ranked very high in terms of human rights: They have a diversity foundation, and they do a lot for the LGBT community. So the times have changed. We've just come so far.*
>
> —Greg Louganis on finally being featured on the Wheaties box, *HBR's 10 Must Reads on Leadership Lessons from Sports*, 2018

Olympic gold medals in 1984, one for the three-meter springboard and one for the ten-meter platform. Six months before the 1988 Olympics, Louganis was diagnosed with HIV. In those games, he duplicated his 1984 wins with two more gold medals. He is the second diver to win gold medals for both the three-meter springboard and the ten-meter platform in consecutive Olympic games, and the first male. Though he was never featured on the Wheaties cereal box at the height of his fame due to homophobia, Wheaties featured him on its box in 2016 as part of its "Legends" initiative to recognize athletes not previously recognized. In 2013, Louganis was inducted into the California Sports Hall of Fame and the National Gay and Lesbian Sports Hall of Fame.

Dorothy "Del" Martin *(San Francisco, CA)* was an LGBT+ activist and cofounder of Daughters of Bilitis, which she started with her wife, Phyllis Lyon, in 1955. Martin and Lyon also started *The Ladder,* the first lesbian magazine with a national audience, which was unafraid to criticize misogyny, even within the gay rights movement. The couple married twice: once in 2004 when San Francisco legalized same-sex marriage, and again in 2008 when the state of California legalized same-sex marriage (because the California Supreme Court nullified their first marriage in 2004). They were the first same-sex couple to marry under each circumstance.

Ray Navarro *(Simi Valley, CA)* was a photographer, videographer, artist, and activist. He studied at Cal Arts in Valencia and later at the Whitney Independent Study Program in New York City. He was an activist

> *[Daughters of Bilitis] was a good coming out place. Where women could get their act together and find out who they were and be able to talk to others and hash it out. We felt that people get themselves together, and they can go out and cope with the world.*
>
> —Dorothy "Del" Marin, *Making Gay History*, interview with Eric Marcus, 1989

with the AIDS Coalition to Unleash Power (ACT UP), and memorably dressed as Jesus Christ while delivering a news report outside a church during the late 1980s Stop the Church protests against Catholic AIDS and anti-contraception rhetoric. Navarro was diagnosed with AIDS around the same time, and soon lost his vision because of it. In 1990, he collaborated on a photo series with Zoe Leonard, which featured mobility devices above sexy captions ("Hot butt" beneath a photo of a wheelchair, for example). Navarro died from AIDS-related illness in 1990 at the age of twenty-six.

Frank Ocean *(Long Beach, CA)* is a musician. He first came into the spotlight as a member of Odd Future, a hip-hop collective. In a 2012 Tumblr post, Ocean said he first fell in love when he was nineteen, and it was with a boy. His first solo album, *Channel Orange,* came out later that year, peaked at second on the Billboard 200, and won a Grammy for Best Urban Contemporary Album. In 2016, he independently released his second album, *Blond*. Ocean has collaborated with other A-list musicians such as Pharrell Williams, John Legend, and Beyoncé.

Monica Palacios *(San Jose, CA)* is a playwright and performance artist. Her long list of works include *BROWNER QUEERER LOUDER PROUDER, Say Their Names, I Kissed Chavela Vargas, Miercoles Loves Luna*, and *Greetings From a Queer Señorita*. Her work has been performed at theaters and universities in California, Texas, London, and Oregon. Palacios is also the author of publications including *Practicing Transgressions* and *Jota Anthology*.

Virginia Prince *(Los Angeles, CA)* was a 1940s transgender rights activist and journalist who lived in San Francisco. Assigned male at birth, Prince dressed in women's clothing from a young age, but resolved to stop once she got married. After earning a PhD in biochemistry, Prince went on to work at the University of California's medical school, where she met and formed a community with transgender patients. Soon, Prince divorced her wife because she was attracted to men. In 1960, Prince founded *Transvestia* magazine, a medium to help transgender people share information and organize, which ran until the early 1980s. Prince also started a sorority for male-to-female crossdressers

that went by two names: Phi Pi Epsilon and Full Personality Expression (FPE). Prince went on to write and advocate for transgender rights through the 1990s. She died in 2009 at the age of ninety-six.

Adrian Ravarour cofounded the gay youth organization Vanguard in 1965. Based in the Tenderloin neighborhood of San Francisco, Vanguard helped young gay people accept their sexuality and organize against discrimination. Ravarour was ordained as a priest in December 1959, and throughout his life worked in both the Mormon and Catholic churches, as well as other spiritual traditions. Ravarour has spent his lifetime dabbling in various arts, from ballet to poetry to musical composition.

Maggi Rubenstein *(San Francisco, CA)* is a sex educator and bisexual activist. She is a founding member of the National Sex Forum and the San Francisco Sex Information Hotline, where she ran workshops on prostitutes' rights and human sexuality. Her workshops became so popular that she founded the Institute for the Advanced Study of Human Sexuality in 1976, which offered academic credit and certification in its classes. Rubenstein also founded the Bisexual Center in San Francisco in the mid-1970s, which spread awareness of bisexuality and fostered community amongst bisexuals. Rubenstein also works as a sex therapist.

Jessica Sabogal *(San Francisco, CA)* is a muralist who was the first woman to receive a commission from Facebook for a mural at its California headquarters. Sabogal didn't initially study art; after college, she was inspired to try stencil art by artists Banksy and Shepard Fairy. She distributed her artwork to every business that would display it, and in 2011 landed a front-page feature on CNN.com for her artwork commemorating the Egyptian Revolution. The next year, Sabogal was commissioned by Penguin Books to design the twentieth anniversary reissue of *Bastard Out of Carolina* by Dorothy Allison. Sabogal, a queer Latina of Colombian heritage, was a keynote speaker at Stanford University's Raza Day High School Conference, where she urged students to take pride in their identities and not let fear stand in their way to success.

Bamby Salcedo *(Guadalajara, Mexico)* is a transgender activist. Salcedo grew up with a difficult childhood—her abusive stepfather and early exposure to drugs impacted her own addiction, causing her to seek treatment after she immigrated to the US. Her journey to health inspired her to help improve the lives of others. Salcedo runs the Angels of Change runway show, which benefits the Los Angeles Children's Hospital's transgender youth health center. She also started the TransLives Matter National Day of Action to advocate against transgender-targeted violence. Salcedo has worked with organizations such as Casa de Esperanza, the Latino Equality Alliance, the Transgender Law Center, AIDS United, and the National LGBTQ Task Force. She currently serves as the president and CEO of the TransLatin@ Coalition in Los Angeles.

George Takei *(Los Angeles, CA)* is an actor and activist who played Mr. Sulu on the original *Star Trek* in the 1960s. Takei has also appeared in *My Three Sons, Mission: Impossible, Hawaii Five-O, General Hospital, Miami Vice, Hey Arnold!, Kim Possible, Adventure Time, Futurama,* and *The Simpsons,* amongst many other roles and cameo appearances. During World War II, Takei and his family were forcibly placed in Japanese American internment camps, first in Arkansas and later in California. Those experiences inspired the

George Takei

2012 musical *Allegiance,* written by Marc Acito and Jay Kuo; Takei played the lead role. As an activist, Takei has worked with the Human Rights Campaign and is the Chairman of the Japanese American National Museum's Board of Trustees. Takei married his husband, Brad Altman, in 2008 at the Japanese American National Museum in Los Angeles.

Anne Tamar-Mattis *(Sonoma County, CA)* is a queer lawyer who is a cofounder and former executive director for Advocates for Informed Choice AIC organization (now known as InterACT). Tamar-Mattis has been an avid writer and activist for queer, trans, and intersex rights, and since 2008 has been an adjunct professor at the University of California–Berkeley School of Law. There, she teaches a course on sexual orientation and the law. She is the partner of intersex activist Suegee Tamar-Mattis (see below).

Suegee Tamar-Mattis *(Sonoma County, CA)* is a pioneer in intersex activism, who declared their intersex identity publicly in the 1990s. After graduating from the College of Osteopathic Medicine at Touro University, Tamar-Mattis opened a transgender clinic in rural

An overlooked group still faces involuntary sterilization. Infants and young children born with intersex conditions—congenital variations of the genitals, chromosomes, or internal sex organs—frequently undergo medically unnecessary sterilization as part of treatment intended to make their appearance match their assigned sex, privileging a normative model of anatomy over the ability of these children to later reproduce.

—Anne Tamar-Mattis, *California Law Review*, 2012

North Bay, California, that provides hormone therapy and emotional support to gender-nonconforming people. With help from the Human Rights Watch, they have spoken with other intersex people to gather evidence of human rights violations against the intersex community. Their research continues to help intersex people heal from trauma. Suegee is married to Anne Tamar-Mattis (see page 224).

Jewel Thais-Williams *(San Diego, CA)* is the founder of one of the first LGBT+ Black spaces in Los Angeles, a disco called Catch One. Growing up, she worked in her uncle's grocery store, which fueled her desire to one day start her own business. After graduating from UCLA, she opened her first business: a dress shop. When the shop struggled, she decided to open a club instead. So, in 1973 she opened Catch One. The bar was intentionally inclusive of racial and LGBT+ diversity; Thais-Williams had been a longtime witness to how homophobia pushed LGBT+ people into underground spaces, and how white LGBT+ people further forced out people of color. As Catch One's popularity grew, it drew visitors such as Madonna and Janet Jackson. In 2000, at the age of sixty, Thais-Williams became a certified acupuncturist and founded the Village Health Foundation, a nonprofit natural healing center.

Peter Thiel *(Frankfurt, Germany)* is a venture capitalist and entrepreneur who is most known for founding PayPal in 1998. A graduate of Stanford University, Thiel has a reputation for being an early investor in successful startups, including Facebook, LinkedIn, and Yelp. In 2003, he cofounded the software company Palantir Technologies, a big data analytics company. His

philanthropy, the Thiel Foundation, invests in breakthrough technology by awarding young entrepreneurs $100,000 to skip school and instead form startup companies. He is a Republican, and endorsed Donald Trump at the Republican National Convention in 2016. In a 2016 interview with *Inc.* magazine, Thiel stated he believes in parabiosis, the practice of receiving blood transfusions from young donors to retain youth and health. His 2014 book *Zero to One: Notes on Startups, or How to Build the Future* was a *New York Times* bestseller.

Alexander Wang *(San Francisco, CA)* is the founder of his namesake fashion label, Alexander Wang, which he started when he was twenty-one years old. After dropping out of Parsons School of Design, Wang launched his label with his family's help. In 2007, his first runway show at New York Fashion Week featured a ready-to-wear women's collection of sleek silhouettes and a monochrome palette. Wang describes his aesthetic as MOD, which stands for "models off-duty." Among his many accolades, Wang has received the Swiss Textiles Award, the title of Swarovski Womenswear Designer of the Year, GQ's Best Menswear Designer of 2011, CFDA's Best Accessory Designer, and also the Vogue/CFDA Fashion Fund's highest honor. He opened his first store in 2012 in Soho, New York, and has since opened stores around the world. From 2012 to 2015, Wang also worked as the creative director of the Spanish/French fashion house Balenciaga.

Mel White *(Santa Clara, CA)* is a religious leader, film and television producer, and activist. As an evangelical Christian pastor, he has ghostwritten the autobiographies of many church leaders, including Billy Graham

> *I had only recognized myself for what I was—being a Black lesbian—a few years prior to opening up the club. And we're talking 1973, when we opened. It wasn't a good time to come out. So, I was closeted at work, closeted at church, closeted at home . . . Closeted everywhere. We had racism, which was rampant in addition to what would happen at the club. There were riots in LA. In 1964, there was another one. Police brutality . . . you hear a lot of about it now because people have cell phones and they can take pictures. But it's been going on for as long as I can remember. We were being killed unnecessarily.*
>
> —Jewel Thais-Williams, AfterEllen.com, 2018

Alexander Wang

and Pat Robertson. In 1965, White started his own production company, Mel White Productions, and has since produced over fifty films on spiritual topics including self-acceptance, the Jonestown massacre, and the Vietnam War. Early in life, White endured religious therapies to rid him of homosexuality, including methods such as shock therapy and exorcism, which only further fueled his advocacy for LGBT+ rights within Christianity. White is the founder of SoulForce, an organization that exposes Christianity's imperial ties and seeks to reclaim an egalitarian Christianity. His influential autobiography, *Stranger at the Gate: To Be Gay and Christian in America*, was published in 1994.

Henry "Hank" Wilson *(Sacramento, CA)* was an LGBT+ activist and teacher. While working as a kindergarten teacher, he protested the 1978 Briggs Initiative, which would have allowed the state of California to fire teachers for being gay. From 1978 to 1996, Wilson also managed the Ambassador, a hotel for AIDS patients, which operated without public funding; he often spent his own money on food, personal care items, and flowers for the hotel's occupants. Wilson himself lived with AIDS for many years. He cofounded the Tenderloin AIDS Network and other LGBT+ rights initiatives such as the Gay Teachers Coalition, the Castro Street Safety Patrol, and the Harvey Milk LGBT Democratic Club. He died of cancer in 2008 at age sixty-one.

We made a conscious decision to work with people with AIDS early on. That was especially important because other agencies wouldn't work with people that had substance abuse and alcohol problems. We had people here who were very sick who were bed-bound and needed attendance and couldn't get support.

—Henry "Hank" Wilson, *Life and Death at the Ambassador Hotel*, 1994

◎ PLACES

The Alice B. Toklas LGBT Democratic Club *(San Francisco, CA)* is the oldest LGBT+ Democratic club in the US. Activists Jim Foster, Del Martin, and Phyllis Lyon founded it in 1971, two years after the Stonewall Riots. The club has worked with many political campaigns and organizers to promote LGBT-supportive legislation. Some past campaigns the club has worked on included that of Harvey Milk, Dianne Feinstein, and Mark Leno, an openly gay California State Senator. The organization continues to promote LGBT+ activism and rights within the Democratic Party.

The Ambassador Hotel *(San Francisco, CA)* was formerly managed by queer activist Henry Wilson, who used the space to care for AIDS patients. Wilson went on to cofound the Tenderloin AIDS Network. The Tenderloin Neighborhood Development Corporation purchased the Ambassador's property in 1999 and renovated the building into low-income housing.

Balboa Park *(San Diego, CA)* was a well-known hangout for gay men from the 1950s to the 1960s. Police swept through the area to arrest them, and on one occasion in 1968, they arrested seventy-five gay

men at once. In 1982, the San Diego History Center relocated to Balboa Park, where it opened an exhibit called "LGBTQ+ San Diego: Stories of Struggles and Triumphs" in 2018.

The Black Cat Café *(San Francisco, CA)* was a bar that opened around 1911 and became increasingly frequented by LGBT+ people after World War II. Unlike many other gay bars that bribed the police to avoid raids, the owner of the Black Cat, Sol Stoumen, refused to pay off the police as a form of resistance. As a result, police regularly raided the bar, but patrons like the drag queen José Sarria found ways to protest. Sarria performed to political songs, often parodies of other songs, and would sing "God Save Us Nelly Queens" in front of police officers. Black Cat closed in 1963.

The Black Cat Tavern *(Los Angeles, CA)* is a gay bar on Sunset Boulevard, as well as a historic city monument. In 1967, police raided the tavern, spurring a riot that spread down the street to different venues and resulted in fourteen arrests. Six weeks later, LGBT+ community members and allies held an organized protest against police brutality. The tavern reopened as a gastropub under the same name in 2008, and is marked with a plaque commemorating the 1967 riot. The plaque, in part, reads: "Site of the first documented LGBT civil rights demonstration in the nation."

Castro Camera *(San Francisco, CA)* was a camera shop run by Harvey Milk from 1972 to 1978. Briefly, Milk lived in the upstairs accommodations with his partner and ran his 1973 city supervisor campaign out of the store. The shop became a space for LGBT+ people to gather and organize. The site of Castro Camera now houses a chapter of the Human Rights Campaign. During the filming of the 2008 film *Milk*, Castro Camera was reconstructed in the original space. Locals who saw the original Castro Camera said the set was nearly identical to the original. The building is a historic landmark, commemorated by a plaque honoring the life and work of Milk.

The Castro Theatre *(San Francisco, CA)* hosts the annual Frameline LGBT+ film festival. The Nassar brothers, a couple of theater entrepreneurs, built the historic building in 1922. Architect Timothy L. Pflueger designed

The Castro Theatre

the building, which features intricate plaster work and art deco details. In 1976, San Francisco made the Castro Theatre its hundredth historical city landmark.

Circus Disco *(Los Angeles, CA)* was an intersectional LGBT+ disco founded in 1975, which remained a disco even after the genre fell from popularity. Circus was critical to the local LGBT+ community as well as local politics. In 1983, labor leader and activist César Chávez gave a talk at Circus Disco to a gay and lesbian business coalition, Project Just Business, about effective fundraising and boycotting. Circus closed in 2016 and was demolished under the initiative of the Lexington Project to redevelop Las Palmas Avenue and Santa Monica Boulevard.

Daughters of Bilitis's publication office *(San Francisco, CA)* was located on Mission Street. It was the office from which the organization distributed the lesbian magazine *The Ladder.* Lesbian couple Del Martin and Phyllis Lyon published the magazine and held meetings for the Daughters of Bilitis at several venues, including venues on Steiner Street and one on Geary Street.

The East Bay Stonewall Democratic Club *(Berkeley, CA)* advocates for LGBT+ rights and visibility. Armand Boulay and Tom Brougham (coiners of

the term "domestic partnership") founded the organization in 1982 to serve their neighborhood's LGBT+ community. The club works with Democratic political organizations and campaigns, builds community, and promotes legislation benefitting LGBT+ individuals and their families.

Gene Compton's Cafeteria *(San Francisco, CA)* was a twenty-four-hour restaurant and, in August 1966, was home to one of the country's first LGBT+ riots. Drag queens and trans women frequented Compton's Cafeteria, which was located in the Tenderloin District, an area known for sex trafficking, drug trafficking, and gambling. It was also one of the only spaces in the city where drag queens and trans women could dress as they pleased. The restaurant's management frequently called the police on patrons who were gay, lesbian, or gender-nonconforming. At the time, police could arrest patrons on the charge of "female impersonation." During the famous 1966 raid, a drag queen threw coffee in an officer's face after he grabbed her, inciting a fight that destroyed a police car, tables, and windows. In the riot's aftermath, the National Transsexual Counseling Network was created.

The GLBT History Museum *(San Francisco, CA)* is a component of the GLBT Historical Society, which was founded in 1985. The museum's permanent exhibit "Queer Past Becomes Present" showcases artifacts from LGBT+ history in the Bay Area that date from 1850 to the present day. The museum also hosts themed seasonal exhibits.

GLIDE Memorial Church *(San Francisco, CA)* was a Methodist Church founded in 1929. In 1966, the church founded the Council on Religion and the Homosexual, which involved multiple other churches. That year, the church also started Vanguard Sweep, an LGBT+ youth organization. The church has continued to take on social justice initiatives, and advocates for issues such as economic justice, racial justice, and the end of racial profiling.

The Great Wall of Los Angeles *(Los Angeles, CA)* is a half-mile long and one of the largest murals in the world. It depicts the chronological history of Los Angeles, with a focus on women and marginalized groups.

GLIDE Memorial Church

Forty artists and forty historians informed the project, designed by Judith Baca. Baca wanted to highlight the histories of all groups outside the dominant historical narrative, including the LGBT+ community, which the mural features in section five. Four hundred community volunteers created the mural over six summers.

Griffith Park *(Los Angeles, CA)* was one of the first sites of "gay-ins," a form of protest against police harassment and discrimination that originated around 1968. Gay-ins were large, community picnics with live music and educational speeches about gay rights and activism. Prior to the gay-ins, Griffith Park was a popular cruising site.

The Hartford Street Zen Center *(San Francisco, CA)* is a Sōtō Zen temple that caters to the local LGBT+ community. Reverend Isaan Dorsey, a former drag queen, opened the center in 1981 as the Gay Buddhist Club. In 1987, the center opened a hospice center for patients suffering from HIV/AIDS, three years before Dorsey himself passed away from AIDS.

Jewel's Catch One *(Los Angeles, CA)* was a club and disco opened by activist Jewel Thais-Williams in 1973. Later known simply as Catch One, it was the first club that provided a safe space for the Black LGBT+ community. Williams operated the bar for forty-two years, and made it a place of refuge during the AIDS crisis.

Las Memorias AIDS Monument *(Los Angeles, CA)*, located in Lincoln Park, commemorates those who died of AIDS. The monument was constructed in 2004,

in part because of the efforts of Richard L. Zaldivar, founder of the Wall-Las Memorias project, which seeks to address substance abuse and HIV prevention in the LGBT+ community. The Las Memorias AIDS Monument was the first publicly funded AIDS monument constructed in the US. Every year on World AIDS Day, new names are inscribed on it in a ceremony called *Noche de Las Memorias*.

Liberace's Palm Springs home *(Palm Springs, CA)* is where he lived from 1968 to 1972, located on North Kaweah road. The home sports a plaque that reads "Piazza de Liberace," and the mailbox is shaped like a grand piano. It is a private residence that new owners have since remodeled, but they have kept key aspects of Liberace's original design, such as gold-plated faucets and a room that is entirely white.

The Los Angeles LGBT Center *(Los Angeles, CA)* is a nonprofit LGBT+ advocacy organization with over six hundred employees. Founded in 1969 as the Gay Community Services Center, it is one of the oldest LGBT+ community centers in the nation. It provides services in four areas: leadership and advocacy, social services and housing, culture and education, and health. The Anita May Rosenstein Campus, opened in April 2019, offers affordable housing for seniors, one hundred beds for homeless youth, a commercial kitchen, and supporting housing for young people. The center has ranked within Charity Navigator's top 3 percent of charities for more than ten consecutive years, under the leadership of Lorri Jean, CEO.

The Millennium Biltmore Hotel *(Los Angeles, CA)* opened in 1923 with a gay-friendly bar. It was also the site of the famous 1971 International Psychologists & Psychiatrists conference, which the Gay Liberation Front interrupted because the conference advocated electroshock therapy as a cure for homosexuality. This sparked a conversation between the two groups in which the GLF protested against the classification of homosexuality as a mental disorder. Two years later, the American Psychological Association removed homosexuality from its diagnostic manual of disorders.

Mission Dolores Park *(San Francisco, CA)*, also known as Dolores Park, has welcomed a diverse range of visitors within the LGBT+, Latinx, and Castro neighborhood communities. Dolores Park, while landlocked, is often referred to as a "gay beach," and is one of the most popular public gathering spaces for LGBT+ people in the city with great views of the city and bay.

The Most Holy Redeemer Catholic Church *(San Francisco, CA)*, since the 1980s, has offered weekly support groups to people affected by the HIV/AIDS crisis. Founded in 1901, the church's history with AIDS activism and inclusivity is documented in the 2007 book *Gays and Grays: The Story of the Gay Community at Most Holy Redeemer Catholic Church* by Friar Donal Godfrey. Most Holy Redeemer Catholic Church continues to welcome people of all sexual orientations and gender identities, and also provides support to sex workers and drug addicts.

The NAMES Project *(San Francisco, CA)* was an AIDS memorial initiative started by activist Cleve Jones in 1986. Jones made a quilt panel to commemorate his friend Marvin Feldman, who had passed away from AIDS complications. The NAMES Project continued making panels to commemorate those lost to AIDS, and had a forty-panel quilt by the 1987 Gay and Lesbian Pride Parade in San Francisco. Four months later, the quilt had 1,920 panels sent in from around the country and spanned the National Mall in Washington. The NAMES Project's venue on Market Street became a gathering space for people to grieve, socialize, and sew. In 1989, the quilt was nominated for a Nobel Peace Prize, and its documentary *Common Threads: Stories from the Quilt* won an Oscar that same year. In 1993, the AIDS Memorial Quilt had thirty thousand panels, and had forty-eight thousand as of 2004. It is the largest community art project to date, and the NAMES Project has raised $3 million for AIDS relief through displays of the quilt.

The Oasis Retreat Center *(Sonoma County, CA)* was the site of the first US intersex conference, and also where the Intersex Society of North America produced the 1997 short film "Hermaphrodites Speak." The video featured ten intersex people from all around world who shared their experiences and talked about the medical abuses intersex people face.

The ONE National Gay & Lesbian Archives *(Los Angeles, CA)* is located at the libraries of the University of Southern California. With over two million items, it is the world's largest collection of materials related to LGBT+ history, and includes films, photographs, letters, artwork, books, and audio recordings. The collection began in 1952 as an initiative of *ONE* magazine from the personal collection of Jim Kepner. In 1994, the collection became a part of ONE Institute, and then moved to the University of Southern California in 2010.

Osento *(San Francisco, CA)* was a Japanese-style bathhouse for women that opened in the 1980s. Lesbians frequented Osento, but the bathhouse was not sexually charged; it was a female-only safe space for relaxation and self-care. Osento closed in 2008.

The Palm Center *(Los Angeles, CA)* is a public policy center and research institute that published "Re-Thinking Genital Surgeries on Intersex Infants," a paper authored by three former US surgeon generals: M. Joycelyn Elders, David Satcher, and Richard Carmona. The paper addresses the practice of cosmetic genital surgery on intersex infants, saying, "Cosmetic genitoplasty should be deferred until children are old enough to voice their own view about whether to undergo the surgery. Those whose oath or conscience says 'do no harm' should heed the simple fact that, to date, research does not support the practice of cosmetic infant genitoplasty." The center is named after Michael D. Palm, a businessman, athlete, and musician who was a member of the board of directors of the Gay Men's Health Crisis.

The Palm Springs Walk of Stars *(Palm Springs, CA)* is lined with stars, one for each of the over four hundred celebrities on the walk. Many LGBT+ celebrities are immortalized here, including Liberace, Drew Barrymore, Lee Daniels, RuPaul, Jodie Foster, Ellen DeGeneres, and more.

The Pendulum *(San Francisco, CA)* was a gay bar in the Castro district that opened to accommodate gay men of color who were barred from other gay spaces. Since its closing in 2005, locals have lamented the loss of Black spaces in the Castro neighborhood.

San Francisco City Hall

The Rainbow Honor Walk *(San Francisco, CA)* is a route through the Castro neighborhood near the intersection of Castro Street and Market Street that honors the community's LGBT+ history. It is lined with forty-four plaques honoring individuals such as Tom Waddell, George Choy, and Oscar Wilde. Local community members lead tours, but maps are also available for self-guided tours.

Rosie the Riveter WWII Homefront National Historical Park *(Richmond, CA)* honors the women whose work contributed to the US efforts in World War II. During the war, many women in Richmond worked in shipyards and other seaside industries, so the park also honors the change in career options that then became publicly acceptable for women. At the time, women increasingly began exploring their sexualities and living on their own or in same-sex residence. The site is recognized by the National Park Service as important to LGBT+ history in the San Francisco Bay Area.

The San Diego LGBT Community Center *(San Diego, CA)* became a nonprofit in 1973, when the center started providing mental health services to the LGBT+ community. It started a twenty-four-hour hotline that LGBT+ people could call for counseling on issues such as discrimination, employment, or housing. Today, the center continues to support the LGBT+ community with family, youth, senior, and counseling services.

San Francisco City Hall *(San Francisco, CA)* was the site of Harvey Milk's assassination in 1978. Harvey Milk was elected as a city supervisor in 1977 as one of the first gay people to be elected to public office. Another city supervisor, Dan White, shot Milk and San Francisco's mayor, George Moscone, on November 27, 1978. Dianne Feinstein, who was then the president of the board of supervisors, found the men's bodies in an office and later publicly announced their deaths. White served a little over five years in prison for the murders. Milk has been commemorated by a bust statue—by the design firm of sculptors Eugene Daub, Rob Firman, and Jonah Hendrickson—which is housed at San Francisco City Hall.

Star Pharmacy *(San Francisco, CA)* was one of the first pharmacies to acknowledge the HIV/AIDS crisis. In 1981, nurse and activist Bobbi Campbell placed flyers in the windows of Star Pharmacy to inform the community about the health crisis after being diagnosed with HIV herself. Campbell died in 1984 at age thirty-two; Star Pharmacy soon closed in 1985. A Walgreens across the street from its former location created a plaque in Campbell's honor.

The Stud *(San Francisco, CA)* is a bar widely known for its drag performances, although it began as a biker bar in the 1960s. Since becoming a gay bar, the Stud has hosted drag queens such as Heklina and RuPaul. It has also held performances by musicians such as Lady Gaga, Bjork, Etta James, the Weather Girls, and Sylvester. In 2016, the Stud's financial hardships almost caused it to close, but the local LGBT+ community rallied together to purchase the bar. With eighteen owners, the Stud is now the first co-op club in the nation.

The Tenderloin Museum *(San Francisco, CA)* documents the history of its namesake neighborhood. From the Prohibition era through the 1980s, Tenderloin was known for gambling, drug trafficking, and sex work. It was frequented by drag queens and transgender women, and was one of the only areas where they lived openly. Uptown Tenderloin Inc., a nonprofit dedicated to educating people on the history of Tenderloin, founded the Tenderloin Museum in 2009.

The Tom of Finland House *(Los Angeles, CA)* honors the work of erotic artist Touko Laaksonen and the work of other erotic artists. Laaksonen traveled between this home and one in Finland, and regularly exhibited work in Los Angeles under the name Tom of Finland. His artwork, which featured men in leather and uniforms, is legendary among the local gay community. Laaksonen and his partner, Durk Dehner, started the Tom of Finland Foundation in 1984 to showcase and preserve his work, as well as the work of others, to promote anti-censorship and liberating portrayals of sexuality. It now possesses one of the largest collections of erotic art in the world.

The Village at Ed Gould Plaza *(Los Angeles, CA)* is part of the Los Angeles LGBT Center, which offers legal, financial, health, and educational assistance to LGBT+ people. Two theaters and two galleries connect to the Village, which have hosted performances and

Will Rogers State Beach

exhibitions by renowned LGBT+ artists and performers. Most gallery shows are free to the public.

West Hollywood *(Los Angeles, CA)* is one of California's most LGBT+ friendly neighborhoods. More than 40 percent of West Hollywood's population identifies as LGBT+, and the neighborhood hosts extravagant Pride and Halloween festivals every year. It is home to many LGBT+ hotels, bars, and cafes, and boasts a design district with famous fashion boutiques, interior design stores, and art galleries.

Will Rogers State Beach *(Los Angeles, CA)*, also known as Ginger Rogers Beach, is an unofficial gay beach that has welcomed LGBT+ people—but mostly gay men—since the 1950s. The beach's namesake, Will Rogers, was a cowboy and Hollywood actor who used to own the land. Rogers died in a plane crash in 1935; the beach became part of a state park in his honor in 1944, when Rogers's wife, Betty, donated the land to the state.

The Woman's Building *(Los Angeles, CA)* was founded in 1973 by the artist Judy Chicago, the graphic designer Sheila de Bretteville, and the art historian Arlene Raven. They also taught many of the building's programs, activities, and artists' group events. The Women's Building was designed as an homage to the architect Sophia Hayden, the first female graduate of a four-year architecture program. For a time, the building hosted one of the first independent art schools for women, the Feminist Studio Workshop. It also rented out studio spaces to female artists. The building closed in 1991.

◎ QUEER FACTS

The *Bay Area Reporter* is a weekly San Francisco newspaper for the LGBT+ community. Bob Ross and Paul Bently founded the *Reporter* in 1971, and it has since become one of the oldest continuously running LGBT+ publications in the country.

"Bisexual Invisibility: Impacts and Regulations" was a report published by the San Francisco Human Rights Commission in 2011. It is the first government document to discuss the visibility of bisexual people. The Lesbian, Gay, Bisexual, and Transgender Advisory Committee approved the report, which says that over half of the LGBT+ community in the US identifies as bisexual, something bisexual activists have long talked about. The report also discusses the high rate of suicidal ideation in the bisexual community, and the pay gap between bisexuals compared to gays and lesbians, who make almost 10 percent more money per year.

The California Legislative LGBT Caucus is a group of openly LGBT+ members of the California State Legislature. Founded in 2002, it is the first group of its kind in the US. In 2017, group membership reached eight people. The caucus seeks to discuss and promote legislation that is supportive of California's LGBT+ community.

California's sodomy laws were instated as early as 1850 through common law. In 1901, a law passed that allowed prisoners to be sterilized if officials deemed them sexual perverts. In 1921, California passed an amendment to made oral sex a crime punishable by up to fifteen years in prison. That same year, California passed another law that any act against public decency would be punished, allowing police to prosecute almost anyone for sexual acts. California decriminalized consensual sodomy and oral sex amongst adults in 1975, but police continued profiling gay men throughout the 1990s.

The Castro Street Fair is a showcase of food, artists, artisans, and other vendors started by Harvey Milk in 1974. The fair occurs every October, and includes many LGBT+ vendors. Proceeds go to local nonprofit organizations, many of which benefit the LGBT+ community.

Demilitarized Fleet Week is an annual event founded by former San Francisco mayor Dianne Feinstein in 1981. The week celebrates the naval history of San Francisco and honors military veterans. It draws huge LGBT+ participation, especially in the years following the repeal of the Don't Ask, Don't Tell policy. Fleet Week includes an air show, an LGBT+ mixer, and a military dog show.

Equality California is an LGBT+ civil rights activist organization that promotes public education and equality for LGBT+ people. With over 800,000 members, it has a long history of successful policy instigation from immigration to marriage equality. In 2017, it passed its 127th piece of LGBT-supportive legislation.

The FAIR Education Act, led by former state senator Mark Leno, passed in 2011 and mandates LGBT+ history be taught in California's school curriculum. It also protects students from educational discrimination because of gender identity or sexual orientation. California is the first state to include LGBT+ history books in its elementary school curriculum, starting in 2017.

The first all-LGBT+ city council was elected to office in 2018 in Palm Springs. The city did not celebrate the milestone, and mayor Robert Moon said he didn't think anything of it until after the election. The council members declared the real victory was that they were all elected on the basis of merit, without advertising their sexualities in their campaigns. The election did not come as a surprise to the residents of Palm Springs, a well-known LGBT-inclusive community.

The first openly gay judge in the US was Stephen Lachs of Los Angeles, whom Governor Jerry Brown appointed as a Superior Court Judge in 1979. Lachs had previously served as a commissioner with the LA County Superior Court. Lachs said that his coming out broke the stereotypes many people held about gay people, and that the more people came out, the more they challenged those stereotypes. In his career, Lachs also was in charge of the fundraiser that created the Municipal Elections Committee of Los Angeles, one of the first gay political committees in the country.

The first openly lesbian official to be appointed to a federal position by the Senate was Roberta Achtenberg, who served as the Assistant Secretary of the US Department of Housing and Urban Development. The Senate appointed her in 1993, making her the first gay or lesbian person appointed to a federal position by the Senate.

The first openly transgender person to serve as a trial court judge of general jurisdiction in the United States was Victoria Kolakowski, who became a judge in 2010. Previously, she served as the cochair for the board of directors at the Transgender Law Center. She is also the former president of the International Association of LGBT Judges.

The first proto-leather bar in San Francisco opened in 1938 and was called the Sailor Boy Tavern. It attracted navymen and set a theme for similar gay bars that later appeared in the area, although the leather scene didn't gain popularity until the 1960s. The Sailor Boy Tavern closed in 1953.

Gay Capital of America is another term for San Francisco, as declared by *LIFE* magazine in the 1964 article "Gay San Francisco."

The Gay Olympics *(now known as the Gay Games)* are a series of sporting events for LGBT+ competitors. Olympic decathlete Tom Waddel and others started the games in San Francisco's Kezar Stadium in 1982, and attracted over 1,300 competitors for its seventeen events. The Gay Olympics are open to people of all sexual orientations, with no requirements dictating who is allowed to compete. Today, the Gay Olympics are held all over the world in cities such as Paris, Hong Kong, and Cleveland.

Health benefits for domestic partnerships first became available in Berkeley, California, which offered them to city employees and their domestic partners starting in 1984.

The HIV/AIDS epidemic began in 1981 in San Francisco, initially called Gay-Related Immuno Deficiency (GRID). It spread throughout the Bay Area, and eventually the country. Although people were wary of the disease, they did not immediately become more cautious, and bathhouses continued operating until 1984. The government proposed creating camps to quarantine people with HIV/AIDS, although it never did. Today, more than half of San Francisco citizens with HIV/AIDS are over the age of fifty. San Francisco is a leader in HIV/AIDS research and preventative care, with a projected zero new infections by 2020.

The LGBT Veterans Memorial was designated in 2018 as the official California monument to honor LGBT+ veterans. It was the first statewide memorial commemorating LGBT+ servicemembers. Prior to its state designation, the venue was established as a local memorial in 2001.

The Log Cabin Republicans is an LGBT+ organization that seeks to build inclusivity within the Republican Party. Its name honors former President Abraham Lincoln, who was born in a log cabin and advocated for liberty and equality during his presidency. The Log Cabin Republicans was founded in the late 1970s after former California governor Ronald Reagan fought the Briggs Initiative, which sought to ban homosexual teachers from public schools. Reagan's work inspired gay Republicans to organize and advocate for their interests. Among its accomplishments, the Log Cabin Republicans helped defeat homophobic Republican presidential candidate Pat Buchanan in 1992 and worked to make President George W. Bush's campaign and presidency more inclusive.

The Mattachine Society was a gay rights organization founded in Los Angeles by activist Harry Hay in 1950. One of the first LGBT+ organizations in the country, it aimed to improve life for gay men. The name was inspired by the French masked group of traveling performers, the Société Mattachine, which spoke out against social injustice, alluding to the fact that gay men were forced to "mask" their authentic lives.

The pride flag

In its Statements of Mission and Purpose, the Mattachine Society vowed to create a gay community and to advocate for gay rights in legislation. Soon, the organization had chapters all over the country. It also originated the gay publication *ONE* magazine, which ran until 1972.

Metropolitan Community Church, the first LGBT+ welcoming Christian denomination, was founded in Los Angeles by Troy Perry in 1968. The MCC has a long history of human rights advocacy beyond LGBT+ issues, and has advocated on climate change, economic justice, and racial justice. It was the first denomination to perform same-sex marriages, and is widely known as the first gay church. Today, there are 160 MCC-affiliated churches across thirty-three countries.

One of the two first openly lesbian rabbis ordained by the Jewish Renewal movement was Chaya Gusfield from Northern California. She and Rabbi Lori Klein, who is also a lesbian, were ordained at the same time in 2006.

Proposition 22 was a California state law that defined marriage as a union between a man and a woman. It passed on the 2000 ballot with 61.2 percent of the vote. California rescinded Proposition 22 in May 2008, but that November, the state passed Proposition 8, which once more banned same-sex marriage. In 2010, a federal judge ruled Proposition 8 unconstitutional. In 2013, the California Supreme Court upheld the 2010 ruling and legalized same-sex marriage statewide.

The rainbow flag was designed by Gilbert Baker in 1978 after Harvey Milk challenged him to create a pride symbol. Baker dyed each section of the flag and sewed them together himself. The eight original colors each held a different meaning: hot pink, sexuality; red, life; orange, healing; yellow, sunlight; green, nature; blue, art; indigo, harmony; violet, spirit. Different versions of the flag were produced throughout the years in varying sizes and colors. In 1994, a mile-long version created to celebrate the twenty-fifth anniversary of the Stonewall riots made the Guinness Book of World Records for the world's longest flag.

The San Francisco Gay Men's Chorus was one of the first choirs comprised of openly gay members, as well as one of the largest male choirs in the world. In 1978, the chorus's first public performance was a candlelight vigil at City Hall after the assassinations of Harvey Milk and George Moscone. Many people credit the San Francisco Gay Men's Chorus as the group that started the national gay chorus trend. Proceeds from its concerts benefit LGBT-supportive organizations.

The San Francisco Trans March promotes transgender visibility, community, equality, and pride. The first march occurred in 2004, and has since been held yearly on the first Friday of Pride weekend. It is one of the largest transgender events in the world, with increasing participation every year.

The School Success and Opportunity Act passed in 2013 to protect transgender students from discrimination. The act states that all K-12 students in California must be "permitted to participate in sex-segregated school programs and activities, including athletic teams and competitions, and use facilities consistent with his or her gender identity, irrespective of the gender listed on the pupil's records."

The Sisters of Perpetual Indulgence is a group of men who dress in drag as nuns and perform pieces that double as activist and charity events. The group started in the Castro neighborhood of San Francisco and now has chapters across the US and the world. The group is also known for its community leadership, especially related to HIV/AIDS awareness and charity work.

Transvestia: The Journal of the American Society for Equality in Dress began in 1952. Virginia Prince, along with other transgender people in Southern California, wrote two issues of *Transvestia*, creating a community of transgender individuals that would help spark the transgender rights movement. The magazine was distributed to the contact list of Louise Lawrence, Prince's mentor.

The White Night riots occurred on May 21, 1979, after Dan White, the man who assassinated San Francisco's mayor George Moscone and Harvey Milk, received the lightest sentence possible for the murders. The LGBT+ community of San Francisco commenced a peaceful protest that ended at City Hall. When they arrived, violence between the police and the protestors resulted in property damage and injuries. Protestors felt angry toward the police because the police had raised $100,000 for White's defense, as he was a former police officer himself. Right after the riot, police raided a gay bar in the Castro district, deepening tensions between the LGBT+ community and the police. Those tensions remained until years later, when mayor Dianne Feinstein appointed a gay-friendly chief of police, who recruited LGBT+ officers.

toward the baker's religious rights. This ruling did not set a precedent, however, as it sidestepped the central conflict of whether the First Amendment protects business owners' rights to refuse to serve certain customers because of their identities, and was instead applied only to this specific case.

The Pit *(Denver, CO)*, Denver's first gay bar, opened in 1939 in downtown Denver on Seventeenth Street. While it was a safe haven for the gay community, patrons still had reason to fear being imprisoned because of police raids. The Pit was the only exclusively, publicly advertised gay tavern until after World War II.

💡 QUEER FACTS

Amendment 2 passed in Colorado in 1992, preventing any city, town, or county in Colorado from taking legislative, executive, or judicial action to recognize gay and lesbian individuals as a protected class. The amendment sparked national outrage and a vocal response from the national entertainment industry, with performers such as Barbra Streisand speaking out against the "hate state." The amendment was repealed in 1996, deemed unconstitutional by the Supreme Court in the case *Romer v. Evans*.

Angie Zapata was murdered in 2008 because of her gender identity. Zapata was an eighteen-year-old transgender woman living in Greeley, Colorado. On June 14, Zapata picked up Allen Andrade, a thirty-one-year-old man she met online, and spent three days with him in her apartment. On the third day, Andrade became aware that Zapata was biologically male. He confronted her and things quickly escalated: he beat her with his fists and eventually with a fire extinguisher until she was dead. In 2009, Andrade was convicted of four charges, including first-degree murder and bias-motivated crime, and was sentenced to life in prison without the possibility of parole. This was the first time a person was convicted of a hate crime in the murder of a transgender person.

Big Mama Rag was a Denver-based lesbian feminist newspaper published from 1972 to 1984 that published articles and editorials to appeal to and educate women. In 1974, *Big Mama Rag* was denied federal tax-exempt status by the IRS, in part because its articles promoted lesbianism. In 1980, the Court of Appeals ruled that the IRS couldn't deny tax exemption

because of the magazine's content, and *Big Mama Rag* won the "right to incorporate."

The Colorado Gay Rodeo Association was founded in September 1982. Initially, the group, more than 200 members large, competed at the Gay Rodeo of Reno. After finding that it wanted clearer competition rules and a greater focus on charity, however, the association promptly began its own rodeo. The association's first rodeo was held in Aurora, Colorado, in June 1983.

Colorado legalized same-sex marriage on October 7, 2014. A few months prior, the Tenth Circuit Court of Appeals (which has jurisdiction over Colorado) had ruled that same-sex marriage bans are unconstitutional. On October 6, 2014, the US Supreme Court refused to hear any appeals on this ruling,

I grew up with a learning disability . . . My passion is budget and numbers. I never dreamt I'd be taking over the gavel and running the chamber. I mean, it wasn't even in my wildest dreams a couple of years ago, let alone when I was a kid.

—Mark Ferrandino, *Out Front*, 2012

essentially finalizing the Circuit Court's rule against the marriage ban. The next day, county clerks began issuing same-sex marriage licenses.

Colorado's first anti-sodomy clause was enacted in 1861 with the Colorado Territorial Laws. Upon the state's formation, it adopted English Common Law, which included an anti-homosexuality clause. The fact that the government explicitly addressed sodomy in its laws suggests that the state was concerned with homosexuality at the time, a fact historians point to as being highly likely because of the area's predominantly male population of miners, railroad workers, military personnel, and cowboys.

Colorado's first openly gay Speaker of the House was Mark Ferrandino. Originally from New York, Ferrandino was first appointed to his role in the House in 2007, and was elected Speaker in 2013. He is known for his work with public health and his advocacy for the Colorado Civil Union Act. Ferrandino reached his term limit in 2015 and went on to become the chief financial officer for Denver Public Schools. He lives in Denver with his partner and their dog.

Denver's first Pride parade was held in 1976, as LGBT+ citizens stepped into the streets from the semi-obscure, half-hidden gay bar scene. It was the first highly visible public statement for the various LGBT+ communities of Denver. The parade was the closing event of a weeklong pride festival put on by the GLBT Community Center of Colorado. It began at Cheesman Park and ran down Franklin Street to Colfax Street, ending up at the Civic Center.

The Gill Foundation was established in 1994, inspired by the 1992 passage of Amendment 2 (see above). Created by Tim Gill, founder of the software company Quark Inc. and an openly gay man, the Gill Foundation aims to advance LGBT+ rights through charity and education. The Gill Foundation prioritizes equal access to employment, housing, and public accommodations, as well as family recognition, safe schools, and local prosperity for LGBT+ people. It has invested more than $345 million in programs and nonprofit organizations throughout the country since its inception.

The Imperial Court of the Rocky Mountain Empire (ICRME), founded in 1973 as a local chapter of the International Imperial Court, is one of Colorado's oldest LGBT+ organizations. ICRME hosts LGBT+ community events and raises money for various charities. Since its inception, it has donated almost one million dollars to various causes, including the Colorado AIDS Project, ICRME's local college scholarship, Freedom Service Dogs of America, and Parkinson's charities. One of its biggest events is the annual Coronation gala, where members elect the new Emperor and Empress to lead the organization for the next year.

The Johnny Cash bus sting operation ran in early 1973 to entrap young gay men. The tour bus, bearing a marquee advertising a Johnny Cash special, typically parked near the state capitol, a popular cruising site. Lured into the bus with the promise of going to a Johnny Cash show, men would then be sexually propositioned—if they showed any interest, they were arrested for offering lewd conduct. In the first three months of 1973, the Denver Police Department vice squad arrested 380 gay men in the operation. The Gay Coalition of Denver appealed to Denver's City Council, arguing that because 100 percent of those arrested for "lewd conduct" were gay and because 99 percent of those arrests were initiated by the police instead of the public, the police had been enforcing discriminatory laws. The GCD and its supporters testified to the City Council for three hours—and were successful. The council agreed to abolish anti-gay laws, leading to the successful repeal of loitering and crossdressing laws in 1973.

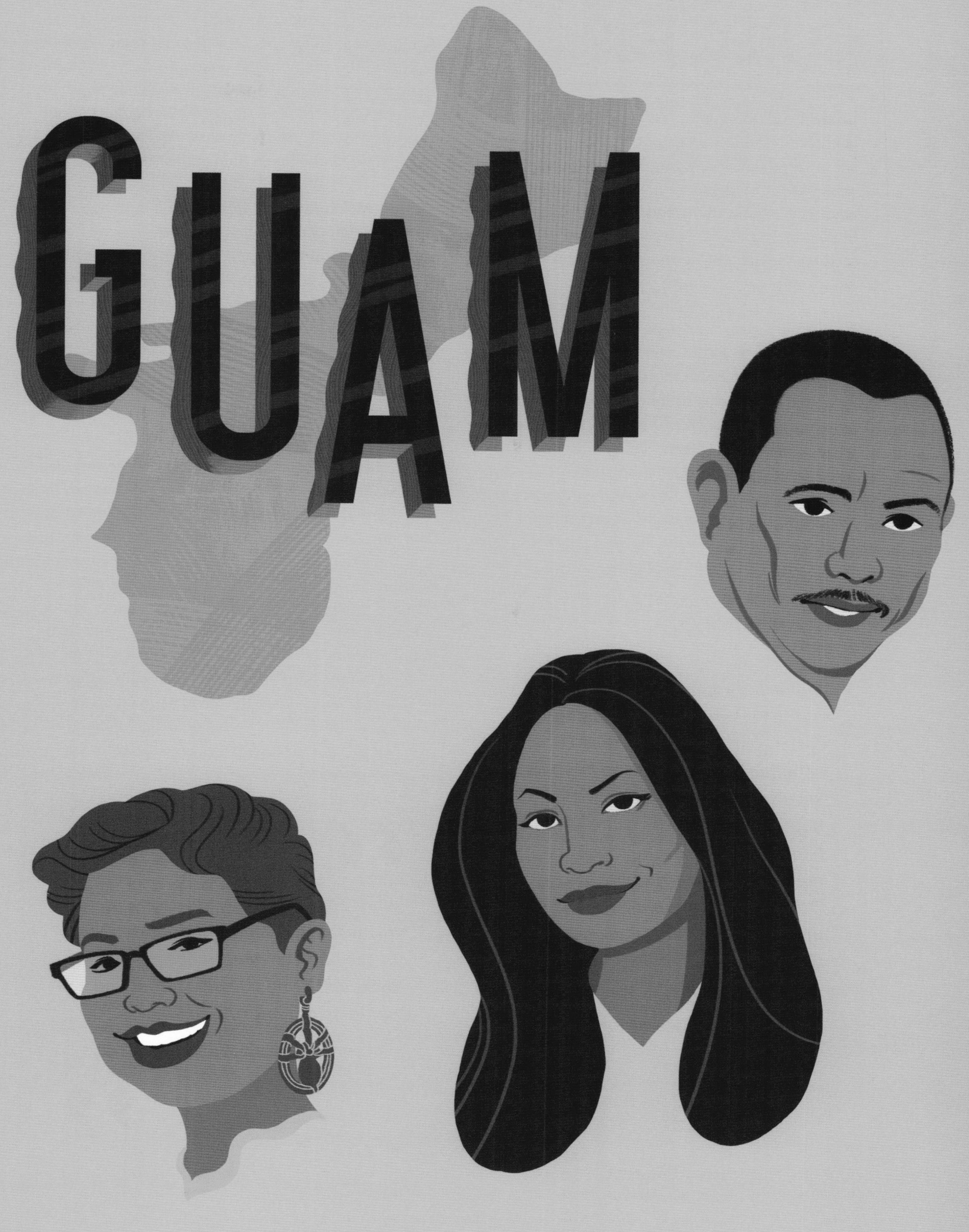
GUAM

👤 PEOPLE

Lasia Casil (*Santa Rita, GU*) became the first transgender politician to run for public office in Guam when she ran for a senator seat in 2018. Previously, Casil had worked with Save Southern Guam, an environmental advocacy organization, and founded Guam's Pride festival in 2016. Casil now serves as the executive director of the Hagåtña Redevelopment and Restoration Authority.

Benjamin Cruz (*Piti, GU*) served as Guam's Chief Justice from 1999 to 2001. He had previously worked as a trial court judge for over thirteen years, and earned his JD from the University of Santa Clara in 1972. He came out as gay in 1995 in *Latte* magazine, but while studying at Claremont McKenna College (then Claremont Men's College) in the 1970s, he started the school's first LGBT+ group. Cruz has served as the director of the Guam Liaison Office, the executive director for the Democratic Party of Guam, and as a Senator of Guam for five consecutive terms.

> 66
>
> *I think it's important to get the word out that there is a safe place here in the Pacific where the LGBTQ+ community can come and feel safe, vacation, relax, and get married. I hope that we can sway closed minds to open up and inspire those in the neighboring countries and islands in Oceana to have confidence and stand up for LGBTQ+ rights and equality in their own communities.*
>
> —Lasia Casil,
> Transnational-Queer-Underground.net,
> 2018
>
> 99

Monaeka Flores is an LGBT+ activist and artist. She has worked for the Legislature of Guam as well as the LGBT+ nonprofit ISA Guam. In 2013, the Guam Council on the Arts and Humanities Agency awarded Flores a fellowship for a conceptual art project about Chamorro identity. She has also worked as the marketing director for the Guam Humanities Council.

Renae McPhearson (*Tumon, GU*) is a transgender burlesque dancer who describes her art as a cabaret twist on strip teasing. "It's suggestive to a certain point, without being too raunchy," she told Guam Pacific Daily News in 2017. Her debut performance, "LOVE, LUST & BURLESQUE," was at the Exit Lounge in Tumon, Guam, on Valentine's Day 2017. McPhearson has also performed at the Globe Ultra Lounge in Tumon for Pride Month, and on the LGBT Float at Guam's Annual Liberation Day Parade.

Josh Tenorio was elected as the first openly gay lieutenant governor of Guam in 2018. Tenorio ran on a platform that included ending LGBT+ discrimination and promoted juvenile and criminal justice reform. In his election, he was the running mate of Lou Leon Guerrero, Guam's first female governor. Previously, Tenorio worked as an administrator of the courts, where he was director of Policy, Planning, and Community Relations. He also served as the director of Guam's Democratic Party and ran the Guam campaign of Barack Obama's 2008 presidential run.

> 66
>
> *What advice I can give to young gay and lesbian potential candidates is: be the best that you can be . . . then there will be no question about your ability to assume any position.*
>
> —Benjamin Cruz, Victory Fund, 2011
>
> 99

◉ QUEER FACTS

Both same-sex parents are listed on the birth certificates of their children in Guam. This policy was instituted in 2017 after Kimberley and Devidene Chargualaf filed a lawsuit because Kimberley's name could not go on the birth certificate. Previously, Guam's birth certificates only allowed one space for the "mother" and one for the "father."

Guam became the first US territory to legalize gay marriage in June 2015, following a court case filed by Loretta Pangelinan and Kathleen Aguero. The couple had applied for a marriage license in April of that year and were denied. The previous year, the Ninth US Circuit Court of Appeals (which has jurisdiction over Guam) had legalized same-sex marriage. When Pangelinan and Aguero sued that they had been unconstitutionally denied a marriage license, Guam's government was quick to comply with the Circuit Courts ruling. The two married a couple days after the ruling.

ISA Guam is an LGBT+ organization that focuses on building community. It also publishes a newsletter and runs a Facebook page with which it informs its members of local LGBT+ events. ISA Guam was founded by Monaeka Flores, Alan Torrado, Lasia Casil, James Servino, Raymond Andersen, and Jason Padua.

Miss Pacificana is Guam's annual transgender beauty pageant that welcomes national contestants. Bobby Solis began the pageant in 1995 to foster LGBT+ community, and the pageant has run on and off ever since. Proceeds benefit AIDS research and health care organizations. Miss Pacificana winners usually become local celebrities and participate in Guam Pride. Contestants are known for their elaborate costumes, such as Jaryna Anjelique Barbas's tropical lizard costume from 2015's pageant. Miss Pacificana teamed up with the Immaculate Heart of Mary Catholic Church in Toto to hold a vigil for those who lost their lives in Florida's 2016 Orlando nightclub shooting.

Workplace anti-discrimination laws against LGBT+ individuals went into effect in Guam on August 11, 2015. Bill 102-33, otherwise known as the Guam Employment Non-Discrimination Act of 2015, bans discrimination on the basis of sexual orientation or gender identity.

◉ PLACES

Denial Bar *(Tamuning, GU)* was a gay nightclub that opened in 2003. It welcomed everybody, gay or straight, and was known for themed parties and over-the-top dancers. Denial ceased operation around 2014.

Guam Alternative Lifestyle Association *(Hagåtña, GU)* is an LGBT+ advocacy organization that promotes sexual diversity and seeks to improve the lives of Guam's LGBT+ community. It has a HIV/AIDS Peer Educator program that seeks to reduce new cases of HIV/AIDS in Guam through a strong community support system and preventative care. It also holds community events such as picnics and movie nights, and participates in Guam Pride.

Guam Pride *(Hagåtña, GU)* is an organization that runs LGBT+ pride events, raises funds for an LGBT+ scholarship, and promotes LGBT+ equality. Each year in June, it throws a reception, party, march, and festival. It also offers free HIV testing during Pride week, and hosts appearances by numerous local and national celebrities.

Jax Lounge *(Tamuning, GU)* is a gay bar with a relaxed atmosphere that opened in 2003. It features a Rainbow Room with multicolored sofas and a dance floor separate from the lounge that is only open on the weekends. It also has a shelf of LGBT+ books and magazines patrons can peruse.

PEOPLE

"

What I do as far as my role in trans activism is be on television, do interviews, and conduct myself in a way that shines a positive light on the trans community. Hopefully doing that will help change the hearts and minds of people.

—Candis Cayne, *HuffPost*, 2015

"

Candis Cayne

Thomas Beatie *(Honolulu, HI)* is a transgender reproductive rights advocate, most famously known as the "Pregnant Man" after he became pregnant in 2008 because his wife was infertile. In early life, Beatie was a Teen Miss Hawaii USA finalist, and went on to graduate from University of Hawaii. Beatie underwent gender-affirming surgery and was recognized as male under Hawaiian law, and eventually gave birth to three kids. When he filed for divorce from his wife in 2012, the case was new legal ground, as there was no legal precedent for who would have custody of the children. In the early 2000s, Beatie served as cochair of the Civil Unions–Civil Rights Movement in Honolulu, lobbying to pass Hawaii's first hate crimes legislation.

Candis Cayne *(Maui, HI)* is an actress most famous for playing Carmelita on the 2007 TV drama *Dirty Sexy Money*. Playing Carmelita made Cayne the first transgender actress to play a recurring transgender character in primetime. Cayne left Hawaii for New York City in the early 1990s, where she worked as a drag performer until discovering her transgender identity. After her breakout role on *Dirty Sexy Money*, she went on to appear in many films and television shows, including *RuPaul's Drag Race*, *Grey's Anatomy*, and *Transparent*.

Scott Coffey *(Honolulu, HI)* is a director, actor, producer, and screenwriter. Coffey is most known for his work with David Lynch in projects such as *Wild at Heart*, *Mulholland Drive*, *Inland Empire*, and the 2017 revival of *Twin Peaks*. Coffey made his directorial debut with the 2005 film *Ellie Parker*, and also directed the 2013 film *Adult World*.

Natasha Kai *(Kahuku, HI)* is a soccer player and Olympic gold medalist. As a college student in the early 2000s, Kai played for the University of Hawaii Rainbow Wahine. In 2004, she joined the Women's National Team as one of its top scorers; she went with the team to the 2008 Beijing Olympics, where Kai was among only three openly gay USA athletes. In 2009, Kai joined the Sky Blue FC, and the Philadelphia Independence in 2011. She rejoined Sky Blue FC in 2017. Kai, who is Polynesian, is recognized for her traditional Polynesian tattoos—she has over fifty-five.

Jiz Lee is a genderqueer adult performer and sex activist. Lee was one of the first genderqueer adult performers to gain popularity, mainly through the 2005 *Crash Pad* web series; they have also appeared in the TV series *Transparent* and *Sense8*. Lee raises money for sex workers and LGBT+ organizations and speaks at academic institutions about queer sexuality. They have been nominated for and won various awards for adult performances, and their writing has been published in *The Feminist Porn Book*, *Best Sex Writing*, *OUT Magazine*, and Jezebel.com, among others. Lee was

Scott Coffey (right)

Jiz Lee

also the editor of the 2015 anthology *Coming Out Like a Porn Star*, which features essays from a gamut of queer adult performers.

Sabrina McKenna *(Tokyo, Japan)* was the first openly gay judge to serve on the Hawaii Supreme Court, and is one of only nine openly LGBT+ judges currently serving on a US state supreme court. McKenna faced only little opposition to her 2011 appointment as judge, but of the five testimonies that opposed McKenna's appointment, four did so because of her sexual orientation. McKenna is a graduate of the University of Hawaii at Manoa, where she served as editor-in-chief of the William S. Richardson Law School's law review journal. Before becoming a Hawaii state trial court judge in 1993, she was a civil litigator, corporate counsel, and law professor. As a trial court judge, she presided in district, circuit, and family courts.

Janet Mock *(Honolulu, HI)* is the former editor of *People* and *Marie Claire* magazines. Mock is an author, TV host, and transgender rights activist, known primarily for her breakout 2014 memoir *Redefining Realness*. Mock, who is part native Hawaiian, spent most of her youth in Honolulu, and studied at the University of Hawaii in Manoa before eventually moving to New York City for her master's degree. In 2011, she came out as transgender in an article for *Marie Claire*. Mock has

> *I look forward to the day that this is no longer something to talk about because nobody says 'heterosexual judge.' People sometimes say woman judge, or African American president. I look forward to the day when people don't need to be qualified in such ways, that people could be judged on their qualifications only.*
>
> —Sabrina McKenna, *Star Advertiser*, 2011

Janet Mock

Esera Tuaolo

received many awards for her activist work, including the Sylvia Rivera Activist Award, the Inspiration Award at the GLSEN Respect Award, and the Stonewall Book Award.

Esera Tuaolo *(Honolulu, HI)* is of Samoan ancestry and was raised in a banana-farming family in Waimanalo, Hawaii. Tuaolo played college football at Oregon State University in the late 1980s, and was a second-round draft pick for the Green Bay Packers in 1990. After leaving the Packers, Tuaolo played for the Minnesota Vikings, Jacksonville Jaguars, Atlanta Falcons, and Carolina Panthers. Tuaolo came out as gay after he retired from football in 2002, and went on to serve as a board member of the Gay and Lesbian Athletics Association. In retirement, Tuaolo settled down in Minnesota, where he performed in small local theater shows. In 2017, he was a contestant on *The Voice*.

Hinaleimoana Wong-Kalu (Kumu Hina) *(Oʻahu, HI)* is a Hula teacher and activist. Wong-Kalu identifies as māhū, the third gender in native Hawaiian culture. In 2014, Wong-Kalu ran for the board of the Office of Hawaiian Affairs, one of the first transgender Hawaiians to seek office. Though her run was unsuccessful,

Hinaleimoana Wong-Kalu

she has chaired the Oʻahu Island Burial Council and cofounded the Kulia Na Mamo, an organization that supports transgender women. Wong-Kalu has also served as the cultural director of Hālau Lōkahi, a Native Hawaiian charter school. She is the subject of the 2014 documentary *Kumu Hina*, which followed a year in her life as an educator in her community as well as her personal life as a māhū person.

PLACES

The Glade Show Lounge (The Glades) *(Honolulu, HI)* was a historic gay bar and drag show lounge. Located on Hotel Street in Chinatown in the 1960s and '70s, the club was frequented by gay men, drag queens, māhū people, and sex workers. The Glades

QUEER FACTS

Aikāne is a native Hawaiian term referring to homosexual men and same-sex relationships in general. It is a combination of the words "ai," meaning sex, and "kāne," meaning man/male. Aikāne were quite common in pre-colonial Hawaiian culture and were granted important political and social roles.

Honolulu Pride, the largest LGBT+ pride celebration in Hawaii, is an annual event put on by the Hawaii LGBT Legacy Foundation. Honolulu Pride is the culmination of two weeks of LGBT-centric events in Wakiki, including pool and dance parties, parades, arts/cultural events, picnics, and athletic events. The celebration is held in October, generally later than most annual pride events.

The Honolulu Rainbow Film Festival is an annual LGBT+ film festival, and one of the longest-running in the country. HRFF presents films in a variety of genres with a special focus on filmmakers from Hawaii. The festival, founded by Jack Law, started in 1989 under the name Adam Baran Honolulu Gay and Lesbian Film Festival; it now operates under the Honolulu Gay and Lesbian Cultural Foundation. Films shown at the festival have gone on to win Peabody and Emmy awards.

The I Am a Boy law, from 1963 to 1972, required all māhū and trans people, as well as drag performers, to wear printed buttons saying "I Am a Boy" or "I Am a Man." The law was designed to regulate gender

Honolulu Pride

expression and let GIs and tourists know who they were dancing with in clubs such as the Glade Lounge. If a person did not comply, they could be arrested and/or fined.

Māhū, in Kanaka Maoli *(Hawaiian)* and Maohi *(Tahitian)* culture, is the term for individuals who exhibit masculine and feminine traits (sometimes also referring to intersex individuals) or identify as transgender or third gender, similar to two-spirit people in Native American cultures. Māhū occupy a sacred space in Hawaiian culture and are usually healers and spiritual leaders; unfortunately, the rise of colonialism has led to more transphobic and Western attitudes toward people of this identity.

Hula's Bar and Lei Stand

was the subject of a 2014 documentary called *The Glades Project* by Hawaiian filmmaker Connie Florez.

Hula's Bar and Lei Stand *(Honolulu, HI)* is the oldest gay bar on O'ahu, open for over forty-two years. Originally located in the Kuhio District in Wakiki under the Big Banyan Tree, in 1998 the bar relocated to its current spot near the Waikiki Grand Hotel. Hula's offers beach views and disco music and hosts weekly drag nights and live music.

The Lavender Center & Clinic *(Honolulu, HI)* is a nonprofit health clinic serving youth and adults in the LGBT+ community. Founded by Samuel Hawk, a doctor who specializes in transgender health, the Lavender Clinic is the only place in Hawaii to offer a full range of services to transgender clients. It also provides free counseling, vocal/speech training, HIV/AIDS testing, youth programs, hormone therapy, education, and primary care.

Queen's Surf Beach *(Honolulu, HI)* is the most popular gay beach in Hawaii, named after the former home of Queen Liliuokalani's beach house and its pier. It's actually a section of Waikiki Beach, located between the Kapahulu Groin and the Waikiki Aquarium. Not associated with any waterfront hotel, its location near a reef makes it ideal for snorkeling and bodyboarding nearby. The area also hosts free outdoor film screenings on weekends.

NeVaDa

⊖ PEOPLE

Nelson Araujo *(Las Vegas, NV)* was elected to the Nevada Assembly in 2014. After serving two terms, he went on to run for Nevada's secretary of state in 2018, though he lost to the incumbent Republican. During his run, he was the first candidate for a secretary of state position to be endorsed by the Human Rights Campaign. Raised by immigrants who fled El Salvador's civil war in the 1980s, Araujo spent his tenure in the Assembly advocating for LGBT+ rights and leading the state's 2017 ban on gay conversion therapy.

Shamir Bailey *(Las Vegas, NV)* (he/him) is a nonbinary musician known mononymously as Shamir. Shamir began performing with friends when he was thirteen years old; before turning twenty, he had signed with Godmode and then XL Recordings. Shamir has released four albums in his career; he was first known for the popular singles "On the Regular" and "Call It Off" from his 2015 debut *Ratchet*. He is known for both his androgynous countertenor voice and appearance.

Shamir Bailey

C. Jay Cox is a director and screenwriter most famous for writing 2002's *Sweet Home Alabama*. He grew up Mormon, but when he came out at nineteen, he chose to leave the church rather than to deny his sexual orientation. Cox's writing and directing credits also include *Latter Days*, a story about a young gay couple, one of whom is Mormon. While Cox claims the movie is not autobiographical, he has said that the story was personal to him.

Thomas Dekker *(Las Vegas, NV)* is an actor. He's best known for his roles in TV shows such as *Honey, I Shrunk the Kids*, *Heroes*, and *Terminator: The Sarah Connor Chronicles*. He is also a singer-songwriter and has released two albums, *Psyanotic* (2008) and *Into the Night* (2018). In 2017, Dekker publicly came out as gay after *Heroes* producer Bryan Fuller indirectly outed him in an awards speech; by then, Dekker had already married his husband a few months earlier.

Nahnatchka Khan *(Las Vegas, NV)* is a TV producer known for *Don't Trust the B---- in Apartment 23* and *Fresh Off the Boat*. Raised in Hawaii by a family of Iranian Americans, Khan's film career has been praised for humorous portrayals of diverse peoples while still being respectful to the represented communities. A lesbian herself, any of Khan's characters subvert tropes about sexual and racial identity. Khan's first writing roles include popular late 1990s and early 2000s shows such as *Recess*, *Pepper Ann*, and *Malcolm in the Middle*.

I never felt like a boy or a girl, never felt I should wear this or dress like that. I think that's where that confidence comes from, because I never felt I had to play a part in my life. I just always come as Shamir.

—Shamir Bailey, the *Guardian*, 2015

Thomas Dekker

When you're none of those things, and you're running zero for three, your expectations are low, but also so is your fear. I got a place at the table, and I'm excited to tell the stories I wanna tell, which are the stories I wanna see.

—Nahnatchka Khan on being a queer woman of color, *Bustle*, 2019

Rutina Wesley *(Las Vegas, NV)* is an actress. Her parents—Cassandra Wesley and Ivery Wheeler—worked in entertainment as a showgirl and tap dancer, respectively. Wesley first starred in the 2007 film *How She Move*, but is best known for her main role in the TV series *True Blood*. Wesley currently stars in *Queen Sugar* and has appeared on shows such as *Hannibal*, *The Walking Dead*, and *Arrow*. In 2013, Wesley divorced her husband, actor Jacob Fishel; she became engaged to a woman named Shonda, a chef, in 2017.

⊙ PLACES

The Gay and Lesbian Community Center of Southern Nevada *(Las Vegas, NV)* provides support and activities to promote and strengthen the local LGBT+ community. Originally founded in 1992, the center's success has required it to move buildings three times to keep up with its growing need for space. Now located in its own recently renovated building, the center hosts meeting and performance spaces, an LGBT+ library, and a computer lab. It also offers office space for many local LGBT+ groups (such as the Nevada Gay Rodeo Association, PFLAG, SAGE, and more). The center was the first safe public space for the LGBT+ community in Las Vegas.

Nahnatchka Khan

⚲ QUEER FACTS

Assembly Bill 99, introduced by Assemblyman Nelson Araujo, passed in the Nevada legislature in 2017. The bill requires government agencies (such as foster agencies and juvenile courts) to respect children's gender identities, and also requires foster parents to receive training on how to work with LGBT+ youth. AB 99 passed simultaneously with SB 201, which banned mental health professionals from providing minors with gay conversion therapy.

The Nevada Equal Rights Commission (NERC) runs Nevada's Equal Employment Opportunity program. The NERC protects against discrimination because of sexual orientation or gender identity, among other things. In 2012, Lauren Scott, a Republican transgender woman, was appointed commissioner of the NERC.

Nevada's first openly gay justice was Lidia S. Stiglich, who was also the second woman on the court. Appointed in 2017 after a successful career in the county courts, Stiglich is a popular judge. During her stint as a county judge, she received a 96 percent approval rating from lawyers.

Nevada's first openly gay lawmaker was David Parks. Born in Boston, Parks was first elected in 1996 to the Nevada State Assembly, where he served for twelve years. In 2008, he was elected to the Nevada Senate, where he continues to serve Nevada's seventh district.

Reno Pride

"Queerest Little City in the World: LGBTQ Reno," by John Jeffrey Auer IV, is a chapter of a theme study done by the National Park Service's LGBTQ Heritage Initiative, which works to provide historical context for LGBT historic places. Auer's chapter focuses specifically on Reno's long LGBT+ history. Although Reno is relatively small, the city's LGBT+ history is large, spanning cross-dressing in the Gold Rush era; the perceived lesbian community that boomed with the "divorce trade" during the 1910s, when Reno was the divorce capital of the world; and drag performances predating World War I.

Reno Gay Pride was an LGBT+ festival held in Reno every year for two decades until it ended in 2018. The festival was held in Wingfield Park.

Liberace Mansion *(Las Vegas, NV)* is the former home of the famous musician and showman Liberace, where he lived part-time from the 1970s until his death in 1987. The mansion was created by combining two existing homes together, resulting in a 14,393-square-foot mansion. The mansion is now privately owned and in the processes of being restored to the same extravagance it held when Liberace lived there, though it remains open for tours. The Liberace Mansion is the first residential property in Clark County, Nevada, to become a historic landmark.

Our Center *(Reno, NV)* supports northern Nevada's LGBT+ community. In 2009, a group of community members realized the area was in need of an LGBT+ safe space and began raising funds to create one. By 2016, the group had finally raised enough to open Our Center. The center offers different events to support wellness, community building, social support, advocacy, education, and volunteerism, and boasts an art room, great room, and library.

⊖ PEOPLE

Maude Adams *(Salt Lake City, UT)* was a Broadway and stage actress in the late 1800s and early 1900s. Her most successful role was the titular character in J. M. Barrie's 1905 Broadway production of *Peter Pan*, but Adams had already achieved success before that, playing various child roles as a young girl. Between 1892 and 1897, she became a "Frohman star," someone known for being cast repeatedly by theatrical director Charles Frohman. Adams is widely considered to have been a lesbian, partially due to her lack of relationships with any men, but mostly because of two long-term relationships with women—the first was with Lillie Florence, and the second with Louise Boynton for over forty-five years until Boynton's passing in 1951.

Mildred Berryman *(Salt Lake City, UT)* was the author of groundbreaking research on homosexuality, an uncompleted thesis titled *Psychological Phenomena of the Homosexual*. Though Berryman never finished the thesis and refused to publish it, quite possibly because

Maude Adams

of rampant anti-gay attitudes during the 1930s when she was writing it, her work contributed valuable insight into the homosexual experience, and challenged the notion that homosexuality was a choice. Berryman had several relationships with women in her lifetime, and at one point ran a business with Ruth Uckerman Dempsey, her partner of over thirty-two years. Berryman was also an accomplished merchant and photographer, and served as president of the Utah Business and Professional Women's Club.

Neal Cassady *(Salt Lake City, UT)* was a 1950s Beat Generation writer and icon. Though he wrote poems and stories of his own, Cassady's name is recognizable for his numerous appearances as a character—or as the likeness of himself—in films, songs, stories, and poems by men and women who cite him as an inspiration and influence, including writers such as Jack Kerouac and Allen Ginsberg. Cassady had a long-lasting relationship with Ginsberg throughout their years in the Beat Generation; "Howl," Ginsberg's most famous poem, is dedicated to him. Cassady died at age forty-one in 1968, having been discovered outside in a coma after leaving a wedding reception while under the influence. His unfinished autobiography, *The First Third*, was published three years later.

Reed Cowan *(Roosevelt, UT)* is a gay journalist and producer. Cowan was raised Mormon, and was told to deny his sexuality. He initially married a woman and they had a son, but he eventually decided to stop living a lie. After divorcing his wife, Cowan reconnected with his high-school sweetheart. The couple married in 2013 and adopted three children. Cowan produced the 2010 film *8: The Mormon Proposition*, which explores the Mormon church's role in the passing of California's Prop 8. Cowan has won numerous Emmy awards and a GLAAD award for journalism. He is a lead anchor for NBC News 3 in Las Vegas.

Steven Fales *(Provo, UT)* is an actor and playwright most known for the show *Confessions of a Mormon Boy*. The play, which he began reading and performing in 2001, is based off of his "bizarre and fantastical" experience of being tried by the Mormon Church for being homosexual. The show has received national acclaim, and expanded into a three-part show known as the

> 66
>
> *I don't have any grandiose ideas that the president of the Mormon Church is going to come out and welcome gays in, what I do hope for is that mothers and fathers will see this film [8: The Mormon Proposition], and they will see that there is something wrong when bigotry is spewed from the pulpit. There is a body count to this war.*
>
> —Reed Cowan, *Daily Herald Ticket*, 2010
>
> 99

Margrethe Mather

Mormon Boy Trilogy. Fales has been nominated for an Outer Critics Circle Award, and also published a companion novel to his stage play, titled *Confessions of a Mormon Boy: Behind the Scenes of the Off-Broadway Hit*, a Lambda Literary Award Finalist for Drama in 2007.

Laci Green *(Salt Lake City, UT)* is the creator of the YouTube sex education series *Sex Plus*, which has led her channel to amass over 1.4 million subscribers since its start in 2008. Green was named one of the thirty most influential people on the internet by *TIME* in 2016, has spoken at dozens of colleges and universities in order to promote healthy sexuality, and has worked with the ACLU and Planned Parenthood. Green identifies as pansexual, a topic she hasn't shied away from discussing on her YouTube channel. Her 2018 young adult nonfiction book, also named *Sex Plus*, was lauded by *Publisher's Weekly* and *Kirkus Reviews* for its in-depth discussion of sexuality. Green has attracted controversy for her statements about transgender individuals, which many have said fall into trans-exclusionary radical feminism.

Kate Kendell *(Ogden, UT)* is the former executive director of the National Center for Lesbian Rights (NCLR), a role she served for over twenty-two years. Kendell started as the NCLR's legal director in 1994, leading the organization through some of the most significant and culture-changing moments in LGBT+ history. From

adoption and child custody issues to wrongful death civil lawsuits, Kendell piloted the NCLR as it advocated in the legal sphere on behalf of LGBT individuals. In 2004, she was instrumental in securing the first marriage licenses for same-sex couples. Kendell stepped down from the NCLR in 2018. She and her wife, Sandy Holmes, have been together for over twenty-five years and have three children.

Margrethe Mather *(Salt Lake City, UT)* was a pictorialist photographer in the early 1900s. Born in 1886, Mather moved to California at a young age, where she worked as a prostitute and an interior designer. She began her photography career as a member of the Los Angeles Camera Club and helped found the Camera Pictorialists of Los Angeles. Mather was known for her artistic adventurousness and her willingness to experiment with photography; she also heavily influenced Edward Weston, a modernist photographer around the same time. Mather was rumored to have been either a lesbian or bisexual with a preference for women. She died in 1952.

Misty Snow *(Salt Lake City, UT)* made history in 2016 as one the first transgender people to run for the US Senate. Snow won the Democratic nomination in the 2016 primary election. At the time, she worked full-time at a grocery store, so she primarily focused her campaign on working-class issues. Ultimately, Snow lost the election to the incumbent. In 2018, she ran for a seat in the Utah House, but later dropped out of the race.

> *And then AIDS—which galvanized our community like nothing else could have, and while it was never worth the death count, it still put in stark relief that being hidden, being silent, being invisible was a matter of life and death. Our visibility, our coming out, our being adamant about our own humanity and demanding that this nation recognize and honor that humanity is how we got to where we are now—in very short order by civil rights-time measurement.*

—Kate Kendell, *Los Angeles Blade*, 2018

> *I guess you could qualify me as pansexual because I really don't care. If a person is great, then a person is great. . . . I guess this is me coming out as pansexual.*

—Brendan Urie, *Paper*, 2018

Wicked, both topped the Billboard chart at number one. Rumors about Urie's sexuality have circulated since the band's first album, and in 2018 Urie confirmed that he was pansexual in an interview with *Paper* magazine. He married his wife in 2013.

Brendon Urie

Brendon Urie *(St. George, UT)* is the lead singer and only remaining member of the band Panic! at the Disco. The band originally started in 2004 by a group of high school friends, and were quickly signed by Fall Out Boy's Pete Wentz to Decaydance Records. The band's first album, *A Fever You Can't Sweat Out,* was a huge success, selling over two million copies. Over the years, the other members of the band left the group, leaving Urie its sole member. The band's fifth album, *Death of a Bachelor,* and its sixth album, *Pray for the*

⊙ PLACES

Encircle *(Provo and Salt Lake City, UT)* offers a wide range of LGBT+ support groups (called "friendship circles") for people of all identities and age groups. Encircle also offers regular programming for community service, art, music, and writing group activities.

Harvey Milk Boulevard *(Salt Lake City, UT),* a twenty-block stretch, was renamed as such in 2016.

Equality Utah first proposed the idea to the city's mayor in 2014, after the city had renamed several streets after other prominent historical figures and had become increasingly supportive of LGBT+ rights. Once the City Council approved the idea, Equality Utah crowdfunded enough money to pay for the new street signs within a week. Jackie Biskupski, Salt Lake City's first lesbian mayor, changed the first street sign herself.

The Utah Pride Center *(Salt Lake City, UT)* was founded in 1992 as the Utah Stonewall Center. After financial difficulties, the center reopened in 1997 as the Gay & Lesbian Community Center of Utah. In 2006, the center changed its name to the Utah Pride Center in an effort to be more inclusive. The center hosts events (such as the Masqueerade Ball) and provides mental health resources, support groups, and a safe space for the local LGBT+ community. It also hosts the annual Utah Pride Festival and Parade.

QUEER FACTS

In 1978, a possibly connected string of murders of gay leaders occurred in Salt Lake City. In November of that year, Tony Adams was murdered in his apartment. Adams was actively involved in the local gay and socialist communities, so friends assumed he was murdered for his connection to those causes. Later that month, Doug Coleman, another gay man, was found murdered in a car. Activists claimed that two additional gay community members were murdered around this time. Local LGBT+ groups pushed the police department to look more carefully into the connection of these crimes out of fear for their safety, but it was to no avail—Tony Adams's case was never solved.

Affirmation is an organization supporting LGBT+ Mormons, which began as informal meetings between Mormon gay men, but solidified into a more formal organization in 1977 under the direction of Mathew Price. Price was determined to build a network of LGBT+ Mormons to foster support in the church, and organized Affirmation's first chapter in Salt Lake City before moving on to Denver and Dallas. The groups initially struggled to gain footing, but over time grew into a strong network. Affirmation is now a global organization with chapters on five continents, and holds conferences around the world in addition to its online community.

Anita Bryant's presence at the 1977 Utah State Fair was protested by the local LGBT+ community.

That year, Dade County in Florida had passed an ordinance to protect the LGBT+ community against discrimination. Anita Bryant, an executive for an orange juice company, began a movement to repeal the protections, successfully leading to the ordinance's repeal. When the Utah State Fair invited Bryant to be a key speaker at the fair, six local organizations rallied to protest. In the months leading up to her appearance, the groups sold merchandise with the slogans "Anita Bryant Sucks Oranges" and "Let he who has not sinned cast the first orange." This culminated in a picket-line protest at the fair, where over one hundred people protested Bryant's presence. Read more about Anita Bryant under Florida.

The first gay mayor of Salt Lake City, and the second woman to hold the position, was Jackie Biskupski. Originally from Minnesota, she was elected in 2015 after beating the two-term incumbent mayor. Prior, Biskupski served thirteen years as a state representative. She became involved in politics after a local high school tried to force its students' Gay Straight Alliance group to close. Biskupski is a strong advocate for women and minorities, as well as the LGBT+ community. In 2016, Biskupski married her long-time partner. The couple has two sons.

The Gay Straight Alliance was banned in 1998 at East High in Salt Lake City. The school administration didn't want to allow a GSA on campus but knew it would face legal repercussions if it explicitly discriminated against only the GSA. So, the school decided to ban all non-curricular student groups. However, when a group of students found out that another non-curricular student group was still meeting on campus, they sued with representation by Lambda Legal. In 1999, Utah's District Courts ruled in favor of the GSA, and all non-curricular student groups (including the GSA) were allowed to meet in the school.

LOVELOUD Fest has been held annually since 2017 by the LOVELOUD Foundation. Dan Reynolds, the lead singer of Imagine Dragons, founded the one-day fest with the aim to foster acceptance and a safe, fun gathering for young LGBT+ people. Proceeds from the festival are donated to local and national LGBT+ charities. The 2019 festival, held at the end of June, featured headliners such as Kesha, Tegan and Sara, and Laura Jane Grace and the Devouring Mothers.

The only people in Utah to treat AIDS during the first years of the 1980s epidemic were Dr. Kristen Ries and Maggie Snyder. Ries moved to Utah in 1981, the same year AIDS/HIV was identified. Most doctors in the state refused to treat patients with AIDS, but Ries made it her mission to treat these patients. She worked alone for the first decade of the epidemic, but Snyder, her partner, eventually joined her as a physician's assistant. Although the couple no longer actively practices medicine, they still advocate for the AIDS community. Ries was present when Utah Senator Jim Dabakis signed an anti-discrimination law to protect the LGBT community in 2015.

Salt Lake City has the highest percentage of gay parents amongst large US cities, according to a 2013 study by the Williams Institute at the UCLA School of Law. The study examined the percentage of gay couples with had children, and showed that 26 percent of gay couples in Salt Lake City have children.

Utah's first openly gay mayor was Willy Marshall, elected in Big Water in 2001. Marshall, a Libertarian originally from Indiana, campaigned door-to-door and ensured that everyone he talked to knew he was gay as a way of preventing his opponents from using his sexuality against him as a scare tactic. In office, after cutting municipal taxes by 50 percent, Marshall moved to decriminalize marijuana, an action that was ultimately overruled by the county. One of the benefits of being mayor in a small town, Marshall has said, is that "people know you and their biases go away."

Utah's first same-sex marriage was between Seth Anderson and Michael Ferguson in 2013. In December 2013, a federal judge ruled against Utah's same-sex marriage ban, citing the precedent of the Supreme Court's ruling against the Defense of Marriage Act. Anderson and Ferguson had been closely following Utah's case, and immediately raced to the city hall after the ruling. At one point, their car got stuck in traffic, and one of them got out and ran to the city hall. They were concerned that the governor would try to halt the granting of marriage certificates (and the state did later push for an emergency stay of the ruling), so they wanted to get their certificate fast. Ferguson was also a plaintiff in *Ferguson vs. JONAH*, a 2015 lawsuit against gay conversion therapy.

Utah passed an LGBT+ anti-discrimination bill in 2015. The bill protected against discrimination in housing or employment because of gender identity or sexual orientation, with an exception for religious organizations. It was backed by the Mormon Church, an unusual break from its anti-LGBT+ rhetoric. When the bill passed, Utah was the only state with a Republican-controlled legislature to pass an LGBT+ non-discrimination bill.

The Utah Pride Festival and Parade began in 1974 and has run annually for over forty-four years. What began as an informal gathering has since flourished, gathering about fifty thousand attendees a year. The Pride Festival includes events, performances, a 5k, Utah Pride awards, a picnic, and the parade.

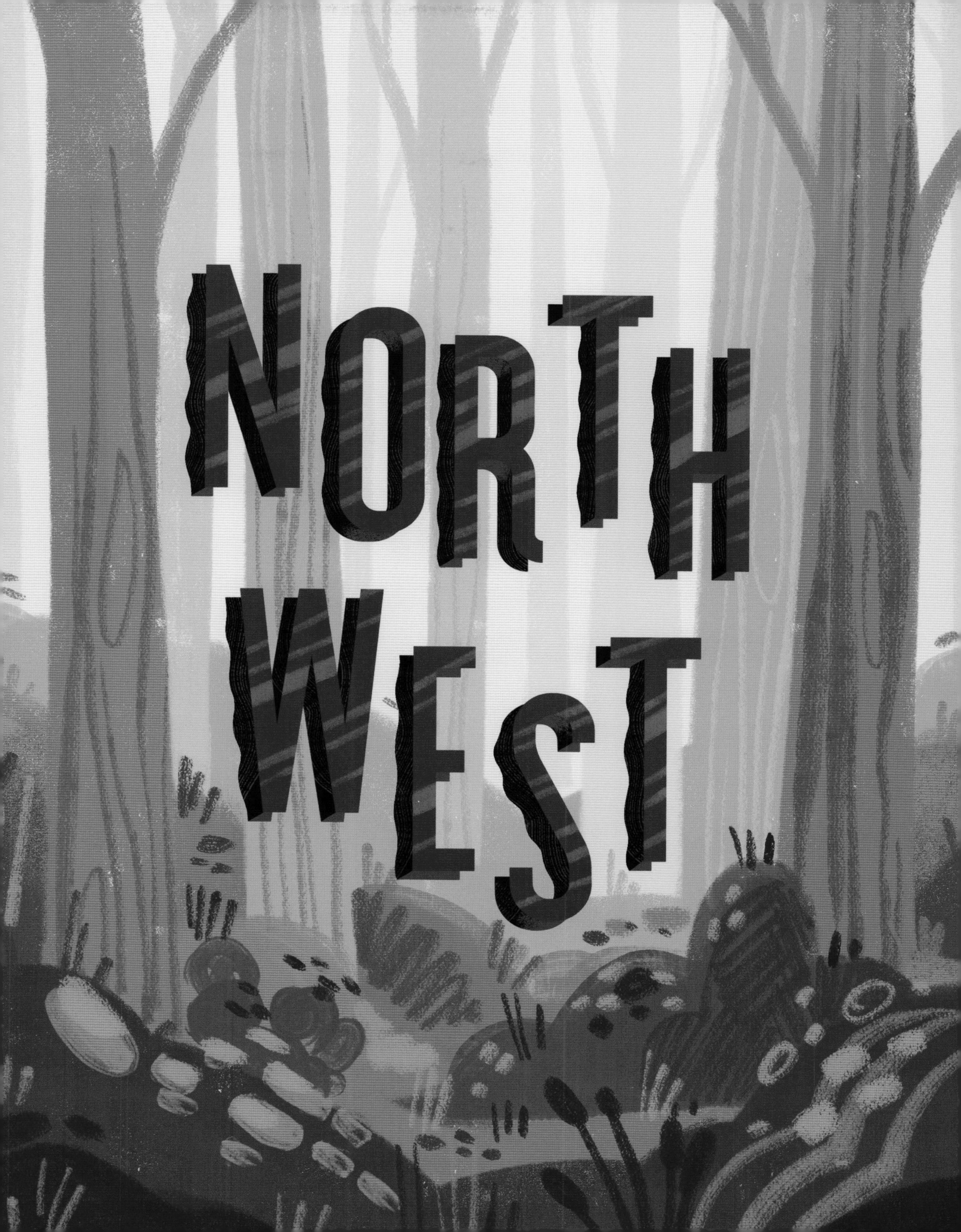
NORTH
WEST

IDAHO

👤 PEOPLE

Jacob Anderson-Minshall *(Inkom, ID)* is an author and queer transgender man. Jacob and his wife have worked on many literary projects together, including founding the lesbian magazine *Girlfriends* and the LGBT+ literary series *QLiterati!*. The Anderson-Minshalls have written many books together, including *Queerly Beloved*, a memoir describing their relationship through Jacob's transition. The couple won a Goldie Award from the Golden Crown Literary Society for the memoir in 2015, making Jacob the first trans man to win the award.

Bruce Bastian *(Twin Falls, ID)*, a gay man, is a noted businessman and philanthropist in the LGBT+ community. In 1979, Bastian cofounded WordPerfect, an early word processing software. After merging with another software company in 1994, Bastian has devoted his time toward supporting the LGBT+ community and the performing arts. He serves on the board of directors of the Human Rights Campaign, and he was appointed to the Presidential Advisory Committee of the Arts by President Barack Obama in 2010.

Bryan Fuller *(Lewiston, ID)* is a gay screenwriter and producer. Fuller has worked in Hollywood since 1993 on a variety of projects, such as *Star Trek: Discovery, Hannibal, American Gods,* and *Pushing Daisies.* He has been nominated for two Emmys, one in 2007 for his work on *Heroes,* and the other in 2008 for *Pushing Daisies.*

Clyde M. Hall *(Fort Hall, ID)* is a Shoshone/Métis Native activist and one of the founders of the modern two-spirit community. Hall was raised by his grandmother on a Shoshone reservation in Idaho. In the 1970s and '80s, he lived in San Francisco, where he joined the Gay American Indians (GAI). He has worked to make reservations more open to and comfortable with two-spirit people. Hall was named on the OUT100 list in 1999. Today, he writes and speaks nationally about Native American culture and is a ceremonial leader for Dance for All People.

Bryan Fuller

> **"** I still feel Mormon. Those men in Salt Lake City can't decide who's Mormon and who isn't.
>
> —Sonia Johnson, *People*, 1980 **"**

Sonia Johnson *(Malad, ID)* is a lesbian who was excommunicated from the Mormon Church after her feminist beliefs conflicted with it. When the Equal Rights Amendment was being debated around 1977, Johnson became actively involved in supporting it, and heavily argued against the LDS, which opposed the bill. Eventually, Johnson was excommunicated from the church, which led her to divorce her husband. Johnson continued to advocate for women's rights and even ran for president in 1984 with the Citizens Party. After her divorce, Johnson began dating women. In 2007, she and her partner opened Casa Feminista, a feminist ranch and hotel, in New Mexico.

Joe Monahan *(Rockville, ID)* was a transgender man living in the western frontier in the late 1800s as a miner and cowboy. Born in New York as a woman, Monahan began to live as a man when he moved West in the 1860s. He worked in Idaho for about thirty years as a single man until his death in 1904. As com-

Joe Monahan

munity members prepared Joe's body for his burial, they discovered that he was anatomically female. It has been suggested that Monahan's neighbors knew he was born female and still accepted him, although there was controversy in the news when his anatomy was discovered.

Paul Popham *(Emmett, ID)* cofounded the Gay Men's Health Crisis, the nation's oldest AIDS organization, with five other men in 1982. Popham served as its president until 1985, when he stepped back due to the severity of his illness. He was also a founder and chairman of the AIDS Action Council. Previously, Popham spent several years in the military, earning a Bronze Star for Valor in the Fifth Air Cavalry during the Vietnam War, and later leading a psychological warfare unit in the Army Reserve. Popham died in 1987 at the age of forty-five.

Qánqon-kámek-klaúlha (Sitting-in-the-Water-Grizzly) *(lower Kootenai River area, ID)* was a two-spirit Kutenai Native American born around 1780. In 1807, Qánqon married a white man from a nearby trading post. She soon returned to her tribe, where she told them she had been transformed into a man by her husband. From then on, she lived as two-spirit. She was a warrior, chief, shaman, and peace messenger. She led multiple excursions of white traders into the West, where she was eventually killed in 1837 in an altercation between two tribes.

Reverend Freda Smith *(Pocatello, ID)* is a lesbian church leader who was active in the early LGBT+ rights movement and officiated the first wedding for a same-sex couple with a legal marriage certificate in 1975. Smith was raised in a religious family and grew up wanting to be a church leader, but she had a

> ❝
> *I really don't like the word berbache, which is French. Indian people don't put labels on themselves; they don't think of themselves as being one way or another.*
>
> —Clyde M. Hall, *Gay Soul*, 1995
> ❞

difficult time reconciling that with her sexuality. After working on Bobby Kennedy's 1968 presidential campaign, Smith came out as a lesbian. Afterward, she worked to decriminalize same-sex relationships in California, where she became actively involved in the Metropolitan Community Church. Smith worked her way up through the mostly male ranks and joined the church's Board of Elders in 1973.

⊙ PLACES

Allies Linked for the Prevention of HIV and AIDS (a.l.p.h.a.) *(Boise, ID)* is an Idaho-based organization that provides sexual health resources, including free AIDS and STI testing. Founded in 2003, the nonprofit also helps community members with housing and runs a food pantry for families affected with AIDS. a.l.p.h.a. currently treats 1,300 people a year and provides over 40,000 pounds of food to those in need.

The Community Center (TCC) *(Boise, ID)* is a nonprofit LGBT+ community center founded in 1983 by a group of people who wanted a center of unity for the area's growing LGBT+ population. The group lacked a physical office for many years and instead focused on building up its library. TCC published *Diversity*, Idaho's first gay publication, for over thirty years. The center has long since secured a physical location, which provides support groups, education, resources, and a safe meeting space for the LGBT+ community.

Shuckey's *(Boise, ID)*, the first gay bar in Idaho, was opened by two men in 1976. The bar helped create an LGBT+ community in the area, giving people a safe location to gather. Soon after it first opened, other LGBT+ organizations emerged in the area. Shuckey's was initially subject to increased scrutiny from the local police, but after a while the community began to accept the presence of the LGBT+ community. The bar closed in 1988.

💡 QUEER FACTS

Gender markers on birth certificates were allowed to be altered for transgender Idahoans in 2018, after a federal judge found the state's restrictions to be unconstitutional in *F.V. v. Barron*. Kansas, Ohio, and Tennessee were the only other states with similar restrictions. The victory was hailed as a significant triumph by transgender activists. The judge asserted that birth certificate discrepancies "can create risks to the health and safety of transgender people" and were "archaic, unjust, and discriminatory."

The Imperial Sovereign Gem Court of Idaho, founded in 1980, is the oldest LGBT+ nonprofit in the state. Via an active social calendar, the ISGCI raises money for the LGBT+ community, providing funds for student scholarships, HIV/AIDS treatment, and a food pantry. The organization also started the Mr., Miss & Mrs. Gay Idaho Foundation, which is now its own independent organization.

My Own Private Idaho is a 1991 film about two male hustlers and best friends, and is one of the first movies in the New Queer Cinema wave. The movie follows the two men along their travels through western United States and then eventually to Italy, and is loosely based off Shakespeare's *Henry IV*. Keanu Reeves and River Phoenix starred in the iconic film, known for its blunt honesty and the way it opened doors for future queer films.

Proposition 1 was a 1994 referendum proposed in Idaho that aimed to restrict gay rights. The referendum would have allowed discrimination against LGBT+ people due to their sexuality and would have banned educators from positively discussing homosexual relationships. A major grassroots campaign, called No on One, organized against the referendum, which was narrowly defeated by a three thousand–vote margin, a victory for the LGBT+ community.

The Sheep Sexuality Experiment was a study that examined the biological root of sheep sexuality, expanding upon research on human sexuality. Many of these experiments were conducted at the US Sheep Experiment Station in Dubois, Idaho. Researchers studied a group of sheep's sexual behavior and then examined their brain structures. The study, published in 2004, found that sheep brain anatomy and hormone production could be responsible for sheep sexuality. This study suggested that sexuality could be biologically predetermined.

Weingartner v. McGriff is an Idaho court case that set a precedent for sexual orientation-based custody cases. Theron McGriff and Shawn Weingartner had been married for years and had two children together before getting divorced in 1997. Afterward, the couple shared joint custody, and Theron came out as gay and began living with his partner. His ex-wife, Weingartner, sued for full custody. In 2002, the court ruled that McGriff could no longer have physical custody of his daughters if he lived with his partner. McGriff appealed, and in 2004 the court ruled that sexual orientation should not be taken into account for custody cases. McGiff was still not granted custody of his children due to other circumstances.

⊖ PEOPLE

Jesse Tyler Ferguson *(Missoula, MT)* is an actor best known for his role on the hit ABC sitcom *Modern Family*. His long career in theater, television, and film has earned him multiple Emmy award nominations. He married his husband, lawyer Justin Mikita, in 2013. The two started a nonprofit called Tie the Knot, whose goal is to advocate for LGBT+ rights throughout the United States and beyond through bowtie sales.

Jesse Tyler Ferguson

Anita Green *(Missoula, MT)* became the first openly transgender person to compete in the Miss Montana USA pageant in 2017. Green was also elected to cast a vote for Bernie Sanders at the Democratic National Convention in 2016. She was sexually assaulted because of her transgender status when she was twenty-one: "In the aftermath of the assault, I decided I'm not going to be ashamed of being a transgender woman, even though that's often the purpose of these kinds of attacks. . . . That realization eventually landed me on a stage in front of a live audience, competing to be Miss Montana USA."

Osh-Tisch was a member of the Aspáalooke (or Crow) tribe who lived in Montana from the 1850s into the 1920s. In the Crow nation, Osh-Tisch was a prominent assigned-male-at-birth baté (two-spirit) member of the tribe. Osh-Tisch's name translates to "Finds Them and Kills Them," a name she earned in the 1876 Battle of the Rosebud during the Great Sioux War. When the US government began forcing the Crow people onto reservations in the 1890s, they also began persecuting two-spirit people and forcing them to wear the haircuts and clothes of their birth genders. As a result, Osh-Tisch was sent to prison, but her community stood by her until she was freed. By the time of her death in 1929, Osh-Tisch was one of the last living baté.

Jeannette Rankin *(Missoula, MT)* was the first woman elected to hold federal office in the United States when she was voted in as a member of the US House of Representatives in 1916. She was a staunch

> *I understand the struggles that members of the transgender community face. I know that it's not easy being transgender but I think it's so important to be true to yourself because in the end, you are the one who's going to make you happy. And the best way we can learn to fight for minority rights is by listening to members of said minority communities; it's important to let minority communities voice themselves and allow them the space to do so.*
>
> —Anita Green, *Cosmopolitan*, 2017

Jeannette Rankin

> ❝You always see people competing in whatever industry you are in and you think I'm not doing well because I'm not in that place. You have to realize you are on your own path.❞
>
> —Jesse Tyler Ferguson, *Forbes*, 2017

narrated from the point of view of a gay track coach. This was the first contemporary gay fiction novel to receive a place on the *New York Times* bestseller list. She spent decades working for *Reader's Digest*. In the 1990s, she volunteered as a commissioner of education in Los Angeles Unified School District over her concerns for LGBT+ youth; a decade later, she ran for City Council in West Hollywood, California.

advocate of women's voting rights, a pacifist, and the only member of Congress to vote against declaring war on Japan after the attack on Pearl Harbor in 1941. Her biographers are split on describing her sexual orientation; she never married, and some characterize her relationships with journalist Katherine Anthony and her life partner, Elizabeth Irving, as lesbian affairs. She had openly lesbian friends and was a pioneer on issues of gender even before women had the right to vote in this country.

Will Roscoe *(Missoula, MT)* is an American activist and author currently based out of San Francisco. In 1975, just six years after Stonewall, he founded the Lambda Alliance at the University of Montana, the first such LGBT+ organization in the state. Roscoe eventually relocated to California, where he worked with Harvey Milk until Milk's assassination in 1978. He also worked closely with Gay American Indians (GAI). Roscoe received a Lambda Literary Award for his books *Jesus and the Shamanic Tradition of Same-Sex Love* and *The Zuni Man-Woman*.

Patricia Nell Warren *(Helena, MT)* is a lesbian poet, novelist, and author of *The Front Runner* (1974), a novel

⊙ PLACES

Gay-friendly vacation spots in Montana include Lazy E-L Ranch and Nez Perce Ranch. These ranches/resorts welcome LGBT+ travelers and even host large groups of gay and lesbian visitors. Lazy E-L Ranch is located in Roscoe, Montana, while the Nez Perce Ranch is located in Darby. Live out your dream of being a Wild West cowboy/cowgirl on a scenic, 12,000-acre ranch complete with stunning mountain vistas and rugged but comfortable lodging.

The Gender Expansion Project provides gender-inclusive education and advocacy for transgender, intersex, and gender-diverse people in Montana, Eastern Washington, Idaho, Wyoming, and the Dakotas. It is based in Missoula, where it shares a location with the Western Montana LGBT+ Community Center. In 2015, it hosted a Gender Expansion Transgender Health Conference, although the organization's website does not indicate whether this will be a recurring event.

☺ QUEER FACTS

Interface Project was cofounded in 2012 by Eden Atwood, a native of Missoula, and Jim Ambrose, born in Baton Rouge, Louisiana. Both are intersex, and their nonprofit publishes stories of people born with intersex traits. Their stories and organization have been featured on CNN, ABC News, and BBC Radio, and have appeared in the *New Yorker*.

The Montana Supportive Business Initiative is a project aimed at bringing awareness to the LGBT+ community and highlighting businesses that are openly supportive of people of all gender identities and sexual orientations. There are over 150 current members of the business network, and the webpage includes a list by major city. This is a great resource for travelers and residents deciding where to do business in Montana.

The Montana Two Spirit Society was formed in 1996 and has organized an annual Two Spirit Gathering every year since. Over one hundred attendees participate every year, and the organization includes individuals from tribes all over the West, not just Montana. A big part of their mission is to "increase visibility of the Two Spirit and Native LGBTI community and restore our traditions."

Out Words is an independent magazine that ran from 2005 to 2014 and sought to represent Montana's LGBT+ community. Luckily, copies of the magazine are still stored in an online, publicly accessible archive on the Western Montana LGBT+ Community Center's website, providing a glimpse into the experiences of queer people across the state in a decade of fundamental change in American culture.

The Montana Human Rights Network LGBT+ Equality Project *(Helena, MT)* was formed over twenty years ago to secure legal protections for LGBT+ Montanans and their families. They work on a state level to add sexual orientation, gender identity, and gender expression to the Montana Human Rights Act and Montana's Bias-Based Crimes statute. The Network has over two thousand members from across the state who actively work to "counter the efforts of militias, freemen and other 'patriots,' anti-Indian groups, anti-environmental activists, and the religious right in Montana."

> *What the university loses when it fails to encompass lesbian and gay studies is not only knowledge of the presence of homosexuality in history and culture . . . but analysis of homophobia and the role it has played in constructing the present . . . These cases underscore how censorship is sometimes omission as well as erasure, how homophobia takes the form of forgetting as well as hating.*
>
> —Will Roscoe, *American Anthropologist*, 1995

OREGON

⊖ PEOPLE

James Beard *(Portland, OR)* is a renowned American chef and television personality. Beard attended Reed College in Portland; he was expelled for his homosexuality in 1922 (according to Reed College, it was because he was a poor student). In 1937, Beard began his first professional food venture, a catering company called Hors d'Oeuvre, Inc. Beard was the first chef to host a cooking show on American television, which aired on NBC starting in 1946. Beard published twenty-six cookbooks, including *The James Beard Cookbook* and *Delights & Prejudices: A Memoir with Recipes*, which Julia Child described as "timeless." Beard founded the James Beard Cooking School in 1955. After his death in 1985, Julia Child called the James Beard Foundation to make sure it preserved his house. The James Beard House is now the site of over two hundred culinary events per year. Beard has become a symbol of American food culture, and helped pioneer America's fascination with culinary excellence. In 1990, his foundation established the James Beard Foundation Award, which has since become one of the most prestigious titles a chef can hold.

James Beard
FOREVER·USA
2014

Kate Brown

Katherine "Kate" Brown *(Torrejón de Ardoz, Spain)* won the 2016 special election for governor, becoming the first openly bisexual person to be elected as governor. Brown said that she hoped her governorship would inspire others in the LGBT+ community because "you can't be what you can't see." As governor, Brown passed a law making it illegal for minors to attend anti-gay conversion therapy. She is an advocate for victims of domestic and sexual violence, based on her own traumas. Brown previously worked in the state House of Representatives, where she was elected in 1991; in 1997 she was elected to the State Senate. She became the state Senate Majority Leader in 2004 and then Oregon Secretary of State in 2009.

Peggy Burton *(Turner, OR)* was a public school teacher who taught math and biology, and was also a sports referee. Burton was the first public school teacher to file a lawsuit on the basis of LGBT+ discrimination, after she was fired in 1970 for being a "practicing homosexual." She took Cascade High School to court with the help of ACLU lawyer Charles Hinkle, where the school was ordered to pay Burton $10,000.

The only thing that will make a soufflé fall is if it knows you're afraid of it.

—James Beard

I carry with me every single day the privilege of white skin and I don't know what it's like to experience racism. I do know, however, what it's like to be terrified going to work every single day, afraid that I might lose my job because someone discovered that my partner was a woman.

—Kate Brown, commencement speech at Willamette University, 2016

Still, Cascade did not allow Burton to continue teaching because she was not tenured, although many other civil cases against teachers reinstated them once they won, regardless of tenure. Burton appealed the court's decision in order to get her job back, but the district cross-appealed to take back its reparations money. The judge denied the cross-appeal because it was not filed on time. Oregon's first civil rights law prohibiting discrimination was passed in 2007.

Khalil Edwards (*Portland, OR*) is an advocate for racial justice and LGBT+ rights. He served as the codirector of the first Black chapter of Parents, Families, and Friends of Lesbians and Gays (PFLAG), which his mother, Antoinette Edwards, helped found. The organization then separated from PFLAG to become its own independent group, called Sankofa Collective Northwest, which delivers support to Black LGBT+ individuals and their families in the Portland area. Under the guidance of Edwards and his codirector, Leila Haile, the organization started a faith outreach program and began to focus on issues like economic disparity and housing justice. Edwards has also served as the racial justice manager of Basic Rights Oregon and works as the development specialist at Power California, which encourages young people of color to participate in government.

Stu Rasmussen (*Silverton, OR*) was the first transgender person to be elected mayor of a US city, when in 1988 he/she (Rasmussen's preferred pronoun) was elected in Silverton. He/she was re-elected in 1990, 2008, 2010, and 2012. During his/her time as mayor, Rasmussen took tight control over the budget to maximize the effectiveness of taxpayer dollars, expanded the library and senior center, and increased tourism.

Rasmussen also served as a city counselor and on the Silver Falls Library Board. He/she owns the Palace Theater with his/her business partner, Roger Paulson, where he/she has worked since youth, when he/she ran the concession stand. Rasmussen cofounded Silverton Cable Television Company and has worked as an engineer with Tektronix, Intel, Phoenix Technologies, and UPS Aviation Technology. In 2013, Intiman Theater in Seattle put on a musical about Rasmussen's life called *Stu for Silverton*.

Nico Santos (*Manila, Philippines*) is an actor and comedian known for his roles in *Paul Blart: Mall Cop 2*, *Superstore*, and *Crazy Rich Asians*. He moved to Gresham, Oregon, from the Philippines when he was sixteen. He later attended Southern Oregon University,

Nico Santos

where he studied acting until one of his professors told him, "You may love the art, but the art does not love you." After his professor's harsh criticism, Santos began to study costume design. He worked at the Oregon Shakespeare Festival in costuming for multiple years until an actor told him that he was so funny he should try stand-up. He moved to California to pursue a career in comedy, and there he found an agent and an acting career. Santos said that he has found it rewarding to play a gay Filipino in *Superstore* as he is one himself.

Tammy Smith *(Oakland, OR)* is a brigadier general in the United States Army in South Korea. Smith called her appointment to the position a "privilege." She has also been the Commanding General of the 98th

> *I'm all about playing queer roles. I want to show people out there that there's such a huge spectrum of people within the queer and Asian community.*
>
> —Nico Santos, *Los Angeles Times*, 2018

Tammy Smith

Training Division, which works with Initial Entry Training, and the United States Army Reserve Deputy Chief of Staff. Smith has said that 1993's Don't Ask, Don't Tell policy was an improvement to the military laws regarding homosexuality that preceded it, because it acknowledged that there were gay people in the military rather than criminalizing their existence. Prior to DADT, the Criminal Investigation Division would read soldiers' diaries and even pose as gay to try to out them as gay so they could be discharged. Still, the policy bothered Smith because the army discharged LGBT+ individuals anyway, and led her to want to retire in 2009. When DADT was repealed in 2010, she decided to stay. She married her wife, Tracey Hepner, in 2012.

◉ PLACES

The former house of James Beard *(Portland, OR)* is located on Southwest Salmon Street, where he was born and raised in the early 1900s. The house has since been converted into apartments. Beard's former home in New York City's Greenwich Village is now the headquarters of the James Beard Foundation culinary institute.

Q Center *(Portland, OR)* is the largest LGBT+ organization in the Pacific Northwest. It provides educational and social events for a variety of subgroups, such as seniors, youth, and affinity groups. It also provides financial support to smaller organizations that help the LGBT+ community, and offers support with mental health and addiction issues.

Ray Leonard's grave *(Lebanon, OR)* is located in the Lebanon Pioneer Cemetery. Leonard was an Oregon pioneer who moved to the state in 1889 and dressed as a man until 1911, when his birth sex was discovered by a doctor after Leonard was committed to an asylum for hallucinations. According to the journals of the doctor who cared for him, Leonard's condition rapidly improved after his identity was revealed. Still, Leonard was required to wear dresses in the asylum, and his 1921 obituary referred to him as female.

⚡ QUEER FACTS

The first transgender man to undergo surgical transition did so in Oregon. Dr. Alan L. Hart graduated from medical school at the University of Oregon in 1917. Afterward, Hart reached out to one of his former professors, J. Allen Gilbert, for psychiatric treatment for homosexuality. Gilbert tried a number of methods, including hypnosis, before Hart convinced Gilbert to give him a hysterectomy. Hart's argument to Gilbert was that he must be sterilized to avoid spreading homosexuality to his offspring. After the surgery, he began to live as a man and married twice. Hart pioneered using X-ray medicine to detect tuberculosis, and spent much of his professional life researching the disease. Hart died in 1962.

Oregon's First Code of Laws was established in 1843 during a gathering of pioneers at Champoeg, and was used as the building blocks of the state's government. Oregon adapted its code from Iowa's, because a member of the community had brought a copy of Iowa's code to Oregon with him. Iowa's laws did not outlaw sodomy, and therefore neither did Oregon's.

The Portland Two Spirit Society is a social group that supports LGBT+ indigenous peoples, as well as their families and friends. Asa Wright started the group in 2004, when it had a membership of about twenty people. Over the years, membership grew, and now over fifty people attend the society's meetings. It hosts a variety of educational and cultural events, such as potlucks and film screenings, and regularly participates in Portland Pride.

The book Sex, *Science and Sin* was published in 1950 and written by Earl Biggs of Portland. The book drew on Biggs's experience as a police officer who investigated sex crimes. After twenty years in the field, Biggs wrote that persecution of homosexuals was illegitimate because sex among them is a consensual behavior. His book drew the attention of Dr. Alfred Kinsey, the famous sexologist who wrote the Kinsey Reports: *Sexual Behavior in the Human Male* and *Sexual Behavior in the Human Female*. Kinsey was so impressed with Biggs's work that he came to Portland to meet Biggs in person.

WomanShare Women's Land Retreat *(Grants Pass, OR)* was a retreat for lesbians and other women away from the pressures of mainstream patriarchal society. It was established in 1974 by three lesbian friends and operated until 1999. The retreat contained twenty-three acres of wooded territory. Membership varied from around four to six women, although there was also a visitor's cabin. The patrons strived to be self-sufficient in all ways, from home and car repair to finances.

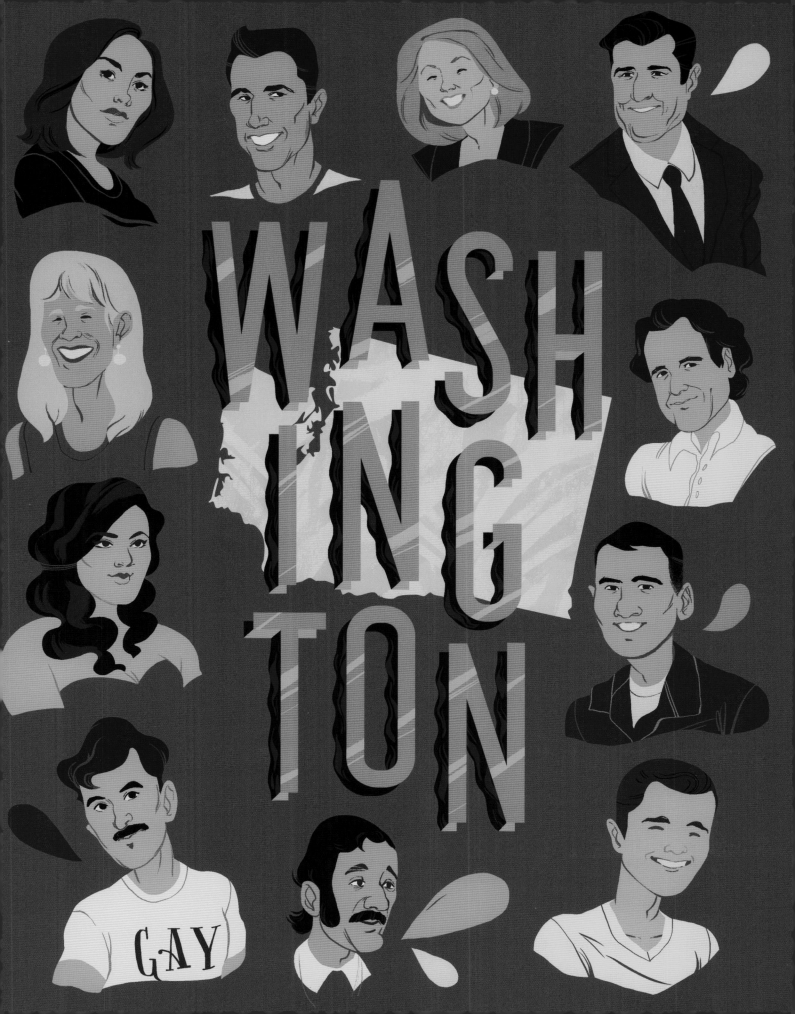

👤 PEOPLE

Graham Ackerman *(Seattle, WA)* is a three-time national gymnastics champion. Ackerman won his first NCAA Men's Gymnastics Championship titles in the floor and vault categories in 2004, and in 2005 in the floor category. In college at the time, he was one of few high-achieving openly gay college athletes.

John Lyon Burnside III *(Seattle, WA)* was a staff scientist for Lockheed and invented the teleidoscope, a type of kaleidoscope. In the 1960s, Burnside was active in the nation's first gay rights demonstrations, which were held in protest of the exclusion of gay people from the military. For almost forty years, Burnside's partner was Harry Hay, a fellow gay rights activist and founder of the Mattachine Society, one of the nation's first gay rights organization.

Jenny Anne Durkan *(Seattle, WA)* was elected mayor of Seattle in 2017, becoming the city's second elected LGBT+ mayor in a row, succeeding Ed Murray, who resigned from the position in 2017 due to several accusations of sexual abuse. Durkan's election broke a ninety-year drought since the last woman had held the position in the 1920s. Prior to her post as mayor, Durkan was nominated by President Barack Obama as the US Attorney for Washington's Western District in 2009.

Stephen Funk *(Seattle, WA)* is a former member of the US Marine Corps. In 2003, he became the first military member to refuse deployment to Iraq. In his application to be a conscientious objector, Funk cited his identity as a gay man for part of the reasoning behind his moral objection to the Iraq War. Funk did not receive objector status and instead spent five months in military prison.

Mary Ann Horton *(Richland, WA)* is a transgender activist and educator. As an internet pioneer, she developed a popular format for email attachments, as well as AT&T's first firewall system. In 2003, Horton was featured in a public service announcement for Stonewall Columbus, an Ohio LGBT+ community center, one

> *War is about destruction and violence and death. It is young men fighting old men's wars. It is not the answer; it just ravages the land of the battleground. I know it's wrong but other people in the military have been programmed to think it is okay.*
>
> —Stephen Funk, *The Guardian*, 2003

Mary Lambert

of the first transgender roles on television actually portrayed by a transgender person.

Mary Lambert *(Seattle, WA)* rose to prominence as a vocalist and collaborator on the song "Same Love," an LGBT+ rights single by Macklemore and Ryan Lewis. Lambert is also a spoken-word poet; her work centers on her experiences as a lesbian raised in a Christian family, as well as body positivity and mental health, among other things.

Conner Mertens *(Kennewick, WA)* made history in 2014, when he came out as bisexual to his teammates on the Willamette Bearcats football team. He was the first active collegiate football player to do so. Mertens is a speaker and advocate for anti-bullying, suicide prevention, and LGBT+ athletics.

Patricia "Patty" Schemel *(Seattle, WA)* was the drummer of the rock band Hole from 1992 to 1998. Schemel's career as a musician is vast, having also performed with fellow Hole member Courtney Love's solo venture, as well as the bands Juliette and the Licks, Upset, and Death Valley Girls, among many others.

Rick Welts *(Seattle, WA)* is the president and COO of the Golden State Warriors NBA team; previously, he was the president and CEO of the Phoenix Suns from 2002 to 2011. Welts served as the NBA's chief marketing officer and executive vice president from 1996 to 1999. Rick publicly came out in a *New York Times* article in 2011, becoming the first prominent male professional sports executive to reveal he is gay.

I was still closeted. It took quite a while because you didn't dare come out back then. It would have been social suicide, job suicide.

—Mary Ann Horton,
The Daily Beast, 2018

 PLACES

The Bailey-Boushay House *(Seattle, WA)* opened in 1992 as the nation's first care facility exclusively for people with HIV/AIDS. The center provides a number of inpatient and outpatient programs and is open to those struggling with mental health, chemical dependency, and homelessness.

Capitol Hill

⚛ QUEER FACTS

Ingersoll v. Arlene's Flowers and *State of Washington v. Arlene's Flowers* center on a florist who refused to sell her flowers for a gay couple's wedding in 2013 due to her religious beliefs. In 2015, a Benton County Superior Court judge ruled that the florist violated Washington's anti-discrimination laws, as well as the Consumer Protection Act. The florist appealed to the US Supreme Court, but in 2018 the case was sent back to the Washington Supreme Court.

The Northwest Lesbian and Gay History Museum Project began documenting the Pacific Northwest's LGBT+ history in 1994. Their collection ranges from oral histories to photos, documents, and objects, preserved with the knowledge that the stories of LGBT+ people often go ignored, unheard, or inaccurately reported. The organization hosts rotating exhibits to ensure the history is accessible to anyone looking to learn more about the region's LGBT+ history and experiences.

Paul Barwick and Faygele ben Miriam were among the first same-sex couples to apply for a marriage license in the United States. Their 1971 request—which was largely motivated to prove that homosexual couples lacked the same rights as heterosexuals—was denied and led to the *Singer v. Hara* lawsuit, which was rejected unanimously in 1974 by the Washington State Court of Appeals.

> *I think there are so many people who grew up in trauma or grew up in houses of turmoil or with parents who were unkind to them who don't know how to accept love because that's what they're used to and that's what they're going to seek out because that's what feels normal. It doesn't feel normal to be treated well or to treat yourself well; you have to learn how to accept love and to learn to take care of yourself.*
>
> —Mary Danielle Lambert, *KEXP*, 2017

The Capitol Hill neighborhood *(Seattle, WA)* is widely regarded as the epicenter of the city's LGBT+ community. The *Seattle Times* reported in 2006 that 12.9 percent of the city's residents identified as LGBT+, one of the largest concentrated populations in the country.

The Casino *(Seattle, WA)* is considered to be one of the first hotbeds of Seattle's gay culture. Joseph Bellotti opened the pool hall and card room in the 1930s, around the time Prohibition was repealed, and the spot quickly became known as a safe space for same-sex dancing, as well as a home to drag performers. The scene eventually migrated upstairs to the Double Header, also owned by Bellotti, who is said to have paid off police in exchange for them leaving the clientele alone. Until it closed in 2015, the Double Header was thought to have been one of the longest-running gay bars in America.

WYOMING

⊖ PEOPLE

Kiyoshi Kuromiya *(Heart Mountain, WY)* was an influential civil rights and gay rights activist. Kuromiya was born at Wyoming's Heart Mountain Relocation Center during the internment of Japanese Americans in World War II. His family eventually returned to their hometown of Monrovia, California, and he later attended the University of Pennsylvania. In 1968, protesting the use of napalm in Vietnam, he handed out pamphlets that stated his intention of burning a dog on the steps of the university's library. Over two thousand people arrived to protest his act, more than any other prior protest. When the crowds appeared, they were handed another pamphlet that said, "You have saved a dog . . . now how about a child, or millions of children." In later years, Kuromiya became a close friend of Martin Luther King Jr., and was an important figure in the gay rights rallies of the early 1960s before helping launch the Gay Liberation Front in Philadelphia. He remained an influential advocate for civil and gay rights until his death in 2000.

Guy Padgett *(Casper, WY)* was formerly a politician in Casper, Wyoming. Padgett came out in 2003 while serving on the city council. In 2005, he was unanimously elected mayor by the city council. At twenty-seven, Padgett became both the city's youngest and first openly gay mayor. He served as mayor until 2009, when he left the position to pursue a graduate degree.

> ❝
> *I'm a twenty-year metastatic lung cancer survivor and a fifteen-year AIDS survivor. And I really believe that activism is therapeutic.*
>
> —Kiyoshi Kuromiya, *Philadelphia LGBT History Project*, 1997
> ❞

Todd Parr *(Rock Springs, WY)* is a children's book author, illustrator, and television producer. He has claimed to have been a difficult student, and received an F in art for not following form. Despite this, he moved to San Francisco to pursue a career in children's illustration. His work on *The Family Book*, a children's book featuring same-sex parents, received some acclaim while also being banned from several school districts. Parr has received many awards and nominations for his work, including the Parents Choice Award for *The Earth Book*, an Emmy nomination for Outstanding Children's Animated Program for his PBS program *ToddWorld*, and a Humanitas Prize nomination for Children's Animation Category for the *ToddWorld* episode "Come Out of Your Shell."

Romaine Patterson is an LGBT+ rights activist who rose to national attention after the murder of her close friend Matthew Shepard. When Fred Phelps of the Westboro Baptist Church organized a hateful protest of Shepard's funeral, Patterson gathered a group of counterprotesters dressed as angels with wings large enough to block out the church's signs. Patterson soon founded Angel Action, an organization for the peaceful counterprotest tactic. She later became involved as a spokesperson for the Matthew Shepard Foundation, as well as several national media campaigns via GLAAD.

Todd Parr

William Panzarella
Scott Parietti
Alexander Petelin
Michael Phair
Brenda Potts
Jim Potts
Kenny Rafowitz
Linda Ranieri

Bertha Reed
Fredrick Roffman
Charlie Rounds
Billy & Sandy Paffen
Allen Selinski
Davis Sensman
St. Louis Park GSA
Rick Stafford

Zaylore Stout
Lo Swan
Vanessa Tennyson
William (Bill) J. Thom
Mike & Dolores Toney
Karl Ulrichs
Rebecca Waggoner-Johnson
Jackie Wanner

Phillip Washington
Yolanda White
Michael White
Victor Wikoli
Oscar Wilde
Trisha Yates

#OGH50S Hall of Fame

Our Gay History in 50 States would not have been possible without the generous support of our early believers. They came from almost every state in this nation and even other countries. Thank you for supporting our Kickstarter!

Sheila A. Bates
Joel A Butler
Alyssa A. Scott
Reggie Acker
Valerie Acklin
Jesse Aguiñaga Sanchez
James Alongi
Cortney Amundson
Chris Anderson
Mark Anthony Lesjak
Nick Azevedo
J. B. Mayo
Tony Bañuelos
Shane Bacon
Jay Balaban
Kim Bartels
Dee Baskin
Yossi & Batia Lindenfeld
Dara Beevas
Jennifer Beightley
Larry Bell
Blake Bitton
David Bloom
Caroline Boehmer
Andrew Bonnington
John Bookwalter Jr.
Ted Bougie
Jack Breckner
Candy Brent
Elijah Brumfield
Rebecca Bryant
Nicolas Burrows
Joel Calhoun
Tommie Casey
Sue Cassidy
Fawn Colombatto
Tim Creagan

The Creative Fund
Lalo Cruz
Andrew Csavoy
Amy Cutler Quale
Darryll D Coleman
Joe D. Metzen
Charles Dailey
Ken Darling
Matthew David
Alvin David
Adrian Davis
Dustyn Davis
Greg Delacerda
Daquent DQ Robinson
Paul Driver
Janet Eckhoff
Elisabeth
Katie Elliott
Marie Ellis
Sarah Erskine
Lauren F. Ignacio
Sheynnon Feder
Steve Field
Nico Figueroa
Alexis Fish
Gage Fisher
Tyrone Folliard
Elliott Foster
Uzodima Franklin Aba-Onu
Addy Free
Karen Frye
Amanda Garcia
Chris Garland
Kim Genelle
Amy Gildemeister
Christina Glad
Tom Glaser

Edgar Gonzalez
Scott Grouell
Tiffany Hanken
David Harrison
Elisabeth Hedman
Howard Held
Keith Hendrickson
Alex Hill
Kitt Hodsden
David Holley Jr.
Holliamari
Derek Holm
James Hood
Sara Howard
Samuel Ingram
Jeremy J. Hundt
Myia Jablonecki
Stacie Jablonecki
Alicia Jackson
Samuel Jacob Doten
Del Jenkins
Michael Jerome
    Folliard-Olson
Annie Jia
Kay Johnson
Tara Jones
Amanda Kabage
Faris Karaman
Karoline Katus
Sean Kennedy
Tracy Kincheloe
David Kohman
Danielle Kotecki
Keith Kozerski
Jeffrey Kranzel
A'kyra Hamilton
Matthew LaMaster

Ben Lambert
Øydis Larsen
Bradley Laurent
Pamela Layton
Marcus Leab
Kervin Leacock
Mariah Leah Jensen
Barry Leavitt
Cory Lefebvre
Robert Leo
Joan & Leon Bates
Laura Leslie
Steven Levy
Paul Lillie
Becky Lindstrom
Taylor Listul
David Lozinski
Cortney Lynn
Shaun M. Parks
Hollie Mae Schultz
Johnny Maio
Maximilian Mantz
Matt Marsh
Max Martin
Jeanne Massey
Carleen Matts
Tracie May-Wagner
Justin McBride
Willard McCloud
Christina Mendez
Chris Metzger
Chris Mitchell
Fernando N. Garcia
Brad Nelson
Rebecca Nguyen
Alex Nugent
Merrilee O'Neil

Rory O'Neil
Victor Olivares
Ron P. Wacks
Tom Pack
Judy Palmer O'Toole
Jerry Pang
Jan Parks
Morgan Pasquier
Trusha Patel Goffe
Jim Patronus
A. Paul Masiarchin
Matthew Paul Schumacher
Bethany Penna
Chuck Peterson
Felipe Pina
Jayson Ponce
Chad Price
Lisa Prosser

Kosta Psiakis
Pyrrhalphis
Ken Rafowitz
William Rand Morris
Casey Rayburg
Russell Ricard
Charlie Rodgers
Ivan Romero
Jesse Sanchez
Billy & Sandi Paffen
Armen Sarkissian
Tim Sauke
Ryan Scheife
Lisa Shaffner
Shey
Summra Shariff
Allyn Shaw
Sarah Slocum

Lisa Sohn
Theresa Stanton
Josh Stewart
Becky Sturm
John Sullivan
Lucy Sullivan
Pete Surdo
J. T. (Julie Thomas)
Rabindra Tambyraja
Jerrell Tate
Michelle Templer
Jamel Thomas
Elizabeth Tisel
Gregory Torrence
Morgan Tupper
Erin Valenciano
Justin Varney
Kelsey Varpness

Seth Viebrock
Matt Wach
Paul Wach
Claire Warren
Libby Waterbury
Edward Weinberg
Jacob Westlund
Adriane Wiggins
Bradford Williams
Patrick Wurst
Richard Xaviar Corral
Yvonne Yeh
Alexander Zachary
Brady Ziegler
Marni Zimlin
Aaron Zimmerman
Eric Zucker

PHOTO CREDITS

A. J. Lopp: 150

Alan Kotok (Flickr): 199

Alan Light (Flickr): 301

Allan Warren: 44, 252

Amirkat1135 (Zedge): xvi (left)

Andrew Rusk (Flickr): 244 (left)

April Brady/Project on Middle East Democracy/POMED (Flickr): 187

Arnold Genthe/Library of Congress: 14 (right)

Beth Mejia: xvii

Carl Van Vechten: 154, 174 (left)

Center for American Progress (Flickr): 109

Christian Wagner (Flickr): xiii (left)

Christopher Macsurak: 38 (right)

CineKink (Flickr): 298 (bottom)

Cliff/Nostri-Imago (Flickr): 146

COD Newsroom: 239

Comisión Interamericana de Derechos Humanos: 127

Dale McDonald Collection (Flickr): 98

Daniel Ramirez (Flickr): 300

David Shankbone: 188 (right), 238

Derek Nance (Flickr): 305

Donna Burton (Flickr): 9

Donna Loring/Jane Peasley: 14 (left)

Ed Ritger/Commonwealth Club: 113 (right)

Elvert Barnes: 200 (right)

Equality California: xi (right)

Eric Bargman: xvi (right)

Eva Rinaldi: 136 (right)

Gage Skidmore (Flickr): xiii (left)

Gareth Watkins: 203 (left)

Governor Mark Dayton (Flickr): 215 (top)

Hans Hillewaert: 244 (right)

Harris & Ewing/Library of Congress: 148

James Cridland (Flickr): 278

Jay Denney: 196 (left)

Jha4ceb: 211

Joe Bielawa (Flickr): 299 (top right)

John Gennusa: 208

John Phelan: 169

Justin Taylor (Flickr): 279

K. Kendall (Flickr): 174 (right)

Kalamazoo Public Library (Flickr): 332

Keith Hinkle (Flickr): 135

Kelly Writers House (Flickr): 232 (right)

Kyle Cassidy: 71

Loop202: 144 (right)

Marion S. Trikosko/Library of Congress: 25

Mayflower Sales Co./Boston Public Library: 27

Myrna Litt (Flickr): 108 (top)

NASA Kennedy: 204

nathanmac87 (Flickr): 85

Ore Lindenfeld: xi (left)

Orlando Fernandez/New York World Telegram and Sun/ Library of Congress: 120

Paul Sableman (Flickr): 228

Pax Ahimsa Gethen: 188 (left)

Peabody Awards (Flickr): 17 (bottom), 319

Phil Duran: xiii (right)

Policy Exchange: 200 (left)

Randy Stern (Flickr): 219 (top)

R0uge: 290

Roger Higgins/New York World Telegram and Sun/Library of Congress: 112

Sara Melikian (Flickr): 4 (left)

Scott McMurren: 258

Sergei Gussev (Flickr): 282

Sergio Ruiz (Flickr): 281

Shutterstock: 3, 4 (right), 5, 10, 13, 18, 19, 20, 24 (both), 33, 34, 36, 38 (left), 39, 40, 45, 46 (both), 48, 49, 54, 56, 62, 65, 66, 67, 81, 82, 86, 90 (right), 91, 93, 94, 95 (both), 96, 97, 99, 100, 103, 104, 105, 108 (bottom), 113 (left), 114, 117, 118, 119, 124 (both), 128, 131, 133, 136 (left), 140, 144 (left), 148, 155, 159, 160, 162 (right), 163, 166, 171, 176, 177 (right), 178 (both), 179, 185, 194, 203 (right), 205, 215 (bottom), 224, 232 (left), 245, 257, 264, 265, 266, 267 (left), 269, 271, 274, 276, 285, 288 (both), 297, 298 (top), 299 (top left), 303, 304 (both), 309, 315, 323 (both), 324, 328, 329,

Stephen Field: xii (top)

Steven Pisano (Flickr): 90 (left)

Ted Van Pelt (Flickr): 76

Todd Van Hoosear (Flickr): 212

Tony Webster (Flickr): 219 (bottom), 220

Unsplash: xii (bottom), xiii (left)

Visible Hand (ItzaFineDay): 161

XPRIZE Foundation (Flickr): 17 (top)

Yuefeng D (Flickr): 230

Zaylore Stout: xii (bottom), xiv (both), xv (all)

WHO INSPIRED YOU?

_____ , born in _____ , _____ ,

is/was _____

_____

_____

_____

_____

_____

_____

_____

_____

_____

_____

_____

DRAW OR ATTACH A PORTRAIT

WHO INSPIRED YOU?

_____ , born in _____ , _____ ,

is/was _____

_____

_____

_____

_____

_____

_____

_____

_____

_____

_____

_____

DRAW OR ATTACH A PORTRAIT

WRITE YOUR OWN HISTORY

I, _____

_____

_____

_____

_____

_____

_____

_____

_____

_____

_____

_____

_____

_____

DRAW OR ATTACH A PORTRAIT

WORKS CITED

Alabama

Aronson, Emily. "Actress and Activist Cox Talks about 'journey to womanhood'." Princeton.edu. November 8, 2015. www.princeton.edu/news/2015/11/18/actress-and-activist-cox-talks-about-journey-womanhood.

Azzopardi, Chris. "Mister Rogers's Gay, Black Friend François Clemmons Wears Tiaras Now." VanityFair.com. June 27, 2018. www.vanityfair.com/hollywood/2018/06/mister-rogers-neighborhood-wont-you-be-my-neighbor-francois-clemmons-officer-clemmons-fred-rogers.

Biography.com Editors. "Tim Cook Biography." Biography.com. April 2, 2014. www.biography.com/people/tim-cook-20967297.

Brumburgh, Gary. "Nell Carter - Biography - IMDb." IMDb.com. www.imdb.com/name/nm0141846/bio.

Chandler, Kim. "Panel Moves to Strike Anti-Gay Phrase in Alabama Sex Ed Law." APNews.com. February 14, 2018. www.apnews.com/6ce4b4c801464aef958aa0e2b7e59a9a.

Cook, Tim. "Tim Cook Speaks Up." Bloomberg.com. October 30, 2014. www.bloomberg.com/news/articles/2014-10-30/tim-cook-speaks-up.

Cox, Laverne. "About + Bio." LaverneCox.com. lavernecox.com/about.

Dunlap, David. "Judge Voids and Alabama Law Against Gay Campus Groups." NYTimes.com. January 31, 1996. www.nytimes.com/1996/01/31/us/judge-voids-an-alabama-law-against-gay-campus-groups.html.

Encyclopedia Britannica. "Tallulah Bankhead." Britannica.com. February 18, 2019. www.britannica.com/biography/Tallulah-Bankhead.

Faulk, Kent. "Alabama Supreme Court Now Recognizes Lesbian Adoption After SCOTUS Opinion." AL.com. May 27, 2016. www.al.com/news/birmingham/2016/05/alabama_supreme_court_vacates.html.

Grayson, Wayne. "UA Student Group for Gays, Lesbians Looks to Broaden Support Citywide." TuscaloosaNews.com. April 24, 2011. www.tuscaloosanews.com/news/20110324/ua-student-group-for-gays-lesbians-looks-to-broaden-support-citywide.

Holden, Stephen. "Nell Carter Is Dead at 54; Star of 'Ain't Misbehavin'." NYTimes.com. January 24, 2003. www.nytimes.com/2003/01/24/arts/nell-carter-is-dead-at-54-star-of-ain-t-misbehavin.html.

IMDb. "Laverne Cox - Awards." IMDb.com. www.imdb.com/name/nm1209545/awards.

Kaczynski, Andrew. "Jeff Sessions Fought As Alabama Attorney General to Keep an LGBT Conference from Meeting on a Public Campus." CNN.com. December 2, 2016. www.cnn.com/2016/12/01/politics/kfile-jeff-sessions-lgbt-conference/index.html.

Lewis, Jone Johnson. "Biography of Angela Davis, Political Activist and Academic." ThoughtCo.com. April 17, 2019. www.thoughtco.com/angela-davis-biography-3528285.

Margolin, Emma. "Roy Moore Suspended From Alabama Supreme Court for Anti-Gay Marriage Order." September 30, 2016. www.nbcnews.com/feature/nbc-out/alabama-chief-justice-suspended-over-gay-marriage-stance-n657511.

Rawls, Phillip. "Alabama Politicians Pressure State University Over Gay Group." April 21, 1992. apnews.com/008a74b1d9c2a9ecd79b41844b1c0fb1.

The New York Times. "Auburn Fight Over Gay Group Shifts to U.S. Court." NYTimes.com. April 29, 1992. www.nytimes.com/1992/03/29/us/auburn-fight-over-gay-group-shifts-to-us-court.html.

West's Encyclopedia of American Law. "Angela Yvonne Davis." Encyclopedia.com. 2005. www.encyclopedia.com/people/history/us-history-biographies/angela-yvonne-davis.

University of Alabama. "UNIVERSITY OF ALABAMA GAY STUDENT UNION ANNIVERSARY T-SHIRT." Apps.Lib.UA.edu. apps.lib.ua.edu/blogs/empoweringvoices/university-of-alabama-gay-student-union-anniversary-t-shirt.

University of Alabama. "UNIVERSITY OF ALABAMA GAY STUDENT UNION PAMPHLET." Apps.Lib.UA.edu. apps.lib.ua.edu/blogs/empoweringvoices/university-of-alabama-gay-student-union-pamphlet.

Wilson, Claire. "Nell Carter." EncyclopediaofAlabama.org. May 26, 2009. www.encyclopediaofalabama.org/article/h-2171.

Alaska

Anchorage PrideFest. "About Anchorage Pride." AnchoragePride.org. anchoragepride.org/about.

Associated Press. "Remote Arctic town hosts Alaska's first known same-sex marriage." CBSNews.com. October 15, 2014. www.cbsnews.com/news/remote-arctic-town-hosts-alaskas-first-known-same-sex-marriage.

Ballotpedia. "Johnny Ellis." Ballotpedia.org. ballotpedia.org/Johnny_Ellis.

Bellware, Kim. "Two Openly Gay Candidates Notch Historic Wins In Alaska Election." HuffPost.com. April 05, 2017. www.huffpost.com/entry/gay-candidates-win-alaska-election_n_58e53b55e4b06a4cb30e9ed9.

Freedom to Marry. "The Freedom to Marry in Alaska." FreedomtoMarry.org. www.freedomtomarry.org/states/alaska.

Hughes, Zachariah. "How LGBT Advocates Scored A Surprising Victory In Alaska." NPR.org. April 11, 2018. www.npr.org/2018/04/11/601097019/how-lgbt-advocates-scored-a-surprising-victory-in-alaska.

Johnson, R.J. "The makeover of Mad Myrna's." AnchoragePress.com. March 15, 2018. www.anchoragepress.com/prismpress/the-makeover-of-mad-myrna-s/article_02a8d328-28bf-11e8-94b6-dba665f784fb.html.

Kelly, Devin. "Anchorage Assembly passes LGBT rights law." ADN.com. September 28, 2016. www.adn.com/anchorage/article/anchorage-assembly-debates-lgbt-rights-law/2015/09/30.

Miller, Jenny Irene. "Continuous." JennyIreneMiller.com. www.jennyirenemiller.com/continuous.

Municipality of Anchorage. "About Us…" Muni.org. www.muni.org/Departments/Assembly/Pages/About%20Us%20-%20Member%20Profiles.aspx.

Pruden, Harlan. "Seeing and Experiencing Alaskan Two-Spirit Pride." TwoSpiritJournal.com. January 12, 2017. twospiritjournal.com/?p=515.

The Identity Center of Anchorage. "The Center—Identity Alaska." IdentityAlaska.org. identityalaska.org/about/community-center.

Towle, Andy. "U.S. Snowboarder Callan Chythlook-Sifsof: I'm Gay." TowleRoad.com. February 10, 2014. www.towleroad.com/2014/02/us-snowboarder-callan-chythlook-sifsof-im-gay.

United States Olympic Committee. "Callan Chythlook-Sifsof." TeamUSA.org. www.teamusa.org/us-ski-and-snowboard/athletes/Callan-ChythlookSifsof.

Wohlforth, Charles. "Sen. Johnny Ellis sacrificed his private life for public service." ADN.com. November 16, 2016. www.adn.com/opinions/2016/11/16/sen-johnny-ellis-sacrificed-his-private-life-for-public-service.

American Samoa

Advocate.com. Editors. "Queer Heroes of America's Territories." Advocate.com. May 22, 2018. www.advocate.com/current-issue/2018/5/22/these-americans-are-our-champions-too.

Amazon. "Samoan Queer Lives." Amazon.com. www.amazon.com/S%C4%81moan-Queer-Lives-Yuki-Kihara/dp/187748427X.

Andrew, Mike. "SGN Exclusive interview: Dr. Vena Sele Samoan activist and Transgender pioneer." SGN.org. web.archive.org/web/20170711091939/www.sgn.org/sgnnews38_25/page3.cfm.

Feagaimaali'i-Luamanu, Joyetter. "Transwoman shares her story." SamoaObserver.ws. March 18, 2018. www.samoaobserver.ws/category/samoa/8594.

Fruean, Adel. "Fa'fafine week campaign kicks off." SamoaObserver.ws. December 02, 2018. www.samoaobserver.ws/category/samoa/1037.

OutRight. "Meet Samoa's Champion of Fa'afafine Rights, To'oto'oali'i Roger Stanley." OutRightInternational.org. November 22, 2017. www.outrightinternational.org/content/meet-samoa-champion-trans-rights-activist-roger-stanley.

OutRight. "Remembering Samoan Fa'afafine Activist To'oto'oali'i Roger Stanley." OutRightInternational.com. January 23, 2018. www.outrightinternational.org/content/remembering-samoan-faafafine-activist-tootooalii-roger-stanley.

PIR Editor. "Transgender American Samoas Hoping To Serve In Military." PIReport.org. June 01, 2016. www.pireport.org/articles/2016/06/01/transgender-american-samoas-hoping-serve-military.

RNZ. "Tuilaepa says no to same sex marriage in Samoa." RadioNZ.co.nz. December 12, 2017. www.radionz.co.nz/international/pacific-news/346017/tuilaepa-says-no-to-same-sex-marriage-in-samoa.

Samoa Faafafine Association Incorporated. "About." Facebook.com. www.facebook.com/pg/sfainc/about/?ref=page_internal.

Samuels, A. J. "Fa'afafines: The Third Gender in Samoa." TheCultureTrip.com. February 09, 2017. theculturetrip.com/pacific/samoa/articles/fa-afafines-the-third-gender.

Sofias. "Vision, Mission & Charity." AsSofias.Webs.com. assofias.webs.com/visionmissioncharity.htm.

Tan, Yvette. "Miss Fa'afafine: Behind Samoa's 'third gender' beauty pageant." BBC.com. September 01, 2016. www.bbc.com/news/world-asia-37227803.

Arizona

ACLU. "ACLU of Arizona to Challenge Phoenix's Unconstitutional Manifesting Prostitution Law in Court." ACLUAZ.org. April 10, 2014. www.acluaz.org/en/press-releases/aclu-arizona-challenge-phoenixs-unconstitutional-manifesting-prostitution-law-court.

Adams, Susan B. "Helen Jacobs, Tennis Champion in the 1930's, Dies at 88." NYTimes.com. June 04, 1997. www.nytimes.com/1997/06/04/sports/helen-jacobs-tennis-champion-in-the-1930-s-dies-at-88.html?mtrref=en.wikipedia.org.

Advocate.com Editors. "Jake Shears Reveals Teenage Harassment." Advocate.com. October 08, 2010. www.advocate.com/news/daily-news/2010/10/08/jake-shears-reveals-teenage-harassment.

Airbus. "Airbus Americas Appoints Amanda Simpson Vice President, Research and Technology." AviationPros.com. June 25, 2018. www.aviationpros.com/tools-equipment/insurance-finance/aircraft/press-release/12418193/airbus-airbus-americas-appoints-amanda-simpson-vice-president-research-and-technology.

Alchetron. "Ken Cheuvront." Alchetron.com. February 06, 2018. alchetron.com/Ken-Cheuvront.

Amazon. "Ben Patrick Johnson." Amazon.com. www.amazon.com/Ben-Patrick-Johnson/e/B001JRZM2O.

AP. "Arizona's Supreme Court Blocks A Special Gubernatorial Election." NYTimes.com. April 13, 1988. www.nytimes.com/1988/04/13/us/arizona-s-supreme-court-blocks-a-special-gubernatorial-election.html.

Arana, Gabriel. "About Me." GabrielArana.com. web.archive.org/web/20130619051120/gabrielarana.com/about-me.

Arana, Gabriel. "My So-Called Ex-Gay Life." Prospect.org. April 11, 2012.

Arizona Archives Online. "BJ Bud Memorial Archives 1966-2015." AZArchivesOnline.org. www.azarchivesonline.org/xtf/view?docId=ead/asu/budd_bj.xml.

Arizona Board of Regents. "Katharine P. 'Kittu' Riddle." Plaza.SBS.Arizona.edu. plaza.sbs.arizona.edu/360.

Arizona PBS. "LGBT Archive." AZPBS.org. April 27, 2017. azpbs.org/horizon/2017/04/lgbt-archive.

Arizona State Legislature. "Member Roster." AZLeg.gov. www.azleg.gov/memberroster/?body=S.

Arizona State University Library. "The Pride of Phoenix." Exhibits.Lib.ASU.edu. exhibits.lib.asu.edu/BjBud/item-set/1364.

Arizona Queer Archives. "Kittu Riddle, Dorothy Riddle, and Lavina Tomer Discussing the Development of Nourishing Space." AZQueerArchives.org. azqueerarchives.org/items/show/359.

Arizona Wildcats. "My-King Johnson." Admin.ArizonaWildcats.com. admin.arizonawildcats.com/roster.aspx?rp_id=9965.

Arnovitz, Kevin. "The Official Coming-Out Party." ESPN.com. October 12, 2016. www.espn.com/espn/feature/story/_/id/17764735/nba-referee-bill-kennedy-long-coming-story.

Austin, Noah. "Arizona women's softball wins big." AZCentral.com. November 12, 2014. www.azcentral.com/story/travel/local/history/2014/11/12/arizona-women-softball-wins-big/18946801.

Bland, Karina and Craig Harris. "Rose Mofford, first woman to serve as Arizona governor, has died." AZCentral.com. September 15, 2016. www.azcentral.com/story/news/politics/arizona/2016/09/15/rose-mofford-arizonas-first-female-governor-has-died/90418304.

Bloomberg. "Pixel Gaiety Costs Job." NYDailyNews.com. December 08, 1996. www.nydailynews.com/pixel-gaiety-costs-job-article-1.749316?barcprox=true.

Brown, Elizabeth Nolan. "Prostitution Precrime? Monica Jones and 'Manifesting an Intent' to Prostitute in America." Reason.com. April 16, 2014. reason.com/2014/04/16/prostitution-thought-crimes-monica-jones.

Buzinski, Jim. "9 inducted into National Gay and Lesbian Sports Hall of Fame." OutSports.com. July 27, 2015. www.outsports.com/2015/7/27/9042113/national-gay-lesbian-sports-hall-fame-megan-rapinoe-robbie-rogers.

Cordova, Randy. "Former Tempe Mayor Neil Giuliano memoir tells trials of being openly gay politician." Archive.AZCentral.com. June 18, 2012. archive.azcentral.com/news/azliving/articles/2012/06/18/20120618neil-giuliano-tempe-mayor-glaad-openly-gay-memoir.html.

Crabapple, Molly. "Project ROSIE Is Arresting Sex Workers in Arizona to Save Their Souls." Vice.com. February 26, 2014. www.vice.com/en_us/article/av4eyb/in-arizona-project-rose-is-arresting-sex-workers-to-save-them.

Crowley, Patrick. "Scissor Sisters' Jake Shears Releases 'Creep City,' Teases Upcoming Solo Record & Cryptic 'Labor Of Love'." Billboard.com. October 31, 2017. www.billboard.com/articles/news/8022037/scissor-sisters-jake-shears-creep-city.

Dorris, Jesse. "Jake Shears." Pitchfork.com. August 10, 2018. pitchfork.com/reviews/albums/jake-shears-jake-shears.

ESPN. "Scott Frantz cherishes acceptance after informing teammates he's gay." ESPN.com. July 13, 2017. www.espn.com/college-football/story/_/id/19983391/scott-frantz-kansas-state-wildcats-details-telling-teammates-gay.

Gay Rodeo History. "The Line of Interesting Facts and Events." GayRodeoHistory.org. 2019. gayrodeohistory.org/timeline.htm.

Graff, E. J. "The Afterlife of Gabriel Arana's Ex-Gay Life." Prospect.org. April 25, 2012. prospect.org/article/afterlife-gabriel-aranas-ex-gay-life.

Greguska, Emma. "ASU Library partners with Phoenix Pride to preserve LGBT history of Arizona." ASUNow.ASU.edu. March 30, 2017. asunow.asu.edu/20170330-arizona-impact-asu-library-partners-phoenix-pride-preserve-lgbt-history-arizona.

Hahnefeld, Laura. "Cheuvront Restaurant in Phoenix to Close at the End of May." PhoenixNewTimes.com. May 02, 2013. www.phoenixnewtimes.com/restaurants/cheuvront-restaurant-in-phoenix-to-close-at-the-end-of-may-6544566.

Hernandez, Daniel Jr. "About." DanielforArizona.org. www.danielforarizona.org/about.

IMDb. "Extra Innings: The Real Story Behind the Bright Lights of Summer." IMDb.com. www.imdb.com/title/tt4145858.

IMDb. "Tony Tripoli—Biography." IMDb.com. www.imdb.com/name/nm2370431/bio?ref_=nm_ov_bio_sm.

Johnson, Ben Patrick. "Ben Patrick Johnson—Biography" IMDb.com. www.imdb.com/name/nm0424570/bio?ref_=nm_ov_bio_sm.

Keen, Lisa. "Obama makes first trans appointments." PrideSource.com. January 07, 2010. web.archive.org/web/20100113010958/www.pridesource.com/article.html?article=39439.

Knipp, Michael A. "Scissor Sister's return." SOVO.com. October 13, 2006. web.archive.org/web/20090111233053/www.sovo.com/2006/10-13/arts/feature/scissor.cfm.

Lebanon Daily News. "Seek to Halt Marriage." Newspapers.com. January 11, 1975. www.newspapers.com/clip/11599022/gay_marriage_sam_burret_tony_secuya.

Martin, Jonathan. "A Senate Candidate's Image Shifted. Did Her Life Story?" NYTimes.com. September 24, 2018. www.nytimes.com/2018/09/24/us/politics/kyrsten-sinema-arizona.html.

Mendelson, Will. "Matt Dallas, Husband Blue Hamilton Adopt Little Boy: Watch the Video!" USMagazine.com. December 22, 2015. www.usmagazine.com/celebrity-news/news/-w160233.

MondoTimes. "Tucson Observer." MontoTimes.com. www.mondotimes.com/1/world/us/3/148/214.

Obert, Richard. "Tempe's My-King Johnson commits to Arizona

Wildcats." AZCentral.com. January 17, 2017. www.azcentral.com/story/sports/high-school/recruiting/2017/01/17/tempe-my-king-johnson-commits-arizona-wildcats-football/96661052.

Oregon Live Comments. "Trail Blazers-Grizzlies: Meet the officials for Game 3, including Scott Foster." OregonLive.com. April 25, 2015. www.oregonlive.com/blazers/2015/04/trail_blazers-grizzlies_meet_the_officials_for_gam_1.html.

Pela, Robrt L. "Under the Sun: Comedian Tony Tripoli Returns Home to Phoenix." PhoenixNewTimes.com. November 19, 2018. www.phoenixnewtimes.com/arts/comedian-tony-tripoli-returns-home-to-phoenix-11040964.

Phoenix Pride. "About Us." PhoenixPride.org. phoenixpride.org/about.

POZ. "San Francisco AIDS Foundation CEO Neil Giuliano to Step Down." POZ.com. August 19, 2015. www.poz.com/article/giuliano-leaves-sfaf-27653-8788.

Riley, John. "Amanda Simpson named Deputy Assistant Secretary of Defense." MetroWeekly.com. September 18, 2015. www.metroweekly.com/2015/09/amanda-simpson-named-deputy-assistant-secretary-of-defense.

Rouse, Wade. "*Kyle XY* Star Matt Dallas Married His Partner over the Fourth of July Holiday." People.com. July 06, 2015. people.com/celebrity/matt-dallas-marries-blue-hamilton-see-the-wedding-photo.

Shao, Chasen. "Mia Yamamoto discusses coming out as a professional lawyer." TheDP.com. April 04, 2016. www.thedp.com/article/2016/04/social-activist-and-transgender-lawyer-mia-yamamoto-at-penn.

Shore, Marshall. "Signs of the Times." EchoMag.com. September 25, 2014. echomag.com/signs-of-the-times-2.

Sieczkowski, Cavan. "Matt Dallas Gay: 'Kyle XY' Actor Comes Out, Announces Engagement." HuffPost.com. January 07, 2013. www.huffpost.com/entry/matt-dallas-gay-kyle-xy-actor-comes-out-engaged_n_2424673.

Smith, Brian. "307 Going Down?" PhoenixNewTimes.com. February 24, 2000. www.phoenixnewtimes.com/music/307-going-down-6417778.

Steinmetz, Katy. "Daniel Hernandez: The Intern Who Helped Rescue Giffords." Content.Time.com. January 13, 2011. content.time.com/time/nation/article/0,8599,2042329,00.html.

Strangio, Chase. "Arrested for Walking While Trans: An Interview with Monica Jones." ACLU.org. April 02, 2014. www.aclu.org/blog/criminal-law-reform/arrested-walking-while-trans-interview-monica-jones.

The Lavender Effect. "Mia Yamamoto." TheLavenderEffect.org. www.thelavendereffect.org/projects/ohp/mia-yamamoto.

The Pride Publishing Company. "The Pride of Phoenix, Vol. 1, Number 1." Exhibits.Lib.ASU.edu. January 13, 1977. exhibits.lib.asu.edu/BjBud/item/1467#?c=0&m=0&s=0&cv=0.

The Yes Men. "Pfizer Drops Drug Prices." TheYesMen.org. April 01, 2016. www.theyesmen.org/pharmagreed.

Thompson, Mark. "Remembering Harry and John." RadFae.org. www.radfae.org/harry-john.

Thompson, Mark. "Remembering Harry." *The Advocate,* January 2003.

Tucson Gay Museum. "About." Facebook.com. www.facebook.com/pg/Tucson-Gay-Museum-200704063352019/about/?ref=page_internal.

Tucson Gay Museum. "Tucson Gay Lesbian Bisexual Transgender Queer Museum." www.tucsongaymuseum.org.

Tucson Gay Newsletter. "1976-1977 *Tucson Gay Newsletter* Publication Archives Collection." TucsonGayMuseum.org. www.tucsongaymuseum.org/tucsongaynewsletter.htm.

Tucson Gay Newsletter. *Tucson Gay Newsletter,* September 1976.

United States Senate. "Kyrsten Sinema (D-AZ)." Senate.gov. www.senate.gov/artandhistory/history/common/image/SinemaKyrsten.htm.

Weisman, Alan. "Up in Arms in Arizona." NYTimes.com. November 01, 1987. www.nytimes.com/1987/11/01/magazine/up-in-arms-in-arizona.html.

Wilkinson, Dot. "A female Yogi." *Sports Illustrated,* October 1960.

WorldCat. "Helen Hull Jacobs." WorldCat.org. www.worldcat.org/search?q=au%3AJacobs%2C+Helen+Hull&d-blist=638&fq=ap%3A%22jacobs%2C+helen+hull%22&qt=-facet_ap%3A.

Arkansas

Allen, Samantha. "University of Arkansas Drops Trans Health Care." TheDailyBeast.com. January 31, 2017. www.thedailybeast.com/university-of-arkansas-drops-trans-health-care.

Associated Press. "Ex-Titans CB Wade Davis comes out." ESPN.

com. June 07, 2012. www.espn.com/nfl/story/_/id/8022419/former-nfl-cornerback-wade-davis-comes-gay.

Barson, Michael. "James Bridges." Britannica.com. December 05, 2012. www.britannica.com/biography/James-Bridges.

Bledsoe, C. L. "Ed Madden." EncyclopediaofArkansas.net. April 09, 2019. www.encyclopediaofarkansas.net/encyclopedia/entry-detail.aspx?entryID=4592.

Brainard, Joe. "Bio." JoeBrainard.org. www.joebrainard.org/BIO_MAIN.htm.

Brewer, Reed. "Ark. protests highlight anti-LGBT bills limiting bathroom access, birth certificates." THV11.com. March 20, 2017. www.thv11.com/article/news/local/ark-protests-highlight-anti-lgbt-bills-limiting-bathroom-access-birth-certificates/424080325.

Brooks, Sarafina. "Black Lives Matter requesting investigation into fatal officer-involved shooting." KATV.com. October 27, 2016. katv.com/news/local/black-lives-matter-requesting-investigation-into-fatal-shooting.

City of Little Rock. "Kathy Webb." LittleRock.gov. www.littlerock.gov/board-of-directors/meet-your-board-members/kathy-webb.

Davis, Wade. "About—Wade Davis." WadeADavis.com. wadeadavis.com/about.

Empire, Kitty. "Coal to Diamonds: A Memoir by Beth Ditto—review." TheGuardian.com. October 20, 2012. www.theguardian.com/books/2012/oct/21/coal-diamond-beth-ditto-review.

Human Rights Campaign. "Equal Care for Equal Lives: About the Conference." HRC.org. www.hrc.org/resources/equal-care-for-equal-lives-about-the-conference.

Hyden, Dan. "Beth Ditto is the cure for everything." ChicagoTribune.com. March 15, 2018. www.chicagotribune.com/entertainment/music/ct-ott-beth-ditto-0316-story.html.

Koon, David. "A transgender Navy sailor comes out." ArkTimes.com. May 21, 2015. www.arktimes.com/arkansas/a-transgender-navy-sailor-comes-out/Content?oid=3856958.

Murphy, Tim. "Meet the Transgender Activist Who Confronted Her Political Opponent—in the Ladies' Room." Yahoo.com. June 20, 2017. www.yahoo.com/lifestyle/meet-transgender-activist-confronted-political-opponent-ladies-room-165326346.html.

NME. "The Cool List 2006: winners revealed." NME.com. November 26, 2006. www.nme.com/news/music/gossip-57-1342170.

Poetry Foundation. "Joe Brainard." PoetryFoundation.org. www.poetryfoundation.org/poets/joe-brainard.

Poets. "Joe Brainard: 'I Remember'." Poets.org. February 21, 2014. www.poets.org/poetsorg/text/joe-brainard-i-remember.

Pruden, William H. III. "Kathy Lynette Webb." EncyclopediaofArkansas.net. June 06, 2016. www.encyclopediaofarkansas.net/encyclopedia/entry-detail.aspx?entryID=7949.

Smith, Stephen. *First Amendment Studies in Arkansas.* Fayetteville, AR: University of Arkansas Press, 2016.

Thompson, W. Brock. "A Crime Unfit to be Named: Arkansas and Sodomy." *The Arkansas Historical Quarterly,* 61, no. 3 (2002): 255-271.

Thompson, Brock. "A place for women." ArkTimes.com. September 02, 2010. www.arktimes.com/arkansas/a-place-for-women/Content?oid=1283784.

Tierney, Keith B. and Mark Sekela. "2, 4, 5-Trichlorophenoxyacetic Acid." ScienceDirect.com. 2013. www.sciencedirect.com/topics/agricultural-and-biological-sciences/2-4-5-trichlorophenoxyacetic-acid.

United States Court of Appeals, Eighth Circuit. "850 F. 2d 361—Gay and Lesbian Student Association v. Gohn." OpenJurist.org. openjurist.org/850/f2d/361/gay-and-lesbian-students-association-v-gohn.

University of Central Arkansas. "James M. Bridges." UCA.edu. uca.edu/gala/alumni/james-m-bridges.

University of South Carolina. "Ed Madden." SC.edu. www.sc.edu/study/colleges_schools/artsandsciences/our-people/faculty-staff/madden_ed.php.

Vagianos, Alanna. "This Gay Former NFL Player Is Using His Privilege To Fight Homophobia." HuffPost.com. June 06, 2018. www.huffpost.com/entry/gay-former-nfl-player-using-his-privilege-to-fight-homophobia_n_5af08f67e4b041fd2d296048.

Zajicek, Anna and Allyn Lord. "Yellowhammer." EncyclopediaofArkansas.net. November 02, 2017. www.encyclopediaofarkansas.net/encyclopedia/entry-detail.aspx?entryID=5382.

California

Alchetron. "Hank Wilson." Alchetron.com. alchetron.com/Hank-Wilson.

Allday, Erin. "Last Men Standing." Projects.SFChronicle.com. March 2016. projects.sfchronicle.com/2016/living-with-aids/story.

American History USA. "Del Martin and Phyllis Lyon." AmericanHistoryUSA. com. www.americanhistoryusa.com/topic/del-martin-and-phyllis-lyon.

Anderson, Laurel and Marina Hinestrosa. "David Campos Appointed to Serve as a Deputy County Executive for the County of Santa Clara." SCCGov. org. March 08, 2017. www.sccgov.org/sites/opa/nr/Pages/David-Campos-Appointed-to-Serve-as-a-Deputy-County-Executive-for-the-County-of-Santa-Clara.aspx.

Anna @ GLAAD. "UPDATE: Military Board Recommends Dismissal of Lt. Dan Choi." GLAAD.org. July 01, 2009. www.glaad.org/2009/07/01/dadt-update-military-board-recommends-dismissal-of-lt-dan-choi.

AP. "Sylvester, Singer and Entertainer, Dies at 42." NYTimes.com. December 18, 1988. www.nytimes.com/1988/12/18/obituaries/sylvester-singer-and-entertainer-dies-at-42.html.

Ballotpedia. "California Proposition 8, the 'Eliminates Right of Same-Sex Couples to Marry' Initiative (2008)." Ballotpedia.org. ballotpedia.org/California_Proposition_8,_the_%22Eliminates_Right_of_Same-Sex_Couples_to_Marry%22_Initiative_(2008).

Ballotpedia. "California Proposition 22, Limit on Marriages (2000)." Ballotpedia.org. 2010. ballotpedia.org/California_Proposition_22,_Limit_on_Marriages_(2000).

Barmann, Jay. "1970's-Era Star Pharmacy, Landmark In The Early Days Of AIDS, Recreated For One Day For Castro Shoot." SFist.com. May 06, 2016. sfist.com/2016/05/06/1970s-era_star_pharmacy_landmark_in.

Bay Area Bisexual Network. "San Francisco's Bisexual Center and the Emergence of a Bisexual Movement." BayAreaBisexualNetwork.org. www.bayareabisexualnetwork.org/sfbc.html.

Berton, Justin. "A new gathering spot for Castro's black gays." SFGate.com. June 24, 2007. www.sfgate.com/living/article/A-new-gathering-spot-for-Castro-s-black-gays-2584624.php.

Bluestein, Greg. "Peter Thiel: The gay tech titan who endorsed Donald Trump at the RNC." AJC.com. July 21, 2016. www.ajc.com/blog/politics/peter-thiel-the-gay-tech-titan-who-endorsed-donald-trump-the-rnc/SpwKs3XkVDexumsquXHMnM.

BMG. "Frank Ocean." BMG.com. www.bmg.com/de/artist/frank-ocean.

Boitano, Brian. "HGTV." BrianBoitano.com. brianboitano.com/hgtv.

Braatz, Rick. "Gloria Johnson: 2009 Person of the Year." GayLesbianTimes. com. December 17, 2009. web.archive.org/web/20101231175949/www.gaylesbiantimes.com/?id=16017.

Bruck, Connie. "The Inside War." NewYorker.com. June 15, 2015. www.newyorker.com/magazine/2015/06/22/the-inside-war.

Buchanan, Wyatt. "S.F. prepares to unveil bust of Harvey Milk." SFGate.com. May 22, 2008. www.sfgate.com/bayarea/article/S-F-prepares-to-unveil-bust-of-Harvey-Milk-3283379.php.

Business of Fashion. "Alexander Wang." BusinessofFashion.com. www.businessoffashion.com/community/people/alexander-wang.

California Legislative LGBT Caucus. "California Legislative LGBT Caucus." lgbtcaucus.legislature.ca.gov.

California Sports Hall of Fame. "Greg Louganis." CaliforniaSportsHalloFame. org. californiasportshalloffame.org/inductees/greg-louganis.

California State Senate. "About Senator Ricardo Lara." SD33.Senate.CA.gov. sd33.senate.ca.gov/biography.

Carroll, Rory. "In gay-friendly Palm Springs, America's first all-LGBT government is no surprise." TheGuardian.com. January 01, 2018. www.theguardian.com/world/2018/jan/01/palm-springs-first-lgbt-gay-city-council-government-interview.

Castro. "Castro Camera: Harvey Milk's Famous Camera Shop and Campaign Headquarters." MyCastro.com. www.mycastro.com/castro-camera.

Castro Street Fair. "Castro Street Fair." castrostreetfair.org.

Castro Theatre. "About Us." CastroTheatre.com. www.castrotheatre.com/aboutus.html.

Charles, RuPaul Andre. "Bio." RuPaul.com. rupaul.com/bio.

Chiland, Elijah. "50 years ago the first major gay rights demonstration happened in Silver Lake." LA.Curbed.com. February 08, 2017. la.curbed.com/2017/2/8/14544806/black-cat-silver-lake-lgbt-gay-rights-protest.

Chiland, Elijah. "Preserving Tom of Finland." LA.Curbed.com. August 26, 2016. la.curbed.com/2016/8/26/12660404/tom-finland-house-los-angeles.

Child, Ben. "Jodie Foster marries partner." TheGuardian.com. April 24, 2014. www.theguardian.com/film/2014/apr/24/jodie-foster-marries-partner.

Cho, Margaret. "Bio." MargaretCho.com. margaretcho.com/bio.

Cindy. "Harvey Milk." ArtandArchitecture-SF.com. January 30, 2014. www.artandarchitecture-sf.com/harvey-milk.html.

Cipriani, Belo Miguel. "About Belo." BeloCipriani.com. belocipriani.com/about-the-author.

City and County of San Francisco. "David Campos." SFBOS.org. sfbos.org/former-supervisor-campos-district-9.

City of Berkeley. "Domestic Partnership Information." CityofBerkeley.info. www.cityofberkeley.info/Clerk/Home/Domestic_Partnership.aspx.

Coachella Valley. "LGBT Veterans Memorial in Cathedral City Could Soon Become the First State LGBT Veterans Memorial in the U.S." CoachellaValley.com. coachellavalley.com/lgbt-veterans-memorial-cathedral-city-soon-become-first-state-lgbt-veterans-memorial-u-s.

Conklin, Lauren and Brock Keeling. "SF Pride: 21 historic LGBTQ sites to visit." SF.Curbed.com. June 15, 2018. sf.curbed.com/maps/san-francisco-gay-pride-lgbtq-landmarks.

County of Los Angeles. "Will Rogers State Beach." Beaches.LACounty.gov. beaches.lacounty.gov/will-rogers-beach.

Cullors, Patrisse. "Bio." PatrisseCullors.com. patrissecullors.com/about.

Desert Sun. "Stephen Lachs made history as openly gay judge." DesertSun. com. May 09, 2014. www.desertsun.com/story/news/nation/lgbt/2014/05/09/stephen-lachs-lgbt-judge-advocate/8900005.

Dignity and Power Now. "Dignity and Power Now." dignityandpowernow.org.

Dillon, Liam. "Ricardo Lara, California's first statewide officeholder to come out as gay, sworn in as insurance commissioner." LATimes.com. January 07, 2019. www.latimes.com/politics/essential/la-pol-ca-essential-politics-may-2018-ricardo-lara-first-statewide-1546904002-htmlstory.html.

Discover Los Angeles. "Discover LGBTQ History in Los Angeles." DiscoverLosAngeles.com. April 09, 2019. www.discoverlosangeles.com/things-to-do/discover-lgbtq-history-in-los-angeles.

East Bay Stonewall Democratic Club. "East Bay Stonewall Democratic Club." www.eastbaystonewalldemocrats.org.

Elders, M. Joycelyn, David Satcher, and Richard Carmona. "Re-Thinking Genital Surgeries on Intersex Infants." PalmCenter. org. June 27, 2017. www.palmcenter.org/publication/re-thinking-genital-surgeries-intersex-infants.

Elliot, Beth. "Buried Treasure." Store.CDBaby.com. 2005. store.cdbaby.com/cd/bethelliott.

Encore. "Jewel Thais-Williams." Encore.org. encore.org/purpose-prize/jewel-thais-williams.

Equality California. "Our Work." EQCA.org. www.eqca.org/our-work.

Estrada, Amy W. and Mark R. Bresee. "New Transgender Student Rights Law to Take Effect on January 01, 2014." AALRR. com. August 16, 2013. www.aalrr.com/EdLawConnectBlog/new-transgender-student-rights-law-to-take-effect-on-january-1-2014.

Familia Trans Queer Liberation Movement. "Staff." FamiliaTQLM.org. familiatqlm.org/staff.

Federation of Gay Games. "Federation of Gay Games." gaygames.org.

Fitz, C. "One Woman, One City, No Fear, 42 Years." www.jewelscatchonedocumentary.com.

Fitzpatrick, Kyle. "Where Is the Asexual Representation in LGBTQ Pride?" Popsugar.com. September 30, 2017. www.popsugar.com/news/What-Asexuality-43580587.

Food Network. "Brian Boitano." FoodNetwork.com. 2010. www.foodnetwork.com/fn-dish/2010/02/brian-boitano-vlogs-from-vancouver.

Forbes. "#40 Peter Thiel." Forbes.com. April 30, 2019. www.forbes.com/profile/peter-thiel/#19e2a04d533a.

Fraley, Malaika. "Meet Judge Victoria Kolakowski, nation's first transgender judge." MercuryNews.com. March 14, 2017. www.mercurynews.com/2017/03/14/meet-judge-victoria-kolakowski-nations-first-transgender-judge.

Freedom to Marry. "The Freedom to Marry in California." FreedomtoMarry. org. www.freedomtomarry.org/states/california.

Garrahan, Matthew. "Megan Ellison: Hollywood's latest player." FT.com. February 21, 2014. www.ft.com/content/8e4526e0-995b-11e3-b3a2-00144feab7de.

Gaycities. "Bet You Don't Know This About the Castro's Fabulous New Sidewalks." SFTravel.com. July 29, 2016. www.sftravel.com/article/bet-you-don%E2%80%99t-know-about-castro%E2%80%99s-fabulous-new-sidewalks.

Gaycities. "Why San Francisco is the World's Gay Mecca." SFTravel. com. September 12, 2017. www.sftravel.com/article/ why-san-francisco-world%E2%80%99s-gay-mecca.

Gerami, Vic. "10 QUESTIONS with VIC: Featuring GREG LOUGANIS." TheBluntPost.com. thebluntpost. com/10-questions-with-vic-featuring-greg-louganis.

Giardina, Henry. "Getting Down in Griffith Park: A History." ThePrideLA.com. May 01, 2017. thepridela.com/2017/05/getting-griffith-park-history.

GLBT Historical Society. "Visitor Info." GLBTHistory.org. www.glbthistory.org/ visitor-info.

Gloria, Todd. "About." ToddGloria.com. toddgloria.com/about.

Gloria, Todd. "Biography." ASMDC.org. a78.asmdc.org/article/biography.

Goode, Morgan. "San Francisco Human Rights Commission Approves Groundbreaking Report: 'Bisexual Invisibility: Impacts and Recommendations'." GLAAD.org. March 10, 2011. www.glaad. org/2011/03/10/san-francisco-human-rights-commission- approves-groundbreaking-report-bisexual-invisibility-impacts-and- recommendations.

Gordon, Rachel. "Hank Wilson dies—gay liberation activist." SFGate.com. November 13, 2008. www.sfgate.com/bayarea/article/Hank-Wilson-dies- gay-liberation-activist-3185940.php.

Grigoriadis, Vanessa. "Caution: Heiress at Work." VanityFair. com. March 2013. www.vanityfair.com/hollywood/2013/03/ megan-ellison-27-producer-zero-dark-thirty.

Hartford Street Zen Center. "History." HSZC.org. hszc.org/about/ history-of-hszc.

Hattenstone, Simon. "Drew Barrymore: 'My mother locked me up in an institution at 13. Boo hoo! I needed it'." TheGuardian.com. October 25, 2015. www.theguardian.com/culture/2015/oct/25/ drew-barrymore-mother-locked-up-in-institution-interview.

Heidemann, Jason. "10 things you probably didn't know about LGBTQ San Francisco." Orbitz.com. May 11, 2017. www.orbitz.com/ blog/2017/05/10-things-probably-didnt-know-lgbtq-san-francisco.

IMDb. "Chaz Bono—Biography." IMDb.com. www.imdb.com/name/ nm0095106/bio.

IMDb. "Drew Barrymore—Biography." IMDb.com. www.imdb.com/name/ nm0000106/bio.

IMDb. "George Takei." IMDb.com. www.imdb.com/name/nm0001786.

IMDb. "Jodie Foster—Biography." IMDb.com. www.imdb.com/name/ nm0000149/bio.

IMDb. "Megan Ellison." IMDb.com. www.imdb.com/name/nm2691892.

InterACT. "Hans Lindahl." InterACTAdvocates.org. interactadvocates.org/staff/ hans-lindahl.

Intersex Society of North America. "Hermaphrodites Speak!" ISNA.org. www. isna.org/videos/hermaphrodites_speak.

Iovannone, Jeffry J. "Dan Choi: Getting Equal." Medium.com. July 10, 2018. medium.com/queer-history-for-the-people/ dan-choi-getting-equal-4501931ba593.

Kamiya, Gary. "Boisterous dive's saga is the story of S.F.'s seamy side." SFGate. com. October 31, 2014. www.sfgate.com/bayarea/article/Boisterous-dive- s-saga-is-the-story-of-S-F-s-5861766.php.

Kaczorowski, Craig. "Mattachine Society." GLBTQArchive.com. 2004. www. glbtqarchive.com/ssh/mattachine_society_S.pdf.

King, Billie Jean. "Biography." BillieJeanKing.com. www.billiejeanking.com/ biography.

King, Mark S. "Feeling the Love for L.A.'s Dearly Departed Circus Disco." Advocate.com. February 04, 2016. www.advocate.com/ commentary/2016/2/04/feeling-love-las-dearly-departed-circus-disco.

Kosoff, Maya. "Peter Thiel Wants to Inject Himself with Young People's Blood." VanityFair.com. August 01, 2016. www.vanityfair.com/news/2016/08/ peter-thiel-wants-to-inject-himself-with-young-peoples-blood.

Krochmal, Shana Naomi. "Billie Joe Armstrong: Idiot Savant." Out. com. March 14, 2010. www.out.com/entertainment/2010/03/14/ billie-joe-armstrong-idiot-savant.

Langley, Garth. "LGBT Military Mixer Celebrates Fleet Week in San Francisco." MilitaryPartners.org. October 17, 2015. militarypartners.org/ lgbt-military-mixer-celebrates-fleet-week-in-san-francisco.

Learning English. "Isadora Duncan, 1877-1927: The Mother of Modern Dance." LearningEnglish.VOANews.com. August 28, 2010. learningenglish. voanews.com/a/isadora-duncan-1877-1927-the-mother-of-modern- dance-101714348/114147.html.

Lindahl, Hans. "About." HansLindahl.com. hanslindahl.com/about.

Litoff, Alyssa and Lauren Effron. "Chaz Bono's 'Transition': Bono Talks About Gender Reassignment Surgery and What It's Done for His Sex Life." ABCNews.Go.com. May 09, 2011. abcnews.go.com/Entertainment/ chaz-bonos-transition-sonny-chers-child-man-sex/story?id=13561466.

Log Cabin Republicans. "Our History." LogCabin.org. www.logcabin.org/ about-us/our-history.

Lori Belilove and the Isadora Duncan Dance Company. "Isadora Duncan." IsadoraDuncan.org. isadoraduncan.org/foundation/isadora-duncan.

Los Angeles Conservancy. "Circus Disco." LAConservancy.org. April 06, 2017. www.laconservancy.org/issues/circus-disco.

Los Angeles Conservancy. "Tom of Finland House." LAConservancy.org. www. laconservancy.org/locations/tom-finland-house.

Los Angeles LGBT Center. "About the Center." LALGBTCenter.org. lalgbtcenter. org/about-the-center/anita-may-rosenstein-campus.

Los Angeles LGBT Center. "At-A-Glance 2019." LALGBTCenter.org. lalgbtcenter. org/images/Downloads/LALGBTC19_AtAGlance_Q1r_v5.pdf.

Los Angeles LGBT Center. "Contact Us." LALGBTCenter.org. lalgbtcenter.org/ about-the-center/facilities.

Louise Lawrence Transgender Archive. "Louise Lawrence Transgender Archive." lltransarchive.org.

Love, Barbara J. Feminists Who Changed America, 1963-1975. Champaign, IL: University of Illinois Press, 2006.

Lovelady, Coty. "Storytelling to End Racial Profiling." Glide.org. www.glide. org/storytelling-to-end-racial-profiling.

Luerssen, John D. "Green Day's Billie Joe Armstrong Says Bisexuality Shouldn't Be an Issue." Spinner.com. March 25, 2010. web.archive. org/web/20120806155541/www.spinner.com/2010/03/25/ green-day-billie-joe-armstrong-bisexual.

Mannen, Amanda. "5 Dark Realities Of Living Through The 1980s AIDS Crisis." Cracked.com. September 07, 2016. www.cracked.com/personal- experiences-2146-living-through-1980s-aids-epidemic-survivors-story. html.

Matzner, Andrew. "Prince, Virginia charles (1913-2009)." GLBTQ.com. web. archive.org/web/20150211063223/www.glbtq.com/social-sciences/ prince_vc,2.html.

Meyerowitz, Joanne J. How Sex Changed. Cambridge, MA: Harvard University Press, 2009.

Michelson, Noah. "28 Stars You Might Not Know Are Bisexual." HuffPost.com. May 30, 2016. www.huffpost.com/entry/bisexual-stars_n_574725bae4b0 3ede44141573.

Michaelson, Noah. "Margaret Cho: 'Nobody Has Ever Really Accepted That I'm Truly Bisexual.'" HuffPost.com. June 19, 2018. www.huffpost.com/entry/ margaret-cho-bisexuality-pride_n_5b27b980e4b0783ae12b754e.

Miles, Milo. "Sylvester: 'Mighty Real' Disco Star Deserves A Modern Spotlight." NPR.org. July 16, 2013. www.npr.org/2013/07/16/202658178/ sylvester-mighty-real-disco-star-deserves-a-modern-spotlight.

National Center for Lesbian Rights. "Remembering Del Martin." Lyon- Martin.org. lyon-martin.org/about-us/the-lyon-martin-story/ remembering-del-martin.

National Park Service. "Rosie the Riveter WWII Home Front." NPS.gov. www. nps.gov/rori/index.htm.

National Park Service. "Great Wall of Los Angeles (Mural)." NPS.gov. www.nps. gov/places/great-wall-of-los-angeles.htm.

O'Hara, Mary Emily. "Californian Becomes Second US Citizen Granted 'Non-Binary' Gender Status." NBCNews.com. September 26, 2016. www. nbcnews.com/feature/nbc-out/californian-becomes-second-us-citizen- granted-non-binary-gender-status-n654611.

O'Hara, Mary Emily. "Nation's First Known Intersex Birth Certificate Issued in NYC." NBCNews.com. December 29, 2016. www.nbcnews.com/feature/nbc-out/ nation-s-first-known-intersex-birth-certificate-issued-nyc-n701186.

Olympic. "Gregory Louganis." Olympic.org. www.olympic.org/ gregory-louganis.

ONE Archives at the USC Libraries. "Lisa Ben Papers Now Available to Researchers." One.USC.edu. April 11, 2016. one.usc.edu/news/ lisa-ben-papers-now-available-researchers.

ONE Archives Foundation. "History." ONEArchives.org. www.onearchives.org/ about/history.

Painter, George. "The Sensibilities of Our Forefathers." GLAPN.org. 1991.

www.glapn.org/sodomylaws/sensibilities/california.htm.

Palacios, Monica. "Bio." MonicaPalacios.com. www.monicapalacios.com/bio.

Parman, Chris. "LGBT Veterans Memorial in Cathedral City Could Soon Become the First State LGBT Veterans Memorial in the U.S." DiscoverCathedralCity.com. May 24, 2018. www.discovercathedralcity.com/lgbt-veterans-memorial-in-cathedral-city-could-soon-become-the-first-state-memorial-in-the-u-s.

Pasulka, Nicole. "Ladies In The Streets: Before Stonewall, Transgender Uprising Changed Lives." NPR.org. May 05, 2015. www.npr.org/sections/codeswitch/2015/05/05/404459634/ladies-in-the-streets-before-stonewall-transgender-uprising-changed-lives.

Peters, Scott H. "Honoring the Life of Gloria Johnson: Congressional Record Vol. 159, No. 153." Congress.gov. October 30, 2013. www.congress.gov/congressional-record/2013/10/30/extensions-of-remarks-section/article/e1618-3?r=104.

Petro, Anthony M. "Ray Navarro's Jesus Camp, AIDS Activist Video, and the 'New Anti-Catholicism'." Academic.OUP.com. May 14, 2017. academic.oup.com/jaar/article-abstract/85/4/920/3797267?redirectedFrom=fulltext.

Ponsonby Productions Limited. "Intersexion." www.intersexionfilm.com.

Purkiss, Nathan. "History of Alice." AliceBToklas.org. www.alicebtoklas.org/history-of-alice.

Rapp, Linda. "Achtenberg, Roberta (b. 1950)." GLBTQArchive.com. 2004. www.glbtqarchive.com/ssh/achtenberg_r_S.pdf.

Ravarour, Adrian and Christopher A. Flores. "Rev. Adrian Ravarour, Ph.D." LGBTQReligiousArchives.org. January, 2008. lgbtqreligiousarchives.org/profiles/adrian-ravarour-ph-d.

Reed, Alex. "This HIV-Positive Olympian Will Finally Be Featured on a Wheaties Box." TakePart.com. April 07, 2016. www.takepart.com/article/2016/04/07/hiv-positive-olympian-wheaties-box.

Revolvy. "Chaya Gusfield." Revolvy.com. www.revolvy.com/page/Chaya-Gusfield.

Rivas, Jorge. "Meet Jennicet, one month after she interrupted President Obama." SplinterNews.com. August 03, 2015. splinternews.com/meet-jennicet-one-month-after-she-interrupted-presiden-1793849645.

Rocha, Michael James. "History Center exhibit explores evolution of San Diego's LGBTQ+ community." SanDiegoUnionTribune.com. July 05, 2018. www.sandiegouniontribune.com/entertainment/visual-arts/sd-et-lgbt-exhibit-20180705-story.html.

Rohrbach, Ben. "5 years later, Jason Collins says NBA is ready for another openly gay player." Sports.Yahoo.com. April 05, 2018. sports.yahoo.com/5-years-later-jason-collins-believes-nba-ready-another-openly-gay-player-172655482.html.

Roscoe, Will. "Mattachine: Radical Roots of the Gay Movement." FoundSF.org. www.foundsf.org/index.php?title=Mattachine:_Radical_Roots_of_the_Gay_Movement.

Ryder, Caroline. "Living With Liberace." PalmSpringsLife.com. November 01, 2012. www.palmspringslife.com/living-with-liberace.

Sabogal, Jessica. "About." JessicaSabogal.com. www.jessicasabogal.com/about-1.

Sabogal, Jessica. "Raza Day." TayoLiteraryMag.com. www.tayoliterarymag.com/jessica-sabogal.

Salcedo, Bamby. "Biography." BambySalcedo.com. bambysalcedo.com/bio.php.

San Diego LGBT Community Center. "Home." www.thecentersd.org.

San Francisco County Planning Commission. "San Francisco Landmark #241 Jose Theater/NAMES Project." NoeHill.com. January 15, 2004. noehill.com/sf/landmarks/sf241.asp.

San Francisco Fleet Week. "San Francisco Fleet Week." fleetweeksf.org.

San Francisco Gay Men's Chorus. "Our Story." SFGMC.org. www.sfgmc.org/about-sfgmc.

San Francisco Travel. "10 Wild Milestones in the Twisted History of San Francisco's Sisters of Perpetual Indulgence." SFTravel.com. November 17, 2016. www.sftravel.com/article/10-wild-milestones-twisted-history-san-francisco%E2%80%99s-sisters-perpetual-indulgence.

San Francisco Travel. "A Brief History of the Rainbow Flag." SFTravel.com. 2018. www.sftravel.com/article/brief-history-rainbow-flag.

San Francisco Travel. "Always Proud, San Francisco: A Brief Gay History." SFTravel.com. April 05, 2019. www.sftravel.com/article/always-proud-san-francisco-brief-gay-history.

Savage, Jon. "Why Frank Ocean is a musical icon." GQ-Magazine.co.uk. April 24, 2017. www.gq-magazine.co.uk/article/frank-ocean-albums.

Schaub, Michael. "California will be the first state to use LGBT-inclusive history textbooks in schools." LATimes.com. November 13, 2017. www.latimes.com/books/jacketcopy/la-et-jc-lgbt-textbooks-20171113-story.html.

Schulman, Michael. "In Drag, It Turns Out, There Are Second Acts." NYTimes.com. February 21, 2014. www.nytimes.com/2014/02/23/fashion/RuPaul-Drag-Race-television.html.

SF Gay History. "South of Market." SFGayHistory.com. www.sfgayhistory.com/neighborhoods/south-of-market.

Smith, Michael J. "The Double Life Of A Gay Dodger." TheStacks. Deadspin.com. May 08, 2013. thestacks.deadspin.com/the-double-life-of-a-gay-dodger-493697377.

Smith, Tiana. "Alicia Garza (1981-)." BlackPast.org. February 04, 2018. www.blackpast.org/african-american-history/garza-alicia-1981.

Soulforce. "Meet Us." Soulforce.org. www.soulforce.org/founders.

Stack, Liam. "Activist Removed After Heckling Obama at L.G.B.T. Event at White House." NYTimes.com. June 24, 2015. www.nytimes.com/2015/06/25/us/politics/activist-removed-after-heckling-obama-at-lgbt-event.html.

Stezano, Martin. "What were the White Night Riots?" History.com. September 01, 2018. www.history.com/news/what-were-the-white-night-riots.

Stud. "About." StudSF.com. www.studsf.com/about.

Sullivan, Elizabeth. "Godmother of SexEd: Maggi Rubenstein." FoundSF.org. www.foundsf.org/index.php?title=Godmother_of_SexEd%3A_Maggi_Rubenstein.

Takei, George. "George H. Takei." GeorgeTakei.com. July 31, 2018. www.georgetakei.com/george-h-takei-2591309480.html.

Talusan, Meredith. "How a Woman-Only Bathhouse Helped Me Find My Female Self." BonAppetit.com. March 13, 2018. www.bonappetit.com/story/osento-bathhouse.

Tamar-Mattis, Anne, Arlene Baratz, Katharine Baratz Dalke, and Katrina Karkazis. "Emotionally and cognitively informed consent for clinical care for differences of sex development." TandFOnline.com. September 17, 2013. www.tandfonline.com/doi/abs/10.1080/19419899.2013.831215.

Tenderloin Museum. "Mission and History." TenderloinMuseum.org. www.tenderloinmuseum.org/board.

Tenderloin Neighborhood Development. "Ambassador Hotel." TNDC.org. February 03, 2012. www.tndc.org/property/ambassador-hotel-55-mason-street.

The Association of LGBTQ Journalists. "Lisa Ben." NLGJA.org. May 2010. www.nlgja.org/blog/2010/05/lisa-ben.

The Bay Area Reporter. "About the BAR." eBar.com. www.ebar.com/about_the_bar.

The City Project. "Robert Garcia." CityProjectCA.org. www.cityprojectca.org/bio-rgarcia.

The NAMES Project Foundation. "The AIDS Memorial Quilt." AIDSQuilt.org. www.aidsquilt.org/about/the-aids-memorial-quilt.

The New York Times. "Glenn Burke, 42, A Major League Baseball Player." NYTimes.com. June 01, 1995. www.nytimes.com/1995/06/01/nyregion/glenn-burke-42-a-major-league-baseball-player.html.

The Wall Las Memorias. "Las Memorias AIDS Monument." TheWallLasMemorias.org. www.thewalllasmemorias.org/las_memorias_aids_monument.

The Woman's Building. "The Woman's Building." thewomansbuilding.org.

Townsend, Jerrald L. "Harry Hay." LGBTQReligiousArchives.org. March 2007. lgbtqreligiousarchives.org/profiles/harry-hay.

Transgender Clinic. "Transgender Clinic." SRFMR.org. www.srfmr.org/project-detail/573534-transgender-clinic.

Trans March. "About." TransMarch.org. www.transmarch.org/about.

Tyson, Chanelle. "Jewel Thais-Williams Changed Nightlife for Black Gays in 1973. She Hasn't Slowed Down Since." Advocate.com. March 22, 2018. www.advocate.com/people/2018/3/22/jewel-thais-williams-changed-nightlife-black-gays-1973-she-hasnt-slowed-down.

University of Victoria. "Virginia Prince." UVIC.ca. www.uvic.ca/transgenderarchives/collections/virgina-prince/index.php.

US News. "Dr. Suegee Tamar-Mattis." Health.USNews.com. health.usnews.com/doctors/suegee-tamar-mattis-641818.

van Gorder, Bryan. "Queer Stars Shine Bright On Hollywood Walk Of Fame." NewNowNext.com. March 16, 2018. www.newnownext.com/celebrities-lgbt-walk-of-fame/03/2018.

VANGUARD. "About." VANGUARD1965.com. www.vanguard1965.com/about.

html.

Visual AIDS. "Ray Navarro." VisualAIDS.org. visualaids.org/artists/ray-navarro.

Vogue. "Alexander Wang." Vogue.com.au. www.vogue.com. au/celebrity/designers/alexander-wang/news-story/ dfb33e7d78f817049d75357977e0ef47.

Wagner, David. "Belo Cipriani, author of 'Blind: A Memoir'." SFGate.com. June 10, 2011. www.sfgate.com/entertainment/article/Belo-Cipriani-author-of-Blind-A-Memoir-2368885.php.

WEHO Ville Staff. "L.A.'s Black Cat, Where the Fight for Gay Rights Got Its Start." WEHOVille.com. June 05, 2014. www.wehoville. com/2014/06/05/l-s-black-cat-fight-gay-rights-got-start.

West Hollywood Marketing Corp. "LGBTQ." VisitWestHollywood.com. www. visitwesthollywood.com/lgbtq.

Wetzstein, Cheryl. "California enacts nation's first law protecting transgender students." WashingtonTimes.com. August 12, 2013. www.washingtontimes.com/news/2013/aug/12/ california-enact-nations-first-law-protecting-tran.

Willis, Raquel. "Alicia Garza Coined 'Black Lives Matter'— And She's Just Getting Started." Out.com. February 12, 2019. www.out.com/out-exclusives/2019/2/12/ alicia-garza-coined-black-lives-matter-and-shes-just-getting-start.

Winder, Andy. "6 Transgender Pioneers Who Helped Change History." StudyBreaks.com. October 01, 2016. studybreaks.com/ culture/6-transgender-pioneers-who-helped-change-history.

Youngmisuk, Ohm. "Jason Collins looks to future as Lakers celebrate their first Pride Night." ESPN.com. October 05, 2018. www.espn.com/nba/story/_/id/24897819/ jason-collins-celebrates-los-angeles-lakers-first-ever-pride-night.

Zach, Elizabeth. "Uncovering Gay History in San Francisco." NYTimes.com. August 16, 2016. www.nytimes.com/2016/08/21/travel/san-francisco-gay-history.html.

Colorado

Asmar, Melanie. "Who was Angie Zapata? Her murderer's trial didn't tell the whole story." WestWord.com. May 28, 2009. www.westword.com/ news/who-was-angie-zapata-her-murderers-trial-didnt-tell-the-whole-story-5103955.

Associated Press. "In a Denver Park, the Past Resurfaces." NYTimes.com. November 15, 2008. www.nytimes.com/2008/11/16/us/16denver.html.

Bartels, Lynn. "Pat Steadman, champion for the underdog." Bartels-On. SOS.State.CO.us. July 09, 2017. bartels-on.sos.state.co.us/index. php/2017/07/09/pat-steadman-champion-for-the-underdog.

Big Mama Rag. "About Big mama rag. (Denver, Colo.) 1972-1984." ChroniclingAmerica.loc.gov. chroniclingamerica.loc.gov/lccn/sn91052503.

Bindel, Paul. "In the Beginning…" OutFrontMagazine.com. December 16, 2015. www.outfrontmagazine.com/trending/in-the-beginning.

Carmichael, James Vinson Jr. *Daring to Find Our Names: The Search for Lebigay Library History.* Westport, CT: Greenwood Publishing Group, 1998.

Colorado Public Radio Staff. "Timeline: Denver's 'Curious And Fascinating' LGBT History." CPR.org. June 29, 2015. www.cpr.org/news/story/ timeline-denvers-curious-and-fascinating-lgbt-history.

Dahir, Mubarak. "The dangerous lives of gay priests: fearing a witch-hunt in the wake of the sex abuse scandal, gay Roman Catholic priests talk of their dedication to their work and their God—and of the secret loves that put their careers at risk." *The Advocate,* July 23, 2002.

Division of Rare and Manuscript Collections at Cornell University Library. "David Goodstein Papers, (ca. 1954-1985)." RMC.Library.Cornell.edu. rmc. library.cornell.edu/EAD/htmldocs/RMM07311.html.

Garcia, Nic and Todd Engdahl. "Colorado speaker Mark Ferrandino to join Denver Public Schools." ChalkBeat.org. June 18, 2014. www.chalkbeat.org/posts/co/2014/06/18/ colorado-speaker-mark-ferrandino-to-join-denver-public-schools.

Gill Foundation. "Priorities." GillFoundation.org. gillfoundation.org/priorities.

Imperial Court of the Rocky Mountain Empire. "About the Imperial Court of the Rocky Mountain Empire." ICRMEDenver.org. www.icrmedenver.org/ about-us.

King, John. "Beginnings of the Gay Rodeo in Colorado." OutFrontMagazine. com. June 21, 2017. www.outfrontmagazine.com/trending/culture/ beginnings-gay-rodeo-colorado.

Liptak, Adam. "In Narrow Decision, Supreme Court Sides With Baker Who Turned Away Gay Couple." NYTimes.com. June 04, 2018. www.nytimes. com/2018/06/04/us/politics/supreme-court-sides-with-baker-who-turned-away-gay-couple.html.

Lomax, John Nova. "This President's Grandson Was More Interesting Than You'll Ever Be." Vice.com. January 13, 2017. www.vice.com/en_us/article/pgp7mv/ this-presidents-grandson-was-more-interesting-than-youll-ever-be.

London, Nell. "As Colorado Swears In An Openly Gay Governor, How One Couple Quietly Changed Minds On LGBT Issues." CPR.org. December 13, 2018. www.cpr.org/news/story/as-colorado-marched-toward-lgbt-rights-the-gill-foundation-quietly-changed-minds.

Luning, Ernest. "BREAKING: Andrade sentenced to life without parole in Zapata killing." ColoradoIndependent.com. April 22, 2009. www.coloradoindependent.com/2009/04/22/ breaking-andrade-sentenced-to-life-without-parole-in-zapata-killing.

Marcus, Aaron. "PrideFest: A History of Denver's Gay Pride Celebration." HistoryColorado.org. June 15, 2017. www.historycolorado.org/story/ hc/2017/06/15/pridefest-a-history-of-denvers-gay-pride-celebration.

MMA Fighting Newswire. "UFC fighters Tecia Torres, Raquel Pennington get engaged." MMAFighting.com. May 14, 2017. www.mmafighting.com/2017/5/14/15637310/ ufc-fighters-tecia-torres-raquel-pennington-get-engaged.

Moore, Keith L. "Queen City of the Plains? Denver's Gay History 1940-1975." Digital.Auraria.edu. 2010. digital.auraria.edu/content/ AA/00/00/15/27/00001/AA00001527_00001.pdf.

Roberts, Michael. "Hate State Amendment 2 After 25 Years—and Why We're Reliving It in 2017." WestWord. com. November 03, 2017. www.westword.com/news/ colorados-hate-state-amendment-2-twenty-five-years-later-9606594.

Sayler, Zoe. "A Brief History of Openly Gay Olympians." Smithsonian. com. February 09, 2018. www.smithsonianmag.com/history/ brief-history-openly-gay-olympians-180968125.

State of Colorado. "Governor Jared Polis." Colorado.gov. www.colorado.gov/ governor/gov-polis.

Steffen, Jordan. "Same-sex marriage in Colorado: 11 answers to commonly asked questions." DenverPost.com. October 18, 2014. www.denverpost. com/2014/10/18/same-sex-marriage-in-colorado-11-answers-to-commonly-asked-questions.

Stokols, Eli. "Sen. Pat Steadman to get Harvey Milk award at White House Wednesday." KDVR.com. May 20, 2013. kdvr.com/2013/05/20/ sen-pat-steadman-to-get-harvey-milk-award-at-white-house-wednesday.

Sylvestre, Berlin. "Scandal and Grief in the Imperial Court." OutFrontMagazine.com. September 17, 2015. www.outfrontmagazine. com/trending/scandal-and-grief-in-the-imperial-court-2.

The Center on Colfax. "Home." lgbtqcolorado.org.

The New York Times. "David Goodstein Dies at 53; Advocate for Homosexuals." NYTimes.com. June 26, 1985. www.nytimes. com/1985/06/26/us/david-goodstein-dies-at-53-advocate-for-homosexuals.html.

Ultimate Fighting Championship. "Raquel Pennington." UFC.com. www.ufc. com/athlete/raquel-pennington.

United States Olympic Committee. "Gus Kenworthy." TeamUSA.org. www. teamusa.org/us-ski-and-snowboard/athletes/gus-kenworthy.

US Court of Appeals for the District of Columbia Circuit. "Big Mama Rag, Inc., a Colorado Nonprofit Corporation, Appellant, v. United States of America et al, 631 F.2d 1030 (D.C. Cir. 1980)." Law.Justia.com. 1980. law.justia.com/ cases/federal/appellate-courts/F2/631/1030/86772.

Watkins, Eli. "Colorado elects nation's first openly gay governor, CNN projects." CNN.com. November 06, 2018. www.cnn.com/2018/11/06/ politics/jared-polis-colorado-gay-governor/index.html.

Connecticut

ACLU. "History of Sodomy Laws and the Strategy That Led up to Today's Decision." ACLU.org. www.aclu.org/other/ history-sodomy-laws-and-strategy-led-todays-decision.

Burtis, Randy. "An Interview with Devin Grayson." ComicBoard.com. August 9, 2004. www.comicboards.com/devin.php.

Connecticut Gay Men's Chorus. "The Connecticut Gay Men's Chorus." CTGMC. org. www.ctgmc.org.

Doris. "She's a Rabbi, She's a Lesbian & She's Ready to Reconstruct

Judaism." TheBlot.com. October 24, 2014. www.theblot.com/
shes-a-rabbi-shes-a-lesbian-shes-ready-to-reconstruct-judaism-7727648.

Furay, Emmett. "Homosexuality in Comics - Part I." CBR.com. July 16, 2007.
www.cbr.com/homosexuality-in-comics-part-i.

Gay History. "Connecticut." GayHistory.Wikidot.com. December 31, 2009.
gayhistory.wikidot.com/connecticut.

Gilbert, Elizabeth. "Bio." ElizabethGilbert.com. www.elizabethgilbert.com/
bio.

Grayson, Devin. "Published Work." DevinGrayson.net. www.devingrayson.
net/published-work.html.

Iqbal, Nosheen. "Photographer David LaChapelle: 'I never wanted to
shoot another pop star—I was tortured by them'." TheGuardian.com.
November 21, 2017. www.theguardian.com/artanddesign/2017/nov/21/
david-lachapelle-photographer-hawaii-warhol.

Jones, Chris. "Joe Alsop's Cold War secrets carry new weight in 'The
Columnist'." ChicagoTribune.com. February 24, 2017. www.chicagotribune.
com/entertainment/theater/reviews/ct-the-columnist-review-ent-0225-
20170224-column.html.

Katz, Jonathan Ned. "Earl Lind: The Cercle Hermaphroditos, c. 1895."
OutHistory.org. outhistory.org/exhibits/show/earl-lind/related/
cercle-hermaphroditos.

Kellaway, Mitch. "Connecticut Makes Changing Birth Certificates
Easier for Trans Folks." Advocate.com. June 30, 2015.
www.advocate.com/politics/transgender/2015/06/30/
connecticut-makes-changing-birth-certificates-easier-trans-folks.

Key Data. "Date Same Sex Marriage Legalized By State." State.1KeyData.com.
state.1keydata.com/date-same-sex-marriage-legalized-by-state.php.

LaChapelle, David. "About." DavidLaChapelle.com. davidlachapelle.com/
about.

LGBT History Month. "Faisal Alam." LGBTHistoryMonth.com.
lgbthistorymonth.com/sites/default/files/wysiwyg_imageupload/2014_
LGBTHM-Bios.pdf.

LGBTQ Religious Archives Network. "Faisal Alam." LGBTQReligiousArchives.
org.
lgbtqreligiousarchives.org/profiles/faisal-alam.

Lawler, Keegan. "Jennie June." AmericanQueer.org. americanqueer.org/
jennie-june-1874-1921.

L'Heureux, Catie. "Eat Pray Love Author Elizabeth Gilbert's Partner Rayya Elias
Has Died." TheCut.com. January 5, 2018. www.thecut.com/2018/01/eat-
pray-love-author-elizabeth-gilbert-mourns-rayya-elias-death.html.

Love, Barbara J. Feminists Who Changed America, 1963-1975. Illinois:
University of Illinois Press, 2006.

Moser, Stephen Macmillan. "Review: Gowns by Adrian." AustinChronicle.
com. June 29, 2001. www.austinchronicle.com/screens/2001-06-29/
gowns-by-adrian.

New England Historical Society. "Adrian, The Hatmaker's Son
Who Dressed America." NewEnglandHistoricalSociety.
com. www.newenglandhistoricalsociety.com/
adrian-hatmakers-son-dressed-america.

Out History. "Michael Wigglesworth: February, 1653." OutHistory.org.
outhistory.org/exhibits/show/the-age-of-sodomitical-sin/1650s/
michael-wigglesworth-februaru-.

PBS News Hour. "Obama selects gay athletes for Sochi Olympics
delegation." PBS.org. December 17, 2013. www.pbs.org/newshour/arts/
obama-selects-gay-athletes-for-sochi-olympic-delegation.

Reconstructionist Rabbinical College. "Meet Our President." RRC.edu. www.
rrc.edu/about/meet-our-president.

The Editors of Encyclopedia Britannica. "Joseph Alsop." Britannica.com.
October 07, 2018. www.britannica.com/biography/Joseph-Alsop.

The Shoeleather History Project. "Kalos Society: Early Gay Liberation."
ShoeleatherHistoryProject.com. shoeleatherhistoryproject.
com/2015/09/16/kalos-society-early-gay-liberation.

Tighe, Mike. "Transgendered folk artist focuses on music to define herself."
LacrosseTribune.com. March 11, 2015. lacrossetribune.com/news/
local/transgendered-folk-artist-focuses-on-music-to-define-herself/
article_86888f2d-724a-59ec-b369-fd50ffd30e72.html.

Toscano, Peterson. "A Reluctant Minister." FriendsJournal.org. June 1, 2018.
www.friendsjournal.org/reluctant-minister.

Toscano, Peterson. "Background." PetersonToscano.com. petersontoscano.
com/background.

Ubuntu Biography Project. "Addie Brown and Rebecca
Primus." UbuntuBiographyProject.com. December
21, 2017. ubuntubiographyproject.com/2017/12/21/
addie-brown-and-rebecca-primus.

United States Olympic Committee. "Caitlin Cahow." TeamUSA.org. www.
teamusa.org/usa-hockey/athletes/caitlin-cahow.

Whiteside, Kelly. "One year later, Caitlin Cahow's life back to
normal following concussion scare." USAToday.com. August 26,
2013. www.usatoday.com/story/sports/olympics/2013/08/26/
concussion-hockey-player-caitlin-cahow/2704169.

Wilkins, Kevin. "A. Hero's Welcome: Brian Anderson Interview."
TheGoodProblem.com. October 19, 2016. thegoodproblem.
com/2016/10/19/a-heros-welcome-brian-anderson-interview.

Wong, Curtis M. "Professional Skateboarding Icon Brian Anderson Comes Out
As Gay." Huffpost.com. September 28, 2016. www.huffpost.com/entry/
skateboarder-brian-anderson-gay_n_57eae21ae4b0c2407cda49ff.

Yardley, William. "Connecticut Approves Civil Unions for Gays." NYTimes.
com. April 21, 2005. www.nytimes.com/2005/04/21/nyregion/connecticut-
approves-civil-unions-for-gays.html.

Delaware

ACLU Delaware. "What We Do and Why We Do It." ACLU-DE.org. www.aclu-de.
org/en/about/history.

Advocate.com Editors. "Delaware City Elects Gay Mayor. Advocate.com.
April 07, 2011. www.advocate.com/news/daily-news/2011/04/07/
delaware-city-elects-gay-mayor.

AIDS Delaware. "Overview." AIDSDelaware.org. aidsdelaware.org/about/
overview.

CAMP Rehoboth Community Center. "CAMP Rehoboth History."
CAMPRehoboth.com. www.camprehoboth.com/camp-rehoboth-history.

Division of Human Relations. "About the Division of Human Relations."
StateHumanRelations.Delaware.gov. statehumanrelations.delaware.gov/
about.

Ehrenfeld, Jesse. "Bio." DrJesse.com. drjesse.com/index.php/bio.

Friess, Steve. "What a connection." The Advocate, March 3, 1998.

Hine, Chris and Phil Thompson. "Elena Delle Donne engaged, comes out:
'I'm not at all going to hide anything'." ChicagoTribune.com. August 3,
2016. www.chicagotribune.com/sports/chicagoinc/ct-elena-delle-donne-
engagement-vogue-20160803-story.html.

Human Rights Campaign. "Sarah McBride." HRC.org. www.hrc.org/hrc-story/
staff/sarah-mcbride.

Karlan, Sarah. "Delaware Passes Trans Protections, With Help From A Young
Advocate." Buzzfeed.com. June 20, 2013. www.buzzfeed.com/skarlan/
delaware-passes-trans-protections-with-help-from-a-young-adv.

Marshall-Steele, Douglas. "Timeline of Delaware's LGBT History."
TowardEquality.org. www.towardequality.org/timeline.html.

McGraw, Patricia Babcock. "Delle Donne opens up about battling Lyme
disease." DailyHerald.com. June 20, 2014. www.dailyherald.com/
article/20140620/sports/140629800.

McKusick, Kirk. "Kirk McKusick's Family and Friends." McKusick.com. www.
mckusick.com/~mckusick/index.html.

Micklos, John. "Aubrey Plaza of NBC's Parks and Recreation: Wilmington
Native Is Building a Buzz in Hollywood." DelawareToday.com. February
16, 2012. www.delawaretoday.com/Delaware-Today/March-2012/Aubrey-
Plaza-of-NBCs-Parks-and-Recreation-Wilmington-Native-Is-Building-a-
Buzz-in-Hollywood/index.php?cparticle=4&amp%3Bsiarticle=3.

Painter, George. "Delaware." GLAPN.org. August 11, 2004. www.glapn.org/
sodomylaws/sensibilities/delaware.htm.

Pesce, Nicole Lyn. "Raul Esparza talks Shakespeare in the Park's
'Cymbeline' and hopes for 'Hannibal' return." NYDailyNews.
com. August 4, 2015. www.nydailynews.com/entertainment/
raul-esparza-talks-shakespeare-park-cymbeline-article-1.2314577.

Special Olympics. "Elena Delle Donne." SpecialOlympics.org. www.
specialolympics.org/about/ambassadors/elena-delle-donne.

Vitali, Ali. "Delaware becomes 11th state to legalize gay marriage."
MSNBC.com. May 07, 2013. www.msnbc.com/the-cycle/
delaware-becomes-11th-state-legalize-gay-m.

Voss, Brandon. "The A-List Interview: Aubrey Plaza." Advocate.com.
July 07, 2016. www.advocate.com/arts-entertainment/2016/7/07/
list-interview-aubrey-plaza.

Wadler, Joyce. "Breaking Character for the First Time in His Life." NYTimes.

com. November 26, 2006. www.nytimes.com/2006/11/26/theater/26wadl. html?pagewanted=all&amp%3B_r=0.

Florida

ACLU. "In re:Gill." ACLU.org. November 16, 2012. www.aclu.org/cases/re-gill.

Alvarez, Lizette and Richard Pérez-Peña. "Orlando Gunman Attacks Gay Nightclub, Leaving 50 Dead." NYTimes.com. June 12, 2016. www.nytimes. com/2016/06/13/us/orlando-nightclub-shooting.html.

Aqua Foundation. "History." AquaFoundation.org. aquafoundation.org/ about/our-history.

Aqua Girl. "AquaGirl." www.aquagirl.org.

Baca, Mandy. "From Pride to The Palace: Miami's LGBT community through the years." TheNewTropic.com. August 06, 2015. thenewtropic.com/ miami-lgbt-history.

Beutke, Allyson A. "Behind Closed Doors." BehindClosedDoorsFilm.com. www.behindcloseddoorsfilm.com/index2.htm.

BiNet USA. "A Brief History of the Bisexual Movement." BiNetUSA.org. www. binetusa.org/bi-history.

Blanco, Richard. "Bio—Richard Blanco." Richard-Blanco.com. richard-blanco. com/bio.

Brewington, Kelly. "Disney World Plays Host to its First Gay Wedding." Sun-Sentinel.com. May 31, 2002. www.sun-sentinel.com/news/fl-xpm-2002-05-31-0205301139-story.html.

Cheltenham, Faith. "The Bisexual History of HIV/AIDS, in Photos." Blog.LGBTHealthLink.org. January 29, 2015. blog.lgbthealthlink. org/2015/01/29/the-bisexual-history-of-hivaids-in-photos.

Clark, Cammy. "A lesbian landmark goes 'all-welcome'." MiamiHerald.com. November 25, 2010. www.miamiherald.com/latest-news/article1937224. html.

Dyer, Tom. "Agents of Change: Equality Florida Executive Director Nadine Smith." WatermarkOnline.com. September 11, 2014. www.watermarkonline.com/2014/09/11/ agents-of-change-equality-florida-executive-director-nadine-smith.

Equality Florida. "Discrimination." EQFL.org. www.eqfl.org/Discrimination.

Equality Florida. "Gina Leigh Duncan." EQFL.org. www.eqfl.org/ gina-leigh-duncan.

Equality Florida. "Nadine Smith." EQFL.org. www.eqfl.org/nadine-smith.

Fantasy Fest. "Official Fantasy Fest Website." fantasyfest.com.

Florida Legislative Investigation Committee. "Reports of Investigators on Meetings of the Southern Christian Leadership Conference and the Ku Klux Klan." FloridaMemory.com. www.floridamemory.com/exhibits/ floridahighlights/investigation.

Gallagher, Kirsten. "Michael Hodge Dies—A Financial Booster of Gay Community." OrlandoSentinel.com. November 24, 1992. www. orlandosentinel.com/news/os-xpm-1992-11-24-9211240620-story.html.

Giuffrida, Angela. "'My life was torn in two when Gianni was shot'—Versace's lover breaks silence." TheGuardian.com. July 29, 2017. www.theguardian.com/tv-and-radio/2017/jul/29/ gianni-versace-murder-lover-slams-american-crime-story-ridiculous.

GLBT History Museum of Central Florida. "About Us." GLBTHistoryMuseum.com. glbthistorymuseum.com/joomla25/index. php?option=com_content&view=article&id=3&Itemid=401&lang=en.

Gourarie, Chava. "Since the 60's, Orlando gay bars have catalyzed a community." Timeline.com. June 13, 2016. timeline.com/since-the-60s-orlando-gay-bars-have-catalyzed-a-community-713ee83d3b09.

Guerrero, Claudia. "Gina Duncan delivers transgender equality speech." TheMinaretOnline.com. October 05, 2017. theminaretonline. com/2017/10/05/gina-duncan-delivers-transgender-equality-speech.

Hamilton, Joe. "Nadine Smith, Founder of Equality Florida." StPetersburgGroup.com. May 31, 2017. stpetersburggroup.com/ podcast-episodes/nadine-smith-equality-florida.

Iovannone, Jeffry J. "Pedro Zamora: Real World Activist." Medium. com. June 21, 2018. medium.com/queer-history-for-the-people/ pedro-zamora-real-world-activist-cf89c5e237ab.

Kennedy, John. "Floria's first openly gay state lawmakers say equality is just part of their priority list." PalmBeachPost.com. December 24, 2012. www. palmbeachpost.com/news/state—regional-govt—politics/florida-first-openly-gay-state-lawmakers-say-equality-just-part-their-priority-list/ C5qT4o5zkvjEwm4lN3kRYL.

Lee, Benjamin. "Moonlight's Tarell Alvin McCraney: 'I never had a coming out moment'." TheGuardian.com. October 21, 2016. www.theguardian.com/ film/2016/oct/21/moonlight-film-tarell-alvin-mccraney-interview.

Lies, Brendon and Landon Woolston. "In Love That Never Dies: Remembering the Legacy of Diana Hemingway." SouthFloridaGayNews.com. December 29, 2016. southfloridagaynews.com/In-Memoriam/in-love-that-never-dies-remembering-the-legacy-of-diana-hemingway.html.

Mayo, Christina. "TRANSART show to spotlight works of transgender artists." MiamiHerald.com. January 16, 2019. www.miamiherald.com/news/local/ community/miami-dade/community-voices/article224639065.html.

Melero, Jillian. "Feature: Bi Pioneers in LGBT Civil Rights." SouthFloridaGayNews.com. September 17, 2015. southfloridagaynews. com/Community/bi-pioneers-in-lgbt-civil-rights.

Metropolitan Community Churches. "About Metropolitan Community Churches." www.mccchurch.org.

Metropolitan Community Church of Tampa. "About Us." MCCTampa.com. www.mcctampa.com/about-us.html.

Miami Beach Pride. "Mission and History." MiamiBeachPride.com. miamibeachpride.com/mission-and-history.

Miami Gay & Lesbian Film Festival. "The Miami Gay & Lesbian Film Festival— Now MiFo." mglff.com.

Monteagudo, Jesse. "The Mariel Boatlift: When Gay Cubans Took Over Miami." SouthFloridaGayNews.com. October 20, 2016. southfloridagaynews.com/ Local/the-mariel-boatlift-the-last-hurrah-of-the-dade-county-coalition-for-human-rights.html.

Mundy, Liza. "Why Janet Reno Fascinates, Confounds and Even Terrifies America?" WashingtonPost.com. January 25, 1998. www.washingtonpost. com/wp-srv/politics/govt/admin/stories/reno012598.htm?noredirect=on.

Navarro, Mireya. "Life of 22 Years Ends, but Not Before Many Heard Message on AIDS." NYTimes.com. November 12, 1994. www.nytimes. com/1994/11/12/us/life-of-22-years-ends-but-not-before-many-heard-message-on-aids.html.

NPR Staff. "Richard Blanco Will Be First Latino Inaugural Poet." NPR. org. January 09, 2013. www.npr.org/2013/01/09/168899347/ richard-blanco-will-be-first-latino-inaugural-poet.

onePULSE Foundation. "onePULSE Foundation Memorial & Museum." onePULSEFoundation.org. onepulsefoundation.org/ onepulse-foundation-memorial.

Odessky, Jared. "Saving Our Children." Columbia.edu. April 3, 2015. asit-prod-web1.cc.columbia.edu/historydept/wp-content/uploads/ sites/20/2016/06/Jared-Odessky.pdf.

One Orlando Alliance. "Coalition." OneOrlandoAlliance.org. oneorlandoalliance.org/coalition.

Out History. "And They Were Wonderful Teachers: Florida's Purge of Gay and Lesbian Teachers." OutHistory.org. outhistory.org/items/show/1317.

Palace. "About." PalaceSouthBeach.com. palacesouthbeach.com/about.

Perry, Troy. "Troy Perry." Facebook.com. www.facebook.com/pg/rev.troy. perry/about/?ref=page_internal.

Pike, William. "Metropolitan Community Churches." Britannica.com. July 23, 2018. www.britannica.com/topic/Metropolitan-Community-Churches.

Portilla, Christian. "TransArt festival seeks to transform, educate in Miami Beach, Wilton Manors." MiamiHerald.com. June 20, 2016. www.miamiherald.com/news/local/community/gay-south-florida/ article84808932.html.

Reading Queer. "About." ReadingQueer.org. readingqueer.org/about.

Road, Cristy C. "malacriancias." CroadCore.org. www.croadcore.org/bio.htm.

Rochman, Bonnie. "Florida's Gay Adoption Ban Crumbles: The Dad Behind the Case Celebrates." HealthLand.Time. com. November 19, 2010. healthland.time.com/2010/11/19/ floridas-gay-adoption-ban-crumbles-the-dad-behind-the-case-celebrates.

Rothaus, Steve. "Herb Sosa of Miami Beach named Hispanic LGBT role model in new video tribute." MiamiHerald.com. November 05, 2014. www.miamiherald.com/news/local/community/gay-south-florida/ article3583514.html.

Rothaus, Steve. "Years after his death, AIDS activist Pedro Zamora is celebrated on film." MiamiHerald.TypePad.com. 2009. miamiherald. typepad.com/gaysouthflorida/2009/03/years-after-his-death-aids-activist-pedro-zamora-is-celebrated-on-film.html.

Schwartz, Elizabeth F. "Elizabeth F. Schwartz, esq.—principal." ElizabethSchwartz.com. elizabethschwartz.com/liz.html.

Smith, Nadine. "Whether or Not Pulse Was a Hate Crime, Hate Still Lives in Florida." Advocate.com. June 12,

2018. www.advocate.com/commentary/2018/6/12/whether-or-not-pulse-was-hate-crime-hate-still-lives-florida.

Springate, Megan E. "LGBTQ Civil Rights in America." NPS.gov. 2017. www.nps.gov/subjects/lgbtqheritage/upload/lgbtqtheme-vol2.pdf.

Stonewall National Museum & Archives. "Archives." Stonewall-Museum.org. www.stonewall-museum.org/the-museum/archives.

Terl, Allan H. "An Essay on the History of Lesbian and Gay Rights in Florida." NSUWorks.Nova.edu. 2000. nsuworks.nova.edu/cgi/viewcontent.cgi?article=1383&context=nlr.

The Greater Miami Convention & Visitors Bureau. "Events." MiamiandBeaches.com. www.miamiandbeaches.com/events.

The Greater Miami Convention & Visitors Bureau. "The White Party. MiamiandBeaches.com. www.miamiandbeaches.com/events/detail/the-white-party/6b105695-847e-4122-ace9-3b6d17a5137c.

The Villa Casa Casuarina. "History." VMMiamiBeach.com. vmmiamibeach.com/history.

Toro, Ana Maria. "Cristy C. Road, a voice for Cuban punk lit." NYDailyNews.com. June 04, 2009. www.nydailynews.com/latino/cristy-road-voice-cuban-punk-lit-article-1.373037.

TransKids Purple Rainbow. "TKPRF Mission Statement & Goals." TransKidsPurpleRainbow.org. www.transkidspurplerainbow.org/about-us.

Underground Books. "The LCN Express: A Loving Committed Network, Lesbian Community Network Newsletter, 24 Issues." UndergroundBooks.net. www.undergroundbooks.net/pages/books/4139/the-lcn-express-a-loving-committed-network-lesbian-community-network-newsletter-24-issues.

Unity Coalition. "UC/CU Meeting Schedule." UnityCoalition.org. www.unitycoalition.org/TransArt.html.

University of California, Berkeley. "Juana María Rodríguez." EthnicStudies.Berkeley.edu. ethnicstudies.berkeley.edu/faculty-profile/juana-maria-rodriguez.

University of Central Florida. "Johns Committee." Guides.UCF.edu. guides.ucf.edu/glbtq/johnscommittee.

University of Southern Florida. "LGBT Collections." Lib.USF.edu. www.lib.usf.edu/special-collections/lgbt-collections.

Vizcaya Museum & Gardens. "About Us." Vizcaya.org. vizcaya.org/about.asp.

Wallace, Carvell. "How Tarell Alvin McCraney Moved From 'Moonlight' to Broadway—and Beyond." NYTimes.com. January 15, 2019. www.nytimes.com/2019/01/15/magazine/tarell-alvin-mccraney-beauty-black.html.

Weaver, Jay and Elinor J. Brecher. "Janet Reno, former Miami-Dade state attorney and U.S. attorney general, dies at 78." Bradenton.com. November 07, 2016. www.bradenton.com/news/politics-government/article113012923.html.

Weaver, Jay. "How Janet Reno handled and bounced back from the biggest cases in her life." MiamiHerald.com. November 07, 2016. www.miamiherald.com/news/state/florida/article113010078.html.

Williams, Jeremy. "Former State Representative Joe Saunders returns to Equality Florida as Senior Political Director." WatermarkOnline.com. August 10, 2017. www.watermarkonline.com/2017/08/10/former-state-representative-joe-saunders-returns-equality-florida-senior-political-director.

Wilton Manors. "LGBT+ Life in Wilton Manors." WiltonManors.com. www.wiltonmanors.com/290/LGBT-Life-in-Wilton-Manors.

Wolf, Colin. "Nearly 48 hours later, Florida Gov. Rick Scott finally acknowledges the LGBT community." OrlandoWeekly.com. June 14, 2016. www.orlandoweekly.com/Blogs/archives/2016/06/14/nearly-48-hours-later-florida-gov-rick-scott-finally-acknowledges-the-lgbt-community.

Yes Institute. "GENDER, ORIENTATION, RESOURCES, EDUCATION." yesinstitute.org.

Georgia

Atlanta Black Pride Weekend. "Atlanta Black Pride Weekend." atlantaprideweekend.com.

Chalmers, Robert. "Legend: Little Richard." GQ-Magazine.co.uk. March 29, 2012. www.gq-magazine.co.uk/article/gq-men-of-the-year-2010-little-richard-legend.

Clarion Call Media. "Laura Jane Grace." ClarionCallMedia.com. www.clarioncallmedia.com/laura-jane-grace-bio.

Hare, Breeanna. "Raven-Symone: I'm not gay, and I'm not African-American." CNN.com. October 06, 2014. www.cnn.com/2014/10/06/showbiz/raven-symone-gay-labels/index.html.

History Commons. "Profile: The Otherside Lounge." HistoryCommons.org. www.historycommons.org/entity.jsp?entity=the_otherside_lounge_1.

HuffPost. "Lawrence D. Mass, M.D." HuffPost.com. www.huffpost.com/author/lawrence-d-mass-md.

Indigo Girls. "Biography." IndigoGirls.com. indigogirls.com/?page_id=13.

Lambe, Stacy. "Where Are They Now: Alan Ball." Out.com. October 28, 2014. www.out.com/out-exclusives/out100-2014/2014/10/28/alan-ball-where-are-they-now-director-producer.

LeonardMatlovich.com. "Leonard Matlovich." www.leonardmatlovich.com.

LeonardMatlovich.com. "Story of His Stone." LeonardMatlovich.com. www.leonardmatlovich.com/storyofhisstone.html.

Neese, Joseph. "Exclusive interview with the founder of Gay Men's Health Crisis." MSNBC.com. December 09, 2014. www.msnbc.com/msnbc/dr-larry-mass-aids-research-pioneer.

Oyez. "Bowers v. Hardwick." Oyez.org. www.oyez.org/cases/1985/85-140.

People of All Colors Together Atlanta. "Chapter Information." BWMTAtlanta.org. www.bwmtatlanta.org/index.php/about-us/club-information.

Recording Academy. "J. Michael Stipe." Grammy.com. www.grammy.com/grammys/artists/j-michael-stipe.

Rock & Roll Hall of Fame. "Little Richard." RockHall.com. www.rockhall.com/inductees/little-richard.

Saunders, Patrick. "Pride School Atlanta shuts down as enrollment dwindles." ProjectQ.US. September 24, 2018. www.projectq.us/atlanta/Pride_School_Atlanta_shuts_down_as_enrollment_dwindles?gid=19255.

The Georgia Voice Editors. "Georgia lesbian lawmaker brings power to the people from within the Gold Dome." TheGAVoice.com. March 18, 2010. thegavoice.com/news/georgia/georgia-lesbian-lawmaker-brings-power-to-the-people-from-within-the-gold-dome.

Willis, George. "Roy Simmons, who came out as gay after NFL career, dead at 57." NYPost.com. February 24, 2014. nypost.com/2014/02/24/roy-simmons-who-came-out-as-gay-after-nfl-career-dead-at-57.

Guam

Advocate.com Editors. "Queer Heros of America's Territories." TheAdvocate.com. May 22, 2018. www.advocate.com/current-issue/2018/5/22/these-americans-are-our-champions-too.

Ammon, Richard. "Gay Guam." GlobalGayz.com. 2008. www.globalgayz.com/gay-guam.

Associated Press. "Guam's gay marriage ban struck down." America.AlJazeera.com. June 05, 2015. america.aljazeera.com/articles/2015/6/5/guams-gay-marriage-ban-struck-down.html.

Barnett, Chris. "Guam's first transgender candidate in the running." KUAM.com. May 17, 2018. www.kuam.com/story/38210025/2018/05/Wednesday/guams-first-transgender-candidate-in-the-running.

Bordallo, Grace Garces. "First gay couple to marry in US territory ties knot in Guam." SanDiegoUnionTribune.com. June 09, 2015. www.sandiegouniontribune.com/sdut-first-gay-couple-to-marry-in-us-territory-ties-2015jun09-story.html.

Cruz, Benjamin J.F. "About." Facebook.com. www.facebook.com/pg/SenatorBenjaminJFCruz/about/?ref=page_internal.

Daily Post Staff. "Leon Guerrero, Tenorio join Pride March." PostGuam.com. June 05, 2018. www.postguam.com/news/local/leon-guerrero-tenorio-join-pride-march/article_5b8058e8-67d2-11e8-a197-dbe28a798454.html.

Guam's Alternative Lifestyle Association. "Who We Are." GalaGuam.Webs.com. galaguam.webs.com/whoweare.htm.

Guam Pride. "About." Facebook.com. www.facebook.com/pg/GuamLGBTQPride/about/?ref=page_internal.

Guam Pride. "Event Info." GuamPride.org. guampride.org/event-info.

Guam Pride. "Faces of Pride: Lasia Casil." Transnational-Queer-Underground.net. transnational-queer-underground.net/guam-pride.

Hernandez, Maria. "LGBT groups, local church unite for vigil." GuamPDN.com. June 14, 2016. www.guampdn.com/story/news/2016/06/14/lgbt-groups-local-church-unite-vigil/85856692.

ISA Guam. "About." Facebook.com. www.facebook.com/pg/ISAGuam/about/?ref=page_internal.

Lee, Sue. "Jaryna Anjelique Balbas is Miss Pacificana." GuamPDN.com. September 01, 2015. www.guampdn.com/story/entertainment/pika-magazine/2015/08/31/jaryna-anjelique-balbas-miss-pacificana/31448983.

Lee, Sue. "The art of teasing: Transgender burlesque 'McPhearson' Punzalan shines." GuamPDN.com. June 08, 2017. www.guampdn.com/story/life/2017/06/08/art-teasing-transgender-burlesque-dancer-renae-mcphearson-punzalan-shines/378562001.

Miller, Hayley. "Guam Takes Step Against LGBT Discrimination in the Workplace." HRC.org. August 12, 2015. www.hrc.org/blog/guam-takes-step-against-lgbt-discrimination-in-the-workplace.

Nicolas, Frank San. "ISA Guam." GuamPDN.com. www.guampdn.com/media/cinematic/gallery/86221798/isa-guam.

Pacific News Center. "VIDEO: Hybridity Exhibit of Local Artist Monaeka Flores Featured at Agana Shopping Center." PacificNewsCenter.com. September 13, 2013. pacificnewscenter.com/hybridity-exhibit-of-local-artist-monaeka-flores-featured-at-agana-shopping-center.

Silva, David. "Cruz control: newly appointed Guam supreme court justice Benjamin Cruz may be the nation's highest-ranking gay judge." Advocate.com. November 25, 1997. web.archive.org/web/20041026083015/www.findarticles.com/p/articles/mi_m1589/is_n747/ai_20013295.

Sobel, Ariel. "5 Things LGBT People Should Know About Guam." Advocate.com. August 09, 2017. www.advocate.com/politics/2017/8/09/5-things-lgbt-people-should-know-about-guam.

Staff Reports. "Guam Pride March and Beach Festival this Saturday, June 2." GuamPDN.com. May 31, 2018. www.guampdn.com/story/life/2018/05/31/guam-pride-march-and-beach-festival-saturday-june-2/658647002.

Weiss, Jasmine Stole. "Court order allows same-sex parents' names on birth certificate." GuamPDN.com. June 16, 2017. www.guampdn.com/story/news/2017/06/16/court-order-allows-same-sex-parents-names-birth-certificate/402234001.

Hawaii

Baxter, Kevin. "U.S. women soccer players get plenty of ink for their accomplishments." LATimes.com. May 28, 2012. www.latimes.com/sports/olympics/la-xpm-2012-may-28-la-sp-oly-soccer-tattoos-20120528-story.html.

Blair, Chad. "Kumu in the Middle." HanaHou.com. 2015. hanahou.com/18.1/kumu-in-the-middle.

Broder Van Dyke, Michelle. "A Brief History Of Sexual Identity In Hawaii." BuzzFeed.com. November 12, 2013. www.buzzfeed.com/mbvd/a-brief-history-of-sexual-identity-in-hawaii.

Chun, Gary. "Remembering the Glades." HawaiiIndependent.net. February 02, 2014. www.hawaiiindependent.net/story/rememering-the-glades.

Hawai'i LGBT Legacy Foundation. "Honolulu Pride 2019." HawaiiLGBTLegacyFoundation.com. hawaiilgbtlegacyfoundation.com/honolulu-pride-2019.

Hawaii News Now. "'I am a boy': The simple button that was Honolulu's scarlet letter." HawaiiNewsNow.com. October 16, 2018. www.hawaiinewsnow.com/2018/10/16/i-am-boy-simple-button-that-was-honolulus-scarlet-letter.

Honolulu Gay and Lesbian Cultural Foundation. "Our History." HGLCF.org. hglcf.org/our-history.

HuffPost Queer Voices. "The Beautiful Way Hawaiian Culture Embraces A Particular Kind Of Transgender Identity." HuffPost.com. April 28, 2015. www.huffpost.com/entry/hawaiian-culture-transgender_n_7158130.

Hula Girl Productions. "Glades." HulaGirlProductions.com. www.hulagirlproductions.com/glades.

Hula's. "About Hula's." Hulas.com. www.hulas.com/about-hulas.

IMDb. "Scott Coffey." IMDb.com. www.imdb.com/name/nm0168892.

Kobayashi, Ken. "Judge secure with sexual orientation." StarAdvertiser.com. January 31, 2011. www.staradvertiser.com/2011/01/31/hawaii-news/judge-secure-with-sexual-orientation.

Kobayashi, Ken. "McKenna is named to state's high court." StarAdvertiser.com. January 26, 2011. www.staradvertiser.com/2011/01/26/hawaii-news/mckenna-is-named-to-states-high-court.

Lavender Center & Clinic. "Lavender Center & Clinic." lavendercenterandclinic.org.

Lee, Jiz. "About Jiz Lee." JizLee.com. jizlee.com/bio.

Mock, Janet and Kierna Mayo. "I Was Born a Boy." MarieClaire.com. May 18, 2011. www.marieclaire.com/sex-love/advice/a6075/born-male.

People Staff. "Gay Man in the NFL." People.com. March 06, 2006. people.com/archive/gay-man-in-the-nfl-vol-65-no-9.

Piepenburg, Erik. "Keep Your Eye on the Road (If You Can)." NYTimes.com. November 06, 2004. www.nytimes.com/2004/11/06/nyregion/keep-your-eye-on-the-road-if-you-can.html?sec=health&pagewanted=1.

TEDx Maui. "Hinaleimoana Wong-Kalu." TEDxMaui.com. 2014. tedxmaui.com/hinaleimoana-wong-kalu.

To Hawaii. "Queen's Surf Beach, Oahu." To-Hawaii.com. www.to-hawaii.com/oahu/beaches/queensbeach.php.

Tsuneyoshi, Sandy. "OSU alum Tuaolo to speak at OSU about NFL, life as gay athlete." Today.OregonState.edu. July 07, 2009. today.oregonstate.edu/archives/2003/may/osu-alum-tuaolo-speak-osu-about-nfl-life-gay-athlete.

Wilson, R.J. "'The First Pregnant Man,' 10 Years Later: Thomas Beatie Reflects On A Difficult Decade." URBO.com. July 12, 2018. www.urbo.com/content/the-first-pregnant-man-10-years-later-thomas-beatie-reflects-on-a-difficult-decade.

Women's Pro Soccer. "Tasha Kai." WomensProSoccer.com. web.archive.org/web/20110703013820/http://www.womensprosoccer.com/philadelphia/players/bios/kai-natasha.

Idaho

Advocate.com Editors. "Historic Night at Golden Crown Literary Awards." Advocate.com. July 28, 2015. www.advocate.com/arts-entertainment/books/2015/07/28/historic-night-golden-crown-literary-awards.

Allies Linked for the Prevention of HIV and AIDS. "About." ALPHAIdaho.org. alphaidaho.org/who-we-are-and-where-we-came-from.

Anderson-Minshall, Jacob. "Swimming Upstream." SwimmingUpstream.life. www.swimmingupstream.life.

Ballotpedia. "Bruce Bastian." Ballotpedia.org. ballotpedia.org/Bruce_Bastian.

Bayly, Michael J. "Clyde Hall: 'All Gay People, in One Form or Another, Have Something to Give to This World, Something Rich and Very Wonderful'." TheWildReed.Blogspot.com. July 10, 2015. thewildreed.blogspot.com/2015/07/clyde-hall-all-gay-people-in-one-form.html.

Belluck, Pam and Adam Liptak. "Split Gay Couples Face Custody Hurdles." NYTimes.com. March 24, 2004. www.nytimes.com/2004/03/24/us/split-gay-couples-face-custody-hurdles.html.

Bold Strokes Books. "Jacob Anderson-Minshall." BoldStrokesBooks.com. www.boldstrokesbooks.com/authors/jacob-anderson-minshall-41.

Burroway, Jim. "Born On This Day, 1825: Karl Heinrich Ulrichs." BoxTurtleBulletin.com. August 28, 2016. www.boxturtlebulletin.com/2016/08/page/2.

Casa Feminista. "Home." CasaFeminista.com. web.archive.org/web/20071122084628/casafeminista.com.

Dance for All People. "About Clyde Hall." DanceForAllPeople.com. danceforallpeople.com/about-clyde-hall.

Dunlap, David W. "THE 1994 ELECTION: HOMOSEXUALS; Gay Politicians Cite Gains Amid Losses." NYTimes.com. November 14, 1994. www.nytimes.com/1994/11/14/us/the-1994-election-homosexuals-gay-politicians-cite-gains-amid-losses.html.

Hagadone, Zach. "The Boys of Boise: 60 Years Later." BoiseWeekly.com. June 17, 2015. www.boiseweekly.com/boise/the-boys-of-boise-60-years-later/Content?oid=3506778.

Iowa State University. "Sonia Johnson." AWPC.CattCenter.IAState.edu. awpc.cattcenter.iastate.edu/directory/sonia-johnson.

Kemp, A. "Bryan Fuller." IMDb.com. www.imdb.com/name/nm0298188/bio.

Lambda Legal. "F.V. v. Barron (formerly F.V. v. Armstrong)." LambdaLegal.org. www.lambdalegal.org/in-court/cases/id_fv-v-armstrong.

Lichtenstein, Grace. "Homosexual Weddings Stir Controversy in Colorado." NYTimes.com. April 27, 1975. www.nytimes.com/1975/04/27/archives/homosexual-weddings-stir-controversy-in-colorado.html.

Metropolitan Community Churches. "Rev Elder Freda Smith—MCC Evangelist." RevElderFredaSmithMCC.com. revelderfredasmithmcc.com.

Oregon Health & Science University. "Biology Behind Homosexuality in Sheep, Study Confirms." News.OHSU.edu. March 05, 2004. news.ohsu.edu/2004/03/05/biology-behind-homosexuality-in-sheep-study-confirms.

Oxley, Chuck. "Gay father loses his bid for custody." Spokesman.com. September 22, 2004. www.spokesman.com/stories/2004/sep/22/gay-father-loses-his-bid-for-custody.

People Staff. "Sonia Johnson." People.com. December 29, 1980. people.com/archive/sonia-johnson-vol-14-no-26.

Portwood, Jerry. "The Enduring Power of My Own Private Idaho." Out.com. October 25, 2015. www.out.com/movies/2015/10/25/

enduring-power-my-own-private-idaho.

Randal, Seth and Alan Virta. "Idaho's Original Same-Sex Scandal." NYTimes.com. September 2, 2007. www.nytimes.com/2007/09/02/opinion/02randal.html.

Romboy, Dennis. "Bastian's profile low & #151; in Utah, at least." DeseretNews.com. June 22, 2003. www.deseretnews.com/article/991843/Bastians-profile-low—in-Utah-at-least.html.

Rosenthal, Andrew. "Paul Popham, 45, A Founder of AIDS Organization, Dies." NYTimes.com. May 08, 1987. www.nytimes.com/1987/05/08/obituaries/paul-popham-45-a-founder-of-aids-organization-dies.html.

Smith, Freda Rev. "Rev. Elder Freda Smith." LGBTQReligiousArchives.org. January 2003. lgbtqreligiousarchives.org/oral-histories/elder-freda-smith.

Springate, Megan E. "LGBTQ America." NPS.gov. 2016. www.nps.gov/subjects/lgbtqheritage/upload/lgbtqtheme-bisexual.pdf.

Stack, Peggy Fletcher. "40 years after her Mormon excommunication, ERA firebrand Sonia Johnson salutes today's 'wonderful' women, says men 'bore' her." SLTrib.com. January 18, 2019. www.sltrib.com/religion/2019/01/18/years-after-her-mormon.

Sundermann, Hannelore. "A re-dress of the West." Magazine.WSU.edu. January 30, 2015. magazine.wsu.edu/2015/01/30/a-re-dress-of-the-west.

The Community Center. "About Us." TCCIdaho.org. tccidaho.org/about-us.

The Imperial Sovereign Gem Court of Idaho, Inc. "The Gem Court." IdahoGemCourt.org. idahogemcourt.org.

Theophanous, Daniel. "Hustler Vibes: My Own Private Idaho And New Queer Cinema." TheQuietus.com. May 06, 2018. thequietus.com/articles/24502-my-own-private-idaho-new-queer-cinema.

Toumayan, Michael. "Elevating Two-Spirit Leaders Across Generations." HRC.org. November 21, 2014. www.hrc.org/blog/two-spirit-leaders.

TV Guide. "Bryan Fuller." TVGuide.com. www.tvguide.com/celebrities/bryan-fuller/bio/286341.

Your Family, Friends and Neighbors. "YFFN: Community." YFFN.org. www.yffn.org/community.htm.

Illinois

Advocates for Youth. "Urooj Arshad." AdvocatesforYouth.org. advocatesforyouth.org/about/our-team/urooj-arshad.

American Battlefield Trust. "Albert Cashier aka Jennie Hodgers." Battlefields.org. www.battlefields.org/learn/biographies/albert-cashier.

Anderson, Melissa. "Lorraine Hansberry's Letters Reveal the Playwright's Private Struggle." VillageVoice.com. February 26, 2014. www.villagevoice.com/2014/02/26/lorraine-hansberrys-letters-reveal-the-playwrights-private-struggle.

Biographical Directory of the United States Congress. "KOLBE, James Thomas, (1942-)." Bioguide.Congress.gov. bioguide.congress.gov/scripts/biodisplay.pl?index=K000306.

Biography.com Editors. "Robert Reed." Biography.com. April 02, 2014. www.biography.com/actor/robert-reed.

Chicago LGBT Hall of Fame. "About the Chicago LGBT Hall of Fame." ChicagoLGBTHallofFame.org. chicagolgbthalloffame.org/about.

Chicago Public Library. "Lorraine Hansberry Biography." ChiPubLib.org. www.chipublib.org/lorraine-hansberry-biography.

Chicago Tribute. "Burr Tillstrom." ChicagoTribute.org. www.chicagotribute.org/Markers/Tillstrom.htm.

Chicago Tribute. "Margaret Anderson." ChicagoTribute.org. www.chicagotribute.org/Markers/Anderson.htm.

Choose Chicago. "Burr Tillstrom Residence." Vamonde.com. www.vamonde.com/posts/burr-tillstrom-residence/2330.

Choose Chicago. "Explore Gay Chicago History: LGBTQ Landmarks Tour." ChooseChicago.com. www.choosechicago.com/things-to-do/lgbtq-chicago/explore-gay-chicago-history-lgbtq-landmarks-tour.

Choose Chicago. "Jane Addams Hull-House Museum." ChooseChicago.com. www.choosechicago.com/listing/jane-addams-hull-house-museum/49058.

Derrick, Ivan. "Taylor Pool patron and gay rights pioneer David Kopay reflects on his time being a gay athlete." TheOccidentalNews.com. November 26, 2018. www.theoccidentalnews.com/sports/2018/11/26/taylor-pool-patron-and-gay-rights-pioneer-david-kopay-reflects-on-his-time-being-a-gay-athlete/2895310.

Directors Guild of America. "Paris Barclay." DGA.org. January 2018. www.dga.org/The-Guild/Members/Profile.aspx?mid=zGnoZaysTnY%3D.

Dunlap, David W. "A Republican Congressman Discloses He Is a Homosexual." NYTimes.com. August 03, 1996. www.nytimes.com/1996/08/03/us/a-republican-congressman-discloses-he-is-a-homosexual.html.

Feinberg, Leslie. "German movement inspired U.S. organizing." Workers.org. March 30, 2005. www.workers.org/2005/world/lgbtseries-0407.

Fox News. "Former Congressman Jim Kolbe To Marry His Longtime Male Partner On Saturday." FoxNews.com. May 15, 2013. www.foxnews.com/politics/former-congressman-jim-kolbe-to-marry-his-longtime-male-partner-on-saturday.

Goldman, Russell. "Transgender Activist CeCe McDonald Released from Prison." ABCNews.go.com. January 14, 2014. abcnews.go.com/blogs/headlines/2014/01/transgender-activist-cece-mcdonald-released-early-from-prison.

Gorey, Edward. Ascending Peculiarity: Edward Gorey on Edward Gorey. Cambridge, MA: Harcourt Brace Academic Publishers, 2001.

Gussow, Mel. "Edward Gorey, Artist and Author Who Turned the Macabre Into a Career, Dies at 75." NYTimes.com. April 17, 2000. www.nytimes.com/2000/04/17/arts/edward-gorey-artist-and-author-who-turned-the-macabre-into-a-career-dies-at-75.html.

History.com Editors. "Rock Hudson announces he has AIDS." History.com. November 13, 2009. www.history.com/this-day-in-history/rock-hudson-announces-he-has-aids.

InterACT. "Georgiann Davis." InterACTAdvocates.org. interactadvocates.org/board/georgiann-davis.

InterACT. "Lynnell Stephani Long." InterACTAdvocates.org. interactadvocates.org/board/lynnell-stephani-long-2.

Jackson, Benjamin. "Meet The Woman Who's Advocating For LGBT Muslim Youth Around The World." TheWindow.Barneys.com. September 25th, 2017. thewindow.barneys.com/urooj-arshad-breaking-dress-code.

LGBT History Month Equality Forum. "Cece McDonald." LGBTHistoryMonth.com. www.lgbthistorymonth.com/cece-mcdonald?tab=biography.

Martinson, David. "Major Donation Will Improve, Sustain Sexual Health Research and Care." SexualHealth.UMN.edu. March 06, 2017. www.sexualhealth.umn.edu/news/major-donation-will-improve-sustain-sexual-health-research-and-care.

Marzulli, John and Barbara Ross. "Obama nominates Asian-American lesbian for federal judgeship." NYDailyNews.com. August 02, 2012. www.nydailynews.com/new-york/obama-nominates-asian-american-lesbian-federal-judgeship-article-1.1128076.

Maxwell, Carrie. "Pidgeon Pagonis: On their film, White House visit, being on 'Transparent'." WindyCityMediaGroup.com. October 26, 2016. www.windycitymediagroup.com/ARTICLE.php?AID=56934.

McHenry, Jackson. "Richard Pryor's Widow on What to Expect From His Diaries, Including His 'Bisexual Experiences'." Vulture.com. February 08, 2018. www.vulture.com/2018/02/richard-pryors-widow-addresses-his-bisexual-experiences.html.

Naito, Joy. "Husky legend and gay icon David Kopay is at peace and at home." Magazine.Washington.edu. magazine.washington.edu/feature/husky-legend-and-gay-icon-david-kopay-is-at-peace-and-at-home.

National Park Service. "LGBTQ Activism: The Henry Gerber House, Chicago, IL." NPS.gov. www.nps.gov/articles/lgbtq-activism-henry-gerber-house-chicago-il.htm.

Orman, Suze. "About Suze Orman." SuzeOrman.com. www.suzeorman.com/about-suze.

Orman, Suze. "Suze's TV + Radio." SuzeOrman.com. www.suzeorman.com/about-suze/tv-radio.

Pagonis, Pidgeon. "Pidgeon Pagonis." PidgeonIsMy.name. www.pidgeonismy.name/about-flatiron.

Painter, George. "The History of Sodomy Laws in the United States—Illinois." GLAPN.org. 1991. www.glapn.org/sodomylaws/sensibilities/illinois.htm#fn73.

Pritzker, Jennifer N. "Jennifer Pritzker: I'm a transgender Republican, but my party is marginalizing me out of existence." ChicagoTribune.com. January 09, 2019. www.chicagotribune.com/news/opinion/commentary/ct-perspec-transgender-republican-jennifer-pritzker-military-gender-0110-20190109-story.html.

Pryor, Richard. "The Official Biography of Richard Pryor." RichardPryor.com. richardpryor.com/biography.php.

Sisters in the Life. "Ruth Ellis." SistersintheLife.com. web.archive.org/web/20071029050149/www.sistersinthelife.com/ruthellis/ruth_ellis.html.

Solomon, Brian. "Jennifer Pritzker Becomes First

Transgender Billionaire." Forbes.com. September 16, 2013. www.forbes.com/sites/briansolomon/2013/09/16/jennifer-pritzker-becomes-first-transgender-billionaire/#4f3fd6e27424.

Teich, Nicholas. *Transgender 101: A Simple Guide to a Complex Issue.* New York, NY: Columbia University Press, 2012.

Ubuntu Biography Project. "Ifti Nasim." UbuntuBiographyProject.com. September 15, 2017. ubuntubiographyproject.com/2017/09/15/ifti-nasim.

Ulaby, Neda. "Paris Barclay: A TV Insider With An Outsider Instinct." NPR.org. January 06, 2011. www.npr.org/2011/01/06/132079148/paris-barclay-a-tv-insider-with-an-outsider-instinct.

United States District Court - Eastern District of New York. "Judge Pamela K. Chen." NYED.USCourts.gov. www.nyed.uscourts.gov/content/judge-pamela-k-chen.

Wilkinson, Kathleen. "Ruth Ellis." CurveMag.com. 2000. web.archive.org/web/20070927011321/www.curvemag.com/Detailed/70.html.

Willis, Raquel. "TransVisionaries: How Miss Major Helped Spark the Modern Trans Movement." Them.us. March 08, 2018. www.them.us/story/transvisionaries-miss-major.

Windy City Times. "Chicago LGBT Hall of Fame restructuring, no event 2018." WindyCityMediaGroup.com. July 11, 2018. www.windycitymediagroup.com/lgbt/Chicago-LGBT-Hall-of-Fame-restructuring-no-event-2018-/63028.html.

Indiana

Bjornstad, William. "James Dean." FindaGrave.com. www.findagrave.com/memorial/267/james-dean.

Brathwaite, Lester Fabian. "The Importance of Being Ernestine Eckstein, Pioneer in the Early Gay Rights Movement." NewNowNext.com. February 27, 2019. www.newnownext.com/ernestine-eckstein-gay-civil-rights-pioneer/02/2019.

Burns, Alexander. "Pete Buttigieg, Mayor of South Bend, Ind., Joins Democratic 2020 Race." NYTimes.com. January 23, 2019. www.nytimes.com/2019/01/23/us/politics/pete-buttigieg-mayor-south-bend-president.html.

Center of Excellence for Transgender Health, University of California, San Francisco. "Bali White." TransHealth.UCSF.edu. transhealth.ucsf.edu/trans?page=ab-white.

Cusac, Anne-Marie. "Meet Pioneer of Gay Rights, Harry Hay." Progressive.org. August 09, 2016. progressive.org/magazine/meet-pioneer-gay-rights-harry-hay.

Dean, James. "Autobiography." JamesDean.com. www.jamesdean.com/biography.

Gent, Jeffrey. "James Dean's Gay Lovers." HomoHistory.com. December 08, 2012. www.homohistory.com/2012/12/james-deans-gay-lovers.html.

Health Resources & Services Administration. "Who Was Ryan White?" HAB.HRSA.gov. hab.hrsa.gov/about-ryan-white-hivaids-program/who-was-ryan-white.

Huffington Post. "Steve Ells, Chipotle Founder And CEO, Honored As Innovator By 'WSJ Magazine'." HuffPost.com. October 24, 2011. www.huffpost.com/entry/steve-ells-chipotle-innovator-wsj-magazine_n_1028416.

Indiana History. "IHS Launches New LGBT Traveling Exhibit." IndianaHistory.org. indianahistory.org/press-release/ihs-launches-new-lgbt-traveling-exhibit.

Indiana History. "Indiana LGBT Collecting Initiative." IndianaHistory.org. indianahistory.org/stories/indiana-lgbt-collecting-initiative.

IndyPride. "Chris Gonzalez Library & Archives." IndyPride.org. indypride.org/library.

James, Andrea. "About." AndreaJames.com. www.andreajames.com/about-2.

Jones, Cleve. "About Cleve." CleveJones.com. www.clevejones.com/about-cleve.

Jones, Kim. "Christian Singer Ray Boltz Comes Out, Says He Lives a Normal Gay Life." LearnReligions.com. September 30, 2018. www.learnreligions.com/christian-singer-ray-boltz-comes-out-709271.

Kinsey Institute. "Kinsey Institute." kinseyinstitute.org.

Leahey, Andrew. "Adam Lambert." AllMusic.com. www.allmusic.com/artist/adam-lambert-mn0001532591/biography.

Marcus, Eric and Marcia Gallo. "Ernestine Eckstein." MakingGayHistory.com. makinggayhistory.com/podcast/ernestine-eckstein.

National Institutes of Health. "Bali White." EDI.NIH.gov. www.edi.nih.gov/

more/team/bali-white.

Nussbaum, Emily. "How Ryan Murphy Became the Most Powerful Man in TV." NewYorker.com. May 07, 2018. www.newyorker.com/magazine/2018/05/14/how-ryan-murphy-became-the-most-powerful-man-in-tv.

Pete for America. "Meet Pete." PeteforAmerica.com. peteforamerica.com/meet-pete.

Publishers Weekly. "When We Rise: My Life in the Movement." PublishersWeekly.com. www.publishersweekly.com/978-0-316-31543-2.

Romeo, Peter. "Remembering the Highs and Lows of Steve Ells' Reign." RestaurantBusinessOnline.com. February 15, 2018. www.restaurantbusinessonline.com/leadership/remembering-highs-lows-steve-ells-reign.

Rose, Lacey. "Ryan Murphy's Professional Highs and Personal Lows: 'I Don't Want to Be That Person Anymore'." October 14, 2015. www.hollywoodreporter.com/features/ryan-murphys-professional-highs-personal-831587.

Rutledge, Stephen. "#BornThisDay: Actor, Will Geer." WorldofWonder.net. March 09, 2016. worldofwonder.net/bornthisday-actor-will-geer.

RyanWhite.com. "Ryan White." ryanwhite.com/index.html.

Song Facts. "Ray Boltz." SongFacts.com. www.songfacts.com/facts/ray-boltz/thank-you.

Songwriters Hall of Fame. "Cole Porter." SongHall.org. www.songhall.org/profile/Cole_Porter.

Teeman, Tim. "Joyce Kazmierski and Sandra Spuzich: A Golf Love Story Comes Out of the Closet." TheDailyBeast.com. October 18, 2015. www.thedailybeast.com/joyce-kazmierski-and-sandra-spuzich-a-golf-love-story-comes-out-of-the-closet.

The Bag Ladies. "History." BagLadiesIndy.org. bagladiesindy.org/who-we-are/history.

The Editors of Encyclopaedia Britannica. "Cole Porter." Britannica.com. July 20, 1998. www.britannica.com/biography/Cole-Porter.

Tri-State Alliance. "About Us." TSAGL.org. tsagl.org/about.html.

Up Closed. "J.C.C. McKinsey." UpClosed.com. upclosed.com/people/john-charles-chenoweth-mckinsey.

USGA. "1966 U.S. Women's Open Champion Sandra Spuzich Dies at 78." USGA.org. October 12, 2015. www.usga.org/articles/2015/10/1966-u-s—women_s-open-champion-sandra-spuzich-dies-at-78.html.

Whitten, Sarah. "Steve Ells wanted to open a fine-dining restaurant, instead he built a burrito empire." CNBC.com. November 29, 2017. www.cnbc.com/2017/11/29/how-steve-ells-built-chipotle-mexican-grill-into-a-burrito-empire.html.

Will Geer's Theatricum Botanicum. "Our Story." Theatricum.com. theatricum.com/our-story.

Iowa

Art Net. "Grant Wood." ArtNet.com. web.archive.org/web/20061019042017/www.artnet.com/Galleries/Artists_detail.asp?gid=267&aid=18073.

Associated Press. "Iowa high court takes on gay marriage." December 07, 2008. www.nbcnews.com/id/28098389/ns/us_news-crime_and_courts/t/iowa-high-court-takes-gay-marriage/#.XNBYypNKjOR.

Associated Press. "Judge Overturns Iowa Ban on Same-Sex Marriage." NYTimes.com. August 31, 2007. www.nytimes.com/2007/08/31/us/31iowa.html.

Associated Press. "Ninety-year-old gay couple marries in Iowa after 72 years together." TheGuardian.com. September 08, 2014. www.theguardian.com/world/2014/sep/08/ninety-year-old-gay-couple-marries-in-iowa.

Blazing Saddle. "The Blazing Saddle." www.theblazingsaddle.com.

Bowers, Marty and Marlys Svendsen-Roesler. "Alice French House Architectural/Historical Survey." NPGallery.NPS.gov. 1983. npgallery.nps.gov/NRHP/GetAsset/NRHP/83002434_text.

Council Bluffs Community Alliance. "Iowa's Progressive History." CouncilBluffsCommunityAlliance.com. councilbluffscommunityalliance.wordpress.com/iowa/iowas-progressive-history.

Crowder, Courtney. "Iowa professor speaks about life after her headline-making transition." DesMoinesRegister.com. October 13, 2016. www.desmoinesregister.com/story/news/2016/10/13/iowa-professor-deidre-mccloskey-making-transition/91874942.

Crowder, Courtney. "LGBTQ clinic at the University of Iowa offers 'relief'." DesMoinesRegister.com. December 15, 2016. www.desmoinesregister.

com/story/news/2016/12/15/iowa-lgbtq-clinic/95393688.

Denler, Heidi Hartwig. "French, Alice." Encyclopedia.com. www.encyclopedia. com/arts/news-wires-white-papers-and-books/french-alice.

Diversity, Equity, and Inclusion at Iowa. "LGBTQ Resource Center." Diversity. UIowa.edu. diversity.uiowa.edu/unit/lgbtq-resource-center.

Diversity, Equity, and Inclusion at Iowa. "UI LGBTQ Clinic." Diversity.UIowa. edu. diversity.uiowa.edu/unit/ui-lgbtq-clinic.

Forman, Ross. "Baseball history includes gay owner of minor league Cubs franchise." WindyCityMediaGroup.com. February 24, 2010. www. windycitymediagroup.com/ARTICLE.php?AID=25640.

Gaines, Steven. "The Man Who Sold His Name." VanityFair.com. September 1991. www.vanityfair.com/news/1991/09/halston-life-story.

Grinnell College. "Biography." Grinnell.edu. www.grinnell.edu/about/ leadership/president/bio.

Grinnell College. "Social Responsibility." Grinnell.edu. www.grinnell.edu/ about/mission/social-responsibility.

Maslin, Janet. "Behind That Humble Pitchfork, a Complex Artist." NYTimes. com. October 03, 2010. www.nytimes.com/2010/10/04/books/04book. html.

McCloskey, Deirdre Nansen. "Curriculum Vitae of Professor Deirdre Nansen McCloskey." DeirdreMcCloskey.com. www.deirdremccloskey.com/main/ vita.php.

Minnesota Transgender Health Coalition. "Discussion." Facebook.com. www. facebook.com/groups/15638628557.

Minnesota Transgender Health Coalition. "Program Personnel." MNTransgenderHealth.org. www.mntransgenderhealth.org/staff.

Moninger, Sara Epstein. "Celebrating points of pride." Now. UIowa.edu. November 10, 2016. now.uiowa.edu/2016/11/ lgbtq-celebrating-points-of-pride.

Oliver, Myrna. "Halston, 57, Icon of the Fashion Industry, Dies." LATimes.com. March 28, 1990. www.latimes.com/archives/la-xpm-1990-03-28-mn-228-story.html.

One Iowa. "About." Onelowa.org. oneiowa.org/about.

One Iowa. "One Iowa's 4th Annual LGBTQ Senior Summit to Focus on Addressing Isolation and Strengthening Connection." Onelowa.org. July 25, 2018. oneiowa.org/2018/07/one-iowas-4th-annual-lgbtq-senior-summit-focus-addressing-isolation-strengthening-connection.

Out History. "LGBTQ Life in Iowa City, Iowa: 1967-2010." OutHistory.org. outhistory.org/exhibits/show/lgbtq-life-in-iowa-city/1970s/1976-1977.

Prairie Lights. "About Us." PrairieLights.com. www.prairielights.com/ about-us.

The Sisters of Perpetual Indulgence, Inc. "sistory." TheSisters.org. www. thesisters.org/sistory.

Thornton, Kelly. "Meet the New U.S. Attorney." VoiceofSanDiego.org. July 05, 2010. www.voiceofsandiego.org/topics/news/meet-the-new-u-s-attorney.

Torchia, Robert and Catherine Southwick. "Grant Wood." NGA.gov. August 17, 2018. www.nga.gov/collection/artist-info.1982.html.

Kansas

Aaron, MTPC Intern. "Alan L. Hart: Pioneer and Physician." MASSTPC.org. March 14, 2014. www.masstpc.org/alan-hart.

Associated Press. "Gay couples marry in Kansas despite legal fight." OregonLive.com. November 14, 2014. www.oregonlive.com/ today/2014/11/gay_couples_marry_in_kansas_de.html.

Baker, Gilbert. "About Gilbert Baker." GilbertBaker.com. gilbertbaker.com/ biography.

Bailey, David and Kevin Murphy. "Kansas ban on same-sex marriage unconstitutional: judge." Reuters.com. November 04, 2014. www.reuters. com/article/us-usa-gaymarriage-kansas/kansas-ban-on-same-sex-marriage-unconstitutional-judge-idUSKBN0IO28H20141104.

Biography.com Editors. "Melissa Etheridge." Biography.com. www.biography. com/people/melissa-etheridge-9542649.

Bunch, Ryan. "'The Wizard of Oz' in the LGBT Community." EPGN.com. October 20, 2016. www.epgn.com/news/ local/11176-the-wizard-of-oz-in-the-lgbt-community.

Cook Walden Funeral Home. "Virgil A. Richard." Legacy.com. September 14, 2013. www.legacy.com/obituaries/statesman/obituary. aspx?page=lifestory&pid=166948495#fbLoggedOut.

Ferruzza, Charles. "Leaders Mark Kansas City's Early Role In The National LGBT-Rights Movement." KCUR.org. October 19, 2016. www.kcur.

org/post/leaders-mark-kansas-citys-early-role-national-lgbt-rights-movement#stream/0.

Finger, Stan and Bryan Lowry. "Same-sex couples apply for marriage licenses at Sedgwick County Courthouse." Kansas.com. November 13, 2014. www. kansas.com/news/local/article3909026.html.

Georgetown University Law Library. "A Brief History of Civil Rights in the United States." Guides.LL.Georgetown.edu. January 24, 2019. guides. ll.georgetown.edu/c.php?g=592919&p=4182201.

Haag, Matthew. "Gilbert Baker, Gay Activist Who Created the Rainbow Flag, Dies at 65." NYTimes.com. March 31, 2017. www.nytimes.com/2017/03/31/ us/obituary-gilbert-baker-rainbow-flag.html.

HRC Staff. "DADT Repeal Advocate Brigadier General Virgil A. Richard Passes Away." HRC.org. September 13, 2013. www.hrc.org/blog/ dadt-repeal-advocate-brigadier-general-virgil-a.-richard-passes-away.

Los Angeles Times. "Obituaries: Ruby Dandridge; Singer, Actress, Mother of Performer Daughters." LATimes.com. October 24, 1987. www.latimes.com/ archives/la-xpm-1987-10-24-mn-3802-story.html.

Mejia, Ari. "Alan L. Hart." OutHistory.org. outhistory.org/exhibits/show/ tgi-bios/alan-l-hart.

Nahmod, David-Elijah. "Rainbow flag creator Gilbert Baker to receive inauguralFounders Award." eBAR.com. June 20, 2012. www.ebar.com/ special_issues/pride//248581.

Nichols, James Michael. "With Your Help, A Pro-Trans House Could Move Right Next To Westboro Church." HuffPost.com. March 30, 2016. www. huffpost.com/entry/pro-trans-house-equality-house_n_56fbfac3e4b0a 06d58044821.

Oz Museum. "Oz Museum." ozmuseum.com.,

Pedraza, Pilar. "Wichita Pride Parade getting younger." KAKE. com. September 30, 2018. www.kake.com/story/39201847/ wichita-pride-parade-getting-younger.

Planting Peace. "About." PlantingPeace.org. www.plantingpeace.org/ about/#about-planting-peace.

Planting Peace. "Mott House." PlantingPeace.org. www.plantingpeace.org/ campaign/transgender-house/#cover.

Quenqua, Douglas. "Turned AWay, He Turned to the Bible." NYTimes.com. September 14, 2012. www.nytimes.com/2012/09/16/fashion/matthew-vines-wont-rest-in-defending-gay-christians.html.

Recording Academy. "Melissa Etheridge." Grammy.com. www.grammy.com/ grammys/artists/melissa-etheridge.

Reese, Diana. "Rainbow house fights Westboro Baptist with love." WashingtonPost.com. March 21, 2013. www.washingtonpost.com/blogs/ she-the-people/wp/2013/03/21/rainbow-house-fights-westboro-baptist-with-love/?noredirect=on&utm_term=.9e31f044b1ad.

Seward County Historical Museum. "Wizard of Oz, Coronado Museum." DorothysHouse.com. www.dorothyshouse.com/home.html.

Spanos, Brittany. "Janelle Monáe Frees Herself." RollingStone.com. April 26, 2018. www.rollingstone.com/music/music-features/ janelle-monae-frees-herself-629204.

Todd, Harry. "Extra Vitamins Leaves Denver, Citing Rising Rent." WestWord.com. January 21, 2019. www.westword.com/arts/ extra-vitamins-leaves-denver-citing-rising-rent-11120532.

Ubuntu Biography Project. "Cornell Gunter." UbuntuBiographyProject. com. November 14, 2017. ubuntubiographyproject.com/2017/11/14/ cornell-gunter.

Ubuntu Biography Project. "Ruby Dandridge." UbuntuBiographyProject. com. March 03, 2018. ubuntubiographyproject.com/2018/03/03/ ruby-dandridge.

Vines, Matthew. "About." MatthewVines.com. www.matthewvines.com/ about.

Waller, Genevieve. "Biography." GenevieveWaller.WordPress.com. genevievewaller.wordpress.com/biography.

Wichita Pride. "Wichita Pride." www.wichitapride.com.

Wong, Curtis M. "The Equality House Needs Your Help After Disgusting Homophobic Attack." HuffPost.com. December 14, 2016. www.huffpost. com/entry/equality-house-graffiti-fundraiser_n_58518de1e4b092f08686 c1fd.

Young, Morgen. "Alan Hart (1890-1962)." OregonEncyclopedia.org. oregonencyclopedia.org/articles/hart_alan_1890_1962_/#.XNBn75NKjOR.

Kentucky

ACLU. "Miller v. Davis." ACLU.org. January 23, 2019. www.aclu.org/cases/miller-v-davis.

Burton, Tara Isabella. "'Welcome home, Matt': Bishop Robinson welcomes Matthew Shepard—and gay Christians—back to the church." Vox.com. October 26, 2018. www.vox.com/2018/10/26/18027342/matthew-shepherd-gene-robinson-interring-lgbtq-christians.

Cratty, Carol. "4 relatives sentenced for kidnap, assault of gay man in Kentucky." CNN.com. June 20, 2013. www.cnn.com/2013/06/20/justice/kentucky-gay-man-attack/index.html.

Del Mar, Pollo. "Grammy-Nominated Singer Joan Osborne Was Uncomfortable with Fame—And Labeling Her Sexuality." HuffPost.com. April 18, 2016. www.huffpost.com/entry/grammynominated-singer-jo_b_9704864.

Garcia, Michelle. "Kentucky: Disabled Gay Couple Ejected From Pool." Advocate.com. June 13, 2011. www.advocate.com/news/daily-news/2011/06/13/kentucky-disabled-gay-couple-ejected-pool.

Jao, Ariel. "Alabama's first openly gay state lawmaker bids farewell." NBCNews.com. March 28, 2018. www.nbcnews.com/feature/nbc-out/alabama-s-first-openly-gay-state-lawmaker-bids-farewell-n860751.

Koeninger, Kevin. "Protesters Challenge Ejection From Ham Breakfast." CourthouseNews.com. October 04, 2018. www.courthousenews.com/protesters-challenge-ejection-from-ham-breakfast.

Pallardy, Richard. "Gus Van Sant." Britannica.com. February 13, 2009. www.britannica.com/biography/Gus-Van-Sant.

Ring, Trudy. "Kim Davis Is Out as Rowan County Clerk." Advocate.com. November 06, 2018. www.advocate.com/election/2018/11/06/kim-davis-out-rowan-county-clerk.

Serchuk, David. "Transgender lawyer JoAnne Wheeler Bland leads the fight for equal rights." InsiderLouisville.com. July 23, 2015. insiderlouisville.com/health/social_good/transgender-lawyer-joanne-wheeler-bland-leads-fight-equal-rights.

Smith, Dinitia. "Finding Homosexual Threads in Lincoln's Legend." NYTimes.com. December 16, 2004. www.nytimes.com/2004/12/16/books/finding-homosexual-threads-in-lincolns-legend.html.

The Original Mickey Mouse Club Show. "Tommy Kirk." OriginalMMC.com. www.originalmmc.com/tomkirk.html.

Louisiana

Alchetron. "Don Lemon." Alchetron.com. February 07, 2018. alchetron.com/Don-Lemon.

Allman, Kevin. "The forgotten inferno: Tinderbox and the Up Stairs Lounge fire." TheAdvocate.com. June 11, 2018. www.theadvocate.com/gambit/new_orleans/news/article_0697007c-ad41-5efc-964d-1a77930fa916.html.

Barnes, Rebecca. "Daughters of Bilitis." Britannica.com. November 21, 2013. www.britannica.com/topic/Daughters-of-Bilitis.

Biography.com Editors. "Truman Capote Biography." Biography.com. April 02, 2014. www.biography.com/writer/truman-capote.

Café Lafitte. "About Us." Lafittes.com. www.lafittes.com/about2.

Chambers, Andrea. "Truman Capote." People.com. January 26, 1981. people.com/archive/truman-capote-vol-15-no-3.

CNN. "Don Lemon." CNN.com. www.cnn.com/profiles/don-lemon-profile#about.

Devor, H. "Reed Erickson (1912-1992): How One Transsexed Man Supported ONE." OnlineAcademicCommunity.UVIC.ca. 2002. onlineacademiccommunity.uvic.ca/ahdevor/wp-content/uploads/sites/2247/2016/12/ReedErickson.pdf.

Divola, Barry. "Big Freedia: The bounce queen of New Orleans." SMH.com.au. November 29, 2018. www.smh.com.au/entertainment/music/big-freedia-the-bounce-queen-of-new-orleans-20181126-p50iex.html.

Fensterstock, Alison. "The Ballad of Big Freedia: How the New Orleans Bounce Icon Was Betrayed By Her City's Housing Crisis." PitchFork.com. August 24, 2016. pitchfork.com/thepitch/1273-the-ballad-of-big-freedia-how-the-new-orleans-bounce-icon-was-betrayed-by-her-citys-housing-crisis.

Klemesrud, Judy. "The Disciples Of Sappho, Updated." NYTimes.com. March 28, 1971. www.nytimes.com/1971/03/28/archives/the-disciples-of-sappho-updated-the-disciples-of-sappho.html.

Kwon, Sarah. "Ti-Grace Atkinson, at home in Cambridge, adds cause to radical feminism: Housing." CambridgeDay.com. January 06, 2016. www.cambridgeday.com/2016/01/06/ti-grace-atkinson-at-home-in-cambridge-adds-cause-to-radical-feminism-housing.

LGBT Community Center of New Orleans. "Home." lgbtccneworleans.org.

NewOrleans.com. "Fat Monday Luncheon." NewOrleans.com. www.neworleans.com/event/fat-monday-luncheon/17742.

NewOrleans.com. "LGBT History in New Orleans." NewOrleans.com. www.neworleans.com/things-to-do/lgbt/history.

Pontchartrain, Blake. "I heard that Truman Capote lived in New Orleans. What did he do here and where did he hang out?" TheAdvocate.net. June 02, 2014. www.theadvocate.com/gambit/new_orleans/news/blake_pontchartrain/article_90b13a12-3193-5a3a-a306-e04f411a0758.html.

Simmons, David Lee. "Cafe Lafitte In Exile." Nola.com. July 15, 2008. www.nola.com/bar-guide/2008/07/cafe_lafitte_in_exile.html.

Southern Decadence. "Southern Decadence." www.southerndecadence.net.

Steven Barclay Agency. "Tony Kushner." BarclayAgency.com. www.barclayagency.com/speakers/tony-kushner.

Stone, Amy L. "Reed Erickson." Britannica.com. August 24, 2016. www.britannica.com/biography/Reed-Erickson.

The Editors of Encyclopaedia Britannica. "Ellen DeGeneres." Britannica.com. December 17, 2008. www.britannica.com/biography/Ellen-DeGeneres.

The Editors of Encyclopaedia Britannica. "Tony Kushner." Britannica.com. April 20, 2009. www.britannica.com/biography/Tony-Kushner.

Transgender Archives, University of Victoria. "Reed Erickson and the Erickson Educational Foundation." UVIC.ca. www.uvic.ca/transgenderarchives/collections/reed-erickson/index.php.

University of New Orleans and Tulane University. "Upstairs Lounge Fire." NewOrleansHistorical.org. neworleanshistorical.org/tours/show/39.

Maine

Baker, Debra Solomon. "After the Silence, We Need Strong Voices." Tolerance.org. April 15, 2011. www.tolerance.org/magazine/after-the-silence-we-need-strong-voices.

Barkley, Jill. "Letter to the editor: Blackstones bar is fine as is: A perfect gathering place." PressHerald.com. March 13, 2015. www.pressherald.com/2015/03/13/letter-to-the-editor-blackstones-bar-is-fine-as-is-a-perfect-gathering-place.

Bouchard, Kelley. "Solomon honored for social justice efforts." PressHerald.com. October 20, 2011. www.pressherald.com/2011/10/20/solomon-honored-for-social-justice-efforts_2011-10-20.

Blackstones. "Welcome to Blackstones.com." Blackstones.com. blackstones.com.

Camp Camp. "About 'Camp' Camp." CampCamp.com. www.campcamp.com/about.

Ekstein, Nikki. "Forget Montauk: Why Maine Should Be Your Modern Summer Retreat." Bloomberg.com. July 8, 2016. www.bloomberg.com/news/features/2016-07-08/maine-s-best-new-hotels-modern-luxurious-and-tied-to-tradition.

English, Bella. "Led by the child who simply knew." Archive.Boston.com. December 11, 2011. archive.boston.com/lifestyle/family/articles/2011/12/11/led_by_the_child_who_simply_knew.

Fecteau, Ryan M. "Representative Ryan M. Fecteau." Legislature.Maine.gov. legislature.maine.gov/housedems/fecteau/index.html.

Gay Ogunquit. "About Ogunquit." GayOgunquit.com. gayogunquit.com/about-ogunquit.

GLAD Legal Advocates & Defenders. "Doe v. Clenchy." GLAD.org. www.glad.org/cases/doe-v-clenchy.

Harrison, Judy, Nick McCrea and Mario Moretto. "Charlie: Why the killing of a young, gay man in Bangor 30 years ago still matters." BangorDailyNews.com. 2014. external.bangordailynews.com/projects/2014/06/charlie/?utm_campaign=refer#.XLS2dpNKjOQ.

Harvie, Ian. "Life." IanHarvie.com. ianharvie.com/life.

Hutchins, Loraine. "Series: LGBTQ America: A Theme Study of Lesbian, Gay, Bisexual, Transgender, and Queer History." NPS.gov. www.nps.gov/articles/lgbtqtheme-bisexual.htm.

Jeltsen, Melissa. "Nicole Maines, History-Making Transgender Teen, Honored By Glamour Magazine." HuffPost.com. November 18, 2014. www.huffpost.com/entry/nicole-maines-glamour_n_6177720.

Keeley, Matt. "The Fate of Charlie Howard Was the Basis for the Tragic Story of the Gay Couple in 'It'." Hornet.com. July 14, 2018. hornet.com/stories/charlie-howard-it-true-story-two.

Office of Governor Janet T. Mills. "Governor Mills Appoints Donna Loring Senior Advisor on Tribal Affairs." Maine.gov. January 23, 2019. www.maine.gov/governor/mills/news/governor-mills-appoints-donna-loring-senior-advisor-tribal-affairs-2019-01-23.

Maine Trans Net. "Our Mission." MaineTransNet.org. www.mainetransnet.org/our-mission.

Maine Trans Net. "Training and Workshop Opportunities." MaineTransNet.org. www.mainetransnet.org/trainings-and-workshops.

Maine Women Writers Collection. "Donna M. Loring: A Penobscot Voice in Politics and Community." UNE.edu. web.archive.org/web/20130322183813/www.une.edu/mwwc/research/featuredwriters/loringdcollectionvisual.cfm.

Muther, Christopher. "Provincetown vs. Ogunquit: Differences more than marginal." Boston Globe.com. August 23, 2014. www.bostonglobe.com/lifestyle/travel/2014/08/23/peace-party-tale-two-gay-resort-towns/s4c9WHhVfqJw01X6zZV3ZI/story.html.

Poets. "Edna St. Vincent Millay." Poets.org. www.poets.org/poetsorg/poet/edna-st-vincent-millay.

Portland Pride. "Portland Pride." Facebook.com. www.facebook.com/pg/pdxpride/about/?ref=page_internal.

Pride Portland. "Pride Portland!" PridePortland.org. prideportland.org.

Reynolds, Daniel. "Trans Actors Ask Hollywood for Roles With Dignity and Depth in Open Letter." Advocate.com. June 20, 2017. www.advocate.com/transgender/2017/6/20/trans-actors-ask-hollywood-roles-dignity-and-depth-open-letter.

Ring, Trudy. "Maine Could Make History With Gay Governor, Youngest Out Legislator." Advocate.com. June 11, 2014. www.advocate.com/politics/election/2014/06/11/maine-could-make-history-gay-governor-youngest-out-legislator.

Solomon, Howard M. "Artist's Statement." HowardSolomon.org. howardsolomon.org/about.

The New York Times. "Edna St. V. Millay Found Dead At 58." Archive.NYTimes.com. October 20, 1950. archive.nytimes.com/www.nytimes.com/learning/general/onthisday/bday/0222.html.

Tuchelske, Eric J. "Summer Camp in Maine Caters to Gays and Lesbians." ChicagoTribune.com. March 25, 2001. www.chicagotribune.com/news/ct-xpm-2001-03-25-0103240217-story.html.

Maryland

Almosthipguy. "John Waters Swears off the word 'Hon' and Honfest." BaltimoreorLess.com. December 11, 2010. www.baltimoreorless.com/2010/12/john-waters-swears-off-hon.

Angier, Natalie. "X + Y = Z." Archive.NYTimes.com. February 20, 2000. archive.nytimes.com/www.nytimes.com/books/00/02/20/reviews/000220.20angiert.html.

Associated Press. "David Reimer, 38, Subject of the John/Joan Case." NYTimes.com. May 12, 2004. www.nytimes.com/2004/05/12/us/david-reimer-38-subject-of-the-john-joan-case.html.

Baltimore Heritage. "LGBTQ Heritage Initiative." BaltimoreHeritage.org. baltimoreheritage.org/project/lgbt-heritage.

Bendix, Trish. "Morning Brew—WNBA star Angel McCoughtry comes out." AfterEllen.com. April 3, 2015. www.afterellen.com/tv/424695-morning-brew-wnba-star-angel-mccoughtry-comes.

Booker, Christopher. "John Waters on the art of shocking audiences." PBS.org. October 7, 2018. www.pbs.org/newshour/show/john-waters-on-the-art-of-shocking-audiences.

Brown, Daniel. "Meet Kristen Beck, the transgender Navy SEAL hero fighting Trump's proposed trans ban." BusinessInsider.com. July 27, 2017. www.businessinsider.com/meet-kristin-beck-2017-7.

Brydum, Sunnivie. "Meet the First Out Trans Soldier in the US Military." Advocate.com. April 10, 2015. www.advocate.com/politics/transgender/2015/04/10/meet-first-out-trans-soldier-us-military?team=social.

Charing, Steve. "Leon's bar in Baltimore celebrates 60 years." WashingtonBlade.com. April 26, 2017. www.washingtonblade.com/2017/04/26/leons-bar-baltimore-celebrates-60-years.

Collins, Andrew. "Baltimore Gay Nightlife Guide." TripSavvy.com. May 22, 2017. www.tripsavvy.com/baltimore-gay-nightlife-guide-1417177.

Crittenton, Anya. "Maryland officially bans conversion therapy for LGBTI minors." GayStarNews.com. May 15, 2018. www.gaystarnews.com/article/maryland-bans-conversion-therapy-lgbti-minors/#gs.572r8v.

Darrach, Brad. "Death Comes to a Quiet Man Who Made Drag Queen History as Divine." People.com. March 21, 1988. people.com/archive/death-comes-to-a-quiet-man-who-made-drag-queen-history-as-divine-vol-29-no-11.

Equaldex. "LGBT Rights in Maryland." Equaldex.com. www.equaldex.com/region/united-states/maryland.

Fenton, Justin and Kevin Rector. "Transgender Woman Killed Tuesday in Northeast Baltimore." BaltimoreSun.com. June 4, 2014. www.baltimoresun.com/news/maryland/crime/bs-md-ci-transgender-homicide-victim-20140604-story.html.

Film Reference. "Darren Star Biography." FilmReference.com. www.filmreference.com/film/66/Darren-Star.html.

Friedman, Devin. "Kristin Beck: A Navy SEAL in Transition." GQ.com. November 25, 2015. www.gq.com/story/kristin-beck-transgender-navy-seal?verso=true.

Gaetano, Phil. "David Reimer and John Money Gender Reassignment Controversy: The John/Joan Case." Embryo.ASU.edu. November 15, 2017. embryo.asu.edu/pages/david-reimer-and-john-money-gender-reassignment-controversy-johnjoan-case.

Hill, Zahara. "15 Queer Black Music Artists Who Are Proudly Living Their Truth." HuffPost.com. June 15, 2017. www.huffpost.com/entry/15-queer-black-music-artists-who-are-proudly-living-their-truth_n_59396cd1e4b0c5a35c9d01eb.

Itzkoff, Dave. "DARREN STAR, creator, 'Beverly Hills 90210'." NYTimes.com. August 29, 2008. www.nytimes.com/2008/08/31/arts/television/31star.html?_r=1&scp=10&sq=Beverly%20Hills,%2090210&st=Search.

Josephs, Brian. "Felicia 'Snoop' Pearson of 'The Wire' Talks Baltimore: 'I Knew Freddie Gray'." Complex.com. May 02, 2015. www.complex.com/pop-culture/2015/05/felicia-snoop-pearson-the-wire-baltimore-riots-freddie-gray-equal-rights.

King, Jay Caspian. "'Our Demand Is Simple: Stop Killing Us'." NYTimes.com. May 4, 2015. www.nytimes.com/2015/05/10/magazine/our-demand-is-simple-stop-killing-us.html.

Kupfer, Ruta. "'Sex and the City' Creator Darren Star: Hollywood Looking to Israel for Ideas." Haaretz.com. February 12, 2008. www.haaretz.com/israel-news/culture/1.5068051.

Lee, Felicia R. "Tickled Red to Be Elmo in a Rainbow World." NYTimes.com. August 23, 2006. www.nytimes.com/2006/08/23/arts/23clash.html?_r=1&adxnnl=1&adxnnlx=1355325456-zWIGyBYSGCaAlL03Rm8veA.

Lee, Trymaine. "Black and Jewish, and Seeing No Contradiction." NYTimes.com. August 27, 2010. www.nytimes.com/2010/08/28/nyregion/28blackjews.html?_r=1.

Martin, Michel. "Activist DeRay McKesson On Why He's Making 'The Case For Hope'." NPR.org. September 8, 2018. www.npr.org/2018/09/08/645895088/activist-deray-mckesson-on-why-hes-making-the-case-for-hope.

McIntosh, Maggie. "About Maggie." DelMaggie.com. www.delmaggie.com/about.

Metz, Nina. "John Waters Loves Christmas. Really." ChicagoTribune.com. December 03, 2010. www.chicagotribune.com/entertainment/ct-xpm-2010-12-03-ct-mov-1203-chicago-closeup-20101203-story.html.

NY Daily News. "Brooklyn, NY—Tale of Tragedy and Triumph for a Struggling Hasidic Black Convert Rap Star." Vosizneias.com. September 14, 2008. www.vosizneias.com/20287/2008/09/14/brooklyn-ny-tale-of-tragedy-and-triumph-for-a-struggling-hasidic-black-convert-rap-star.

Ortega, Shane Alejandro. "Shane Alejandro Ortega." NYTimes.com. 2015. www.nytimes.com/interactive/2015/opinion/transgender-today/stories/shane-alejandro-ortega.

Pilkington, Ed. "Fear and violence in transgender Baltimore: 'It's scary trusting anyone'." TheGuardian.com. August 1, 2014. www.theguardian.com/world/2014/aug/01/murder-transgender-women-baltimore-heighten-fears-mia-henderson.

Portwood, Jerry. "Y-Love is Ready for Love." Out.com. May 15, 2012. www.out.com/entertainment/music/2012/05/15/y-love-yitz-jordan-hip-hop-jewish-gay.

Rector, Kevin. "Effort to preserve Baltimore's gay history is underway." BaltimoreSun.com. September 20, 2013. www.baltimoresun.com/features/gay-in-maryland/bs-md-gay-history-project-20130915-story.

html.

Reeves, Ronke Idowu. "Q&A: Kevin Clash on Being Elmo." BET.com. November 6, 2011. www.bet.com/news/celebrities/2011/11/07/q-a-kevin-clash-on-being-elmo.html.

Riley, John. "Maryland's Gay Wunderkind." MetroWeekly.com. August 29, 2013. www.metroweekly.com/2013/08/marylands-gay-wunderkind.

Sentementes, Gus G. and Julie Bykowicz. "Error frees city murder suspect." BaltimoreSun.com. October 31, 2006. www.baltimoresun.com/news/bs-xpm-2006-10-31-0610310070-story.html.

Sports Reference. "Angel McCoughtry." Sports-Reference.com. www.sports-reference.com/olympics/athletes/mc/angel-mccoughtry-1.html.

Strasdauskas, Anne. "Anne Strasdauskas, Maryland, 1998." OutHistory. org. www.outhistory.org/exhibits/show/out-and-elected/1998/anne-strasdauskas.

Sullivan, Kathleen J. "Stanford junior wins 2018 Truman Scholarship for graduate studies." News.Stanford.edu. April 13, 2018. news.stanford.edu/2018/04/13/truman-scholar.

Terris, Ben. "Meet Kristin Beck, a transgender former Navy SEAL running for Congress." WashingtonPost.com. June 22, 2015. www.washingtonpost.com/lifestyle/style/meet-kristin-beck-a-transgender-former-navy-seal-running-for-congress/2015/06/22/299006e4-0b87-11e5-9e39-0db921c47b93_story.html?noredirect=on&utm_term=.3fab7e2ba2a9.

The Baltimore Sun. "A gay history of Maryland in photos." BaltimoreSun.com. www.baltimoresun.com/entertainment/bal-a-gay-history-of-maryland-in-photos-photogallery.html.

The Baltimore Sun. "Digest." BaltimoreSun.com. September 24, 2007. www.baltimoresun.com/news/bs-xpm-2007-09-24-0709240116-story.html.

The New York Times. "Divine, Transvestite Film Actor, Found Dead in Hollywood at 42." NYTimes.com. March 8, 1988. www.nytimes.com/1988/03/08/obituaries/divine-transvestite-film-actor-found-dead-in-hollywood-at-42.html.

The PRIDE Center of Maryland. "Arts and Culture—GLCCB." GLCCB.org. www.glccb.org/programs/arts-culture.

The PRIDE Center of Maryland. "THE PRIDE CENTER OF MARYLAND." PrideCenterMD.org. www.pridecentermd.org.

TV Guide. "John Waters Biography." TVGuide.com. www.tvguide.com/celebrities/john-waters/bio/279296.

Vote Smart. "Maggie McIntosh's Biography." VoteSmart.org. votesmart.org/candidate/biography/6188/maggie-mcintosh#.XLTIBpNKjOQ.

WNBA. "Angel McCoughtry." WNBA.com. www.wnba.com/player/angel-mccoughtry/#/bio.

Massachusetts

Buck, Stephanie. "An out lesbian and abortion rights activist, Marie Equi got locked up for espionage." Timeline.com. October 2, 2017. timeline.com/marie-equi-abortion-activist-b712c6ef2656.

Driver, Betsy. "The origins of Intersex Awareness Day." IntersexDay.org. October 14, 2015. intersexday.org/en/origin-intersex-awareness-day.

Dunlap, David W. "John E. Boswell, 47, Historian Of Medieval Gay Culture, Dies." NYTimes.com. December 25, 1994. www.nytimes.com/1994/12/25/obituaries/john-e-boswell-47-historian-of-medieval-gay-culture-dies.html.

Eaton, Perry. "A gay feminist badass from Massachusetts wrote 'America the Beautiful'." Boston.com. June 30, 2015. www.boston.com/culture/entertainment/2015/06/30/a-gay-feminist-badass-from-massachusetts-wrote-america-the-beautiful.

InterACT Advocates. "interACT Advocates." InteractAdvocates.org. interactadvocates.org.

InterACT Advocates. "Intersex Awareness Day." InteractAdvocates.org. interactadvocates.org/intersex-awareness-day.

Kerman, Piper. "About the Author." PiperKerman.com. piperkerman.com/orange/bio.

Koenig, Kailani. "Ten years ago, Massachusetts introduced us to gay marriage." MSNBC.com. May 16, 2014. www.msnbc.com/msnbc/ten-years-ago-massachusetts-introduced-us-gay-marriage.

Krone, Mark Thomas. "Boston Queer History. MarkThomasKrone. Wordpress.com. November 21, 2014. markthomaskrone.wordpress.com/2014/11/21/1950s-gay-boston.

Lewis, Jone Johnson. "15 Surprising Facts About Susan B. Anthony." ThoughtCo. July 31, 2017. www.thoughtco.com/surprising-facts-about-susan-b-anthony-3528409.

Marusic, Kristinia. "Trans Pioneer HOlly Boswell, Who Created The Transgender Symbol, Passes Away at 66." NewNowNext.com. August 16, 2017. www.newnownext.com/holly-boswell-creator-of-transgender-symbol-obituary/08/2017.

Mezey, Susan Gluck. "Hurley v. Irish-American Gay, Lesbian and Bisexual Group of Boston (1995)." MTSU.edu. www.mtsu.edu/first-amendment/article/65/hurley-v-irish-american-gay-lesbian-and-bisexual-group-of-boston.

Monroe, Irene. "Remembering Trans Heroine Rita Hister." HuffPost.com. November 19, 2010. www.huffpost.com/entry/remembering-trans-heroine_b_785829.

Provincetown Chamber of Commerce. "Provincetown: Cape Cod's Most Popular Vacation Destination!" PTownChamber.com. ptownchamber.com.

Roddy, Michael. "Bernsetin in letters—gifted, gay and loved by his wife." Reuters.com. April 11, 2014. www.reuters.com/article/us-books-music-bernstein/bernstein-in-letters-gifted-gay-and-loved-by-his-wife-idUSBREA3A0J720140411.

Sheridan, Chris. "Amaechi becomes first NBA player to come out." ESPN.com. February 9, 2007. www.espn.com/nba/news/story?id=2757105.

Stokes, Wendy. "A Brief History Of 'Boston Marriages'." TheFrisky.com. August 8, 2018. thefrisky.com/a-brief-history-of-boston-marriages.

Sullivan, Robert David. "Last Call." Archive.Boston.com. December 2, 2007. archive.boston.com/bostonglobe/ideas/articles/2007/12/02/last_call.

Terence. "Angelina Weld Grimké." QueerHistory.Blogspot.com. February 27, 2013. queerhistory.blogspot.com/2011/02/angelina-weld-grimke-1880-1958-african.html.

The History Project. "Home." HistoryProject.org. www.historyproject.org/index.php.

The New York Times. "Miss Susan B. Anthony Died This Morning." Archive.NYTimes.com. March 13, 1906. archive.nytimes.com/www.nytimes.com/learning/general/onthisday/bday/0215.html.

Trans Equality. "Raffi Freedman-Gurspan." TransEquality.org. transequality.org/about/people/raffi-freedman-gurspan-sheherhers.

Wicked Queer. "About Us." WickedQueer.org. www.wickedqueer.org/about-us.

Zvonkin, Judith. "Angelina Weld Grimke." DCLibrary.org. 029c28c.netsolhost.com/blkren/bios/grimkeaw.html.

Michigan

Admin. "Miss Ruby's Flaming Star." OurCommunityRoots.com. June 10, 2017. ourcommunityroots.com/?p=56676.

Affirmations. "Serving People of all Sexual Orientations & Gender Identities." GoAffirmations.org. www.goaffirmations.org/about-us

Andrews, Travis M. "Dana Zzyym doesn't identify as male or female, so can't get a passport." WashingtonPost.com. July 21, 2016. www.washingtonpost.com/news/morning-mix/wp/2016/07/21/dana-zzyym-doesnt-identify-as-male-or-female-so-they-cant-legally-leave-the-country.

Associated Press. "Federal Judge Rules Dana Zzyym, Intersex Person, Can't Be Denied Passport." CPR.org. September 20, 2018. www.cpr.org/news/story/federal-judge-rules-dana-zzyym-intersex-person-can-t-be-denied-passport.

Associated Press. "Mich. man in '95 talk show murder case released." DetroitNews.com. August 22, 2017. www.detroitnews.com/story/news/local/michigan/2017/08/22/talk-show-slaying/104848614.

Bernhard, Sandra. "Biography." SandraBernhard.com. www.sandrabernhard.com/bio.

BTL Staff. "Gay rodeo gears up for July." PrideSource.com. April 21, 2011. pridesource.com/article/46610.

BTL Staff. "Hotter Than July burns up Detroit's Palmer Park." PrideSource.com. July 19, 2007. pridesource.com/article/26095.

Burack, Cristina. "Who is Richard Grenell, the US ambassador to Berlin?" DW.com. April 06, 2018. www.dw.com/en/who-is-richard-grenell-the-us-ambassador-to-berlin/a-39797271.

Burns, Gus. "Three LGBT homicides at Detroit's Palmer Park recorded in less than two years." MLive.com. August 10, 2015. www.mlive.com/news/detroit/2015/08/three_lgbt_homicides_at_detroi.html.

BWW News Desk. "Who Wants Cake? Hosts THE BOYS IN THE BAND Reading 12/6." BroadwayWorld.com. November

18, 2009. www.broadwayworld.com/detroit/article/ Who-Wants-Cake-Hosts-THE-BOYS-IN-THE-BAND-Reading-126-20091118.

DeVito, Lee. "Menjo's is making a museum of Detroit's gay history." MetroTimes.com. March 03, 2015. www. metrotimes.com/the-scene/archives/2015/03/03/ menjos-is-making-a-museum-of-detroits-gay-history.

Ellison, Garret. "After 40 years, the Apartment Lounge, Michigan's oldest gay bar, is finally changing owners." MLive.com. September 19, 2012. www.mlive.com/business/west-michigan/2012/09/after_40_years_the_ apartment_l.html.

Fox, Emily. "How the largest gay resort in the Midwest is in Michigan's 'Bible belt'." MichiganRadio.org. January 11, 2016. www.michiganradio.org/post/ how-largest-gay-resort-midwest-michigans-bible-belt.

Gasaway, Lee. "Poet & Activist, Terri Jewell, Dies." MichiganLGBTQRemember. Files.Wordpress.com. January 1996. michiganlgbtqremember.files. wordpress.com/2016/11/jewell-obit-btl-199601p28.pdf.

Gay Saugatuck Douglas. "Your Travel Guide To The Gay Friendly Small Towns Of Saugatuck And Douglas, Michigan." gaysaugatuckdouglas.com.

Grant, Japhy. "Think Harvey Milk Was the First Openly-Gay Politician? Think Again." Queerty.com. January 21, 2009. www.queerty.com/think-harvey-milk-was-the-first-openly-gay-politician-think-again-20090121.

Grierson, Beth and Carrie Snyder. "Routsong, Alma." Encyclopedia.com. www.encyclopedia.com/arts/news-wires-white-papers-and-books/ routsong-alma.

Helling, Steve. "Inside the Career of Eden Lane, TV's First Transgender Reporter." People.com. February 21, 2015. people.com/celebrity/ eden-lane-first-transgender-reporter-on-tv.

HQ WWTLC. "What About the Michigan Womyn's Music Festival?" WWTLC.org. September 07, 2018. wwtlc.org/faq-items/ what-about-the-michigan-womyns-music-festival.

Jao, Ariel. "Openly gay U.S. ambassador to Germany makes Republican history." NBCNews.com. April 27, 2018. www.nbcnews.com/feature/nbc-out/ openly-gay-u-s-ambassador-germany-makes-republican-history-n869641.

Jones, Tom. "LA Times snags LZ Granderson as new sports and culture columnist." Poynter.org. January 09, 2019. www.poynter.org/business-work/2019/ la-times-snags-lz-granderson-as-new-sports-and-culture-columnist.

Kohler, Will. "Gay History—September 16th: Maria Callas, NAMBLA, Wilheim Von Gloeden, and the 'Little Faggot Truck'." Back2Stonewall.com. September 16, 2018. www.back2stonewall.com/2018/09/today-gay-history-september-16th.html.

Kuruvilla, Carol. "6 Questions With A Gay Imam, Daayiee Abdullah." HuffPost.com. April 10, 2015. www.huffpost.com/entry/ gay-imam-daayiee-abdullah_n_7043502.

Lambda Legal. "Victory! State Department Cannot Rely on its Binary-Only Gender Policy to Deny Passport to Nonbinary Intersex Citizen." LambdaLegal.org. September 19, 2018. www.lambdalegal.org/ blog/20180919_victory-state-department-cannot-rely-on-binary-only-gender-policy.

Lesbian Herstory Archives. "LHA Daughters of Bilitis Video Project: Alma Routsong." Herstories.PrattInfoSchool.nyc. herstories.prattinfoschool. nyc/omeka/collections/show/57.

LGBT Detroit. "Hotter Than July." LGBTDetroit.org. www.lgbtdetroit.org/ hotterthanjuly.

LGBTQ Religious Archives Network. "Imam Daayiee Abdullah." LGBTQReligiousArchives.org. lgbtqreligiousarchives.org/profiles/ daayiee-abdullah.

Menjos. "Menjos Gay Entertainment Complex." NewMenjosComplex.com. www.newmenjoscomplex.com/menjos.

Mesli, Rostom and Brian Whitener. "The Flame: The Gay Bar of Ann Arbor, MI, 1949-1998." OutHistory.org. outhistory.org/exhibits/show/ the-flame-ann-arbor/the-flame.

Michigan LGBTQ Remember. "Diplomat." MichiganLGBTQRemember.com. michiganlgbtqremember.com/tag/diplomat.

Michigan State University Libraries. "Isabel Miller (Alma Routsong)." SPCEExhibits.Lib.MSU.edu. spcexhibits.lib.msu.edu/html/materials/ collections/michcoll/miller.jsp.

Millich, Gretchen. "East Lansing Marks 40th Anniversary of Gay Rights Ordinance." WKAR.org. March 06, 2012. www.wkar.org/post/ east-lansing-marks-40th-anniversary-of-gay-rights-ordinance#stream/0.

Nelson, David. "DAVID NELSON—A Perspective On Hotter Than July (Feature)." TheLGBTUpdate.com. July 22, 2015. www.thelgbtupdate.com/ david-nelson-a-perspective-on-hotter-than-july-feature.

Notable Kentucky African Americans Database. "Jewell, Terri Lynn." NKAA. UKY.edu. February 27, 2018. nkaa.uky.edu/nkaa/items/show/2764.

Opalewski, Kate. "The Ringwald Celebrates 10th Season of Unpredictable Theatre." PrideSource.com. September 01, 2016. pridesource.com/ article/77909-2.

Opalewski, Kate. "Transgender Michigan Celebrates 20 Years." PrideSource. com. August 10, 2017. pridesource.com/article/82507-2.

Piper, Matthew. "Palmer Park's turnaround and neighborhood revival." ModelDMedia.com. January 28, 2014. www.modeldmedia.com/features/ palmerpark12814.aspx.

Poetry Foundation. "Beth Brant." PoetryFoundation.org. www. poetryfoundation.org/poets/beth-brant.

Rapp, Linda. "Radicalesbians." GLBTQArchive.com. 2004. www.glbtqarchive. com/ssh/radicalesbians_S.pdf.

Retzloff, Tim. "Remembering Beth Brant." PrideSource.com. August 08, 2018. pridesource.com/article/remembering-beth-brant.

Rupersburg, Nicole. "RIP: 9 shuttered Detroit bars & restaurants that we'll miss." Thrillist.com. December 31, 2014. www.thrillist.com/eat/detroit/ detroit-bars-and-restos-that-have-closed.

Ruth Ellis Center. "The Legacy of Ruth Ellis." RuthEllisCenter.org. www. ruthelliscenter.org/who-we-are/legacy2.

Segal, Mark. "LGBT History: It's Not What You've Been Told." EPGN.com. January 21, 2016. www.epgn.com/opinion/ mark-my-words/9894-lgbt-history-it-s-not-what-you-ve-been-told.

Swenson, Kyle. "A 1995 TV Show Surprised Him With His Gay Secret Admirer: This Week He Leaves Prison." WashingtonPost.com. August 23, 2017. www. washingtonpost.com/news/morning-mix/wp/2017/08/23/a-1995-tv-show-surprised-him-with-his-gay-secret-admirer-this-week-he-leaves-prison/.

The Apartment Lounge. "The Apartment Lounge." www.apartmentloungegr. com.

The Association of LGBTQ Journalists. "LZ Granderson - 2011 Winner." NLGJA. org. 2011. www.nlgja.org/blog/2011/07/lz-granderson-2011-winner.

Transgender Michigan. "Transgender Michigan." www.transgendermichigan. org/Index.html.

University of Michigan. "Michigan's LGBT Heritage: Event Timeline: 1970s." Lib.UMich.edu. www.lib.umich.edu/online-exhibits/exhibits/show/ lgbtheritage/1970/1970timeline.

University of Michigan. "Michigan's LGBT Heritage: Event Timeline: 1990s." Lib.UMich.edu. www.lib.umich.edu/online-exhibits/exhibits/show/ lgbtheritage/1990/1990timeline.

U.S. Department of State. "Richard Grenell." State.gov. www.state.gov/r/pa/ ei/biog/281314.htm#.

Wax, Emily. "Imam Daayiee Abdullah welcomes gay Muslims to worship, marry." WashigtonPost.com. April 17, 2013. www.washingtonpost.com/ lifestyle/style/imam-daayiee-abdullah-welcomes-gay-muslims-to-worship-marry/2013/04/17/3ebcab3a-a5db-11e2-b029-8fb7e977ef71_ story.html?utm_term=.dad7a3d4d717.

WestWord. "Best Old-New Denver Tour: 1600 block of Wazee Street." WestWord.com. 2015. www.westword.com/best-of/2015/ shopping-and-services/best-old-new-denver-tour-6612755.

Williams, Cristan. "Michigan Womyn's Music Festival." TransAdvocate.com. April 09, 2013. www.transadvocate.com/michigan-womyns-music-festival_n_8943.htm.

Woods, Alan. "The 7 Best Towns in Michigan for LGBT Families." Movoto.com. www.movoto.com/guide/mi/ the-7-best-towns-in-michigan-for-lgbt-families.

Minnesota

Abadi, Mark. "New Land O'Lakes CEO Beth Ford just became the first openly gay woman to lead a Fortune 500 company —take a look at her career so far." BusinessInsider.com. August 01, 2018. www.businessinsider.com/ beth-ford-land-o-lakes-ceo-2018-7.

Bakst, Brian. "Dayton MN Supreme Court pick is court's first openly gay justice." MPRNews.org. January 22, 2016. www.mprnews.org/ story/2015/01/22/dayton-pick-first-openly-gay-mn-supreme-court-judge.

Bancroft, Ann. "About Ann Bancroft." AnnBancroftFoundation.org. www. annbancroftfoundation.org/about/ann.

Baran, Madeleine. "Once-thriving Mpls. LGBT center faces identity crisis." MPRNews.org. January 07, 2011. www.mprnews.org/story/2011/01/07/district-202.

Baran, Madeleine, Sasha Aslanian, and Curtis Gilbert. "Minnesota voters reject marriage amendment." MPRNews.org. November 07, 2012. www.mprnews.org/story/2012/11/06/politics/elex-night-marriage-amendment.

Belstler, Dot. "2018 Pride Guide; The Twin Cities Pride Magazine." Issuu.com. May 31, 2018. issuu.com/dotbelstler/docs/2018_prideguide_final.

Birkey, Andy. "Bragging on Minneapolis: The top 10 ways the city made LGBT history." TheColu.MN. July 15, 2014. thecolu.mn/12876/bragging-minneapolis-top-10-ways-city-made-lgbt-history.

Bisexual Organizing Project. "About the Bisexual Organizing Project." BisexualOrganizingProject.org. www.bisexualorganizingproject.org/about.html.

Bisexual Organizing Project. "Because." BisexualOrganizingProject.com. www.bisexualorganizingproject.org/because.html.

Blount, Rachel. "Transgender athlete Allums opens new doors." StarTribune.com. November 14, 2010. www.startribune.com/transgender-athlete-allums-opens-new-doors/107820834.

Bromstad, David. "About." Bromstad.com. bromstad.com/about.

Brown, Curt. "Now the real gay marriage fight is on." StarTribune.com. September 02, 2012. www.startribune.com/now-the-real-gay-marriage-fight-is-on/122426949.

Bush Foundation. "Rainbow Health Initiative." BushFoundation.org. www.bushfoundation.org/rainbow-health-initiative.

Carlson, Angie. "Sex Becomes Him." IndyWeek.com. August 08, 2001. web.archive.org/web/20090226213555/www.indyweek.com/gyrobase/Content?oid=oid%3A16264.

CNN Library. "Prince Fast Facts." CNN.com. September 02, 2018. www.cnn.com/2015/08/23/us/prince-fast-facts/index.html.

Collins, Jon. "Transgender candidates win Mpls. City Council seats, make history." MPRNews.org. November 08, 2017. www.mprnews.org/story/2017/11/08/minneapolis-elects-transgender-candidates-to-city-council.

Compton, Julie. "Gay Couple Pens Memoir After 45 Years of Marriage." NBCNews.com. October 10, 2016. www.nbcnews.com/feature/nbc-out/gay-couple-pens-memoir-after-45-years-marriage-n660831.

Constitutional Law Reporter. "Baker v. Nelson: The Often Forgotten Supreme Court Same-Sex Marriage Case." ConstitutionalLawReporter.com. December 20, 2012. constitutionallawreporter.com/2012/12/20/baker-v-nelson-the-often-forgotten-supreme-court-same-sex-marriage-case.

Cruikshank, Margaret. "Fierce with Reality: Literature on Aging." CriticalGerontology.com. February 24, 2017. criticalgerontology.com/author/mcruikshank.

Dupuy, Beatrice. "Pipeline protesters angry with Hennepin County sheriff pack Minneapolis City Hall." StarTribune.com. October 29, 2016. www.startribune.com/pipeline-protesters-pack-minneapolis-city-hall/399110951/#1.

Dyslin, Amanda. "Human rights activist Jacob Reitan has led nationwide battles." MankatoFreePress.com. May 29, 2017. www.mankatofreepress.com/news/local_news/human-rights-activist-jacob-reitan-has-led-nationwide-battles/article_76f90532-4183-11e7-95cb-7394718a5e15.html.

Farrow, Kenyon. "Tori Fixx: Hip Hop's Homo Revolution." NewNowNext.com. March 22, 2007. www.newnownext.com/tori-fixx-hip-hops-homo-revolution/03/2007.

Freedom to Marry. "The Freedom to Marry in Minnesota." FreedomtoMarry.org. www.freedomtomarry.org/states/minnesota.

Goodrich, Kristine. "MSU's pioneering LGBT Center celebrates 40 years." MankatoFreePress.com. April 12, 2018. www.mankatofreepress.com/news/local_news/msu-s-pioneering-lgbt-center-celebrates-years/article_9d0e6e00-3df5-11e8-ab61-07288d61c779.html.

Haggerty, George and Bonnie Zimmerman. Encyclopedia of Lesbian and Gay Histories and Cultures. New York, NY: Garland Publishing Inc., 2000.

Holdgrafter, George. "Quatrefoil Library Moves to Minneapolis: Outstanding GLBT Resource Serves as Community Gathering Space." LavenderMagazine.com. November 27, 2013. www.lavendermagazine.com/our-affairs/quatrefoil-library-moves-to-minneapolis-outstanding-glbt-resource-serves-as-community-gathering-space.

Huffington Post. "Jacob Reitan." HuffPost.com. www.huffpost.com/author/jacob-reitan.

IMDb. "Chi Chi LaRue." IMDb.com. www.imdb.com/name/nm0479001/?ref_=tt_ov_dr.

IMDb. "David Bromstad." IMDb.com. www.imdb.com/name/nm2303410/?ref_=nv_sr_1.

Indigenous Peoples Task Force. "About IPTF." IndigenousPeoplesTF.org. indigenouspeoplestf.org/about-iptf.

Just Us Health. "Minnesota AIDS Project and Rainbow Health Initiative Merge." JustUsHealth.org. May 02, 2018. www.justushealth.org/news/minnesota-aids-project-and-rainbow-health-initiative-merge.

King, Maraya. "UMN Tretter Collection finds national recognition." MNDaily.com. June 08, 2017. www.mndaily.com/article/2017/06/university-tretter-collection-receives-national-award.

LaBaton, Stephen. "Military Rebuffed by Appeals Court over Homosexuals." NYTimes.com. November 17, 1993. www.nytimes.com/1993/11/17/us/military-rebuffed-by-appeals-court-over-homosexuals.html.

Lavender Magazine. "About Lavender." LavenderMagazine.com. www.lavendermagazine.com/media-kit/about.

LaRue, Chi Chi. "About Me." ChiChiLaRue.com. www.chichilarue.com/about-me.

Lee, Ryan. "Godfather of gay rap." Southern Voice. December 12, 2008. archive.is/20081215151645/www.southernvoice.com/2008/12-12/arts/music/9570.cfm.

Lesbian, Gay, Bisexual, Transgender Center at the University of Minnesota, Mankato. "Jim Chalgren." MNSU.edu. www.mnsu.edu/lgbtc/imhalgren.html.

Margolin, Emma. "How Minneapolis Became First U.S. City to Pass Trans Protections." NBCNews.com. June 03, 2016. www.nbcnews.com/feature/nbc-out/how-minneapolis-became-first-u-s-city-pass-trans-protections-n585291.

Minneapolis City Council. "About Andrea Jenkins." CI.Minneapolis.MN.US. September 17, 2018. www.ci.minneapolis.mn.us/ward8/about-andrea.

Minnesota Legislative Reference Library. "Clark, Karen J." Leg.State.MN.us. www.leg.state.mn.us/legdb/fulldetail?id=10101.

Molloy, Parker Marie. "Going to a Prison Made CeCe McDonald Want to Fix Them." Advocate.com. July 30, 2014. www.advocate.com/40-under-40-emerging-voices/2014/07/30/40-under-40-prison-turned-cece-mcdonald-activist.

National Women's Hall of Fame. "Ann Bancroft." GreatWomen.org. web.archive.org/web/20130404160154/www.greatwomen.org/women-of-the-hall/search-the-hall/details/2/15-Bancroft.

Nevius, C. W. "James Hormel to be honored as early hero of gay rights." SFChronicle.com. March 04, 2016. www.sfchronicle.com/bayarea/nevius/article/Hormel-heir-to-be-honored-for-gay-rights-fight-6871408.php.

Office of Communications at Humphrey School of Public Affairs. "Former Humphrey School Assistant Dean Named to the Minnesota Supreme Court." HHH.UMN.edu. January 26, 2016. www.hhh.umn.edu/news/former-humphrey-school-assistant-dean-named-minnesota-supreme-court.

OutFront Minnesota. "Leading MN Towards LGBTQ Equality." www.outfront.org.

OutFront Minnesota. "Legal Help." OutFront.org. www.outfront.org/legal-help.

Paisley Park. "About Paisley Park." OfficialPaisleyPark.com. officialpaisleypark.com/pages/about.

Poetry Foundation. "Danez Smith." PoetryFoundation.org. www.poetryfoundation.org/poets/danez-smith.

Poetry Foundation. "Hieu Minh Nguyen." PoetryFoundation.org. www.poetryfoundation.org/poets/hieu-minh-nguyen.

Pride Institute. "Our Locations." Pride-Institute.com. pride-institute.com/about/lgbt-treatment-centers-locations.

Pride Twin Cities. "Twin Cities Pride." tcpride.org.

Quatrefoil Library. "History." QLibrary.com. www.qlibrary.org/about-the-library/history.

Reclaim. "Project Clear." www.reclaim.care/project-clear/project-clear.html.

Reclaim. "What We Do." Reclaim.care. www.reclaim.care/what-we-do/overview.html.

Rivas, Jorge. "Activist and Poet William Brandon Lacy Campos Dies at 35." ColorLines.com. November 12, 2012. www.colorlines.com/articles/activist-and-poet-william-brandon-lacy-campos-dies-35.

Rosengren, John. "Sacred Rights of the International Two Spirit Gathering." UTNE.com. 2009. www.utne.com/mind-and-body/sacred-rights-of-the-international-two-spirit-gathering-lgbt-native-american-indian-community.

Schmalz, Jeffrey. "On the Front Lines With: Joseph Steffan; From Midshipman To Gay Advocate." NYTimes.com. February 04, 1993. www.nytimes.com/1993/02/04/garden/on-the-front-lines-with-joseph-steffan-from-midshipman-to-gay-advocate.html.

Smith, Danez. "Bio." DanezSmithPoet.com. www.danezsmithpoet.com/bio-encore.

Solomon, Akiba. "CeCe McDonald: Attacked for Her Identity, Incarcerated for Surviving." Ebony.com. May 04, 2012. www.ebony.com/news/cece-mcdonald-bias-attack.

Steinmetz, Katy. "Meet The First Openly Transgender NCAA Division I Athlete." Time.com. October 28, 2014. time.com/3537849/meet-the-first-openly-transgender-ncaa-athlete.

The Bridge for Youth. "LGBTQ Youth and their Families." BridgeforYouth.org. bridgeforyouth.org/find-help/support-groups/lgbt-youth-and-their-families.

The Bridge for Youth. "Our History." BridgeforYouth.org. www.bridgeforyouth.org/behind-the-bridge/history.

The Family Partnership. "2012 Annual Report." TheFamilyPartnership.org. 2012. www.thefamilypartnership.org/wp-content/uploads/2016/02/50657_TFP_2012_Annual_FINAL-Second_Print.pdf.

The New York Times. "In a Lost Legal Battle, Gay Activist Sees Potential Gain." NYTimes.com. November 16, 1997. www.nytimes.com/1997/11/16/nyregion/in-a-lost-legal-battle-gay-activist-sees-potential-gain.html.

Twin Cities Gay Men's Chorus. "38 years of music worth coming out for." TCGMC.org. tcgmc.org/about-us/a-brief-history.

Ubuntu Biography Project. "Andrea Jenkins." UbuntuBiographyProject.com. May 10, 2017. ubuntubiographyproject.com/2017/05/10/andrea-jenkins.

Ubuntu Biography Project. "William Brandon Lacy Campos." UbuntuBiographyProject.com. August 31, 2017. ubuntubiographyproject.com/2017/08/31/william-brandon-lacy-campos.

UMaine Center on Aging. "Margaret (Peg) Cruikshank." MaineCenteronAging.UMaine.edu. mainecenteronaging.umaine.edu/people/margaret-peg-cruikshank.

University of Minnesota Libraries. "The Jean-Nickolaus Tretter Collection in Gay, Lesbian, Bisexual and Transgender Studies." Lib.UMN.edu. www.lib.umn.edu/tretter.

US Department of State. "Biography: James C. Hormel." 1997-2001.state.gov. 1997-2001.state.gov/about_state/biography/hormel_james.html.

Waldron, Travis. "Major League Soccer Player Collin Martin Comes Out As Gay." HuffPost.com. June 29, 2018. www.huffpost.com/entry/collin-martin-mls-comes-out-as-gay_n_5b364d8ae4b08c3a8f69c3e5.

Mississippi

Academy of Television Arts & Sciences. "Jonathan Murray." Emmys.com. www.emmys.com/bios/jonathan-murray.

Al-Mohamed, Day. "Black #Disability History: Richmond Barthé, Sculptor of the Harlem Renaissance." LeadOnNetwork.org. February 13, 2016. leadonnetwork.org/wordpress/2016/02/13/black-disability-history-richmond-barthe-sculptor-of-the-harlem-renaissance.

Barnett, Todd. "Tennessee Williams (1911-1983)." SHSMO.org. shsmo.org/historicmissourians/name/w/williams.

Bass, Erin Z. "Douglas Ray's Queer South." DeepSouthMag.com. April 17, 2014. deepsouthmag.com/2014/04/17/douglas-rays-queer-south.

BBC. "Mississippi man jailed for transgender killing." BBC.com. May 16, 2017. www.bbc.com/news/world-us-canada-39938428.

BBC. "UK warns gay travellers about US anti-LGBT laws." BBC.com. April 21, 2016. www.bbc.com/news/world-us-canada-36104879.

Biography.com Editors. "Robin Roberts Biography." Biography.com. April 29, 2014. www.biography.com/personality/robin-roberts.

Biography.com Editors. "Tig Notaro Biography." Biography.com. August 20, 2015. www.biography.com/performer/tig-notaro.

BTL Staff. "Terri O'Connell races toward the checkered flag." PrideSource.com. October 18, 2007. pridesource.com/article/27373.

Campbell, Larrison. "HB 1523 ruling spurs federal judge to revisit gay marriage case." MississippiToday.org. October 02, 2017. mississippitoday.org/2017/10/02/hb-1523-ruling-spurs-federal-judge-reopen-gay-marriage-case.

Campbell, Larrison. "'Religious freedom' law upheld by federal appeals court." MississippiToday.org. June 22, 2017. mississippitoday.

org/2017/06/22/5th-circuit-dismisses-case-against-house-bill-1523.

Clark, Jeff. "16-year-old trans graduate made history at Pass High. Here's why he's leaving Mississippi." SunHerald.com. May 18, 2018. www.sunherald.com/news/local/education/article211325904.html.

Ellis, Ralph, Emanuella Grinberg and Janet DiGiacomo. "Mississippi man sentenced for hate-crime killing of transgender woman." CNN.com. May 16, 2017. www.cnn.com/2017/05/15/us/transgender-hate-crime-murder-sentence-mississippi/index.html.

Food Network. "Cat Cora Bio." FoodNetwork.com. www.foodnetwork.com/profiles/talent/cat-cora/bio.

Grace House Services. "About." GraceHouseMS.org. gracehousems.org/about.

Hayden, Erik. "Robin Roberts Publicly Mentions Relationship With Longtime Girlfriend." HollywoodReporter.com. December 29, 2013. www.hollywoodreporter.com/live-feed/robin-roberts-publicly-mentions-relationship-667862.

IMDb. "Cat Cora." IMDb.com. www.imdb.com/name/nm1752094/bio.

IMDb.com. "Patrik-Ian Polk." IMDb.com. www.imdb.com/name/nm0689319/bio?ref_=nm_ov_bio_sm.

IMDb.com. "Tig Notaro." IMDb.com. www.imdb.com/name/nm0449299/bio?ref_=nm_ov_bio_sm.

Livability. "Tennessee Williams' First Home is Columbus, MS Welcome Center." Livability.com. April 28, 2011. livability.com/ms/columbus/things-to-do/tennessee-williams-first-home-is-columbus-ms-welcome-center.

Martin, Phillip. "ON FILM: Community and Courage." ArkansasOnline.com. August 10, 2007. www.arkansasonline.com/news/2007/aug/10/film-community-and-courage-20070810/?entertainment/movies.

Middleton, Josh. "Trans Organist Desiree Hines Dies of Cancer." PhillyMag.com. January 25, 2013. www.phillymag.com/news/2013/01/25/memoriam-desiree-hines.

Miller, Joshua Rhett. "Bullies drove boy to suicide after he came out as bisexual: family." NYPost.com. March 13, 2018. nypost.com/2018/03/13/bullies-drove-boy-to-suicide-after-coming-out-as-bisexual-family.

Mississippi Rainbow Center. "Lighthouse Community Church." MSRainbowCenter.org. www.msrainbowcenter.org/lighthouse-community-church.

NPR Staff. "Tig Notaro On Her Terrible Year In 'I'm Just A Person'." NPR.org. June 15, 2016. www.npr.org/2016/06/15/482058688/tig-notaro-on-her-terrible-year-in-im-just-a-person.

Parents, Families and Friends of Lesbians and Gays. "PFLAG of Jackson, Mississippi." pflagjacksonms.wordpress.com.

PBS. "Alice Walker: Beauty in Truth." PBS.org. February 14, 2014. www.pbs.org/wnet/americanmasters/alice-walker-biography-and-awards/2894.

PGN Staff. "T. Desiree Hines, Organist and Trans Activist, 33." EPGN.com. January 31, 2013. www.epgn.com/news/obituaries/5550-21574595-t-desiree-hines-organist-and-trans-activist-33.

Poetry Foundation. "Alice Walker." PoetryFoundation.org. www.poetryfoundation.org/poets/alice-walker.

Rose, Lacey. "Reality TV Pioneer Jonathan Murray Talks 'Real World,' Kim Kardashian Marriage Fallout." HollywoodReporter.com. March 30, 2012. www.hollywoodreporter.com/news/bunim-murray-25-years-the-real-world-jonathan-murray-306327.

Shapiro, Lila. "How An 'Anti-Gay' Mississippi Town Stopped A Gay Bar From Opening." HuffPost.com. November 04, 2013. www.huffpost.com/entry/shannon-mississippi-gay-bar_n_4183751.

Summers, Martin. "Richmond Barthé (1901-1988)." BlackPast.org. November 19, 2007. www.blackpast.org/african-american-history/barthe-richmond-1901-1988.

The Columbus-Lowndes Convention and Visitors Bureau. "Tennessee Williams Home & Welcome Center." VisitColumbusMS.org. www.visitcolumbusms.org/places-to-visit/tennessee-williams-home-and-welcome-center-c-1875.

The Editors of Encyclopaedia Britannica. "Alice Walker." Britannica.com. January 12, 2000. www.britannica.com/biography/Alice-Walker.

The Editors of Encyclopaedia Britannica. "Richmond Barthé." Britannica.com. February 15, 2016. www.britannica.com/biography/Richmond-Barthe.

The Spectrum Center. "The Spectrum Center." hattiesburgpride.com.

University Press of Mississippi. "A celebration of the African American modern sculptor." UPress.State.ms.us. www.upress.state.ms.us/books/1122.

Wong, Curtis M. "Lance Bass: 'I Thought I'd Never Be Able To Tell Anyone' I Was Gay." HuffPost.com. May 01, 2018. www.huffpost.com/entry/lance-bass-coming-out-gay-speech_n_5ae8796fe4b02baed1be3a56.

Missouri

Adler, Eric. "Threats, bullying hit family of KC transgender girl on cover of National Geographic." KansasCity.com. December 22, 2016. www.kansascity.com/news/local/article122430344.html.

Admin. "In Loving Memory of Midnight Annie." OurCommunityRoots.com. May 10, 2016. ourcommunityroots.com/?p=34239.

America's Library. "Langston Hughes Was Born February 1, 1902." AmericasLibrary.gov. www.americaslibrary.gov/jb/progress/jb_progress_hughes_2.html.

America's Library. "The Peanut Man." AmericasLibrary.gov. www.americaslibrary.gov/aa/carver/aa_carver_peanut_3.html.

Asher, Levi. "William S. Burroughs." BeatMuseum.org. www.beatmuseum.org/burroughs/williamsburroughs.html.

Baker, Chris. "Dani Bunten Berry: Pioneering Game Designer." Wired.com. January 30, 2007. www.wired.com/2007/01/dani_bunten_ber.

Barnes, Cleve. "Ted Shawn 1891-1972." NYTimes.com. January 16, 1972. www.nytimes.com/1972/01/16/archives/ted-shawn-18911972.html.

Beeson, Dan. "A brief history of George Washington Carver: the greatest 'bisexual' black scientist of his time." GayStarNews.com. February 08, 2018. www.gaystarnews.com/article/george-washington-carver-facts/#gs.bz6633.

Bendix, Trish. "The Fight Over Leslie Feinberg's 'Stone Butch Blues'." IntoMore.com. March 26, 2018. www.intomore.com/culture/The-Fight-Over-Leslie-Feinbergs-Stone-Butch-Blues.

Boom. "About #Boom." Boom.LGBT. June 18, 2014. www.boom.lgbt/index.php/boom-info/about-boom.

Boykin, Keith. "Biography." KeithBoykin.com. www.keithboykin.com/bio.

Breslauer, Jan. "HIV-Positivist: Michael Kearns has made a stage career of his activism, and a successful life in Hollywood—saying the heck with homophobia." LATimes.com. July 03, 1994. www.latimes.com/archives/la-xpm-1994-07-03-ca-11423-story.html.

Business of Home. "Melvin Dwork, interior designer and gay rights icon, dies at 94." BusinessofHome.com. June 20, 2016. businessofhome.com/articles/melvin-dwork-interior-designer-and-gay-rights-icon-dies-at-94.

Cassandra, Rachel and Katie Wudel. "5 Romance Tips From The World's Most Famous Asexual." Good.IS. July 04, 2016. www.good.is/articles/the-sexless-relationship-guru.

Carver, George Washington. "1897 or Thereabouts." NPS.gov. www.nps.gov/gwca/learn/historyculture/upload/1897-Or-Thereabouts-English-8-2010-final.pdf.

CBC Arts. "Decades before Fortnite, Dani Bunten Berry saw the future —and built games to bring people together." CBC.ca. June 21, 2018. www.cbc.ca/arts/decades-before-fortnite-dani-bunten-berry-saw-the-future-and-built-games-to-bring-people-together-1.4716790.

Cinema St. Louis. "QFest St. Louis." CinemaStLouis.org. 2019. www.cinemastlouis.org/qfest.

CMG Worldwide. "Josephine Baker." CMGWW.com. www.cmgww.com/stars/baker/about/biography.

Crossroads College Preparatory School. "Graduate David Jay to Speak at Crossroads." CrossroadsCollegePrep.org. April 08, 2015. crossroadscollegeprep.org/archives/5024.

Daues, Jessica. "NGA's Olympian: Librarian was two-time gold medalist, world-record holder." Medium.com. August 05, 2016. medium.com/@NGA_GEOINT/ngas-olympian-librarian-was-two-time-gold-medalist-world-record-holder-804256a5bde4.

Engel, Elizabeth. "Langston Hughes." SHSMO.org. shsmo.org/historicmissourians/name/h/hughes.

Engel, Elizabeth. "Thomas A. Dooley III (1927–1961)." SHSMO.org. shsmo.org/historicmissourians/name/d/dooley.

Feinberg, Leslie. "Self." LeslieFeinberg.net. www.lesliefeinberg.net/self.

Fenske, Sarah. "JJ's Clubhouse Is for Sale." RiverFrontTimes.com. March 22, 2019. www.riverfronttimes.com/artsblog/2019/03/22/jjs-clubhouse-is-for-sale.

Fine, Howard. "FIDM Fashion School Names Verreos, Paul Co-Chairs of Design Program." LABusinessJournal.com. August 01, 2018. labusinessjournal.com/news/2018/aug/01/fidm-fashion-school-names-verreos-paul-co-chairs-d.

Fox, Margalit. "Thomas Morgan, a Journalist and Activist, Dies at 56." NYTimes.com. December 27, 2007. www.nytimes.com/2007/12/27/nyregion/27morgan.html.

Freedom for All Americans. "Longtime LGBTQ Advocate Masen Davis to Serve as New Freedom for All Americans CEO." FreedomforAllAmericans.org. October 25, 2017. www.freedomforallamericans.org/longtime-lgbtq-advocate-masen-davis-to-serve-as-new-freedom-for-all-americans-ceo.

Frost, Karen. "Bisexual Civil Rights Champion Josephine Baker." AfterEllen.com. December 07, 2017. www.afterellen.com/people/527011-queer-history-josephine-baker.

Gorenfeld, John. "Get behind the M.U.L.E." Salon.com. March 19, 2003. www.salon.com/2003/03/18/bunten.

Holmes, Elizabeth. "Andy Cohen Is Tired of Being 'Dad Shamed' by 'Momsplainers'." NYTimes.com. March 16, 2019. www.nytimes.com/2019/03/16/style/andy-cohen-is-tired-of-being-dad-shamed-by-momsplainers.html.

Huffington Post. "Masen Davis." HuffPost.com. www.huffpost.com/author/masen-davis.

Huntington Theatre Company. "John McDaniel." HuntingtonTheatre.org. October 2018. www.huntingtontheatre.org/artists/john-mcdaniel.

Jacob's Pillow Dance. "Modern Dance Pioneer Ted Shawn." JacobsPillow.org. www.jacobspillow.org/about/pillow-history/ted-shawn.

James, Danielle. "Fashion Designer Nick Verreos Talks 'Passion For Fashion' And How To Achieve Fashion Success." TheBeatDFW.com. September 2016. thebeatdfw.com/2920024/fashion-designer-nick-verreos-talks-passion-for-fashion-and-how-to-achieve-fashion-success.

JJ's Clubhouse. "Welcome Home Bears and Cubs!" JJsClubhouse.com. www.jjsclubhouse.com.

Johnson, Chris. "Former Obama LGBT liaison named PFLAG executive director." WashingtonBlade.com. January 17, 2019. www.washingtonblade.com/2019/01/17/former-obama-lgbt-liaison-named-pflag-executive-director.

King, Mark S. "The Truth is Bad Enough: What Became of the Happy Hustler?" MarkSKing.com. marksking.com/my-fabulous-disease/the-truth-is-bad-enough-what-became-of-the-happy-hustler.

Lambda Literary Foundation. "In Memoriam: Betty Berzon, Anyda Marchant." LambdaLiterary.org. May 14, 2019. web.archive.org/web/20060709125252/www.lambdaliterary.org/memoriam.html.

Macmillan Speakers. "Andy Cohen." MacmillanSpeakers.com. www.macmillanspeakers.com/andycohen-1.

Masterworks Broadway. "John Kander." MasterworksBroadway.com. masterworksbroadway.com/artist/john-kander.

McDaniel, John. "Bio." JohnMcDaniel.com. johnmcdaniel.com/bio.

McFadden, Robert D. "Melvin Dwork, Once Cast From Navy for Being Gay, Dies at 94." NYTimes.com. June 16, 2016. www.nytimes.com/2016/06/17/obituaries/melvin-dwork-once-cast-from-navy-for-being-gay-dies-at-94.html.

Meinzer, Melissa. "Happy Big 3-0, St. Louis LGBT Media!" RiverFrontTimes.com. January 14, 2011. www.riverfronttimes.com/newsblog/2011/01/14/happy-big-3-0-st-louis-lgbt-media.

Moore, Doug. "'World's Oldest Drag Queen' has a Purple Heart and a broken heart—but no plans to leave the stage." STLToday.com. www.stltoday.com/news/local/metro/world-s-oldest-drag-queen-has-a-purple-heart-and/article_e9489a25-e121-50cd-b88d-81b39ab42b12.html#2.

O'Neil, Tim. "A Look Back: The jungle doctor, Tom Dooley, succumbs to cancer in 1961." STLToday.com. January 18, 2014. www.stltoday.com/news/local/govt-and-politics/a-look-back-the-jungle-doctor-tom-dooley-succumbs-to/article_bec381d7-2c9c-5875-a6e1-8d7776342afd.html.

PBS. "John Kander and Fred Ebb." PBS.org. www.pbs.org/wnet/broadway/stars/john-kander-and-fred-ebb.

Penguin Random House. "Keith Boykin." PenguinRandomHouse.com. www.penguinrandomhouse.com/authors/2959/keith-boykin.

PFLAG. "Brian Bond Named New Executive Director of PFLAG National." PFLAG.org. January 17, 2019. pflag.org/press-releases/brian-bond-named-new-executive-director-pflag-national.

Poets. "Langston Hughes." Poets.org. www.poets.org/poetsorg/poet/langston-hughes.

POZ. "The Passing of a Veteran HIV-Positive Journalist." POZ.com. December 28, 2007. www.poz.com/article/thomas-morgan-obit-13740-7622.

Pride St. Louis. "PrideCenter of St. Louis." PrideSTL.org. pridestl.org/community/center.

Publishers Weekly. "Obituary: Barbara Grier, Founder of Naiad Press." PublishersWeekly.com. November 11, 2011. www.publishersweekly.com/

pw/by-topic/industry-news/people/article/49469-obituary-barbara-grier-founder-of-naiad-press.html.

Reigns, Steven. "About Steven." StevenReigns.com. www.stevenreigns.com/about.

Reigns, Steven. "Steven Reigns' Therapy for Adults." TherapyforAdults.com. www.therapyforadults.com.

Schjeldahl, Peter. "The Outlaw." NewYorker.com. January 26, 2014. www.newyorker.com/magazine/2014/02/03/the-outlaw-2.

Scolieri, Paul A. "Ted Shawn (1891-1972)." DanceHeritage.org. 2012. new.danceheritage.org/html/treasures/shawn_essay_scolieri.pdf.

Shameless Grounds. "About" ShamelessGrounds.com. shamelessgrounds.com/about.

Skrivan, Laurie. "World's Oldest Drag Queen." STLToday.com. 2018. www.stltoday.com/news/multimedia/pictures/world-s-oldest-drag-queen/collection_c5f67d0e-7af9-52a0-b003-37a34e127e43.html#8.

Stiles, Nancy. "Clementine's, St. Louis' Oldest Gay Bar, is Closing Sept. 28." RiverFrontTimes.com. September 26, 2014. www.riverfronttimes.com/foodblog/2014/09/26/clementines-st-louis-oldest-gay-bar-is-closing-sept-28.

St. Louis LGBT History Project. "About." StLouisLGBTHistory.com. www.stlouislgbthistory.com/about.html.

St. Louis LGBT History Project. "The St. Louis LGBT History Project." stlgayhistory.livejournal.com.

The Grove. "About." TheGroveSTL.com. thegrovestl.com/about.

The New School Archives Digital Collections. "Melvin Dwork." DigitalArchives.Library.NewSchool.edu. digitalarchives.library.newschool.edu/index.php/Detail/people/239.

The Transgender Institute. "About Us." TransInstitute.org. transinstitute.org/about-us.

The Vital Voice. "History." TheVitalVoice.com. www.thevitalvoice.com/about-us/history.

Trans-Parenting. "Trans-Parenting." www.trans-parenting.com.

Trout, Carilynn and Jillian Hartke. "Helen Stephens (1918-1994)." SHSMO.org. shsmo.org/historicmissourians/name/s/stephens.

Walsh, Chris M. "Chely Wright Comes Out As Country Music's First Openly Gay Singer." Billboard.com. May 04, 2010. www.billboard.com/articles/news/958369/chely-wright-comes-out-as-country-musics-first-openly-gay-singer.

Woo, Elaine. "Betty Berzon, 78; Writer, Psychotherapist, Activist Helped Establish L.A. Gay & Lesbian Center." LATimes.com. January 25, 2006. www.latimes.com/archives/la-xpm-2006-jan-25-me-berzon25-story.html.

Wright, Chely. "Biography." Chely.com. www.chely.com/biography.

Wright, Chely. "Confessions of a Gay Christian Country Singer." HuffPost.com. June 24, 2011. www.huffpost.com/entry/gay-christian-country-singer_b_880736.

Montana

Bitter Root Cabins. "Nez Perce Ranch." BitterRootCabins.com. bitterrootcabins.com/nez-perce-ranch.

Gender Expansion Project. "Gender Expansion Project." genderexpansion.tumblr.com.

Lazy E-L Ranch. "Lazy E-L Ranch." LasyEL.com. www.lazyel.com.

Montana Human Rights Network. "LGBTQ Equality Project." MHRN.org. mhrn.org/equality-project.

Swan-Perkins, Samuel White. "5 Two-Spirit Heroes Who Paved the Way for Today's Native LGBTQ+ Community." KQED.org. November 20, 2018. www.kqed.org/arts/13845330/5-two-spirit-heroes-who-paved-the-way-for-todays-native-lgbtq-community.

Nebraska

ACLU. "Stewart and Stewart v. Heineman." ACLU.org. August 05, 2015. www.aclu.org/cases/stewart-and-stewart-v-heineman.

Associated Press. "Pastor Defrocked for Holding Gay Marriage." NYTimes.com. November 18, 1999. www.nytimes.com/1999/11/18/us/pastor-defrocked-for-holding-gay-marriage.html.

Blay, Zeba. "Roxane Gay Is The Lead Writer Of A Marvel Comic. Here's Why That's Huge." HuffPost.com. July 29, 2016. www.huffpost.com/entry/roxane-gay-is-the-lead-writer-of-a-marvel-comic-heres-why-thats-huge_n_579b9aefe4b08a8e8b5df764.

Campaign for Nebraska. "Student awarded first Louis Crompton Scholarship; organizers hope to endow scholarship this year." CampaignforNebraska.org. August 07, 2013. web.archive.org/web/20140223142330/campaignfornebraska.org/stories/-/asset_publisher/qFL02b8zoBTe/content/student-awarded-first-louis-crompton-scholarship-organizers-hope-to-endow-scholarship-this-year.

Creech, Jimmy. "Jimmy Creech." LGBTQReligiousArchives.org. February 06, 2003. lgbtqreligiousarchives.org/profiles/jimmy-creech.

Criss, C.C. Dr. and Mabel L. Criss. "GAY FREEDOM, Issue #1." QueerOmahaArchives.Omeka.Net. August 19, 1972. queeromahaarchives.omeka.net/items/show/3207.

Daehn, Veronica. "Sigma Nu refuses to comment about article on gay member." DailyNebaskan.com. October 19, 2000. www.dailynebraskan.com/sigma-nu-refuses-to-comment-about-article-on-gay-member/article_c1af0635-e368-5134-a783-3ce819d2d70c.html.

Das, Lina. "I felt raped by Brando." DailyMail.co.uk. July 19, 2007. www.dailymail.co.uk/tvshowbiz/article-469646/I-felt-raped-Brando.html.

Feeney, Nolan. "This 66-Year-Old Woman Is Suing All Gay People—Yes, All of Them." Time.com. May 06, 2015. time.com/3848666/nebraska-woman-sues-gays.

Gabriel, Davina Anne. "Brandon Teena Murderer Sentenced." BrandonTeena.org. February 21, 1996. brandonteena.org/?option=com_content&view=article&Itemid=120&id=57:brandon-teena-murderer-sentenced.

Gugliemi, Jodi. "Did Richard Pryor and Marlon Brando Have Sex? What We Know About the Rumor Rocking Hollywood." People.com. February 13, 2018. people.com/movies/richard-pryor-and-marlon-brando-everything-we-know.

Huffington Post. "Eric Lueshen." HuffPost.com. www.huffpost.com/author/eric-lueshen. —

Imperial Court of Nebraska. "ICON History." ImperialCourtofNebraska.org. www.imperialcourtofnebraska.org/history.

Jerrett, Greg. "Dominique Morgan." OmahaMagazine.com. January 15, 2016. omahamagazine.com/articles/tag/queer-people-of-color-qpoc.

Kelly, Michael. "A trailblazer reaches the end of one trail." Omaha.com. May 15, 2014. www.omaha.com/eedition/sunrise/articles/a-trailblazer-reaches-the-end-of-one-trail/article_25209d7b-6ee1-53da-a9d6-40b0e51a63ca.html.

Laird, Cynthia. "Gay studies expert Louis Crompton dies." eBAR.com. July 29, 2009. www.ebar.com/news///240087.

Lincoln Bi Community. "About." Facebook.com. www.facebook.com/pg/lincoln.bi.community/about/?ref=page_internal.

Lueshen, Eric. "The Gay Kicker and the Homophobe." OutSports.com. November 03, 2014. www.outsports.com/2014/11/3/7079073/eric-lueshen-gay-nebraska-football-player-homophobia-profile.

Martin, Michel. "Malcolm X's Daughter Disputes Claims in New Bio on Father." NPR.org. April 20, 2011. www.npr.org/2011/04/20/135570322/malcolm-xs-daughter-addresses-controversial-claims-in-new-bio-on-father.

McArdle, Molly. "The Rise of Roxane Gay." BKMag.com. February 22, 2017. www.bkmag.com/2017/02/22/rise-roxane-gay.

Mink, Jessica. "Jessica D. Mink." Harvard.edu. November 13, 2015. tdc-www.harvard.edu/mink.

Minkowitz, Donna. "How I Broke, and Botched, the Brandon Teena Story." VillageVoice.com. June 20, 2018. www.villagevoice.com/2018/06/20/how-i-broke-and-botched-the-brandon-teena-story.

Nebraska AIDS Project. "Nebraska AIDS Project." www.nap.org.

NPR/TED Staff. "Roxane Gay: What Does It Mean To Identify As A Feminist?" NPR.org. June 15, 2018. www.npr.org/2018/06/15/619933829/roxane-gay-what-does-it-mean-to-identify-as-a-feminist.

OutLinc. "OutLinc Expanding to OutNebraska." OutLinc.org. outlinc.org/outlinc-expanding-to-outnebraska.

Painter, George. "The Sensibilities of Our Forefathers." GLAPN.org. August 10, 2004. www.glapn.org/sodomylaws/sensibilities/nebraska.htm.

Panic Bar. "Panic!" PanicBar.com. www.panicbar.com.

Patrice, Joe. "Surprisingly, Lawsuit Against 'All Homosexuals' Summarily Dismissed." AbovetheLaw.com. May 07, 2015. abovethelaw.com/2015/05/surprisingly-lawsuit-against-all-homosexuals-summarily-dismissed.

Queer Omaha Archives. "Queer Omaha Archives." queeromahaarchives.omeka.net.

Queer People of Color Nebraska. "About." Facebook.com. www.facebook.com/pg/QPOCNebraska/about/?ref=page_internal.

Revolvy. "Jessica Mink." Revolvy.com. www.revolvy.com/page/

Jessica-Mink?cr=1.

Roper & Sons. "Dr. Louis Crompton." RoperandSons.com. roperandsons.com/dr-louis-crompton.

Schulberg, Budd. "The King Who Would Be Man." VanityFair.com. March 2005. www.vanityfair.com/news/2005/03/brando200503?verso=true.

Star City Pride. "About." Facebook.com. www.facebook.com/pg/starcitypride/about/?ref=page_internal.

Star City Pride. "Star City Pride." starcitypride.org.

Tatchell, Peter. "Malcolm X was bisexual. Get over it." TheGuardian.com. October 20, 2009. www.theguardian.com/commentisfree/cifamerica/2009/oct/20/malcolm-x-bisexual-black-history.

Tetreault, Pat and Jacy Farris. "40 Years of History in the Heartland: UNL and Lincoln, Nebraska." OutHistory.org. outhistory.org/exhibits/show/unl/2000s.

The Daily Nebraskan. "No comment." DailyNebraskan.com. October 19, 2000. www.dailynebraskan.com/no-comment/article_87c13854-3610-5737-8f01-a5a3ca8a28fe.html.

TransLNK. "About." Facebook.com. www.facebook.com/pg/translnk/about/?ref=page_internal.

Urban League of Nebraska. "Youth Diversity Leadership Summit: Growing Roots." UrbanLeagueNeb.org. April 29, 2016. www.urbanleagueneb.org/event/youth-diversity-leadership-summit-growing-roots.

Wegener, Luke. "LGBTQ+: Interview with Meredith Bacon." QueerOmahaArchives.Omeka.Net. September 21, 2016. queeromahaarchives.omeka.net/items/show/3286.

WGLE. "WGLE interviews: Jessica Mink." SGMA.AAS.org. sgma.aas.org/interview_mink_full.html.

Nevada

Araujo, Nelson. "We've Reached Landmark Decisions For The LGBTQ Community. Let's Move Forward, Not Backwards." HuffPost.com. October 03, 2016. www.huffpost.com/entry/weve-reached-landmark-decisions-for-the-lgbtq-community_b_57f2a06be4b0972364deba77.

Auer, Jeff. "READING: 'Queerest Little City in the World: LGBT Reno During the 1960s." SundanceBookstore.com. www.sundancebookstore.com/natlparks.

Auer, John Jeffrey IV. "Queerest Little City in the World: LGBTQ Reno." NPS.gov. www.nps.gov/articles/lgbtqtheme-reno.htm.

Ballotpedia. "David Parks." Ballotpedia.org. ballotpedia.org/David_Parks.

Ballotpedia. "Lauren Scott." Ballotpedia.org. ballotpedia.org/Lauren_Scott.

Cherub, Sandra. "New Nevada Supreme Court justice has 'pursuit of justice' in her heart." ReviewJournal.com. March 09, 2017. www.reviewjournal.com/news/politics-and-government/nevada/new-nevada-supreme-court-justice-has-pursuit-of-justice-in-her-heart.

Dummy. "Shamir interview: 'I was that kid who would play with action figures, then my Easy-Bake Oven'." DummyMag.com. May 15, 2013. www.dummymag.com/features/shamir-bailey-interview.

Gilchrist, Tracy E. "True Blood's Rutina Wesley Comes Out in Heartfelt Instagram Engagement Post." Advocate.com. November 20, 2017. www.advocate.com/television/2017/11/20/true-bloods-rutina-wesley-comes-out-heartfelt-instagram-engagement-post.

Hill, Libby. "'Fresh Off the Boat' showrunner Nahnatchka Khan keeps cool no matter how rocky things might get." LATimes.com. March 24, 2016. www.latimes.com/entertainment/tv/la-ca-st-conversation-20160327-story.html.

Housman, Steven M. "C. Jay Cox: Man With A Mission." StevenHousman.com. January 2004. www.stevenhousman.com/Profiles/CJayCox.html.

HRC Staff. "A Banner Day for LGBTQ Civil Rights on Equality Day in Nevada." HRC.org. April 07, 2017. www.hrc.org/blog/a-banner-day-for-lgbtq-civil-rights-on-equality-day-in-nevada.

HRC Staff. "Human Rights Campaign Endorses Nelson Araujo for Nevada Secretary of State." HRC.org. March 22, 2018. www.hrc.org/blog/hrc-endorses-nelson-araujo-for-nv-secretary-of-state.

Lamphier, Jason. "Hot List: Shamir." Out.com. May 07, 2015. www.out.com/hot-list/2015/5/04/hot-list-shamir.

Mizoguchi, Karen. "Heroes Alum Thomas Dekker Reveals He's Gay After He Says a 'Prominent Gay Man' Tried to Out Him." People.com. July 13, 2017. people.com/celebrity/thomas-dekker-reveals-hes-gay.

Nevada Department of Employment, Training, and Rehabilitation. "Nevada Equal Rights Commission." DETR.State.NV.us. detr.state.nv.us/nerc.htm.

Nevada Legislative Counsel Bureau. "AB99 Overview." Leg.State.NV.us. 2017. www.leg.state.nv.us/App/NELIS/REL/79th2017/Bill/4812/Overview.

Our Center. "Welcome to Our Center." ourcenterreno.org.

Rahman, Ray. "The Executive Producer with a Fresh Perspective." TIME.com. 2017. time.com/collection/american-voices-2017/4480476/nahnatchka-khan-fresh-off-the-boat.

Reno Gay Pride. "The Reno Gay Pride Festival." renogaypride.com.

The Gay and Lesbian Community Center of Southern Nevada. "Mission and History." TheCenterLV.org. thecenterlv.org/about/mission.

The Liberace Mansion. "About The Liberace Mansion." TheLiberaceMansion.com. theliberacemansion.com/about-us.

Up Closed. "About Thomas Dekker." UpClosed.com. upclosed.com/people/thomas-dekker-1.

Us Weekly Staff. "Rutina Wesley: 25 Things You Don't Know About Me." UsMagazine.com. June 28, 2013. www.usmagazine.com/celebrity-news/news/rutina-wesley-25-things-you-dont-know-about-me-2013286.

Willis, Stacy J. "Despite 12 years of service, gay state senator David Parks still faces many hurdles in Nevada." LasVegasSun.com. January 26, 2010. lasvegassun.com/news/2010/jan/26/despite-12-years-service-gay-state-senator-david-p.

New Hampshire

Ballotpedia. "David Pierce." Ballotpedia.org. ballotpedia.org/David_Pierce_(New_Hampshire_Senate).

Ballotpedia. "Raymond Buckley." Ballotpedia.org. ballotpedia.org/Raymond_Buckley.

Equality Health Center. "About." EqualityHC.org. www.equalityhc.org/about.html.

Gates, Anita. "A Musical's Star Plays, and Admires, Warhol." NYTimes.com. December 11, 2009. www.nytimes.com/2009/12/13/nyregion/13actorct.html?_r=2.

Griffith, John. "Paul Goodman." FindaGrave.com. www.findagrave.com/memorial/404/paul-goodman.

Johnson, Chris. "Buoyed by Dem wins in NH, Buckley seeks DNC chair post." WashingtonBlade.com. December 22, 2016. www.washingtonblade.com/2016/12/22/buoyed-democratic-wins-buckley-seeks-dnc-chair.

MacDowell Colony. "MacDowell Colony." MacDowellColony.org. www.macdowellcolony.org/about.

Mitovich, Matt Webb. "USA Network's Mr. Robot Adds Shield, Queer as Folk and Smash Alums." TVLine.com. May 1, 2015. tvline.com/2015/05/01/usa-networks-mr-robot-cast-recurring.

Out History. "1940 Defense of Homosexuality: 'MILLIONS OF QUEERS (Our Homo America)'." OutHistory.org. outhistory.org/exhibits/show/1940-defense/intro-bernstein.

Phelps, Rob. "Openly transgender candidate elected to Somersworth, NH school board." BostonSpiritMagazine.com. November 13, 2017. bostonspiritmagazine.com/2017/11/openly-transgender-candidate-elected-to-somersworth-nh-school-board.

Radner, Joan. "Interview with Allen Irvin Bernstein [5/16/2012]." Memory.LOC.gov. May 16, 2012. memory.loc.gov/diglib/vhp-stories/loc.natlib.afc2001001.04938/transcript?ID=sr0001.

Robinson, Charlotte. "Maura Healey Talks Historic Campaign for Attorney General in Massachusetts." HuffPost.com. March 13, 2014. www.huffpost.com/entry/maura-healey_b_4947975.

Schoenberg, Shira. "Massachusetts Attorney General candidate Maura Healey says experience in AG's office prepared her for the top job." MassLive.com. October 21, 2013. www.masslive.com/politics/2013/10/massachusetts_attorney_general_4.html.

Scott, A. O. "Gadfly of the '60's, Getting His Due." NYTimes.com. October 18, 2011. www.nytimes.com/2011/10/19/movies/paul-goodman-changed-my-life-directed-by-jonathan-lee-review.html?mtrref=en.wikipedia.org.

Seacoast Outright. "About." SeacoastOutright.org. www.seacoastoutright.org/about.

Tischler, Doug. "Opera's Lesbian Divas." AfterEllen.com. April 20, 2008. www.afterellen.com/people/31274-operas-lesbian-divas.

Women Singing Out. "Women Singing Out!" Facebook.com. www.facebook.com/pg/Women-Singing-Out-83070201223/about/?ref=page_internal.

New Jersey

Alam, Rumaan. "Malcolm Forbes, 'More Than I Dreamed." NYTimes.com. June 8, 2016. www.nytimes.com/2016/06/12/magazine/malcolm-forbes-more-than-i-dreamed.html.

Allen Ginsberg Project. "Bio." AllenGinsberg.org. allenginsberg.org/?page=bio.

Andreeva, Nellie. "Michael Ausiello Teams With Bad Robot for '80s Dramedy Based On His Childhood." Deadline.com. July 24, 2018. deadline.com/2018/07/michael-ausiello-bad-robot-80s-dramedy-based-on-his-childhood-jj-abrams-1202432348.

Back Up. "Alan Keyes' Daughter Coming Out." CBSNews.com. February 13, 2005. www.cbsnews.com/news/alan-keyes-daughter-coming-out.

Becker, Aliza. "Marcia Freedman." AJPeaceArchive.org. August 26, 2015. ajpeacearchive.org/peace-pioneers1/marcia-freedman-2.

Berkowitz, Richard. "Safe Sex Positive." RichardBerkowitz.com. 2018. richardberkowitz.com.

Biography.com Editors. "Kate Pierson." Biography.com. April 2, 2014. www.biography.com/people/kate-pierson-17178786.

Biography.com Editors. "Nathan Lane." Biography.com. April 2, 2014. www.biography.com/people/nathan-lane-9542438.

Board of Governors of the Federal Reserve System. "Federal Reserve Board—Federal Reserve Bank of Atlanta." FederalReserve.gov. www.federalreserve.gov/aboutthefed/federal-reserve-system-atlanta.htm.

Boykin, Keith. "Crossing Jordan." KeithBoykin.com. November 14, 2006. web.archive.org/web/20090222230029/www.keithboykin.com/arch/2006/11/14/crossing_jordan_1.

Brathwaite, Les Fabian. "Saving All Her Love: A New Doc Tackles Whitney Houston's Sexuality." Out.com. August 31, 2017. www.out.com/popnography/2017/8/31/saving-all-her-love-new-doc-tackles-whitney-houstons-sexuality.

Breaking Media. "About." AbovetheLaw.com. March 8, 2010. abovethelaw.com/about.

Buzinski, Jim. "Gay Athlete Climbs Mountains For A Cause." OutSports.com. March 14, 2013. www.outsports.com/2013/3/14/4101450/gay-athlete-cason-crane-mountain-climber-trevor-project-suicide-prevention.

Courage to Connect NJ. "Board of Directors." CouragetoConnectNJ.org. www.couragetoconnectnj.org/board_of_directors.

CTOTOGO. "Jersey City To Become 1st City in New Jersey to Offer Trans-Inclusive Health Benefits." HudsonPride.org. September 25, 2015. hudsonpride.org/2015/09/25/trans-inclusive-health-benefits.

Dale, James. "Why did I challenge the Boy Scouts' anti-gay policy? Because I am a loyal Scout." WashingtonPost.com. February 8, 2013. www.washingtonpost.com/opinions/why-did-i-challenge-the-boy-scouts-anti-gay-policy-because-i-am-a-loyal-scout/2013/02/08/346ebab2-7159-11e2-a050-b83a7b35c4b5_story.html?amp;utm_term=.5aa3001db8b3&noredirect=on&utm_term=.e630ed913b5d.

Davis, Peter. "Amanda Lepore, Confessions From Loving Life as a Living Doll." Observer.com. April 20, 2017. observer.com/2017/04/amanda-lepore-discusses-sex-change-and-more-in-new-book.

Decker, Julie Sondra. "Julie Sondra Decker." JulieSondraDecker.com. juliesondradecker.com/?page_id=247.

Deiorio, Joseph. "Author Michael Ausiello, Spoiler Alert: A Hero Dies." Tapinto.net. November 11, 2017. www.tapinto.net/towns/roselle-roselle-park/categories/press-releases/articles/author-michael-ausiello-spoiler-alert-a-hero-d.

Esnaashari, Farbod. "Fred Rosser drives forward, continues outreach despite leaving Darren Young and WWE behind." ESPN.com. March 9, 2018. www.espn.com/wwe/story/_/id/22702163/even-darren-young-wwe-fred-rosser-continues-lgbtq-anti-bullying-outreach.

Felsenthal, Daniel. "The Baroque Splendor of Christianity Meets East Village Bohemia." HyperAllergic.com. November 30, 2018. hyperallergic.com/473835/thomas-lanigan-tenemental-howl-happening.

Fitness, Shaun T. "Shaun T Fitness." ShaunTFitness.com. shauntfitness.com.

Frey, Jennifer. "Introducing Kwame Anthony Appiah." Blogs.Law.NYU.edu. 2014. blogs.law.nyu.edu/magazine/2014/introducing-kwame-anthony-appiah.

Garden State Equality. "Garden State Equality." GardenStateEquality.org. www.gardenstateequality.org.

Gay Activist Alliance in Morris County. "About GAAMC." GAAMC.org. www.gaamc.org/about.

Gianoulis, Tina. "Gay and Lesbian Alliance Against Defamation." GLBTQ.com. 2012. web.archive.org/web/20121002144000/www.glbtq.com/social-sciences/gay_lesbian_alliance.html.

Ginsberg, Johanna R. "NJ native to lead rabbinical association." NJJewishNews.TimesofIsrael.com. March 20, 2013. njjewishnews.timesofisrael.com/nj-native-to-lead-rabbinical-association.

GLSEN. "GLSEN NJ CELEBRATES NEW AFFIRMING LAW." GLSEN.org. July 24, 2017. www.glsen.org/central-new-jersey-chapter-northern-new-jersey-chapter/article/glsen-new-jersey-chapters-celebrate.

Goldman, Bruce. "Neuroscientist Ben Barres, who identified crucial role of glial cells, dies at 63." Med.Stanford.Edu. December 27, 2017. med.stanford.edu/news/all-news/2017/12/neuroscientist-ben-barres-dies-at-63.html.

Grossman, Anna Jane. "Chris Barley and Marc Kushner." NYTimes.com. April 13, 2012. www.nytimes.com/2012/04/15/fashion/weddings/chris-barley-and-marc-kushner-vows.html.

Hampton, Wilborn. "Allen Ginsberg, Master Poet Of Beat Generation, Dies at 70." NYTimes.com. April 6, 1997. www.nytimes.com/1997/04/06/nyregion/allen-ginsberg-master-poet-of-beat-generation-dies-at-70.html.

Hevesi, Dennis. "Kermit Love, Costume Creator, Dies at 91." NYTimes.com. June 24, 2008. www.nytimes.com/2008/06/24/arts/24love.html.

Holden, Stephen. "Portrait of an Activist." NYTimes.com. June 11, 2009. www.nytimes.com/2009/06/12/movies/12posi.html.

Hudson Pride Center. "Cultural Sensitivity Training." HudsonPride.org. hudsonpride.org/training.

James, George. "Malcolm Forbes, Publisher, Dies at 70." NYTimes.com. February 26, 1990. www.nytimes.com/1990/02/26/obituaries/malcolm-forbes-publisher-dies-at-70.html.

Karni, Annie. "Jim McGreevey 10 years after resigning: 'It's been a messy journey, but I believe this is where I was always meant to be'." NYDailyNews.com. August 09, 2014. www.nydailynews.com/news/politics/jim-mcgreevy-10-years-resigning-nj-governor-meant-article-1.1898226.

Kinsey Institute. "Dr. Alfred C. Kinsey." KinseyInstitute.org. www.kinseyinstitute.org/about/history/alfred-kinsey.php.

Kuperinsky, Amy. "How celebrity trainer Shaun T went from Camden survivor to fitness superstar." NJ.com. August 08, 2016. www.nj.com/entertainment/2016/08/shaun_t_insanity_cize_beachbody_hip_hop_abs.html.

Lane, Julie. "Feminist leader dies at 76." TimesReview.com. June 27, 2008. web.archive.org/web/20111003161111/www2.timesreview.com/ST/Stories/T052208_Alexander_jal.

LeBlanc, M. A. "Orlando Jordan." OnlineWorldofWrestling.com. February 16, 2018. www.onlineworldofwrestling.com/bios/o/orlando-jordan.

Liang, Ellis. "21 Questions With… Carson Crane '17." UniversityPressClub.com. April 1, 2012. www.universitypressclub.com/archive/2012/04/21-questions-with-cason-crane-17.

Lisowski, Joshua. "Walt Whitman's Grave in Harleigh Cemetery." PhiladelphiaEncyclopedia.org. philadelphiaencyclopedia.org/whitman-2.

Martin, Michael. "Guillermo Diaz: Angel of Mercy." Out.com. March 27, 2011. www.out.com/entertainment/television/2011/03/27/guillermo-diaz-angel-mercy.

Miller, Jonathan. "He Fought the Law. They Both Won." NYTimes.com. January 22, 2006. www.nytimes.com/2006/01/22/technology/he-fought-the-law-they-both-won.html.

Mosbergen, Dominique. "Battling Asexual Discrimination, Sexual Violence And 'Corrective' Rape." HuffPost.com. June 20, 2013. www.huffpost.com/entry/asexual-discrimination_n_3380551?1371733068=.

New Jersey Gay Men's Chorus. "New Jersey Gay Men's Chorus." NJGMC.org. www.njgmc.org.

New Jersey Hills. "Gina Genovese elected as Long Hill Mayor." NewJerseyHills.com. January 11, 2006. www.newjerseyhills.com/gina-genovese-elected-as-long-hill-mayor/article_d4eecca8-559e-5de7-b333-3d8db3c23e9e.html.

NewsPlanet Staff. "Frank Part of Starr Review." PlanetOut.com. September 9, 1998. web.archive.org/web/20050129132007/www.planetout.com/news/article-print.html?1998%2F09%2F09%2F5.

Nordyke, Kimberly. "'Star Trek' Star Claims Kevin Spacey Made a Pass at Him at Age 14; Spacey Apologizes, Comes Out as Gay." HollywoodReporter.

com. October 29, 2017. www.hollywoodreporter.com/news/star-trek-star-claims-kevin-spacey-made-a-pass-at-him-at-age-14-1052828.

O'Bryan, Will and Randy Shulman. "Maya Keyes." MetroWeekly.com. February 23, 2005. www.metroweekly.com/2005/02/maya-keyes.

Olya, Gabrielle. "Celebrity Fitness Trainer and Creator of Popular INSANITY Workout Shaun T Responds to Body Shamers Who Called Him Too Skinny." People.com. October 20, 2015. people.com/bodies/shaun-t-responds-to-body-shamers-who-called-him-too-skinny.

Out. "OUT100 2017." Out.com. November 8, 2017. www.out.com/out100-2017/2017/11/08/out100-2017.

Pareles, Jon and Adam Nagourney. "Whitney Houston, Pop Superstar, Dies at 48." NYTimes.com. February 11, 2012. www.nytimes.com/2012/02/12/arts/music/whitney-houston-dies.html?pagewanted=print.

Pavel Zoubok Gallery. "Thomas Lanigan-Schmidt." PavelZoubok.com. pavelzoubok.com/artist/thomas-lanigan-schmidt.

Pierson, Kate. "Kate's Lazy Meadow." LazyMeadow.com. www.lazymeadow.com/index.php?page=story-of-kate-s-lazy-meadow.

Puente, Maria. "Kevin Spacey scandal: A complete list of the 15 accusers." USAToday.com. November 7, 2017. www.usatoday.com/story/life/2017/11/07/kevin-spacey-scandal-complete-list-13-accusers/835739001.

Rapp, Linda. "Frank, Barney (b. 1940)." GLBTQArchive.com. 2004. www.glbtqarchive.com/ssh/frank_b_S.pdf.

Reilly, Richard Byrne. "With $2M in the bank, Architizer hopes to digitize architecture and construction." VentureBeat.com. February 11, 2014. venturebeat.com/2014/02/11/with-2m-in-the-bank-architizer-hopes-to-digitize-architecture-and-construction.

Rishon, Shais. "Black Jews You Should Know, Part 4." TabletMag.com. www.tabletmag.com/scroll/197992/blackjew-you-should-know-4.

Rutledge, Stephen. "#LGBTQ: Doc Film, 'The Death and Life of Marsha P. Johnson' Debuts at Tribeca Film Fest." WorldofWonder.net. April 6, 2017. worldofwonder.net/comingattractions-death-life-marsha-p-johnson.

Saar, Tzafi. "The American Jewish Woman Who Brought Feminism to Israel." Haaretz.com. August 3, 2010. www.haaretz.com/1.5038363.

Schlessigner, Burd. "Dolores Alexander Papers." Asteria.FiveColleges.edu. 2007. asteria.fivecolleges.edu/findaids/sophiasmith/mnsss427.html.

Schnurr, Samantha. "Nathan Lane Marries Devlin Elliott After 18 Years of Dating." EOnline.com. November 20, 2015. www.eonline.com/news/717715/nathan-lane-marries-devlin-elliott-after-18-years-of-dating.

Schudel, Matt. "Ben Barres, transgender brain researcher and advocate of diversity in science, dies at 63." WashingtonPost.com. December 30, 2017. www.washingtonpost.com/amphtml/local/obituaries/ben-barres-transgender-brain-researcher-and-advocate-of-diversity-in-science-dies-at-63/2017/12/30/3b697cba-ebea-11e7-9f92-10a2203f6c8d_story.html.

Signorile, Michelangelo. "The Other Side of Malcolm." *OutWeek,* March 18, 1990.

Speak Out. "Helen Zia." SpeakOutNow.org. www.speakoutnow.org/speaker/zia-helen.

Stenovec, Timothy. "Keith Rabois, COO Of Square, Resigns After Relationship With Employee, Harassment Allegations." HuffPost.com. January 26, 2013. www.huffpost.com/entry/keith-rabois-square-resigns_n_2559017.

Stanford Law and Business Association. "Lunch Talk with Keith Rabois on a Career in Law, Startups and Venture Capital." Law.Stanford.edu. 2015. law.stanford.edu/event/lunch-talk-with-keith-rabois-on-a-career-in-law-startups-and-venture-capital.

The College of Wooster. "Dario Hunter." Wooster.edu. www.wooster.edu/bios/dhunter.

The Paris Review. "A Humorist at Work." TheParisReview.org. 1993. www.theparisreview.org/miscellaneous/1931/a-humorist-at-work-fran-lebowitz.

The Pride Center of New Jersey. "Home." PrideCenter.org. www.pridecenter.org.

Tungol, J. R. "LGBT History Month Icon Of The Day: Marsha P. Johnson." HuffPost.com. October 15, 2012. www.huffpost.com/entry/lgbt-history-month-icon-marsha-p-johnson_n_1955668.

Tyler Clementi Foundation. "Tyler Clementi's Story." TylerClementi.org. tylerclementi.org/tylers-story.

Vilanch, Bruce. "Lane." *Advocate,* February 2, 1999.

Women's Media Center. "Helen Zia: A Disobedient Daughter and Her Passion For Justice." WomensMediaCenter.com. September 9, 2009. web.archive.org/web/20150721210538/www.womensmediacenter.com/blog/entry/helen-zia-a-disobedient-daughter-and-her-passion-for-justice.

Woo, Elaine. "Dr. Joel D. Weisman dies at 66; among the first doctors to detect AIDS." LATimes.com. July 23, 2009. www.latimes.com/nation/la-me-joel-weisman23-2009jul23-story.html.

Yuan, Jada and Aaron Wong. "The First Black Trans Model Had Her Face on a Box of Clairol." TheCut.com. December 14, 2015. www.thecut.com/2015/12/tracey-africa-transgender-model-c-v-r.html.

Zernike, Kate and Marc Santora. "As Gays Wed in New Jersey, Christie Ends Court Fight." NYTimes.com. October 21, 2013. www.nytimes.com/2013/10/22/nyregion/christie-withdraws-appeal-of-same-sex-marriage-ruling-in-new-jersey.html?_r=0.

New Mexico

Aaron, MTPC intern. "Transgender Spotlight: We'wha." Masstpc.org. April 28, 2014. www.masstpc.org/wewha.

ACLU. "Griego v. Oliver—Freedom to Marry in New Mexico." ACLU.org April 25, 2014. www.aclu.org/cases/griego-v-oliver-freedom-marry-new-mexico?redirect=lgbt-rights/griego-v-oliver.

Apache, Crisosto. "Lozen and Dahteste." CrisostoApache.com. December 08, 2011. crisostoapache.com/lozen-and-dahteste.

Bannerman, Ty. "Silent No More: A new monument honors LGBT veterans." Alibi.com. 2014. alibi.com/feature/47040/Silent-No-More.html.

Biography.com Editors. "Neil Patrick Harris Biography." Biography.com. April 01, 2014. www.biography.com/actor/neil-patrick-harris.

Brewer, Graham Lee. "Why marriage equality is a matter of tribal sovereignty." HCN.org. March 30, 2018. www.hcn.org/articles/indian-country-news-why-marriage-equality-is-a-matter-of-tribal-sovereignty.

Bryan, Susan Montoya. "Same-Sex Couples Line Up in Sadoval County To Get Married." ABQJournal.com. February 20, 2004. www.abqjournal.com/news/state/apwed02-20-04.htm.

Common Bond New Mexico. "U-21—Common Bond New Mexico." CommonBondNM.org. commonbondnm.org/u21.

DeBiase, Johanna. "Famous ballet artist retires to Eagle Nest." TaosNews.com. April 27, 2016. taosnews.com/stories/famous-ballet-artist-retires-to-eagle-nest,25730.

Franzen, Trisha. "Differences and Identities: Feminism and the Albuquerque Lesbian Community." *Signs: Journal of Women in Culture and Society* 18, no. 4 (1993).

Garcia, Michelle. "Santa Fe Selects Its First Gay Mayor, Javier Gonzales." Advocate.com. March 05, 2014. www.advocate.com/politics/election/2014/03/05/santa-fe-selects-its-first-gay-mayor-javier-gonzales.

Georgia O'Keeffe Museum. "About the Museum." OKeeffeMuseum.org. www.okeeffemuseum.org/about-the-museum.

Goldman, Carrie. "Generation Bullied 2.0 Book Review." ChicagoNow.com. August 22, 2013. www.chicagonow.com/portrait-of-an-adoption/2013/08/generation-bullied-2-0-book-review.

Graver, David. "'Drunktown's Finest' Director Sydney Freeland On Growing Up Navajo and Trans." Vice.com. February 22, 2015. www.vice.com/en_us/article/xd5n54/trans-and-navajo-drunktowns-finest-999.

Hickey, Nora. "Saying Social: Albuquerque's oldest LGBT club is still going strong." Alibi.com. alibi.com/feature/47053/Staying-Social.html.

Jusino, Teresa. "Interview: *Her Story* Director Sydney Freeland on Trans People Telling Trans Stories." TheMarySue.com. September 09, 2015. www.themarysue.com/tms-interview-her-story-director-sydney-freeland.

Kuffer Law. "The History of LGBT Rights in New Mexico." KufferLaw.com. May 25, 2016. www.kufferlaw.com/the-history-of-lgbt-rights-in-new-mexico.

Kisselgoff, Anna. "Not Only a Partner, a Dynamic Interpreter." NYTimes.com. June 18, 2005. www.nytimes.com/2005/06/18/arts/dance/not-only-a-partner-a-dynamic-interpreter.html.

Last, T.S. "Former mayor is in 'an exciting space'." ABQJournal.com. March 23, 2018. www.abqjournal.com/1149519/in-an-exciting-space-ex-former-sf-mayor-javier-gonzales-considers-his-legacy-ponders-his-future.html.

Loomis, Steve LTC. "New Inclusive Memorial Honors LGBT Veterans." GayMilitarySignal.com. 2014. www.gaymilitarysignal.com/1406Loomis.html.

McCoy, Micah. "Civil Rights Groups Hail Massachusetts Decision Allowing NM Same-Sex Couples to Marry." ACLU-NM.org. May 05, 2010. www.aclu-nm.org/en/news/civil-rights-groups-hail-massachusetts-decision-allowing-nm-same-sex-couples-marry.

Miller, sj. "Gender Identity Expert, sj Miller." sjMiller.info. www.sjmiller.info/about.html.

Nussbaum, Emily. "High-Wire Act." NYMag.com. September 11, 2009. nymag.com/arts/tv/profiles/59002.

Ojibwa. "Hosteen Klah: Navajo Healer, Artist." NativeAmericanNetRoots.net. December 21, 2009. nativeamericannetroots.net/diary/320.

Out History. "Paula Gunn Allen." OutHistory.org. outhistory.org/items/show/1599.

Out History. "Victoria Sigler, Florida, 1995." OutHistory.org. outhistory.org/exhibits/show/out-and-elected/1995/victoria-sigler.

Quintana, Chris. "Zia Regional Rodeo has family feel for gay community." SantaFeNewMexican.com. August 04, 2012. www.santafenewmexican.com/news/local_news/zia-regional-rodeo-has-family-feel-for-gay-community/article_04e64627-ce0b-5305-94fc-74afb857de42.html.

Santos, Fernanda. "New Mexico Becomes 17th State to Allow Gay Marriage." NYTimes.com. December 19, 2013. www.nytimes.com/2013/12/20/us/new-mexico-becomes-17th-state-to-legalize-gay-marriage.html.

Stewart, Jocelyn Y. "Champion of Native American literature." LATimes.com. June 07, 2008. www.latimes.com/archives/la-xpm-2008-jun-07-me-allen7-story.html.

Stockel, H. Henrietta. *Chiricahua Apache Women and Children: Safekeepers of the Heritage.* College Station, TX: Texas A&M University Press, 2000.

Swan-Perkins, Samuel White. "5 Two-Spirit Heroes Who Paved the Way for Today's Native LGBTQ+ Community." KQED.org. November 20, 2018. www.kqed.org/arts/13845330/5-two-spirit-heroes-who-paved-the-way-for-todays-native-lgbtq-community.

The New Mexico Gay Rodeo Association. "About Us." NMGRA.org. January 13, 2014. nmgra.org/about.htm.

The University of New Mexico. "History of the LGBTQ Resource Center." LGBTQRC.UNM.edu. lgbtqrc.unm.edu/about/history.html.

Up Closed. "Victoria Sigler." UpClosed.com. upclosed.com/people/victoria-sigler.

Women's Resource Center. "History of the Women's Resource Center." Women.UNM.edu. women.unm.edu/about/index.html.

Woods, Marco. "U-21 Opens the Door for LGBT Youth." NewMexicoNewsReport.com. April 02, 2018. www.newmexiconewsport.com/u-21-opens-door-lgbt-youth.

Zuni Pueblo Department of Tourism. "Experience Zuni." www.zunitourism.com.

New York

ACT UP. "Capsule History." ACTUPNY.org. www.actupny.org/documents/capsule-home.html.

Alice Austen House. "About the Museum." AliceAusten.org. aliceausten.org/organization.

Ali Forney Center. "About Us." AliForneyCenter.org. www.aliforneycenter.org/about-us.

Amazon. "In the Night Kitchen (Caldecott Collection)." Amazon.com. www.amazon.com/Night-Kitchen-Caldecott-Collection/dp/0064434362.

Amazon. "Pierre: A Cautionary Tale in Five Chapters and a Prologue." Amazon.com. www.amazon.com/Pierre-Cautionary-Tale-Chapters-Pro-logue/dp/0064432521/ref=sr_1_2?keywords=pierre+maurice+senda-k&qid=1551126638&s=books&sr=1-2.

Armus, Teo. "Was Walt Whitman 'gay'? New textbook rules spark LGBTQ history debate." NBCNews.com. November 22, 2017. www.nbcnews.com/feature/nbc-out/was-walt-whitman-gay-new-textbook-rules-spark-lgbtq-history-n821636.

Barajas, Stephanie. "Christine Jorgensen." OutHistory.org. outhistory.org/exhibits/show/tgi-bios/christine-jorgensen.

Baseline Studio Systems. "Harvey Fierstein." PBS.org. www.pbs.org/wnet/broadway/stars/harvey-fierstein.

BET. "BET: C. Riley Snorton is 1 of 10 Transgender People You Should Know." UPress.UMN.edu. June 11, 2014. www.upress.umn.edu/press/press-clips/bet-c-riley-snorton-is-1-of-10-transgender-people-you-should-know.

BiNet USA. "BiNet USA." BiNetUSA.org. www.binetusa.org.

Bluestockings. "About Bluestockings." Bluestockings.com. bluestockings.com.

Bowman, Mark. "Father Mychal Judge—Profile." LGBTQReligiousArchives.org. October 2011. lgbtqreligiousarchives.org/profiles/mychal-judge.

Bradshaw, Don T. "Bio de Bruce." WeGotBruce.com. wegotbruce.com/bio.

htm.

Brantley, Ben. "Her Sequins, Plumes and Foghorn Voice." NYTimes.com. March 28, 2011. www.nytimes.com/2011/03/29/theater/harvey-fierstein-joins-la-cage-aux-folles.html.

Browne, David. "Six Things You Didn't Know About Clive Davis." RollingStone.com. March 04, 2013. www.rollingstone.com/music/music-news/six-things-you-didnt-know-about-clive-davis-194379.

Brumburgh, Gary. "Luther Vandross—Biography." IMDb.com. www.imdb.com/name/nm0005526/bio.

Bullough, Vern L. *Homosexuality: A History.* New York: New American Library. 1979.

Bush, John. "Frankie Knuckles—Biography." AllMusic.com. www.allmusic.com/artist/frankie-knuckles-mn0000793821/biography.

Business of Fashion. "Michael Kors." BusinessofFashion.com. www.businessoffashion.com/community/people/michael-kors.

Callen-Lorde. "About Us." Callen-Lorde.org. callen-lorde.org/about.

Chan, Sewell. "Venerable Bookstore to Close in Village." NYTimes.com. February 3, 2009. www.nytimes.com/2009/02/04/nyregion/04bookstore.html.

Cills, Hazel. "Legendary House DJ Frankie Knuckles Dies at 59." Gawker.com. web.archive.org/web/20140401194819/gawker.com/legendary-house-dj-frankie-knuckles-dies-at-59-1555847551.

Claire, Marie. "Grace Jones' incredibly glamorous life in iconic pictures." MarieClaire.co.uk. May 20, 2016. www.marieclaire.co.uk/news/celebrity-news/inside-the-glamorous-world-of-grace-jones-8312.

Codrea-Rado, Anna. "A Timeline of Christopher Street, New York LGBTQ Nightlife's Most Storied Thoroughfare." Vice.com. June 26, 2016. www.vice.com/en_us/article/d7jdnv/christopher-street-timeline-pride-2016-history.

Colapinto, John. "The Harvey Milk School Has No Right to Exist. Discuss." NYMag.com. February 7, 2005. nymag.com/nymetro/news/features/10970/index5.html.

Commins, John. "Struggling St. Vincent's Hospital is Closing." HealthLeadersMedia.com. April 07, 2010. www.healthleadersmedia.com/strategy/struggling-st-vincents-hospital-closing.

Cook-Daniels, Loree. "Living Memory LGBT History Timeline Current Elders Would Have Been This Old When These Events Happened…" Forge-Forward.org. 2007. forge-forward.org/wp-content/docs/LGBT_elder_timeline_FINAL.pdf.

Cornell University. "C. Riley Snorton." Africana.Cornell.edu. africana.cornell.edu/c-riley-snorton.

Coscarelli, Joe and Sydney Ember. "Jann Wenner and His Biographer Have a Falling Out." NYTimes.com. October 18, 2017. www.nytimes.com/2017/10/18/books/jann-wenner-biography-joe-hagan.html.

Cruz, Eliel. "Remembering Brenda: An Ode to the 'Mother of Pride'." Advocate.com. June 17, 2014. www.advocate.com/bisexuality/2014/06/17/remembering-brenda-ode-%E2%80%98mother-pride%E2%80%99.

Cruz, Wilson. "What am I? Actor Wilson Cruz: My identity is my sword." NBCLatino.com. May 13, 2013. nbclatino.com/2013/05/13/what-am-i-actor-wilson-cruz-my-identity-is-my-sword.

Cumming, Alan. "What I've Won: 2010s." AlanCumming.com. www.alancumming.com/2010s-a.

Cumming, Alan. "Full bio." AlanCumming.com. www.alancumming.com/bio.

Cummings, Mike. "Defending an 'Indecent' play: 'The God of Vengeance' in the Yale University Library archives." News.Yale.edu. October 15, 2015. news.yale.edu/2015/10/15/defending-indecent-play-god-vengeance-yale-university-library-archives-0.

Curbed Staff. "Unraveling the History of Central Park's Bethesda Fountain." NY.Curbed.com. July 16, 2014. ny.curbed.com/2014/7/16/10074022/unraveling-the-history-of-central-parks-bethesda-fountain.

Davis, Clive. "Clive Davis Biography." CliveDavis.com. www.clivedavis.com/bio.

DiMarco, Nyle. "About." NyleDiMarco.com. www.nyledimarco.com/about.

Early, Gerald. "About Countee Cullen's Life and Career." English.Illinois.edu. www.english.illinois.edu/maps/poets/a_f/cullen/life.htm.

Edevane, Gillian. "Who Is Cynthia Nixon's Wife, Christine Marinoni? Actor Announces New York Governor Run." NewsWeek.com. March 19, 2018. www.newsweek.com/who-christine-marinoni-cynthia-nixon-wife-governor-833050.

Encyclopedia of AIDS. "Silence = Death." ACTUPNY.org. www.actupny.org/reports/silencedeath.html.

Equality Forum. "Brenda Howard." LGBTHistoryMonth.com.

lgbthistorymonth.com/brenda-howard?tab=biography.

FDR Library & Museum. "Eleanor Roosevelt Biography." FDRLibrary.org. fdrlibrary.org/er-biography.

Feinberg, Scott. "SXSW: Tab Hunter Opens Up About Life As a Closeted Gay Star During Hollywood's Golden Age." HollywoodReporter. com. March 13, 2015. www.hollywoodreporter.com/race/tab-hunter-opens-up-life-781046.

Fox, Margalit. "Maurice Sendak, Author of Splendid Nightmares, Dies at 83." NYTimes.com. May 8, 2012. www.nytimes.com/2012/05/09/books/maurice-sendak-childrens-author-dies-at-83.html.

Flanagan, Andrew. "Jann Wenner, 'Rolling Stone,' And The Decline Of Rock 'N' Roll." NPR.org. November 2, 2017. www.npr.org/sections/therecord/2017/11/02/561591591/jann-wenner-rolling-stone-and-the-decline-of-rock-n-roll.

Friess, Steve. "From the Poker Table to Wall Street." NYTimes.com. July 27, 2018. www.nytimes.com/2018/07/27/business/vanessa-selbst-poker-bridgewater.html.

Goddard College. "H. Sharif 'Herukhuti' Williams." Goddard.edu. www.goddard.edu/people/h-sharif-williams.

Gonzales, Erica. "This Is How Close Lady Gaga Is to EGOT Status." HarpersBazaar.com. February 24, 2019. www.harpersbazaar.com/celebrity/latest/a25994587/lady-gaga-egot.

GLSEN. "Women's History Month Heroes: Urvashi Vaid." GLSEN.org. www.glsen.org/blog/womens-history-month-heroes-urvashi-vaid.

GMHC. "About Us." GMHC.org. gmhc.org/about-us.

Gray, Sarah. "Here's What You Need to Know About Cynthia Nixon's History of Political Activism." TIME.com. March 19, 2018. time.com/5206095/cynthia-nixon-politics.

Greatest Physiques. "Chris Dickerson." GreatestPhysiques.com. www.greatestphysiques.com/male-physiques/chris-dickerson.

Greenwell, Garth. "James Baldwin's Giovanni's Room: an antidote to shame." TheGuardian.com. November 19, 2016. www.theguardian.com/books/2016/nov/19/james-baldwin-giovannis-room-garth-greenwell-60th-anniversary-gay-novel.

Guardian Film. "Oscar winners 2019: complete list." TheGuardian.com. February 25, 2019. www.theguardian.com/film/2019/feb/25/oscar-winners-2019-the-full-list-live.

Hallowell, Billy. "A Safe Haven for Gay People: Do You Know the History Behind NY's 'Secret' Gay Resort Community?" TheBlaze.com. July 03, 2013. www.theblaze.com/news/2013/07/03/a-safe-haven-for-gay-people-do-you-know-the-history-behind-nys-secret-gay-resort-community.

Hamm, Mia. "Abby Wambach." TIME.com. April 16, 2015. time.com/collection-post/3823298/abby-wambach-2015-time-100.

Hartocollis, Anemona. "The Decline of St. Vincent's Hospital." NYTimes.com. February 2, 2010. www.nytimes.com/2010/02/03/nyregion/03vincents.html.

Herman, Robin. "'No Exceptions,' and No Renee Richards." Archive.NYTimes.com. August 27, 1976. archive.nytimes.com/www.nytimes.com/packages/html/sports/year_in_sports/08.27.html.

Herrera, Ana. "Willi Ninja: Voguing Butch Queen." OutHistory.org. outhistory.org/exhibits/show/tgi-bios/willi-ninja.

Higginbotham, Adam. "Cumming out on top." TheGuardian.com. February 16, 2003. www.theguardian.com/books/2003/feb/16/fiction.film.

History.com Editors. "Eleanor Roosevelt." History.com. November 9, 2009. www.history.com/topics/first-ladies/eleanor-roosevelt.

History.com Editors. "The Stonewall Riots." History.com. May 31, 2017. www.history.com/topics/gay-rights/the-stonewall-riots.

History of American Women. "Emma Stebbins." WomenHistoryBlog.com. May 2015. www.womenhistoryblog.com/2015/05/emma-stebbins.html.

Holland, Brynn. "How Activists Plotted the First Gay Pride Parades." History.com. June 9, 2017. www.history.com/news/how-activists-plotted-the-first-gay-pride-parades.

Holson, Laura M. "The Diarist of a Scene That Never Gets Old." NYTimes.com. January 29, 2010. www.nytimes.com/2010/01/31/fashion/31musto.html.

Housing Works. "About Us." HousingWorks.org. www.housingworks.org/about-us.

Human Rights Watch and interACT. "'I Want to Be Like Nature Made Me'." HRW.org. July 25, 2017. www.hrw.org/report/2017/07/25/i-want-be-nature-made-me/medically-unnecessary-surgeries-intersex-children-us.

IMDb. "Bruce Vilanch." IMDb.com. www.imdb.com/name/nm0897358/?ref_=fn_al_nm_1.

IMDb. "Cynthia Nixon—Biography." IMDb.com. www.imdb.com/name/nm0633223/bio.

IMDb. "David Geffen—Biography." IMDb.com. www.imdb.com/name/nm0311691/bio.

IMDb. "Felipe Rose." IMDb.com. www.imdb.com/name/nm0741377/?ref_=nmbio_bio_nm.

IMDb. "Gore Vidal—Biography." IMDb.com. www.imdb.com/name/nm0000683/bio.

IMDb. "Harvey Fierstein—Biography." IMDb.com. www.imdb.com/name/nm0001213/bio?ref_=nm_ov_bio_sm.

IMDb. "Kate McKinnon." IMDb.com. www.imdb.com/name/nm0571952/?ref_=nmbio_bio_nm.

IMDb. "Leslie Gore—Biography." IMDb.com. www.imdb.com/name/nm0330753/bio.

IMDb. "Michael Kors—Biography. IMDb.com. www.imdb.com/name/nm1824476/bio?ref_=nm_ov_bio_sm.

IMDb. "Michael Musto." IMDb.com. www.imdb.com/name/nm0616003/?ref_=nmbio_bio_nm.

IMDb. "Octavia St. Laurent." IMDb.com. www.imdb.com/name/nm0820732/?ref_=nmbio_bio_nm.

IMDb. "Parvez Sharma." IMDb.com. www.imdb.com/name/nm2204599.

IMDb. "Tab Hunter—Biography." IMDb.com. www.imdb.com/name/nm0002147/bio.

International Federation of Bodybuilding and Fitness. "Chris Dickerson." IFBBPro.com. www.ifbbpro.com/chris-dickerson.

Intersex Campaign for Equality Admin Author. "NYC Issues Second Intersex Birth Certificate!" IntersexEquality.com. June 21, 2017. www.intersexequality.com/nyc-issues-second-intersex-birth-certificate.

INTO. "New Jersey Elects First-Ever Intersex Person to Hold Public Office in U.S." IntoMore.com. November 9, 2017. www.intomore.com/impact/New-Jersey-Elects-FirstEver-Intersex-Person-to-Hold-Public-Office-in-US/3b58450f57784745.

Key Speakers. "Abby Wambach." KeySpeakers.com. keyspeakers.com/bio.php?3730-abby-wambach.

Kilcooley-O'Halloran, Scarlett. "Michael Kors." Vogue.co.uk. January 24, 2013. www.vogue.co.uk/article/michael-kors.

Klebine, Anna. "'Hell Hath No Fury like a Drag Queen Scorned': Sylvia Rivera's Activism, Resistance, and Resilience." OutHistory.org. outhistory.org/exhibits/show/tgi-bios/sylvia-rivera.

Knight, Kyle, Suegee Tamar-Mattis, and MJ Movahedi. "A Changing Paradigm: US Medical Provider Discomfort with Intersex Care Practices." HRW.org. 2017. www.hrw.org/sites/default/files/report_pdf/us_intersex_1017_web.pdf.

Kreps, Daniel. "Lesley Gore, 'It's My Party' Singer, Dead at 68." RollingStone.com. February 16, 2015. www.rollingstone.com/music/music-news/lesley-gore-its-my-party-singer-dead-at-68-166857.

Lambda Legal. "Lambda Legal History." LambdaLegal.org. www.lambdalegal.org/about-us/history.

Lesbian Herstory Archives. "A Brief History." LesbianHerstoryArchives.org. www.lesbianherstoryarchives.org/history.html.

Leslie-Lohman Museum. "Education." LeslieLohman.org. www.leslielohman.org/education.

Lieberman, Charlotte. "Audre Lorde." WritingonGlass.com. www.writingonglass.com/audre-lorde.

Mariner, David. "Wilson Cruz Biography." IMDb.com. www.imdb.com/name/nm0190497/bio.

McDonald, Dionn. "Audre Lorde." OutHistory.org. outhistory.org/exhibits/show/aa-history-month-bios/audre-lorde.

McGrath, Charles. "Gore Vidal Dies at 86; Prolific, Elegant, Acerbic Writer." NYTimes.com. August 1, 2012. www.nytimes.com/2012/08/01/books/gore-vidal-elegant-writer-dies-at-86.html.

McGrath, Kathryn. "Pushed to the Margins." BitchMagazine.org. web.archive.org/web/20071021165745/www.bitchmagazine.org/archives/07_03margins/margins.shtml.

McQuiston, John T. "Christine Jorgensen, 62, Is Dead; Was First to Have a Sex Change." NYTimes.com. May 4, 1989. www.nytimes.com/1989/05/04/obituaries/christine-jorgensen-62-is-dead-was-first-to-have-a-sex-change.html.

Monaghan, Terry. "Obituary: Willi Ninja." TheGuardian.com. September 13, 2006. www.theguardian.com/news/2006/sep/13/guardianobituaries.usa.

National Park Service. "History & Culture—Eleanor Roosevelt." NPS.gov. February 26, 2015. www.nps.gov/elro/learn/historyculture/index.htm.

National Park Service. "Stonewall National Monument." NPS.gov. June 2016. www.nps.gov/places/stonewall-national-monument.htm.

National Women's Hall of Fame. "Our History." WomenoftheHall.org. www.womenofthehall.org/about-the-hall/our-history.

NBC. "Kate McKinnon." NBC.com. www.nbc.com/saturday-night-live/credits/repertory-player/kate-mckinnon.

New Fest. "What We Do." NewFest.org. newfest.org/mission.

News Staff. "June 1972: The Ithaca Statement." BiMedia.org. February 10, 2012. bimedia.org/1984/june-1972-the-ithaca-statement.

New York City AIDS Memorial. "About." NYCAIDSMemorial.org. nycaidsmemorial.org/about.

Nichols, Claire. "Eleanor Roosevelt and journalist Lorena Hickok's love affair addressed in novel White Houses." ABC.net.au. June 28, 2018. www.abc.net.au/news/2018-06-28/eleanor-roosevelt-lorena-hickok-white-houses-love-affair/9918614.

Nittle, Nadra Kareem. "Biography of Artist Jean-Michel Basquiat." May 02, 2018. www.thoughtco.com/jean-michel-basquiat-biography-4147579.

NYC LGBT Historic Sites Project. "Audre Lorde Residence." NYCLGBTSites.org. www.nyclgbtsites.org/site/audre-lorde-residence.

NYC LGBT Historic Sites Project. "James Baldwin Residence." NYCLGBTSites.org. www.nyclgbtsites.org/site/james-baldwin-residence.

NYC LGBT Historic Sites Project. "Lesbian Herstory Archives." NYCLGBTSites.org. www.nyclgbtsites.org/site/lesbian-herstory-archives.

NYC LGBT Historic Sites Project. "Mattachine Society & Daughters of Bilitis Offices." NYCLGBTSites.org. www.nyclgbtsites.org/site/mattachine-society-daughters-of-bilitis-offices.

NYC LGBT Historic Sites Project. "Oscar Wilde Memorial Bookshop." NYCLGBTSites.org. www.nyclgbtsites.org/site/oscar-wilde-memorial-bookshop.

NYC LGBT Historic Sites Project. "Starting Point of First NYC Pride March." NYCLGBTSites.org. www.nyclgbtsites.org/site/starting-point-of-nycs-first-pride-march.

NYC LGBT Historic Sites Project. "Studio 54." NYCLGBTSites.org. www.nyclgbtsites.org/site/studio-54.

NYC LGBT Historic Sites Project. "Transy House." NYCLGBTSites.org. www.nyclgbtsites.org/site/transy-house.

Office of the City Clerk. "Marriage Equality in New York City: Questions and Answers for Same-Sex Couples and All Those Who Wise to Marry Here." CityClerk.NYC.gov. www.cityclerk.nyc.gov/html/marriage/same_sex_couples_faq.shtml.

Ogunnaike, Lola. "Willi Ninja, 45, Self-Created Star Who Made Vogueing Into an Art, Dies." NYTimes.com. September 6, 2006. www.nytimes.com/2006/09/06/arts/dance/06ninja.html.

Panisch, Alex. "Visit Site of James Baldwin's Home in New York's West Village." OutTraveler.com. October 08, 2015. www.outtraveler.com/destination-guide/new-york-city/2015/10/08/visit-site-james-baldwins-home-new-york%E2%80%99s-west-village.

PBS. "About the Author." PBS.org. August 22, 2013. www.pbs.org/wnet/americanmasters/james-baldwin-about-the-author/59.

PFLAG New York City. "About PFLAG NYC." PFLAGNYC.org. www.pflagnyc.org/about.

PMK/HBH and Anastasia Andrew Veno. "Wentworth Miller—Biography." IMDb.com. www.imdb.com/name/nm0589505/bio.

Poetry Foundation. "Countee Cullen." PoetryFoundation.org. www.poetryfoundation.org/poets/countee-cullen.

Poetry Foundation. "James Baldwin." PoetryFoundation.org. www.poetryfoundation.org/poets/james-baldwin.

Poets. "Walt Whitman." Poets.org. www.poets.org/poetsorg/poet/walt-whitman.

Polchin, James. "The Baldwin of Giovanni's Room." GLReview.org. October 29, 2014. glreview.org/article/the-baldwin-of-giovannis-room.

Price, Kenneth M. and Ed Folsom. "About Walt Whitman." English.Illinois.edu. 1995. www.english.illinois.edu/maps/poets/s_z/whitman/bio.htm.

Prickett, Sarah Nicole. "Who Is Marc Jacobs?" NYTimes.com. August 20, 2015. www.nytimes.com/2015/08/20/t-magazine/who-is-marc-jacobs.html.

Queer Music Heritage. "Hamilton Lodge Ball." QueerMusicHeritage.com. November 2014. www.queermusicheritage.com/nov2014hamilton.html.

Recording Academy. "Luther Vandross—Awards." Grammy.com. www.grammy.com/grammys/artists/luther-vandross.

Restauri, Denise. "Top Poker Player Wins $11.6 Million And Goes To Work Thinking She's A Loser." Forbes.com. June 14, 2016. www.forbes.com/sites/deniserestauri/2016/06/14/top-poker-player-wins-11-6-million-and-goes-to-work-thinking-shes-a-loser/#7a63a17254fb.

Reuters. "Luther Vandross Dies At 54." Billboard.com. July 4, 2005. www.billboard.com/articles/news/62200/luther-vandross-dies-at-54.

Reyes, Raul A. "A Forgotten Latina Trailblazer: LGBT Activist Sylvia Rivera." NBCNews.com. October 6, 2015. www.nbcnews.com/news/latino/forgotten-latina-trailblazer-lgbt-activist-sylvia-rivera-n438586.

Reynolds, Daniel. "Is Lady Gaga LGBT or an Ally?" Advocate.com. March 27, 2017. www.advocate.com/media/2017/3/27/lady-gaga-lgbt-or-ally.

Ringel, Lance. "Great Expectations, Unexpected Impact." Stories.Vassar.edu. February 16, 2018. stories.vassar.edu/2018/180216-great-expectations-unexpected-impact.html.

Rock & Roll Hall of Fame. "Clive Davis." RockHall.com. www.rockhall.com/inductees/clive-davis.

SAGE. "Advocating for LGBT Seniors." SAGEUSA.org. www.sageusa.org.

Samuels, Wilfred D. "James Baldwin." BlackPast.org. January 23, 2007. www.blackpast.org/african-american-history/baldwin-james-1924-1987.

Scutti, Susan. "'The protocol of the day was to lie': NYC issues first US 'intersex' birth certificate." CNN.com. January 2, 2017. www.cnn.com/2016/12/30/health/intersex-birth-certificate/index.html.

Shafer, Jack. "The Licentious Life and Times of Jann Wenner." NYTimes.com. November 27, 2017. www.nytimes.com/2017/11/27/books/review/sticky-fingers-joe-hagan-jann-wenner-biography.html.

Sibilla, Nick. "How Liquor Licenses Sparked the Stonewall Riots." Reason.com. June 28, 2015. reason.com/2015/06/28/how-liquor-licenses-sparked-stonewall.

Simmons, Aishah Shahidah. "Feminists We Love: Gloria I. Joseph, Ph.D." TheFeministWire.com. February 28, 2014. www.thefeministwire.com/2014/02/feminists-love-gloria-joseph-ph-d.

Society of Fellows in the Humanities. "Gloria I. Joseph." SocietyofFellows.Columbia.edu. societyoffellows.columbia.edu/speakers/gloria-i-joseph.

Sorway, Bibby. "Marc Jacobs." Vogue.co.uk. March 07, 2012. www.vogue.co.uk/article/marc-jacobs-biography.

Springate, Megan E. "LGBTQ America." NPS.gov. 2016. www.nps.gov/subjects/lgbtqheritage/upload/lgbtqtheme-bisexual.pdf.

Stabbe, Oliver. "Queens and queers: The rise of drag ball culture in the 1920s." AmericanHistory.SI.edu. April 11, 2016. americanhistory.si.edu/blog/queens-and-queers-rise-drag-ball-culture-1920s.

Status PR. "Nyle DiMarco." IMDb.com. www.imdb.com/name/nm6667669/bio.

St. John, Keith. "Keith St. John, New York, 1989." OutHistory.org. outhistory.org/exhibits/show/out-and-elected/late-1980s/keith-st-john.

Struby, Tim. "Her poker face." ESPN.com. June 27, 2013. www.espn.com/poker/story/_/page/Selbst/how-vanessa-selbst-became-best-female-poker-player-all-espn-magazine.

Sylvia Rivera Law Project. "About SRLP." SRLP.org. srlp.org/about.

The Art Story. "Jean-Michel Basquiat." TheArtStory.org. www.theartstory.org/artist-basquiat-jean-michel-life-and-legacy.htm.

The Center. "About." GayCenter.org. gaycenter.org/about.

The Asexual Visiblity and Education Network. "Welcome." Asexuality.org. www.asexuality.org.

The Audre Lorde Project. "About ALP." ALP.org. alp.org/about.

The Franciscans Communications Office. "About Father Mychal." MychalsMessage.org. 2002. www.mychalsmessage.org/aboutfrm/aboutfrm.htm.

The History Makers. "Frankie Knuckles's Biography." TheHistoryMakers.org. www.thehistorymakers.org/biography/frankie-knuckles.

The Local. "AfD youth wing furious over Berlin pride parade ban." TheLocal.de. July 17, 2018. www.thelocal.de/20180717/afd-youth-wing-furious-over-berlin-pride-ban.

The National First Ladies' Library. "First Lady Biography: Eleanor Roosevelt." FirstLadies.org. www.firstladies.org/biographies/firstladies.aspx?biography=33.

The New York Times. "Audre Lorde, 58, A Poet, Memoirist And Lecturer, Dies." NYTimes.com. November 20, 1992. www.nytimes.com/1992/11/20/books/audre-lorde-58-a-poet-memoirist-and-lecturer-dies.html?sq=%22audre+lorde%22&scp=1&st=cse.

The Nyle DiMarco Foundation. "About the Foundation." NyleDiMarcoFoundation.com. nyledimarcofoundation.com/about.

The Trevor Project. "About the Trevor Project." TheTrevorProject.org. www.

thetrevorproject.org/about/#sm.0000t9eed313p1e7lrqxm3742ikc5.

The University of Chicago. "C. Riley Snorton." English.UChicago.edu. english. uchicago.edu/c-riley-snorton.

TIME. "TIME Magazine Covers." Content.TIME.com. May 17, 1963. content. time.com/time/covers/0,16641,19630517,00.html.

Tisdale, Walker III. "Exclusive Conversation with Chris Dickerson." HealthyBlackMen.org. March 20, 2011. web.archive.org/ web/20140804060733/healthyblackmen.org/2011/03/20/ talking-truth-with-chris-dickerson.

Turner, Allison Marie. "Queer History 101: Ali Forney." CampusPride.org. October 13, 2015. www.campuspride.org/queer-history-101-ali-forney.

Tutelian, Louise. "Eleanor Roosevelt's Place Apart." NYTimes.com. December 17, 2004. www.nytimes.com/2004/12/17/travel/escapes/eleanor-roosevelts-place-apart.html.

Vaid, Urvashi. "About." UrvashiVaid.net. urvashivaid.net/wp/?page_id=2.

Vario, Anthony Ronald. "Anthony Perkins." IMDb.com. www.imdb.com/name/ nm0000578/bio?ref_=nm_ov_bio_sm.

Vario, Anthony Ronald. "Grace Jones—Biography." IMDb.com. www.imdb. com/name/nm0005063/bio.

Viloria, Hida. "About." HidaViloria.com. hidaviloria.com/about.

Walker, Rebecca. "New Again: Wentworth Miller." InterviewMagazine. com. March 29, 2017. www.interviewmagazine.com/culture/ new-again-wentworth-miller.

Wallenberg, Petter. "Octavia St. Laurent's last interview." DazedDigital. com. November 20, 2014. www.dazeddigital.com/artsandculture/ article/22663/1/octavia-st-laurents-last-interview.

Weber, Carol Ruth. "Felipe Rose Sparks Energy Beyond Village People." Medium.com. September 14, 2018. medium.com/@carolruthweber/ felipe-rose-sparks-energy-beyond-village-people-interview-cf509da9289c.

Weinraub, Bernard. "Anthony Perkins's Wife Tells of 2 Years of Secrecy." NYTimes.com. September 16, 1992. www.nytimes.com/1992/09/16/arts/ anthony-perkins-s-wife-tells-of-2-years-of-secrecy.html.

Weinraub, Bernard. "Geffen Is Said To Be Angered By Biography." NYTimes. com. March 6, 2000. www.nytimes.com/2000/03/06/business/geffen-is-said-to-be-angered-by-biography.html.

Williams, H. "Herukhuti" Sharif, PhD, MEd. "Dr. Herukhuti's 2018 New York City Pride Rally Speech." SacredSexualities. org. June 24, 2018. sacredsexualities.org/2018/06/24/ dr-herukhutis-2018-new-york-city-pride-rally-speech-full-text.

Wolde-Michael, Tsione. "A Brief History of Voguing." NMAAHC.SI.edu. nmaahc. si.edu/blog-post/brief-history-voguing.

Woodruff, Sheryl. "Before Stonewall: The 'Sip In' at Julius'." GVSHP.org. August 30, 2012. gvshp.org/blog/2012/08/30/ before-stonewall-the-sip-in-at-julius.

Zax, Talya. "The Last Time We Saw 'God of Vengeance' on Broadway, the Whole Cast Got Arrested." Forward.com. January 13, 2017. forward.com/ culture/359653/the-last-time-we-saw-god-of-vengeance-on-broadway-the-whole-cast-got-arrest.

North Carolina

Barr, Jeremy. "Chris Hughes steps down as editor of The New Republic, names Vidra C.E.O." Politico.com. September 17, 2014. www.politico.com/ media/story/2014/09/chris-hughes-steps-down-as-editor-of-the-new-republic-names-vidra-ceo-002862.

Bellamy, Cammie. "The Carolina Gay Association, Organizing and Opposition, 1974-1989." OutHistory.org. 2012. outhistory.org/exhibits/show/nc-lgbt/ campus-activism/carolina-gay-association.

Clarkson, Frederick. "Christian right undermines marriage equality with religious supremacism." LGBTQNation.com. October 26, 2014. www. lgbtqnation.com/2014/10/christian-right-undermines-marriage-equality-with-religious-supremacism.

Duke University Libraries. "Lesbian & Gay Pulp Fiction: Gay Pulp Fiction." Guides.Library.Duke.edu. January 14, 2019. guides.library.duke.edu/ queerpulps/gaypulps.

Elliott, Leah. "LGBTQ Vigil in response to 1981 Hate Crime." DurhamCivilRightsMap.org. www.durhamcivilrightsmap.org/ places/24-lgbtq-vigil-response-to-1981-hate-crime.

Fallon, Kevin. "America's Favorite Loser: Why It's Time to Take Clay Aiken Seriously." TheDailyBeast.com. April 03, 2015. www.thedailybeast.com/ americas-favorite-loser-why-its-time-to-take-clay-aiken-seriously.

Forbes. "Chris Hughes." Forbes.com. December 12, 2016. www.forbes.com/ profile/chris-hughes/#4c53a50137d2.

Galassi, Josh. "First openly gay NASCAR driver talks racing, homophobic fans, and vodka cranberries." Queerty.com. October 14, 2018. www.queerty. com/first-openly-gay-nascar-driver-talks-racing-homophobic-fans-vodka-cranberries-20181014.

Gonzalez, Carolina Dalia. "Former Columbia Rugby player is proposed to at the Rio Olympics." ColumbiaSpectator.com. March 02, 2017. www.columbiaspectator.com/spectrum/2016/08/09/ former-columbia-rugby-proposed-rio-olympics.

Hanna, Jason, Madison Park and Eliott C. McLaughlin. "North Carolina repeals 'bathroom bill'." CNN.com. March 30, 2017. www.cnn. com/2017/03/30/politics/north-carolina-hb2-agreement/index.html.

Jenkins, Jack. "The Unlikely Story Of How Religion Helped Bring Same-Sex Marriage To North Carolina." ThinkProgress.org. November 18, 2014. thinkprogress.org/the-unlikely-story-of-how-religion-helped-bring-same-sex-marriage-to-north-carolina-c3884a574dc3.

Mungello, D. E. Remember This: A Family in America. Lanham, MD: Rowman & Littlefield, 2016.

NBC. "Welcome to Queer 2.0!" NBCNews.com. June 03, 2016. www.nbcnews. com/video/welcome-to-queer-2-0-698560067526.

NWPA Pride. "LGBT History Month—Jackie 'Moms' Mabley— Comedian." NWPAPride.org. www.nwpapride.org/article. php?recordid=201510momsmabley.

Price, Mark. "UNC Charlotte launches LGBT history collection." CharlotteObserver.com. April 08, 2016. www.charlotteobserver.com/ news/local/article70707177.html.

Qnotes. "About." GoQNotes.com. goqnotes.com/about.

Reddy, Luke. "Rio Olympics 2016: Venue worker's marriage proposal to Brazil player accepted." BBC.com. August 09, 2016. www.bbc.com/sport/ olympics/37018532.

Stern, Randy. "Stephen Rhodes: Out Racing For Equality." LavenderMagazine. com. March 19, 2015. www.lavendermagazine.com/our-homes/ meet-our-next-out-and-proud-sports-hero-a-racing-driver.

Terris, Ben. "'American Idol' made Clay Aiken a star. But he knows it won't make him a congressman." WashingtonPost.com. September 18, 2014. www.washingtonpost.com/lifestyle/style/american-idol-made-clay-aiken-a-star-but-he-knows-it-wont-make-him-a-congressman/2014/09/18/028c9630-3e63-11e4-b03f-de718edeb92f_story. html?utm_term=.8528458e960f.

Tobia, Jacob. "Bio." JacobTobia.com. jacobtobia.com/Bio.

University of North Carolina at Charlotte. "Goldmine: Repository at UNC Charlotte." goldmine.uncc.edu.

University of North Carolina. "Carolina Gay Association." Museum. UNC.edu. museum.unc.edu/exhibits/show/student-organizations/ carolina-gay-association.

Yahoo! Movies. "Evan Rachel Wood—Biography." Movies.Yahoo.com. web. archive.org/web/20120208102944/movies.yahoo.com/person/evan-rachel-wood/biography.html.

North Dakota

ACLU. "ACLU Secures Historic Custody Win for Lesbian Mother." ACLU. org. November 14, 2003. www.aclu.org/press-releases/aclu-secures-historic-custody-win-lesbian-mother?redirect=news/ aclu-secures-historic-custody-win-lesbian-mother.

Boschee, Josh. "About Josh." JoshforND.com. joshfornd.com/about.

Dominus, Susan. "Rape Worn Not on a Sleeve, but Right Over the Heart." NYTimes.com. April 04, 2008. www.nytimes.com/2008/04/04/ nyregion/04bigcity.html.

Eriksmoen, Curt. "Libbie Custer's laundress actually a man." BismarkTribune. com. January 15, 2012. bismarcktribune.com/news/columnists/curt-eriksmoen/libbie-custer-s-laundress-actually-a-man/article_33e41b80-3e26-11e1-8096-001871e3ce6c.html.

EqualDex. "LGBT Rights in North Dakota." EqualDex.com. www.equaldex. com/region/united-states/north-dakota.

Fargo-Moorhead Pride. "FM Pride Week." FargoMoorhead.org. www. fargomoorhead.org/event/fm-pride-week.

Fargo-Moorhead Pride. "Home." fmpride.com.

Freedom for All Americans. "North Dakota." FreedomforAllAmericans.org. www.freedomforallamericans.org/category/states/nd.

Henry, Jennifer. "Williston's Heartbreakers has liquor license revoked." KFYRTV.com. October 10, 2018. www.kfyrtv.com/content/news/Willistons-Heartbreakers-has-liquor-license-revoked-496790671.html.

Kerzman, Kristopher. "Throwback Thursday: Fargo's first gay pride week." Inforum.com. August 13, 2015. www.inforum.com/news/3817014-throwback-thursday-fargos-first-gay-pride-week.

Lang, Nico. "The boom and bust of North Dakota's only gay bar." Vox.com. August 25, 2016. www.vox.com/2016/8/25/12639490/north-dakota-gay-bar-heartbreakers-williston.

Lawlor, David. "Mrs. Nash, the Transvestite with Custer's Seventh Cavalry." HistoryWithaTwist.Wordpress.com. August 11, 2013. historywithatwist.wordpress.com/2013/08/11/mrs-nash-the-transvestite-with-custers-seventh-cavalry.

National Center for Transgender Equality. "North Dakota Name Change Laws." TransEquality.org. April 2019. transequality.org/documents/state/north-dakota.

National Public Media. "The Face Behind The Voice: NPR Radio Host Ari Shapiro." NationalPublicMedia.org. July 2016. www.nationalpublicmedia.com/news/npr-radio-host-ari-shapiro.

NDHRC Admin. "North Dakota LGBTQ Summit: United Across North Dakota." NDHRC.org. September 07, 2018. www.ndhrc.org/2018/09/07/north-dakota-lgbtq-summit-united-across-north-dakota.

Nicholson, Blake. "Gay marriage ban approved in North Dakota." BismarkTribune.com. November 01, 2004. bismarcktribune.com/news/state-and-regional/gay-marriage-ban-approved-in-north-dakota/article_94bc1ce1-c5df-5dc0-b6fa-d1f2fac3b5fb.html.

North Dakota Human Rights Coalition. "North Dakota Human Rights Coalition." NDHRC.org. www.ndhrc.org.

North Dakota Legislative Branch. "Representative Josh Boschee." Legis.ND.gov. www.legis.nd.gov/biography/josh-boschee.

North Dakota Safe Zone. "Contact." RuscoWindows.WixSite.com. ruscowindows.wixsite.com/ndsafezone/contact.

North Dakota Safe Zone. "Goals." RuscoWindows.WixSite.com. ruscowindows.wixsite.com/ndsafezone/goals.

NPR. "Ari Shapiro." NPR.org. www.npr.org/people/2101154/ari-shapiro.

Painter, George. "The Sensibilities of Our Forefathers." GLAPN.org. 2001. www.glapn.org/sodomylaws/sensibilities/north_dakota.htm.

Pride Minot. "About." Facebook.com. en-gb.facebook.com/PrideMinot.

Pride Minot. "About Us." www.prideminot.org/aboutus.

Richman, Kimberly D. *Courting Change: Queer Parents, Judges, and the Transformation of American Family Law.* New York, NY: NYU Press, 2008.

Soderholm, Anna. "FM Pride Collective And Community Center Relocates." MSumAdvocate.com. September 12, 2014. msumadvocate.com/2014/09/12/fm-pride-collective-and-community-center-relocates.

South Dakota Film Festival. "In Front of Us: The Invisible Problem." SouthDakotaFilmFest.org. southdakotafilmfest.org/films/in-front-of-us-the-invisible-problem.

South Dakota Film Festival. "Joseph-Katrina Koesterman." SouthDakotaFilmFest.org. southdakotafilmfest.org/guests/joseph-katrina-koesterman.

Streetman, Jonathan. "Ten Percent Society asks UND to fund LGBT center." GrandForksHerald.com. April 29, 2016. www.grandforksherald.com/news/4021561-ten-percent-society-asks-und-fund-lgbt-center.

Tristate Transgender. "Home." Facebook.com. www.facebook.com/TristateTrans.

Tristate Transgender. "Home." tristatetransgender.weebly.com.

University of North Dakota. "Ten Percent Society." www1.UND.edu. www1.und.edu/orgs/ten-percent-society.

Vote Smart. "Randy Boehning's Biography." VoteSmart.org. votesmart.org/candidate/biography/41688/randy-boehning#.XOyTapNKjOR.

Welker, Emily. "North Dakota lawmaker who voted against gay rights comes out as gay." BismarkTribune.com. April 28, 2015. bismarcktribune.com/news/state-and-regional/north-dakota-lawmaker-who-voted-against-gay-rights-comes-out/article_a7b04654-ba11-5bf6-b74a-94724ed2c754.html.

Wellesley Centers for Women. "Jennifer Baumgardner Named Editor in Chief of Women's Review of Books." WCWOnline.org. March 05, 2018. www.wcwonline.org/2018/jennifer-baumgardner-named-editor-in-chief-of-women-s-review-of-books.

Ohio

Associated Press. "World War II POW, 92, fought enemy overseas, gay policy at home." CBSNews.com. November 11, 2014. www.cbsnews.com/news/world-war-ii-pow-92-fought-enemy-overseas-gay-policy-at-home.

Biography.com Editors. "Tracy Chapman Biography." Biography.com. April 02, 2014. www.biography.com/musician/tracy-chapman.

Carras, Christi. "'Transparent' Trace Lysette on Accusing Jeffrey Tambor of Sexual Harassment: 'It Was Hell'." Variety.com. August 07, 2018. variety.com/2018/tv/news/transparent-trace-lysette-jeffrey-tambor-sexual-harassment-1202898144.

Cenziper, Debbie. "Love Wins: The Lovers and Lawyers Who Fought the Landmark Case for Marriage Equality." Amazon.com. www.amazon.com/Love-Wins-Landmark-Marriage-Equality/dp/0062456105.

Conliffe, Ciaran. "Natalie Clifford Barney, Queen of The Paris Lesbians." HeadStuff.org. September 25, 2017. www.headstuff.org/culture/history/natalie-clifford-barney-queen-of-the-paris-lesbians.

Daily Voice. "Happy Birthday to Danbury's Tracy Chapman." DailyVoice.com. March 30, 2014. dailyvoice.com/connecticut/danbury/neighbors/happy-birthday-to-danburys-tracy-chapman/441215.

Duignan, Brian. "Judith Butler." Britannica.com. February 14, 2012. www.britannica.com/biography/Judith-Butler.

Dunne, Matthew W, "Homophobia, Housewives and Hyper-Masculinity." In *The Routledge History of Gender, War, and the U.S. Military,* edited by Kara D. Vuic. New York, NY: Routledge, 2018.

Encyclopedia of Cleveland History. "Oven Productions." Case.edu. case.edu/ech/articles/o/oven-productions.

Fantz, Ashley. "An Ohio transgender teen's suicide, a mother's anguish." CNN.com. January 04, 2015. www.cnn.com/2014/12/31/us/ohio-transgender-teen-suicide/index.html.

Feingold, Eric. "The David Zimmer Collection." GOHI.org. 2017. gohi.org/david-zimmer-collection.

Fleming, Amy. "The quiet revolutionary." TheGuardian.com. October 30, 2008. www.theguardian.com/lifeandstyle/2008/oct/31/tracy-chapman-women-pop-usa.

Fox, Fallon. "Leelah Alcorn's Suicide: Conversion Therapy Is Child Abuse." Time.com. January 08, 2015. time.com/3655718/leelah-alcorn-suicide-transgender-therapy.

Fresh Speakers. "Elle Hearns." FreshSpeakers.com. www.freshspeakers.com/speakers/elle-hearns.

Hearns, Elle. "About Elle." ElleHearns.com. ellehearns.com/about.

Hirshberg, Debra. "How Gay Are We: Oven Productions Has Been Celebrating Female Pride for Nearly 40 Years." ClevelandMagazine.Blogspot.com. August 15, 2014. clevelandmagazine.blogspot.com/2014/08/how-gay-are-we-oven-productions-has.html.

Kellaway, Mitch. "After Years of Hiding in Hollywood, Trans Actress Trace Lysette Is Finally 'Living Out Loud'." Advocate.com. April 15, 2015. www.advocate.com/politics/transgender/2015/04/15/after-years-hiding-hollywood-trans-actress-trace-lysette-finally-liv.

Mattson, Greggor. "Before It Was Hingetown." BeltMag.com. June 15, 2016. beltmag.com/before-it-was-hingetown.

O, Scott. "Cleveland LGBT History—Hingetown." ToursofCleveland.com. October 15, 2018. toursofcleveland.com/cleveland-lgbt-history-hingetown.

Oven Productions. "Oven Productions 43rd Annual Womyn's Variety Show." Eventbrite.com. 2018. www.eventbrite.com/e/oven-productions-43rd-annual-womyns-variety-show-tickets-43298920236.

PBS News Hour. "John Yang." PBS.org. www.pbs.org/newshour/author/john-yang.

Pulitzer Center. "John Yang." PulitzerCenter.org. pulitzercenter.org/user/239010.

Robinson, Franklin A. Jr. "Guide to the Corbett Reynolds Papers." SOVA.SI.edu. 2016. sova.si.edu//record/NMAH.AC.1390.

Sakar, Anne. "Stretch of I-71 where Warren County teenager died is part of the Adopt-A-Highway program." Cincinnati.com. November 20, 2015. www.cincinnati.com/story/news/2015/11/20/stretch—71-where-warren-county-teenager-died-part-adopt—highway-program/76119898.

Schneck, Ken. *LGBTQ Cleveland.* Mount Pleasant, SC: Arcadia Publishing, 2018.

Sega, Lauren. "Grassroots: Black Queer & Intersectional

Columbus Redefines Liberation." ColumbusUnderground. com. July 21, 2017. www.columbusunderground.com/ grassroots-black-queer-intersectional-columbus-redefines-liberation-ls1.

Stonewall Columbus. "Rupert 'Twink' Starr—2014 Featured Veteran." StonewallColumbus.org. stonewallcolumbus.org/veteransmonth/ rupert-starr.

The Editors of Encyclopaedia Britannica. "Natalie Barney." Britannica.com. March 28, 2013. www.britannica.com/biography/Natalie-Barney.

Totenberg, Nina. "Legal Battle Over Gay Marriage Hits The Supreme Court Tuesday." NPR.org. April 27, 2015. www. npr.org/sections/itsallpolitics/2015/04/27/402456198/ legal-battle-over-gay-marriage-hits-the-supreme-court-tuesday.

Usmani, Josh. "Deidre McPherson." CleveScene.com. July 27, 2016. www. clevescene.com/cleveland/deidre-mcpherson/Content?oid=4941991.

Wright-Patterson Air Force Base. "Wright-Patterson Air Force Base." www. wpafb.af.mil.

Oklahoma

Blecha, Peter. "Tipton, Billy (1914-1989): Spokane's Secretive Jazzman." HistoryLink.org. September 17, 2005. www.historylink.org/File/7456.

Custer, Jane. "The Empowered (Not Defeated) Queeroes of Melanie Gillman." OutFrontMagazine.com. September 07, 2016. www.outfrontmagazine. com/trending/empowered-not-defeated-queeroes-melanie-gillman.

Freedom Oklahoma. "Freedom Oklahoma." www.freedomoklahoma.org.

Gillman, Melanie. "*As the Crow Flies.*" MelanieGillman.com. www. melaniegillman.com/?page_id=14.

Kaufman, Gil. "Former YouTube Star Greyson Chance Comes Out." Billboard. com. July 20, 2017. www.billboard.com/articles/columns/pop/7873383/ greyson-chance-comes-out.

Martin, Douglas. "Cris Alexander, Actor and Photographer, Dies at 92." NYTimes.com. March 24, 2012. www.nytimes.com/2012/03/25/arts/cris-alexander-actor-and-photographer-dies-at-92.html.

National LGBTQ Task Force. "About: Mission & History." TheTaskForce.org. www.thetaskforce.org/about/mission-history.html.

Oklahoma City. "LGBT OKC." VisitOKC.com. www.visitokc.com/lgbt.

Oklahoma Hall of Fame. "Knie, Roberta." OklahomaHoF.com. oklahomahof. com/member-archives/k/knie-roberta-1982.

Oklahomans for Equality. "OKEQ—Oklahoma's resource for LGBT persons and their families." www.okeq.org.

Oklahomans for Equality. "Our Story." OKEQ.org. www.okeq.org/about-us. html.

PFLAG. "About PFLAG Oklahoma City." PFLAGOklahomaCity.org. pflagoklahomacity.org/about.

Smith, Dinitia. "Billy Tipton Is Remembered With Love, Even by Those Who Were Deceived." Archive.NYTimes.com. June 02, 1998. archive.nytimes. com/www.nytimes.com/library/books/060298tipton-biography.html.

Stearns, David Patrick. "Roberta Knie, leading Wagnerian soprano and Philadelphia voice teacher." Philly.com. March 28, 2017. www.philly. com/philly/obituaries/Roberta-Knie-leading-Wagnerian-soprano-and-Philadelphia-voice-teacher.html.

Tapley, Kristopher. "Gender-Fluid Actor Kelly Mantle Makes Oscar History." Variety.com. December 09, 2016. variety.com/2016/film/awards/ oscars-gender-fluid-actor-kelly-mantle-1201938597.

The Gayly. "Informing the Fabulous South-Central United States." Gayly.com. www.gayly.com/index.php.

Thrillist Travel. "The Most LGBTQ-Friendly City in Every Red State in America." Thrillist.com. March 31, 2017. www.thrillist.com/travel/nation/ most-gay-friendly-city-in-every-red-state-in-america.

Wadewitz, Mikel. "THE RIGHT KIND OF ATTENTION." KellyMantle.com. November 01, 2013. web.archive.org/web/20131101144639/www. kellymantle.com/frontiers2.html.

Oregon

Chibbaro, Lou Jr. "Sex with minor charges dropped against Terry Bean." WashingtonBlade.com. September 2, 2015. www.washingtonblade. com/2015/09/02/sex-with-minor-charges-dropped-against-terry-bean.

Fitzgibbon, Joe. "Stu Rasmussen (1948-)." OregonEncyclopedia.org. March 17, 2018. oregonencyclopedia.org/articles/rasmussen_stu_1948_/#. XLzRVpNKjOQ.

Gay & Lesbian Archives of the Pacific Northwest. "Oregon Gay History Timeline." GLAPN.org. www.glapn.org/6020timeline.html.

Gay & Lesbian Archives of the Pacific Northwest. "Peggy Burton." GLAPN.org. www.glapn.org/6316PeggyBurton.html.

Givens, Orie. "Yes, There Are Black Queers in Oregon and They Need Help." Advocate.com. August 25, 2016. www.advocate.com/race/2016/8/25/ yes-there-are-black-queers-oregon-and-they-need-help.

The James Beard Foundation. "About Us." JamesBeard.org. www. jamesbeard.org/about.

Johnson, Chris. "Kate Brown becomes first openly LGBT person elected governor." WashingtonTable.com. November 8, 2016. www.washingtonblade.com/2016/11/08/ kate-brown-becomes-first-openly-lgbt-person-elected-governor.

Legislative Counsel Committee of Oregon. "2017 ORS 659A.403 Discrimination in place of public accommodation prohibited." OregonLaws.org. 2017. www.oregonlaws.org/ors/659A.403.

Martinac, Paula. *The Queerest Places.* New York, NY: Henry Holt and Company, 1997.

Mayes, Steve. "Alleged victim in Terry Bean sex case disappears, trial now in doubt." OregonLive.com. July 31, 2015. www.oregonlive.com/ portland/2015/07/victim_in_terry_bean_sex_case.html.

Miller, Timothy. *The 60's Communes: Hippies and Beyond.* Syracuse, NY: Syracuse University Press, 1999.

Nicola, George T. "Rediscovering Family: Antoinette, Keith, and Khalil Edwards." GLAPN.org. January 10, 2018. www.glapn. org/6060KeithAntoinetteKhalilEdwards.html.

NPR Staff. "Americas, Just Get Over It And Make The Souffle." NPR. org. April 10, 2014. www.npr.org/2014/04/10/300306564/ americans-just-get-over-it-and-make-the-souffle.

Oberle, Tim. "Eighth Army Welcomes First Female Deputy Commanding General." Military.com. July 12, 2016. www.military.com/daily-news/2016/07/12/eighth-army-welcomes-first-female-deputy-commanding-general.html.

Parks, Casey. "In Orlando's shadow, Native American Two Spirit group brings light to Pride." OregonLive.com. June 18, 2016. www.oregonlive.com/ portland/2016/06/portland_pride_2016_two_spirit.html.

Portland Two Spirit Society. "Portland Two Spirit Society—About." Facebook. com. www.facebook.com/pg/Portland2Spirits/about/?ref=page_internal.

Power California. "Khalil Edwards." PowerCalifornia.org. powercalifornia.org/ people/2018/10/30/khalil-edwards.

Q Center. "About Q Center." PDXQCenter.org. www.pdxqcenter.org.

Rasmussen, Stu. "Stu Rasmussen for Mayor of Silverton. StuRasmussen.com. www.sturasmussen.com/about.htm.

Special to The Oregonian. "How Nico Santos went from a Gresham 'band of freaks' to NBC and comedy." OregonLive.com. April 22, 2017. www. oregonlive.com/events/2017/04/nico_santos_bridgetown_comedy_ festival.html.

United States Court of Appeals, Ninth Circuit. "Peggy BURTON, Plaintiff-Appellant, v. CASCADE SCHOOL DISTRICT UNION HIGH SCHOOL NO. 5 et al, Defendants-Appellees." OpenJurist.org. March 28, 1975. openjurist. org/512/f2d/850/burton-v-cascade-school-district-union-high-school-no.

University of Oregon. "Oregon Lesbian Land Manuscript Collections in Special Collections." ResearchGuides.UOregon.edu. January 26, 2018. researchguides.uoregon.edu/lesbian-lands.

US Army Reserve. "Brigadier General Tammy S. Smith." USAR.Army. mil. www.usar.army.mil/Leadership/Article-View/Article/580319/ brigadier-general-tammy-s-smith.

Williamette University. "Kate Brown at Willamette." Vimeo.com. 2016. vimeo. com/166836336.

Williams, Chuck. "Sunday Interview with Brig. Gen. Tammy Smith: 'I did my work on Army installations, but my life occurred off of the installation'." Ledger-Enquirer.com. July 16, 2016. www.ledger-enquirer.com/news/ local/military/article90106842.html.

WomenShare. "WomenShare records, 1974-1999." ArchivesWest. OrbisCascade.org. archiveswest.orbiscascade.org/ark:/80444/xv08663.

Yamato, Jen. "'Crazy Rich Asians': Nico Santos is here for queer representation." LATimes.com. August 10, 2018. www.latimes.com/ entertainment/movies/la-et-mn-crazy-rich-asians-nico-santos-20180810-story.html.

Young, Morgen. "Alan Hart (1890 - 1962)." OregonEncylopedia.org. March 17, 2018. oregonencyclopedia.org/articles/hart_alan_1890_1962_/#.

XLy6OZNKjOQ.

Zé, Lucas Aka. "Nico Santos." IMDb.com. www.imdb.com/name/nm4456672/bio?ref_=nm_ov_bio_sm. D

Zohn, Alexandra and Peggy Grodinsky. "James Beard's Books." JamesBeard.org. www.jamesbeard.org/about/james-beard-books.

Pennsylvania

Academy of Motion Picture Arts and Sciences. "The 82nd Academy Awards: 2010." Oscars.org. 2010. www.oscars.org/oscars/ceremonies/2010.

Artavia, David. "Rep. Brian Sims to Introduce Marriage Bill in Pennsylvania." Advocate.com. June 27, 2013. www.advocate.com/politics/marriage-equality/2013/06/27/rep-brian-sims-introduce-marriage-bill-pennsylvania.

Bendix, Trish. "'The L Word' creator Ilene Chaiken on what fans can expect from the reboot." NBCNews.com. February 17, 2019. www.nbcnews.com/feature/nbc-out/l-word-creator-ilene-chaiken-what-fans-can-expect-reboot-n972271.

Blumgart, Jake. "Philadelphia was likely first city to have a gayborhood." PhillyVoice.com. April 01, 2016. www.phillyvoice.com/philadelphia-was-first-city-have-gayborhood.

Bolcer, Julie and GO Staff. "Rainbow Street Signs Dedicated in Philadelphia's 'Gayborhood'." GoMag.com. July 12, 2007. gomag.com/article/rainbow_street_signs_dedi.

Bruno, Katie. "Carlett Brown: The Extreme Marginalization of Transwomen of Color." OutHistory.org. outhistory.org/exhibits/show/tgi-bios/carlett-brown.

Delaware Valley Legacy Fund. "HISTORY." DVLF.org. www.dvlf.org/history.

Gates, Henry Louis Jr. "Who Designed the March on Washington?" PBS.org. www.pbs.org/wnet/african-americans-many-rivers-to-cross/history/100-amazing-facts/who-designed-the-march-on-washington.

Gillespie, Tyler. "The Last Day at Giovanni's Room, America's Oldest Gay Bookstore." RollingStone.com. May 21, 2014. www.rollingstone.com/culture/culture-news/the-last-day-at-giovannis-room-americas-oldest-gay-bookstore-94901.

Hornsby-Gutting, Angela. "Deborah Batts." Blackpast.org. May 19, 2007. www.blackpast.org/african-american-history/batts-deborah-1947.

Human Rights Campaign. "Candace Gingrich." HRC.org. www.hrc.org/staff/candace-gingrich.

Human Rights Campaign. "Philadelphia, Pennsylvania: 2018 Municipal Equality Index Scorecard." HRC.org. 2018. assets2.hrc.org/files/assets/resources/MEI-2018-Philadelphia-Pennsylvania.pdf.

IMDb. "Ilene Chaiken." IMDb.com. www.imdb.com/name/nm0149669.

Kennedy, Randall. "From Protest to Patronage." TheNation.com. September 11, 2003. www.thenation.com/article/protest-patronage.

McFadden, Robert D. "Edith Windsor, Whose Same-Sex Marriage Fight Led to Landmark Ruling, Dies at 88." NYTimes.com. September 12, 2017. www.nytimes.com/2017/09/12/us/edith-windsor-dead-same-sex-marriage-doma.html.

Philly Pride. "Annual Reminder, 50th Anniversary." PhillyGayPride.org. www.phillygaypride.org/annual-reminders-50th-anniversary.

Out.com Editors. "Out100: Lee Daniels." Out.com. November 13 2013. www.out.com/out-exclusives/out100-2013/2013/11/13/out100-lee-daniels.

Out History. "Marc Stein: 50th Anniversary Annual Reminders, Philadelphia, July 4, 1965 - July 4, 1969." OutHistory.org. outhistory.org/exhibits/show/50th-ann/intro.

Reynolds, Daniel. "From L Word to Empire: Ilene Chaiken Has Changed Television Twice." Advocate.com. September 21, 2016. www.advocate.com/people/2016/9/21/l-word-empire-ilene-chaiken-has-changed-television-twice.

Seelye, Katharine Q. "Speaker's Sister Now Speaking Out." NYTimes.com. March 6, 1995. www.nytimes.com/1995/03/06/us/speaker-s-sister-now-speaking-out.html?sec=health&emc=rss&partner=rssnyt&mtrref=en.wikipedia.org.

Siddiqui, Sabrina. "Brian Sims, Openly Gay State Rep., Urges Pat Toomey To Support ENDA." HuffPost.com. November 1, 2013. www.huffpost.com/entry/pat-toomey-enda_n_4192491.

Sims, Brian. "About Brian." Sims4PA.com. web.archive.org/web/20111101193606/www.sims4pa.com/Bio.

The Andy Warhol Foundation for the Visual Arts. "Andy Warhol Biography."

WarholFoundation.org. warholfoundation.org/legacy/biography.html.

The Keith Haring Foundation. "Bio." Haring.com. www.haring.com/!/about-haring/bio#.XLYvK5NKjOQ.

The Warhol. "LGBTQ+." Warhol.org. www.warhol.org/lgbtq.

Queer Books. "History." QueerBooks.com. www.queerbooks.com/mission/about-us.

Ubuntu Biography Project. "Billy Porter." UbuntuBiographyProject.com. September 21, 2017. ubuntubiographyproject.com/2017/09/21/billy-porter.

Ubuntu Biography Project. "Ethel Waters." UbuntuBiographyProject.com. October 31, 2017. ubuntubiographyproject.com/2017/10/31/ethel-waters.

White, Claytee D. "Ethel Waters." BlackPast.org. February 11, 2007. www.blackpast.org/african-american-history/waters-ethel-1896-1977.

William Way LGBT Community Center. "Mission." WayGay.org. www.waygay.org/mission-history.

Puerto Rico

Biography.com Editors. "Ricky Martin." Biography.com. April 02, 2014. www.biography.com/musician/ricky-martin.

Centro Comunitario LGBTT de Puerto Rico. "CCLGBTTPR." centrolgbttpr.org.

Cho, Hahna. "Luisa Capetillo: Feminism and Labor in Puerto Rico." BackStoryRadio.org. September 07, 2018. www.backstoryradio.org/blog/luisa-capetillo-feminism-and-labor-in-puerto-rico.

Costantini, Cristina. "Pedro Julio Serrano: 'Unteaching' an Island." ABCNews.Go.com. February 11, 2013. abcnews.go.com/ABC_Univision/profile-pedro-julio-serrano-puerto-ricos-prominent-human/story?id=18458343.

CyberNews. "The Historic New Presidency of the Bar Association." Noticel.com. September 08, 2012. www.noticel.com/ahora/histrica-la-nueva-presidencia-del-colegio-de-abogados/608635848.

El Nuevo Día. "Woman of Intersections." ElNuevoDia.com. May 27, 2012. www.elnuevodia.com/estilosdevida/hogar/nota/mujerdeintersecciones-1264798.

Ferrer, Norma Valle. Luisa Capetillo, Pioneer Puerto Rican Feminist. New York, NY: Peter Lang Publishing, 2006.

Florio, John and Ouisie Shapiro. "Orlando Cruz Fights to Become Boxing's First Openly Gay Champion." NewYorker.com. November 25, 2016. www.newyorker.com/sports/sporting-scene/orlando-cruz-fights-to-become-boxings-first-openly-gay-champion.

HRC Staff. "Gay & Lesbian Sports Hall of Fame Prepares to Induct Inaugural Class." HRC.org. August 02, 2013. www.hrc.org/blog/gay-lesbian-sports-hall-of-fame-prepared-to-induct-inaugural-class.

National Park Service. "Edificio Comunidad de Orgullo Gay de Puerto Rico." NPS.gov. www.nps.gov/places/edificio-comunidad-de-orgullo-gay-de-puerto-rico.htm.

Negrón-Mutaner, Frances. "About." FrancesNegronMuntaner.com. www.francesnegronmuntaner.com/about.

Serrano, Pedro Julio. "About me." PedroJulioSerrano.com. pedrojulioserrano.com/yo.

Staff Reports. "Puerto Rico dedicates first LGBT monument." WashingtonBlade.com. July 06, 2016. www.washingtonblade.com/2016/07/06/puerto-rico-dedicates-first-lgbt-monument.

Rhode Island

Adler, Melissa A. "The ALA Task Force on Gay Liberation: Effecting Change in Naming and Classification of GLBTQ Subjects." Journals.Lib.Washington.edu. 2013. journals.lib.washington.edu/index.php/acro/article/viewFile/14226/12086.

BBC. "HP Lovecraft: The man who haunted horror fans." BBC.com. March 22, 2012. www.bbc.com/news/magazine-17472580.

Brenkert, Ben. "Franklin D. Roosevelt's Forgotten Anti-Gay Sex Crusade." TheDailyBeast.com. June 23, 2015. www.thedailybeast.com/franklin-d-roosevelts-forgotten-anti-gay-sex-crusade.

Brown University. "About the LGBTQ Center." Brown.edu. www.brown.edu/campus-life/support/lgbtq/about.

Cain, Sian. "Ten things you should know about HP Lovecraft." TheGuardian.com. August 20, 2014.

Carlos, Wendy. "Wendy Carlos Biography." WendyCarlos.com. www.wendycarlos.com/biog.html.

Dartmouth College Department of English and Creative Writing. "Alexander Chee." English.Dartmouth.edu. english.dartmouth.edu/people/alexander-chee.

Fagan, Kate. "Bio." ByKateFagan.com. www.bykatefagan.com/about.

Fricke, Aaron. "LGBT Anti-Bullying Aaron Fricke Publishes Expanded Version of Acclaimed Memoir." OutwordMagazine. com. www.outwordmagazine.com/inside-outword/music-and-books/1335-lgbt-anti-bullying-pioneer-aaron-fricke.

GLAD. "Aaron Fricke v. Richard B. Lynch." GLAD.org. www.glad.org/cases/aaron-fricke-v-richard-b-lynch.

Gray, Channing. "Where are they now: After Trinity, Anne Bogart's career has soared." ProvidenceJournal.com. December 2, 2017. www.providencejournal.com/news/20171202/where-are-they-now-after-trinity-anne-bogarts-career-has-soared.

Harmetz, Aljean. "Van Johnson, Film Actor, Is Dead at 92." NYTimes.com. December 12, 2008. www.nytimes.com/2008/12/13/movies/13johnson.html?_r=1&ref=obituaries.

House, Wes. "We Can't Ignore H.P. Lovecraft's White Supremacy." LitHub.com. September 26, 2017. lithub.com/we-cant-ignore-h-p-lovecrafts-white-supremacy.

Journal Staff. "TIMELINE: Gay and lesbian history in Rhode Island, and nationally." ProvidenceJournal.com. July 27, 2014. www.providencejournal.com/news/20140727/timeline-gay-and-lesbian-history-in-rhode-island-and-nationally.

Kim, Crystal Hana. "The trailblazing writing life of Alexander Chee." WashingtonPost.com. April 20, 2018. www.washingtonpost.com/entertainment/books/the-trailblazing-writing-life-of-an-openly-gay-korean-american-writer/2018/04/20/401a80f0-434d-11e8-bba2-0976a82b05a2_story.html?utm_term=.bd7b3897be5b.

Locus Magazine. "Caitlin R. Kiernan: Transmutations." LocusMag.com. December 31, 2008. www.locusmag.com/2008/Issue12_Kiernan.html.

Loewe, Emma. "How the Ultimate Wellness Couple Is Prepping For revitalize." MindBodyGreen.com. September 7, 2017. www.mindbodygreen.com/articles/how-kathryn-budig-and-kate-fagan-pack-for-revitalize.

Malsbury, Susan. "Israel David Fishman papers." Archives.NYPL.org. archives.nypl.org/mss/1012.

Petenbrink, Troy. "World's Best Destinations for LGBT Pride Celebrations." NationalGeographic.com. June 9, 2018. www.nationalgeographic.com/travel/lists/lgbt-best-places-to-go-pride-month-parades.

Reed, Susan. "After a Sex Change and Several Eclipses, Wendy Carlos Treads a New Digital Moonscape." People.com. July 01, 1985. people.com/archive/after-a-sex-change-and-several-eclipses-wendy-carlos-treads-a-new-digital-moonscape-vol-24-no-1.

Rhode Island Pride. "About Us." PrideRI.org. www.prideri.org/about.

The AIDS Memorial Quilt. "The AIDS Memorial Quilt." AIDSQuilt.org. www.aidsquilt.org/about/the-aids-memorial-quilt.

The Kennedy Center. "Anne Bogart." Kennedy-Center.org. www.kennedy-center.org/Artist/A82975.

Vallance, Tom. "Evie Wynn Johnson." Independent.co.uk. August 28, 2004. www.independent.co.uk/news/obituaries/evie-wynn-johnson-550363.html.

VanderMeer, Jeff. "Interview: Caitlin R. Kiernan on Weird Fiction." WeirdFictionReview.com. March 12, 2012. weirdfictionreview.com/2012/03/interview-caitlin-r-kiernan-on-weird-fiction.

Woo, Elaine. "Bob Hattoy, 56; witty and outspoken advocate for the environment, AIDS research." LATimes.com. March 06, 2007. www.latimes.com/archives/la-xpm-2007-mar-06-me-hattoy6-story.html.

Youth Pride, Inc. "About Youth Pride, Inc." YouthPrideRI.org. www.youthprideri.org/about-youth-pride-inc.

South Carolina

Allison, Dorothy. "Bio." www.dorothyallison.com.

Arnold, Jenny. "USC Upstate students to protest lawmakers plan to cut funding over gay-themed programs." GoUpstate.com. April 16, 2014. www.goupstate.com/news/20140416/usc-upstate-students-to-protest-lawmakers-plan-to-cut-funding-over-gay-themed-programs.

CNN. "CNN—Elections 2006." CNN.com. 2006. www.cnn.com/ELECTION/2006/pages/results/ballot.measures.

Dys, Andrew. "Five charged in beating of SC gay man." HeraldOnline.com. April 30, 2011. www.heraldonline.com/latest-news/article12272993.html.

Ghorayshi, Azeen. "A Landmark Lawsuit About An Intersex Baby's Genital Surgery Just Settled for $440,000." BuzzFeedNews.com. July 26, 2017. www.buzzfeednews.com/article/azeenghorayshi/intersex-surgery-lawsuit-settles.

Licata, Salvatore J. and Robert P. Petersen. Historical Perspectives on Homosexuality. Philadelphia, PA: Haworth Press, 1980.

McDermott, Maeve. "Miss Missouri Erin O'Flaherty tells her coming out story: 'It was really hard.'" USAToday.com. September 08, 2016. www.usatoday.com/story/life/entertainthis/2016/09/08/miss-america-missouri-erin-oflaherty-tells-her-coming-out-story/90009344.

NBC Los Angeles. "Comedian Andy Dick Faces Sexual Harassment Allegations." NBCLosAngeles.com. July 02, 2018. www.nbclosangeles.com/news/local/Comedian-Andy-Dick-Faces-Sexual-Harassment-Allegations-487142621.html.

Norton, Rictor. "Writhing Bedfellows." RictorNorton.co.uk. 1998. rictornorton.co.uk/withers.htm.

O'Brien, Ken. "Humor in the Extreme." ChicagoTribune.com. December 13, 1998. www.chicagotribune.com/news/ct-xpm-1998-12-13-9812130118-story.html.

Parker, Adam. "New LGBTQ archive at College of Charleston receives grant to help document neglected era of history." PostandCourier.com. February 03, 2018. www.postandcourier.com/features/new-lgbtq-archive-at-college-of-charleston-receives-grant-to/article_89813778-0768-11e8-8c02-7f62c7fd868e.html.

South Carolina Black Pride. "About." SouthCarolinaBlackPride.com. www.southcarolinablackpride.com/about.html.

South Carolina Division of the Sons of Confederate Veterans. "Signer of the SC Ordinance—Judge Thomas Jefferson Withers." SCSCV.com. February 14, 2014. scscv.com/2014/02/14/signer-of-the-sc-ordinance-2.

South Carolina Equality. "Our History." EqualMeansEveryone.org. www.equalmeanseveryone.org/get-to-know-us/our-history.

Southern Poverty Law Center. "M.C. v. Aaronson." SPLCenter.org. www.splcenter.org/seeking-justice/case-docket/mc-v-aaronson.

Stein, Marc. "Anita Cornwell, October 06, 1993." OutHistory.org. 2017. outhistory.org/exhibits/show/philadelphia-lgbt-interviews/interviews/cornwell.

Townsend, Jerry. "Dr. Rembert Truluck." LGBTQReligiousArchives.org. December, 2005. lgbtqreligiousarchives.org/profiles/rembert-truluck.

Ward, Justin. "Remembering Sean Kennedy Five Years Later." GLAAD.org. May 16, 2012. www.glaad.org/blog/remembering-sean-kennedy-five-years-later.

WYFF. "Defendant In Gay Man's Death Gets 2.5 Year Sentence." WYFF4.com. June 13, 2008. www.wyff4.com/article/defendant-in-gay-man-s-death-gets-2-5-year-sentence/6986701.

WYFF. "Gay Man's Killer Released After 1 Year." WYFF4.com. July 03, 2009. www.wyff4.com/article/gay-man-s-killer-released-after-1-year/6989216.

South Dakota

Advocate Contributors. "Forty Under 40." Advocate.com. April 07, 2010. www.advocate.com/print-issue/cover-stories/2010/04/07/forty-under-40?pg=1#article-content.

Black Hills Center for Equality. "Black Hills Center for Equality." www.bhcfe.org.

Botelho, Greg and Wayne Drash. "South Dakota governor vetoes transgender bathroom bill." CNN.com. March 02, 2016. www.cnn.com/2016/03/01/us/south-dakota-transgender-bathroom-bill.

Buhl, Angie. "About Angie." AngieBuhl.com. web.archive.org/web/20121102134045/http://angiebuhl.com/about.

City of Brookings. "Brookings, SD." www.cityofbrookings.org.

Holland, Jim and Scott Feldman. "Rapid City women first to obtain same-sex marriage license, marry in South Dakota." RapidCityJournal.com. June 27, 2015. rapidcityjournal.com/news/local/rapid-city-women-first-to-obtain-same-sex-marriage-license/article_d9dde9e5-0195-54fe-9d56-de3ac99460eb.html.

Huffington Post. "Coya White Hat-Artichoker." HuffPost.com. www.huffpost.com/author/coya-white-hatartichoker.

Marcus, Eric. "Episode 07—Chuck Rowland." MakingGayHistory.com. makinggayhistory.com/podcast/episode-1-7.

Monahan, Terry. "Law-Abiding Sioux Falls Makes Room for Gays at the Prom." WashingtonPost.com. May 24, 1979. www.washingtonpost.com/archive/

politics/1979/05/24/law-abiding-sioux-falls-makes-room-for-gays-at-the-prom/c22469d8-9969-43fe-ba19-48e1c0c99586/?noredirect=on&utm_term=.8f42c0977bf9.

Nagle, Rebecca. "The Healing History Of Two-Spirit, A Term That Gives LGBTQ Natives A Voice." HuffPost.com. June 30, 2018. www.huffpost.com/entry/two-spirit-identity_n_5b37cfbce4b007aa2f809af1.

Sioux Falls Pride. "About Sioux Falls Pride." SiouxFallsPride.org. www.siouxfallspride.org/about-sioux-falls-pride.

Taylor, Jesse. "South Dakota's first out gay college athlete plays basketball for Dakota Wesleyan University." OutSports.com. August 14, 2015. www.outsports.com/2015/8/14/9152149/jesse-taylor-gay-south-dakota-basketball.

The Center for Equality. "The Center for Equality." SiouxFallsFreeThinkers.com. www.siouxfallsfreethinkers.com/the-center-for-equality.html.

Tennessee

Addams, Calpernia. "Biographical Information for Press." Calpernia.com. www.calpernia.com/aboutme/press-bio.

Cady, Jennifer. "Megan Fox Talks Bisexuality for Guys, Robert Pattinson for Ladies." EOnline.com. May 11, 2009. www.eonline.com/news/123257/megan-fox-talks-bisexuality-for-guys-robert-pattinson-for-ladies.

Campaign for Southern Equality. "Tennessee." SouthernEquality.org. southernequality.org/legal-resources/tennessee.

East Tennessee Faith for Equality. "Welcoming and Affirming Lesbian, Gay, Bisexual, and Transgender Persons and Families." etnfaith4equality.weebly.com.

Fallon, Kevin. "'Don't Say Gay' Is Back: 5 Things to Know About the Tennessee Bill." TheDailyBeast.com. January 31, 2013. www.thedailybeast.com/dont-say-gay-is-back-5-things-to-know-about-the-tennessee-bill.

Hankinson, Bobby. "Gay Iconography: Bessie Smith's Queer Blues." Towleroad.com. May 02, 2015. www.towleroad.com/2015/05/gay-iconography-bessie-smiths-queer-blues.

Hollingsworth, Barbara. "Gay Couples Ask Federal Court to Force Tennessee To Issue Them Marriage Licenses." CNSNews.com. November 21, 2013. www.cnsnews.com/news/article/barbara-hollingsworth/gay-couples-ask-federal-court-force-tennessee-issue-them-marriage.

Kee, Lindsay. "67,000+ Petition Signers Ask Lawmakers to Veto 'Bathroom' Legislation." ACLU-TN.org. April 18, 2016. www.aclu-tn.org/67000-petition-signers-ask-lawmakers-veto-bathroom-legislation.

Kee, Lindsay. "Giles County Schools To Stop Censoring Pro-LGBT Speech." ACLU-TN.org. August 15, 2016. www.aclu-tn.org/giles-county-schools-stop-censoring-pro-lgbt-speech.

Lady Bunny. "Lady Bunny Bio." LadyBunny.net. ladybunny.net/bio.

Movoto Real Estate. "The 7 Best Towns in Tennessee for LGBT Families." Movoto.com. www.movoto.com/guide/tn/the-7-best-towns-in-tennessee-for-lgbt-families.

Norris, John. "Miley Cyrus Breaks Silence on Rootsy New Music, Fiance Liam Hemsworth & America: 'Unity Is What We Need'." Billboard.com. May 03, 2017. www.billboard.com/articles/news/magazine-feature/7783997/miley-cyrus-cover-story-new-music-malibu.

Schulman, Michael. "Lady Bunny Is Still the Shadiest Queen Around." NYTimes.com. September 29, 2018. www.nytimes.com/2018/09/29/style/lady-bunny-drag-queen.html.

Steinmetz, Katy. "Miley Cyrus: 'You Can Just Be Whatever You Want to Be'." Time.com. June 15, 2015. time.com/3918308/miley-cyrus-transgender-rights-instapride.

Truth in Progress. "Jazz Vocalist, Intersex Rights Advocate Eden Atwood joins film to bring soundtrack tunes!" TruthinProgress.com. July 10, 2014. www.truthinprogress.com/truth-in-progress1/2014/07/jazz-vocalist-intersex-rights-advocate-eden-atwood-joins-film-to-bring-soundtrack-tunes.

Texas

Advocate Contributors. "Tom Ford Tells All." Advocate.com. November 09, 2009. www.advocate.com/arts-entertainment/film/2009/11/09/visionary-tom-ford.

Advocate. "Wilmer 'Little Ax' Broadnax." Advocate.com. 2018. www.advocate.com/media-gallery/detail/1018246/1298021.

Alvin Ailey American Dance Theater. "Alvin Ailey American Dance Theater." www.alvinailey.org.

Avery, Dan. "Logo Announces Contestants For 'RuPaul's All Star Drag Race' Season 2." NewNowNext.com. June 17, 2016. www.newnownext.com/logo-rupauls-all-star-drag-race-season-2/06/2016.

Babb, Kent. "Transgender wrestler Mack Beggs identifies as male. He just won the Texas state girls' title." TexasTribune.org. February 26, 2017. www.texastribune.org/2017/02/26/transgender-wrestler-mack-beggs-identifies-male-he-just-won-texas-stat.

Barrios, Gregg. "Taming of the Sexual Outlaw: 25 Years After 'City of Night,' John Rechy Searches for a New Recognition With a Novel About Monroe." LATimes.com. September 07, 1988. www.latimes.com/archives/la-xpm-1988-09-07-vw-1509-story.html.

BBC. "Big Bang Theory star Jim Parsons marries partner Todd Spiewak." BBC.com. May 15, 2017. www.bbc.com/news/entertainment-arts-39920429.

Biography.com Editors. "Tom Ford Biography." Biography.com. April 01, 2014. www.biography.com/fashion-designer/tom-ford.

Carpenter, Dale. Flagrant Conduct: The Story of Lawrence v. Texas. New York, NY: W. W. Norton & Company, 2012.

Clines, Francis X. "Barbara Jordan Dies at 59; Her Voice Stirred the Nation." NYTimes.com. January 18, 1996. www.nytimes.com/1996/01/18/us/barbara-jordan-dies-at-59-her-voice-stirred-the-nation.html.

Connelly, Shea. "Raising Awareness of Intersex Issues." TMC.edu. October 03, 2017. www.tmc.edu/news/2017/10/raising-awareness-intersex-issues.

Dance Informa. "Ailey Receives Presidential Medal of Freedom." DanceInforma.us. November 15, 2014. danceinforma.us/articles/ailey-receives-presidential-medal-of-freedom.

Dubin, Jared. "Michael Sam, first openly gay player, retires for mental health reasons." CBSSports.com. August 14, 2015. www.cbssports.com/nfl/news/michael-sam-first-openly-gay-player-retires-for-mental-health-reasons.

D'Zurilla, Christie. "Designer Tom Ford reveals he and Richard Buckley are married." LATimes.com. April 08, 2014. www.latimes.com/entertainment/gossip/la-et-mg-tom-ford-married-richard-buckley-20140408-story.html.

Erbland, Kate. "Gothams 2017 Host John Cameron Mitchell Opens With Incendiary Speech: 'Everything's F**ked Up'." IndieWire.com. November 27, 2017. www.indiewire.com/2017/11/gothams-2017-host-john-cameron-mitchell-speech-1201901448.

Fisher, Marc and Sue Ann Pressley. "Crisis of Sexuality Launched Strange Journey." WashingtonPost.com. March 29, 1997. www.washingtonpost.com/archive/politics/1997/03/29/crisis-of-sexuality-launched-strange-journey/3709d9ff-51ee-4f50-a9cd-a45525d7ad8f/?utm_term=.5c487bde88ab.

Gaydos, Steven. "Director-Choreographer-Performer Tommy Tune Talks About the Start of His Stage Career." Variety.com. January 02, 2018. variety.com/2018/legit/features/stage-star-tommy-tune-1202651253.

Gellman, Alan. "Historian and Founder of Gay Archives in Dallas, Phil Johnson." HoustonLGBTHistory.org. April 1984. www.houstonlgbthistory.org/misc-johnson2.html.

Gettell, Oliver. "Little Axe illuminates transgender gospel singer Willmer Broadnax." EW.com. March 01, 2016. ew.com/article/2016/03/01/little-axe-transgender-gospel-singer-short-film.

GLSEN. "State Maps." GLSEN.org. www.glsen.org/article/state-maps.

Hafford, Michael. "Heaven's Gate 20 Years Later: 10 Things You Didn't Know." RollingStone.com. March 24, 2017. www.rollingstone.com/culture/culture-news/heavens-gate-20-years-later-10-things-you-didnt-know-114563.

Houston LGBT History. "Mary's Naturally Bar—History." HoustonLGBTHistory.org. www.houstonlgbthistory.org/houston-marys-history.html.

Houston LGBT History. "Texas Gay Conferences." HoustonLGBTHistory.org. www.houstonlgbthistory.org/misc-tgc.html.

Human Rights Campaign. "Profile: Barbara Jordan (1936-1996)." HRC.org. November 14, 2008. web.archive.org/web/20081114152344/www.hrc.org/issues/3554.htm.

IMDb.com. "Justin Simien." IMDb.com. www.imdb.com/name/nm2282177/?ref_=nmbio_bio_nm.

Johnson, Phil. "Letter from Phil Johnson to Circle of Friends board members." TexasHistory.UNT.edu. texashistory.unt.edu/ark:/67531/metadc304822.

Kuser, Daniel A. "17 years after deadly shooting in Reverchon Park, victim all but forgotten." DallasVoice.com. January 30, 2008. www.dallasvoice.com/17-years-after-deadly-shooting-in-reverchon-park-victim-all-but-forgotten.

Low, Florence. "'End Gender': US Gender Non-Conforming Activist and Artist Visits Yerevan." HETQ.am. May 03, 2017. hetq.am/en/article/78366.

Macaulay, Alastair. "Alvin Ailey Dancers Return Like Conquering Heroes." NYTimes.com. December 04, 2017. www.nytimes.com/2017/12/04/arts/dance/alvin-ailey-city-center.html.

Malkin, Marc. "Jim Parsons Opens Up For the First Time About Relationship With Longtime Boyfriend." EOnline.com. October 19, 2013. www.eonline.com/news/472109/jim-parsons-opens-up-for-the-first-time-about-relationship-with-longtime-boyfriend.

Mindock, Clark. "Gloria E Anzaldúa: 5 facts about the cultural scholar you need to know." Independent.co.uk. September 26, 2017. www.independent.co.uk/news/world/americas/gloria-e-anzald-a-who-is-she-life-career-google-doodle-today-cultural-scholar-immigration-borders-a7968441.html.

Mitchell, Robert. "As first American injured in Iraq, Eric Alva addresses other issues." News.Harvard.edu. April 07, 2017. news.harvard.edu/gazette/story/2017/04/eric-alva-shares-story-of-being-gay-a-marine-and-changing-history.

Morris, Mike. "Former Houston mayor Annise Parker to lead Victory Fund." Chron.com. December 08, 2017. www.chron.com/news/politics/houston/article/Former-mayor-Parker-to-lead-Victory-Fund-12416282.php.

Olsen, Mark. "With 'Dear White People,' Justin Simien wants to start conversations." LATimes.com. October 10, 2014. www.latimes.com/entertainment/movies/la-et-mn-ca-dear-white-people-20141012-story.html

Oyez. "Lawrence v. Texas." Oyez.org. www.oyez.org/cases/2002/02-102.

Page, Jason. "Opinion: Why Michael Sam Is a Footnote in History, Not a Trailblazer." NBCNews.com. August 23, 2016. www.nbcnews.com/feature/nbc-out/opinion-why-michael-sam-footnote-history-not-trailblazer-n634786.

PBS. "Tommy Tune." PBS.org. www.pbs.org/wnet/broadway/stars/tommy-tune.

Pollock, Cassandra. "Who is Lupe Valdez, the Dallas County sheriff running for governor?" TexasTribune.org. December 06, 2017. www.texastribune.org/2017/12/06/who-lupe-valdez-dallas-county-sheriff-running-democrat-texas-governor.

Pomerantz, Dorothy. "Todrick Hall's Great Hollywood Adventure." Forbes.com. January 09, 2014. www.forbes.com/sites/dorothypomerantz/2014/01/09/todrick-halls-great-hollywood-adventure/#4eee76ee54ac.

Rechy, John. "After the Blue Hour." Goodreads.com. www.goodreads.com/book/show/30622617-after-the-blue-hour.

Rees, Christina. "Meet Sandy, Galveston's Newest Pink Resident." Glasstire.com. July 18, 2014. glasstire.com/2014/07/18/meet-sandy-galvestons-newest-pink-resident.

Robbins, Liz. "Swoopes Says She Is Gay, and Exhales." NYTimes.com. October 27, 2005. www.nytimes.com/2005/10/27/sports/basketball/swoopes-says-she-is-gay-and-exhales.html.

Robert's Lafitte. "Galveston's Original Show Bar!" RobertsLatiffe.Weebly.com. robertslafitte.weebly.com/index.html.

Romano, Andrew. "The True Story Behind Dallas Buyers Club: Meet the Real Ron Woodruff." TheDailyBeast.com. November 03, 2013. www.thedailybeast.com/the-true-story-behind-dallas-buyers-club-meet-the-real-ron-woodruff.

Rose, Steve. "Justin Simien: 'I'm black, I'm a man, I'm gay, but I'm more than all of those things'." TheGuardian.com. June 25, 2015. www.theguardian.com/film/2015/jun/25/justin-simien-im-black-im-a-man-im-gay-but-im-more-than-all-of-those-things.

Ruiz-Grossman, Sarah. "Lupe Valdez Makes History In Texas By Winning Democratic Nod For Governor." HuffingtonPost.com.au. May 23, 2018. www.huffingtonpost.com.au/entry/lupe-valdez-win-texas-democratic-primary-governor_n_5afcac91e4b06a3fb50d613c.

Simonson, Robert. "Tommy Tune Receives 2003 National Medal of Arts." Playbill.com. November 12, 2003. www.playbill.com/article/tommy-tune-receives-2003-national-medal-of-arts-com-116310.

Small, Zachary. "Why Can't the Art World Embrace Robert Rauschenberg's Queer Community?" Artsy.net. May 19, 2017. www.artsy.net/article/artsy-editorial-art-embrace-robert-rauschenbergs-queer-community.

Smith, Brandi. "Should LGBTQ history be taught in Houston public schools?" KHOU.com. June 22, 2017. www.khou.com/article/news/local/should-lgbtq-history-be-taught-in-houston-public-schools/451357669.

Stern, Mark Joseph. "Is MoMA Putting Artists Back in the Closet?" Slate.com. February 26, 2013. slate.com/culture/2013/02/moma-closets-jasper-johns-and-robert-rauschenberg-why.html.

The Houston Intersex Society. "The Houston Intersex Society." October 23, 2015. thehoustonintersexsociety.wordpress.com.

Townsend, Brad. "Flashback: With UIL days behind him, transgender wrestler Mack Beggs looks ahead to college, competing against men." Sportsday.DallasNews.com. February 22, 2018. sportsday.dallasnews.com/high-school/high-schools/2018/02/22/transgender-wrestler-mack-beggs-one-year-later-difficulty-defiance-new-uil-drama.

University of Houston Libraries. "LGBT History Research Collection." Libraries.UH.edu. libraries.uh.edu/branches/special-collections/lgbt.

University of North Texas. "Hugh Callaway." Exhibits.Library.UNT.edu. exhibits.library.unt.edu/resource-center-exhibit/hugh-callaway.

University of North Texas. "Lesbian, Gay, Bisexual and Transgender Archive." Library.UNT.edu. library.unt.edu/special-collections/collections/lgbt-archive.

Vaid-Menon, Alok. "ABOUT—ALOK." AlokVMenon.com. www.alokvmenon.com/about.

Van Natta, Don Jr. "Babe Didrikson Zaharias's Legacy Fades." NYTimes.com. June 25, 2011. www.nytimes.com/2011/06/26/sports/golf/babe-didrikson-zahariass-legacy-fades.html.

Vargas, Jose Antonio. "Defending His Country, but Not Its 'Don't Ask, Don't Tell' Policy." WashingtonPost.com. February 28, 2007. www.washingtonpost.com/wp-dyn/content/article/2007/02/27/AR2007022701589.html.

Vilkomerson, Sarah. "Michelle Rodriguez answers gay rumors." CNN.com. October 01, 2013. www.cnn.com/2013/10/01/showbiz/celebrity-news-gossip/michelle-rodriguez-gay-rumors/index.html.

Weber, Bruce. "A Minimalist Actor Now Warms to Excess." NYTimes.com. November 04, 1992. www.nytimes.com/1992/11/04/theater/a-minimalist-actor-now-warms-to-excess.html.

Weller, Sheila. "Discovering the Vulnerable Woman Behind Janis Joplin's Legend." VanityFair.com. November 27, 2015. www.vanityfair.com/culture/2015/11/janis-joplin-little-girl-blue-documentary-interviews.

White, Edmund. "The Making of John Rechy." NYBooks.com. April 03, 2008. www.nybooks.com/articles/2008/04/03/the-making-of-john-rechy/?pagination=false.

Woerner, Meredith. "A Look Inside The World of 'Dear White People's' Justin Simien." Variety.com. June 19, 2018. variety.com/2018/tv/news/dear-white-people-justin-simien-thats-life-1202851067.

Wolf, Brandon. "Mary's Infamous Mural: Iconic Art for an Iconic Bar." OutSmartMagazine.com. December 01, 2011. www.outsmartmagazine.com/2011/12/mary%E2%80%99s-infamous-mural-iconic-art-for-an-iconic-bar.

Zaharias, Babe Didrikson. "Record of Achievement." BabeDidriksonZaharias.org. web.archive.org/web/20070927080531/www.babedidriksonzaharias.org/achievements.cfm.

Zeigler, Cyd. "Mack Beggs wins 2nd state title, promptly gets booed by idiots." OutSports.com. February 25, 2018. www.outsports.com/2018/2/23/17042524/mack-beggs-wrestling-texas-trans-high-school.

US Virgin Islands

Benfield, Edward. "LGBTQ Community See Losses in Territory, But Reason for Hope." StThomasSource.com. July 31, 2017. stthomassource.com/content/2017/07/31/lgbtq-community-see-losses-in-territory-but-reason-for-hope.

Carribean Alliance for Equality. "Leadership." CarribbeanAllianceforEquality.org. web.archive.org/web/20150212205800/caribbeanallianceforequality.org/leadership.

Ellis, Susan. "Joseph Memorializes Audre Lorde in 'The Wind is Spirit'." StJohnSource.com. April 19, 2016. stjohnsource.com/2016/04/19/joseph-memorializes-audre-lorde-in-the-wind-is-spirit.

Ellis, Susan. "Women's Sexuality Conference Advocates for LGBT Rights." StJohnSource.com. October 06, 2016. stjohnsource.com/2016/10/06/womens-sexuality-conference-advocates-for-lgbt-rights.

Jao, Ariel. "#Pride30: Senator Janelle Sarauw is breaking barriers in U.S. Virgin Islands." NBCNews.com. May 31, 2018. www.nbcnews.com/feature/nbc-out/pride30-senator-janelle-k-sarauw-breaking-barriers-u-s-virgin-n872981.

McRae, Donald. "The night boxer Emile Griffith answered gay

taunts with a deadly cortege of punches." TheGuardian.com. September 10, 2015. www.theguardian.com/sport/2015/sep/10/boxer-emile-griffith-gay-taunts-book-extract.

Poets. "Adrienne Rich." Poets.org. www.poets.org/poetsorg/poet/adrienne-rich.

Pugmire, Lance. "Emile Griffith dies at 75; champion boxer struggled with his sexuality." LATimes.com. July 23, 2013. www.latimes.com/local/obituaries/la-me-emile-griffith-20130724-story.html.

Ring, Trudy. "Amid Threat of Massacre, St. Croix Holds First Pride Parade." Advocate.com. June 11, 2018. www.advocate.com/pride/2018/6/11/amid-threat-massacre-st-croix-holds-first-pride-parade.

Sarauw, Janelle. "Bio." JanelleKSarauw.com. www.janelleksarauw.com/bio.

Source Staff. "Conservationist Jon Stryker Donates $1.275 Million for Expansion of National Park." StJohnSource.com. January 23, 2017. stjohnsource.com/2017/01/23/conservationist-jon-stryker-donates-1-275-million-for-expansion-of-national-park.

Source Staff. "Not for Profit: Liberty Place." StCroixSource.com. February 25, 2013. stcroixsource.com/2013/02/25/not-profit-liberty-place.

St. Croix Pride. "Home." www.stxpride.org.

Telegraph. "Adrienne Rich." Telegraph.co.uk. March 29, 2012. www.telegraph.co.uk/news/obituaries/9174640/Adrienne-Rich.html.

Women's Coalition of St. Croix. "About Us." WCSTX.org. wcstx.org/about-us.

Utah

ACLU. "GSA Court Victories: A Guide for LGBT High School Students." ACLU.org. www.aclu.org/other/gsa-court-victories-guide-lgbt-high-school-students.

Affirmation. "Our History." Affirmation.org. affirmation.org/who-we-are/our-history.

Asher, Levi. "Neal Cassady." BeatMuseum.org. www.beatmuseum.org/cassady/nealcassady.html.

Ballotpedia. "Misty Snow." Ballotpedia.org. ballotpedia.org/Misty_Snow.

Burt, Brandon. "Utah's Gay Mayor." GaySaltLake.com. May 13, 2004. gaysaltlake.com/news/2004/05/13/utahs-gay-mayor.

BWW News Desk. "MORMON BOY TRILOGY to Head Off-Broadway Following Bay Street Run." BroadwayWorld.com. July 17, 2018. www.broadwayworld.com/article/MORMON-BOY-TRILOGY-to-Head-Off-Broadway-Following-Bay-Street-Run-20180717.

Calvey, Mark. "LGBTQ activist Kate Kendell reflects on marriage equality as she steps down." BizJournals.com. March 19, 2018. www.bizjournals.com/sanfrancisco/news/2018/03/19/lgbtq-nclr-kate-kendell-marriage-equality-lgbt.html.

Cassell, Heather. "Kendell confident in NCLR's future." eBAR.com. December 26, 2018. www.ebar.com/news/news//270023.

Caulfield, Keith. "Panic! at the Disco's 'Pray for the Wicked' Debuts at No. 1 on Billboard 200 Albums Chart." Billboard.com. July 01, 2018. www.billboard.com/articles/columns/chart-beat/8463542/panic-at-the-disco-pray-for-the-wicked-debuts-no-1-billboard-200.

Clay, Joanna. "Love story survives time and tragedy." OCRegister.com. September 18, 2013. www.ocregister.com/2013/09/18/love-story-survives-time-and-tragedy.

Encircle. "Our Programs." EncircleTogether.org. encircletogether.org/programs.

Fales, Steven. "When All Else Fales." stevenfales.blogspot.com.

Free, Cathy. "Salt Lake City Voters Elect the City's First Openly Gay Mayor Jackie Biskupski." November 05, 2015. people.com/politics/salt-lake-city-voters-elect-the-citys-first-openly-gay-mayor.

Gephardt Daily Staff. "Salt Lake City Mayor Biskupski marries." GephardtDaily.com. August 15, 2016. gephardtdaily.com/top-stories/salt-lake-city-mayor-biskupski-marries.

Green, Laci. "About." LaciGreen.tv. www.lacigreen.tv/about.

HarperCollins Publishers. "Laci Green." HarperCollins.com. www.harpercollins.com/author/cr-131843/laci-green.

Hazlehurst, Beatrice. "Brendon Urie Lays It All Out." Papermag.com. July 06, 2018. www.papermag.com/brendon-urie-lays-it-all-out-2584081623.html?rebelltitem=5.

HuffPost Queer Voices. "Gay Parents In The U.S.: Salt Lake City Has Highest Percentage Of Same-Sex Couples Raising Kids." HuffPost.com. May 22, 2013. www.huffpost.com/entry/gay-parents-salt-lake-city-_n_3314969?guccounter=1.

Jensen, Maren. "Person 2 Person: Dr. Kristen Ries." KUTV.com. June 18, 2017. kutv.com/features/person-2-person/person-2-person-dr-kristen-ries.

Knight, Christopher. "It's her show." LATimes.com. December 17, 2003. www.latimes.com/archives/la-xpm-2003-dec-17-et-knight17-story.html.

Lambda Legal. "East High Gay Straight Alliance v. Board of Education of Salt Lake City School District." LambdaLegal.org. www.lambdalegal.org/in-court/cases/east-high-gsa-v-board-of-ed-salt-lake.

Love Loud Festival. "FAQ." LoveLoudFest.com. loveloudfest.com/frequently-asked-questions.

Margolin, Emma. "Utah legislature passes Mormon-backed LGBT nondiscrimination law." MSNBC.com. March 12, 2015. www.msnbc.com/msnbc/utah-legislature-passes-mormon-backed-lgbt-nondiscrimination-law.

McDonald, Joel. "Maude Adams: Mormon, Lesbian and the Broadway's First Peter Pan." Affirmation.org. February 07, 2019. affirmation.org/maude-adams-mormon-lesbian-and-the-broadways-first-peter-pan.

Neal & Carolyn Cassady. "Neal Cassady." NealCassadyEstate.com. www.nealcassadyestate.com/neal.html.

News 3 Live. "Reed Cowan." News3lv.com. March 16, 2012. news3lv.com/archive/reed-cowan.

Ocamb, Karen. "NCLR's Kate Kendell steps down and into LGBT history." LosAngelesBlade.com. March 18, 2018. www.losangelesblade.com/2018/03/18/nclrs-kate-kendell-steps-down-and-into-lgbt-history.

Photography News. "Remembering photographer Margrethe Mather." Photography-News.com. March 04, 2017. www.photography-news.com/2011/03/remembering-photographer-margrethe.html.

Rogers, Melinda. "New University of Utah Project Will Document History of HIV/AIDS in Utah." UNews.Utah.edu. September 09, 2015. unews.utah.edu/new-university-of-utah-project-will-document-history-of-hivaids-in-utah.

Shannon, Jake. "Willy Marshall, America's first elected Libertarian mayor." IndependentPoliticalReport.com. 2015. independentpoliticalreport.com/2015/12/willy-marshall-americas-first-elected-libertarian-mayor.

Signorile, Michelangelo. "The First Trans U.S. Senate Candidate Is Already Making History." HuffPost.com. July 10, 2016. www.huffpost.com/entry/misty-k-snow-transgender_n_577fd846e4b01edea78dad24?guccounter=1.

Snow, Misty K. "About." www.mistyksnow.com.

The Editors of Encyclopaedia Britannica. "Maude Adams." Britannica.com. March 11, 1999. www.britannica.com/biography/Maude-Adams.

The J. Paul Getty Museum. "Margrethe Mather." Getty.edu. www.getty.edu/art/collection/artists/1713/margrethe-mather-american-1885-1952.

Utah Pride Center. "About the Festival." UtahPrideCenter.org. utahpridecenter.org/festival/about-the-festival.

Utah Pride Center. "About." UtahPrideCenter.org. utahpridecenter.org/about.

Utah Pride Center. "Events." UtahPrideCenter.org. utahpridecenter.org/events.

Villarreal, Yezmin. "Lesbian Mayor Installs 'Harvey Milk Boulevard' Sign in SLC." Advocate.com. May 14, 2016. www.advocate.com/politics/2016/5/14/lesbian-mayor-installs-harvey-milk-boulevard-sign-slc.

Whitaker, Morgan. "Meet the first same-sex couple in Utah to get a marriage license." MSNBC.com. December 22, 2013. www.msnbc.com/melissa-harris-perry-4.

Williams, Ben. "Anita Bryant Sucks Oranges." QSaltLake.com. December 14, 2017. qsaltlake.com/news/2017/12/14/hurricane-anita.

Williams, Ben. "The Murder of Tony Adams." QSaltLake.com. November 07, 2009. qsaltlake.com/news/2009/11/07/the-murder-of-tony-adams.

Williams, Troy. "A (Virtual) Walk Down Salt Lake City's Harvey Milk Blvd." Advocate.com. May 19, 2016. www.advocate.com/commentary/2016/5/19/virtual-walk-down-salt-lake-citys-harvey-milk-blvd.

Wood, Stacy, Sabrina Ponce, and Caroline Cubé. "Finding Aid for the Mildred Berryman papers 1937-1999 LSC.2170." OAC.CDLIB.org. January 03, 2018. oac.cdlib.org/findaid/ark:/13030/c87s7qx2/entire_text.

Vermont

Abel, David. "Vermont legalizes same-sex marriage." Archive.Boston.com. April 8, 2009. archive.boston.com/news/local/massachusetts/articles/2009/04/08/vermont_legalizes_same_sex_marriage.

Advocate.com Editors. "40 Under 40." Advocate.com. April 27, 2013. www.advocate.com/print-issue/current-issue/2013/04/17/40-under-40?page=full.

Dougherty, Mike. "DMV will implement third gender option with reboot of licensing system." VTDigger. org. January 10, 2018. vtdigger.org/2018/01/10/dmv-looks-to-state-law-as-it-mulls-third-gender-option-on-licenses.

Faerie Camp Destiny. "What Is Faerie Camp Destiny?" FaerieCampDestiny.org. www.faeriecampdestiny.org/drupal/about_destiny.

Gates, Gary J. "Vermont Leads States in LGBT Identification." News.Gallup. com. February 6, 2017. news.gallup.com/poll/203513/vermont-leads-states-lgbt-identification.aspx.

Green Mountain Crossroads. "Green Mountain Crossroads' Andrew's Inn Oral History Project." GreenMountainCrossroads.org. www.greenmountaincrossroads.org/andrews-inn-oral-history-project.html.

Henry Sheldon Museum. "Sylvia and Charity: A Vermont Love Story For The Ages." HenrySheldonMuseum.org. April 30, 2009. henrysheldonmuseum.org/sylvia-and-charity-a-vermont-love-story-for-the-ages.

InterACT. "Kimberly Zieselman, JD." InterACTAdvocates.org. interactadvocates.org/staff/kimberly-zieselman-jd.

Kroll, Andy and Patrick Caldwell. "Robby Mook Just Took the Hardest Job in Politics—Saving the Clintons From Themselves." MotherJones. com. April 9, 2015. www.motherjones.com/politics/2015/04/robby-mook-hillary-clinton-campaign-manager-profile.

McCullum, April. "Christine Hallquist: What you need to know about the first transgender nominee for governor." BurlingtonFreePress.com. August 14, 2018. www.burlingtonfreepress.com/story/news/politics/government/2018/08/14/christine-hallquist-first-transgender-governor-nominee-vermont-democrat-what-know/993980002.

McDonald, James. "Five Things We Know About Robby Mook, Hillary Clinton's Openly Gay Campaign Manager." Out.com. April 20, 2015. www.out.com/news-opinion/2015/4/20/five-things-we-know-about-robby-mook-hillary-clintons-openly-gay-campaign.

Northern Vermont University. "Lyndon State Senior Justin Chenette Elected State Rep. in Maine." NorthernVermont.edu. November 7, 2012. www.northernvermont.edu/about/news-events/news-center/lyndon-state-senior-justin-chenette-elected-state-rep-maine.

Outright Vermont. "Home." OutrightVT.org. www.outrightvt.org.

Patty Sheehan & Friends. "About." PattySheehanandFriends.org. pattysheehanandfriends.org/about.

Pride Center of Vermont. "Pride Center of Vermont." PrideCenterVT.org. www.pridecentervt.org.

Prism Center at UVM. "On This Day in #UVM History." Facebook.com. January 25, 2019. www.facebook.com/PrismUVM/photos/a.104390649916487/756385131383699/?type=3&amp%3Btheater.

The Ladies Professional Golf Association. "Patty Sheehan." LPGA.com. www.lpga.com/players/patty-sheehan/81929/overview.

The VT Bear Film Festival. "About the Festival." VTBearFilm.com. vtbearfilm.com/about.

Thomas, Nick. "Carleton Carpenter turns 90." TheSpectrum.com. July 7, 2016. www.thespectrum.com/story/entertainment/2016/07/07/carleton-carpenter-turns-90/86748358.

Very Vermont. "The Life and Death of Fearless Stagecoach Driver, Charley Parkhurst." DailyUV.com. 2016. dailyuv.com/842027?type=news.

Yoked, Tzach. "'After Transitioning, Everything Seems Easier': Meet Christine Hallquist, Who May Become America's First Trans Governor." Haaretz.com. August 24, 2018. www.haaretz.com/us-news.premium.MAGAZINE-meet-christine-hallquist-who-may-become-first-trans-governor-1.6411518.

Zieselman, Kimberly Mascott. "I was an intersex child who had surgery. Don't put other kids through this." USAToday.com. August 9, 2017. www.usatoday.com/story/opinion/2017/08/09/intersex-children-no-surgery-without-consent-zieselman-column/539853001.

Virginia

Akron Community Foundation. "Local gay rights pioneer leaves lasting legacy." AkronCF.org. www.akroncf.org/ContactUs/NewsEvents/ViewArticle/tabid/96/ArticleId/1429/Local-gay-rights-pioneer-leaves-lasting-legacy.aspx.

ACLU. "History of Sodomy Laws and the Strategy That Led Up to Today's Decision." ACLU.org. www.aclu.org/other/history-sodomy-laws-and-strategy-led-todays-decision.

Barton, Rachel. "Walking Tour: Gentrification and Queer Erasure in Roanoke, Virginia." NotchesBlog.com. April 27, 2017. notchesblog.com/2017/04/27/walking-tour-gentrification-and-queer-erasure-in-roanoke-virginia.

Barton, R.M. "Intersectional Activism & Early Gay Liberation in Southwest Virginia." WussyMag.com. October 18, 2017. www.wussymag.com/all/2017/10/17/gay-activism-is-southwest-virginia.

Better Housing Coalition. "Greta J. Harris." BetterHousingCoalition.org. www.betterhousingcoalition.org/person/greta-j-harris.

Birchmeier, Jason. "Kevin Aviance." AllMusic.com. www.allmusic.com/artist/kevin-aviance-mn0000067314/biography.

Brookhaven National Laboratory. "Benjamin Banneker (1731-1806)." BNL. gov. www.bnl.gov/bera/activities/globe/banneker.htm.

Classical Place. "Tona Brown." ClassicalPlace.com. www.classicalplace.com/tonabrown/bio.html.

Dickens, Tad. "Killer at Gay Club Gets Life Sentences: Ronald Edward Gay Says His Shooting Rampage, Which Left One Person Dead and Three Others Injured, Was Motivated by His Hatred of Gays." Greensboro.com. July 23, 2001. www.greensboro.com/killer-at-gay-club-gets-life-sentences-ronald-edward-gay/article_9feb1df9-3525-53b4-be71-450c9fe34011.html.

Diversity Richmond. "About Diversity Richmond." DiversityRichmond.org. diversityrichmond.org/who-we-are.html.

Erotic Art Collection. "George Quaintance." EroticArtCollection.com. www.eroticartcollection.com/George_Quaintance/George_Quaintance.html.

Equality Virginia. "Who We Are." EqualityVirginia.org. www.equalityvirginia.org/about-ev/who-we-are.

Equality Virginia. "Dr. Christine M. Robinson." EqualityVirginia.org. 2016. www.equalityvirginia.org/dinner-2016/outstanding-virginians/christine-robinson.

Equality Virginia. "Jeff Trammell." EqualityVirginia.org. 2014. www.equalityvirginia.org/dinner-2016/outstanding-virginians/jeff-trammell.

Equality Virginia. "Greta J. Harris." EqualityVirginia.org. 2014. www.equalityvirginia.org/dinner-2016/outstanding-virginians/greta-j-harris.

Equality Virginia. "Robin Gorsline." EqualityVirginia.org. 2016. www.equalityvirginia.org/dinner-2016/outstanding-virginians/robin-gorsline.

Fahim, Kareem and Sarah Garland. "Fourth Man Is Arrested After Attack on a Dance Recording Artist in the East Village." NYTimes.com. June 12, 2006. www.nytimes.com/2006/06/12/nyregion/12beating.html.

Frank, Priscilla. "Meet The First African American Transgender Performer To Take The Stage At Carnegie Hall." HuffPost.com. May 23, 2014. www.huffpost.com/entry/tona-brown_n_5373411.

Gearhart, Sally Miller. "Sally's Story." SallyMillerGearhart.net. sallymillergearhart.net/sallys-story.

Health Brigade. "History." HealthBrigade.org. www.healthbrigade.org/history.

Kirst, Seamus. "Celebrity Gossip Guru B. Scott On The Business Of Pop Culture Blogging." Forbes.com. February 25, 2016. www.forbes.com/sites/seamuskirst/2016/02/25/celebrity-gossip-guru-b-scott-on-the-business-of-pop-culture-blogging/#592e57d9647d.

LeonardMatlovich.com. "Leonard Matlovich." www.leonardmatlovich.com.

LeonardMatlovich.com. "Story of His Stone." LeonardMatlovich.com. www.leonardmatlovich.com/storyofhisstone.html.

Machi, Sara. "Virginia may be getting first LGBT historical marker in Roanoke." WDBJ7.com. March 22, 2017. www.wdbj7.com/content/news/Roanoke-group-wants-to-get-historical-marker-416889843.html.

National Park Service. "Benjamin Banneker and the Boundary Stones of the District of Columbia." NPS.gov. www.nps.gov/places/sw-9-intermediate-boundary-stone-of-the-district-of-columbia.htm.

Nationz Foundation. "About." NationzFoundationRVA.org. www.nationzfoundationrva.org/about.

O'Brien, Kimberly. "Police: Backstreet Cafe gunman hunted gays." Roanoke. com. September 24, 2000. www.roanoke.com/news/crime/roanoke/police-backstreet-cafe-gunman-hunted-gays/article_092a6657-057a-5ea5-901a-b52bed518c5b.html.

Olivo, Antonio. "Danica Roem of Virginia to be first openly transgender person elected, seated in a U.S. statehouse." WashingtonPost.com. November 08, 2017. www.washingtonpost.com/local/virginia-politics/danica-roem-will-be-vas-first-openly-transgender-elected-official-after-unseating-conservative-robert-g-marshall-in-house-race/2017/11/07/d534bdde-c0af-11e7-959c-fe2b598d8c00_story.html?utm_term=.c11304cc4d3f.

Out History. "The Gay Community Center of Richmond." OutHistory. org. outhistory.org/exhibits/show/rainbow-richmond/in-the-twenty-first-century/gccr.

Richmond Triangle Players. "About Richmond Triangle Players." RTriangle. org. www.rtriangle.org/about-rtp.html.

Roem, Danica. "About Danica." DanicaRoem.NGPVANHost.com. danicaroem. ngpvanhost.com/about-danica.

Sessoms, Brandon Scott. "About B. Scott." LoveBScott.com. www.lovebscott. com/about-b-scott.

Side by Side. "Mission & History." SidebySideVA.org. www.sidebysideva.org/ about-1.

Southwest Virginia LGBTQ+ History Project. "Library." LGBTHistory.Pages. Roanoke.edu. lgbthistory.pages.roanoke.edu/library.

Sullivan, Patricia. "'In love with a community': Longtime Arlington politician will retire, but 'he's not leaving." WashingtonPost.com. December 22, 2017. www.washingtonpost.com/local/virginia-politics/in-love-with-a-community-arlingtons-longest-serving-politican-will-retire-but-wont-leave/2017/12/22/aedd8226-e42a-11e7-a65d-1ac0fd7f097e_story. html?utm_term=.d3e4eddc394f.

Sykes, Wanda. "Bio." WandaSykes.com. www.wandasykes.com/bio.php.

TASCHEN Books. "George Quaintance." TASCHEN.com. www.taschen.com/ pages/en/search/george-quaintance.

Ubuntu Biography Project. "Kevin Aviance." UbuntuBiographyProject.com. June 22, 2017. ubuntubiographyproject.com/2017/06/22/kevin-aviance.

Up Closed. "Jay Fisette." UpClosed.com. upclosed.com/people/jay-fisette.

Virginia Department of Historic Resources. "Timeline of LGBT History in Virginia and the United States." DHR.Virginia.gov.

Wydra, Elizabeth B., Doug Kendall, Judith E. Schaeffer, David H. Gans, and Ilya Shapiro. "Bostic v. Shaefer." TheUSConstitution.org. www. theusconstitution.org/litigation/bostic-v-schaefer-4th-cir.

Washington

Bailey-Boushay House. "Bailey-Boushay House." www.baileyboushay.org.

Hale, Lara. "Capitol Hill." VisitSeattle.org. www.visitseattle.org/ neighborhoods/capitol-hill.

McNichols, Joshua. "A Walk Through Seattle's LGBT History." KUOW.org. June 27, 2013. kuow.org/stories/walk-through-seattles-lgbt-history.

Paulson, Don. "Seattle Gay History—The Spinning Wheel Cabaret." SGN.org. May 2, 2008. www.sgn.org/sgnnews36_18/page12.cfm.

Washington, DC

Adkins, Judith. "'These People Are Frightened to Death.' Congressional Investigations and the Lavender Scare." Archives.gov. 2016. www.archives. gov/publications/prologue/2016/summer/lavender.html.

Archer, Michael. "Gospel According To Deacon." PublishersWeekly.com. August 25, 2003. www.publishersweekly.com/pw/print/20030825/22003-gospel-according-to-deacon.html.

Bailey, Amber. "HABS Survey Nob Hill DC." NPS.gov. 2016. www.nps.gov/ places/upload/Nob-Hill-1.pdf.

Bianco, David. "Frank Kameny." BNL.gov. www.bnl.gov/bera/activities/globe/ kameny.htm.

Brown, Lydia X. Z. "About." AutisticChoya.com. www.autistichoya.com/p/ about.html.

Canfield, Kevin. "The FBI's Spying on Writers Was Literary Criticism at Its Worst." TheDailyBeast.com. September 08, 2018. www.thedailybeast.com/ the-fbis-spying-on-writers-was-literary-criticism-at-its-worst.

Clark, Philip. "'Accept Your Essential Self': The Guild Press, Identity Formation, and Gay Male Community." Academia.edu. 2013. www. academia.edu/9728447/_Accept_Your_Essential_Self_The_Guild_Press_ Identity_Formation_and_Gay_Male_Community.

Dalphonse, Sherri. "You Must Remember… Deacon Maccubbin and Jim Bennett." Washingtonian.com. October 12, 2015. www.washingtonian.com/2015/10/12/ washington-dc-legends-jim-bennett-and-deacon-maccubbin.

DiGuglielmo, Joey. "Meshell's magic." WashingtonBlade.com. November 10, 2011. www.washingtonblade.com/2011/11/10/ meshell%E2%80%99s-magic.

Dunlap, David W. "Franklin Kameny, Gay Rights Pioneer, Dies at 86." NYTimes. com. October 12, 2011. www.nytimes.com/2011/10/13/us/franklin-kameny-gay-rights-pioneer-dies-at-86.html.

Friedman, Vanessa. "André Leon Talley's Next Act." NYTimes. com. May 24, 2018. www.nytimes.com/2018/05/24/style/ andre-leon-talley-documentary.html.

Gandhi, Lakshmi. "Autistic Activist Lydia X. Z. Brown Is Fighting 'Violence Affecting Disabled Folks'." NBCNews.com. August 15, 2016. www.nbcnews. com/news/asian-america/how-austistic-activist-lydia-x-z-brown-fighting-violence-affecting-n626266.

Gay Travel 4 U. "High Heel Drag Queen Race 2019 Washington." GayTravel4U.com. 2019. www.gaytravel4u.com/event/ washington-dc-high-heel-drag-queen-race.

Gleason, James. "LGBT History: The Lavender Scare." NGLCC.org. October 03, 2017. www.nglcc.org/blog/lgbt-history-lavender-scare.

Gunn, Tim. Gunn's Golden Rules: Life's Little Lessons for Making It Work. New York, NY: Simon & Schuster, 2010.

Historical Society of Washington, D.C. "DC Gay Liberation Front (GLF) Collection." DCHistory.PastPerfectOnline. com. dchistory.pastperfectonline.com/archive/ DA95E8C9-4208-41B7-81D0-322345725692.

Latino GLBT History Project. "Our Story." LatinoGLBTHistory.org. www. latinoglbthistory.org/our-story.

Nauert, Heather. "In Recognition of Intersex Awareness Day." State.gov. October 26, 2017. www.state.gov/r/pa/prs/ps/2017/10/275098.htm.

Ndegeocello, Meshell. "About." Meshell.com. www.meshell.com/about-1.

Newbold, Alice. "Unmasking The Private and Public Selves Of André Leon Talley." Vogue.co.uk. September 28, 2018. www.vogue.co.uk/article/ andre-leon-talley-interview.

Orton, Kathy. "A poet's rowhouse in Northwest Washington has a renaissance." WashingtonPost.com. June 01, 2018. www.washingtonpost. com/news/where-we-live/wp/2018/06/01/a-poets-rowhouse-in-northwest-washington-has-a-renaissance/?utm_term=.dc8d04f34a9c.

Rainbow History Project. "About Us." www.rainbowhistory.org.

Rainbow History Project Digital Collections. "Deacon Maccubbin." Archives. RainbowHistory.org. 2007. archives.rainbowhistory.org/exhibits/show/ pioneers/2007awardees/maccubbin.

Revolvy. "Tynan Power." Revolvy.com. www.revolvy.com/page/Tynan-Power.

Ring, Trudy. "LGBT Muslims Make Progress on the Path to Acceptance." Advocate.com. September 23, 2013. www.advocate.com/politics/religion/2013/09/23/ lgbt-muslims-make-progress-path-acceptance?page=full.

Samuels, Wilfred D. "Richard Bruce Nugent (1906-1987)." BlackPast. org. October 10, 2012. www.blackpast.org/african-american-history/ nugent-richard-bruce-1906-1987.

Sopelsa, Brooke. "Justice Department Ordered to Release 1950s Gay 'Purge' Documents." NBCNews.com. August 03, 2017. www.nbcnews.com/ feature/nbc-out/court-tells-justice-department-release-1950s-gay-purge-documents-n789056.

Sophie's Parlor Women's Radio Collective. "Forty Years Later—Are We Taking Care of Ourselves?" SophiesParlor.Blogspot.com. 2013. sophiesparlor. blogspot.com/2013/01/forty-years-later-are-we-taking-care-of.html.

Stern, Simon. "Manual Enterprises v. Day (1962)." MTSU.edu. www.mtsu.edu/ first-amendment/article/395/manual-enterprises-v-day.

Ubuntu Biography Project. "Richard Bruce Nugent." UbuntuBiographyProject. com. July 01, 2017. ubuntubiographyproject.com/2017/07/01/ richard-bruce-nugent.

Vallese, Zach and Andrea Swalec. "Photos: Drag Queens Strut and Sprint at DC High Heel Race." NBCWashington.com. October 30, 2018. www. nbcwashington.com/entertainment/the-scene/Photos-Drag-Queens-Sprint-to-Finish-Line-in-DC-High-Heel-Race-499046791.html.

West Virginia

Appalachian Queer Film Festival. "About Us." AQFF.org. aqff.org/about-us.

Bendix, Trish. "Queer Women History Forgot: Ada 'Bricktop' Smith." GoMag.com. March 31, 2017. gomag.com/article/ queer-women-history-forgot-ada-bricktop-smith.

Diaz, George. "Christy Martin, still standing strong after attempted murder, years of domestic violence." OrlandoSentinel.com. July 31, 2018. www. orlandosentinel.com/opinion/os-ae-christy-martin-boxer-domestic-violence-murder-20180730-story.html.

Eskridge, William N. Dishonorable Passions: Sodomy Laws in America, 1861-2003. London, UK: Penguin, 2008.

Fairness West Virginia. "About." FairnessWV.org. fairnesswv.org/about.

Freedom to Marry. "The Freedom to Marry in West Virginia." FreedomtoMarry.

org. www.freedomtomarry.org/states/west-virginia.

Georgia House of Representatives. "Rep. Karla Drenner." House.GA.gov. www. house.ga.gov/Documents/Biographies/drennerKarla.pdf.

IMDb. "Tom McBride." IMDb.com. www.imdb.com/name/nm0564381/bio.

Jacobs, Andrew. "Gay Legislator at the Center of a Storm in Georgia." NYTimes.com. March 09, 2004. www.nytimes.com/2004/03/09/ us/gay-legislator-at-the-center-of-a-storm-in-georgia. html?scp=3&sq=Karla%20Drenner&st=cse.

LaBorde, Monique. "Huntington Mayor Champions LGBT Inclusion." WVPublic.org. July 03, 2018. www.wvpublic.org/post/ huntington-mayor-champions-lgbt-inclusion#stream/0.

Lavers, Michael K. "W. Va. voters elect first openly gay state lawmaker." WashingtonBlade.com. November 09, 2012. www.washingtonblade. com/2012/11/09/w-v-voters-elect-first-openly-gay-state-lawmaker.

Leichner, Helen. "Ada 'Bricktop' Smith (1894-1984)." BlackPast.org. January 06, 2013. www.blackpast.org/african-american-history/ smith-ada-bricktop-1894-1984.

Living AIDS Memorial Garden. "Living AIDS Memorial Garden." livingaidsmemorialgarden.org.

Moser, Laura. "In the Backwoods of Lost River, a Gay Retreat." NYTimes. com. October 30, 2013. www.nytimes.com/2013/11/03/travel/in-the-backwoods-of-lost-river-a-gay-retreat.html.

Ohlheiser, Abby. "All five residents of a West Virginia town voted to ban LGBT discrimination." WashingtonPost.com. February 12, 2015. www.washingtonpost.com/news/morning-mix/wp/2015/02/12/ all-five-residents-of-a-west-virginia-town-voted-to-ban-lgbt-discrimination/?utm_term=.27784b41844d.

Quinn, Ryan. "Study: WV has nation's highest percent of teens who identify as transgender." WVGazetteMail.com. March 01, 2017. www.wvgazettemail. com/news/education/study-wv-has-nation-s-highest-percent-of-teens-who/article_d5080981-91d8-5490-b8ed-e80c57348bd1.html.

Rader, Jan. "Faith Fuels This Fire Chief's Fight Against the Opioid Epidemic." GuidePosts.org. January 25, 2018. www.guideposts. org/better-living/health-and-wellness/addiction-and-recovery/ faith-fuels-this-fire-chiefs-fight-against.

Rainbow Pride of West Virginia. "About Us." WVPride.org. www.wvpride.org/ about-us.html.

Shugerman, Emily. "LGBT attacks not hate crimes, West Virginia court rules." Independent.co.uk. May 12, 2017. www.independent.co.uk/news/world/ americas/lgbt-hate-crimes-west-virginia-court-ruling-a7733086.html.

Skinner, Stephen. "Attorney Stephen Skinner." SkinnerFirm.com. skinnerfirm. com/about-us/stephen-skinner.

Sparkes, Sam. "These Are The 10 Gayest Places In West Virginia For 2019." RoadSnacks.net. December 19, 2018. www.roadsnacks.net/ gayest-places-in-west-virginia.

The Electric Dirt Collective. "About." QueerAppalachia.com. www. queerappalachia.com/who-why.

Thompson, Ronnie. "The Lambda Society at Marshall meets for the first time this semester." MarshallParthenon.com. January 27, 2015. marshallparthenon.com/2009/news/ the-lambda-society-at-marshall-meets-for-the-first-time-this-semester.

Wisconsin

Baldwin, Tammy. "About Tammy Baldwin." Baldwin.Senate.gov. www. baldwin.senate.gov/about.

Barron, James. "Liberace, Flamboyant Pianist, Is Dead." NYTimes.com. February 05, 1987. www.nytimes.com/1987/02/05/obituaries/liberace-flamboyant-pianist-is-dead.html.

Biography.com Editors. "Liberace Biography." Biography.com. April 02, 2014. www.biography.com/musician/liberace.

Boughner, Terry. "Two Fallen Heros." The Wisconsin Light. March 1995. www. mkelgbthist.org/media/print/wis-light/covers-v06-10/light-v08-05-fons. pdf.

Doylen, Michael. "Donna Burkett." MkeLGBTHist.org. 2012. www.mkelgbthist. org/people/peo-b/burkett_donna.htm.

Fortin, Jacey. "Transgender Student's Discrimination Suit Is Settled for $800,000." NYTimes.com. January 10, 2018. www.nytimes. com/2018/01/10/us/transgender-wisconsin-school-lawsuit.html.

Georgetown Institute of Politics and Public Service McCourt School of Public Policy. "Mary Cheney." Politics.Georgetown.edu. politics.georgetown.edu/ mary-cheney.

History of Gay and Lesbian Life in Milwaukee, Wisconsin. "Christopher Fons." MkeLGBTHist.org. 2006. www.mkelgbthist.org/people/peo-f/ fons_christopher.htm.

History of Gay and Lesbian Life in Milwaukee, Wisconsin. "Miriam Ben Shalom." MkeLGBTHist.org. 2012. www.mkelgbthist.org/people/peo-b/ benshalom_miriam.htm.

May, Meredith. "Retired Navy Cmdr. Zoe Dunning fought ban on gays." SFGate.com. March 22, 2012. www.sfgate.com/LGBT/article/Retired-Navy-Cmdr-Zoe-Dunning-fought-ban-on-gays-3425458.php.

Mosiman, Dean. "Proposed landmark would be most prominent recognition of an LGBT site in city history." Madison.com. January 06, 2018. madison. com/wsj/news/local/govt-and-politics/proposed-landmark-would-be-most-prominent-recognition-of-an-lgbt/article_2c4fd360-503c-53fa-9cc5-bf8e6b4a61af.html.

Nabozny, Jamie. "Jamie Nabozny Bio." JamieNabozny.com. www. jamienabozny.com/assets/jamienaboznybio.pdf.

NE Wisconsin LGBT History Project, Paul "Cricket" Jacob and Lloyd Schaefer. "Argonauts Leather Club." MkeLGBTHist.org. 2013. www.mkelgbthist.org/ organiz/leather/argonauts.htm.

OutReach Magic Festival. "History of PRIDE in Madison." OutReachMagicFestival.org. 2019. www.outreachmagicfestival. org/a-history-of-pride.

Pappas, Alex. "Exclusive: Mary Cheney Marries Longtime Partner Heather Poe." DailyCaller.com. June 22, 2012. dailycaller.com/2012/06/22/ exclusive-mary-cheney-marries-longtime-partner-heather-poe.

Rottmann, Andrea. "AB70—Wisconsin's Gay Rights Law." MkeLGBTHist.org. 2012. www.mkelgbthist.org/events/community/ab70.htm.

Schwamb, Don and Michail Takach. "Mint Bar." MkeLGBTHist.org. 2016. www. mkelgbthist.org/business/bars/mint.htm.

Terry, Don. "Suit Says Schools Failed To Protect a Gay Student." NYTimes. com. March 29, 1996. www.nytimes.com/1996/03/29/us/suit-says-schools-failed-to-protect-a-gay-student.html.

Takach, Michail. "Milwaukee's magnificent Mint Bar lit the LGBTQ beacon." OnMilwaukee.com. April 11, 2017. onmilwaukee.com/history/articles/ mint-bar-history.html.

Tipler, Gary. "Making History." OurLivesMadison.com. March 2018. ourlivesmadison.com/article/making-history.

Wisconsin Women Making History. "Miriam Ben Shalom." WomeninWisconsin. org. womeninwisconsin.org/miriam-ben-shalom.

Wyoming

Advocate.com Editors. "Family Guy." Advocate.com. April 10, 2006. www. advocate.com/politics/commentary/2006/04/10/family-guy.

Advocate.com Editors. "Annie Proulx tells the story behind 'Brokeback Mountain'." Advocate.com. December 17, 2005. www.advocate. com/arts-entertainment/entertainment-news/2005/12/17/ annie-proulx-tells-story-behind-brokeback.

Cathy Connolly for House District 13. "Biography." ConnollyforHouse.com. www.connollyforhouse.com/biography.php.

Eder, Richard. "Don't Fence Me In." NYTimes.com. May 23, 1999. www.nytimes.com/1999/05/23/books/don-t-fence-me-in. html?pagewanted=all&src=pm.

Italie, Leanne. "In Todd Parr's world, it's OK to make mistakes." DailyHerald. com. August 1, 2014. www.dailyherald.com/article/20140801/ entlife/140809969.

Jackson, David. "Obama signs hate-crimes law rooted in crimes of 1998." Content.USAToday.com. October 28, 2009. content.usatoday.com/ communities/theoval/post/2009/10/620000629/1#.XLzkcJNKjOQ.

Johnson, Kirk. "Very Much at Home: A Gay Mayor in Wyoming." NYTimes.com. December 16, 2005. www.nytimes.com/2005/12/16/us/very-much-at-home-a-gay-mayor-in-wyoming.html.

KUTV. "Utah Theater Balks at 'Brokeback Mountain'." KUTV.com. January 10, 2006. web.archive.org/web/20070926211849/kutv.com/topstories/ local_story_007175321.html.

Ling, Susie. "The Kuromiyas of Monrovia: A Family of Unsung Heroes." Rafu.com. September 20, 2016. www.rafu.com/2016/09/ the-kuromiyas-of-monrovia-a-family-of-unsung-heroes.

Matthew Shepard Foundation. "Our Mission." MatthewShepard.org. www. matthewshepard.org/about-us.

Meyer, Liz. "Out in the Equality State." SGN.org. March 6, 2009. web.archive.
org/web/20110606073625/www.sgn.org/sgnnews37_10/page12.cfm.

Najafi, Yusef. "Avenging Angel." MetroWeekly.com. November 7, 2007. www.
metroweekly.com/2007/11/avenging-angel.

National Park Service. "LGBTQ Memorials: Matthew Shepard Memorial,
Laramie, WY." NPS.gov. www.nps.gov/articles/lgbtq-memorials-matthew-
shepard-memorial-laramie-wy.htm.

Padgett, Guy. "Guy Padgett." Trib.com. December 5, 2008. trib.com/words_
of_wisdom/guy-padgett/article_5220670c-3ff4-59f1-8d51-573759be9ac1.
html.

Parr, Todd. *The I LOVE YOU Book.* Boston, MA: Little, Brown and Company,
2009.

Parr, Todd. "Todd Parr." HachetteBookGroup.com. www.hachettebookgroup.
com/contributor/todd-parr.

Sosa, Alfredo. "Kiyoshi Kuromiya." CritPath.org. 2010. critpath.org/about-us/
kiyoshi-kuromiya.

Stein, Marc. "Kiyoshi Kuromiya, June 17, 1997." OutHistory.org. 2009.
outhistory.org/exhibits/show/philadelphia-lgbt-interviews/interviews/
kiyoshi-kuromiya.

The Patterson Family. "Welcome to the World of Romaine Patterson!"
EatroMaine.com. www.eatromaine.com/1/index-family.html.

The White House Office of the Press Secretary. "Remarks by the President at
Reception Commemorating the Enactment of the Matthew Shepard and
James Byrd, Jr. Hate Crimes Prevention Act." ObamaWhiteHouse.Archives.
gov. October 28, 2009. obamawhitehouse.archives.gov/the-press-office/
remarks-president-reception-commemorating-enactment-matthew-
shepard-and-james-byrd-.

The Wyoming Gay-Straight Alliance Network. "About Us." WYGSANetwork.org.
www.wygsanetwork.org/about-us.

Vaughan, Roger. "The Defiant Voices of S.D.S." *Life Magazine,* October 1968.

Wong, Curis M. "Gay Historical Sites, Past And Present: A Look At LGBT
Relevant Places Across America." HuffPost.com. February 02, 2016. www.
huffpost.com/entry/gay-sites-then-and-now_n_5526577.

Wyoming Equality. "About—We're Queer. And We've Always Been Here."
WyomingEquality.org. www.wyomingequality.org/about.

Wyoming Equality. "About—Rendezvous." Rendezvous Wyoming.org. www.
rendezvouswyoming.org/about.